Revolution

Revolution

Structure and Meaning in World History

SAÏD AMIR ARJOMAND

The University of Chicago Press
Chicago and London

The University of Chicago Press, Chicago 60637
The University of Chicago Press, Ltd., London

Published 2019
Printed in the United States of America

28 27 26 25 24 23 22 21 20 19 1 2 3 4 5

ISBN-13: 978-0-226-02683-1 (cloth)
ISBN-13: 978-0-226-02684-8 (e-book)
DOI: https://doi.org/10.7208/chicago/9780226026848.001.0001

Library of Congress Cataloging-in-Publication Data

Names: Arjomand, Said Amir, author.
Title: Revolution : structure and meaning in world history / Saïd Amir Arjomand.
Description: Chicago ; London : The University of Chicago Press, 2019. | Includes bibliographical references and index.
Identifiers: LCCN 2018043828 | ISBN 9780226026831 (cloth : alk. paper) | ISBN 9780226026848 (ebook)
Subjects: LCSH: Revolutions—History—To 1500. | Revolutions—Philosophy.
Classification: LCC HM876 .A75 2019 | DDC 303.6/4—dc23
LC record available at https://lccn.loc.gov/2018043828

♾ This paper meets the requirements of ANSI/NISO Z39.48-1992 (Permanence of Paper).

CONTENTS

ABBREVIATIONS

Akhbār	*Akhbār al-dawla al-ʿAbbāsiyya wa fihi akhbār al-ʿAbbās wa waladihi*. 1971. Edited by ʿA.-ʿA. al-Duri and ʿA.-J. al-Mutallabi. Beirut.
Annals	Cornelius Tacitus. 1942. *The Annals*. In *The Complete Works of Tacitus*, edited by M. Hadas, 1–416. New York: Modern Library.
Ansāb 3	Ahmad b. Yahyā b. Jābir al-Balādhuri. 1978. *Ansāb al-Ashrāf*. Vol. 3. Edited by ʿA.-ʿA. al-Duri. Beirut.
Antiquities	Flavius Josephus. 1971. *The Second Jewish Commonwealth (Being Books XII–XX of the "Jewish Antiquities")*. Translated by N. N. Glatzer. New York: Schocken.
BSOAS	*Bulletin of the School of Oriental and African Studies*
CM	Constitution of Medina. References are to the paragraphs of documents A–H as edited in M. Lecker, *The "Constitution of Medina": Muhammad's First Legal Document* (Princeton, NJ: Darwin Press, 2004).
Gregory	E. Emerton, ed. (1932) 1969. *The Correspondence of Pope Gregory VII: Selected Letters from the Registrum*. New York: W. W. Norton.
History	Cornelius Tacitus. 1942. *The History*. In *The Complete Works of Tacitus*, edited by M. Hadas, 417–673. New York: Modern Library.
Ibn Isfandiyār	Muḥammad Ibn al-Ḥasan Ibn Isfandiyār. 1941 (AH 1330). *Tārikh-e Tabarestān*. Tehran: Ramazāni.
JAOS	*Journal of the American Oriental Society*

JESHO	*Journal of the Economic and Social History of the Orient*
Jewish War	Flavius Josephus. (1959) 1981. *The Jewish War.* Translated by G. A. Williamson. Rev. ed. Harmondsworth, UK: Penguin.
JNES	*Journal of Near Eastern Studies*
Jovayni	ʿAlāʾ al-Din ʿAtā-Malek Jovayni. 1911. *Tārikh-e Jahān-goshā.* Edited by M. Qazvini. 3 vols. Leiden: E. J. Brill.
JRS	*Journal of Roman Studies*
JSAI	*Jerusalem Studies in Arabic and Islam*
Khaldun	ʿAbd al-Rahmān Ibn Khaldun. 1992. *Kitāb al-ʿibar (Tārikh Ibn Khaldun).* 7 vols. Beirut: Dār al-kutub al-ʿIlmiyya. Vol. 1 edited and translated by F. Rosenthal as *The Muqaddimah,* 3 vols. (Princeton, NJ: Princeton University Press, 1967).
Life	Muhammad Ibn Ishāq. 1858–60. *Sīrat Rasūl Allāh.* Edited by F. Wüstenfeld. Göttingen. Translated by A. Guillaume as *The Life of Muhammad* (London: Oxford University Press, 1955). Page references are to the English translation, which gives the references to the Arabic text in the margins.
Mostawfi	Hamdallāh Mostawfi. 2000 (AH 1389). *Zafarnāma.* Vol. 8, *Qesm-e Soltāniyya.* Edited by N. Zākeri. Tehran: Pazhuheshgāh-e ʿOlum-e Ensāni va Motāleʿāt-e Farhangi.
Nihāya	*Nihāyat al-ʿirab fi akhbāri'l-Furs wa'l-ʿArab.* Unpublished manuscript partially translated in G. Widengren, "The Establishment of the Sasanian Dynasty in the Light of New Evidence," in *La Persia nel Medioevo* (Rome: Accademia nazionale dei lincei, 1971), 711–84.
Q.	Qurʾān
Rashid al-Din	Rashid al-Din Fazlallāh Hamadāni. 1994 (AH 1373). *Jāmeʿ al-Tavārikh.* Edited by M. Rawshan and M. Musavi. 4 vols. Tehran: Alborz.
Shāhnāma	Ferdawsi. 1995 (AH 1374). *Shāhnāma.* Moscow ed. 8 vols. Tehran: Nashr-e Dād.
Sib. Or.	J. J. Collins, ed. and trans. 1983. *Sibylline Oracles.* In *The Old Testament Pseudepigrapha,* edited by J. H. Charlesworth, 1:317–472. New York: Doubleday.

ŠKZ	Šapur Kaʿba-ye Zardosht: Shāpur I's rock relief inscriptions published in various collections; most recently, P. Huyse, *Die dreisprachige Inschrift Šābuhrs I. an der Kaʿba-i Zardušt (ŠKZ)* (London: School of Oriental and African Studies, 1999).
Suet.	Suetonius. 1957. *The Twelve Caesars*. Translated by R. Graves. Harmondsworth, UK: Penguin.
Tabari	Muhammad b. Jarir al-Tabari. 1879–1901. *Ta'rikh al-rusul va'l-muluk*. Edited by M. J. de Goeje. 15 vols. Leiden. Annotated English translation in *The History of al-Tabari*, 40 vols. (Albany: State University of New York Press, 1985–2007). Page references are to the English translation, which gives the references to the Arabic text in the margins.

INTRODUCTION

Revolution in Comparative and Historical Sociology

The collapse of communism in 1989 closed two centuries of modern revolutions on the bicentennial of the French Revolution of 1789. Revolution is a modern concept that acquired its new meaning and definitive form as a result of the chain of events in France in 1789 that became known as the Great Revolution. The French Revolution thereby gave birth to the modern myth of revolution during the Jacobin Reign of Terror in 1793–94. Revolution was a single logical and coherent step in the march of human progress (Furet 1981:82, 88) that disparaged attempts to hinder it as reactionary counterrevolution doomed to failure (Doyle 1991). The Thermidorian Reaction to the Reign of Terror further generated a revolutionary faith among those determined to save the revolution—a system of belief in the regeneration of man or his salvation through revolution. The revolutionary faith was sustained by generation after generation of young intellectuals who constituted the "prophets and priests of this new secular religion . . . largely crying through the wilderness throughout the nineteenth century" (Billington 1980:8). A class of professional revolutionaries thus emerged in Western Europe. The myth of revolution espoused by this new generation of revolutionary intellectuals included a modernized republicanism shaped by the strong Classicist echoes of that of the first Roman revolution, immortalized by the great painter of the French Revolution Jacques-Louis David,[1] which motivated the Revolution of 1830 in France—the next in the epicycle of modern revolutions. The myth of revolution, however, remained sociologically innocent. The young Alfred de Musset, writing his play *Lorrenzaccio* (1834) during the revolutionary process, would make his protagonist into a "modern Brutus," and one now disillusioned with Liberty, "a most seductive demon" that had set the 1830 revolution in motion (Musset 1991:126–27, 133). It was left to the young Karl Marx, a professional revolutionary of the next revolution in the modern epicycle, that of 1848, to remedy the sociological innocence of the myth of revolution. Marx thus adapted the Jacobin idea of revolution to his hallmark conception of class struggle and the historic mission of the proletariat as the new revolutionary class on the model of the bourgeoisie of the French Revolution.

The process of the revolution in France was thus transformed into the autonomous cultural form I call the modern myth of revolution. As an autonomous cultural form, it had a subsequent life of its own through an emergent social group and a new organization that acted as its social and institutional bearers. In the early 1860s, the Russian revolutionaries corrected Marx's erroneous identification of the cultural bearers of revolution with the proletariat by borrowing a term coined in Poland: the intelligentsia (Billington 1980:400–402). By the turn of the century, V. I. Lenin had made significant changes to the idea of revolution, while mobilizing the Russian intelligentsia in its support and recruiting a cadre of revolutionary professionals. With this move, the Communist Party became the vanguard of revolution and so inscribed into its modern myth the instrument of the "[r]evolutionary-democratic dictatorship of the proletariat and peasantry" (Tucker 1969:129).[2]

In the era inaugurated by the Russian Revolution of 1917 and continued with the Chinese Revolution of 1949 and the Cuban Revolution of 1959, the modern myth of revolution underwent further modification. Mao Tse-tung (1970) made the peasantry the revolutionary class and modified the revolutionary process into warfare waged by it from the countryside against the cities. The modern myth of revolution was thus militarized, acquiring the Asian communist form of guerrilla warfare (Tucker 1969:155–62). The neo-Jacobin, Marxist-Leninist idea of revolution also underwent a far-reaching modification in the rest of the so-called Third World after World War II, whereby the Marxian revolutionary class was replaced by the masses of the non-European world who were victims of Western imperialism (Kedourie 1991:197). The utopian myth of revolution expired with the dystopian post-1989 revolutions of central Eurasia. But myth in its Marxist-Leninist form had in fact expired a decade earlier in January 1979 with the collapse of Democratic Kampuchea and was partially supplanted a month later by a new myth of the Islamic state and revolution born in the Islamic Revolution of February 1979.

The Islamic Revolution in Iran was the last in the two-century cycle of modern revolution with a common origin in the modern myth of revolution in its last, late twentieth-century version. Although a powerful new idea of Islamic revolution had been added to it and Qur'anic terms used to repackage the script for Third World revolution as the struggle of the Disinherited (*mustaz'afin*) against the imperialism of the new arrogant idol (*tāghut*), the Great Revolution script survived in it, enabling the Islamic revolutionaries to indiscriminately label their sundry opponents as counter-revolutionaries and enemies of the people.

When the myth of revolution became an autonomous modern cultural form, it was transformed from a consequence of one (French) revolution to a cause of subsequent ones. In this way, causality was reversed, and the idea of revolution became one of its causes in the following two centuries. In formal terms, whenever we find *uniformity of consequences* but *variety* in the factors causing them, a teleological explanation seems in order. In such a teleological explanation, "reverse causality" obtains, and consequences serve as causes (Stinchcombe 1968:80).[3] As we shall see, after producing revolution after revolution for two centuries, the myth of revolution in its Marxist version expired with the Khmer Revolution in Kampuchea and, in its Islamic revolution form, did not survive long after the Islamic Revolution in Iran. The teleology of subsequent revolutions followed a different pattern.

The revolutions in Eastern and Central Europe after 1989 resulted in fundamental changes in state and society, while firmly rejecting this modern myth of revolution. "The study of revolution," wrote Jack Goldstone (2001:140), "may be reaching an impasse, in which it is simply overwhelmed by the variety of cases and concepts it seeks to encompass." Although one of the late S. N. Eisenstadt's last books (2006) had "Great Revolutions" in its title, it covered a variety of great transformations and civilizational trends other than political revolutions in the narrow sense. Then came the Arab revolutions of 2011, which did not replicate the Great Revolution script at all but, rather, followed the pattern of the European revolutions of 1848—that is, of revolution in a civilizational zone or world region with varied outcomes in its different countries.

Instead of despairing and being overwhelmed by the variety of revolutions, however, I have sought to come to terms with it in the pages that follow. To understand the contemporary version, I am offering a typology of revolutions reaching back way beyond 1789 and indeed to the dawn of history. The book of history needed to be reopened at long last—to be precise, after two hundred years—to reread the past for the construction of a new conception of revolution and a typology adequate to its historical variety from the globally broadened perspective of the present. In this volume, I am accordingly not concerned with the facts of the French Revolution, with the extremely distorted Marxian reading of that event as the bourgeois revolution, or with the atrocities committed on the basis of that reading against the bourgeoisie as counterrevolutionaries in Russia after 1917 and Cambodia after 1975, both episodes misleadingly and aspirationally presented as the revolution of the proletariat. My starting point for rereading history is rather the script of the Great Revolution and the modern myth of revolution whose expansion it was. My theoretical mission is to challenge this script, which has distorted the reading of the subsequent revolutions of the next two centuries, and to demystify the myth by locating earlier instances of radical transformation of the political order and its social base in world history.

The Modern Idea of Revolution and Rereading the Past

No secret needs to be made of the fact that my conception of ancient and medieval revolutions in this study is anachronistic. This anachronism is the inevitable result of the fact that the time of my theoretical initiative is what Paul Ricoeur calls a "present of attention" with essential reference to the past and the future. Forming the idea or constructing a narrative of a revolution involves the constitution of the present of attention with essential reference to the past of memory and the future of expectation.[4] This means rereading the past and scripting the future.

The utopian myth of (the Great) Revolution as the regeneration of man and total transformation in the forward march of history was indeed a secular apocalypse born of the French Revolution of 1789 (Lasky 1976:30–59), and it remained prevalent throughout the short twentieth century (1917–89), scripting an epicycle of revolutions that ended with the collapse of communism; and each occurrence in the cycle of modern revolutions imposed a forced rereading of the past. In Latin America, as part of the Western civilizational zone already in the nineteenth century, and in the rest of the globe in the course of decolonization in the mid-twentieth century, the modern myth of revolution generated coups d'etat, "wars of national liberation," and a few political and social revolutions, until what appears to be its expiration in 1989.

The rise of social sciences itself was the epistemic revolution of the European Age of Revolution. As the great theorist of this epistemic revolution, Reinhart Koselleck (1985:46–47), who reopened the book of history in light of new concepts engendered by this revolution, saw clearly: "Revolution assumes a transcendental significance; it becomes a regulative principle of knowledge." The sociophilosophical conception of revolution as a coherent collective singular serving as a regulative principle of knowledge informed the modern historiography of revolution. In the first place, "to assume their meaning as the French Revolution," a chain of events had to be ordered within a master narrative of time and place, "constructing their significance and relationship one to another, inventing a logic that might hold them together or set them apart, inscribing them within a script for the past, present and future" (Baker 1990:204). One should add that the script was extended as what was now the revolution unfolded, producing, in the most popular version, a ten-year script: the Great French Revolution, 1789–1799.

In the *Communist Manifesto* of 1848, the revolutionary *terrible simplificateur* Karl Marx simplified the French Revolution script in accordance with his universal law of class struggle as engine of world history: the new script for the future revolution was the apocalyptic clash of the bourgeoisie and the proletariat (Tucker 1969:126–27). Revolution thus conceived was made the pivot of the impressive mix of prophecy and social science called Marxism.

Once the Great French Revolution was constructed as an idea, not only did it lay claims to a new understanding of future events—indeed, a new recipe for future events—but it also reopened the past by establishing a new criterion for selectively investing it with significance. We begin to look for similar patterns of interconnected events in the past by attending closely to features of different periods which did *not* have the same significance to those who lived in them (Gallie 1968:120). We as theorists of revolution now have available to us knowledge of new events that is logically outside the order of a prior sequence of events that we describe as revolution (Danto 1985:356). We can now make sense of some earlier sequence of events as revolution on the basis of adequate similarity and should expand our historical knowledge by striving toward "a sort of pluralistic unity." The present would thus become the time of theoretical initiative, time to rediscover in history "the dialectic of the past and the future and their exchange in the present" (Ricoeur 1984–88:3.207).

With the notion of the Great French Revolution in place, the first sequence of prior events to suggest itself is the Great Rebellion in England in the mid-seventeenth century. The understanding of that event had already crystallized into a new meaning of the word "revolution" in the English language. The 1st Earl of Clarendon had still used the term "revolution" somewhat literally for the restoration of 1660, but when John Evelyn wrote in his diary on December 2, 1688, that "the Papists in offices lay down their commissions and fly. . . . It looks like a Revolution," he was clearly anticipating a repetition of the pattern of events that had begun in 1640 (*Oxford English Dictionary*, compact edition, s.v. "revolution"). The English Revolution did acquire a new meaning after 1789, but one that was congruent with the historical record.

Needless to say, there is no compelling or good reason for stopping our search for revolutionary patterns in 1640. What Francis Bacon had written in one of his great essays half a century earlier applies very well to the English and French Revolutions as well as to the subsequent ones: "The causes and motives of seditions are, innovation in religion; taxes; general oppression; advancement of unworthy persons; strangers; dearths; disbanded soldiers; factions grown desperate; and *whatever, in offending people, joineth and knitteth them in a common cause*" (1994:38, emphasis added). Bacon goes on to say that great troubles in state are marked by the mobilization of both the upper and the lower classes of society: "for common people are of slow motion, if they be not excited by the greater sort; and the greater sort are of small strength, except the multitudes be apt and ready to move of themselves" (1994:39). Last, Bacon emphasizes that princes need "some great person . . . of military valor, near unto them, for the repressing of seditions *in their beginnings*" (1994:41, emphasis added).

In these few words, we have a causal theory of revolution which goes far in explaining subsequent revolutions, including those of the twentieth century. Bacon uses the term "sedition" (as the Romans used *seditio*; the Greeks, *stasis*; and the Muslims, *fitna*) to refer to major political upheavals, "tempests in state." These obviously have something in common with modern revolutions; otherwise, the explanatory power of Bacon's enumeration of causes would be puzzling indeed. The same is true of the consequences of revolutions, which were not a matter of concern for Bacon. If the structure of authority and the political community in which it prevailed were altered after the collapse of the state and a period of intense political mobilization during the Great French Revolution, we would be justified, not to say impelled, to look for comparable prior sequences of events with similar consequences.

What makes Bacon's observation so apposite for the tempest in the Stuart state that was to come within a generation and for the revolution in France a century and a half later, however, is the intimate connection between modern revolution and the concentration of authority in the modern state that is captured by the ideal type of revolution I shall call Tocquevillian. Martin Luther's posting of the Ninety-Five Theses in 1517 and his burning of the papal bull and books of canon law at the gates of Wittenberg in 1520 were certainly acts of sedition, but the revolutionary tempest they caused was not one in state, because the authority structure he challenged and shook was that of the Catholic Church. The Holy Roman Empire under which he lived was not a state resembling the centralizing early modern states of England and France. Although Luther sought to exploit the amorphous authority structure of the Holy Roman Empire in his *Address to the Nobility of the German Nation* in 1520, a year after Charles V was elected emperor, it was not until 1546 that the latter could put together an army to confront the Protestant princes of the Schmalkaldic League. The Holy Roman Empire was not the only premodern polity with a fragmentary power structure in which a revolution could occur, however. As we shall see, most of our premodern cases of revolution occurred in fragmented polities whose integration was religiocultural. But, especially for the papal revolution of Gregory VII covered in chapter 9, we cannot rely on Bacon's observations to understand their nature and require other models or ideal types such as the ones offered below.

Revolutions after the French Revolution similarly lead to the reopening of the past in the search for their meaning by comparison. When the script for revolution was reenacted throughout Europe in 1848, it did not fail to stimulate a rereading of the distant past in search of comparable patterns. Two great historians of antiquity who had experienced the revolutions of 1848, Theodor Mommsen and N. D. Fustel de Coulanges, independently found the concept of revolution applicable to ancient history. Mommsen entitled book 4 of his *History of Rome* (1854–56), covering the period from the Gracchi to the Sullan restoration (133–79 BCE), "The Revolution." Fustel similarly devoted book 4 of *The Ancient City* (1864) to the treatment of the progressive breakdown of particularism and the reconstruction of more inclusive and integrated communities.[5] It was entitled "The Revolutions," covering four types that constituted the four stages of the revolutionary transformation of the social, political, and religious organization of the city-states of Greco-Roman antiquity that was completed in the fifth century BCE: dispossession of kings, change in the constitution of the family, the entry of the plebs into the city, and the establishment of democracy.

Nor did the revolutions of the twentieth century fail to generate a similar search. Just as Mommsen and Fustel were influenced by the revolutions of 1848, Ronald Syme was thinking of the interwar communist and fascist revolutions, and in particular of Mussolini's, when he entitled his book on the transition from the republic to the principate from 60 to 23 BCE *The Roman Revolution* (1939).

My own experience of revolution began late in 1978, and my interest in it was aroused by the incipient Islamic revolution in Iran. I vividly recollect hearing late at night on the BBC World News on December 23, 1978, while waiting to interview Ayatollah Ruhollah Khomeini in Neauphle-le-Château near Paris before his return to Iran,[6] that Malcolm Caldwell, a British Marxist academic and well-wisher of the Red Khmer Revolution in Cambodia, had been murdered in Phnom Penh. Years later, I read that Caldwell had "returned delighted" from an interview with Pol Pot hours before his murder by the Red Khmer (Chandler 1991:309–10). In January 1979, Pol Pot fled Phnom Penh and the shah of Iran left Tehran. A revolution collapsed and another triumphed.

The events in Iran were a full reenactment of the modern myth of revolution, but one with particular added features that resulted in the establishment of the first Shiʿite theocracy in history. I sought to understand it as a modern revolution in comparative perspective (Arjomand 1986, 1988), while also drawing a parallel (Arjomand 1980) between its clericalist outcome and the consolidation of hierocratic authority in medieval Christianity that resulted from what Berman (1983) popularized as the papal revolution. In this work, I study this parallel further in chapter 9, while seeking parallels and contrasts with older revolutionary patterns in Iranian and Islamic history in chapters 6 and 8. Fortunately for my understanding of revolution, time would not stand still but generate new revolutionary patterns at great variance with the "Great Revolution" type of the French and Iranian Revolutions but quite close to that of the European revolutions of 1848. The Arab Revolution of 2011 thus prompted me to locate it in a comparative and historical perspective once its pattern emerged reasonably clearly by the end of 2013 (Arjomand 2015).

Revolution and Theory

The first sociological model of revolution in the twentieth century was directly inspired by the modern myth of revolution. It was based squarely on the script of the Great French Revolution, and was first developed in the analytical tradition initiated by Lyford Edwards's *The Natural History of Revolution* in 1927. He and other exponents of the natural history of revolutions, such as Brinton (1938) and Hopper (1950), treated revolutions as regular sequences of events whose common narrative was generalized into a pattern consisting of successive stages. Revolution was now conceptualized as a process. The process of revolution was treated as an autonomous process with its own predictable dynamics, whatever causes might set it in motion. This is an important contribution in identifying a common sequence and many of the major features of the sociological dynamics of revolutionary process, which Goldstone (1982:189–92) concisely summarizes as a sequence of ten stages. Although, as we shall see, the exact sequence they identified occurs in only one of the types of revolution that I have distinguished, most of its elements can be found in somewhat different sequences in other types of revolution as well.

This basic idea has recently been repackaged as a "robust process," defined as "a sequence of events that has unfolded in similar (but neither identical nor fully predictable) fashion in a variety of different historical contexts" (Goldstone 1991b:57). The conceptualization of a generic revolutionary process is nevertheless highly problematic in that it requires a forced reading of the later revolutions as following the script of the French (and Russian) Revolution. It is now badly in need of historicization, as new patterns of revolution have since appeared in global history.

The basic problem with the old, natural history approach to the "revolutionary process" is not that it does not fit a number of cases, such as the revolutions of Mexico (Knight 1990a, 1990b) and Iran (Arjomand 2009), but rather that it is generic and does not in any way capture the partially varying directionality of different historical revolutions. Selbin (1999:12–20) attempts to rectify this defect by making a distinction between "institutionalization," meaning the process of putting a new government in place, and "consolidation," meaning achieving the goals of the revolution. When specifying the latter, however, he can come up with only the alleged goals of the revolutionary project, generically conceived as common to all revolutions and blandly referred to as "healthcare, education, justice . . . [and] a better life!" or, even more elusively, "the soul of the people" and their vision (Selbin 1999:13, 20). All this, needless to say, derives from the modern myth of revolution and not from any actual or historicized revolution. If historicized, actual revolutions do not share a generic vision, but each of them has its own; and different visions set the varying directionality of each. And it is likewise with the soul of the revolutionaries.

A second sociological model of revolution that emerged in the mid-twentieth century focused not so much on its process or sequence of stages but on the violence generated by it. The close association of revolution with violence underlies this seemingly passing trend in research on "collective violence" in the social sciences. The focus on violence, too, highlights generic causes at the expense of the diversity of consequences or variety in the goals and direction of revolutionary social change. The combination of the obsession with causes and the conception of revolution as collective violence explains a tendency in comparative studies of revolution to highlight similarities at the expense of differences. What little attention has been paid to the typology of revolutions (e.g., Pettee 1966) has been very rudimentary and inadequate for representing the diversity of outcomes. For this and other reasons explained in the next section, we must put aside the natural history/anatomy and the collective violence models rather than trying to build on them. The two related main goals of the present study are to rectify these shortcomings by historicizing the process of revolution and by focusing on the consequences, meaning, and typology of revolutions.

The third sociological model of revolution was more significant, however, and therefore is worth retaining. The Marxian version of the myth of revolution proved immune to the overwhelming empirical evidence disproving it for very long, and when it gave way to a new paradigm in the last quarter of the twentieth century, the source of the latter was obscured by a last-ditch effort to continue crediting the modern myth of revolution to Marx. At the close of the twentieth century, the renowned sociologist Randall Collins claimed that a paradigm shift in the sociology of social revolutions had put an end to this prehistory of the social-scientific study of revolution. Celebrating the conventional wisdom of the last quarter of that century in the field he described as macrohistory, Randall Collins (1999:3) stated that "the most striking accumulation of knowledge has taken place on Marx's favorite topic, revolution!" This prodigious accumulation of knowledge was the result of the state-centered perspective, introduced by the groundbreaking work of Charles Tilly (1978) and Theda Skocpol (1979), which was said to have "created a paradigm revolution in the theory of revolution." This self-congratulatory statement mischievously hides Alexis de Tocqueville (d. 1866) as the true author of the state-centered "paradigm revolution" in question by an irrelevant profession of faith in Marx, which in turn inadvertently betrays a deeply rooted Eurocentrism, as Marx could not conceive of non-European revolutions.

Tocqueville is not so much as mentioned in *States and Social Revolutions* (1979) by Theda Skocpol, who is credited with "bringing the state back in," presumably for the benefit of those who had not heard of Tocqueville. Yet, for those of us who have read him, Tocqueville's state-centered theory of revolution remains unsurpassed. On the other hand, to acknowledge her Marxian inspiration, Skocpol (1979:4) added "class-based revolt from below" to her definition of social revolution as "the basic transformation of a society's state and class structure." Following in her footsteps, Jack Goldstone (1991b) identified the causes of state breakdown: (1) demographic pressure causing fiscal crisis, (2) elite alienation and rebellions, and (3) the potential for political mobilization, which resulted from social mobility and the rise of aspiring new elites in early modern Europe. He claimed that these three factors held for the twentieth-century revolutions as well, though downplaying demographic pressure as the cause of fiscal crisis (Goldstone 1991a:37–40).

The main problem with this conceptualization is, however, its tautological circularity or, more precisely, its "definition-qua-explanation" (Motyl 1999:4). Revolution is defined as state breakdown, and state breakdown is its main direct cause. State breakdown is hypothetically measured by fiscal crisis and military weakness, but these are the very causes of revolution itself.

Meanwhile, the students of revolution in Latin America (Goldfrank 1979; Farhi 1990) and the Caribbean (Meeks 1993) had added peripherality in the world system to the causal conditions of revolution (Goldfrank 1979; Farhi 1990; Meeks 1993). State crisis causing revolution in this world region stems from "their weak and dependent capitalist relation" (Meeks 1993:188). This sets the stage for the "fourth-generation" theories of revolution to posit the "permissiveness of the world system" as a formal cause of revolution (Foran 1993). One cannot ask for a better theory of everything, as everything happening in the world conceptualized as a system occurs because it meets the condition of its permissiveness! This most synthetic approach sees "revolutions as conjunctural amalgams of systemic crisis, structural opening, and collective action, which arose from an intersection of international economic, political and symbolic factors" (Lawson 2016:106–7). In his sprawling analysis of forty-six cases of "third-world revolutions," the fourth-generation theorist John Foran (2002) highlights the interaction of five conditions said to be indispensable: dependent development; exclusionary, paternalistic regimes; economic downturns; and a world-system opening (Lawson 2016:119). A tighter analysis of the international dimension of revolutions, highlighting such phenomena as the export of revolution and revolution by design and international support for it, is offered by Fred Halliday (1999). Most recently, George Lawson (2017) highlights the polycentric character of the revolutions of the global age and interdependence among them across time and space. This much is implicit in my account of the major modifications of the modern myth of revolution, with each modification motivating an epicycle of revolutions. As we shall see in the chapters that follow, interdependence across time also obtains for ancient and medieval revolutions in world history.

As I have dealt with what I saw as the inadequacy of the state breakdown theories of Skocpol (Arjomand 1988; epilogue below) and Goldstone (Arjomand 1992) in the third generation of theorists of revolution, and of that of Foran in the fourth (Arjomand 2006), what remains to be done for completing this brief survey is to engage with Charles Tilly's third-generation theory hailed for contributing to the paradigm shift celebrated by Collins. Although Tilly's (1978) distinction between a "revolutionary situation" and a "revolutionary outcome" proved fruitful in stimulating much research in historical sociology, it is hard to see its theoretical import. In his survey of European revolutions between 1492 and 1992, he counts between 30 and 50 revolutionary outcomes out of a total of 707 revolutionary situations (Tilly 1993:243). Shortly before his death, I sent him my paper on the rise of Safavid Shah Esmāʿil in 1501 as a Mahdist revolution and suggested that he consider it an exotic addition to his 30–50 cases of European revolutionary outcomes; he firmly resisted.[7] One may therefore wonder about the comparative import of his European finding, even if one were not to question the relevance of his over 650 cases of failed European revolutions to the global study of revolution.

Revolution and Meaning in History

The word "revolution" lost its original meaning of return to the starting point in modern times and became synonymous with great change. The new sense of the term has informed many studies of revolution in the nineteenth and twentieth centuries. This means that we naturally think of revolution in terms of its consequences. Yet, the sociology of revolution has grossly neglected its consequences. To be more precise, in so defining the so-called Great Revolutions, unspecified socioeconomic and cultural changes that were qualified as fundamental were implicitly and uncritically attributed to them, but the real concern of the sociology of revolution so far has been to identify their alleged causes. Sociologists' surprising omission of specific and historically plausible consequences of revolutions can be attributed to the conception of revolution as a thing according to Durkheim's first rule for sociological method and to the correspondingly naive notions of causality along positivistic lines. This neglect of consequences can also be said to stem from the more fundamental neglect of the relation between the concept of revolution and the thorny issue of meaning in history.

Revolution itself is history in the making, and its conception is intimately connected with the understanding of history. Its meaning and emergent norms take shape as it historically unfolds. Great Revolutions as ideas or collective representations are themselves ex post facto constructions of meaning in national histories and global history and are so constructed on account of the significance attached to them. This significance depends heavily on the *consequences* of a revolutionary rupture, or more precisely on whether it opens a new developmental path for institution building and social reconstruction. The possibility of such constitutional reconstruction depends on the self-understanding of the historical actors. At the same time, those who win the revolutionary power struggle (and sometimes those who lose it in the short run) reopen the past for self-understanding, and their interpretation of it thus becomes a social myth and scripts the future, generating a distinctive cycle of revolutions that eventually ends when that myth expires.

The great sociologist who required adequacy at the level of meaning for the proper study of social action, Max Weber, produced no theory of revolution. Weber not only lived through the two Russian Revolutions but also learned Russian and wrote two book-length essays on the Russian Revolution of 1905 and its aftermath (Weber [1906] 1995). He did so, however, before he had developed his main concepts in political sociology, and before he had developed a sociological methodology for dealing with meaning in his comparative study of world religions. Furthermore, the historical significance, as Weber (1904) conceived it, is inevitably retrospective, and that of the Russian Revolutions of 1905 and 1917 could not have been clear as he was living through them. The resulting work of Weber is quite disappointing in retrospect, and even at the time. Weber knew that his essays on contemporary Russian events were basically works of journalism, and he did not "consider them scholarly achievements" (Radkau 2009:234). Unlike Randall Collins (2005), I cannot in good conscience give Weber a better grade for them than he himself did. It is true, though, that we find undeveloped insights here and there in his subsequent writing. Weber discussed the medieval revolutions in Italian cities in comparison to the lack thereof in Oriental cities, thereby analyzing them in the light of their world-historical significance. His discussion of plebiscitary or leader-democracy (*Führerdemokratie*) as "a variant of charismatic authority" (Weber 1978:268–69) also shows Weber's awareness of the importance of revolutionary charismatic leadership, seeing "a highly emotional type of devotion to and trust in the leader" as "a natural basis for the utopian component which is found in all revolutions." (I have tried to develop this insight in my analysis of the routinization of revolutionary charismatic leadership as the constitutional politics in the struggle for the reconstruction of political order after the Islamic Revolution of 1979 in Iran [Arjomand 2009].)

Weber outlived the 1917 Russian Revolution by only two turbulent years but recorded his famous prediction on its significance in world history—namely, that, instead of withering away as predicted by Lenin, the bureaucratic state would grow monstrously by swallowing the economy as well. Nevertheless, he did not explain revolution as meaningful social action in his interpretive sociology. Nor did he integrate revolution into his political sociology or into the analysis of the eruption of charisma as a new starting point for the developmental process of institutional rationalization. The absence of revolution thus leaves a major gap in Weber's political sociology, even though he cannot be held responsible for the continued neglect of meaning in the sociology of revolution.

Like all social action, revolutionary action is meaningful to the historical actors—what Weber (1978:1.4) called its subjective meaning. But revolution, intuitively thought of in terms of its consequences, also has an objective meaning in history. For Weber ([1904] 1949), the objective meaning of a major event was indeed conceived in terms of its consequences and consisted in its cultural and historical significance. This methodological insight was, incidentally, not much applied by Weber himself, but it will be developed in this study. It implies that a revolution could be of interest as a subject of sociological study because of the relevance of the value-ideas that it shaped or reshaped and that are tantamount to its cultural significance.

The addition of the dimension of meaning to the conception of revolution thus reopens the fundamental issues of definition and conceptualization of process as a typical sequence of events and their causation and consequences in comparative and historical sociology. More importantly, it raises the question of the significance of revolutions as groundbreakers in world history.

Definition and Architectonics of the Concept of Revolution

Revolution is a major instance of discontinuity in history that results in the replacement of one political order by another. It consists of a complex of meaningful events that transform the constitution of the structure of authority and political community through political mobilization and often acquire cultural significance. More formally, revolution can be defined as a culturally significant and complex event that greatly increases the political mobilization of society and thereby results in major changes in its political organization or the structure of authority (the state, when the term applies) and/or its social base (i.e., the political community). Breaking this definition into its components and drawing out their methodological implications:

1 Revolution is a complex event and its analysis requires historicization. This means that the analysis of the process of revolution requires its periodization.

2 Revolution involves an intense political mobilization that subsides but results in a lasting transformation of the constitution of the political community and/or its form of government and structure of authority.

3 The implication of the above two points combined is that the analysis of revolution as a process should distinguish between two overlapping stages: the revolutionary power struggle among the contenders in the competition engendered by political mobilization and the constitutional politics of postrevolutionary political and social reconstruction. Each of these two phases of the process of revolution needs to be historicized through the periodization of revolution.
4 The outcome of the struggle for political order consists of changes in political and social organization. The enlargement of the political community and the changes in the structure of power are the two structural outcomes of revolutions. They are subject, each and in combination, to a range of variation that can be divided heuristically into a typology.
5 The meaning of a particular revolution is not confined to its structural outcomes but includes its cultural significance in world history generated by its prefigured or emergent value-ideas. The cultural significance of a revolution is determined by its distinctive pattern and directionality, which I shall call its teleology.

This definition expresses a fundamentally political conception of revolution and makes the political factors included in the definition the focal point of its explanation (Kraminick 1972:62–63). It also points beyond causes, process, and structural outcomes to culturally significant consequences that may be prefigured in the ideas and symbols that set revolutionary change in motion but are anyway increasingly crafted in its course and thereby determine the distinctive pattern and directionality of specific revolutions that endow them with significance in world history. Defining revolution thus by its consequences requires putting the historicized and specific teleology of a particular revolution in a much broader, indeed global, historical and comparative, typologically ordered range of variation.

In line with this proposed reconstruction of the concept of revolution on the basis of its consequences, the typology of revolutions offered in this book is designed to capture the range of variation in the structural consequences of revolutions. The causes and preconditions of revolutions should be considered only if they have a direct bearing on the consequences of the revolutions. Socioeconomic and cultural causes and preconditions can vary, but there is constancy in the political factors that are the defining features of revolution. I do not wish to suggest that reductive socioeconomic explanations of revolutions are illegitimate or inappropriate. In fact, some aspects of the social structure will turn out to be highly relevant in my analysis, as will aspects of culture, and as we shall see, there is remarkable patterning in the clustering of such factors. Nevertheless, economic, social, and cultural factors can cause a revolution only through their impact on the political process and structure. This impact can be theoretically abstracted from socioeconomic and cultural contexts by focusing on the political order—that is, on the constitution of political community and its authority structure and political contentions to change them.

Let me take an example of a causal explanation of revolution to illustrate the proper analytical organization of social and political factors. According to Arthur Stinchcombe (1975:583–84), a revolution can be set in motion by the impact of social mobilization upon a rigidly restrictive structure of authority. In this explanation, the difference between the rates of mobilization and incorporation causes the development of revolutionary situations: "If the rate of mobilization of the population is high, due to urbanization and the extension of literacy, and the rate of the population's incorporation into the governing structure is low, we will expect the number of people available for revolution to increase." The failure of the regime to open in time and incorporate these potential revolutionaries then results in revolution (Stinchcombe 1975:582).

The general point illustrated by this example is that the social, economic, and cultural causes and preconditions, such as urbanization and the spread of literacy, even when correctly identified, still operate through the more immediately pertinent political factors of the kind highlighted by Aristotle's conception of revolution as a change in the constitution of the polity, which is determined in part by its very structure. The Marxian conception of the "Great Revolution"—that is, the notion of "social revolution" as the transformation of the mode of production and class structure—makes too many unproven assumptions about the relation between political order, the social structure, and the economy, called the (real) infrastructure, while neglecting the political order itself by dismissing it as a (mere) superstructure. The revisionist Marxian idea of the "relative autonomy" of the state still remains reductive and fails to analyze the political structure as Aristotle did.

The same lack of any sharp differentiation between the political and other factors, this time cultural and civilizational, is true of the much rarer formulation of the idea of the Great Revolution in terms of its consequences, such as Eisenstadt's (1978) notion of the fundamental transformation of the symbolic and institutional structure of society and economy that generates what he called the Civilization of Modernity (Eisenstadt 2006). By contrast, the Aristotelian notion of revolution as a change in the constitution of the polity will be shown to provide us with a better starting point for any rigorous analysis of revolution, because it sharply separates the immediately relevant changes of political structure from the much broader contextual factors and conditions, some of which may be shown to be causally relevant by comparative analysis.

Three features of my definition require comment. The first is the absence of reference to violence. Violence does accompany such radical change, to a varying extent, and is often its most dramatic feature; but it should not be made its defining feature (Bienen 1968). Violence is endemic to virtually all types of political order without necessarily, or even usually, changing its structure. Therefore, recurrent typical patterns of violence that pertain to different types of political regimes (Gluckman 1965) must be kept distinct from the phenomenon of revolution, which I propose to characterize by its consequence—namely, the transformation of the polity. The way violence is relevant to the consequence of revolution is by the concentration and temporary monopolization of its legitimate use by the winners of the revolutionary power struggle, who can thereby bring it to an end. As early as 1948, Gerth and Mills understood Weber to have "rounded out" Marx's economic determinism by partial military determinism of social action. Yet, military sociology has to my knowledge spectacularly failed to systematically link the noted importance of military action for the outcome of revolutions to the changes in the military and political organization of respective societies. This will be illustrated in chapter 10, on the Mongol Revolution.

Meager results obtained after generations of positivistic research on "collective violence" (surveyed in Rule 1988) strongly suggest that we would do better to make the degree and significance of change, and not the magnitude of violence accompanying it, our defining criterion. Furthermore, we have recently witnessed a set of remarkably bloodless revolutions resulting from the collapse of communism in Central and Eastern Europe (M. Kennedy 1999).

Second, although this volume will end in the fourteenth century, my definition is broad enough to include, as well as the constitutional revolutions of the first decade of the twentieth century in Iran and the Ottoman Empire (Sohrabi 2011), cases of radical transformation through "constitutional" seizure of power and cases of "revolution through coup d'etat" (Janos 1964:134–35), typical of the century's second quarter in Italy and Germany, "velvet" or "negotiated revolutions" of its last quarter in Eastern Europe and South Africa (M. Kennedy 1999; Lawson 2005), and the Arab Revolution of 2011 (Arjomand 2014), so long as they involve significant change.[8] I hope to demonstrate this range in the epilogue. Furthermore, the definition leaves open the possibility that the revolutionary process may be initiated either from the top by the collapse of authority at the center or from the bottom by social and political oppositional action on the periphery. In other words, it can in principle accommodate both the older, society-centered notion of revolution as the uprising of the masses and the newer, statist notion of revolution as "state breakdown" (Goldstone 1991b).

Finally, I have defined revolution not only by its consequence—transformation of the political order—but also by its phenomenological coherence as a process or an extended event. Sociologists and political scientists have shown an obsession with the causes of revolution in general but have had no interest in periodization of particular revolutions as events. The result has been a gross neglect of the systematic treatment of revolutions as patterned sequences of events with precise beginnings and ends (Zimmermann 1983:407). Historians, by contrast, have naturally been concerned with periodization of particular revolutions but have rarely given the matter systematic and comparative attention. The periodization of revolution as a series of events with a beginning and an end and its conception as a process with a specific direction must go hand in hand in order to bring about the historicization of the conception of revolutionary process, which has never been done before.

This makes the conceptualization of revolution as an event a central theoretical task, essential for establishing *what* we want to explain. The exploration of the epistemological and methodological implications of "aggregating occurrences into conceptual events" (A. Abbott 1992:76) in the social sciences is recent. These implications are crucial for the study of revolution. As Motyl (1999:2) put it, "only through an act of conceptual will are such disparate real events roped together to become a 'revolution.'" By collocating a set of events as constituents of a revolution, we are already explaining the connection among them. An important contribution of the comparative historian may in fact be the presentation of a systematic rationale for these connections with the help of theory as attempted in the pages that follow.

This last feature of my definition has important analytical entailments. Revolution as an *explanandum* must be a coherent whole. "Now a thing is a whole," Aristotle tells us (*Poetics* 50b26; Ricoeur 1984–88:1.38), "if it has a beginning, a middle, and an end." As Paul Ricoeur comments aptly with regard to poetic composition (1984–88:1.39), the ideas of beginning, middle, and end are not taken from the experience of succession in any real action but are the effects of ordering. A revolution as a complex event has a beginning and an end, and further, "both the beginning and the end are part of the *explanandum*." What is to be explained is the *connection* among a set of events, the first and the last of which are connected as "end-points of a temporally extended change—as beginning and end of a temporal whole"

(Danto 1985:234–35). Periodization becomes indispensable because our *explanandum* depends on it.[9] The recasting, reorientation, and regrouping of facts and issues that are necessary for making revolutions intelligible as temporal wholes are important aspects of the theorist's construction of a revolution.

To give one example from chapter 8 below, no historian as far as I know has connected the murder of Caliph al-Walid in the Syrian desert in 744; the rebellion of the chiliastic palace guards in Hāshimiyya, Iraq, in 758–59; the rebellion of ʿAbd al-Jabbār, the first revolutionary chief of police and the governor of Khorasan (in northeastern Iran and Transoxania) in 760; and, finally, the rebellion of the early ʿAlid rival of the ʿAbbasid victors, Muhammad b. ʿAbdallāh b. al-Hasan, the Mahdi of the house of Muhammad in 762. The connection among these temporally and spatially separated events by mostly unconnected groups of historical actors is established by my conceptual reconstruction of the history of the complex of events during this period of nineteen years as "the ʿAbbasid Revolution: 744–63."

Periodization also entails historicizing the concept of the revolution as a process, which is done with the help of the contemporary theory of narrative. My theoretical model should present the process of revolution as a temporal whole both chronologically as an episode and logically as a structured configuration. The two aspects should be interwoven in order to historicize process as a general conceptual category built on the basis of historically specific instances. This would be tantamount to the analytical refiguration of the temporal experience of the revolutionary generation through what might be called "secondary narrativization" with the help of sociological theory (Ricoeur 1984–88:3.3). To do so, however, social theory faces the daunting task of extending the refiguration of temporal experience from individual to society. In refiguring the collective experience of time in the analytically posited event of revolution by means of secondary narrativization, the social theorist has to supply the sociological criteria of aggregation, elimination, and closure other than those implicit in the temporal experience of the diversity of geographically separated historical actors. Narratives of revolution by winners and losers in the revolutionary power struggle abound. These figurations of the revolutionary episode are, however, neither consistent with one another nor necessarily shared by the nonrevolutionaries who were significant historical actors. More fundamentally, individual narratives do not capture the conceptual interconnections that make revolution a coherent, extended event that separates a before and an after marked by a major change in the political order and/or its social base. In other words, the interconnection has to come from our sociological typology of revolution. The requisite coherence as a logical configuration must derive from a model or a typology that represents the dynamics of violent interaction among social forces within a crumbling societal structure of domination.

Conceptions of Revolution in the Ancient and Medieval World

Although I shall begin with the analysis of the rise of Sargon of Akkad as a revolution and speak of a subsequent cycle of revolutions in ancient Mesopotamia, there is no evidence of a Mesopotamian conception of revolution. Ancient Greek thinkers, by contrast, not only were familiar with the phenomenon of revolution but also wrote about it.

The oldest conception of revolution discussed in this study—that found in ancient Greece—was sharply focused on the politically pertinent structural factors and is therefore worth recovering as our point of departure. Plato, Aristotle, and Polybius shared a fundamentally political conception of revolution that related revolutionary change to certain inherent characteristics of political regimes. Revolution was a reversal of constitutions (*metabolé politeion*).[10] The likelihood and character of revolution therefore depended on the constitution of the polity in which it took place. Using this common concept, Plato and Aristotle offered important insights into the causation of revolution. According to Plato: "Is it not a simple fact that in any form of government revolution always starts from the outbreak of internal dissension in the ruling class? The constitution cannot be upset so long as that class is of one mind, however small it may be" (*Republic* 8.545; Plato 1941:262).

We can read Aristotle to be saying that proneness to revolution in a state, conceived as *metabolé tes politeias* (constitutional change), is due to the character and structural properties of political regimes. According to Aristotle, oligarchies and aristocracies are prone to revolution because of those whom they *exclude* from the political society. Impoverished members of the governing class become revolutionary leaders; the regime is undermined by persons who are wealthy but excluded from office; and sedition arises when the circle of government is too narrow and "the masses of a people consist of men animated by the conviction that they are as good as their masters in quality" (*Politics* 8.3; Aristotle 1962:221). From these considerations it would follow that the type of revolution to which oligarchies and aristocracies are prone is what I shall call *integrative revolution,* revolution that enlarges the political community, broadening the franchise and/or other political rights, notably access to power.[11]

Contrary to widespread prejudices, the Qur'an pays no attention to the organization of the state (Donner 1998). Nor does it contain any significant notion of political revolution. The political revolution in seventh-century Arabia was an indirect consequence of the rise of monotheism[12] and was therefore not seen as political. Nevertheless, an ancient notion of revolution as the transfer of world power or empire (*šolṭān*) from one nation to another, as elaborated in the book of Daniel and passed on to Western Christendom as *translatio imperii* (transfer of sovereignty),[13] is implicit in the Qur'an (3.134–35). This ancient conception came to the fore with Islam's social revolution in the mid-eighth century, now commonly called the 'Abbasid Revolution.[14] It was elaborated as the notion of *dawla*, the (divinely ordained) turn in power, whose original sense of rotation was to recede over the centuries until the word assumed the meaning of "the state." The term, however, can be translated as "revolution" without any violence to its original sense. When the ninth-century historian al-Ya'qubi (1960:2.393) spoke of "those who are knowledgeable about the revolution" (*ahl al-'ilm bi'l-dawla*), there was only one turn in power that could be so referred to. The change of dynasty in the mid-eighth century was thus seen as epochal by contemporaries. Indeed, it generated a remarkable adaptation of Sasanian political astrology that can be traced firmly to Māshā'allāh, the Jewish astrologer who advised Caliph al-Mansur, the consolidator of the 'Abbasid Revolution, on the time and location of the new City of Peace (*madinat al-salām*, Baghdad). In a passage that draws on the astrological works of Māshā'allāh and Abu Ma'shar and has remained virtually unknown, Ibn Abi Tāhir Tayfur (d. 893) saw the heavenly revolution of the stars replicated in a Great Revolution in the kingdom. Anticipating a similar transposition in Europe by centuries, he stated that the Great Conjunction of Saturn and Jupiter at the vernal equinox in 749 determined "the general revolution in religion and the state" (*al-inqilāb al-kulli fi'l-din wa'l-mulk*). Tayfur's political astrology was indeed accompanied by a moral theory of revolution as God's removal of powerful dynasties who had become oppressors. But Māshā'allāh and Tayfur, while producing a distinctive conception of revolution I have called "Persianate" (Arjomand 2012), did not generate an autonomous sociological theory of revolution. Theory came from Aristotle and was developed by Ibn Khaldun (Dale 2006).

In his commentary on Plato's *Republic*, the great Andalusian philosopher Abu'l-Walid Muhammad Ibn Rushd (Averroës) (d. 1198) discussed the Greek notion of revolutionary transformation as change in the constitution of the polity from one type to another and, when applied to the decay of regimes in Muslim Spain, as the lapse from timocracy to oligarchy and from democracy to tyranny (Averroës 1966:206–37). This was an attempt to shore up the Greek typology of political regimes and did not fit the Andalusian cases he had in mind. Theoretical innovation came with another thinker from the Maghreb, ʿAbd al-Rahmān Ibn Khaldun (d. 1406), who criticized Averroës precisely for not seeing that timocracy was a bad definition for the urbanized nobility of Muslim Spain, who, as a result of sedentarization, had lost the group solidarity on which honor is based (Khaldun, 1.143–44; trans. 1.275–76). Ibn Khaldun's theory of the cycles of rise, senility, and disintegration of dynastic states is well known in itself, though not its conscious Greek derivation. In fact, he explicitly discussed Aristotle's rhetoric and political science as the two branches of knowledge closest to his new positive science of history (Khaldun, 1.39–42; trans. 1.77–83; Mahdi 1957:125, 157; Dale 2006:435–38). As we shall see, it is as a good empirically minded Aristotelian that Ibn Khaldun explains cyclical change in terms of the structural properties of historical Muslim polities, which are grounded in a dual social organization. The social structure he portrays consists of urban centers of civilization and tribal peripheries. Its political order rests on two distinct elements: ruling authority (*mulk*) and the instrument for gaining it, which is group solidarity (*ʿasabiyya*). According to Ibn Khaldun, both these elements are generated in tribal societies but become separated with the complexity of civilization. Ruling authority is transferred to the urban centers, while group solidarity is sustained and reproduced only in the tribal periphery. A cyclical motion of rise and fall of tribally originating dynastic states is generated by the interaction between the centers of civilization, in which group solidarity is weakened, and the tribal societies of the periphery, where strong group solidarity is constantly reproduced. It is important to note that Ibn Khaldun's term that I have translated as "dynastic state" is none other than the abovementioned *dawla*, the term for revolution in the sense of "turn in power" that first gained currency in reference to the ʿAbbasid Revolution and later came to mean "the state" (whose turn in power was divinely ordained, the claim made by all states).

In Aristotelian terms, as explicated by Ibn Khaldun in the model to be discussed below, the properties of the regime are its "essential accident" that follow upon the type and are *not* external to it so as to count as its "causes" (Dale 2006:435). The modern literature on revolutions, by contrast, postulates causes and preconditions for revolution that pertain to the political structure as well as to the economic, social, and cultural structures or spheres of life. This mixing of the alleged economic, social, and political "causes" has resulted in much confusion, which can be clarified only by making a sharp distinction between the political factors, which are pertinent at the phenomenal level whose incidence defines revolution, and social, cultural, and economic factors that are external to the phenomenon of revolution itself but can account for and explain its causes. A variety of reductive underlying causes and preconditions are thus offered in explanations of revolution that are in fact interchangeable. To avoid confusion when adducing these causal factors, as I argued in the previous section, we must separate them from the definitional properties or necessary attributes that are entailed by and follow upon the *concept* of revolution. Such conceptual properties of revolution would indeed be its essential accidents in Aristotelian-Khaldunian terms as distinct from its causes. For instance, "state breakdown" cannot then be given as one of revolution's "causes," as is done by Goldstone and others. It is an essential accident or definitional attribute of the concept of revolution.

As we shall see presently, both the Aristotelian and the Khaldunian conceptions of revolution offer important insights that are incorporated into my typology.

Causes, Process, and Consequences of Revolutions Reconsidered

According to the architectonic conception outlined above, revolutions are a complex sequence of extended events separated from earlier events, from events before their *outbreak* (beginning). Their complexity can be described as a *process* (middle) that produces a distinct *outcome* (end). That outcome makes for the closure of revolution as an extended event or sequence.[15]

Redundant causality is a feature that explanations of revolutions share with those of many other social phenomena. In all such explanations, we need to separate the important and the trivial causes; and what is important or trivial depends entirely on one's definition of the object of explanation. As MacIver ([1942] 1964:149) put it, "the search for causes is the search for differences within comparable situations." A contrast space for comparable situations is therefore needed, based on actual as well as counterfactual "objectively possible" cases—that is, what happened as well as what could plausibly have happened. This contrast space should be built into the structure of the explanation in order to limit the range of *relevant* alternatives. In practice, it would consist of all historical cases to date that fall under the definition of revolution as realized cases of major transformations of the political order and its social base by mass mobilization. The definition itself, however, represents the common denominator of extended events we have constructed as logically configured temporal wholes that resemble one another, and therefore, it depends on the salient revolutions at the time of our theoretical initiative in the dialectic of the past and the future. The phenomenological coherence of revolutions as extended events has implications beyond what actually happened for the post hoc coherence attributed to them first by the historical actors in retrospect and then similarly by their historians. The presumption of the coherence of a revolution's narrative involves the making sense of a revolution by the historical actors as well as by the subsequent historians. This is the unavoidable entailment of the significance of revolutions as a component of their meaning in world history, which is inevitably ex post facto. It also means that my scheme is open-ended: a revolution of sufficient significance can happen tomorrow, adding a new realized case and thus changing the composition of the contrast space. This open-endedness is in line with the nature of historical knowledge and the construction of ideas in world history that I have touched upon.

Needless to say, the comparative spectrum or contrast space would have been very different if I had chosen "collective violence" as the historically invariant object of explanation (e.g., Gurr 1980). Pragmatic consideration, too, suggests the utility of a shift of focus away from violence to change, as it greatly expands the contrast/comparative space for what Pierce called abductive analysis as a step in theorizing (Tavory and Timmermans 2014).

Once revolutions are constructed as integral events with historical hindsight, they can be thus systematically compared. Comparisons are useful for establishing what the things compared have in common, and they are useful for bringing out the singular features that distinguish any one of the things compared from the others. Common patterns connecting the causes and consequences can be constructed as ideal types or models within a typology of revolutions. This leaves certain singular features of revolutions that are historically unique. What the comparative analysis can do here is to sharpen the distinctive outcomes of different historical revolutions—or cycles of revolution ideographically—that is, by contrasting their respective teleologies as instances of meaningful collective social action.

By opening up a new contrast space, each new revolution forces us to reread the past. The final success of the Communist Revolution in China thus changed the contrast space that was at the time dominated by the French and Russian Revolutions. The rereading of those earlier Great Revolutions was what Samuel Huntington (1968) did upon reflection on the Chinese Revolution led by Mao Tse-tung. Huntington thus produced a crude typology of revolution by noting a sharp contrast between the revolution in China, which he took as the prototype of the "Eastern" revolution, and the Western type familiar from the French and Russian cases: "In the Western revolution, political mobilization is the consequence of the collapse of the old regime; in the Eastern revolution, it is the cause of the destruction of the old regime" (Huntington 1968:267). Further: "In the Western revolution, the revolutionaries fight their way out of the capital to capture control of the countryside. In the Eastern revolution, they fight their way from the remote areas of the countryside and eventually capture control of the capital" (Huntington 1968:271).

Huntington contrasted this pattern of "Western revolution," corresponding to my Tocquevillian type, with that of "Eastern revolution," or the type of revolution I will call Khaldunian or neo-Khaldunian. In the latter type, the insurgent leaders "withdraw from central, urban areas of the country, establish a base area of control in a remote section, struggle to win support of the peasants through terror and propaganda, slowly expand the scope of their authority. . . . The origins of the revolt are lost in the obscurity of the jungle and the mountain. The end of the revolutionary process, on the other hand, can be precisely dated . . . by the final conquest by the revolutionaries of the capital of the regime" (Huntington 1968:270–71). This new type of revolution by design was perfected by Mao, who adopted the strategy of conducting a protracted military and political struggle from the countryside against the government in the cities in China (DeNardo 1985:25–31). Writing on the "laws of revolutionary war" in 1936, Mao substituted warfare from the countryside, to which the Communist Party had withdrawn in the Long March, for the revolutionary struggle. Mao merged the political work and the military work in winning over the masses. The Communist Party was to lead an agrarian revolution in which the peasantry replaced Marx's industrial proletariat (Mao 1970:415). Last but not least, he correctly predicted that it was "impossible for the Chinese Red Army to grow very rapidly or defeat its enemy quickly" (Mao 1970:416).

Charles Ragin's (1987) qualitative methodology led to approaching revolutions as emergent processes of multiple, interchangeable causes in varying conjunctures. He highlighted the multiple and conjunctural character of causality in historical and comparative sociology in general, but his conclusions discredited the prevalent approach in the sociology of revolution in particular. Causes of revolutions are multiple (either A or B can cause a revolution) and conjunctural (A can cause a revolution in combination with B but *not* with C). This means that the vain search for an invariant set of causes of revolution that has vitiated theories of revolution from Gottschalk (1944) to Skocpol (1979) is methodologically too crude (Ragin 1987:37–38) and should be given up. Similar methodological conclusions were reached by Andrew Abbott, who consonantly highlighted the order and sequence in the bundles of events that add up to the process called revolution. Abbott claimed to uncover a theoretical revolution that was very different from Collins's alleged Copernican paradigm shift. Speaking of the "exhaustion of our old paradigm," he hailed sequence analysis and event history analysis as especially fruitful for the study of revolution and as amounting to "a quiet revolution . . . underway in social sciences" (1995:93).

By foregrounding the consequences of revolution in my definition, I do not mean to reject causal analysis but only make it secondary. In fact, the structural typology used in this volume rests squarely on clustering causes in close connection with consequences, which vary according to a small number of ideal types. Invariant relations between a cluster of causes and a particular outcome can still be sought, however, but within different *types* of revolution and as a means of distinguishing between the types. They are useful for constructing a typology of revolution. His contribution to the alleged paradigm shift in macrohistory notwithstanding, Tilly (1993:5) concluded from his survey of European revolutions that different kinds of states produce different kinds of revolution: "revolutions are no longer what they were because states are no longer what they were." In one of his last papers, Tilly came to an appreciation of Aristotle's typology of governments for showing "regimes as having their own characteristic forms of contention and changes of regime as resulting largely from political contention" (Tilly 2005:425). To this late restatement of the Greek idea, we should add that different kinds of society and culture produce different kinds of revolution! There are different *types* of revolution, each type with a distinct cluster of causes and consequences punctuated by their narrative as extended events. This implies that it is pointless to seek an adequate causal analysis of revolutions without an accompanying typological one.

One important implication of the autonomy of the revolutionary process, which was implicit in the mid-twentieth-century conception of revolution as a process but has rarely been made explicit, is the *disjunction* between the consequences of revolution and the causes of its outbreak. The intervening factors are (*a*) the revolutionary power struggle and (*b*) the value-ideas drawn upon for postrevolutionary reconstruction, which sometimes take the form of ideologies.

Sudden outbreaks of revolution sharpen the disjunction between their causes and consequences. Some contemporary works in mathematical sociology explain the sudden outbreak of revolution—in other words, its beginning—in terms of the aggregation of heterogeneous preferences through interdependent decisions in collective acts (Granovetter 1978). Repression makes people falsify their political preferences in conformity with the status quo, but doubts raised about its effectiveness, especially by the outspoken behavior of a few, may induce many to cross the threshold to open rebellion in accordance with their true preferences (Kuran 1989). Timur Kuran (1992) further demonstrates that it is not possible to detect what Edwards (1927) called "preliminary" and "advanced" symptoms of revolution because of the way preferences are falsely expressed—and the more so the less democratic and open the regime. This explanation confirms the time-honored precept of raising the cost of being the first to protest openly (Rule 1988:29–30, 53), which informed Bacon's judgment on the expediency of swift military action at the inception of sedition.

The narrative of a revolution proper as an event must anyway begin with the moment of revolutionary liminality, the great opening for the freedom of action created by the disintegration of the political structure. Liminality means the removal of structural constraints upon human agency. It can, to varying degrees, be accompanied by a collective "sentiment of empowerment, which occurs in certain moments, transforms the group into a charismatic community, transforms, ultimately, social structure into agency" (Tiryakian 1995:274). The quest for meaning is built into human agency at this liminal stage and shapes the ends of revolutionary collective action—its teleology. Revolution marks a break with the past and a new beginning for intense vitality and activism but is marked by a political and conceptual struggle among contending forces. Teleology can explain the emergent properties of revolutions that derive from goal-directed social action in history and that can*not* be accounted for by reductive causality. It can address the issues of intentionality and agency in revolutionary action and thus capture the distinctive cultural creativity of each revolution (Sewell 1995).

The middle part of our narrative traces the process of revolution. Huntington (1968:270) has observed that the process of revolution also gives rise to the competitive mobilization of new groups by revolutionary contenders. Tilly and Rule (1965) have noted a corollary of this feature, namely, that the revolutionary process—or, more precisely, the power struggle among contenders—generates much more violence than the collapse of the old regime and the outbreak of the revolution (Rule 1988:177–78). Stinchcombe (1990) has focused on the differential instrumentality of crowds and bureaucratic organization and the increasing reliance on the latter in the process of institutional change after the outbreak of revolution. Last but not least, Furet (1981), focusing on the cultural aspect of the revolutionary process, has offered us a valuable analysis of the progressive autonomy of the revolutionary ideology—the emergence of Jacobinism—as an outcome of the revolutionary process in France. This autonomy in the developmental path of the value-ideas generated by a specific revolution is what I term its *teleology*.

The objective of the natural history approach had been the analytical delimitation of revolution as a temporal whole, an extended event or sequence, by setting its beginning, stages, and end. The newer approach to the revolutionary process adopted in this study, by contrast, tends to link the process to the *consequences* of revolutions. The concept of consequences brings us back from the realm of liminality in moments of enthusiasm into the structural constraints determining the process of institutionalization. Here the teleology of a revolution blends with the cultural, social, and political factors that are external to its value-ideas and their teleology. This study historicizes the consequences of different revolutions instead of deriving them abstractly as the end point of a general process. The idea of the mere end of an unhistoricized temporal sequence or, worse still, of the return to normalcy after the "fever" of revolution is over (Brinton [1938] 1965:16–17) is highly misleading because the body politic after the revolution does not have the same constitution as the one before. To be specific, Huntington's observation points to the enlargement of political community as a consequence of the process of revolutionary mobilization, Rule's and Tilly's to the concentration of power as a means of bringing the revolutionary struggle to an end, and Furet's to the generation of the autonomous myth of revolution that was to serve as the recipe for a long cycle of subsequent modern revolutions. What I add in historicizing the consequences of revolution is the outcome of the struggle for a new political order, which depends not only on the power coefficient of the contending groups and forces but also on what Weber called their ideal interest. The consequences of a revolution are thus not just a generic end state but the outcome of particular constitutional politics set in motion by each revolution.

Consequently, the model of process that shapes the logical configuration of my secondary narrativization of the revolutionary event has two foci. On the one side, it traces the course of competitive mobilization and the revolutionary power struggle that ends with the restructuring of the political community and the redistribution of power within it. On the other, it follows the process of institutionalization of competing principles of order that ends with the restructuring of the system of authority and its legal basis. This conception of process as constitutional politics makes possible the closure of my analysis of specific revolutions with reference to these two sets of end results. We can then proceed with comparisons and a causal explanation.

A Structural Typology of Revolutions: Explaining Common Patterns

To make significant comparisons and causal inferences, we need a comparative spectrum or contrast space. This comparative spectrum can be structured with the help of a small number of types. Causation and typology, etiology and taxonomy, are often treated as separable and separate. The two tasks, however, are intertwined, and the clarification of types is the prerequisite for analysis of causation (MacIver [1942] 1964:160, 367). Typology is one of the most important methodological tools of historical and comparative sociology—and, unfortunately, one that is badly neglected. An ideal type is a perfect heuristic device for modeling a sequence of events such as a revolution with a built-in explanation in terms of causes, intervening process, and outcome. What makes typology especially indispensable as an analytical device for the study of revolution is the multiple and conjunctural causation of revolution.

My typology is designed both to highlight the political nature of the phenomenon of revolution and to remedy the neglect of its outcomes. It is based on the two typical structural end results of revolution that have emerged from my historical survey: centralization of power, which is well known, as it is the key feature of the modern state, and enlargement of the political community, which is not widely recognized, as it typically occurs in premodern fragmented or segmentary polities. The present study will show that the construction of larger, more integrated communities or the enlargement of existing ones is the older and the more general of the two end results of revolution. The integrative dimension of revolution can be found not only in modern societies with centralized states but also in ancient and medieval societies without centralized states. In fact, it is in some of the important revolutions of the ancient and medieval world and in societies without centralized states that we can more clearly observe the relationship between revolution and integration, because it is not yet entangled with complicating features that stem from the relationship between revolution and centralization of power.

I will accordingly call this older, premodern, and more basic type of revolution type I, integrative revolution, and subdivide it into three ideal types or models, types I.1–3, which are designed to cover the range of variation in the relation between revolution and the enlargement of the political community: (1) the revolutionary construction of an integrated political community from segmentary tribal societies or self-contained city-states;

(2) the opening of oligarchies in the course of the expansion of city-states into empires; and (3) the integration achieved through the invasion of the center by a mobilized political island on the periphery. A fourth model will represent the newer and better-explored relationship between centralization of power and revolution in the modern world and constitute my second type of revolution (type II).

Integrative Revolution I.1: Constitutive Revolution

Radical change in the political order may result from the incongruence between cultural and political integration. This can arise in a culturally unified society where the structure of authority remains segmented—confined to tribes or city-states. The larger society is culturally unified while political authority is segmented, except under martial emergency, and political integration remains either intermittent, in the form of ad hoc confederations of tribes and city-states, or weak, based solely on networks of personal ties among patrons and clients across the segments (Balandier 1985:318–22). Such societies, including the "segmentary states" that are found to be prone to rebellions (Fallers 1968:80), can be restructured through revolution. The type of revolution that occurs in these societies is an integrative revolution that constitutes a new political order by concentrating coercive power into a permanent army and by institutionalizing central political authority and unifying administration, thus integrating the segments into a single political community. This ideal type will accordingly be called a "constitutive revolution." The first revolution in world history, the Akkadian Revolution in the second half of the second millennium BCE, belongs to this constitutive type.[16]

Integrative Revolution I.2: Aristotelian-Paretan Revolution

Aristotle's idea of integrative revolution in oligarchies can serve as the starting point for my second model. Among the moderns, Vilfredo Pareto's theory of revolution comes closest to Aristotle's idea.[17] Put simply, his theory is as follows: If access to the political class, the ruling elite, is blocked for energetic and resolute individuals, whom he called lions, from the lower classes, and if the ruling elite becomes weak and incapable of stern repression—because of an increase in the proportion of foxes to lions in its composition—a revolution is likely to occur (Pareto [1917–19] 1968:1555–56, no. 2227). In this situation, socially upwardly mobile individuals who are excluded from power become a revolutionary counter-elite that eventually seizes power and makes history the graveyard of yet another aristocracy (Pareto [1917–19] 1968:1304–5, nos. 2053–57).

Oligarchies are not the only kinds of political regimes whose capacity for incorporation is limited. Other personalistic, nonmobilizational regimes have the same property. In the twentieth century, we find a startling difference in the fragility of political regimes and their susceptibility to revolutions. Mobilization, partial and total, and pluralism, even when "limited," act as powerful antidotes to revolution (Linz 1975). By contrast, those regimes that remain personalistic despite some bureaucratization of administration—in terms of Linz's (1975:259–64) classifications of regimes, the "Caudillistic" (or "caciquistic") regimes of prerevolutionary Mexico and Nicaragua and the "Sultanistic" ("neo-patrimonial" in my [1988, 2014] terminology) regimes such as Iran under the last shah (1941–79), Ben ʿAli's Tunisia, and Mubarak's Egypt down to 2011—are found most prone to revolution.[18] In these regimes, too, the same set of causes and consequences of revolution obtains. The postrevolutionary regimes develop greater absorptive capacity by becoming, in Dahl's (1975:121) typification, either "competitive oligarch[ies]," as in Mexico, or "inclusive hegemonies," as in Russia, China, and Iran.[19] It is this greater absorptive capacity of the integrative revolution through the enlargement of the political community that accounts for what Tilly (2000:13–14) sees as the propensity of revolutions for democratization.

The Aristotelian-Paretan model can be applied to medieval and modern revolutions as well, but to do so we need to modify and extend it a little further. The condition for a revolution is that the counter-elite mobilizes a significant segment of society; if they seize power without doing so, we would have circulation of elites without revolution. The most important demand the counter-elites need to satisfy in order to mobilize their constituencies is the desire for incorporation into the political community, for citizenship, when the term applies. It should be noted in passing that the Aristotelian-Paretan type of revolution also fits the construction of alternative political communities by modern revolutions of national liberation and independence. In these cases, the counter-elite are the native aspirants to rule who mobilize a wide constituency on the promise of enfranchisement and incorporation into a new national political community. Our most interesting ancient case is perhaps the creation of alternative national political communities in the cycle of Roman revolutions.[20] In more general sociological terms, this type of integrative revolution aims at greater vertical integration of society. The upward social mobility and integration into the political class of the aspiring counter-elite as representatives of a rising class—in the Roman case, the equestrian order, or knights—enhance the vertical integration of society.

Integrative Revolution I.3: Khaldunian Revolution

Integrative revolutions can begin in the center, or they can begin in the periphery. The periphery of an empire is by definition loosely integrated politically but culturally oriented and fiscally linked to its center. The integration brought about by the takeover of the center by the periphery produces a distinct type of revolution, one that students of contemporary revolutions have often misconstrued as "peasant revolution." Medieval Islam offers us the possibility of a better understanding of this type of integrative revolution, which is brought about by nomads and not by peasants and which I propose to call Khaldunian. It is put forward as my third structural ideal type of integrative revolution.

Ibn Khaldun, as we have seen, offered as a structural precondition of dynastic change the endemic translocation of ruling authority and group solidarity between the periphery and the center in a dual social structure. He also paved the way for a theoretical move from dynastic change to revolution by considering the *superimposition* of new religiously (or, by modern extension, ideologically) based solidarity upon existing, tribal group solidarity (*ʿasabiyya*). A religious cause and movement, therefore, need group solidarity if they are to succeed: "Religious mission cannot materialize without group solidarity. This is so because any mass [political] undertaking by necessity requires group solidarity." The prophets and religious reformers who fail are precisely those who do *not* recognize the significance of group solidarity. Those who succeed are the ones who do (Khaldun, 1.168–71). Notable examples of the latter studied by Ibn Khaldun and considered in my forthcoming book, *Apocalypse and Social Revolution in Islam*, are two urban-educated religious reformers: the Almoravid leader Yahyā Ibn Yāsin (d. 1059) and the Almohad leader the Mahdi Ibn Tumart (d. 1130), whose movements in the Maghreb unified the tribes of the periphery and established puritanical empires of virtue in North Africa and Spain. Ibn Khaldun's idea is confirmed by recent sociological research that shows groups with high solidarity to have greater capability for mobilization than others (Oberschall 1978:306–9). Ibn Khaldun's model of revolutions from the periphery can therefore be slightly modified by making some admixture of preexisting solidarity (*ʿasabiyya*) and party discipline on the basis of religion—or a religious ideology or political religion in modern times—the functional equivalents required for revolutionary mobilization.

Ibn Khaldun brings in religion explicitly to explain the major cases of dynastic change, which approximate our modern concept of revolution. Revolutions can be said to occur when the movement that begins in the periphery and conquers the center is not merely tribal but motivated by a religious mission. Revolution, then, is a special case of cyclical dynastic change, one in which religion plays an important role. One of his relevant chapters is entitled "The [Dynastic] States with Broad Domination and Great Ruling Authority Have Their Origin in Religion, Be It Either Prophethood or a Calling to God" (Khaldun, 1.167). The revolt against the dynastic state begins in the remote periphery with the religious leaders who have mobilized solidary tribes. Their victory does not come suddenly but only after many indecisive battles until senility takes hold of the ruling dynasty, resulting in the weakening of its group solidarity and a sharp decline in its fiscal power.

These then are the essentials of the Khaldunian type of revolution. It begins in the periphery with a militarized solidary group that is united on the basis of a religious cause. The key factor for explaining the failure of the regime and the success of the insurgents is differential solidarity. The urban base of the regime lacks social cohesion while the already-strong group solidarity of the insurgents is strengthened by a unifying religious cause. The revolutionaries progress gradually with a series of attacks on governmental forces. The end comes after a long time with the military defeat of the dynasty and the capture of its capital and other major cities.

Does this not remind you of a major pattern of revolution in the twentieth century? Replace religion by political religion in the form of communist ideology, and the tribe by the party as the solidary group unified on its basis, and you have Huntington's abovementioned type of "Eastern revolution." My major medieval case of Khaldunian revolution, however, is the Eurasian revolution of Chinggis Khan, who unified the Turko-Mongolian tribes of the steppe on the periphery of the Muslim and Chinese empires to conquer both.

What is most interesting in this Khaldunian type of revolution is not new at all. In China, its prototypes account for state formation in northern China after the fall of the Tang dynasty. In the Muslim world, the ʿAbbasid revolutionary agents organized a clandestine religiopolitical revolutionary party on the basis of an Islamic mission to include the Muslims of the periphery. It comprised a mixture of tribal and settled groups in Khorasan, with fewer clandestine cells in Iraq and southern Iran; and it was the Khorasanian wing from the eastern periphery of the Umayyad Empire that was decisive for the military victory of the revolution (see ch. 8).

We could say, in the language of multiple and conjunctural causality, that a strong dose of either preexisting solidarity or party discipline, or both, in conjunction with either a religious mission or a revolutionary ideology (political religion), or both, will produce a Khaldunian revolution.

Type II: Tocquevillian Revolution

The Tocquevillian ideal type, based on his study of the Great French Revolution, is the one most familiar to us. There is no need of justification for relabeling it a "Western" type of revolution, as Huntington did. In this modern type of revolution, a centralized state is already in place. In fact, revolution takes the form of the disintegration of the authority of the state, resulting from weakened legitimacy and lack of commitment on the part of its upholders, and the collapse of the established political order at the center. As we shall see, most integrative revolutions also have centralization as a consequence of the termination of revolutionary power struggle. What is distinctive about my type II revolution is that centralization also appears as a *cause* of revolution.

Hannah Arendt ([1963] 1979:116) inferred, from the "amazing ease" with which those who make revolutions "pick up the power of a regime in plain disintegration," that revolutions "are the consequences but never the causes of the downfall of political authority." Arendt ([1963] 1979:260) adduced Tocqueville's observation in 1848 that the regime fell "before rather than beneath the blows of the victors, who were astonished at their triumph as were the vanquished at their defeat." The progressive sapping of authority of the old regime is central not only to Tocqueville's analysis of the French Revolution but also, on close reading, to Trotsky's analysis of the Russian Revolution (Stinchcombe 1978). Tocqueville showed how the growth of the centralized bureaucratic state dissolved the group solidarity necessary for routine concerted political action and thus caused periodic revolutionary explosions that paralyzed the state temporarily. He was also the first to point to the central paradox of the French Revolution: namely, that it made the absolutist state it wanted to destroy all the stronger. Weber predicted the same paradoxical result for the Bolshevik Revolution, and Jouvenel (1949) highlighted the concentration of power and the growth of centralized government as the general consequence of all revolutions in history. Centralization of the structure of authority was thus both the cause and the consequence of the revolution for Tocqueville.

However, the Tocquevillian model, too, is in need of elaboration, especially if we wish to apply it to premodern revolutions. I propose two modifications. The first is to replace the notion of the state by the structure of authority. With this modification, the crumbling of any structure of authority from within, if followed by its (re)centralization, can be considered a Tocquevillian revolution. In France, too, what preceded the revolution was a breakdown in the authority structure of the ancien régime, a composite and quite chaotic authority structure in which the absolutist state apparatus was superimposed upon the medieval *Ständesstaat*. Going further back in history as we are about to, we can recognize similar breakdowns in the authority structure of the city-state of Rome, owing to the strain of imperial expansion, and of the Umayyad Empire as a result both of military overextension and of the pressure of increasing conversion to Islam. Focusing on the structure of authority instead of the state enables us to consider religious, as well as political, structures of authority. In fact, the former becomes our primary focus of analysis in chapter 9, on the papal revolution of the eleventh and twelfth centuries in Europe, where integration was the result of the strengthening and centralization of hierocratic, in contrast to political, authority.

The second modification is focused on the consequences of the concentration of power in the state for its social foundations—namely, the social groups that are included in the political community. Tocqueville does mention the reaction of the French nobility against the growing power of the state which manifested itself in the aristocratic prerevolution of the *parlements*. But he does not have a systematic treatment of the revolutionary role of the groups that are dispossessed by the growing state. More recent neo-Marxian analyses of the state and revolution similarly neglect the considerable revolutionary role of *declining* classes and of solidary groups dispossessed by centralizing states or threatened by socioeconomic change. My own analysis of the impact of the state formation on Iranian society as a cause of the Islamic Revolution focused on the role of the adversely affected but solidary social groups, most notably the religious estate (Arjomand 1988).

The Analytical Relationship among the Ideal Types of Revolution

The second modification of the Tocquevillian model is particularly important in showing a common cause in the Tocquevillian and Aristotelian-Paretan types of revolution. Concentration of power in a centralized state reduces political participation and deprives many social groups of access to political power, thereby creating the potential for excluded counter-elites.

Pareto's notion of a revolutionary counter-elite implies their leadership in mass mobilization against a ruling elite maintained by the armed forces of the state. This allows us complete flexibility in assigning relative weights to state crisis and mass political mobilization. The conjuncture of these two factors has long been noted in the literature. Lenin considered it indispensable for the occurrence of revolutions (Hobsbawm 1986:19–20). The "crisis of the upper classes" was already identified as the cause of revolution by Plato; Lenin added the rebellion of the masses: "Only when the *'lower classes' do not want the old way*, and when the 'upper classes' *cannot carry on in the old way*—only then can revolution triumph" (as cited in Tucker 1969:150). There is also the additional requirement that aspiring elites lead the mass mobilization; these aspiring elites are much better described as "revolutionary counter-elites" in our Aristotelian-Paretan ideal type.

The common feature of the Tocquevillian and the Khaldunian types of revolution is the prior existence of a centralized authority structure. In modifying Pareto's idea of revolution, I suggested that the circulation of elites per se is not a revolution, but an ideology or a religious movement can help it become one. In a parallel way, it can be stated that the Khaldunian change of dynasties is not a revolution per se but can become one only through the implantation of a religious mission or, its modern equivalent, a political religion (Voegelin 1952). In these cases, it is religion or ideology that brings about the integrative expansion of the political community over and above the change of dynasty or the circulation of elites.

The difference between the Aristotelian-Paretan and Khaldunian types of integrative revolution is better conceived in terms of vertical, rather than horizontal, integration. The integration of the peoples of the periphery into societies of an ecumene through a common high culture or religion is horizontal integration, and the enlargement of political community through the empowerment of groups and individuals formerly excluded from the political class represents a vertical form of integration.

The society-centered, integrative Aristotelian-Paretan model and the state-centered Tocquevillian model are by no means mutually exclusive. Rather, they are complementary, as they capture different aspects of revolution that are often found together. One could even say that the integrative model makes possible a systematic treatment of "fraternity," the missing element in Tocqueville's otherwise-brilliant analysis of the tension between liberty and equality as inconsistent goals of modern revolutions. The importance of the quest for fraternity within an enlarged political community or, less idealistically, for a wider distribution of political rights through enfranchisement is proven not only by the revolutionary patterns of the ancient world but also by the quest for religious fellowship in the medieval world and by the nationalist, fascist, and Islamic revolutions of the nineteenth and twentieth centuries, all of which are motivated, to a significant degree, by the quest for imagined or real community on the basis of authenticity: the authenticity of blood, nationality, religion, or culture.

Furthermore, there can be considerable tension between the integrative and centralizing dimensions of revolutions highlighted by our two models. In fact, this tension is akin to the tension Tocqueville himself saw between liberty and equality as the two contradictory principles of revolution and underlies its paradoxical consequence. Borkenau (1937:67) saw the clash of the two forces depicted in our two models as "the law of twofold development of modern revolutions." He maintained that the tension would inevitably be resolved to the benefit of the forces of centralization, thereby explaining the abovementioned Tocquevillian paradox that was later generalized by Jouvenel.

More generally, more than one ideal type of revolution can be used to explain each case of revolution. Many of our cases are in fact mixed types. (See table 3 in the conclusion.)

Religion, Ideology, and the Motivation of Revolution

Religion and ideology can provide important sources of motivation to revolutionary action in integrative revolutions. In the Aristotelian-Paretan type of integrative revolution, for instance, success depends on the counter-elite's ability to generate a political motive for opposing the regime. This political motive can be combined with moral motives into an ideology. The oppositional ideology then reinforces the moral motives for denying the legitimacy of the established political order and for seeking to overthrow it. Once an oppositional ideology spreads, the moral motives make co-optation difficult, even if the regime is willing to broaden access to power during crisis. In the Khaldunian integrative revolution, reformist religion is necessary to supplement tribal solidarity and neutralize its segmental character. Thus, religion plays a critical role in the constitutional reconstruction resulting from the revolution. In the case of the Sasanian Revolution in Iran, Zoroastrian religion was a major constituent of the pan-Iranian imperial ideology of the revolution, while in the rise of Islam and the papal revolution, it was the substance of the revolution itself.[21]

Pareto, wanting to outdo the Marxists, often discounted ideology as a mere mask for the counter-elite's lust for power. But this misses the point. Religious propaganda, nationalism, and ideology are important because they constitute the crucial link between the revolutionary counter-elite and the constituencies they succeed in mobilizing.[22] This explains the fact, noted by Tocqueville (1955:13, 156) and even by Pareto himself ([1917–19] 1968:1301–3, nos. 2048–50), that the integrative dimension of modern revolutions makes them akin to the great religious movements of the past.

Religious motives, when and if they are found at the inception of revolutions, as was the case with the messianism of the failed Maccabean revolt,[23] the monotheism of Islam, and the struggle for the freedom of the church in the papal revolution, give a distinctive direction to a revolution's developmental path. This aspect by no means exhausts the subject, however. The study of revolution as meaningful social action also requires an examination of its source of motivation. To this enormously important subject I have devoted a companion volume (Arjomand, forthcoming) on the origins and development of political messianism in the Judaeo-Christian-Islamic tradition. It unearths the archetype of the modern myth of revolution with which I began this introduction.

Teleology of Revolutions and Their Significance

The disjunction between causes and consequences of revolution has other important implications. The preconditions and causes of a revolution do *not* determine its distinctive direction or its teleology and cannot predict its nongeneric consequences that account for its specific cultural significance. In this study, teleology will *not* be used in the strict Aristotelian sense but rather as a term denoting the directionality of revolution.

What is not captured by my structural ideal types is the contribution of religion and ideology to the teleology of revolutions. It is possible to have revolutions whose outcome is generic but which lack any distinctive teleology. In such cases, the outcome—radical change in the political order—is due entirely to the unintended consequences of the revolutionary process to which our structural typology is applicable. In other cases when it applies, however, teleology can be thought of as the distinctive direction of a revolution, its intended or intentionally prefigured consequences.

I have argued (1986) that ideologies, as distinct from the loss of legitimacy and moral indignation, cannot account for the collapse of the established political order to any significant degree. But the value-ideas that form their normative foundation and are progressively defined and formulated during the revolutionary process *do* shape the political order installed by the revolution to a significant extent. Eisenstadt is one of the very few students of the Great Revolutions to approach them both typologically and from the viewpoint of their consequences. Observing that the Great Revolutions have occurred only in "imperial" and "imperial-feudal" societies, he offers us a useful set of sociological conditions for their occurrence that can be interpreted as conditions for their transformative impact—that is, for determining the likelihood that major institutional change will result from the breakdown of the state or system of authority. At the cultural level, he points to the tension between the mundane and the transcendental realms found in the civilizations built around the world religions of salvation. At the structural level, he mentions the existence of distinct centers continuously penetrating the periphery, the existence of distinct cultural and religious collectivities and institutions, and, above all, the existence of autonomous social strata—primary and secondary elites—capable of acting independently from one another. These cultural and structural factors together make for the coalescence of protest movements, institution-building ventures, and the ideological articulation that is necessary if the breakdown of central authority is to result in lasting institutional change and restructuring (Eisenstadt 1978:esp. 245–49; 2006). In other words, the conditions that Eisenstadt specifies for the Great Revolutions really are the sort of conditions that determine whether a revolution is teleological in my sense—that is, whether or not, in the turnover of power, a set of value-ideas finds effective social bearers to constitute the telos of the revolution. Only when such conditions are satisfied can we speak of the teleology of a revolution as partially intended consequences, prefigured in the religious ideas or political myths of the contenders in the revolutionary power struggle that become embodied in enduring institutions in the course of political reconstruction under the contingent constraints of revolutionary power struggle.

Those who overthrow a regime at an opportune moment have moral and material motives for doing so. They may be motivated by material interests or by normative principles, value-ideas, or by both. Usually, by interweaving the two, they enter the revolutionary process with a project, or soon develop one. If successful, their project can explain certain consequences of the revolution that correspond to their intentions. As different actors have different and often contradictory projects, however, the revolutionary process of aggregation also has unintended consequences of the kind built into my typology. But the value-ideas of the victors, and occasionally those of the vanquished too, can determine the direction of institutional change that the process produces—that is, the teleology of the revolution.

The value-ideas that constitute the telos of a revolution can be progressively articulated by the historical actors into an ideology that emerges in the course of the revolution but survives it as an autonomous cultural form. This autonomous cultural form is the collective representation of that revolution and therefore the vehicle of its cultural significance in subsequent history. The democratic revolution in Athens established a blueprint for government that became the project of the revolutionary parties in the Greek city-states during the Peloponnesian War, as did the life and deeds of Muhammad for the ʿAbbasid and subsequent revolutions in Islamic history.

As we have seen in the above discussion of the modern myth of revolution, only in modern times does the idea of revolution itself become a cause of revolution. Only then do we find the autonomous idea of revolution and ideologies derived from it going hand in hand with a new philosophy of history that considers revolution a hallmark of the forward march of progress. The teleology of our premodern revolutions, by contrast, is motivated by religious and cultural beliefs among which the notions of politics and of revolution itself are heteronomous. As we shall see, millennial beliefs, astral determination of the rise and fall of empires, and the idea of the freedom of the church from earthly powers have been the major religious and cultural beliefs that have brought about revolutionary change in the political order in the ancient and medieval world.

In studying the teleology and the cultural significance of revolutions, comparisons also serve an important purpose. Different institutional arrangements can be meaningfully compared as solutions to the same set of problems (McDaniel 1978). To give a grandiose example, Max Weber compared the institution of the world religions as different solutions to the problem of meaning and the quest for salvation. The institutionalization of the basic value-ideas of different revolutions can similarly be compared as different answers to the common question of right order. Revolutions are moments of freedom and agency when the possibility of a radical break with the past is real. The realization of this freedom can take different directions, and this can be shown only by comparing concrete historical cases. The purpose of such comparisons is to comprehend how the "laws of freedom," to use a Kantian term, or the ends of collective agency, to use my own, can be differently constituted as the moral principles for the construction of a new political order in different revolutions whose success or failure depends on the contingencies of the revolutionary power struggle.

Last but not least, we can meaningfully contrast the cultural significance of specific revolutions and their latecomer epigone in the cycle. Such contrasts are our only means for the cognitive appropriation of world history in its uniqueness. In fact, what forces us to reopen the book of history and reread it anachronistically is precisely the significance in world history of revolution in the modern sense of major transformation. Our approach to the analysis of the structure of meaning supplies the institutional underpinning that perpetuates the value-ideas through embodiment in institutions set up to defend them as their vested interests. Institutional underpinning of value-ideas thus endows world history with meaning and significance. Among other things, it immunizes civilizational analysis (Arjomand and Tiryakian 2004) against culturalist misinterpretations as well as unwarranted retrojection of modernization theory.

The revolution of the "True [Legitimate] King" in Akkad, who was soon to be transformed into the King of the Four Quarters, thus established the value-idea of universal/imperial monarchy. The argument can be made that the highly distinctive axial breakthrough in ancient Greece was the this-worldly discovery of "the political" (Raaflaub 2005). The Cleisthenian Revolution elaborated the political into a constitutional form of the rule of law (as against government by men) and achieved the institutionalization of democracy as a universalizable value-idea. The Roman revolutions universalized the value-idea of citizenship while incorporating it into that of imperial monarchy, while the Sasanian Revolution in ancient Persia elaborated the idea of universal monarch into the king of kings of Iran and Non-Iran and the emperor of the center and the periphery of an aristocratic empire. The next two revolutions that I discuss, in which religion was the autonomous factor and the political was the heteronomous factor, bridge the ancient and the medieval world, as they do the transcendent and the immanent. But as they both occurred in the context of ancient civilizations, their supreme value-idea of a transcendent God (the Qur'an's "King of the Heavens and the Earth") blended with the Persian imperial monarch as the king of kings. The Gregorian Revolution further institutionalized the spiritual sword of early Christianity, transforming it into the medieval Catholic Church. Chinggis Khan's revolution finally appropriated the blended value-idea of Persian and Chinese universal monarchy for his nomadic patrimonial empire as the world-conquering Lord of Auspicious Conjunction (*sāheb qerān*), while setting in motion a long-sustained intercivilizational encounter between the Chinese and the Islamicate civilizations.

ONE

The Akkadian Constitutive Revolution and the Establishment of Universal Monarchy in Mesopotamia

Revolution, defined as structural transformation that is outstanding because of the significance of its consequences in world history, though a phenomenon of infrequent occurrence, is nevertheless as old as civilization. According to this definition, the rise of Sargon of Akkad and the unification of the parochial city-states of Mesopotamia around 2340 BCE constitute the first documented revolution in world history. Our information about this momentous event at the dawn of the historical age is extremely scant and fragmentary. The dire necessity of making do with bare facts, however, can be turned into an advantage. Rich documentation often induces historians to compile an infinitely regressive list of causes of revolutions which matter very little, given the multiple and conjunctural nature of the causality involved. Lack of information on the specific antecedents upon which Sargon's success was contingent may in fact be a blessing, as it eliminates such a distraction. By precluding a detailed causal analysis, the documents force us to focus our attention on the consequences of revolution as an abrupt change in the structure of political power that opened a new developmental path in world history. The Akkadian Revolution stands out in its basic outlines as an integrative revolution that broke down the insular barriers of the local Mesopotamian temple polities and unified them into a much larger political community, perhaps an empire, on the basis of the novel idea of universal monarchy. It was a constitutive revolution that, to an unprecedented extent, concentrated power in Mesopotamia in a newly founded (imperial) center, Agade.

Political Structure of Mesopotamian City-States and Their Common Culture

In the mid-third millennium BCE, southern Mesopotamia (Sumer) consisted of a number of contiguous agrarian city-states on the plain between the rivers Tigris and Euphrates. Land was irrigated by a network of canals from the rivers and their tributaries. Each city-state was a single temple community. The god of the city-state was its proprietor. The capital city and its surroundings were the exclusive domain of the god's family, while junior gods owned smaller domains around towns and villages (Jacobsen 1976:81–84). An official called *ensi* ruled the city-state as the steward and representative of its god.[1] However, Sumer was a culturally integrated society; the gods of the city-states were all united under the overlordship of the god of Nippur, Enlil (god of storm), as the paterfamilias of an extended divine clan (Frankfort 1951; Steinkeller 1992).

No natural barriers defended Mesopotamia from invaders; and common dependence on the same source of water locked the cities in continuous struggle over irrigation. It is reasonable to attribute the emergence of kingship to these ecological conditions. With the increased use of metal in warfare, kingship stabilized itself in Sumer by superimposing military relationships upon the religiopolitical order of the temple communities (McNeill 1963:56–58). Presumably owing to its origin in military emergency, the office of the king had a limited tenure, being in principle revertible to the assembly of elders (Jacobsen 1943; Frankfort 1951:68–70), and the king held a secular title, *lugal*, which meant "great man" and also "owner." At the same time, the ownership of the city-states by the extended families of gods clearly implied that the borders between them were divinely sanctioned, making territorial expansion virtually impossible despite endemic intercity warfare (Steinkeller 1992). Given these features of the Sumerian culture, kingship remained a problematical institution and failed to become an instrument of unity (Frankfort 1951:70).

The cities of northern Mesopotamia (Akkad) had a different political system. Though pervaded by the influence of Sumerian culture, the temple played a more restricted role in socioeconomic life, and secular kingship was much more powerful and authoritarian. As a long-term consequence of the domination of the south by the northern city of Kish (2700–2600 BCE), the northern conception of kingship began to have an impact in the south, where several rulers are known to have assumed the title *lugal Kish* (king of Kish), very probably as a generic term for a new type of hegemonic kingship (Steinkeller 1993:120). The practice of hegemonic kingship grew as Uruk replaced Ur as the dominant southern city and culminated in the reign of Lugalzagesi, which marks the first step in the transition to empire. Several Uruk rulers used the title *lugal kalam-ma* (king of the Land). Nevertheless, they emphasized that they held two separate kingships—of Uruk and of Ur (Steinkeller 1993:129). The unification of the south under Lugalzagesi, the *ensi* of the city of Umma, who later became the king of Uruk, though a dramatic break with the past in practice, did not remove the ideological barriers to empire. This was to be done by a northern upstart, Sargon.

While Lugalzagesi was nurturing expansionist designs in Umma, Urukagina, the *ensi* of the neighboring city of Girsu, emerged as an upholder of the Sumerian theocratic political tradition (Frankfort 1951:72; Westenholz 1993:164). Like other local rulers, he was defeated by Lugalzagesi. The latter became the king of Uruk and claimed to have been legitimized by the patriarch of gods, Enlil, as the "king of the Land." Lugalzagesi further asserted that Enlil had rendered the foreign lands subject at his feet from the rising to the setting sun (Gadd 1971b:420–21). Nevertheless, his violation of the territorial integrity of the city-states counted against him. Though victorious, he was still denounced as follows: "Offense there was none in Urukagina, king of Girsu, but for Lugalzagesi, governor of Umma, may his goddess Nisaba make him carry his sin upon his neck" (cited in Gadd 1971a:143). She did, but only after he had reigned for twenty-five years. Further, though Lugalzagesi paid for his sin, the man who made him pay was but a holier sinner. History was for Sargon as tradition was against him.

The independent city-states of the third millennium BCE were nevertheless religioculturally unified. The standardization of writing and the numerical system and the technical repertory of material culture facilitated the prevalence of a common culture in the land between the two rivers. A similar standardization of the god lists of the city-states into a unified and hierarchical pantheon completed Mesopotamian cultural unity at the highest symbolic level. Mesopotamian city-states constituted an interacting "peer polity" system that consolidated this cultural unity by generating distinctive institutional homologies (Renfrew 1986). The formation of pan-Mesopotamian cultural institutions thus generated the ideal of unified government embodied in a universal monarch. "The absence of such a political entity," as Yoffee (2005:56) puts it, "did not preclude the conception that there should be a political domain to match and concretize the cultural ideal of a single Mesopotamian political system." The cultural unification of Mesopotamia in the third millennium BCE must therefore be considered the precondition sine qua non of the political unification brought about by the first revolution in world history—namely, that of Sargon of Kish.

The fundamental precondition of the Akkadian constitutive revolution was thus the lack of congruence between the Mesopotamian political order and its social and cultural foundations. The problem of effective government was at the core of this as of all subsequent revolutions. The political order—the system of autonomous petty city-states with its parochial theocratic authority structure and problematic, weakly legitimated kingship—was inadequate for Mesopotamia as a culturally homogeneous unit with economically interdependent irrigation networks and developed intercity trade. Religious sanctification of the borders of the god-owned cities made the system stable but also plagued it with warfare arising from endemic conflict over the control of water. Imperial kingship instituted by Sargon's revolution was an effective solution to the chronic political problem of the Sumerian city-states. In other words, unification of government through the enhancement of the authority of the hegemonic king was a solution to endemic conflict among the agrarian, interdependent city-states. The immediately pertinent precondition of this political unification was the religious and cultural homogeneity of Mesopotamia; the chief obstacle to it was the divine ownership of the city-states and its sanctification of city borders. This obstacle to political unity was overcome by the idea of universal monarchy and its subsequent institutionalization.

Revolutionary Unification of Mesopotamia and Transition to Empire

According to legend, Sargon was the unwanted son of a priestess by a wandering father and was found in a basket in a river by a palm gardener, who raised him and taught him the same profession. He became the cupbearer of the king of Kish, Ur-Zababa, but refused to carry out the king's sacrilegious order to "change the drink offering of E-sagila." Divine favor was consequently transferred from the offending king of Kish to his cupbearer, who is referred to in the Sumerian Sargon legend as "Sargon, chosen of the gods" (cited in Cooper 1993:18). With this divine sanction, Sargon defected to found his own capital city of Agade. With the foundation of his new city, Sargon assumed the name "True [Legitimate] King" (*sharru-kin* = Sargon) (Gadd 1971b:420).[2]

Sargon's unification of Mesopotamia was in no sense a conquest by foreigners or members of a different race (Jacobsen 1939). What is true is that the northern city of Kish was on the periphery of the Mesopotamian civilized universe, and it is reasonable to assume that the city of Agade, which has not yet been discovered, was even more so. It is therefore correct to state that "the Akkadians were in a favorable position to unite barbarian prowess with civilized technique to form a powerful military force; and in fact, Sargon was only one of the earliest of a long line of Lords Marchers who created empires by successfully exploiting a similarly strategic position on the frontier between civilization and barbarism" (McNeill 1963:61). This fact makes Sargon's conquests the first instance of a gradually progressing revolution which deliberately starts from the periphery but is constantly oriented toward the center of society.

The rise of Sargon was slow, and the unfolding of the Akkadian Revolution, gradual. While Lugalzagesi was building his empire in the south, Sargon was gradually gaining ascendance in the north. Sargon did not overthrow Ur-Zababa, after whom five more reigns in the same dynasty are recorded. This very number, however, indicates the instability that must have accompanied the rise of Sargon. Be that as it may, Sargon's power grew and he sought recognition from Lugalzagesi. Messengers were exchanged between them, but Lugalzagesi would not accept Sargon's overweening demands. Sargon stormed the city of Uruk and defeated its military commander, who was reportedly aided by the forces of fifty town-governors, before Lugalzagesi himself reached the battlefield to suffer the same fate. Sargon then completed the unification of the north and the south with the conquests of Ur, Lagash, and, finally, Umma. Another inscription records that he won thirty-four battles, as a result of which the Persian Gulf region was now in his power. He thus unified the north and the south into an empire ruled from his new capital, Agade. Though political unification stopped at the borders of "the Land"—that is, the civilized world between the two rivers—territorial expansion did not. After the unification of Mesopotamia, military mobilization was harnessed for imperial expansion. Sargon conquered the foreign land of the northwest, reaching as far north as Anatolia, though probably not as far south as Syria as claimed by the legend, and completing the circle with the conquest of Elam, an area on the eastern and southeastern periphery that had been penetrated by the Uruk expansion (Liverani 1993:53–54; Michalowski 1993:79–84; Steinkeller 1993:110–16). Sargon's instrument was the largest standing army ever assembled; with his retinue and army, "5400 men ate bread daily before him" (Gadd 1971b:424).

Sargon's firm orientation toward central Mesopotamian tradition is evident throughout the war of unification. After the conquest of Uruk, Sargon captured Lugalzagesi and brought him in a yoke to the gate of Enlil at Nippur as a trophy to the national god. The former king was thus shown to have forfeited Enlil's mandate to rule to Sargon, his new representative on earth as *ensi-gal Enlil* (Jacobsen 1939). After the conquest of Umma, Lugalzagesi, the *ensi* of Umma, and probably other captured local governors were led in triumph to mark the unification of Mesopotamia (Gadd 1971b:420–22). Southern city-states were turned into provinces but retained much of their independence. Sargon upheld the religion and culture of the fallen cities and enhanced the cultural homogeneity of Mesopotamia by introducing a uniform calendar (Frankfort 1951). Sargon's campaigns thus entailed no mere subjugation of Sumer by brute force. They were his main instrument for a constitutive revolution that integrated the hitherto-fragmented Mesopotamian political community under a single imperial monarchy.

Sargon's integrative revolution was not merely extensive but also had an intensive aspect. He made a bid for the loyalty of the lower classes by enhancing their legal rights. He changed the formula for oaths; the king's name could be invoked alongside the gods. This made the king the patron of all who swore by his name and made it possible for the common people—those without a patron to "overshadow" them—to find satisfaction in court for the first time (Frankfort 1951).

Mesopotamian Value-Ideas and the Ideology of the Akkadian Revolution

The cornerstone of the ideology of the Akkadian Revolution was the idea of universal monarchy. According to this ideology, the ruler was the charismatic center of a universal society. Sargon clearly claimed divine election and made "True King" his epithet. His rule was in accordance with the just command of the gods and was legally sanctioned by them. Using technical legal terms, Sargon's victory over Lugalzagesi was described as Enlil's "judgment" upon Sargon's law case (Jacobsen 1976:86). Sargon also appropriated the office of the high priestess of Nanna at Ur, establishing a tradition that was continued for centuries by the ruling kings of Sumer (Michalowski 1987). Last but not least, he called himself "he who rules the Four Quarters" (Frankfort 1948:228). His grandson and most important successor Naram-Sin made this phrase into the enduring title of King of the Four Quarters (*shar kibratim arba'im*). The long, baroque string of epithets of the pre-Sargonic kings was replaced by the terse regal titles of the dynasty of Agade that denoted sovereignty over the four quarters of the universe (Seux 1967:11nn3–4, 305–7).[3]

The notion of universal kingship was conjoint with that of a universal political community. "The Land" already connoted such universality. It was reinforced by the idea of "the totality" (*kishshatu*).[4] To this end, Sargon assumed the title of king of the Totality (*sharr kishshati*) (Seux 1967:308n233). The new political community constructed by the Akkadian Revolution was the whole land, constituting the totality that comprised the four quarters of the civilized universe.

Another element of the Sargonic ideology was the justification for revolutionary change of dynastic rule. Though heteronomous, this implicit idea of revolution was not unimportant. The old idea of kingship as a temporary office, *bala*, was modified into a conception of legitimate dynastic rule of one city over the whole of Mesopotamia. The gods granted kingship to one city and its god for a time and then transferred it to another city and god. The dominion of Akkad was thus legitimated as "the term (*bala*) of Inanna [its goddess]" (Jacobsen 1943:167). The overthrow of an established dynasty was thus justified as the judgment of the assembly of gods upon the doomed imperial city whose god's mandate to rule had expired (Jacobsen 1976:87–91). Like other elements of the Sargonic heritage, this theory of the divine shift of sovereignty from one dynasty to another very likely was elaborated during the Third Dynasty of Ur, at the end of the third millennium, when the lament known as the "Curse of Agade" tells us that because of the sins of Naram-Sin in Nippur (the city of Enlil, the god who had killed Kish like the "Bull of Heaven" and given kingship to Sargon), "political legitimacy was removed from Agade." The great gods then "direct[ed] their face to the city [and] curse[d] Agade with a baleful curse" (Pritchard 1955:646–51 [lines 2–6], 142–47, 222–23; Cooper 1993:17).

Consequences and Significance of the Akkadian Revolution

Sargonic contemporary propaganda and later, anachronistic legends are inextricably interwoven in the ancient and modern historiography of Akkad as "the first universal empire" (Michalowski 1993:69). Even though the universal empire in fact collapsed after three generations, the idea it had realized was perpetuated as the core of Mesopotamian historical memory by imperial scribes' celebration of the exploits of the Akkadian dynasty (Yoffee 2005:144). If this concord across time needed reinforcement, curious attestation to the impact of the Akkadian Revolution is provided by the prominent place of Sargon in the Babylonian science of divination. Signs of divine determination of worldly affairs that diviners claimed to read upon the liver and other organs of sheep include a large number of omens relating to Sargon—for example, "omen of Sargon who became the master of the land" (Gadd 1971b:423–24). The perpetuated prominence of Sargon as the recipient of divine favor cannot be accidental. It cannot be attributed solely to the propaganda of his successors and must surely attest to the revolutionary legitimacy of the True King as the divine instrument of unification of the Mesopotamian city-states, as the charismatic leader, in our terminology, of the first documented constitutive revolution in world history.

The consequences of the Akkadian Revolution establish its world-historical significance. The most important of these has already been mentioned. The Akkadian Revolution marked an important step in the expansion of civilization: "The sociological barrier which had hitherto restricted civilized life to communities organized and led by priesthoods was for the first time transcended" (McNeill 1963:63). This was done by the institution of universal monarchy. The title King of the Four Quarters was assumed by the next unifier of Mesopotamia in the twenty-second century BCE, Shulği, and by subsequent claimants to universal monarchy and empire builders. Sargon II of Assyria (722–705 BCE) assumed it together with the very name True King. Thus, the idea of universal monarchy, instituted by the Akkadian ideological revolution and publicized through a program of inscribed monuments (Cooper 1990), time and again acted as the instrument for the reconstruction of a unified political community (Cooper 1993; Liverani 1993:48–51).

A second consequence, perhaps equally important, was the concentration of power in the hands of the ruler. Sargon's presumably armed retinue of 5,400 represented the greatest concentration of manpower recorded up until then. The military and administrative organizations of the Sargonic empire were closely interlinked (Foster 1993:26–28). Sargon founded a new city for the central, imperial administration in order to detach his men from local ties and prevent them from putting down roots in existing city-states. He also appointed them as royal officials alongside local rulers of the conquered city-states, putting them in charge not only of collecting food and other materials for his army but also of "breaking down the boundaries between the city-states" (Yoffee 2005:142). The Akkadian regime was sustained by a militaristic culture and heroic ideology that were in sharp contrast to the orderly nomocratic culture of Sumer. The Sargonic administrative system was based on a highly *personal* principle of loyalty. The surviving letters of the kings and imperial elite to local officials demonstrate a new patrimonial style of centralized administration in the unified empire (Westenholz 1993).

As the ensuing pages will demonstrate, all subsequent revolutions share at least one of these two outcomes with the Akkadian Revolution: the enlargement of the political community and the concentration of power in the government. Furthermore, like most subsequent revolutions, the Akkadian Revolution was incomplete and set in motion a cycle of revolutions to overcome reversals and amplify the two abovementioned consequences.

Sargon's integrative revolution was not entirely successful. Widespread local rebellions probably occurred at the end of his own reign and certainly greeted all his successors upon ascension to the throne. Centrifugal tendencies and parochial loyalties survived and destroyed the empire after the thirty-seven-year reign of Naram-Sin. The centralization of power under Sargon was crude and impermanent. It was not until Naram-Sin replaced the local rulers by royal appointees chosen from among his own kinsmen and styled "slaves of the king" and created Crown land for distribution among the officials in exchange for services that administrative centralization became appreciable (Frankfort 1951:74; Steinkeller 1992). Furthermore, definitive administrative centralization in Mesopotamia did not occur until the next integrative revolution, which established the empire of the Third Dynasty of Ur (2112–2004 BCE). It was the second ruler of that dynasty and its true empire builder, Shulği, who created a standing army, a unified bureaucratic system, and a scribal school for training bureaucrats and revived the policy of assigning newly created Crown land in exchange for services. This centralization of power was accompanied by a radical reform of the writing system, the introduction of a new calendar and a new accounting system, and the reorganization of weights and measures (Steinkeller 1987:20–21; Yoffee 2005:144–47).

Nor were the ideological foundations of Sargon's universal monarchy entirely solid. It was left to Naram-Sin to assume the title King of the Four Quarters and, further, to claim divinity. He became god of Agade upon the request of its citizens to the great gods. His officials gave their children names that included the king's name as a divine element (Michalowski 1987). Nevertheless, the ideological consolidation resulting from Naram-Sin's deification was somewhat inconsistent, as it identified him with a particular city. It was Shulği, the next unifier of Mesopotamia some two centuries later, who completed the ideological consolidation of universal monarchy in Mesopotamia by his more universalistic deification as god of the Land (*dingir kalam-ma*) (Steinkeller 1987:20; 1992). Officials, including those from the middle and lower echelons, changed their own names to include the king's name as a divine element. The cult of divine kings, living and deceased, became widespread. As Michalowski (1987:56) puts it, "the new concept of divine kingship, which began with Naram-Sin but which acquired new ideological features under Shulği and his successors, was created in order to provide a broader vision of societal center, one which overcame localized forms which had been anchored in the city, the temple, and the city ruler." The Sargonic ideological revolution was now completed, and universal monarchy was institutionalized by a cycle of revolutions in Mesopotamia.

Note that the consequences of the Akkadian and the Third Dynasty of Ur revolutions were brought about not by the founders but by the consolidators of the respective monarchies, a fact that strongly argues for the disjunction between the causes and outcomes of revolutions and for the independence of their teleology from the violence generated in their process.[5]

Dynastic Cycles and the Emergence of a New Revolutionary Pattern in Ancient Mesopotamia

Under the socioeconomic conditions of the ancient world, military and administrative centralization was possible to achieve but impossible to sustain for long—hence the cycle of Mesopotamian revolutions creating a succession of centralized empires that disintegrated within a few generations. With the definitive bureaucratic centralization and ideological consolidation of divine monarchy in the Third Dynasty of Ur state, there came into being a blueprint for imperial state formation. This dynasty, too, was short-lived, like the Akkadian one, but its institutional paradigm survived its collapse and guided the teleology of the cycle of later Mesopotamian revolutions, beginning with the Isin dynasty, which followed the house of Ur (Michalowski 1987:57), through the rise of the Babylonian Empire, which was created by the Amorites from the periphery of the Syrian desert under Hammurabi (1792–1750 BCE), to the rise of the Assyrian Empire under Sargon II in the eighth century BCE (Oppenheim 1964:52; Mann 1986:1.ch. 5).

The rise of the Old Babylonian Empire under Hammurabi is particularly important in the cycle of Mesopotamian integrative revolutions not only historically but also from the viewpoint of my typology. It did have the feature of concentration of power, which was accompanied by obvious legal consolidation, as demonstrated by the Law Code of Hammurabi. Furthermore, it was a typologically interesting instance of a revolution beginning on the periphery of a disintegrating empire.

Lugalzagesi, Sargon's predecessor and rival in empire building, unified Mesopotamia from the south, which was at the center and not on the periphery, as the founders of the Third Dynasty of Ur were to do two centuries later. As a revolution beginning in the periphery but with a firm orientation toward the cultural center, the rise of Akkad shares a common feature with the Khaldunian type of revolution. Although there is indirect evidence to suggest that the Gutians, who overthrew the Akkadian empire, were nomads, it is not until the kings of Larsa, who bore the additional title of chiefs of the Amorites (*rabi'in Amurrim*) after 2025 BCE, that we have firm historical evidence for the existence of nomadic pastoralism on the fringes of Mesopotamian urban society (Rowton 1973b:207, 214). The existence of this "enclosed nomadism" within the Mesopotamian empires of the second millennium BCE gave these empires a "dimorphic structure" which persisted in western Asia until the twentieth century CE (Rowton 1973a) and bears closely on the pattern of dynastic change and revolution. Four features of this structure, termed "dimorphic" by Rowton (1973b:202) so as to define "the double process of interaction between nomad and sedentary, between tribe and state," stand out from our perspective: (1) Nomadic enclaves were found on the edges of city-based empires and seasonally penetrated the sedentary zones. In addition to seasonal migration, there was also (2) a process of sedentarization which reinforced the tribes' interconnection with the larger society. To these social aspects of the dimorphic structure should be added two political aspects: (3) the nomadic enclaves were autonomous chiefdoms, whose chiefs were, however, appointed by the imperial ruler. Finally, (4) the nomadic pastoralist tribe was "a paramilitary unit in a permanent state of partial mobilization" (Rowton 1973a:254).

These features capture the social connectedness and loose political integration of the pastoralist tribes in Mesopotamian (and later western Asian) empires. Once we consider the dynamics of the decline and disintegration of these empires as a result of the "dissipation" of centralized power into local structures (Mann 1986:1.ch. 5) and the ease with which permanently paramilitary pastoralist tribes could be mobilized, the potential of these autonomous chiefdoms on the periphery for initiating dynastic change—and, on occasion, revolution—becomes clear. Hammurabi belonged to the sixth generation of local kings and autonomous chiefs who bore the title chief of the Amorites (Rowton 1973b:214) and was the first to shed his Akkadian name for an Amorite one (Oppenheim 1964:156–57, 337). The formation of the Old Babylonian Empire by him can therefore be considered the first major historical instance of the Khaldunian type of revolution in the Middle East and North Africa.

TWO

The Athenian Constitutive Revolution and Subsequent Revolutions of Ancient Greece

The significance of the sixth-century-BCE political evolution of Athens in world history is due to the establishment of democracy in that city-state. It is therefore understandable that the Athenian constitutional development in the late seventh and sixth centuries is usually seen as the growth of democracy. Nevertheless, with ample sociological justification, one historian goes so far as to assert that "the Athenians were engaged in the far more important business of building a unified body politic" (Sealey 1976:134). These two aspects of the Athenian constitutional development are not incompatible, and Cleisthenes's genius in fact makes them complementary. In fact, these twin consequences make the constitutive revolution led by Cleisthenes in the closing decade of the sixth century BCE the culmination of a long period of change.

There were over two hundred city-states in Greece in the first half of the first millennium BCE. Greece was thus a much more fragmented system of "interacting peer polities" than Mesopotamia a millennium and a half earlier but just as unified linguistically and culturally, if not more so. Snodgrass (1986) highlights two distinctive features of the pan-Hellenic institutional homologies generated and sustained by peaceful interaction and warfare among the Greek city-states: the *polis* itself, which emerged as the standard polity in the eighth century BCE, and the spread of codified law from one city-state to another in the subsequent two centuries. Raaflaub (2005) similarly highlights as the pan-Hellenic features of the same axial age (800–500 BCE) the formation of the polis and the emergence of "the political" as its modus operandi (Raaflaub 2005:254–55), along with a strong and distinctive conception of the law: "'Nomos,' thus Pindar, is *basileus* (king) of all, mortal and immortal alike" (cited in Raaflaub 2005:274).

These preconditions of the Cleisthenian Revolution can more generally be considered those of the distinctiveness that Jaspers (1949) called the breakthrough to transcendence in the axial age through philosophy and that Voegelin (1956) more elaborately characterized as the breakthrough from the cosmological symbolization of order in the ancient Near Eastern empires to the symbolization of the polis as a *macroanthropos*. This "anthropocentric" symbolization of transcendent order through philosophy is in turn contrasted with the "theocentric" symbolization of the ultimate source of order through revelation in ancient Israel. Whereas in the theocentric mode of establishing transcendent truth, the political is subordinated to the religious, in the anthropocentric, Hellenic mode, as Raaflaub and others emphasize, the political acquires full autonomy. As Aristotle was to put it famously in the opening paragraph of *Politics*, it is in the political association, the polis, that the most sovereign good attainable by mankind is pursued. For our narrower viewpoint, the pan-Hellenic formation of the polis and the concomitant conception of the rule of law are what made the constitutive revolution of Cleisthenes in Athens also a constitutional revolution.

Constitutive Revolution and the Establishment of Democracy in Athens

The legendary history attributes the unification of the twelve cities of Attica and the creation of the Council of the Areopagus in Athens as its political center to Theseus at the time of the Trojan War. The kings were gradually demoted and their place taken by archons whose tenure was reduced from life to ten years, and eventually to one year, the first annual archon being Creon (683/682 BCE).

What we know from the historical record is that in the seventh century there were nine archons, elected annually, one of whom bore the title *basileus* (king) (Aristotle, *Athenian Constitution*, ch. 57). The Council of the Areopagus consisted of the ex-archons. What the archons and the council held together was a fragmented polity resting on kinship. Its basic unit was the patriarchal household (*oikos*). Beyond the household, there was the clan (*genos*), which took precedence over the tribe (*phratria*). Dracon's legislation on homicide in 621/620 significantly strengthened public authority by restricting family feuds, setting up homicide courts and thus asserting the right of the Athenian state to deal with homicide. During the first quarter of the sixth century, Solon, who liberated all those enslaved for debt and was later called the first "champion of the people," was the great legislator and creator of political community. Solon set up the timocratic system of government with its Council of Four Hundred, presumably elected by the four classes of the census ratings (*timai*), which were based on wealth, and a popular court of law to hear appeals against the decisions of the magistrates (Hornblower 1992:4–7). His codification of customary law significantly increased the salience of public law and thus enhanced public authority. He further reduced the power of the clan by modifying inheritance laws (Gaudemet 1982:154). The long tyranny of Peisistratus and his sons in the second half of the sixth century entailed some concentration of power and much de facto integration of the Athenian political community. Nevertheless, by the late sixth century BCE in Athens, as in the rest of Greece, the political community was still less important than the aristocratic family—the dominant clan of the tribe—and its clients (Sealey 1976:124–28; Lintott 1982:46–50, 75).

Solon's constitutional reforms set in motion the trends that were to find their culmination in Cleisthenes's constitutional revolution. Meanwhile, the monetization of the Greek economy and the growth of trade during the second half of the sixth century had generated considerable upward and downward social mobility. As shown in the poems of Theognis of Megara (ca. 550–500 BCE), wealth had thrown lineage into confusion (Gouldner 1965:15), thereby creating the preconditions for revolution mentioned by Aristotle (1962:203–7): an old nobility reacting to dispossession while the new rich were clamoring for inclusion in the sphere of law and authority.

> Those who before knew nothing of lawsuits, nothing of laws,
> who went about in goatskins . . . , like wild deer,
> these are now The Great Men. . . . Our former nobles are Rabble now.

Theognis is haunted by the specter of civil discord, when "base men take to disorderly ways, . . . and give rights to the unrighteous," causing bloodshed and destruction. "But pray that our city may never be such" (R. Lattimore 1960:27). Theognis's prayer was unanswered, and as we shall see, his city of Megara succumbed to the cycle of revolution and counterrevolution that swept through the Greek world in the latter part of the fifth century BCE.

Herodotus (5.63) tells us that "the liberation of Athens from the despotic rule" of the house of the last tyrant, Peisistratus, was achieved by the exiled Cleisthenes with the help of other exiles. Cleisthenes was the scion of the aristocratic Alkmeonid family and had served as archon in 525/524 (Sealey 1976:136–37). The Alkmeonid guerrilla warfare against the Peisistratidae was launched in or before 514 BCE. A drinking song describes his followers as "Good warriors and well-born / Who showed then what stock they came of" (Aristotle 1984:61). Association of tyranny with foreign domination by

Persia and Sparta made it unpopular and conversely increased the popularity of the Alkmeonid cause. Religion played an important role in the early stage of the Cleisthenian Revolution. Under the Peisistratidae, the Alkmeonidae had obtained a contract to build the temple at Delphi, and Cleisthenes enlisted the support of the Delphic priestess for their cause, allegedly through bribery. Delphi was the only pan-Hellenic institution above the city-states, all of which recognized the authority of its oracles, which often concerned legal and political matters (Snodgrass 1986:54–55). The priestess reportedly told those Spartans who consulted the oracle that it was their duty to liberate Athens by overthrowing the house of Peisistratus (Herodotus, 5.64). This the Spartans did; Peisistratus's son Hippias was expelled from Athens by them in 510. In the course of the revolutionary power struggle between Cleisthenes and Isagoras, who was backed by the Spartans and by the former supporters of the tyrants in the eastern districts, "Cleisthenes, who was getting the worst of it, managed to win popular support. He then changed the number of Athenian tribes from four to ten and abolished the old names." This reform was inspired by a more limited reconstruction of the tribal system pioneered elsewhere by Cleisthenes's maternal grandfather, Cleisthenes, the tyrant of Sicyon (Herodotus, 5.67–68). The revolutionary slogans that can be firmly associated with Cleisthenes are *isegoria* (equality of speaking) and *demokratia* (power of the people), though *isonomia* (equality of political rights) is also attributed to him (Hornblower 1992:8). Cleisthenes gave these political slogans institutional embodiment upon victory. He thus "reorganized the Athenians into tribes and instituted the system of popular government (*demokratia*) in Athens" (Herodotus, 6.131).

The achievement of Cleisthenes, the "champion of the people" (*prostates tou demou*) and "the first Athenian to win a civil war with a program of political reform" (Lintott 1982:50, 55), was momentous. It established a new political order—the system of government that came to be called democracy some half a century later—and greatly broadened the social foundations of government by enlarging the political community and enhancing its integration. According to Aristotle, the measures introduced by Cleisthenes meant "that a number of new tribes and clans should be instituted by the side of the old; that private cults should be reduced in number and conducted at common centers; and that every connivance should be employed to make the citizens mix, as much as they possibly can, and to break down their old loyalties" (*Politics* 6.4.19; 1962:266). As Aristotle states in the *Athenian Constitution* (ch. 21; 1984:64, emphasis added), "He refused to divide the Athenians into twelve tribes, to avoid allocating them according to the already existing thirds: the four tribes were divided into twelve thirds, and *if he had used them he would not have succeeded in mixing the people up."* The four traditional real tribes were replaced by ten artificial tribes, each with subdivisions. The basis for membership in the new tribes was territorial—in other words, the place of residence. The new tribes were also made the basis of training and military organization. Each new tribe was made up of a fixed number of *demes* (districts). Many of the demes were already existing geographic units, but new ones were also created.[1] Of the 139 attested demes, perhaps some 30 were new ones, set up by Cleisthenes (Traill 1975:81, 101). Furthermore, each of the new artificial tribes consisted of three elements called *trittyes,* which were even more artificial and were geographically defined as areas of the city, the inland, and the coast (Hornblower 1992:8). Perhaps the most fundamental aspect of the Cleisthenian political reconstruction was his making the demes the basis of the personal identity of Athenian citizens. According to Aristotle, "He made the men living in each deme fellow-demesmen of one another, so that they should not use their fathers' names and make it obvious who were the new citizens *but should be named after their demes*: this is why the Athenians still call themselves after their demes" (*Athenian Constitution,* ch. 21; 1984:64, emphasis added). This lasting consequence of the Cleisthenian reform was due to the fact that the deme was constitutionally defined as a group of citizens who bore the same demotic. The demotic was assigned upon enrollment in the deme register. Those coming of age (at eighteen) almost invariably registered in their father's district, regardless of domicile, and acquired franchise by being given the same demotic (Traill 1975:73–74).

The tribal assemblies were to meet in Athens. The Council of the Areopagus remained. In addition, Cleisthenes established a new Council of Five Hundred, whose members were annually drawn by lot from the ten tribes in equal numbers. The council's important function was the preparation of business for the popular assembly of the entire body of citizens (30,000) which required a quorum of 6,000 and met less frequently. Council members could serve only twice in a lifetime. The development of law in the preceding century had evidently given the Cleisthenian ideology a pronounced constitutionalist character. The Cleisthenian settlement has been dated to 503/2, in preference to the date given in Aristotle's *Athenian Constitution* (508/7); and the new Council of Five Hundred was sworn in in 501/500 (Sealey 1976:146–57).

The artificial new tribal system became the basis of the Athenian democratic constitution. The tribe-kings became mere dignitaries, and the influence of powerful families, like Cleisthenes's own family, was disrupted, enabling recent immigrants into Attica "to be incorporated more easily into the voting population" (Lintott 1982:54). As Aristotle stated, all citizens were identified by their demes, and the newly enfranchised citizens, including slaves, could no longer be recognized and segregated. Although the citizens appeared to have kept their fathers' names, they ceased to record those of their clans (*genos*), and their civic identity became primary. Family names were ignored, and every Athenian without distinction coupled with his own name the name of his deme. Indeed, the most famous Alkmeonid of the postrevolution era did not identify himself as such but "went under the name of Pericles, son of Xanthippus, of the deme of Cholargus" (Glotz as cited in Gouldner 1965:20). Last but not least, the institution of the new tribes shattered the exclusiveness of the old tribal religion, whose cult centers often became centers of deme government (Traill 1975:101), offering the chance to worship to those who had previously been excluded (Fustel de Coulanges [1864] 1900:282–83).

Religion, as we have seen, was used tactically and for mobilizing support for revolution, but it did not supply the directive elements of revolutionary action, as the religious was teleologically subordinate to the political. Nor was there any explicit justification of revolutionary change and revolution. It was not religion, nor any divinely ordained mandate for change, but the democratic political ideology that determined the direction, the teleology, of the Cleisthenian Revolution. Only after democracy had been firmly established were sacrifices made on its behalf, and only in the fourth century BCE do we see a cult of Demokratia (Hornblower 1992:15).

Consequences of the Cleisthenian Revolution

The consequences of the Cleisthenian Revolution proved lasting. His radical constitutional reconstruction of Athens remained definitive and shaped Athenian political life in the fifth century. The enlargement of the political community was irreversible, as was its constitutional restructuring. Although Athenian politics was dominated by the demes in or near the city, access to power was open to all citizens. In fact, Themistocles, archon in 493/92 and the next Athenian political leader of a comparable stature to Cleisthenes, came from a peripheral deme (Sealey 1976:184–85, 257, 303). Not only was membership in the political community broadened, but the trend was set for increasing actual political participation and power sharing. Whereas before 500 BCE, the people (*demos*) were usually spectators, they were often drawn into the struggles of the powerful (*dunatoi*) after that date (Lintott 1982:261). Popular political participation was significantly enhanced by the transference of some of the judiciary powers of the archons and the Council of the Areopagus to popular jury courts, while archonship was opened to the lower two classes of census ratings by Ephialtes around 462 BCE. In the 450s, Pericles made access to office more practical for the majority of citizens by introducing regular payment, from the proceeds of the Athenian overseas empire, for jury members, the Council of Five Hundred, and most magistracies. With the councils, the jury courts, and some seven hundred offices, every Athenian citizen in the mid-fifth century had the chance to hold office at least once in his lifetime (Sealey 1976:258–61, 298–301). The mode of politics, too, was permanently affected. It became markedly constitutional; constitutional procedures acquired uncontested and exclusive legitimacy.

The Athenian construction of a larger political community out of a segmentary tribal society dominated by aristocratic clans had its obvious limits: the territory of the city. The well-known remarks on the small size of the ideal city by Plato and similar ones by other philosophers were not greatly at variance with the actual population of the city-states and point to the rather narrow limits of the integrative potential of the Athenian democratic revolution. Greek political culture did not generate the integrative principles for the imperial society of the Hellenistic period that were brought back by Alexander from the East. On the other hand, it resulted in active democratization in contrast to the passive democratization that accompanied imperial integrative revolutions in Rome.[2]

The Cleisthenian constitutional revolution established democracy as a political regime with a long life in world history, and more immediately, it ushered in nearly a century of democratic government during which Athens was remarkably free from civil strife (*stasis*). Its long-term consequences, however, were not confined to Athens but affected the entire Greek world through an epicycle of democratic revolutions and oligarchic counterrevolutions.

Ideology, Organization, and the Cycle of Greek Revolutions and Counterrevolutions during the Peloponnesian War

The Thirty Years' Peace, dominated by Pericles's Athens, came to an end, and the Peloponnesian War (431–404 BCE) produced a cycle of revolutions and counterrevolutions in ancient Greece. The Peloponnesian War increased the frequency of foreign interventions; and war between the Greek cities acted as a powerful stimulus to revolutions and civil wars within cities, which had the consequence of further standardizing the polis. Meanwhile, the wooing of people with political programs had become common ever since the onset of constitutional politics in Cleisthenes's Athens. But the detractors of democracy, too, were formulating their objections with increasing coherence. In the last quarter of the fifth century, this antidemocratic oppositional ideology was presented as a rival political doctrine: *aristokratia*, or government by the best (Lintott 1982:168–73). Political programs became the hallmark of the revolutions that took place in the Greek city-states under the stimulus of the Peloponnesian War. Revolutionary ideology emerged as an important factor in Hellenic international political culture and international—strictly speaking, inter-city-state—politics, producing a cycle of revolutions and counterrevolutions. Thucydides tells us how the revolution of 427 BCE in Corcyra ushered in an intercity wave of revolutions and how political programs were borrowed by the latecomers, with Athens and Sparta supporting the democratic and the oligarchic revolutions respectively.

Rival intervention by Corinth and Athens in the affairs of Corcyra set in motion the first and most savage revolution of this cycle in 427 BCE. The trouble began with 250 prisoners, returned to act as a fifth column for the Corinthians, who charged the leader of the democratic party with enslaving Corcyra to Athens. There followed a bloody struggle, confused by the intermittent appearance of Peloponnesian and Athenian fleets, which ended with the elimination of the antidemocratic party. "There were fathers who killed their sons; men were dragged from the temples or butchered on the very altars." Mobilization by both parties was so intense and extensive that not only women but also slaves joined in the fighting, the latter being offered their freedom by both sides in competitive bidding. Violence eventually came to an end "since of the two parties one had practically ceased to exist" (Thucydides, 3.5, 4.3).[3]

The revolution in Corcyra was also important for its interstate consequences and can be taken as the prelude to the Peloponnesian War itself. As such, it shows the possibility of the "primacy of foreign policy" for the latecomers to a cycle of revolutions. Corcyra occupied a significant position in relation to the two power blocs; and the polarization of the two factions, the oligarchs and the democrats, was thorough as a result of respective identification with the two blocs. Both sides expected foreign help. All this accounts for their ruthlessness and explains why the revolution ended with the complete elimination of one of the two parties (Heuss 1973:24–34).

Thucydides interrupts his account of the events in Corcyra to digress on the advent of revolutionary parties and ideologies in the Hellenic world of his time. Party membership had become stronger than family ties. The new revolutionary parties represented a contemporary transformation of the sixth-century aristocratic coteries or clubs (*hetaireia*): "These parties were not formed to enjoy the benefits of the established laws [as had been the *hetaireiai* previously], but to acquire power by overthrowing existing regimes; and the members of these parties felt confidence in each other not because of any fellowship in a religious communion, but because they were partners in crime" (3.82). Thucydides's invidious contrast with fellowship in a religious communion gives us a better clue to the nature of the bond among the revolutionaries, stemming from a shared ideology, than his moral condemnation of revolutionary activity as criminal. With the coming of revolutions, "words, too, had to change their usual meaning." Moderation was considered a disguise for cowardice. "Fanatical enthusiasm was the mark of a real man, and to plot against an enemy behind his back was perfectly legitimate self-defense." Conversely, refusal to believe or engage in conspiracies was considered disruption of the unity of the party. "Leaders of parties in the cities had programs which appeared admirable—on one side political equality for the masses, on the other the safe and sound government of the aristocracy—but in professing to serve the public interest they were seeking to win the prizes for themselves" (3.82). "As a result of these revolutions, there was a general deterioration of character throughout the Greek world. . . . Society had become divided into two ideologically hostile camps, and each side viewed the other with suspicion" (3.83).

The advent and international currency of political programs and techniques of revolutionary organization thus made possible the occurrence of counterrevolutions against democratic governments. One such was the revolution in Megara in the summer of 424. According to Thucydides (4.5), "the Megarians in the city of Megara were suffering badly from the war with Athens, since the Athenians invaded their country twice a year in full force. They were also hard pressed by their own exiles at Pegae who had been driven out in a revolution by the democratic party and were causing trouble by acts of brigandage." The democratic party was tainted by its collaboration with the Athenians, and the exiles were recalled from Pegae and seized power. They broke their solemn oaths against recrimination for the past and condemned about a hundred men to death as collaborators with the Athenians. The (counter)revolution of 424 BCE in Megara established a strict oligarchy in that city-state. "It was a change of government made after a revolution by a very few people, and yet it lasted for a very long time."

Much more noted than the Megarian revolution was the oligarchic (counter)revolution of 411 BCE in Athens. Its program was aristocracy, government by the best, and it was carried out by an organized minority against popular government. There is no denying that the well-documented oligarchic (counter)revolution of 411 has some fascinating features. The foremost of these is the conversion of the *hetaireiai* (social coteries cum political associations) and *symposia*—sworn brotherhoods or "clubs that already existed in Athens for mutual aid in lawsuits and in getting appointments" (Thucydides 1954:519)—into a revolutionary political party. The oligarchists' systematic underground organization of terror for the elimination and intimidation of opponents makes them the forerunners of the nineteenth-century revolutionaries. It also highlights the importance of party discipline and systematic organization of violence long before Leninism. Regarding discipline, it is interesting to note that the members had to commit, first, sacrilegious vandalism and, later, murder to demonstrate their commitment to the cause by burning their bridges to normal life (Lintott 1982:134, 137). It is equally interesting to note that *hetaireiai* (*collegia* in Latin) and *symposia* remained potential centers of sedition into the early Roman Empire, as documented in Philo's report on the archdemagogue Isidore of Alexandria (Bowersock 1986b:312–13). Plotting and conspiring in caucus also find ample documentation. Nor is it without interest that to these innovations a subsequent oligarchic coup in 404 added the typically modern phenomenon of retaining a sham legal constitutional facade for arbitrary rule (Lintott 1982:esp. 160). Nevertheless, the above features do not alter the basic fact that the oligarchic counterrevolution of 411 was a failure, as was its sequel in 404. The oligarchs were overthrown in the late summer of 411. The "intermediate regime" that followed did not last, and democracy was fully restored in 410. Although the abovementioned counterexample of Megara cannot be ignored, it is tempting to speculate on this failure. Unlike the situation in Megara, it was not the democratic but the oligarchic group that was associated with foreign (Persian) domination. Given that patriotism worked not for but against them, the failure of the oligarchs can be further explained by the fact that their aims were contrary not to one but to both natural outcomes of the revolutionary process: the enlargement of the political community and the concentration of power—the Four Hundred of 411 or even the Thirty of 404 were a far cry from the extensive, albeit passive, democratization under the monarchies of Sargon and Augustus.

In short, the Athenian democratic ideology and the Spartan-sponsored oligarchic counterpart supplied the blueprints for the later revolutions and counterrevolutions among the interacting peer polities of ancient Greece, as the Sargonic monarchical ideology had done for the latecomers in ancient Mesopotamia.

In ancient Greece, the citizenry and the hoplite army were either identical or widely overlapping, and citizenship went hand in hand with possession of arms. Relatively broad distribution of power was characteristic of oligarchies as well: the oligarchic group could consist of some one thousand men or an eighth of the male adult citizens of a medium-sized city-state (Lintott 1982:261). Private use of violence to recover debts and enforce court judgments was encouraged or permitted. The absence of a concentration of power in the coercive arm of government made violence endemic and political revolutions likely. An important consequence of this dispersion of the means of coercion was the institution of exile and ostracism. There was no organized police force—and, of course, no secret police—to keep the opposition repressed at home. They had to be exiled. The role of exiles in Greek revolutions is striking, even more so than in modern revolutions: Cleisthenes launched his revolutionary bid for power in exile, revolution in Corcyra began with prisoners of war returning from Corinth, and that in Megara was the work of exiles. The salience of exiles is easy to explain in terms of my model. The exiles had every reason to attempt to return home and regain power by revolutionary means. Their motive for doing so was stronger than that of the other excluded groups mentioned by Aristotle, as was their sense of entitlement. Unlike the latter, the exiles' exclusion from the political community meant actual dispossession, the forfeiture of the rights of membership they had enjoyed in the past.

The Constitutive Revolution of the Roman Ancient Republic: A Comparison

The history of Rome around 500 BCE is shrouded in mystery. Yet it is entirely possible—and indeed quite likely—that the expulsion of the Etruscan kings and the foundation of the republic by Brutus around 500 BCE constituted an integrative revolution that replaced the old tribal curiae with the tribes and centuries of the hoplite army that made up the central organ of the political system of republican Rome.[4] The resemblance of this result to the Cleisthenian reforms is striking:

> The three old tribes were superseded by new ones based on place of residence, the city itself being divided into four tribes, and the land outside the walls originally perhaps to a further sixteen [later thirty-one]. Residence, not kinship, was thus the basis of the new organization, and the consuls (and after them the censors) would . . . have the power of enrolling immigrants into

> the tribes when they made the census. . . . The new tribes existed only for political purposes and as a basis for taxation; unlike the *curiae*, they had no self-government and no *sacra*. (Jolowicz and Nicholas 1972:20)

Thus, in the new constitution, which remained anachronistically attributed in its entirety to the last but one of the seven kings, Servius Tullius (mid-sixth century BCE), artificial tribes on the basis of residence replaced natural tribes on the basis of kinship, opening the way for further incorporation of immigrants, and the religious and political self-sufficiency of the tribes was abrogated.

This system was modified during the revolutionary epicycle around 450 BCE, the revolution that recognized the plebeians as a corporation and integrated their institutions into the Roman political system. They also acquired the right to convene the Senate. Two important plebeian institutions became an integral part of the political system of the Roman republic: the ten tribunes (originally four, the representatives of the four plebeian tribes) and the *consilium plebis*, whose enactments (*plebiscita*) became equally valid with laws (*leges*) early in the third century BCE. The ban on marriages between patricians and plebeians was also repealed (Rostovtzeff [1927] 1960:29–30; Jolowicz and Nicholas 1972:14–15, 24–25).

The incorporation of the plebeian institutions, further enhanced during the struggle between the orders in the fourth century BCE, introduced anarchical elements into the Roman political structure. One strange result of this amalgamation was that there were three bodies equally capable of legislation: *comitia centuriata*, *comitia tributa*, and *consilium plebis*. These bodies were also charged with the election of the magistrates of the Roman republic. The *comitia centuriata* and the *comitia tributa* consisted entirely of the same people but were organized differently; the *consilium plebis*, yet again consisting by and large of the same people as the patrician bodies, must have become numerically insignificant by the third century (Jolowicz and Nicholas 1972:25–26). A more serious result was that tremendous legal powers were conceded to the tribunes. Not only did they enjoy inviolability (*sacrosanctitas*) and the general power of *coercitio*, but they also had the power to initiate legislation as presidents of the *consilium plebis*. Furthermore, each one of the ten tribunes had the veto power (*intercessio*) over legislation. This power, together with the power of *auxilium*—the power to help and protect the oppressed—had its origins in the fact that the plebs had entered the Roman polity as a defeated people in need of protection (Betti and Crifò [1914] 1982:57–63), but it could nevertheless bring the business of government to a standstill (Jolowicz and Nicholas 1972:54–55). Although the tribunes, being typically younger members of the noble plebeian families in the early stages of their political careers, were as a rule easily managed by the Senate; their office built a potential for anarchy in the constitution of the Roman republic. As we shall see, this potential was actualized by the Gracchi and the other revolutionary tribunes of the late republic. The Senate, originally the patrician preserve, was in theory only an advisory council of the ex-magistrates, an aristocracy of office, without legislative power. In practice, however, it became the governing body of the Roman republic, officially designated as the Senate and People of Rome (in that order). In particular, it controlled the finances and the foreign affairs of the empire.

As Gaetano Mosca (1939:361) observed, in the third century BCE, Rome already had found "a way to snap the fatal circle that prevented the Greek city from expanding." The broadening of the right of citizenship made possible the extension of political society beyond the city. The right of citizenship was differentiated into a number of more specific prerogatives that formed the basis of categories of partial citizenship. People who lived far from Rome could be granted citizenship and incorporated into the Roman political system. Some 292,000 men were thus enrolled as Roman citizens in 265 BCE.[5] Furthermore, two additional categories of rights made possible the partial integration of a much larger population. Of these, the Latin rights (*ius Latii*) came closest to citizenship and were to be used as a halfway house to it (Jolowicz and Nicholas 1972:61). A less favorable status was granted to (other) Italians as *socii* (allies; allied city-states). Nevertheless, Roman territorial possessions and the population subject to its rule expanded phenomenally during the second century BCE. The political institutions of the Roman city-state, too, were inadequate for the vast society on which it was superimposed by the latter part of the century. As events were to prove, the city-state could not be shored up and gave way to the empire.

Conclusion

In chapter 1, we saw the emergence of the integrative paradigm of universal monarchy in Akkad and its dissemination throughout the Mesopotamian world by a cycle of revolutions. The Athenian constitutional revolution similarly generated a cycle of revolutions and counterrevolutions in the Hellenic world through its interacting peer polities (Renfrew 1986).

There appears to be no necessary correlation between the amount of violence generated in the process of a revolution and the extent and significance of change it produced in Greece. The Cleisthenian Revolution was not particularly violent, but the changes it produced were momentous and its consequences are still with us today. The later revolutions of Corcyra and Megara were more proficient in their techniques of revolutionary agitation and much more violent, but they did not modify the existing democratic and oligarchic blueprints and had no effect beyond those city-states. The greatest Greek political theorist, Aristotle of Stagira, who was a *metic* (and not a citizen) in Athens, accordingly made a distinction between the common term *stasis* (sedition, strife), which corresponds fairly closely to the current sociological concept of collective violence, and his theoretical concept of *metabolé tes politeias* (constitutional change) as revolution in the state, in order to define revolution in terms of its consequence—namely, political transformation (Meier 1984:664). Regime change thus became the defining feature of his conception of revolution and has been incorporated into my Aristotelian-Paretan type of integrative revolution. Thus, Aristotle was also theorizing the competing regime blueprints that served as the ideological basis of the revolutions and counterrevolutions of the Hellenic ecumene in the fifth century BCE.[6]

THREE

Revolution in the Roman Republic

Social scientists would be puzzled by historians' current use of the term "Roman revolution" to cover the full span of the last century of the republic. A central unifying theme in this cycle of revolutions and civil wars can, however, be found, even though it has not been so identified by the historians. The theme is the enlargement of the political system of the Roman city-state, in violent spasms, to include new cities and peoples, on the one hand, and new social classes and groups, on the other. In geographical terms, Roman political society came to incorporate first the Latins, then the Italian allies (*socii*), then the whole of Italy. In social structural terms, it came to incorporate first the knights, then the soldiery. This common theme allows us to speak of Roman integrative revolutions in accordance with the Aristotelian-Paretan criterion. In addition, the Tocquevillian theme of increasing centralization of authority is present in its last phase—that is, in the transition from republic to empire from the time of Julius Caesar onward. By the same token, however, the periods of civil strife from the fall of Nero to the rise of Vespasian (68–70 CE) and from the fall of Commodus to the rise of Septimius Severus (192–97 CE) must also be treated as revolutions—and they have not been so treated to my knowledge. The integrative and centralizing consequences common to these latter instances of dynastic change qualify them as revolutions according to my definition.

Prelude to Revolution: 126–122 BCE

The tribunate of Tiberius Gracchus in 133 BCE is usually considered the beginning of the Roman revolutions (Mommsen 1854–56:vol. 3; Badian 1972b). The year marks the break in the concord between the tribunate and the Senate and the onset of popular mobilization by revolutionary tribunes.

It is true that by deposing another tribune who had blocked him by exercising the *intercessio*, Tiberius Gracchus transgressed the traditional Roman principle of inviolability and autonomy of the office of tribune.[1] Although the Gracchan agrarian law of 133 for the distribution of public land was important,[2] the limited redistribution it achieved (Badian 1972b:681; Stockton 1979:59) had, at best, an indirect effect on revolution. The emergence of revolutionary tribunes in this period was more a symptom than a cause of the incipient breakdown in the authority structure of republican Rome. However, the fundamental cause of the political crisis of the late Roman republic that was present before and persisted long after the agrarian law was a different one. The institutional structure of the Roman polity was increasingly at variance with the size and structure of the society it was superimposed upon and it sought to govern. The dynamics of the long series of revolutions and counterrevolutions set in motion by the inadequacy of the political system of the Roman city-state for governing the Latin cities and Italian cities and finally the empire was the step-by-step enlargement of political community.

The first movement toward this enlargement of the Roman political community beyond the city of Rome begins in the period of the Gracchi. The Gracchan party was well disposed to the Latins and the Italians. Tiberius Gracchus, already in 133 BCE, had spoken of the Italians as the kinsmen of the Romans (Sherwin-White 1973a:138). In 126 BCE, his younger brother, Gaius Gracchus, as *quaestor*, spoke against an act by the tribune Pennus expelling all aliens from Rome. The circumstances of the act make it clear that its passing was due to the fear of support for the Gracchan party by Latins and Italians. Well-to-do Latins, whose prosperity Polybius attributed to the public contract system, had been flocking to Rome as early as 187 BCE (Badian 1972b:683), and measures had been taken to restrict migration in 187, 177, and 172 BCE (Brunt 1988:95). These measures could not have been very effective, and by 122 the Roman plebs feared they could be crowded out by the Latins (Keaveney 1987:54). In 125 BCE, M. Fulvius Flaccus, the leading member of the Gracchan party, and of the triumvir in charge of the distribution of the public land instituted by the Gracchan agrarian law of 133, was elected consul and proposed a radical bill. As a Gracchan, Flaccus upheld the principle of the sovereignty of popular assemblies against constitutional practice, at least implicitly by deposing a tribune, as Tiberius Gracchus had done (Betti and Crifò [1914] 1982:70–71). Flaccus's momentous proposal, which can be presumed to have been put forward the previous year in concert with Gracchus's speech against Pennus, was to grant the Italian allies citizenship or, if they preferred, the right of *provocatio* (protection against Roman magistrates), in exchange for their acquiescence in the redistribution of the public land held by them.[3] Flaccus's proposal stirred popular support and senatorial hostility. It was abandoned in the face of senatorial opposition when Flaccus left Rome for Massilia during a military emergency (Badian 1958:176–79).

According to Appian, Flaccus "incited" the Italians to demand citizenship. This implies that they preferred citizenship to land and considered their political gain to outweigh their economic loss. Be that as it may, Flaccus's failure to enact his bill resulted in considerable discontent among the Italians, and a revolt broke out in the Latin colony of Fregellae in 125 BCE. It is interesting to note that fifty years earlier, in 177, some four thousand families of *socii* had immigrated to Fregellae to upgrade themselves to the status of Latins (Keaveney 1987:52, 65). The fact that Gaius Gracchus was accused of conspiring to bring about a revolt of the allies, and not just of complicity in the defection of a single Latin city, indicates that discontent was not confined to Fregellae—and so does the swift and heavy-handed reaction of the Senate. L. Opimius razed the city to the ground to set an example, we may assume, to deter other Italian communities and nip in the bud a more general insurrection against the Roman state. The grant of citizenship *per magistratum* (through magistracy) to the Latins was probably made at this time as a concession to win over the aristocracies of other Latin cities (Brunt 1988:94–97).

In 123 BCE, Gaius Gracchus became tribune with an ambitious program for social, political, and economic reform. He was impressed by Greek political ideas, especially the unconditional sovereignty of the popular assemblies and a "balanced constitution" (Nicolet 1967:153–63, 192–203), and wished to transform the tribunate into a quasi-monarchical office that was based on popular support. Although he was a major founding figure of the *populares* faction of the late republic (Betti and Crifò [1914] 1982), his own ideas for political reform had the distinctive goal of opening up the Roman oligarchy and included designs for creating a balanced constitution, as recommended by Polybius, and for enlarging the Roman political community. As one of the last measures during his second term as the tribune of the people (122 BCE), Gaius Gracchus, in concert with Flaccus, proposed a bill offering full citizenship to the Latins and Latin right to the Italian allies. Once more, land was to be bartered for political rights (Mommsen 1854–56:3.362). His competitor for tribuneship, Livius Drusus, whose son was to play an important role in the revolutionary crisis of 91 BCE, offered the Latins the right of *provocatio* at home and abroad. Consul Fannius at once took restrictive measures in anticipation of an influx of Italians into the city of Rome in support of Gracchus's enfranchisement proposal (Keaveney 1987:47–48, 62–63). Gracchus also sought to increase the confidence of the Italian allies in Roman justice by introducing a law allowing the provincials to prosecute (Badian 1962:204). But the time for revolution had not yet come. Gracchus was defeated by Drusus and was no longer tribune in 121. Opimius, the destroyer of Fregellae, was now consul and armed with the first *Senatus consultum ultimum* (declaration of a state of emergency) in history, but lacking any police force, he called upon the senators and the knights to present themselves and their armed attendants to defend the state against the aspirant to tyranny. Many did. Gaius Gracchus and Fulvius Flaccus perished side by side, together with three thousand of their supporters, and their bodies were thrown into the Tiber (Stockton 1979:196–98).

Gaius Gracchus also took measures that directly or indirectly affected the social group that gradually came to constitute the second stratum of Roman society, the knights (*equites*). Until 129 BCE, the senators and the knights constituted the upper and lower ranks of the same class, the official class, distinguished from the rest of the citizenry by the "public horse" conferred by the censors (Nicolet 1974). In line with the timocratic character of the Roman political system, where public office was unpaid, the officer class consisted of the rich; and the eighteen centuries of cavalry, the *equites equo publico* (knights with the public horse), were manned from a broader census category of property owners. As distinct from the cavalry as a military and legal order in the strict sense, the census category designated the knights as a social class. The Roman concept of *imperium* united civil and military authority in its holder; and the officer class was also the political class and supplied the magistrates (Gelzer [1912] 1969; Badian 1972a:50). In 129 BCE, a law was passed that required the senators to give up the public horse. This was the first step by the Gracchan politicians to give the *equites* a distinct corporate identity as a counterweight to the Senate. Further measures were taken by Gaius Gracchus, tribune in 123 and 122 BCE, to institutionalize this distinct corporate identity and to give the equestrian order an independent institutional base and therefore distinct interests (Badian 1972a:58–61, 65–66). He embarked on reform to preserve or restore the "balanced constitution" by strengthening the middle elements (*equites*) and the lower classes (Rowland 1965:372–73), setting up a permanent extortion court (*quaestio perpetua repetundarum*) to hear complaints of extortion and misgovernment against magistrates, and choosing 450 knights as its jurors, excluding fathers, brothers, and sons of magistrates, senators, and even ex-senators (Gelzer [1912] 1969:11; Stockton 1979:140–46). The knights thus acquired an institutional base under their exclusive control independently of the Senate, and their other judiciary functions as jurors in other courts were enlarged and enhanced (Brunt 1988:ch. 4). They now had the power of judgment over the senatorial class, who composed the magistracy. In Appian's words, Gracchus "made the knights look like masters, and the senators their subjects"; and in Diodorus's, "he made the inferior element in the state master over the superior" (cited in Nicolet 1967:188; Stockton 1979:114). Gaius's appointment of the 450 knights as jurors also gave them another important political asset: judiciary immunity (Nicolet 1967:188). The most important long-term effect of the reform was the creation of a distinct social group which came to be referred to as the Gracchan jurors (*iudices Gracchani*). The Gracchan jurors came to constitute the core of a new social class (Badian 1972a:65).

Gaius Gracchus's other policies were also highly beneficial to the knights. His *lex de provincia Asia* gave them an important fiscal role and a lucrative enterprise in tax collection. Access to the revenue of this very rich province (Pergamon), unlike that of the province of Sicily, was to be contracted out in Rome and not locally. It was henceforth auctioned off by the censors to the great joint-stock companies of the *publicani*, who belonged to the equestrian class (Badian 1972a; Stockton 1979:154–55). His corn law (*lex frumentaria*) provided for the regular monthly distribution of subsidized grain to Roman citizens and is remembered as the first step in the process of making the inhabitants of Rome in effect state pensioners (Hopkins 1978:14–15; Stockton 1979:126–29). But it was also a boon to the knights who imported grain (Rowland 1965:370), and so was his program of public works, contracted to the companies of the *publicani*.

Except for the anachronism of arguing from effect, Varro and Appian were partially right in seeing the creation of the equestrian courts by Gracchus as tantamount to giving the state two heads and thus opening the floodgates of civil war. Although Gracchus's aim may have been to create the balanced constitution of Polybius by incorporating the knights into the Roman polity, the mode of incorporation, pitting judicial against political power, was potentially conflictual. In this sense, too, the Gracchan period was a prelude to revolution: the *concordia* between the upper and lower ranks of the political class, the officer class, was destroyed.[4] Henceforth, an increasingly distinct line was drawn between the senatorial political class and a predominantly apolitical class of well-to-do knights, some of whom engaged as *publicani* in tax farming and in directing companies that contracted with the state, while others managed their estates in the countryside.[5]

Despite his impressive reforms through legislation and his programs of public works and colonization, Gracchus's was a failed revolution in that it succeeded neither in changing the political regime in the direction of Greek democracy nor in moving in the direction of monarchy by upgrading the office of the tribune. The collegial character of the tribunate made such changes difficult; and the tribunes never acquired military command. Nor did he succeed in enlarging the political community to include the Latins and the Italians. His one measure that altered the power structure of Rome was the politically consequential integration of the knights into the judiciary structure. This was the first step in the integrative revolution in social structural terms, one that, furthermore, inserted yet another potentially conflict-producing element into the Roman authority structure.

Extension of Roman Citizenship through the Social and Civil Wars: 91–84 BCE

Political Crisis and the Onset of Civil War

Two unrelated events in 95 BCE mark the onset of the crisis that led to the first cycle of revolutions and counterrevolutions in Roman history from 91 to 82 BCE. The first was trouble in Asia, where the *publicani* were the most powerful, and was serious enough to justify the dispatch of Consul Mucius Scaevola Pontifex, a distinguished jurist, with Consul Rutilius Rufus, an equally distinguished jurist, as his legate. The reform and reorganization of the province of Asia in the following years brought Scaevola and Rutilius into a head-on clash with the *publicani*, the richest and only organized section of the new equestrian class. This was the culmination of over a decade of aggressive political activity by the *equites* against senatorial domination (Sherwin-White 1956:2–5). In 92 BCE, the *publicani* found an ally in the Senate, Rutilius's old enemy Marius, and shamelessly abused their judiciary power to put Rutilius on trial in the extortion court and convict him (Badian 1972a:89–94; Brunt 1988:152). The senatorial and equestrian classes were thus seriously divided, a condition Plato considered necessary for the occurrence of revolution.

The second event of 95 BCE was the passing of the *lex Licinia Mucia*. The law established a judicial procedure for depriving of citizenship those who had claimed it illegally. Its enactment showed the Roman political system to be a restrictive oligarchy that barred socially powerful groups from political power, a condition Aristotle considered conducive to revolution in oligarchies. During the preceding decade, Gaius Marius, himself a new man from the town of Arpinum, which had received citizenship some two generations earlier, had shown a readiness to reward Italians who had served in the military with citizenship (Keaveney 1987:77). The *lex Licinia Mucia* was an attempt to reverse this trend; and its consequences were disastrous. Asconius knew that the Italian aristocracy passionately desired citizenship, and a great number of them posed as citizens; the law so provoked the Italian *principes* as to cause the war of the Italian *socii*, the Social War, some three years later (Brunt 1988:100).

The *lex Licinia Mucia* must have caused considerable discontent and anxiety among the Italian upper class in the ensuing years; a tradition relates that Poppaedius Silo, the leader of the Marsi in their imminent rebellion, marched on Rome to demand citizenship with ten thousand men fearing judicial investigation (Brunt 1988:101). The waves of unrest produced by the conviction of Rutilius among the senatorial class and by the *lex Licinia Mucia* among the Italians were thus joined by the year 91. Livius Drusus the Younger tried to ride both waves. On the first count, he proposed to deprive the knights of the judiciary power they had abused in exchange for three hundred seats in the Senate, a measure that would have doubled the Senate's size. On the second count, he followed his father's footsteps in reviving Gracchus's enfranchisement proposal and offered citizenship to the Latins and the Latin right to the Italian *socii*. The Italians firmly supported Drusus. Only the Etruscans and the Umbrians opposed his package deal, but this was probably because they considered the price Drusus set for citizenship in terms of redistribution of their public land too high. (They did avail themselves of citizenship when it was offered free of this charge a year later; Badian 1962:226–27.) Drusus failed, however. He was assassinated before the end of the year, the night after postponing the vote on his proposal. His proposal was dropped and the Italian leaders took up arms as their demand for citizenship had not been met. The Social War thus broke out and plunged Rome into civil strife for almost a decade. Twelve Italian allied city-states rose up against Rome. Even though the Italian allies lost the war, the restrictive barriers of the Roman oligarchy were shattered forever. The Social War was the first integrative revolution of the late Roman republic.

It is interesting to note that the Latins remained loyal to Rome during the Social War. This can be explained by the fact that the grant of citizenship through magistracy—in all probability a concession made as a result of the revolt of Fregellae—had opened up an important avenue to Roman citizenship for those who had held local magistracies. The numbers involved were small, and many Latins must have remained disaffected. Nevertheless, the Latin aristocracies, which enjoyed or had easy access to citizenship, remained loyal to Rome when the Italian aristocracies fought to gain the same right and privilege (Stockton 1979:189–94; Keaveney 1987:119).

If the division of the Roman upper class in 91 BCE made revolution a possibility, the political motive of the excluded municipal upper class to gain access to power made it an actuality. The evidence shows that the Italians were organized and ready to take up arms if Rome rejected their demand for citizenship (Keaveney 1987:91–92). The Italians demanded and were prepared to fight for citizenship not merely because it was beneficial to them but because they felt entitled to it. Their sense of entitlement is not difficult to understand.

The Short Life of the First New Nation

The Romanization and Latinization of Italy had been proceeding for centuries. To this process, the Latins had contributed their language, and the Romans their political institutions and imperial expansion. There were close patron-client ties between the Roman and Italian aristocracies and some intermarriage. Roman rule had unified Italy and superimposed upon regional patriotism a strong pan-Italianism through identification with Rome. The Roman army, in particular, had acted as a powerful mechanism for the unification of the peoples of the peninsula (Gabba 1976:28, 187n61). The result was the linguistic, cultural, and political homogeneity of Italy by 91 BCE. Not only did the Latins and *socii* share a cultural community with Rome; they also shared a common political destiny: the Italians carried a heavier military burden in the Roman imperial expansion in the second century, contributed more men to the legions than did the Romans, and continued to be taxed after the Romans were freed of the *tributum* in 167 (Brunt 1988:126n109; Keaveney 1987:15). They had defended Italy valiantly against the Cimbri and Tutones under Marius as recently as 102 BCE, and they reminded the Romans in 91 how much the empire owed to Italian arms (Brunt 1988:129). Their participation in empire was particularly significant, as the provincial subjects did not differentiate between them and the Romans. The experience of military life in the provinces of the empire had taught them to identify with the Romans and consider themselves their equals (Keaveney 1987:8–13). In short, there was considerable equalization of condition while the differences in legal status persisted. Against this background, the demand of the Italians for inclusion in the Roman political community makes perfect sense and seems more than justified. The desired political integration, to be more precise, meant freedom from subjection to the unchecked *imperium* of the Roman magistrates (which was the lot of the provincials and the conquered peoples), the right to vote, and the right to hold office. In the Roman timocratic system, where municipal votes counted heavily by Cicero's time, the right to vote was a considerable asset (Brunt 1988:126–27). The right to hold office in the Roman state was an obvious asset, all the more so in that it had no obvious cost in terms of local power: the Roman concept of *municipium* implied a double citizenship, both national and local, because it included minor rights of self-government (Jolowicz and Nicholas 1972:63; Sherwin-White 1973a:ch. 6).

The twelve rebellious allies set up the unified state of Italia, modeled after the Roman state, with Corfinium, renamed Italica, as its federal capital, and struck their own coins. An interesting fact that rules out an economic interpretation of the Social War is the leadership of the Marsi, whose public land had remained unaffected by redistribution under the Gracchan agrarian law. Even more interesting is the very fact of setting up an independent replica of the Roman polity as a confederation. This fact illustrates the two modalities of integrative revolution as alternatives. The constitution of a new Italian federal political order here appears as a substitute for integration into the old Roman one. If the Italian demand for citizenship and equality could not be met by the integration of its upper classes into the Roman political system, independence from Rome and the building of a new Italian federal polity constituted an alternative way of achieving liberation—that is, political entitlement (Keaveney 1987:ch. 3). This early attempt at the creation of a new nation in the vicinity of old Rome, however, was doomed to failure.

The Extension of Roman Citizenship despite the Defeat of the Rebel States

With the *lex Iulia de civitate* of 90 BCE, after one year of fighting, Rome offered the choice of citizenship to loyal Latins and to the allies who had not joined the rebels to obtain it. The news was hastily sent to troubled Etruria and Umbria and presumably to other waverers. The Etrurians and the Umbrians were thus dissuaded from joining the rebels, as they were about to do, and accepted Roman citizenship instead. In 89 BCE, the widespread massacre of Roman and Italian officials and traders alike in the East at the instigation of Mithradates IV, king of Pontus, created a desperate situation, making it imperative for the Senate to settle the war in Italy. A further enfranchisement law (*lex Plautia Papiria*) was passed in that year, extending the provisions of the *lex Iulia* to all Italians who would surrender by a specified date. The legal foundations for the extension of Roman citizenship to the Italians were laid. The Italian communities accepted Roman citizenship, changing their status from allied (sovereign) states to *municipia* (Brunt

1988:105–6; Keaveney 1987:142, 170–71). The inhabitants of present-day Italy north of the Po (Gallia Transpadana) were granted the Latin right. The war ended in 88 BCE, though scattered fighting continued into 87.

Both in its causes and in its consequences, the Social War demonstrates Aristotle's proposition that aristocracies and oligarchies that exclude men of substance and social influence are prone to revolution. After 89, the Italians entered Roman political life immediately and on an enormous scale (Gabba 1976:96–100, 236–37n204). There was considerable overlap between the geographical and social structural dimensions of this integrative consequence of the Social War. The *equites*, though opposed to Drusus for wanting to deprive them of their judiciary power, had looked kindly on the demands of the *socii* (Gabba 1976:88). This is hardly surprising if we bear in mind their social composition. The Italian aristocracies belonged to the equestrian class and, in fact, weighed heavily in that class. The importance of Italian recruitment into the equestrian order is incontestable, though we also have records of some knights from the colonies and provincial cities, especially from Spain (Nicolet 1974:1.387, 416–22 [table 7]). The Italian allies were granted citizenship not as individuals but as communities. Nevertheless, enfranchisement had greater benefits for the upper classes. By integrating the upper class of the Italian *municipia* into the Roman political system, the Social War at the same time enhanced the political integration of the *equites*. The municipalization of Italy that resulted from the Social War entailed considerable uniformity in administration through the introduction of the *quattuorviri* as magistrates in all *municipia* (Sherwin-White 1973a:165–66). Not only did this measure promote the unification of Italy, but it also assured the preponderance of the *municipia* within the Roman state and thus the political integration of the municipal *equites*.

The end of the Social War was not the end of revolution. On the contrary, the shock of the absorption of the Italians set in motion long-lasting revolutionary turmoil. What Mommsen called "the Sulpician revolution" was nothing but the continuation of the integrative revolution. In 88 BCE, the tribune of the plebs, Publius Sulpicius Rufus, consciously set out to complete Drusus's proposed reforms. Rome was proposing to register the newly enfranchised Italians in a few new tribes that would have voted last in the assemblies. This would have made the newly granted citizenship fairly worthless and was unacceptable to the Italians, who were demanding registration in all the tribes (Salmon 1958). Sulpicius took up their cause. Having met with senatorial recalcitrance, he turned to the aged Marius, who was well disposed toward the Italians. Sulpicius succeeded in passing a law equalizing the rights of the old and new citizens by distributing the latter among all the tribes of the assembly. Furthermore, he gave the same right to vote in all the tribes to the freedmen. Sulpicius courted the knights by introducing legislation favorable to them. He had an armed retinue of three thousand freedmen and six hundred knights, which he mockingly called his anti-Senate (Betti and Crifò [1914] 1982:119). This retinue made him master of the streets of Rome. Competitive mobilization was drawing new strata into the revolutionary power struggle, thus extending the integrative revolution into the lower ranks of the social structure (Mommsen 1854–56:2.531–35; Keaveney 1987:172–74). Sulpicius's alliance with Marius had added Marian veterans to the mobs which supported him. This spelled serious trouble. The hero of the last phase of the Social War, Lucius Cornelius Sulla, had become one of the two consuls for 88 and was given the mission against Mithradates in the East by lot. The Marian veterans wanted the commission for their general, as they were excluded from Sulla's army. Sulla marched on Rome with his six legions, even though all but one of his officers refused to accompany him. This march on Rome was successful, the mob being no match for Sulla's soldiers. Sulpicius was put to death, and his laws were nullified. Marius fled. The Roman tradition forbade the legions from setting foot in the city of Rome and the area surrounding the walls, where civil authority alone prevailed. In 88 BCE, Sulla breached this military inviolability of the city of Rome and ushered the armies into Roman politics. The new client army, as distinct from the old contingents of armed citizenry, had been created but not so exploited by Marius; Sulla used it as a political instrument for the first time in Roman history. The lesson was not lost even on the old Marius, who was to follow Sulla's example in the last year of his life. The age of the popular revolutionary tribunes—the Gracchi, Saturninus, who will be mentioned later, and Sulpicius—had come to an end, and the era of the contumacious generals inaugurated (Seager 1969:xi). Nevertheless, Sulla's march on Rome was only an indication of what was to come; the army did not produce its integrative revolution until some four decades later. And it did not end the revolution in 88.

The Italians found a new champion in the consul of 87, Cinna. With Sulla and his army safely out of the way in the East, Cinna gathered the followers of Marius and Sulpicius and began mobilizing the new citizens and encouraging them to revive their demand for redistribution among the thirty-five tribes. The influx of new citizens to Rome to press this demand alarmed the senators; violence broke out and Cinna was forced to flee. Competitive mobilization intensified, making the defeated Italians one of the decisive forces in Roman politics. Cinna recruited aggressively among the Italians, and Marius began recruiting in Etruria to join forces with him.

The Senate was forced to concede citizenship even to the Italians who had not surrendered by the date specified in the *lex Plautia Papiria*, though this gained few friends. The Samnites demanded the same for themselves and all deserters on their side; this was granted by Marius and Cinna. The latter also recruited widely among the slave population, even breaking into *ergastula* (underground prisons for slaves) in search of able bodies. With his legions thus put together, Cinna retook Rome, still in 87 BCE, and remained its master until his death in 84 BCE.

Once in power, Cinna paid less attention to the Italians, whose redistribution among the tribes was not carried out (Keaveney 1987:180–85). Instead, he instituted the first revolutionary reign of terror, using bands of slaves, whom he had set free, to massacre hundreds of his political opponents, mostly senators and knights. Marian veterans were also used as instruments of terror, as were the equestrian courts for the banishment of the lesser victims (Rostovtzeff [1927] 1960:112).

Meanwhile, competitive mobilization in the revolutionary power struggle on behalf of Sulla continued throughout Italy. The redistribution of the new citizens among all the thirty-five tribes was carried out in 84 BCE, apparently by a decree of the Senate (Gabba 1976:95). Sulla wrote from the East to reassure the new citizens, while his agents were actively courting them. The courting of the Italians intensified when Sulla landed in Italy in 83 BCE and began to advance toward Rome. Both Cinnans and Sullans were lobbying the Italians. Sulla himself signed a treaty with some Italian nations guaranteeing their newly won political rights (Gabba 1976:124; Keaveney 1987:186–87).

The Italians had lost the Social War but won their objectives, and their gains were consolidated by the ensuing civil war. The gains from the integrative revolution were irreversible.

Sulla and the Counterrevolution: 82–79 BCE

Civil war ended with Sulla's retaking of Rome in November 82 BCE. He refined and formalized Cinna's haphazard revolutionary terror into "proscription." He publicly posted a list of names of the proscribed, confiscating their property and fixing rewards for their heads, which were to be publicly exposed. By the time of its closure on June 1, 81, the list included 4,700, including about forty senators and 1,600 knights. With this massive purge instituted, Sulla was immediately proclaimed *dictator rei publicae constituendae* (dictator for the regulation of the commonwealth) and proceeded with his main task of the restoration of the republic. He abdicated his dictatorship at the end of 81, becoming one of the two consuls of *res publica restituta* in 80 and, finally, a private citizen in 79.

Two momentous reforms by Sulla completed the first integrative revolution of Rome, as Gaius Gracchus had dimly envisioned and the elder Drusus had sought to forestall and as the younger Drusus had proposed and Sulpicius had failed to accomplish. He institutionalized the integration of the Italians into the Roman political system, and he organized the integration of the knights in a less contentious manner than before. "Among the first acts carried out by Sulla when he landed in Italy was to recognize the legitimacy and absolute necessity of the demand of the *novi cives* by distributing them among the thirty-five tribes. It is a fact that Sulla, both explicitly and implicitly, legitimized everything the allies had done to achieve what they wanted against the view of the Senate: that is, the war itself" (Gabba 1976:97).

To this geographical extension of Roman political society, Sulla added an overlapping social structural dimension. According to Appian, "To the Senate, which had been much thinned by the sedition and the wars, he added about 300 members of the best of the *equites*. . . . To the plebeians he added more than 10,000 slaves of the men who had been killed, choosing the youngest and the strongest, to whom he gave freedom and Roman citizenship, and he called them Cornelii after himself" (cited in Lewis and Reinhold 1951:1.271). Of the two measures, the more important measure by far was the enlargement of the Senate. As Gabba (1976:142–50) has painstakingly shown, Sulla followed Drusus's scheme of doubling the size of the Senate from three hundred to six hundred, making three hundred knights senators; and he raised the number of quaestors from eight to twenty to ensure the orderly future replenishment of the Senate. The Senate had been drastically depleted by the losses during the social and civil wars, perhaps by one-half; and this gave Sulla the opportunity to promote perhaps as many as one hundred and fifty of his officers to senators. The *equites*, it is very true, had to pay for the three hundred seats in the Senate by losing the extortion courts. But this loss, partially restored in 70 BCE, did produce the result Drusus and Sulla had intended: the Polybian ideal, to be revived by Cicero, of a balanced polity based on the concord between the upper classes of the enlarged Roman society. Sulla's judiciary reform, it should be added, had a rationalizing as well as a political motive: the number of jury courts was greatly increased, and judicial commissions and permanent and special courts were reorganized or created on the basis of specialization of function. He also furthered the integration of Italy into the Roman polity by setting up a municipal system modeled on earlier Latin communities and by setting up a municipal council of one hundred modeled on the Roman Senate (Mommsen 1854–56:4.117, 128–33). Furthermore, Sulla reduced the power of the office of the revolutionary tribunes and restricted the right of *intercessio*, subjected plebiscites to approval by the Senate, and made the office less attractive to ambitious politicians by making it incompatible with subsequent occupation of *curule* offices. Some administrative reorganization thus went hand in hand with the integration of the allied states into Rome that took place following the Social War.[6]

Sulla the nullifier of Sulpicius's law presided over the incorporation of the Italians and the freedmen into the Roman political system; Sulla the champion of the Senate promoted three hundred knights and many common soldiers into their ranks; Sulla the inventor of proscription abolished capital punishment for political offenses; Sulla the violator of Rome's military sanctity made the Rubicon the boundary of a much-extended demilitarized Roman territory subject to civil authority on which no troops could be stationed (Mommsen 1854–56:4.123–24, 130). He even followed Drusus's Gracchan step of founding colonies (Gabba 1976:136). The enigma of Sulla, a constant subject of fascination for historians, is none other than the paradox of counterrevolution. Mommsen (1854–56:3.372) knew this when he said that restoration is always revolution.

Transformation of the Republic into Monarchy: 52–27 BCE

Imperial expansion had a profound impact on the character of the Roman army and the structure of authority in the Roman city-state. Originally, civil and military *imperia* were conjoint in each of the two annually elected consuls, as the people of Rome conferred *imperium militiae* on the supreme magistrate by a *lex curiata de imperio*. Imperial expansion required extension of military command beyond the two consuls. It became necessary to confer *imperium consulare* (*militiae*) upon other ex-magistrates and the privilege of *imperium proconsulare* (authority on behalf of the consul) upon private citizens. This extension implied a violation of the republican constitution but was necessary to create authority "independent of the *imperium militiae* of the supreme civil magistracy" (Betti and Crifò [1914] 1982:48). Furthermore, the armies commanded by generals with proconsular authority constituted an emerging social formation with a profoundly unsettling impact on Roman society and polity.

After 88 BCE, the place of the pre-Sulla revolutionary tribunes was taken by army commanders with proconsular, and occasionally consular, authority, who, in the long run, proved to be the successful agents of the revolutionary transformation of the republican city-state into an imperial monarchy. "The revolution moves from the *forum* of the city to the provinces of the empire" (Betti and Crifò [1914] 1982:52). It is to this "proconsular revolution," which is at the same time the integrative revolution of the Roman army, that we can now turn.

The period of civil strife between Pompey and Julius Caesar, the latter's dictatorship and murder, followed by a longer civil war that ended with the battle of Actium in 31 BCE and was celebrated by the conferment of the title Augustus upon Octavian in 27 BCE is one of the best known in world history. This second phase of Roman revolution has two interesting features. First, it was an integrative revolution that accelerated the integrative processes of extension of citizenship and political integration of Italy and enhanced the integration of the *equites* into the Roman authority structure. In one respect, however, its integrative dimension went significantly beyond the trends already in place: the integration of the newly professionalized army into the Roman social and political structure. Second, the transition from republic to empire was a centralizing revolution: Caesar and Augustus fundamentally altered the Roman polity by concentrating power in the hands of a monarch without a formal office who became known as the *princeps* (first citizen), the emperor, the Caesar.

It has been estimated that throughout the last two centuries BCE, commonly some 100,000 to 130,000 Italians, or over 10 percent of the adult male population, served in the armies (Hopkins 1978:4, 56); and probably 200,000 Italians were under arms when Caesar was murdered (Campbell 1984:157). The intimate relationship between military and political organization, between citizenship and military service, in the ancient "Servian constitution" will be recalled. Military service was a fundamental duty of all citizens. However, as all soldiers had to equip themselves with arms, military service was in practice compulsory only for the five classes of propertied citizens (*adsidui*); citizens without property (*proletarii*) who lacked the means to arm themselves were ordinarily exempted. The second century witnessed a fundamental change in Roman military organization: the citizens' militia was gradually replaced by armies of volunteers recruited from two overlapping categories: the proletariat and the rural population. This fundamental reform, usually associated with Marius's reform of 107 BCE, had in fact been in the making for decades. By the mid-second century BCE, there were not enough propertied citizens to meet the military needs of the Roman state. In 129 BCE, the census qualifications for the fifth propertied class were lowered, permitting an artificial conversion of 76,000 *proletaries* to *adsidui*. There may also have been a decline in the population and an increase in the number of the proletariat and the lowest census class; this proletarianization of the *adsidui* would also have meant proletarianization of the militia. Even so, the militia was not adequate to the needs of the expansive republic. In 134 BCE, Scipio had to take an army of clients and volunteers to Spain. In 107, Marius institutionalized regular recruitment of proletarian volunteers, and in 103 and 100 BCE, through the tribune Saturninus, he established the practice of distributing land to the veterans. He also improved the training programs (Gabba 1976:ch. 1).

The task of recruiting and maintaining volunteer armies naturally devolved upon the general, who could not be changed frequently, as had been the case. The soldiers' pay was meager, even when supplemented by booty at irregular intervals. Furthermore, serving in the army was ruinous to smallholders and was bound to reduce them to proletarians even if they had been petty *adsidui*. The soldiers of the new volunteer armies, therefore, clamored for land upon discharge and looked to their generals to get it for them. Given the formalized nature of the patron-client relationship in Roman society, it is hardly surprising that the soldiers became the military *clientela* of the generals en masse. The new volunteer armies were thus, from the beginning, client armies of the nonrotating generals; and the allotment of land was the chief obligation of the generals to their soldier-clients upon discharge. In this fashion, a new class of soldiers erupted onto the Roman political scene as supporters of their generals: Sulla, followed by the old Marius, then Pompey and Caesar (Gabba 1976:26–27; Brunt 1988:265–66). The nucleus of Pompey's army was, in fact, the private army recruited by his father during the Social War. One can therefore speak no longer of the Roman army but rather of the armies of Marius, Sulla, Pompey, and Caesar. Sulla discharged his obligation as the patron of his veterans by massive settlement of his veterans in Italy. Given the scarcity of land in Italy, however, Sulla's solution could not be repeated often.

A satisfactory solution to the veteran problem was found not by the Senate but by Julius Caesar and was left for Augustus to complete: massive settlement of veterans as colonists in the provinces of the empire (Gabba 1976:37–52; Hopkins 1978:13, 68 [table I.2, sec. F]). Under Caesar, furthermore, the process of professionalization of career officers, begun under Marius and Sulla, advanced very considerably. When Sulla marched on Rome in 88, all but one of his officers refused to follow him; when Caesar crossed the Rubicon into the demilitarized Roman territory, all but one of his officers *did* follow him (L. de Blois 1987:15–16). If Sulla's officers were still overwhelmingly citizens on military duty, Caesar's were overwhelmingly military men with few civil scruples. Though Brunt (1988:256, 268) correctly objects to the notion of professional armies, because most soldiers did not desire to remain in the army for the whole of their active lives and looked forward to discharge and settlement on land, the evidence for the increasing professionalization of a distinct class of career officers is clear. Of course, the ex-centurions may well have looked forward to gaining equestrian status in the census and even becoming senators, as many of them did under Sulla and Caesar. This orientation may not indicate the sense of identity implied by the term *homo militaris* (Gabba 1976:35). Nevertheless, lack of strict professionalization did not impede the identification of soldier-clients with their generals. In fact, the veterans of Sulla's and Caesar's armies were commonly referred to as such for more than a decade after their patron's death (L. de Blois 1987:5).

Breakdown of the Authority Structure of the Late Republic and the Victory of Julius Caesar: 52–44 BCE

The army was already the decisive factor in Roman politics in the 80s BCE. The rise of Pompey owed much to Sulla's favor and to the private army raised by his father. However, as consul in 70 BCE, he made a significant overture to the *populares* by annulling, with Caesar's vigorous help (Suet., *J. Caesar* 5), Sulla's restriction of the power of the tribunes.[7] Caesar survived Sulla's repression and reemerged as a leader of the *populares*. Though a patrician who reckoned his descent from the goddess Venus, Julius Caesar was the son-in-law of Cinna (Suet., *J. Caesar* 1, 6) and availed himself of what had survived of the latter's political network in Rome, where he became aedile in 65 BCE and began scheming with Marcus Crassus. In 63, Cicero, as consul, uncovered the Cantilinarian conspiracy and executed its leaders with the approval of the Senate. Caesar opposed the death penalty and was forcefully ejected from a session for obstructing the procedure. Though well connected with the *populares*, Caesar's sociopolitical base was not by any means confined to the city of Rome. He took over Marius's clientele in Africa and built his own in Transpadane Gaul and in Spain, where he served as magistrate in 68 and 61 (Gaudemet 1982:446). Caesar married his daughter to Pompey and crafted the first triumvirate with him and Crassus in 60, becoming consul in 59 BCE.

The political and fiscal institutions of the Roman republic were hopelessly inadequate for solving the problem of maintaining standing volunteer armies for the empire. This was shown clearly when Pompey failed to reward the veterans through the Senate and proper constitutional channels in 60 BCE, whereas Caesar did it for him as consul in 59 by having the veterans improperly intervene in the assemblies (Gabba 1976:43–44). The armies drew the lesson that they could not look to the Senate to solve their problems and were entirely dependent on their generals. Incidentally, in that year Caesar also followed Tiberius Gracchus's example of removing a tribune who opposed him by the vote of the assembly.

The triumvirate fell apart after the death of Caesar's daughter while he had embarked upon the conquest of Gaul with proconsular *imperium*. The series of special commands that had to be created for Pompey, Caesar's accession to the consulate and proconsulate of Gaul in 59 BCE, and the de facto triumvirate itself were indicative of the inadequacy of the republican authority structure to the Roman Empire of conquest. As the arrangement between Pompey and Caesar fell apart,[8] with the former in Spain and the latter in Gaul—the provinces they respectively held with proconsular mandates—the breakdown of the Roman authority structure produced a revolutionary crisis.

The 50s BCE witnessed a marked increase in civil violence in the city of Rome. As had been the case in Greece, there was no proper police force in Rome, and the magistrates were without adequate executive power. Since the violent suppression of Tiberius Gracchus, violence in political and private disputes was fostered by law and constitutional precedent. Furthermore, the law itself became highly politicized. Partisan legislation became frequent, and the criminal courts were used as an instrument in the political struggle (Gruen 1974:506–7). Furthermore, the lack of even a minimal concentration of legalized coercive power now was aggravated by the alarming growth of gangs—formed mostly of freedmen and slaves by such politicians as Publius Clodius and Titus Annius Milo. Furthermore, the *plebs urbana*, which included army veterans as well as dispossessed and uprooted peasants, was generally available for mobilization as mobs (Lintott 1968; 1982:175). "Unseemly violence prevailed almost constantly, together with shameful contempt for law and justice." Appian goes on to state that faction leaders refused to disband troops entrusted to them by the state and even hired forces (Lewis and Reinhold 1951:1.251–52). Endemic violence thus increased sharply.

As a result of armed clashes between the gangs of Clodius and Milo, no consuls or praetors could be elected at the beginning of 52 BCE. Even the nomination of an interrex was prevented by the veto of the tribune acting under Pompey's direction. Rome was thus in a state of complete anarchy, with the system of public authority broken down and armed gangs in control of the streets. Clodius was murdered on January 18. Two days later, the Senate nominated Lepidus as interrex. The Senate declared a state of emergency, entrusting the protection of the state to Pompey as proconsul *ad urbem*.[9] In February, avoiding the title of dictator made infamous by Sulla, Pompey was made the sole consul (*consul sine collega*), retaining his proconsular mandate for Spain and Africa. In contravention of constitutional norms (Mommsen 1887:517), consular and proconsular authority were thus amalgamated to save Rome from anarchy (Betti and Crifò [1914] 1982:365–75).

Caesar reacted by seeking to add consulate to his proconsulate for Gaul. A plebiscite[10] conceded to him the right to run for consulate on the condition that he would reenter the city. In September 51, Consul M. Marcellus proposed terminating Caesar's proconsular *imperium* in Gaul. The consul and the Senate thus joined in a legislative battle against Caesar and the pro-Caesar tribunes. In 50 BCE, Pompey was given two legions to oppose Caesar; Caesar moved his troops to the border of Italy and threatened to intervene if violence was used against Caesarian tribunes. On January 7, 49, the new consul, Lentulus, ignored the *intercessio* of the tribunes M. Antonius and Q. Cassius, ejecting them from the curia by force, and obtained the Senate vote on a declaration of a state of emergency (Betti and Crifò [1914] 1982:381–414). On January 10, Caesar and his army crossed the Rubicon, the boundary set for the demilitarized zone by Sulla. The pro-Caesar tribunes who had fled Rome were welcomed by Caesar on the bank of the Rubicon. Supported by a supernatural apparition, Caesar proceeded toward Rome. Pompey and many of the senators fled to the Adriatic coast. Caesar marched on Rome, then left it in a hurry for Spain, Pompey's province, where most of his forces were stationed, saying: "I am off to meet an army without a leader; when I return I shall meet a leader without an army" (Suet., *J. Caesar* 34). This latter he did in August 48, defeating Pompey in Pharsalus in Thessaly.

Caesar brought civil strife to a speedy end by concentrating all power in his own hands. To achieve this, he adopted the twin strategy of, on the one hand, cumulating ordinary offices with the extraordinary office of dictatorship and, on the other, weakening the Senate and the elective magistracies. He was accordingly recognized as dictator in November 49; held the consulate from 48 to the end of his life, being made the sole consul in 45; obtained the tribunician power (*tribunicia potestas*) for life after Pharsalus; and imitated Sulla in having himself proclaimed *dictator rei publicae constituendae* in 47, his dictatorship being confirmed for ten years in 46 and for life in 45 or 44 BCE. He had been acclaimed *pontifex maximus* in 50 BCE and retained that supreme religious office. At the same time, he undermined the authority of the magistracies by obtaining, after Pharsalus, the right to designate the candidates for consulate and other magistracies and by multiplying their occupants. He weakened the Senate by flooding it with knights and military officers (increasing the number of its members to nine hundred), by taking over the right to nominate the provincial governors as dictator, and by depriving it of much of its financial power (Gaudemet 1982:447–48).

Julius Caesar's assumption of the tribunician power[11] for life was consistent with his contemptuous treatment of certain tribunes and with his general strategy of stripping away the authority of all established offices. But as we shall see, with this idea he stumbled upon an ingenious means of appropriating the palladium of democracy in the city-state for imperial monarchy. Caesar's concentration of power went hand in hand with legal reform, consisting of "the reduction of the Civil Code to manageable proportions" (Suet., *J. Caesar* 44), the reform of the calendar on the basis of the solar year (in 46 BCE), and rationalization of municipal and imperial administration and, through the use of his slaves, of financial administration. Nevertheless, Caesar's solution to the breakdown of the authority structure of Rome was not radical reorganization but concentration of power through the cumbersome procedure of ad hoc cumulation of offices and titles, together with the weakening of the Senate and the magistracies.

Although he refused the title of king, Julius Caesar departed sharply from the republican tradition by installing a golden throne in the Senate house, by striking coins bearing his effigy, by setting up altars, temples, and priests for his own cult, and by changing the name of the seventh month to July (Suet., *J. Caesar* 76).

In the course of competitive mobilization required by the revolutionary process, Julius Caesar had acted vigorously to promote the enlargement of the Roman political community. He permitted those Italians who had been proscribed or otherwise excluded by Sulla on account of their Marian or Cinnan affiliations to enter Roman political life, and he granted citizenship to many colonists[12] and to the legionaries he had raised in Transalpine Gaul (Suet., *J. Caesar* 24). In geographical terms, he lavishly distributed Roman franchise beyond Italy. We cannot be certain about Caesar's vision of the imperial polity. "But one point is not doubtful: he meant to extend the Roman and Latin franchise as widely as possible among the inhabitants of the provinces" (Rostovtzeff [1927] 1960:136). In 49, Caesar extended Roman citizenship to Transpadane Gaul. In all probability, he also set in motion a machinery for the collection and transmission of financial statistics by the municipal censors that also served as a mechanism for the registration of citizens qualified to vote. He certainly furthered the municipalization of Italy and the establishment of uniform administrative procedures, even though he did not live to complete his plans for completing the establishment of uniform procedures in municipal administration (Sherwin-White 1973a:157–59, 170–71). In social structural terms, too, he created new citizens out of not only his soldiers but also physicians and teachers resident in Rome (Suet., *J. Caesar* 42) and set in motion considerable upward social mobility by appointing many knights and upstarts, especially military officers, to the Senate.

Failure of Republican Constitutionalism and the Posthumous Political Triumph of Caesar's Army: March 44–October 42 BCE

The revolution that followed the murder of Caesar was started by exponents of the republican tradition with the support of most of the old senators, who correctly saw that the increase in Caesar's power meant the decline of the power of the Senate. It was thus a revolution set in motion by a declining senatorial class in reaction to its progressive political dispossession by a tyrant, a centralizer. Roman resentment toward the new citizens, and toward Caesar for "admitting to the Senate men of foreign birth, including semicivilized Gauls, who had been granted Roman citizenship" (Suet., *J. Caesar* 76), must also have been a factor of considerable significance. The outcome of the revolution, however, was not what the republican constitutionalists could have desired, or anyone could have foreseen. A certain Gaius Octavianus, a young man adopted by Julius Caesar, unexpectedly entered the political scene as his heir, and through him, after a decade and a half of immense civil strife and bloodshed, Caesar's work of integration and centralization was completed. Caesar the dictator for life became Caesar the emperor; and the timocratic political order of the republic was replaced by the more broadly based imperial political order of the principate. Let us examine the three crucial phases of this revolutionary transition separately.

The conspirators who murdered Caesar in the Senate on the ides (15th) of March, 44 BCE, were led by Cassius and Brutus. They were both praetors, and Marcus Brutus was the nephew of Cato and a descendant of the legendary founder of the republic and of *libertas* in Rome. The Liberators, as they styled themselves, were met with a cool reception when they appealed to the populace in the Forum; and a speech delivered in the Capitol by Brutus the next day fell flat; even in the Senate, the proposal to award them special honors for tyrannicide on March 17 failed to carry. Brutus and Cassius traveled to the small towns of Latium and gathered some adherents from the local aristocracies, but the new recruits' devotion to the republican cause was never put to the test, as the praetors soon departed for the East. The conspirators numbered about sixty and had the support of most of the old senators. What the Liberators expected, and did not find, was popular support outside the Senate; and there is no evidence that they used the techniques of the demagogic tribunes of the preceding era. Instead, they relied on the Senate and adopted the strategy of gaining control of the eastern legions. What they had not taken into account was being confronted with the vested interests of Caesar's veterans. Marcus Antonius (Marc Antony), himself a Caesarian general, wasted no time cultivating the veterans and spent a whole month (mostly May) setting up military colonies and allotting land to veterans. He returned to Rome with an escort of veterans; a few days later a law was passed permitting all ex-centurions to serve on juries. Antony, whose life had been spared at Brutus's insistence, had played his hand very well and had reached an accommodation with the Liberators and the Senate. Now he alarmed them by his escort of veterans. On June 5, the Senate voted commissions for Brutus and Cassius that amounted to honorable exile. But Antony was consul for 44, and decisive action by his unexpected rival Octavian had to be postponed until his term ended. (In fact, it was to begin on January 1, 43 BCE.) Meanwhile, Caesar's heir had put in his bid for the support of the veterans, and intense mobilization and countermobilization of soldiers had set in.[13]

In sharp contrast to the Liberators, Octavian began his efforts at mobilizing the plebs and the veterans by organizing games and festivals. Veterans pressured Antony toward accommodation with Octavian to avoid a split in the Caesarian party. Octavian was drawing on his inheritance and could also claim the services of Caesar's wealthy freedmen. According to Syme (1939:130), he was "attracting all the enemies of society—old soldiers who had dissipated gratuities and farms, fraudulent financiers, unscrupulous freedmen, ambitious sons of ruined families from the local gentry of the towns of Italy." On November 10, Octavian occupied the Forum with some three thousand of the veterans he had recruited; but his coup failed, as the veterans refused to fight Antony and his Macedonian legions. Caesar's veterans now had two champions; the Senate could play a role. Cicero, the venerable consul for 63, had emerged as the leader of the Senate after the departure of Cassius and Brutus. After some hesitation, he decided to use Octavian, his famous saying, "*Cedant arma togae*" (Let arms cede to the toga!), notwithstanding. Rumors later reported Cicero as having said that the youth was to be praised, uplifted, and lifted off (Syme 1939:181–82). A fateful error, as it turned out; lifted off Octavian could not be.

With two new consuls loyal to the Senate, Cicero opened the year 43 BCE with a severe attack on Antony according to a program made public on December 20. Cicero had taken over the leadership of the republican constitutionalists and had decided on a tactical alliance with Octavian to split the Caesarians. The youth had been courting him for a while, but Cicero had not been won over while Antony was in office and would have nothing to do with the failed November coup. Now he had Octavian elected to the Senate, with the title of propraetor, and given direction of the military operations against Antony along with the new consuls, Hirtius and Pansa. The soldiers were promised donatives, and two legions were recalled to the standards by Octavian, with land allotments (Brunt 1988:266). The Senate also backed Decimus Brutus in his refusal to hand over the command of his army in the Cisalpina to Antony. Meanwhile, Marcus Brutus and his agents were campaigning in Greece and Macedonia, and Cassius was doing the same in Syria, evidently in coordination with Cicero; early in February came news of their successes. Cicero spoke for Brutus and secured his appointment as proconsul of Macedonia. The republican constitutionalists levied a property tax, raised troops, and dispatched them under the consuls to confront Antony in March, together with Octavian and Decimus Brutus. Lepidus and another general, Plancus, were also summoned from the west to support the armies of the republic against Antony. The decisive battles took place in April, the last one in Mutina. The republic won and Antony fled west. The cost of victory, however, was tremendous. Both consuls had fallen, and casualties among the raw levies had been very heavy. The remnants of the consuls' armies mostly joined Octavian's, with very few going to Decimus Brutus. On April 27, all Rome celebrated the victory of Mutina. But the political cost of losing both consuls soon became evident, as no new ones were elected. Before the end of May, Cicero would find that "the Senate was a weapon that had broken to pieces in his hands" (Syme 1939:181).

Cicero's plans foundered on the unnatural alliance between the republican constitutionalists and the heir and veterans of Caesar. Solidarity with Antony, as a Caesarian general, had outweighed the duties of citizenship and loyalty to the republic for Lepidus and Plancus. Lepidus chose to be a Caesarian leader and co-presider over the destruction of the republic. By June, Antony and Lepidus were acting in concord. More ominous still were the movements of Octavian and his augmented army. In July, four hundred centurions and soldiers met with the Senate and demanded the consulate for Octavian and the promised donative for themselves. Upon the Senate's refusal, Octavian followed the examples of Sulla and Caesar, crossing the Rubicon and marching on Rome. The legions of the republic went over to him, and he was elected consul on August 19, 43 BCE, when he was not yet twenty.

A part of Caesar's army asserted its political clout by marching on Rome with Octavian. Octavian gave each soldier a donative amounting to more than ten years' pay out of the treasury. All that was left was to reunite with other parts of Caesar's army in political supremacy. Octavian, Antony, and Lepidus met to shape the future of the Roman state for a decade: "the Caesarian leaders were drawn irresistibly together. They were instruments rather than agents. Behind them stood the legions and the forces of revolution" (Syme 1939:188). Caesar's abolished dictatorship was revived as a triumvirate; a law on November 27, 43, established the three leaders of the Caesarian professionalized army as *tresvir rei publicae constituendae* (triumvirate for the regulation of the commonwealth) for five years. It was to be renewed for another five-year term in 37 BCE. Proscriptions followed, claiming Cicero's life, among others. Many of the proscribed fled, either east to Brutus and Cassius or west to Pompey's son. Having thus abolished the republic in Rome, the triumvirate prepared to confront Brutus and Cassius in the East during the summer of 42. The definitive defeat of republican constitutionalism and the physical destruction of Brutus, Cassius, and the old Roman aristocracy were accomplished at the battle of Philippi in Macedonia in October 42 BCE (Syme 1939:chs. 14–15).

The revolution of the Caesarian army had triumphed. The remaining republicans were routed in 41, and the score with Pompey's son was definitively settled in 37 BCE. The accommodation and final destruction of Pompey's son requires a brief comment. Pompey had been Caesar's archrival, with his own client army and a constituency of Italians, new citizens, and Cisalpines very much like Caesar's. After the defeat of Pompey, many of the pardoned Pompeians joined Caesar's service and played a major role in the conspiracy to murder the latter. Pompey's army, on the other hand, transferred their loyalty as his *clientela* to his son, Sextus Pompeius, who forced the triumvir to acknowledge him as a major partner in 40 BCE. In 37 BCE Octavian inflicted a series of stunning defeats on Pompey's son, destroying his army, and had him executed. Thus, there was only one professional army left, Caesar's, to become *the* Roman army under Augustus.

Caesar's triumphant army discharged its obligation to its deceased patron. On January 1, 42 BCE, Julius Caesar was deified, and a temple was erected for him in the Forum. The triumviral version of dictatorship spelled the death blow to the authority of consuls, who were henceforth handpicked in advance. The authority of praetors, too, was drastically devalued, as the number of praetors was increased from sixteen to sixty-seven in one year. The number of senators soon exceeded a thousand. During the proscription, many powerful figures outside Rome were also expelled from Italy. A new political elite was installed, almost all with non-Latin names. Under the triumvirate and during the civil wars, many non-Romans (*peregrini*) had been recruited into the legions, thereby gaining citizenship, and many auxiliary soldiers were granted citizenship (Wiseman 1969:71, 74–75). Furthermore, the machinery created by Julius Caesar for registration of municipal voters must surely have been used by Octavian's agents for mobilization of support for him in Italy. Revolution was thus acting as a powerful agent of circulation of elites. Caesar's favored Cisalpine Gaul was made a part of Italy, and its inhabitants were granted citizenship (Syme 1939:199–201, 207). Augustus's later restrictive citizenship policy for non-Italians during the principate was a retrenchment, one that brings out all the more the unintended consequences of the inevitably competitive revolutionary mobilization.

This phase of the revolution already brought about two changes that proved irreversible: (1) the republican authority structure was fundamentally altered and its social base practically destroyed; and (2) the armies were institutionally incorporated into the Roman political system, and the soldiers as a class were integrated into Roman society. The profound impact of the incorporation of the army upon the authority structure of Rome is admirably captured by Betti and Crifò ([1914] 1982:576–77): the man who received *imperium militiae* through the salutation of the army, later confirmed by the Senate, could be a private citizen (as was Scipio in 211, Marius in 88, Pompey in 82, 77, 67, and 66, and Octavian in 43 BCE) and not a magistrate of the city-state elected by the people. The army, with the endorsement of the Senate, had usurped the jurisdiction of the "old people" of the city of Rome. "The army was the new people." The salutation by the army and the Senate henceforth conferred supreme magistracy on a *princeps designatus*. The subsequent *lex de imperio* of the people merely confirmed the person so designated. Thus, with the establishment of monarchy in the form of the "principate" under Octavian, who assumed the title Augustus, the city-state had been transformed into an imperial monarchy.

In the process of competitive mobilization, rhetoric and slogans are freely appropriated. The *libertas* and *virtus* of the republican constitutionalists, like the democratic rhetoric of the *populares*, meant little to Caesar's veterans. But to broaden their popular appeal, Caesar and his adopted son absorbed and neutralized the political tradition and rhetoric both of the *populares* and of the republican constitutionalists. Julius Caesar claimed to have crossed the Rubicon in order to restore liberty to the people who were oppressed by the opposing political faction. The formula was to be taken up by Augustus (*Res gestae* 1.1): "At the age of nineteen I raised an army . . . , and by means of this army I restored to liberty the Republic, which was oppressed by the tyranny of a faction" (Lewis and Reinhold 1951:1.562, trans. modified).

Tota Italia *for Imperator Caesar, Son of the God Julius; or, The Triumph of the Italian Core over the Eastern Periphery: 36–31 BCE*

Octavian consolidated his position with the army. He took immediate advantage of the deification of Caesar and began calling himself *divi filius* (son of god). In 38 BCE, he was using Caesar as a family name (*gentilicum*) and took the striking step of converting the military title of imperator into his forename (praenomen). Henceforth, he called himself Imperator Caesar, maximizing his identification with the army and its deified patron (Syme 1958).

Augustus was also conscious of the importance of building a constituency beyond the army and concentrated his efforts in municipal Italy and in the military colonies. Turning to the colonies of the veterans, who had returned to civilian pursuits, was a natural first step beyond the army itself. Italy was also a natural constituency for Octavian, who belonged to the municipal equestrian elite by birth. By contrast, Antony's ties were increasingly with the eastern provinces. In 36 BCE, he threw in his lot with Cleopatra, and as her husband, he stood for the East. Octavian championed Italy against Cleopatra.

As we shall see, political oracles, often attributed to various Sibyls, became a major ideological weapon for opposition to Hellenistic and later Roman domination in the Near East. Cleopatra's ambition was to rule over the Roman Empire from its Egyptian periphery, in the tradition of Alexander, and she accordingly named her son by Antony Alexander Helios (*Sib. Or.*, p. 358). A political oracle put in circulation by her before the battle of Actium (*Sib. Or.* 3.350–80, p. 370) exploits the typical Sibylline anti-Roman motif but ends not with the total destruction of Rome but with its subjugation, which is followed by peace and concord. The oracle is particularly vehement in subjecting Octavian's Italians to the vengeance of Asia:

> However much wealth Rome received from tribute-bearing Asia,
> Asia will receive three times that much again from Rome . . .
> Whatever number from Asia served the house of the Italians,
> twenty times that number of Italians will be serfs
> in Asia, in poverty, and they will be liable to pay ten-
> thousandfold. (*Sib. Or.* 3.350–55)

As the second term of the triumvirate expired and the two pro-Antony consuls for 32 BCE called for a return to constitutional government, Octavian appealed to all of Italy. He later claimed: "All of Italy of its own accord swore an oath of allegiance to me and chose me as its leader in the war which I won at Actium" (cited in Syme 1939:184). An oath of personal allegiance to the revolutionary leader was taken throughout Italy in defiance of constitutional authorities, and the towns of Italy offered public vows for his safety. He prepared for war by claiming revolutionary legitimacy on the basis of the consent of *tota Italia*. The authority of Imperator Caesar, son of the god Julius, was augmented by that of the revolutionary leader of the Italian nation against foreign interests. The national pride of a more deeply united Italy was no doubt aroused by the victory against Antony at the battle of Actium in 31 BCE and constituted a solid basis for the Augustan principate. Actium was Italy's victory. It was two centuries too early for the domination of the Roman center by the eastern periphery, which had to await the last revolution of the Roman Empire.[14]

This phase of the revolution, too, was a period of great social mobility for all of Italy. It was a period of great advancement for the soldiery in the form of settlement in veterans' colonies in Italy and the provinces and entry into the equestrian order and the Senate. The freedmen also did very well. But above all, this phase deepened the political integration of Italy, hand in hand with the reaffirmation of the boundaries that set it apart from the provinces of the Roman Empire. It is worth recalling that Sulla had demilitarized Rome up to the Rubicon. Augustus demilitarized the whole of Italy; no legions were to be stationed there. Access both to the Senate and to state offices was opened to the inhabitants of all of Italy. Municipal men from areas close to Rome had been conspicuous in the Senate for some time, but now they came from a much broader area covering the entire peninsula (Syme 1939:ch. 24).

Since 52 BCE, the fate of revolution had often been decided in the provinces, the most decisive battles having been fought in Pharsalus, Philippi, and Actium. But the secret of the empire was not yet out. It had to await another revolution, which came a century later.

The Augustan Settlement and the Cumulative Consequences of the Revolutions of the Late Republic

Imperator Caesar divi filius chose the year 27 BCE for the legal settlement that would mark the end of civil strife and the restoration of peace and stability. The restoration of the republic was proclaimed with great flourish, with the imperator as its first citizen (*princeps*). On the ides (13th) of January, the Senate conferred upon him the title Augustus, which had an aura of sanctity. Thus was inaugurated the peculiar form of monarchy in the Roman Empire that survived Augustus's death in 14 CE and is known as the principate. Both the authority structure of the principate and its social base were radically different from the republican political order. All but in name, the latter had undergone a revolutionary transformation whose two dimensions can be examined separately.

Concentration of Power and Transformation of the Authority Structure

Octavian had held the consulate since 31 BCE without interruption and had been granted a number of other prerogatives. With the title Augustus, he was given ten provinces as proconsul in 27. Reacting to a foiled conspiracy in 23, Augustus resigned his consulship in favor of an admirer of Brutus and instead followed Caesar's example and received the tribunician power (*tribunicia potestas*) for life. He dated his reign from its receipt and made definitive the abstraction of the tribunician power from the tribunate, which was thus appropriated for imperial monarchy as a symbol of passive democratization. Furthermore, Augustus's proconsular *imperium* was made superior to that of other proconsuls (*imperium maius*) and was valid (unlike that of other proconsuls) even in the city of Rome. This, in effect, reduced all other proconsuls governing the provinces to the legates of Augustus. In 19 BCE, Augustus was given "the *imperium* of the consuls for life, so that he should use twelve *fasces* always and everywhere and should sit on his curule chair between the two consuls for the time being" (Dio, cited in A. Jones 1960:13). He was also given censorial powers as the supervisor of morals for five years. Upon Lepidus's death in 12 BCE, Augustus also became the supreme pontiff (*pontifex maximus*).[15] Of this assortment of offices, two were fundamental. "The two pillars of his rule, proconsular *imperium* and the tribunician powers, were the Revolution itself—the Army and the People. On them stood the military and monarchic demagogue" (Syme 1939:337).

The discrepancy between form and content in the principate is jarring. This discrepancy is best captured by Dio's reversal of the formula used by Augustus when he states that, by the settlement of 27, "the whole power of the people and the Senate passed to Augustus and from this time there existed what was really a monarchy" (cited in Wells 1984:55). Augustus preferred the more elusive but also more secure supreme authority and influence (*auctoritas*) of the *princeps* to the more concrete legal power (*potestas*) of dictatorship chosen by Julius Caesar, but he was also appreciative of the legitimatory benefits that would result from decorating his power with a smattering of formal offices. Thus, "in the last resort, the magistracies were arranged not to give Augustus power, but to clothe his power in decent and traditional garments" (Wells 1984:61–62).

Dio knew that behind the republican facade, Augustus's monarchical power rested on his control of finances and of the army (Wells 1984:55). The public treasury (*aerarium*) had been managed by quaestors during the republican era, and its control, as we have seen, was one of the major sources of the Senate's power. Augustus brought it under his control by appointing first a prefect and then a praetor over it, and he took an interest in its efficient management, often subsidizing it from his private purse (*fiscus*) (A. Jones 1960:106–7). "But the chief innovation on the republican system was this—that military affairs were now withdrawn entirely from the competence of the Senate and the popular assembly. Nor were such matters any concern of the annual magistrates, the consuls and the praetors; they were reserved exclusively for the emperor to deal with." Furthermore, the armies were stationed in the provinces governed by Augustus (Rostovtzeff [1927] 1960:170–71).

Augustus transformed the client army he had inherited from Caesar into a standing army of twenty-five legions, consisting of some 180,000 Roman citizens, and he set up a second army recruited from among Roman subjects, the *auxilia*. Three Urban Cohorts under the urban prefect were quartered in the city of Rome, constituting the first effective police force in Roman history. Last but not least in its dire long-term consequences, he set up a palace guard for the emperor under a knight as their Praetorian prefect. This Praetorian Guard consisted of nine (later ten) cohorts, each of one thousand men, recruited from the barbarians, mostly Germans (Rostovtzeff [1927] 1960:169–70). Julius Caesar had doubled the soldiers' pay in 49, just before the war with Pompey. Augustus further improved the pay and conditions of the troops and undertook their settlement on a massive scale. The cost of maintaining the standing army was enormous, and Augustus forced his well-to-do Italian supporters to pay for peace and prosperity by reintroducing direct taxation. He also made a large contribution out of his *fiscus*. In 6 CE, he created a military treasury (*aerarium militare*) to pay the soldiers' discharge benefits, with a large gift from his purse and a promise of further annual contributions. Augustus personally controlled military pay and benefits. No one else was allowed to gain favor as a benefactor of troops. "The army was the emperor's personal possession," and the emperor was the sole paymaster and benefactor of the army (Campbell 1984:159, 185).

Augustus also made great strides in centralizing administrative authority. He set up a continuous imperial administration, manned largely from his slaves and freedmen, with knights as heads of its departments. To the *scribae*, who had constituted the civil service under the republic, were added the imperial slaves and freedmen assisting secretaries and procurators, on the one hand, and military clerks, on the other. Civil and military administrative procedures were rationalized and centralized (A. Jones 1960:ch. 10, esp. 158–59). This process included the establishment of special commissions that were assigned particular administrative tasks and were responsible to the emperor. All this eroded the authority of the Senate and the elected magistrates who had survived the republican period (Wells 1984:62). Concentration of power affected other spheres of life as well. Under the republic, all Roman jurists with an established reputation for learning could issue *responsa* when asked for their opinion. Augustus required that *responsa* be given "with his authority" and under seal. The right to issue *responsa* became a privilege (*beneficium*) granted by the emperor (Jolowicz and Nicholas 1972:359). The granting of this right of *publicly* giving opinions (*publice respondere*) was an important step in the institutionalization of judiciary authority under the monarch. Augustus also rationalized court procedures through extensive legislation (Kunkel 1972:107, 125).

The right of free association, too, was affected. Under the Twelve Tables, citizens were free to form associations (*collegia*). The Senate had dissolved the *collegia* after riots in 64 BCE, but the right of association had been restored in 58. "Caesar dissolved all workers' guilds except the ancient ones" (Suet., *J. Caesar* 42). Augustus and his successors followed Caesar in imposing new restrictions on *collegia*, which now required a government license (Brunt 1988:306). Nor would Augustus leave intact the ideological oppositional weapon of the periphery. As the supreme pontiff, Augustus destroyed two thousand subversive prophetic and Sibylline verses in Greek and Latin and even edited the official Sibylline Books containing the oracles before depositing them in two gilded cases (Suet., *Augustus* 31, 71). The Augustan Age itself was the new golden age of the oracle of the Sibyl of Cumae, as interpreted by Virgil in the Fourth Eclogue in 4 BCE, and the Augustan empire itself the earthly realization of eschatology.

The power structure of the principate was thus fundamentally different from that of the republic it had replaced: there was much greater concentration of power in the standing army under the exclusive and permanent control of a nonrotating monarch—the *princeps*, the emperor. Nevertheless, the reality was that the polity was awkwardly represented by the nonlegal notion of the first citizen and such titles as imperator, Caesar, and Augustus borne as names. No wonder the republican constitutionalism of the losers survived, in form if not in content, as the patina masking the monarchy of Augustus; and like Sulla but without his sincerity, Augustus celebrated the restoration of the republic. As we shall see, the half-life of the republican tradition continued down to 70 CE.

The Extension of Roman Citizenship, the Political Integration of Italy, and the Equestrian Order

It is time, in conclusion, to provide an overview of the progressive extension of citizenship as a result of the two stages of integrative revolution (see table 1). On the basis of these figures, it can be stated that the size of Roman political society doubled as a result of the first revolution (the Social War) and increased again more than fourfold mainly as a result of competitive mobilization during the second revolution. There are a number of difficulties with these census figures,[16] but they indubitably show the enlargement of Roman political society as a result of the two-step integrative revolution

I have surveyed the incorporation of the knights of the towns of Italy into the Roman polity, which resulted from the Social War and was confirmed by Sulla. Sulla did proscribe many knights, but in this regard, he was evenhanded, as a sizable proportion—perhaps a quarter—of the surviving senators were also proscribed. On the other hand, like Caesar after him, Sulla flooded the Senate with knights. This process of political incorporation is all the more remarkable in view of the lack of organized political activities on the part of the equestrian order in this period.[17] In the earlier period, it may

Table 1 Integrative revolution and the extension of Roman citizenship

Year of census	Number of citizens	Main cause of change
234 BCE	270,212	
154–153 BCE	324,000	
131–130 BCE	318,823	Demographic
115–114 BCE	394,336	
86–85 BCE	463,000[a]	
70–69 BCE	910,000[b]	The Social War
28 BCE	4,063,000	The second Roman revolution
14 CE	4,937,000	Demographic reformist policy of Emperor Claudius
48 CE	5,894,000	

Source: Nicolet 1967:app. 2; Jolowicz and Nicholas 1972:12.
[a]Though the Italians had legally gained citizenship by this date, they were not yet properly registered by any means (Brunt 1988:135–36).
[b]900,000 according to some sources.

be recalled, the main cause of conflict between the *equites* and the senators was the judiciary power granted the former by Gracchus. Once their incorporation into the Roman body politic was achieved in the 80s, the knights became politically passive. Sulla, however, wounded them by depriving them of this judiciary power. This source of tension was removed by the compromise enacted in the *lex Aurelia* of 70 BCE, which mandated the sharing of jury duties between the senators and the *equites* (Gruen 1974:500). Henceforth, the two orders acted in concord, and the knights were as divided in the subsequent civil wars as were the senators. Even at the height of their political activism, the *equites* had not constituted a united pressure group, only the *publicani* had. Caesar abolished tax farming in the province of Asia and entrusted the collection of taxes to his agents. This removed the chief cause of unity for political pressure within the equestrian class. Yet Caesar did not humble the *equites* but rather created opportunities for them in his financial and political administration (Syme 1939:71; Badian 1972a:116–17). Sulla had doubled the size of the Senate to six hundred; Caesar increased it further to nine hundred. In all, he appointed some four hundred new senators, all upwardly mobile elements, mostly knights and mostly Italian. Many of the knights excluded by Sulla because of their Marian or Cinnan sympathies thus returned to active political life and entered the Senate under Caesar (Syme 1939:ch. 6; Gabba 1976:37). But he also opened the equestrian order to people of humbler origins. The equestrian class was thus greatly enlarged, to the chagrin of the higher-status knights and the delight of those of humbler status, especially those military men who became knights. Incidentally, under Sulla and Caesar, the incorporation of the knights and the army officers went hand in hand. Military men from humble origins were appointed to the equestrian order, and many of the newly knighted military men then became senators. Augustus reintroduced stratification within the equestrian class, re-creating an elite of *equites equo publico*, with the right to wear the golden ring (Henderson 1963:65, 71). More important, Augustus directly continued Caesar's opening of administrative careers to the knights. In his new order, the military, judiciary, and financial functions of the knights were reorganized in the service of the state (Broughton 1962:157).

The rise of Augustus was the culmination of the process of integration of the knights into the Roman political system. Augustus himself was a knight by birth and the grandson of a small-town banker and was very much a municipal man in his cautious orientation and puritanical tastes; and he was solidly supported by the knights of Italy. The defeated Antony represented the provinces, whose full integration had to await another revolution. It is interesting to note that in his *Res gestae* Augustus mentions the equestrian order alongside the Senate and the Roman people as giving him the title of father of the country (*pater patriae*) in 2 BCE (Lewis and Reinhold 1951:2.19, no. 35). Indeed, it has been argued that Augustus maintained the pretense of restoring the republic and sustained an elaborate republican facade in order to appeal to this class of new men from the *municipia* and the colonies who had been enfranchised in the Social War and who venerated the republican tradition of Rome (A. Jones 1960:4). In any event, it is clear that Augustus gave the knights open access to positions in the Senate and in military and provincial administration, notably making the prefectships of Egypt and of the Praetorian Guard their preserves (Broughton 1962:157–60; Brunt 1988:191–93).

In short, the Augustan Revolution completed the process set in motion by the first phase of the integrative revolution in the 80s BCE and accelerated by Julius Caesar.

FOUR

Revolution in the Roman Principate and Its Transformation into Imperial Constitutional Autocracy

The Authority Structure of the Principate

The revolution of Caesar and Augustus had changed the authority structure of the Roman republic profoundly and irreversibly. In chapter 3, I identified tribunician power and the proconsular *imperium* as the foundations of Augustus's rule. The tribunes had been neutralized by the emperor's assumption of tribunician power. The assumption of tribunician power was indicative of the concentration of power in the hands of the emperor and, after the Flavian Revolution, served as the foundation of his legislative power. However, as Mommsen (1887:840–41) has pointed out, tribunician power was the consequence and not the basis of Caesardom. The *imperium*, the true foundation of monarchical power, meant exclusive command over the soldiers of the whole empire. It was defined as proconsular—that is, technically held on behalf of the consuls. Proconsular authority, hitherto conferred in extraordinary ways, became an element of the ordinary constitution. It was thus regularized into the legal basis of the emperor's rule (Mommsen 1887:840–45).

Nevertheless, the term *imperator* had no legal, constitutional significance and was not even a title; Octavian had borne it as a forename (praenomen). It was only after the Flavian Revolution and with Vespasian that Imperator Caesar became a regular title (Syme 1958:184–85). The authority structure of the Roman monarchy, the principate, had a fundamental flaw that stemmed from its revolutionary origins. The problem of succession remained unresolved, and the republican authority structure had to be temporarily resuscitated at the death of each emperor. The irregularity of succession among the Julio-Claudians is striking. Tiberius used the tribunician power already granted him to convene the Senate. Claudius and Nero were hailed imperator by the Praetorian Guard. Vespasian, as we shall see, dated his rule from his acclamation as imperator by his army. Thereafter, this haphazard method of the election of the Caesar was established. Though confirmed by a resolution of the Senate, election could occur when the troops of any army designated someone imperator and could be initiated by any soldier. The emperor could then assume the names of Caesar and Augustus (Mommsen 1887:774–75; Heuss 1974:86–88). The Senate would have to recognize the choice of the army, and the popular assembly would have to ratify its resolution through the grant of tribunician power (Mommsen 1887:1143–47; Heuss 1974:80–85). The principate was thus "an autocracy tempered by legally permanent revolution" (Mommsen 1887:1133).

It has been argued that because the authority of the emperor could not be legally based, it depended on the consensus of three elements in the Roman polity: the army, the Senate, and the *plebs urbana*. The consent of these three elements was the sociological basis of "the acceptance system" of the principate. The acclamation by the army would initiate the rule of the emperor, while the legal categories of *imperium* (*consulare* and *proconsulare*) and *tribunicia potestas* signified the consent of the Senate and the *plebs urbana* respectively (Flaig 1992:esp. 183–84). This picture of the social balance of power behind the principate implies that the withdrawal of consent by any of the three elements could produce a crisis of legitimacy by exposing the shaky legal foundations of imperial authority.

This vulnerability of the authority structure of the principate is the crucial factor in accounting for the occurrence of the two revolutions of the Roman Empire.[1] On these two occasions, the legally permanent possibility of revolution at the time of the death of an emperor unleashed ferocious civil strife that could not be stayed by the formal resuscitation of the republic at the point of succession, irreversibly altered the Roman authority structure and its legal framework, and further enlarged the Roman political community in two significant steps.

The First Year of the Four Emperors and Revolutionary Power Struggle

The turmoil that shook the Roman Empire after the fall of Nero in 68 CE is one of the best-documented periods in Roman history. Yet no one has risen to the challenge of analyzing it as a political revolution. The challenge must now be met.

Dispossession of the Aristocracy, Loss of Legitimacy, and the Fall of Nero

The half-life of the tradition of republican constitutionalism was prolonged by Augustus's decision to hide the reality of monarchy behind the constitutional facade of the restored republic. However, the weakness of social support for this republican tradition was demonstrated when Caligula was murdered in January 41, and the flaw in the structure of authority of the principate gaped wide. The attempt at the restoration of the republic was a fiasco. The murderers from the Praetorian Guard had had no particular candidate in mind. The senators, relying on the Urban Cohorts, opted for restoring the republic. The consuls summoned the Senate to the Capitol.[2] Dissension among the senators continued unabated for two days, while the crowds surrounding the building demanded monarchy, asking for Caligula's surviving uncle, Claudius (Suet., *Gaius* 60; *Claudius* 10–11). The people thus did not identify with the republicanism of the senators. The army remained loyal to the Julio-Claudian house. Claudius, now the choice of the army and the people, became emperor. The senators, abandoned by the Urban Cohorts, gave up the idea of restoring the republic and paid him homage in the Praetorian camp (Momigliano [1934] 1961). According to Josephus, the people saw in the emperors a restraint on the rapacity of the senators. In the following year, the governor of Dalmatia attempted to restore the republic but was abandoned by his soldiers (Ste. Croix 1981:362). Thereafter, revolution was forestalled for a generation by Claudius's policies of administrative rationalization and vigorous extension of Roman citizenship.

In the year 60, a comet blazed in the sky, "which in popular opinion always portends revolution to kingdoms, so people began to ask, as if Nero was already dethroned, who was to be elected" (*Annals* 14.22). Nero, however, was still under the beneficial influence of his Spanish teachers, Burrus and Seneca. At the close of 64, "people talked much about prodigies, presaging impending peril," including the appearance of a comet, "for which Nero propitiated with noble blood" (*Annals* 15.47). The decimation of the aristocracy had set in, unprecedented use being made of the law of treason for this purpose.[3] After the death of Burrus in 62 and the forced retirement of Seneca, Nero began to deprive the Senate of importance and embarked on the physical extermination of prominent members of the aristocracy who could be elected emperor, including members of the royal family. He also began to make systematic use of confiscation as a fiscal instrument, making regular the practice of confiscating the estates of the "ungrateful." From 66 onward, men began using Nero's fiscal greed to settle private scores (Griffin

1985:204–5). These confiscations affected the propertied provincial as well as the Romans (Suet., *Nero* 38; Brunt 1959:557). Temples, too, were plundered for gold, a move offensive to the religious. At the same time, Nero was giving the highest posts in the empire to Orientals, especially freedmen who were entirely dependent on him. According to Suetonius (*Nero*, 37), Nero often hinted broadly that it was not his intention to spare the remaining senators but would one day wipe out the entire senatorial order and let knights and freedmen govern the provinces and command the armies instead. In his announcement at the Isthmus Canal project, to a huge crowd, he loudly voiced the hope that it might benefit himself and the Roman people, but he made no mention of the Senate.[4]

The alarm of the Roman aristocracy could only have been increased by Nero's megalomaniac projects. He deified his wives, changed the name of the month of April to Neroneus, identified himself with Hercules on his coins, and planned to call Rome Neropolis (Momigliano 1934:732–33).

Nero's manner of concentration of power, typical of tyrants, meant the dispossession and destruction of the aristocracy, which gathered to conspire under the banner of the restoration of republican freedom and the Stoic hatred of tyranny. Nero's former tutor and minister Seneca joined a conspiracy of senators, knights, and one of the two prefects of the Praetorian Guard, with the aim of restoring public liberty (*Annals* 15.52, 59). The conspirators planned to replace Nero with the old Roman aristocrat C. Calpurnius Piso or perhaps with Seneca, who was "but an equestrian and from a provincial family."[5] Nero uncovered the Pisonian conspiracy in 65, executed nineteen persons, exiled thirteen, enlarged the number of secret informers, and redoubled his efforts to destroy the aristocracy (Momigliano 1934:726–30).

Weak though it was, republican constitutionalism, tinged with Stoic ideas, was the only available platform for opposition to the Julio-Claudian dynasty. "Nero, after having butchered so many illustrious men, at last aspired to extirpate virtue itself, by murdering Thrasea Paetus and Barea Soranus" (*Annals* 16.21). In 66, these Stoic constitutionalists were put on trial for treason before the Senate. Nero had to resort to physical intimidation of the Senate and heavy bribery of the prosecutor (*Annals* 16.27, 33). It is interesting to note that a young tribune of the people who was an admirer of Thrasea offered to block the sentence of the Senate but was dissuaded from doing so by Thrasea (*Annals* 16.26). Thrasea obviously realized that the days of the revolutionary tribunes of the distant past could not be brought back.

Nero might have succeeded in destroying the Senate had he not neglected and then offended the army. He had rewarded the Praetorian Guard with a generous donative for their loyalty at the time of the Pisonian conspiracy.

He was, however, in arrears with the pay of the army (Suet., *Nero* 32; Brunt 1959:533). The army, furthermore, found his effeminacy and histrionics deeply offensive, as it did his mockery of military honors and triumphal insignia (Griffin 1985:230–31). Nero had been appearing frequently on the public stage (*Annals* 15.33) and had "stooped to marry himself to one of that filthy herd, by name Pythagoras, with all the forms of regular wedlock. The bridal veil was put over the emperor" (*Annals* 14.37). In the speech attributed to the rebel Vindex, much is made of this effeminacy, and Nero is called a woman. In any event, Nero did not trust the legionaries to arrest Piso (*Annals* 15.59). Corbulo, the popular general and victor of the wars in the East, visited Rome in May 66 during the trial of the Stoic constitutionalists Thrasea Paetus and Barea Soranus, and it is quite probable that he was involved in the Vinician conspiracy (presumably so named after his son-in-law) of the ensuing months (Griffin 1985:178–79). Before the end of the year, not only Corbulo but also the Scribonii brothers, who commanded the armies of Upper and Lower Germany, had been lured away from their armies to Greece to see the emperor and given orders to take their own lives. Nero's belated assumption of *imperator* as a forename (Campbell 1984:124) and his decision to strike coins of the military type (Kraay 1949:133) could not have had much effect in allaying discontent among the legions. Alarmed by the deaths of Corbulo and the Scribonii, the armies of the provinces were ready to unmake the lyre-playing emperor. The man who set out to rouse them to do so was a Romanized Gaul and governor of Lugdunensis (Lyon), Julius Vindex.

Revolution for the Restoration of Liberty

Cicero still considered the Gauls of Narbonensis barbarians (Alföldy 1988:91). As we have seen, Julius Caesar enabled the Gallic soldiers and tribal aristocracies to enter Roman political society. The revolution that began with the fall of Nero was to be their integrative revolution as much as that of the provincial armies. Julius Vindex, who set it in motion, was an Aquitanian prince, born and educated in Rome and now a senator and governor, who appropriately bore Caesar's first name as a mark of his family's enfranchisement.[6]

In the latter part of 67, Vindex began spreading his conspiratorial propaganda among the army commanders, from Vespasian in Judaea to Galba in Spain. Most of the commanders remained cautious, and some informed Rome. Titus Vinius, the legate of Aquitanian Gaul, however, responded enthusiastically and pressed Servius Galba, the governor of Nearer Spain, to accept the leadership of the movement for restoration of public liberty (Nicolas 1979:1.272–74, 295–99). Helius, the freedman Nero had left in charge of Rome when he himself left for his long visit to Greece in September 66, hurried there in desperation in January 68 to plead with Nero to return, informing him of Vindex's activities. Nero agreed to return but landed in Naples, and not in Rome, around March 20. There, he heard the news of the Gallic revolt on the anniversary of his mother's murder. He reacted phlegmatically, tarrying in Naples for two more weeks. When he eventually returned to Rome, his first priority was to demonstrate a new type of water organ to the leading citizens invited to the palace. He then dismissed the two consuls, assuming sole consulship himself, and whimsically suggested that he would also dismiss all army commanders and provincial governors (Suet., *Nero* 42).

The absence of violence in the events that preceded the fall and suicide of Nero contrasts sharply with the bloodshed that followed it. What we witness in Rome during the two months after Nero's return in April is not violence but the disappearance of the awe of authority and the thorough discrediting and thus delegitimization of the ruler by graffiti and lampoons. One doggerel reminded the Romans that the numerical value of Nero's name was the same as "murdered his own mother"; another invidiously contrasted his unmanly histrionics with the manly virtues of the Parthian king; while graffiti scrawled on columns played on the term *galli*, which means both "cocks" and "Gauls," by saying that his crowing had aroused even the cocks (Suet., *Nero* 39, 45). "In his military preparations," remarks Suetonius (*Nero* 44) sarcastically, he was mainly concerned with finding enough wagons to carry his stage equipment and arranging, for the concubines who would accompany him, to have male haircuts and be issued with Amazonian shields and axes. When all this was settled, Nero called the Roman populace to arms; but no eligible recruits came forward, so he forcibly enlisted a number of slaves.

It can be said more neutrally that Nero failed in his attempt to recruit an army in the face of the insolence of the Senate and the opposition of the assemblies and their refusal to authorize new taxes. The prefect of the Praetorian Guard, Nymphidius Sabinus, lost his nerve and made a deal with the partisans of Galba, promising the guard a donative on the latter's behalf that they were never to receive. The Senate declared Galba emperor and Nero the enemy of the public. In this revolutionary crisis the resuscitation of the authority structure of the republic thus immediately *preceded* the demise of the emperor. Deserted by his own bodyguard and dreading the punishment "in the ancient style" prescribed for a public enemy, Nero took his own life, with the famous words "what an artist dies in me" (*qualis artifex pereo*), on

June 9, 68. "In the widespread general rejoicing, citizens ran through the streets wearing caps of liberty" (Suet., *Nero* 57).

Vindex, the architect of the revolution for the restoration of liberty, had perished a month earlier in confrontation with the army of Upper Germany under circumstances which remain obscure, but the commander of the army, Virginius Rufus, had declared himself loyal not to Nero but to the Senate as the body with the authority to appoint a new emperor; and Galba, the leader Vindex had designated for the task of restoration of liberty, had received the Senate's endorsement.

When the established authority crumbles from within and collapses, it is usual for more than one contender to arise. So it was with the collapse of Nero's rule. Clodius Macer rebelled against Nero in Africa, independently of Galba and Vindex, styling himself the legate of the Senate and people of Rome (for numismatic evidence, see Kraay 1949; Nicolas 1979). Very probably, Virginius Rufus did likewise. Although he was frequently saluted as emperor by his soldiers, his response was to leave the choice to the Senate and people of Rome, which did not preclude his own confirmation. Virginius made his troops swear allegiance to Galba, following the example of the first legion of Lower Germany. Clodius Macer never did so and was eventually murdered by Galba's agents in October 68 (Nicolas 1979:1.236–37, 483–85). The fact remains, however, that Vindex was the first to rise as the champion of liberty against the tyrant.

Vindex's name—meaning "avenger" or "champion"—admirably suited his role as the champion of liberty (*adsertor libertatis*), as he was referred to on his coins and by that Flavian admirer Pliny the Elder. In Roman law, the *adsertor* was the man who, by means of a *vindicta*, freed before a magistrate one wrongfully enslaved; and Vindex was the champion of the Roman people wrongfully enslaved by Nero. Vindex's coins also offer fascinating evidence of his constitutionalist propaganda. "Rome Restored," "Rome Renascent," "Liberty of the R[oman] P[eople] Restored," "Liberator," "Avenger [*vindex*] of the Liberty of the R[oman] P[eople]," and "*Adsertor* of Public Liberty," are all revealing legends. Equally striking is the legend "Salvation of the Human Race,"[7] especially in light of the discovery of an altar dedicated to *Salus generis humani* in the area of Vindex's revolt (Kraay 1949:138–40). It should be noted, however, that by this time, the restoration of public liberty meant the restoration of the constitutional principate of Augustus, the *libertas Augusta*. Both Vindex and Galba issued series of deified Augustus coins (Nicolas 1979:2.1321–27) and appealed to other Augustan symbols.

Although the unfortunate Vindex perished while confronting or negotiating with Virginius Rufus, Galba, a man who had studied law, remained faithful to Vindex's ideal of constitutionalism and restoration of public liberty (Mommsen 1965:335–39; Kraay 1949:146–49). His commitment to the same political principles was underlined during his first public act as the head of the movement for the restoration of liberty, when, in Suetonius's (*Galba,* 10) words, "Galba took his place on the tribunal, *as though going about the business of freeing slaves,* but before him were ranged statues and pictures of Nero's prominent victims. . . . Galba was at once hailed Imperator, and accepted the honor, announcing that he was now the representative of the Roman Senate and People" (emphasis added).

Galba began to recruit legions and auxiliaries, and "he chose the most intelligent and oldest noblemen available as members of a kind of Senate" (Suet., *Galba* 10). On July 6, 68, while Galba was still in Spain and waiting for Virginius Rufus to acknowledge him as emperor, Tiberius Julius Alexander, the governor of Egypt and one of the key actors in the revolution, welcomed him with an edict stating that "the gods have reserved for this very sacred moment the security of the inhabited world" and praising "the one who, for us, has illuminated the way to the salvation of the whole human race, our benefactor Augustus Imperator Galba" (trans. in Sherk 1988:119). Verginius's legions swore allegiance to Galba at about the same time or shortly thereafter. Galba set out for Rome after meeting the delegates of the Senate near Narbonne in the latter part of August (Nicolas 1979:1.521).

The new political elite brought to power by Galba reflected the coalition of social forces which had supported him or were sympathetic to his cause. Galba's Narbonnesian partisans are conspicuous in this new elite, as are Spanish supporters more generally. Provincials from Spain who had been on the rise under the influence of Burrus and Seneca, but whose new access to positions of power had been blocked in Nero's latter years, thus became integrated into the highest levels of Roman political community. Galba's partisans also included a number of important Gauls (Syme 1982). He had celebrated the "Concord of Spain and Gaul" on his coins (Kraay 1949:141), honored the memory of Vindex, and rewarded the Gallic states who had supported him with a grant of citizenship and remission of tribute (Brunt 1959:545).[8] Foremost among his partisans was Antonius Primus, a Gaul from Toulouse, who was to play a crucial role in the Flavian Revolution. The last group to gain power under Galba consisted of aristocrats who had been dispossessed and exiled by Nero and who, like Galba himself, subscribed to the tradition of republican constitutionalism. Foremost among this group was Piso Licinianus, whom Galba was to adopt and choose as his successor (Syme 1982:461, 479). The one group left out in Galba's distribution of the spoils of office was the army.

The Secret of the Empire

Tacitus, himself the product of the Flavian Revolution (*History* 1.1), wrote some forty years later in the great book devoted to it that the "Year of the Four Emperors" had revealed the secret of the empire: "Welcome though the death of Nero had been in the first burst of joy, yet it had not only roused various emotions in Rome, . . . it had also excited all the legions and their generals; for now had been divulged that secret of the empire that emperors could be made elsewhere than at Rome" (*History* 1.4). The senators were the first to rejoice, and the knights fully sympathized with them (*History* 1.4), but it was the legions who were to have the last say.

Galba vetoed the donative promised by Nymphidius to the Praetorian Guard. The latter perished in his attempt to become the master of Rome, and thousands of his unarmed soldiers were slaughtered (*History* 1.6). Nor did Galba forget that the Upper German legions had opposed Vindex. He entered the city of Rome with his Spanish troops, who mingled with those who had been recalled from the Caspian expedition by Nero. "Rome was full of strange troops. . . . Here were vast materials for a revolution, *without a decided bias towards any one man*" (*History* 1.6, emphasis added). The dour Galba did not realize this: "'I choose my soldiers, I do not buy them,' noble words for the commonwealth, but fraught with peril for [Galba] himself" (*History* 1.5). This attack on the army was a fateful mistake because it was an attempt to undo the tacit pact between the emperor and the army on which the principate rested (Flaig 1992:176). In January 69, disaffected soldiers in Upper Germany and then in the capital selected as emperors, in preference to Galba, two men who were "the most worthless of mortals" (*History* 1.50). The Year of the Four Emperors began with the refusal of the legions of Upper Germany to swear allegiance to Galba on January 1, 69. Following Virginius's formula, the choice of the new emperor was left to the Senate and the people of Rome (*History* 1.12). Two days later, the soldiers gave up this obsolete political superstition and proclaimed their lackluster commander, Aulus Vitellius, emperor. On January 15, the Praetorian Guard chose Marcus Otho, Nero's governor of Lusitania, who had been the first provincial governor to join Galba and was miffed at being bypassed as his successor. Galba and his successor-designate, Piso, were then murdered during a public ceremony. The Senate confirmed the choice of Otho and voted him the honors and powers pertaining to the emperor. Civil war ensued. Otho was defeated by forces of Vitellius at Bedriacum before his Danubian legions could reach him and committed suicide on April 16. Vitellius was then confirmed as emperor and voted the usual honors in Rome by the Senate. Before long, however, in the first days of July, Flavius Vespasianus, the commander of the Roman army in the First Jewish-Roman War, was acclaimed emperor by the legions of the East. The year closed with the capture of Rome by the Flavian forces on December 21, 69, and the Senate's confirmation of Vespasian as emperor with extensive powers immediately thereafter.

The soldiers who made Otho emperor were not submissive to authority. On the contrary, they told their commanders what to do. "Everything was then ordered according to the will of soldiery. The Praetorians chose their own prefects." They also appointed Flavius Sabinus, Vespasian's brother, prefect of the city (*History* 1.46). Although Otho lavished favors upon them, the soldiers in the capital continued to be disorderly and restless (*History* 1.80–83; Syme 1939:154). Things were even worse in the army of Vitellius, where "all was disorder and drunkenness, more like a nocturnal feast and revel than a properly disciplined camp" (*History* 1.68). There was a serious breakdown of discipline in the armies of Germany and clashes among the Gallic auxiliaries and between the legions and the auxiliaries. These gave even Otho grounds for praising the martial youth of Rome and sons of Italy, in contrast to Vitellius's native tribes and their semblance of an army (Syme 1939:155). Disorder among the Vitellian forces in Italy grew worse in the last months and was marked by a mutiny of the fleet at Ravenna and its defection to the Flavians (*History* 2.94, 3.12–13). Furthermore, the Praetorians, who had been the mainstay of Otho, had been discharged and became supporters of Flavius Sabinus, whom they had chosen as prefect of the city and who retained his post. Financial stringency now required further discharge of legionaries and auxiliaries, and dismissals were indiscriminate (*History* 1.67–69). Thus, an indefinite number of discharged soldiers were added to some nine thousand former Praetorians as supporters of the Flavian party in Rome. The emperor, however, was to be made elsewhere than in Rome.

The secret of the empire was out indeed. Vespasian's sponsor and subordinate commander of the legions in Syria, Mucianus, knew it as he was organizing the Flavian party among the provincial legions in the spring and summer of 68, and he made it explicit when openly inviting Vespasian to become emperor: "That an emperor can be created by the army, Vitellius is himself a proof. . . . You have from Judaea, Syria and Egypt, nine fresh legions, unexhausted by battle, uncorrupted by dissension" (*History* 2.76).

Vespasian's own officers, too, knew the secret of the empire. According to Josephus, who was then a prisoner in Vespasian's camp, "his officers and men in informal groups were already talking openly of revolution." They were envious of the no-good soldiers in Rome who could "vote anyone they fancy on the throne. . . . We, who have toiled and sweated and grown old in the service, let others enjoy this privilege, even when we have in our own camp a candidate with much stronger claims" (*Jewish War* 257). The army could choose an emperor anywhere it liked; it was about time the legions in the eastern periphery did so. In a well-coordinated move, the governor of Egypt, Tiberius Alexander, made the legions of Alexandria swear allegiance to Vespasian on July 1; and his own soldiers in Judaea impulsively saluted him as emperor on July 3 (*History* 2.79–80).[9] According to Josephus, Vespasian first declined the acclamation, but the officers would not take no for an answer, "and the rank and file surrounded him sword in hand, and threatened to kill him if he refused" (*Jewish War* 258). Be that as it may, the army of Syria under Mucianus swore allegiance to Vespasian in mid-July. The control of Egypt, the granary of Rome, was crucial to Flavian strategy, and Vespasian decided to go there in person while dispatching Mucianus to Rome.

The Third Legion in the Danubian army, one of the oldest eastern legions, declared itself for Vespasian in the beginning of August. By mid-August, Antonius Primus, the commander of Galba's 7th Legion, had swayed the rest of the Danubian army to the Flavian cause.[10] However, this latter army, which conquered Italy for Vespasian, could not, by any stretch of the imagination, be considered "uncorrupted by dissension."

Already with the breakdown of discipline after Otho's defeat, some two thousand men in the three legions in Moesia who had acknowledged him were unwilling to switch allegiance to the choice of the German army. They, too, had intuited the secret of the empire: "They felt they were in no way inferior to the troops in Spain who had appointed Galba; and the Guards who had appointed Otho; and the troops in Germany who had appointed Vitellius. So they went through the whole list of provincial governors of consular rank . . . , until in the end they unanimously chose Vespasian—on the strong recommendation of some Third Legion men" (Suet., *Vespasian* 6). This was a few months before the Flavian party was ready to strike, but the incident was obviously not forgotten. Flavian agents remained active among the Danube legions, and "the Flavian party was the strongest among the common soldiers" (Nicols 1978:145). When Antonius Primus began to use his oratory to advocate switching allegiance to Vespasian, the politicization of the soldiery had already gone quite far, and "the centurions and some of the common soldiers had intruded themselves into the deliberations" (*History* 3.3). Primus acquired commanding authority over the Danubian army only by yielding to the demands of the soldiers. The latter demanded to march on Italy, apparently against Vespasian's orders, and Primus obliged by leading them (Nicols 1978:176). After their victory over the Vitellian army in Cremona on the last day of October or in the first days of November, the soldiers of the Danubian army became even more unruly and were "ready to break through all discipline, unless they were led as they wished" (*History* 3.19). Even promotion became politicized, and new centurions to replace those killed in the war were elected by soldiers (*History* 3.49).

As Primus's soldiers plundered their way down the Italian peninsula to Rome, Vespasian's older brother, Flavius Sabinus, slowly negotiated with Vitellius, who agreed to abdicate in favor of Vespasian. This agreement for a peaceful transfer of power among the leaders of the contending parties was wrecked at the last minute by Vitellius's irate supporters. Violent clashes ensued, the Capitol was burned to the ground, and Sabinus perished just before the troops of Antonius Primus entered the city. Vitellius was lynched; Vespasian's younger son, Domitian, was hailed Caesar. Mucianus had set out from Syria and was on his way to the capital at top speed. When he arrived in January 70, he found himself in the midst of a power struggle among the commander of the occupying Flavian forces, Antonius Primus; the young and ambitious son of the emperor, Caesar Domitian; the Praetorian prefect, Arrius Varus; and the Senate. He needed all his considerable political ability to assert his paramount authority on behalf of the new emperor, who was in Alexandria. Mucianus could not, however, give this matter his undivided attention, as grim news continued to arrive, in January and February, of the disintegration of the armies of Germany, the murder of the commanders Flaccus and Vocula by the soldiers, and widespread revolts of the Batavians, the Germans, and the Gauls.

The undisciplined and politicized army of Antonius Primus had won a revolution. The undisciplined and politicized German army which had elected Vitellius, by contrast, was destroyed by its own auxiliaries. In 69, at least seven of the twenty-nine legions of the Roman army were stationed in the frontier regions of Upper and Lower Germany.[11] These armies of the Rhine had over the years become regionalized and de-Romanized, and now contained many native officers. In addition to the legions, there were some eight auxiliary units recruited from the local population under the command of Gallo-Germanic officers. These had been regularized under Augustus and provided channels for upward social mobility to the local subjects.

Julius Civilis, a Batavian prince and officer in the army of the Rhine, had been sent to Rome in chains as a rebel—in all probability for his implication in the rebellion of Vindex—and was restored to his command of the Batavian auxiliaries by Galba in October 68 (Nicolas 1979:2.1200–1202). Knowing him to be a friend of Vespasian's, Antonius Primus had incited him to begin pro-Flavian agitation in the latter part of August 69 (*History*

5.26).[12] Civilis approached both the Gauls and the Germans to build a wider coalition. He reminded them of the evils of overtaxation and conscription that were the consequence of Roman rule and assured them that "never has the power of Rome been more depressed" (*History* 4.14). Around the core of eight thousand Batavians (the eight cohorts of Vitellius's army that had been sent back to the Rhine after Bedriacum), Civilis gathered Canninefates and Frisians and other Germans into an army, "in which now the banners of the Roman cohorts stood by the side of the animal standards from the sacred groves of the Germans" (Mommsen 1968:140). Julius Civilis swore in Roman troops in Vespasian's name in October. He then besieged the legionaries who remained loyal to Vitellius in Vetera. The news of the disastrous defeat of the Vitellian forces in Cremona resulted in the complete demoralization of the legionaries and the total collapse of Roman military power on the Rhine, leaving Civilis's army the most effective force in the region (Drinkwater 1983:46). In December 70, he forswore allegiance to Rome and vowed to grow his hair long (*History* 4.61) as the champion of Celtic liberty.

The coalition sought by Civilis, however, was very fragile, resting on unbridgeable ethnic diversity, and was uneasily maintained by frequent use of hostages as surety (*History* 4.61, 79). The Gauls, in particular, were unwilling to accept Batavian supremacy. In January 70, Julius Classicus, Julius Tutor, and Julius Sabinus, all native Gallo-Roman aristocrats whose families had received citizenship from Julius Caesar or Augustus, as was the case with Julius Vindex and Julius Civilis, decided to set up their own state. The first two were Treverans and officers in the army of the Rhine who had entered secret negotiation with Civilis, the last a Lingonian. Classicus had his Roman commander, Vocula, treacherously murdered and proclaimed the Gallic Empire (Imperium Galliarum) around February 1, 70. The besieged Roman legionaries were forced to swear allegiance to the Gallic Empire but were nevertheless massacred. Later in the month, Tutor obliged other units of the army of the Rhine, together with the inhabitants of Cologne, to swear allegiance to the Gallic Empire. Disappointed with the Gauls, Civilis drew closer to his German allies, most notably the German prophetess Veleda. Meanwhile, Mucianus was putting together a Roman army to suppress the rebellion, and he set out for Gaul with the new emperor's son, Domitian, in the spring of 70.

As had been the case with the Italian confederacy of 89 BCE,[13] the Romanized elite of the Gallic Empire displayed striking attachment to the Roman tradition. Sabinus boasted descent from a bastard of Caesar's and named himself Caesar; Classicus assumed the insignia of Roman magistracy

(*History* 4.59, 67; Mommsen 1968:145–46). Their coins bore such legends as "*Libertas Restituta*" and "*Adsertor Libertatis*" (Nicolas 1979:2.1331). The Gallic Empire, however, was short-lived. The Gallic tribes did not constitute a unified nation. Sabinus was defeated by the Sequani, who remained faithful to Rome, in April; and in May, an assembly of the Gallic peoples in Rheims could not forget that the Treverans and the Lingones, who now formed the Gallic Empire, had opposed Vindex and refused to recognize him (*History* 4.69). Finally, on June 10, 70, Trier fell to the Flavian general Cerialis, and the Gallic Empire came to an end. Classicus, Tutor, and the 112 Treveran senators were treated as traitors, as was Sabinus, who was put to death after nine years in hiding. Civilis, by contrast, was able to remind Cerialis of his earlier service to the Flavian cause and was offered peace on generous terms. Roman rule was reestablished in the Rhine by the time Vespasian made his triumphant entry into the city of Rome toward the end of October 70 (*History* 4.55–79, 5.14–26; Nicolas 1979:2.1217–40, 1270–75; Wells 1984:176).

Mucianus had returned to Italy in September to welcome the new emperor and deliver Rome to him. Relying on the legions he had brought from Syria and whatever units he could reorganize, he had won the revolutionary power struggle at the crucial military level by tactfully removing Varus and Primus[14] and by amusing Caesar Domitian while checking his ventures in Germany. He had also won the revolutionary power struggle at the political level and established mastery over the Senate by exploiting the division between the republican constitutionalists and those compromised by their subservience to Nero. The mantle of Stoic constitutionalism had now fallen upon the shoulders of Thrasea's son-in-law, Helvidius Priscus, who was elected praetor for 70. The republican constitutionalists, basking in the enhanced authority of the Senate since Galba, wanted to give it a greater weight in government and were voicing the public outcry against the secret informers. The Senate prevailed in obtaining the abolition of Nero's secret service. Mucianus, however, succeeded in muting the constitutionalists' ardor for public liberty and in curbing the growing authority of the Senate by suggesting that some matters were too important to be left to the Senate and should be deferred until the arrival of the emperor (*History* 4.5–10, 39–45). It is interesting to note that before Mucianus's arrival, Helvidius sought to assert the authority of the Senate in fiscal matters through the praetors, but a tribune of the people "put his veto on any resolution being adopted in so important a matter in the absence of the emperor" (*History* 4.9). One could not ask for a more symbolic transfer of power than that from the tribune, the anarchic, revolutionary office of the late republic, to the emperor as the victor of the revolution of 68–69. Helvidius Priscus, however, remained undaunted. He was the only man to greet Vespasian by his private name when he returned to Rome and, "throughout his praetorship, omitted all courteous mention of [Vespasian] from official orders" (Suet., *Vespasian* 15). Vespasian had been Thrasea's and Soranus's friend (*History* 4.7) and followed Galba's platform of a constitutional principate. He was therefore patient with Helvidius and did not condemn him to death until 75. Meanwhile, on Mucianus's advice, the emperor banished the subversive elements, calling them "philosophers and astrologers," in 71 and again in 74 (Lucrezi 1982:103).

From the beginning, Vespasian made his older son, Titus, who returned in triumph from Jerusalem in 70, a close partner in his rule, thereby anticipating an easy solution to the problem of succession. Titus succeeded Vespasian in due course in 79 and was in turn succeeded, after his untimely death in 81, by his brother Domitian, who ruled until 96. The revolution caused by the fall of Nero was over by the end of 69, the Year of the Four Emperors. Its consequences, however, unfolded during the quarter century of Flavian rule.

The Flavian Consolidation of Revolution and Constitution of Imperial Autocracy

The revolution of 69 was the revolution of the army, but it was not a revolution for the army. The army was too divided—both vertically and horizontally, into legionaries and auxiliaries and into various regional and linguistic groups—and too poor in distinctive ideology and political culture to supply the teleology of the revolution it had caused.[15] Other factors set the direction of the revolution, making it a revolution for the provinces and for strong centralized government by the emperor, or what can be termed constitutional autocracy. Of these factors, only one was conscious and deliberate. Purposeless strife and violence without direction under Otho and Vitellius, which had been generated by a divided and later disintegrating army against the background of the collapse of central authority, gave way to an orderly sense of direction under Vespasian. Vespasian began his rule with a clear plan for the integration of the provincial client states and for administrative centralization (Flaig 1992:406–7). He also resumed the broken teleology of the constitutionalist revolution of Vindex and Galba by continuing their coin types such as *"Adsertori Libertatis Publicae"* and *"Pax Augusta"* (Kraay 1949:148–49). The first type in particular sought to revive the legendary tradition of the republic founded on the basis of liberty by Brutus. One of the first acts of the Flavians was "to examine and restore to their place the brazen tables of the laws, which had fallen down through the ages" (*History* 4.40). Constitutionalism, however, as had been the case with Augustus, was put at the service of concentration of power. The paradoxical consequence of making the principate subject to legal regulation was to place the prince constitutionally above the law.

Augustus and the Julio-Claudian emperors had maintained a republican facade and a confused legal/constitutional basis for their authority. The *lex de imperio Vespasiani* (*l.d.i.V.*), ratified by the popular assembly on behalf of the people in the received form of an opinion of the Senate (*Senatus consultum*), probably in January or February 70 (Lucrezi 1982:152–53), definitively made the principate an institution in public law for the first time (Levi 1938a).[16] It was revolutionary in gathering a number of experimentally granted concessions to earlier emperors and making them the objects of conferment by a single law (Lucrezi 1982:163). Through amalgamating the prerogatives of the preceding emperors, the *l.d.i.V.* definitively legitimized the supreme authority of the emperor in constitutional law. The first clause of the law thus gave Vespasian the right to conclude treaties; clause 4 converted the right of designation of candidates, granted to Caesar ad hoc in 44 BCE,[17] into a regular appointive right;[18] and clause 5 gave Vespasian authority to extend the boundary of the city of Rome for the first time. With this formal legal legitimization, Imperator Caesar Vespasian Augustus no longer needed the Augustan array of magistracies to disguise his power in traditional forms. Indeed, he was in no hurry to assume the tribunician power. Augustus had counted his reign from the assumption of the tribunician power as the day of *imperium* (*dies imperii*). Vespasian took the revolutionary step of dating his reign from his appellation by the soldiers, thereby degrading the tribunician power and the Senate's ratification as legal pillars of imperial authority. His day of *imperium* was July 1, 69. In December 69, he was already addressing the Senate as *princeps* (*History* 4.34); and clause 8 of the *l.d.i.V.* confirmed this newly introduced principle, retroactively giving all his acts and orders since that date the force of law.[19] The *l.d.i.V.* thus reflected a profound change in the Roman structure of authority. The emperor was the center of power, with the Senate shorn of some of its prerogatives. The people of Rome and the popular assemblies had disappeared in all but name.

The perfunctoriness of the formally legislative comitial proceedings is evident from the unaltered formal character of the *l.d.i.V.* as an opinion of the Senate (Brunt 1977:95). The *l.d.i.V.* is indeed of capital importance in that it marks the transfer of the legislative power of the people to the emperor. As

Mommsen (1887:876–79) pointed out, the proconsular mandate obtained by the emperors from the Senate could not confer any legislative competence. Legislative power could have been derived only from the *lex de imperio*, passed by the *comitia tribuniciae potestatis* as expressing the will of the people. Augustus had strictly used the *plebiscita* of the popular assemblies for his extensive enactments (Kunkel 1972:125). In the second century, by contrast, imperial legislation became frequent, and the legislative power of the *princeps* was derived from the *lex de imperio*. The constitutions of the emperors thus took the place of the *lex* and *plebiscita* of the popular assemblies of the republican era (Brunt 1977:110–15; Gaudemet 1982:581).

Hand in hand with the legal institution of imperial autocracy went the reestablishment of military discipline and considerable administrative centralization, made possible by Vespasian's important fiscal reform. The lessons of the revolutionary upheaval were not lost on Vespasian, who was determined to bring the armies under firm centralized imperial control. He stopped the practice of giving command of the auxiliary units to officers from their own native nobility (Mommsen 1968:150–51). He also moved soldiers from their native provinces, created ethnically mixed units, and instituted a system of rotation of officers to forestall excessive influence over the legionaries (Lucrezi 1982:109–11).[20] One of the earliest bones of contention between the Flavians and Helvidius Priscus during the revolutionary power struggle pertained to the power of the public treasury (*aerarium*) controlled by the Senate through the praetors. Vespasian made the imperial treasury (*fiscus*) the main organ of government finances, established provincial *fisci*, and centralized their control by establishing a procurator in Rome (A. Jones 1960:110–11). He also reorganized the imperial estates in the provinces; and he and Titus converted them from the property of individual emperors to Crown property (Griffin 1985:206–7).

Thus, the *l.d.i.V.* brought the revolution of 68–70 to an end and ushered in the era of strong imperial government. It was a milestone in the degradation of the deliberations of the popular assemblies and the first recognition of the supremacy of the will of the emperor in public law. Aiming at making the principate subject to public law and thus establishing the constitutional principle of *leges super principem* (the laws above the prince), the *l.d.i.V.* paradoxically became the progenitor of the legislative competence of the *princeps*. The Julio-Claudian emperors still considered themselves bound by common rules in civil law. This changed with Domitian, who took the *lex de imperio* to authorize the prince to disregard the law, to be above the law (Pliny, cited in Brunt 1977:109; Gaudemet 1982:587–88).[21] Domitian was also the first emperor to assume the title of Lord and God (*dominus et deus*) (Suet., *Domitian* 309; Dio, cited in Lewis and Reinhold 1951:2.560). To understand this assumption of divinity, however, we need to look at the integrative consequences of our revolution.

As had been the case with the civil wars of the late republic, civil strife and competitive mobilization among the contenders in the revolutionary power struggle resulted in considerable enlargement of the political community. Galba, as we have seen, granted citizenship to the Gallic supporters of Vindex. He also gave citizenship to the British auxiliaries (*History* 1.43). Otho sought to win support by granting Roman citizenship to a number of colonies and to the Gallic Lingones (*History* 1.78). Such ad hoc measures culminated in the systematic policies of the Flavians. Vespasian, Titus, and Domitian widely extended citizenship to the urban communities of the Romanized provinces. This is reflected in the large number of persons named Flavius after the enfranchising emperor. Furthermore, they made extensive use of the granting of Latin rights (and full citizenship through magistracy) as a mode of "collective naturalization" (Saumagne 1965:ch. 2). They promoted urbanization, settled the veterans in colonies, and gave civic autonomy to local communities that became municipalities and were given charters modeled on the Italian municipal constitutions (Lewis and Reinhold 1951:2.129–30, 320–26). Pliny's assertion that Vespasian granted Latin rights to the whole of Spain is borne out by epigraphic evidence. There was vigorous and systematic promotion of the *municipia Flavia*. This municipalization and granting of *jus Latii* resulted in the integration of Spain into the Roman political community (Saumagne 1965:76–78). The Flavian Revolution thus integrated the newly municipalized Spain, as the earlier revolutions had integrated municipal Italy. This process gave the provincials access to political power: not only the Senate but also emperorship. From the Flavian period on, the provincials, especially from Spain and southern Gaul, formed an influential grouping in the senatorial order (Alföldy 1988:103), and the formerly very limited number of Greek senators increased (Griffin 1985:212; Wells 1984:146). Three of the four emperors of 69 came from equestrian families of the Italian municipalities integrated into the Roman political system by the revolution of Augustus (Syme 1939:361); provincials from municipal Spain who entered the Senate under Vespasian included the father of Emperor Trajan and the grandfather of Marcus Aurelius (Lucrezi 1982:107); Hadrian was also a Spaniard. In fact, the families integrated into the Roman aristocracy by the Flavians supplied the emperors from 97 to 192, the onset of our next and last revolution (Flaig 1992:410). Although our documentation is scant, the integration of Syria on the eastern periphery into the Roman Empire was also considerably enhanced, interestingly by a Spaniard who had served in the Jewish war under Vespasian, M. Ulpius Traianus, who built roads and promoted urbanization with vigor, paving the way for the annexation of Arabia by his son, Trajan, in 106 (Bowersock 1973).

The Flavian Revolution was also an integrative revolution in social structural terms. It opened the Senate to commanders of legions and other military men for the first time since Julius Caesar (Flaig 1992:408–9). The Senate had been depleted by Nero and the civil war to perhaps as few as two hundred. In 73–74, Vespasian and Titus, as censors, increased the number of senators, perhaps fivefold. Many *equites*, military men, and provincials thus entered the senatorial order (Lucrezi 1982:105–6). Those elected to the Senate included the first future African consul (Duncan-Jones 1967:154). The *equites* also began to play a greater role in imperial administration, replacing some of the freedmen (Wells 1984:179).

An interesting aspect of the integrative revolution is the impact of the political culture and the cultural influence of the eastern periphery of the Roman Empire on its central tradition. The cults of monarchs and rich men and women, who were called "saviors," "benefactors," and "founders," were a feature of social life in the cities of the Hellenistic East. Under Roman rule, the honor was extended to the Roman magistrates. Under Augustus, nondynastic cults of the Roman magistrates were gradually transformed into the dynastic cult of the Julio-Claudian house. In 11 CE, Augustus forbade such honors to provincial governors; the words "savior" and "founder" disappeared from the honorific inscriptions of the magistrates, only the title "benefactor" being allowed (Bowersock 1965:118–19). This concentration of prestige in the imperial house gradually resulted in the spontaneous phenomenon of emperor worship at the grass roots in the eastern provinces. With the Flavian Revolution, this eastern cultural trend significantly contributed to the institution of imperial autocracy in Rome.

The contribution of the eastern periphery to the Flavian propaganda was considerable. In Alexandria, sacrifices were offered on behalf of Vespasian (*Jewish War* 259), and he was acclaimed as "the one savior and [benefactor!], son of [Amm]o[n] rising up . . . god Caesar Vespasian" (papyrus, trans. in Sherk 1988:123). During his long stay in that city, "envoys came from all over the world to congratulate their new sovereign, so that the city—bigger than any but Rome—proved too small for the swollen population" (*Jewish War* 262). As we have seen, the governor of Egypt, Tiberius Alexander, had been a key figure in the Flavian party. Tiberius Alexander was Philo's nephew and a Hellenized Jew who had given up his ancestral religion to serve the imperial government. He had been dispatched to Palestine as procurator by Emperor Claudius and, as governor of Alexandria in 66, had quickly and heavy-handedly suppressed sympathetic Jewish unrest in that city at the onset of insurrection in Judaea; he returned to Judaea as chief of staff to Titus in 70 (*Jewish War* 131, 158–60; *Antiquities* 20.5, p. 505). He was evidently familiar with Jewish messianism, which was intense in this period,[22] and must have drawn upon it along with other religious themes in his orchestration of Flavian propaganda. Vespasian himself must have seen value in appropriating the same while conducting the war against the Jewish rebels. During his first critical postacclamation meeting with Mucianus, he released from prison a Jewish revolutionary turncoat who had sought to ingratiate himself by prophesying that God had chosen Vespasian to be the ruler of the world and was "foreshadowing the scepter by other portent" (*Jewish War* 203). This turncoat, Joseph son of Matthias, or Flavius Josephus, as he renamed himself after his new patron, who must have given him Roman citizenship, clearly appropriated the "ambiguous oracle" that foretold to the Jews that "one from their country would become ruler of the whole world," which was in his opinion the major stimulus for the Jewish revolt again Rome in 66 CE (*Jewish War* 328). From Qumran, whose settlement Vespasian destroyed, we have what are most probably the fragments of this oracle, which must refer to the ruler of the fourth world empire, Rome (Kittim), who is brought before the Jewish Messiah (4Q285, frag. 4.10; Vermes 1992:89–90), at which point "the Prince of Congregation, the Br[anch of David] will kill him" (4Q285, frag. 5; Vermes 1995:150). Josephus was put on the staff of Vespasian's son Titus and accompanied them to Alexandria.[23] Josephus must have promoted, with some eventual success,[24] the idea that the expected Messiah was none other than Vespasian (*Jewish War* 407). Through Tiberius Alexander and Josephus, there was thus some partial Flavian appropriation of Jewish royal messianism into the dominant Hellenistic notions of sacral kingship. Other Oriental trends, too, were incorporated into the Flavian ideological propaganda. Vespasian was presented as the savior of the world and its lord (*dominus*) by divine will and Tyche/Fortune; and his alleged miracles were publicized. During the revolutionary process, these Oriental ideas were useful for underlining the sacred and providential sanction of the coming Flavian *imperium*. The sacralization of Flavian rule proved lasting: Vespasian and Titus wore the crown, and Domitian, as we have seen, assumed the title Lord and God (Lucrezi 1982:58–88).

FIVE

The Last Roman Integrative Revolution

The last and final Roman revolution was set in motion by the fall of Commodus on the last day of 192 CE in a strikingly parallel fashion to that of Nero. Bloody purges of the Senate were the immediate background of both revolutions. Both revolutions were facilitated by loss of legitimacy resulting from the flagrant immorality of the emperor and were fueled by hatred for the freedmen in control of the government, the male paramours and concubines surrounding young megalomaniac emperors, and the same hatred for secret informers. Commodus did not share Nero's passion for acting and playing the lyre but instead loved to appear in the public arena as a gladiator. Finally, 193 was also a year of four emperors, three of whom were recognized by the Senate.

Loss of Legitimacy and Commodus's Purge of the Senate and His Murder

Ever since he became emperor in 180, Commodus, son of that wisest of emperors, Marcus Aurelius, had surrounded himself by favorites and concubines and was hated by the senatorial order, whose members incessantly plotted against him. In 182, Commodus's male lover Saoterius was successfully murdered, but an attempt on the life of the emperor, who was not yet twenty, failed. The assailant had, however, allegedly taken time to proclaim, "This dagger the senate sends you" (*Augustan History*, cited in Birley 1976:164).[1] Commodus fully returned the deep hatred of the Senate, and their mutual hostility continued unabated throughout his reign. Some senators were subjected to judiciary persecution by the (equestrian) Praetorian prefects.[2] To make mockery of the constitutional authority structure, Commodus created twenty-five consuls for 190 (instead of two). One of the twenty-five, who were "appointed by Cleander," the chamberlain (Dio, cited in Birley 1976:128), was the future emperor Septimius Severus. The beginning of the end came in 190. Cleander's enemies in government had caused a corn shortage and ordered the Urban Cohorts to take the side of the crowd against the Praetorian Guard when riots broke out in Rome. In a panic, Commodus had Cleander beheaded. This caving in could only have emboldened his enemies. Commodus, nervous and assertive, began a bloody purge of the Senate that claimed many lives over the next two and a half years and was comparable to Nero's (Birley 1976:132; Alföldy 1988:164). It is important to note that some of the most powerful of Commodus's senatorial victims were also commanders of the army (Millar 1964:127). In August 192, he extorted contributions from the senators for his birthday and forced them to applaud him in the arena, brandishing his sword at them and cutting the head off an ostrich as a forewarning of their fate (Millar 1964:132–33). Commodus's megalomania was also similar to Nero's: he increasingly identified himself with Hercules, renamed Rome *colonia Commodiana*, and had all the months of the year and all kinds of institutions and places named after his names and epithets.

In reaction, a conspiracy was hatched and effectively executed by the city prefect, Publius Helvius Pertinax, and the new Praetorian prefect, Aemilius Laetus. The latter was from Africa and secured the appointment of a fellow African colonist, Clodius Albinus, to Britain and of the Severi brothers to the two Danubian provinces, which together had eight legions (Birley 1971:ch. 10). Laetus had Commodus murdered on the evening of December 31, 192, and with the Roman people who loved Pertinax for his years of service as their city prefect already massed raucously around their camp, Laetus brought Pertinax to the Castra Praetoria and had him acclaimed imperator by the guards in unison with the people that night (Herodian, 2.2.7–9).

The Senate enthusiastically approved the choice of Pertinax and rejoiced at the murder of Commodus. Its decree declared him the enemy of the fatherland: "The executioner of the Senate is the enemy of the gods; the murderer of the Senate is the enemy of the gods! He that killed the Senate, let him be dragged by the hook." It further ordered, at least twice, "informers to the lions!" (*Augustan History*, as cited in Birley 1976:176–77).

Pertinax, son of a freedman who had been elevated to the equestrian order and then to senatorial rank, displayed reverence toward the Senate; sought to prevent the revolutionary power struggle from contaminating the Senate when it was about to declare one of its members a public enemy and have him put to death; abolished treason trials; restored the exiles; and rehabilitated the memory of those unjustly executed. But the violent end of the Antonine era, after nearly a century of unparalleled stability, released turbulent forces that could not be so easily stayed. Pertinax identified with the declining element of the imperial polity (the Senate) and ignored its ascending element (the army). He had assumed the title *princeps Senatus* and, to his peril, remained its steadfast champion to the very end (Dio, 74.5.1, 8.5; 1927:130–31, 138–39; Howe 1942:41; Millar 1964:134–36). Furthermore, he posed as the restorer of the ancient liberty of the Roman people and championed the constitutional tradition of Marcus Aurelius. He refused to follow the latter in initiating his own dynasty, however, and even refused to allow his name to be stamped on imperial property, which he considered common and public property (Herodian, 2.4.2, 7). On the other hand, Pertinax repeated Galba's mistake of resisting the soldiers' demands. After two attempted coups by the Praetorian Guard had failed, a mutiny of the troops, who were disgruntled because of Pertinax's parsimony, put an end to his short rule on March 28. Pertinax was struck down and his head fastened to a spear (Dio, 74.10.3; 1927:142).

Two Praetorian tribunes then began looking for a candidate for emperorship outside the Senate and found a senior consular, Didius Julianus, who had been restive or, as Cassius Dio (74.11.2; 1927:143) put it, "eager for revolution and hence had been exiled by Commodus." The city prefect was also interested in the job. The soldiers put the empire up for auction; and the two men started bidding (Dio, 74.11.3–5; 1927:143). Julianus offered a higher donative and, having the additional advantage of not being the dead emperor's father-in-law, was acclaimed emperor by the guards. He was escorted to the Senate by the guards in military formation and carrying standards and was declared emperor. The crowds, however, shouted insults and threw stones at him and rioted in favor of the governor of Syria, Pescennius Niger (Millar 1964:136–38). More ominously, the provincial armies, which knew the secret of the empire from a century earlier, did not feel themselves bound by the choice of the Praetorian Guard in Rome. On April 9, Septimius Severus was saluted imperator by his troops and began preparing to march on Rome as the avenger of Pertinax. Severus had received the news of the election of his former superior and ally, Pertinax, with delight and claimed that he had at night dreamt that the sixty-six-year-old Pertinax had fallen from his horse and that Severus himself mounted it. Before he could set out, however, he heard that Niger had been proclaimed emperor in Antioch by the Syrian army and acknowledged in Egypt.

Severus was not deterred, however, and began marching to Rome at top speed. Julianus had Severus's friend, Laetus, murdered, but his situation was nevertheless desperate. The Praetorian Guard took the law into their own hands, choosing their own prefects, one of whom made overtures to Severus but was killed (Howe 1942:41–42, 68). As defections of the guards to Severus's side began, however, the Senate anxiously sent him envoys. The Praetorians soon obeyed his order to arrest the murderers of Pertinax. On June 1, 193, with Severus encamped fifty miles north of the city, Consul Silius Messala convened the Senate. Septimius Severus was proclaimed emperor; Julianus was proclaimed a public enemy and condemned to death and then was killed by a common soldier. A deputation of one hundred senators immediately set out to greet the new emperor at his camp. They were followed by the entire palace staff. Severus ordered the Praetorian Guard to take an oath of allegiance to him and then to assemble unarmed outside the city to greet him. At the gathering, surrounded by the Danubian legionaries, some five thousand guards heard the new emperor's harsh address and were disbanded, surrendering their uniforms and ceremonial daggers. Thus was disbanded the only remaining military unit manned by Italians, as by then Romans and Italians had virtually disappeared from the legions. To the horror of Senator Cassius Dio (75.2.6; 1927:165), Severus filled "the city with a throng of motley soldiers most savage in appearance, most terrifying in speech, and most boorish in conversation." He recruited his bodyguard from the same motley crew.

Before entering the city, Severus dismounted from his horse and exchanged his uniform for civilian clothes. The soldiers escorting him, however, were fully armed. While he was addressing the Senate, the soldiers demanded the same bounty that had been granted to Octavian's soldiers in 43 BCE, but they eventually settled for much less. Severus then ordered the state funeral and deification of Pertinax. He did not, however, repeat the latter's mistake and identified himself with the army rather than the Senate. On the contrary, he exiled some senators and confiscated the property of many (Dio, 75.8.4; 1927:180–81). In a shrewd move in anticipation of the continuation of the many-sided revolutionary power struggle, Severus made his fellow African Clodius Albinus his junior partner in rule and gave him the title Caesar (Dio, 75; Birley 1971:ch. 11).

Septimius Severus and the Revolutionary Power Struggle, 193–197

Severus left Rome within a month to fight Pescennius Niger, a knight and a relative of Albinus (Dio, 75.6.1–2; 1927:172–73) who had proclaimed himself emperor in Syria after the death of Pertinax. From this moment on, the revolutionary development set in motion by prominent African members of the imperial elite in Rome shifts to the eastern periphery of the empire, and Syria becomes the main arena of Roman politics. One curious by-product of the revolution of 68–70 had been the myth of the return of Nero from the East. The fact that Nero had not been killed but had committed suicide made it all the easier to deny his death.[3] In any event, the first rebel claiming to be the returning Nero had appeared within a year of Nero's death, and two more false Neroes had made their appearance in the 80s (Bowersock 1986b:309–11). Thereafter, the myth of Nero redivivus became absorbed into the *Sibylline Oracles* and the developing apocalyptic lore of the Antichrist (J. Collins 1984).[4] In a region known for the use of political oracles, the apocalyptic Nero myth must have played a role in Niger's bid for emperorship. Now a new oracle, expressing the envy and *ressentiment* of the provincials, predicted the return of Nero redivivus and the destruction of Rome in 195–96:

> No longer will the plain of luxuriant Rome be victorious when he
> comes from Asia, conquering with Ares . . .
> . . . the man of secret birth,
> riding a Trojan chariot from the land of Asia
> with the spirit of fire (*Sib. Or.* 8.145–46, 153–55, p. 421)[5]

The Sibyl was wrong about the precise outcome, however. By the end of April or the beginning of May 194, Severus had won the civil war against Niger and his nine eastern legions completely. His army, the instrument of this victory, gained immediate recognition from him through the grant, on April 14, of the title *mater castrorum* (mother of the camp) to the powerful empress, Iulia Domna, who was accompanying the emperor and the army (Birley 1971:182). He had also taken the offspring of the governors of the eastern provinces into custody in Rome as hostages to make sure there would be no trouble in securing the governors' submission after the disposal of Niger (Herodian, 3.2.5). The Parthian king Vologases V, who had promised Niger support, instigated the rebellion of Abgar VIII of Osrhoene, who massacred the Roman soldiers Severus had garrisoned against Niger during the civil war, but that rebellion, too, was suppressed (Dabrowa 1984:156). In 195, Severus decided to break with Albinus, who was popular with the senators in their desperate struggle against the emperor (Herodian, 3.5.2), and to establish his own dynasty. He proclaimed himself the son of Marcus Aurelius by adoption, renamed his elder son Marcus Aurelius Antoninus after the deceased emperor, and gave him the title Caesar (Birley 1971:184). Albinus, who had remained in Britain, was thus deprived of the title Caesar and was left with few options. He proclaimed himself emperor. Albinus, it will be recalled, came from Africa and shared the same original constituency with Severus. Civil war against Severus was thus very much a part of the revolutionary power struggle within the winning revolutionary faction. Civil war in the West came to an end with the final defeat of Albinus and his troops in Lugdunum (Lyon) in February 197. The battle, the first led by Severus as emperor, was devastating for both sides, and his commander of the cavalry, Maecius Laetus, almost let Severus die in battle so that he could pick up the pieces. Severus was, however, too weakened to deal with Laetus immediately and had to wait some two years before having him put to death in Mesopotamia (Dio, 76.6.8, 10.3; 1927:210–11, 220–21).

Severus immediately proceeded to purge the Senate and government of Albinus's supporters, however, arresting sixty-four senators and executing twenty-nine of them, thus breaking the oath he had taken four years earlier not to condemn any senators to death. He did so, however, apparently after trials and conviction according to the due process of law (Dio, 77.7.3; 1927:252–53). The property of the victims was confiscated (Herodian, 3.8.2). In all, the revolutionary power struggle among the four contenders for the imperial purple had taken a little over four years.

The executions of the senators who had supported Albinus made Severus's break with the Senate in 197 definitive and his reliance on the army complete. He flooded it with Syro-Phoenician *adlecti* (Bowersock 1982). In Gibbon's words, "the Senate was filled with polished and eloquent slaves from the eastern provinces who justified personal flattery . . . and descanted on the inevitable mischiefs of freedom" (cited in M. Grant 1996:37). Among Severus's successors, only Iulia Mamaea, the mother of the last Severan emperor, was conciliatory toward the Senate and enlarged the presence of the senators in the imperial council; but that created no countervailing power to the army. Nor did it prevent her murder and that of the "son of Mamaea," as Alexander Severus was scornfully referred to, by the legionaries in 235 (M. Grant 1996:48).

Severus would not waste the military mobilization he had achieved in fighting his rivals in the civil wars and took his armies back east for a march down the Euphrates for conquest. He defeated the Parthians and captured and sacked their capital, Seleucia, in December 197. In December 198, Severus assumed the title Parthicus Maximus to mark the victory. He made Osrhoene a Roman province in 199 and created three new legions in Mesopotamia (Bivar 1983:94; Dabrowa 1984:157; Millar 1993:125–26; M. Grant 1996:8). Septimius Severus had the luxury of thinking of his empire as universal and global as the Parthian Empire was taking its expiring gasps. But as we shall see in the next chapter, a new empire was already being born in Persia, and it began asserting itself vigorously before the end of the Severan dynasty.

The Severan Consolidation of Revolution

Septimius Severus, the African emperor, made C. Fulvius Plautianus, his trusted kinsman and aide in the civil wars, the Praetorian prefect, and he had the Senate declare his son Antoninus (known to history by his nickname, Caracalla) first Caesar and then Augustus (emperor designate). Over the next quarter century, under Severus until 211 and under Caracalla until 217, the legal foundations of autocracy were developed independently of the Senate. Throughout the period, the powerful presence of Septimius's Syrian wife, Iulia Domna (d. 217), was conspicuous. She was the daughter of the high priest of the sun god, Elagabalus (al-Jabal), in Emesa (Homs), whose ancestor is epigraphically attested as the priest-ruler (*rex magnus*) under Augustus (Teixidor 1997–98:717). She herself was given the title Augusta by her husband and ruled the empire with her son Caracalla, completing the Severan consolidation of the revolution. The rule of the Punic(African)-Syrian Severan dynasty signaled the completion of the cycle of Roman integrative revolutions and was appropriately crowned by Caracalla's *constitutio Antoniniana* (212), which did away with the gradations of civic rights and universalized Roman citizenship throughout the empire (M. Grant 1996:30–31).[6] But it also resulted in the centralization of power and the legal consolidation of autocracy.

The Severan Revolution was led by a man whose native city, Lepcis (Leptis) Magna in Africa, had been given the status of *colonia* by Trajan in 110, thirty-five years before his birth, and who had married the young and brilliant daughter of the high priest of Emesa,[7] was acclaimed imperator by the army on the Danube frontier in Pannonia, and enlarged the Roman Empire in Tripolitana and further west in Mauretania. Severus was the great expander of the empire, Propagator Imperii, as printed on his coins and medallions, and spoke of it in global, universal terms as *genus humanum* and *orbis* (M. Grant 1996:28–29). The revolution had been won by the provincial armies, which, in contrast to those in 69 CE, had remained intact and maintained their discipline. It was an integrative revolution of an unusual kind in which the center of the empire was dominated by two regions of the periphery—Africa and Syria. Septimius Severus paid only four short visits to Rome during his first decade as emperor (Birley 1971:20–42, 124, 216). He probably had an African accent, as his sister certainly did (M. Grant 1996:8). In his son Caracalla, the hostile consul from the province of Asia Cassius Dio detected "the harshness and cruelty of Africa and the craftiness of Syria" (78.6.1a).[8] Even the last Severan emperor, Alexander Severus (222–35), despite his impeccable Roman education, was unhappily self-conscious about his Syrian speech and manner (M. Grant 1996:26).

In 217, the equestrian lawyer and Praetorian prefect Macrinus instigated the murder of Caracalla and took over as emperor. Marcus Opellius Macrinus was from a poor family in Mauretania who had risen to knighthood. He added Severus to his name and assumed the title Augustus, appointing his son, Diadumenian, who was thirteen, Caesar, as the dynastic principle had evidently taken root (M. Grant 1996:22–23). Iulia Domna committed suicide, but her sister, Iulia Maesa Augusta, aided by her daughter, Iulia Sohaemus, and the latter's lover, used the Syrian troops around Emesa to defeat and kill Macrinus, and imperial rule returned to the Severan house in 218. Iulia Sohaemus, capitalizing on the enormous popularity of the murdered Caracalla, claimed that her son, Bassianus, was Caracalla's illegitimate son, accordingly changing his name to that of his alleged father, Antoninus. He was soon nicknamed Elagabalus, after the god of his maternal family. He was murdered in 222 by order of his maternal grandmother, Iulia Maesa Augusta, and replaced by his younger cousin, Alexianus, who was likewise a priest of the temple of the sun god in Emesa, which enshrined a black meteorite not unlike that enshrined in the Ka'ba at Mecca (Herodian, 5.3.5; Bowersock 1975:233–34). Alexianus was also said to be the illegitimate son of Caracalla. Postrevolutionary Severan reconstruction was resumed and continued by Maesa's other daughter, Iulia Mamaea, as Augusta and mother of the new emperor, renamed Alexander Severus (222–35). The rule of the Severan dynasty came to a violent end in just over four decades with the murder of the mother and son by the German legionaries in 235, but the consequences of the Severan Revolution were deep and long-lasting.

Consequences of the Severan Revolution

The Legal Consolidation of Autocracy and the Rule of Roman Law

The Severan conclusion of the revolution of 193–97, much more so than the Flavian conclusion of the revolution of 68–70, resulted in increased centralization of military power and in the legal consolidation of imperial authority. During the second century, many administrative and legal reorganizations and rationalizations had taken place through reform and not revolutions. Notable among these had been Trajan's transformation of imperial administration into a civil service, which led to the growth of administrative law modeled on Roman criminal law (Sirks 2015:338) and Hadrian's expansion of the equestrian offices, and the increasing judiciary functions of the emperor's council (*consilium principis*) and the related growth of Roman law (Kunkel 1972:109–10). The Severan Revolution gave this process of centralization a tremendous boost. The greater centralization of imperial administration was reflected in the more extensive employment of procurators to administer imperial finances and in the creation of a new department of imperial domains for the management of confiscated land (Jolowicz and Nicholas 1972:337). Furthermore, Severan military reforms resulted in the creation of three new legions, reaffirmation of the army's role in the choice of the emperor at the expense of the Senate, and some militarization of government.[9] But the main significance of the Severan period consists in the reform and rationalization of Roman law and the consolidation of constitutional autocracy.

Septimius Severus had in all probability studied and briefly taught law at the school of Scaevola, with his friend and very likely fellow Libyan (T. Honoré 1994:80) Papinian (Aemilius Papinianus),[10] the greatest jurist of his reign, whom he appointed Praetorian prefect and kept close at hand to the very end of his rule (Dio, 77.10.7, 14.5; 1927:260–61, 268–69). Like Papinian, Severus began his *cursus honoris* under Marcus Aurelius as an *advocatus fisci*, typical for law graduates going into imperial administration (A. Honoré 1962:163, 205). He remained keenly interested in the law as emperor and attended to his legal functions twice a day, as judge in the morning and as jurisconsult in the evening. Once he had won the revolutionary power struggle and civil wars, Severus also vigorously engaged in imperial legislation, issuing twenty-four imperial rescripts (constitutions) in 197, a number that increased after his death to seventy-one in 213 under Caracalla (A. Honoré 1962:177). But already in 197, Tertullian could write of the attempt to reform contradictory legal traditions by this "most conservative of princes" (cited in R. Grant [1970] 1990:97).

The republican constitutional organs maintained and progressively appropriated by Augustus (Sirks 2015:333) had disappeared or were completely dilapidated by the end of the second century, except for the Senate, which received its near-lethal blow from Severus. The last plebeian institution, the *plebiscita,* had expired with the Flavian Revolution, and the *Senatus consultum* as an instrument of legislation virtually lapsed after the Severan Revolution, ceding its place to imperial addresses to a passive Senate and to the *constitutiones* of the emperor framed by the imperial council (Howe 1942:43).

Under Severus, the office *a libellis,* which issued rescripts on behalf of the emperor in response to inquiries and was manned by professional lawyers (T. Honoré 1994:73),[11] showed great vigor and had a lasting impact on the growth of Roman civil law. Severus also centralized the administration of criminal justice by abolishing the cumbersome republican criminal commissions and transferring their functions to imperial officials and by giving unlimited jurisdiction for Rome to the urban prefect and for Italy to the Praetorian prefect (Howe 1942:43; T. Honoré 1981:15; 1982:3).[12] Ulpian (Domitius Ulpianus), who began his brilliant career in law under Severus, contributed *De appellationibus* (On appeals) to rationalize the law of procedure. Ulpian greatly enhanced the judicial functions of the Praetorian prefect, partly in connection with the extension of the jurisdiction of the imperial council, of which he was a member (Howe 1942:ch. 4). The Praetorian prefect had his own court of appeal and became the key figure in this centralized judiciary system.[13]

Severus appears to have appointed more lawyers to important posts than any emperor before him. Papinian and Ulpian, two of the greatest authorities in Roman law of all time, played a prominent political as well as intellectual role in the establishment and consolidation of the Severan state. Paul (Julius Paulus), the third great lawyer of that generation, was the emperor's legal adviser as a member of the imperial council and served as either a Praetorian or a lesser prefect (Howe 1942:44, 46; M. Grant 1996:50). Papinian was the head of the rescript office from 195 until 202, where Ulpian and Paul served as his assessors, and was succeeded by Ulpian, whose style dominates the rescripts down to May 209 (A. Honoré 1962:207, 217; T. Honoré 1982:ch. 3). Papinian was appointed the Praetorian prefect in 205 and held that position until he perished in 213, when Caracalla eliminated his younger brother, Geta, and the latter's supporters. Papinian must have sided with Geta and thereby lost his life. Ulpian most likely took Caracalla's side and flourished during the remainder of his reign.

Ulpian, Papinian's student and a protégé of Iulia Domna and her sister and niece, was from a patrician family of Syro-Phoenician Tyre (Sur). He was most probably author of the *constitutio Antoniniana* and embarked on his monumental work on Roman law to complete Caracalla's revolutionary project of legal rationalization (T. Honoré 1982:26–29). Iulia Maesa, who ran the Severan state after ending the interval of Macrinus's emperorship, subscribed to Roman constitutional law to the extent of claiming the quaint tribunician power for her grandson Elagabalus when she was putting him on the throne and would not allow any extraconstitutional persecution of him (Dio, 80.2.2–3.2; 1927:440–43). Ulpian also had excellent relations with Caracalla's cousin Iulia Mamaea and was appointed the Praetorian prefect under her young son, Alexander Severus (222–35), who called him "my parent" (T. Honoré 1982:36–37). Ulpian was killed by the Praetorian Guard after they rioted in August 223. His legal work, however, was continued by his students, Marcianus and Modestinus, both of whom were knights like their master (A. Honoré 1962:212–17). Nevertheless, Ulpian's murder by the Praetorians signaled the failure of the Severans to put the guards under civilian control and to subject them and the army to the rule of law. Alexander Severus was forced to acknowledge this defeat by reverting the prefectship of the Praetorians to military men (M. Grant 1996:17, 51).

To enhance the authority of the imperial officials, Ulpian wrote *De officio proconsulis* (On the proconsul's office) and included the prefects, alongside consuls and proconsuls, among the magistrates possessing *imperium* (Howe 1942:39, citing *Digest* 2.4.2). Nor is it an accident that it was Ulpian who definitively enshrined the imperial constitutions and established the legal principle that the emperor was above the law (*princeps legibus solutus*).[14] Finally, Ulpian made definitive the transfer of the legislative power of the people to the emperor with the legal fiction of empowerment through the *lex de imperio*: "Whatever the emperor has decided has the force of law [*quod principi placuit, legis habet vigorem*]; in as much as through the law which was passed concerning his *imperium*, the people confers all its power and authority on him and in him" (*Digest* 1.4.1).

It would be wrong to assume, however, that the Severan lawyers remained subservient to the constitutional autocrat. This was certainly not so after Septimius Severus. Ulpian at times referred to Caracalla as plain Antoninus, without any imperial or other titles, and had a condescending attitude to the emperor's rescript, which he sometimes characterized as "correct" or "quite right" (*imperatorrecte / rectissime rescripsit*); he believed that nothing became the emperor so much as abiding by the law (T. Honoré 1982:45, 141–42, 165). Paul freely criticized the emperors' constitutions (A. Honoré 1962:217–18) and argued in the imperial council of Alexander Severus that the emperor should obey the laws (M. Grant 1996:51). Their fellow equestrian lawyer Macrinus, who became emperor briefly in 217–18, similarly put the law above the emperor and went much further in rejecting imperial constitutions as the source of law while ridiculing the rescripts of his predecessors Commodus and Caracalla (*Augustan History* 2.76–77; Macrinus, 13.1; A. Honoré 1962:191). The Severan lawyers definitively furthered their own professional interest by establishing the opinions of the jurists (*prudentes, iuris auctores*) as the source of law, alongside custom (A. Honoré 1962:228–31). Their achievement remained definitive. The Code of the Emperor of the East Theodosius II (429 CE) states categorically, "We confirm all the writings of Papinian, Paul, Gaius (the only non-Severan), Ulpian and Medisetinus" (clause 1.4.3, as cited in Sirks 2015:337). Papinian wrote thirty-seven books of quaestiones and nineteen books of responsa (M. Grant 1996:50), while the bulk of the texts in the *Digest* of the Justinian Code are attributed to Ulpian (41 percent) and Paul (17 percent) (T. Honoré 1982:47).

Septimius Severus did not rely exclusively on lawyers to find a constitutional basis for his legitimacy and dynastic ambitions. As a victor of the first round of civil wars in the revolutionary power struggle with no hereditary claim to rule, Severus first celebrated his divine election by the gods, most notably Jupiter, who is depicted on a coin issued in 194 in the same size as Severus and clasping his right arm, the two holding an orb between them. Severus's divine election was foretold by *omina imperii* (imperial omens); to commemorate some of them, monuments were built (Herodian, 2.9.3–4; Fears 1977:258–62). According to the neo-Pythagorean theory of divine election of kings (*peri basileias*), as stated by Galen of Pergamon (d. 200 CE) and (Pseudo-)Ecphantus, kings imitate the gods who elect them, thereby mediating the latter's benefaction to men. Divine and royal virtue are unified, and the welfare of the subjects is the foremost duty of mimetic kingship (Buraselis 2007:14–21).

The text of the *constitutio Antoniniana* is found in a well-studied papyrus (Papyrus Gissen 40.1). Caracalla and the Roman gods appear to be the sponsors of the *constitutio*, as it makes the *oikoumene* the common fatherland of all (Oliver 1978:408). The text is consonant with the political theology of *peri basileias*. "After offering thanks to the immortal gods I [Marcus Aurelius Augustus Antoninus] lead [to their sanctuaries] my people . . . [and] I grant all those under my rule in the oikumene Roman citizenship" (Oliver 1989:499–500). Here Caracalla uses the traditional phrase "all those under my rule" to signify that he is the universal patron of all provincials (Oliver 1978:407), mediating between the gods and his subjects in delivering the *constitutio Antoniniana* as a "divine-imperial gift (*theia dōrea*)." No wonder we have a prayer of thanksgiving offered to the "saving Fortune of our lord the invincible Severus Antoninus [Caracalla] which saved you" (cited in Frend 1984:300–301n16). With the legal consolidation of autocracy buttressing the idea of sacral monarchy under the Severans, a new era began. *Dominus* (lord or master [over slaves]) became the official title of the later Severan emperors, who further instituted the official declaration of *devotion*, readiness to surrender life, for the army and civic communities (Alföldy 1988:183).

Let us summarize the changes in the Roman structure of authority made definitive by the Severan Revolution. With the greatly reduced importance of Rome,[15] the *plebs urbana* lost its significance after securing the acclamation of Pertinax at the end of 192. The army, by contrast, now became the foremost element in the polity, with the much-weakened Senate lagging far behind as its second element. Dominating the polity was the autocratic emperor. The military aspect of the late imperial polity predominated over the legal. In all probability, the great jurist Ulpian lost his life for trying to subjugate the army to the newly rationalized rule of law (Howe 1942:52). Nevertheless, the rule of law was institutionalized, as legal science ceased to grow and became petrified. The twin military and legal authority of the autocratic emperor remained distinctive of the later empire, which is known as the dominate.

The Integrative Revolution and Its Consequences

Not only were the emperors being made elsewhere than at Rome, but now ordinary consuls began assuming their office elsewhere. The triumph of the periphery over the center was marked by Emperor Severus and his son Antoninus (Caracalla) inaugurating the year 202 as consuls in Antioch. In the following year, the royal family intended to visit Lepcis Magna to celebrate the tenth year of Severus's reign, and two natives, the emperor's elder son Geta and his kinsman Plautianus, inaugurated the year as consuls in their home town (Birley 1971:211, 219).

The remarkable freedom of the Roman Empire in the second century from revolutionary upheavals had been, to no small extent, due to the openness of access to the ruling class and continuous effective administration. Unlike the senatorial aristocracy of the republic, the emperors had no vested interest in restricting access to the Senate. Patronage worked effectively as a mechanism for the integration of provincials across the empire into the imperial ruling class through the mediation of senators and governors. Provincial privileged classes were thus linked to the imperial center. As Severus and Albinus were both Africans, this made for the effective integration of the provinces, including North Africa, into the imperial polity, which also meant the effective integration of the North African *equites* (Saller 1982:esp. ch. 5). The African *equites* had begun to appear on the periphery of Roman political society only in the middle of the second century (Alföldy 1988:125; Duncan-Jones 1967:esp. 154). Of Septimius Severus's Praetorian prefects after the end of the civil wars, Plautianus (197–205) and very probably Papinian (205–11) were from Africa (T. Honoré 1994:80). With the Syrian princesses, Iulia Domna and her sister and nieces, the integration of the Syrian and Phoenician knights continued throughout the Severan period and beyond. The new political elite was thus overwhelmingly recruited from the African and Syro-Phoenician peripheries of the empire instead of Italy and Spain. Whereas over half of the political elite of the Antonine regime of old came from Italy (Birley 1971:282), well over half of the Severan political and administrative elite came from the East and Africa. This is shown in table 2.

Table 2 Composition of the Roman elite under Septimius Severus

Origin	Governors of military provinces (*N* = 34)	Procurators (*N* = 106)
Italy	4	19
Spain and Gaul	1	7
The East	1	15
Africa	6	35
Total	12	76

Source: Birley 1972:336–58. "Military provinces" refers to those with two or three legions. The origins of the officeholders are identified by Birley with strong probability. For a description of the office of procurator, see Jolowicz and Nicholas 1972:336–37.

The integration of the eastern provinces was more consequential in the long run, presaging the replacement of Rome by Constantinople within a century. In fact, already in 211 or 212, when Caracalla and Geta were forced to live close to each other by their mother, Iulia Domna, the former was to have his headquarters in Byzantium and the latter in Chalcedon, on opposite sides of the straits, and the latter wanted either Antioch or Alexandria as his capital, as neither was inferior to Rome (Herodian, 4.3.6–7). It is surely telling of the long-term consequences of the Severan Revolution that the millennial anniversary of the foundation of Rome in 247–48 was celebrated by the one and only Arab Roman emperor, Philip the Arab (Bowersock 1983:124).

Septimius Severus granted *ius coloniae* and *ius Italicum*—which implied complete assimilation to the status of the Italian colonies, in particular immunity from taxation—not only to Greek but also to Semitic cities and principalities of the East, notably Tyre and Laodicea. He deepened the Romanization and integration of Egypt by setting up city councils in that country, and he heavily fortified the eastern provinces against the Parthian Empire, notably Palmyra (Tadmor) in Syria and Dura-Europus in Mesopotamia (M. Grant 1996:28–29). He and his son Caracalla adopted imperial victory titles that included Arabicus, Adiabenicus, and Parthicus; gave the annexed Mesopotamian cities and principalities the title of Roman colonies, hitherto reserved in the eastern provinces for veteran settlements; and similarly granted the status of colonies to the settlements of the auxiliaries (and not just of legionaries) (Millar 1993:121–24, 137–39). Caracalla extended *ius Italicum* to Antioch and Emesa (Homs), the city of his mother; and he or his father made Palmyra a *colonia*. During the Severan era, five Mesopotamian cities were granted the status of *colonia*: Edessa, Carrhae, Reshina, Singara, and Nisibis (Millar 1993:141–44). Furthermore, Septimius Severus gave Alexandria a municipal constitution, introduced urban councils in many other areas, and fostered the development of municipal life in Egypt (Sherwin-White 1973a:275–78; Millar 1964:144; Frend 1974:343). The East was represented at the apex of imperial power by the Syrian empress (Augusta), who was an indefatigable partner to the emperor. She remained fully identified with the twin pillars of Severan propaganda: the dynasty, as *Augusta* and later *mater Augustorum*, and the army, as *mater castrorum* (mother of the camp) (Ghedini 1984:188–91).

The Severan integrative revolution marks a decisive point in Roman constitutional history. Though the trend had already been set, "it is only Severus who rounds the last mark and drives straight for the complete balance and equalization, and even the fusion of the Greek and Latin elements of the Roman world" (Sherwin-White 1973a:275). This statement can be improved only by pointing out that the integrative revolution went even further. The support for the new dynasty in fact came from areas that were not wholly Roman or Greek and whose cultures were respected. The Severans thus allowed the use of Punic and Aramaic ("Assyrian") in addition to Latin and Greek for legal purposes (T. Honoré 1982:4). The Jews were among the eastern supporters of the regime and had expressed their devotion to Septimius Severus and Iulia Domna in an inscription in Palestine at the end of the civil wars in 197 (R. Grant [1970] 1990:98). Severus and Caracalla did not require the observance of the imperial cults by the Jews in view of their religion (Bowersock 1983:174). What nevertheless remained was the legal distinction between foreigners (*peregrini*) and Roman citizens; and it was this distinction that was abolished by Caracalla's edict, which established universal franchise and completed the long series of integrative revolutions since the Social War by extending Roman citizenship to the whole of the Roman Empire. There can be no doubt of the value of Roman citizenship as an asset at the beginning of the third century (Sherwin-White 1973b), all the more so because the principle of dual citizenship remained in force, and the grant of universal citizenship did not affect the status of the municipal communes. Nor can there be much doubt that the grant increased the number of citizens very considerably, a fact reflected in the tremendous increase in the incidence of Aurelius as a second name in honor of the enfranchising emperor. The universalization of citizenship not only elevated the status of many individuals but also opened access to the new imperial legal machinery, thus stimulating tremendous growth of civil law (Sherwin-White 1973a:386–87, 392–93).

The victory of the African emperor with a vigorous Syrian empress installed a political elite originating from the Roman colonies in Africa and Syria. Furthermore, Septimius Severus introduced municipal self-government in Egypt and enabled Egyptians to enter the Senate (Wells 1984:286). The

Roman colonies of Africa were especially overrepresented in imperial administration and governorships under Septimius Severus because they had formed the core of the conspiratorial, revolutionary counter-elite that gained power in the summer of 193. Syria had been won over from Niger after the first civil war, and its elite must have been integrated a little later, becoming especially prominent in the emperor's legal service. Tyre was the founding city of Carthage, and Lepcis Magna, also founded by Tyre, had commemorated this with a monumental statue with inscriptions in Latin and Greek erected in Tyre (Millar 1993:118, 292). Tyre had supported Severus during the civil war and was granted *ius Italicum*, and "on account of its outstanding loyalty to the *res publica* and to the *imperium Romanum*," as its native Ulpian proudly put it, it was made the capital of a new province of Syria, called Phoenicia (cited from the *Digest* in Millar 1993:291). Severus settled his veterans there and called it *colonia Septimia Severa metropolis* (T. Honoré 1982:11).

The last Roman revolution was thus integrative not only geographically but also in terms of social structure. The Severan Revolution socially integrated the huge Roman army by increasing pay and elevating the status of the soldiers, since the army was the main avenue of upward social mobility for the lower ranks of the population throughout the empire. It also enhanced the integration of the equestrian order, giving the knights greater access to the highest offices than ever before. And finally, it integrated women into the highest echelon of imperial political structure and society (M. Grant 1996:45–48). It was, as we have seen, a revolution carried out by the provincial armies. Furthermore, unlike the revolution of 68–70, it was also a revolution for the soldiers and not just for the legion commanders.

Caracalla was not a military man himself but knew his crucial dependence on the army. He identified with the soldiers, looked after their interests, and granted them indulgences (see his rescripts from 212–13, cited in T. Honoré 1994:21). This identification was mutual, with adverse long-term consequences: from the time of Caracalla, the army designated itself as soldiers of the Caesar (rather than of the Roman state) (Mommsen 1887:848). There was substantial improvement in military pay. A legionary soldier's pay had been 900 sesterces a year under Augustus and had been raised to 1,200 by Domitian. Septimius Severus raised this pay, probably to 2,000, and Caracalla, to 3,000. The pay of the auxiliaries (five-sixths that of the legionaries) was similarly improved. Caracalla also increased the discharge *premia* substantially.[16] The soldiers also enjoyed the right of marriage for the first time (Campbell 1984:161–62, 409). The Severan Revolution thus consolidated, if not created, a new social estate with esprit de corps, associations (*scholae* or *collegia*), and emergent common military cults (Alföldy 1988:172; M. Grant 1996:34–36).

This brings us to another major social force mobilized by the Severan Revolution: the equestrian order, to which the lawyers invariably belonged. Access to the equestrian order for the promoted centurions, and through it to some of the highest offices of the empire, had been opened since the time of Hadrian.[17] To the offices of the prefects of the Praetorian Guard, of Egypt, and of the fleet that were the preserves of the equestrian order, Severus added the prefectship of the new province of Mesopotamia. He also put three legions under equestrian prefects rather than senatorial legates. In addition, there are seven known cases of appointment of *equites* as lieutenants of (theoretically senatorial) governors (Campbell 1984:404–8; Alföldy 1988:167, 171). Furthermore, the expanding legal machinery of the empire under the Severans provided an important institutional niche for the *equites*. The best known Severan jurists—Papinian, Paul, Tryphoninus, Messius, Menander, Ulpian, and Modestinus—were all knights (T. Honoré 1982:3). Furthermore, they were all provincial *equites*, and alongside them there appears a substratum of provincial lawyers (Kunkel 1972:121). The Severan Revolution thus inaugurated the century of the rise of the *equites* to the highest level of political power. The Severan lawyer Macrinus, who, as the prefect of the Praetorians, had Caracalla murdered and replaced him in 217, was the first knight (and the first Mauretanian) to become emperor without ever having been raised to the senatorial order. However, "as the power of the Senate waned or was deliberately undermined, the emperor depended more and more on the equestrian order in ruling an ever more centralized state" (Howe 1942:48). Once more, we see the same phenomenon we encountered in the aftermath of the Flavian Revolution. The nonsolidary equestrian order—or, sociologically speaking, stratum—was drawn upon for the weakening and dilution of the senatorial order, which was much smaller, more cohesive, and solidary. In both cases, revolution resulted in the simultaneous growth of autocracy and passive democratization.

I have discussed the important role of the knights of the Latin and the Italian cities in the transition from the Roman republic to empire in chapter 4. The knights of the equestrian order constituted the second stratum of Roman imperial society, the first being the senatorial order, and with their gradual rise, they may well have felt some relative deprivation and *ressentiment* toward their senatorial betters, even though their access to the higher order was by no means blocked. Given the underrepresentation of the eastern provinces of Syria, Judaea, and Arabia in the senatorial order, the knights were for all practical purposes the upper stratum of these provinces, and a few of them harbored the highest aspirations. One C. Avidius Cassius from Cyrrhus in northern Syria, son of an equestrian, had moved up to the senatorial order and to provincial governorship and even attained the general command of "all Asia / the East" under the coemperor Verus. He proclaimed himself emperor in Egypt in 175, but his three-month reign ended in his murder as Marcus Aurelius became sole emperor (Millar 1993:115–17). When Septimius Severus divided Syria in two, creating the new province of Phoenicia and celebrated its founding parenthood of his own Punic native land, the knights were in fact the aristocracy of Syria and Phoenicia. The husband of his sister-in-law, Iulia Maesa, was a knight from Emesa,[18] and those of the latter's daughters, Iulia Sohaemus and Iulia Mamaea, were knights from Apamea and Arca (Caesarea ad Libanum) respectively (Millar 1993:119–20). They certainly did not help the Senate in its desperate struggle against Severus. By contrast, the equestrian lawyers joined the latter's imperial service and acted as bearers of the rule of law and sustainers of his invigorated constitutional autocracy.

In doing so, they greatly enlarged the Roman political community by progressive extension and finally the universalization of citizenship. More consequential than Ulpian's epitomization of the established fact of constitutional autocracy was his certification of the novel universal enfranchisement by Caracalla: "In orbe Romano qui sunt ex constitutione imperatoris Antonini cives Romani effecti sunt" (Those who have been made Roman citizens in the Roman world by the constitution of Emperor Antoninus) (*Digest* 1.5.17). The significance of the *constitutio Antoniniana* is evident from ancient sources: Aurelius Victor a century and a half later and especially Justinian in the sixth century acknowledged its importance.[19] Direct evidence is even more compelling. The (*gentilicum*) names born by different generations of enfranchised Roman citizens constitute important markers of the cycles of the Roman integrative revolution. In the third century, the number of Aurelii (so named after Caracalla's middle name in celebration of the *constitutio Antoniniana*) vie with the number of Iulii (named after *lex Iulia*) for first place, with the majority of the former in eastern provinces, followed by Flavii (named after Vespasian) and Claudii (named after Claudius) and Aelii (named after Hadrian), enfranchised in the middle of the two earlier cycles respectively (Buraselis 2007:98–102). A drastic upsurge in the number of Aurelii new citizens in the provinces, especially in Greek-speaking Macedonia, Asia, and Syria, is proven by Buraselis's (2007:94–120, esp. 118) painstaking counting of the persons who integrated this name into their traditional identity. Because many of the new citizens, unlike the patriciate of Roman cities, belonged to disprivileged classes, they did not leave spectacular memorials to express their gratitude, but there are a large number of Caracalla portraits in private domains, and his popularity and legitimacy lasted long after his murder (Buraselis 2007:118–19).

Our most striking evidence, however, comes from a papyrus dated 215, in which the name Aurelius is explicitly linked to the *constitutio Antoniniana*, which is referred to in terms of Severan political theology as "the divine [meaning the imperial] gift" (Buraselis 2007:114–15).

Equal protection under the law in general empowered the lower strata, while specific laws of the period weakened masters' and patrons' rights and declared the *honestiores* and *humiliores* alike equal before the Natural Law (M. Grant 1996:52). Paul and Ulpian invalidated transactions involving coercion and intimidation of private persons (Buraselis 2007:61, 66) and allowed defendants not to appear in court if they feared tyranny or enemy attack (T. Honoré 1982:33). The great enhancement of the civil rights of the free population of the empire resulted from the equalization and standardization of legal rights; and the unification of Roman law throughout all the provinces of the empire resulted in fiscal equalization (Buraselis 2007:120–57). This passive democratization resulting from equality of all citizens before the law was enhanced by the Severan ideology and political theology of divine monarchy underlying the *constitutio Antoniniana*, which resulted in the leveling of all citizens as subjects of the emperor, whose duty was the benefaction of all men in imitation of gods (Buraselis 2007:88–93).

Perhaps the most eloquent epitome to the last Roman integrative revolution from the periphery, M. Iulius Philippus, from a distinguished family of provincial knights, was the second knight and the first and only Arab to become emperor (244–49). His brother was the prefect of Mesopotamia, and he himself became the Praetorian prefect and was an army commander under Gordian III when the latter fell in battle against Shāpur I of Persia in 243. Philip the Arab was hailed imperator by the Roman army in Mesopotamia in 244 and is the last emperor known to have created a *colonia* in the provinces—Philippopolis (Shahbā), named after himself and located in present-day Syria on the edge of the Hauran plateau and the Arabian Desert (Bowersock 1983:124–27; Millar 1993:156).

Cultural and Religious Consequences of the Severan Revolution

With the last Roman integrative revolution, the Roman world was inundated by the culture of the periphery. As we have seen, Cassius Dio could not withhold his contempt for the motley of barbarian soldiers, savage in speech and appearance, who occupied Rome when Septimius Severus came to power. Plautianus, the Libyan Praetorian prefect and allegedly a boyhood lover of Caracalla, kept his daughter in seclusion, with secretly castrated Roman noblemen serving her as eunuchs, and threw a lavish wedding party for her marriage to Caracalla, "partly in royal, partly in barbarian style" (Dio 1927:229, 235, 239). The cultural influence of the periphery began with the introduction of foreign wisdom by the Sophists at the court of Iulia Domna, who had an intellectually brilliant circle to which Dio belonged and that offered an imaginary debate on the Roman constitution between Octavian's counselors and the Sophist Philostratus, who wrote a biography of the first-century Orientalizing sage of Tyana, Apollonius, later known in the Arab world as the Lord of the Talisman (Dio, 52.78.171–78; Teixidor 1997–98:716; Kemezis 2014:165–67; Al-Azmeh 2014:94). If the city of Rome itself was so deeply affected, it is not surprising that the provinces of the East experienced what amounted to a cultural and religious revolution.

The cultural dimension of the Severan integrative revolution is of primary importance and reflects a much stronger impact of the eastern periphery upon the increasingly cosmopolitan culture of the Roman Empire. The empress, now Iulia Augusta, who was presented in a variety of divine forms in her lifetime, personified this new cosmopolitan universalism, perhaps best in an inscription dated 214 from the time of her son, Caracalla, where she is presented as Tyche (goddess of fortune) of the *oikoumene* (Ghedini 1984:143–44, 191). The imperial cult under her direction was capable of assimilating other polytheistic cults and could serve as a focus for polytheistic identity while at the same time being universalist and integrative (Ghedini 1984:123–93; Fowden 1993:38). The Severan period witnessed a gradual, spontaneous, and sporadic diffusion of Oriental cults and the growth of the cult of the emperor. The image of the emperor changed from a potential to an actual god, and the cult of the emperor spread from the East to the rest of the empire, including Africa. The arch in Lepcis Magna presents Septimius Severus as Jupiter and Iulia Domna as Juno, thus transmitting the idea of the emperor as a living god to Africa (Ghedini 1984:188–90, figs. 2 and 11). The thanksgiving prayer for salvation by the Fortune of Emperor Caracalla has already been mentioned. It is indeed tempting to argue, along Durkheimian lines, that the urge to consolidate the unity of the increasingly integrated empire was translated into the spread and growing strength of the cult of the emperor (Hopkins 1978:ch. 5).

It has been suggested (T. Honoré 1982:29) that the universalist religions that were widespread in Syria indirectly influenced Ulpian in the monumental work of rationalization and systematization of law that he most probably undertook at the bidding of Caracalla and Iulia Domna. Nor can there be doubt regarding the influence of the Stoic concept of the *ius gentium*, and the idea of human brotherhood in the Roman family of nations, in the fragments of Ulpian's substantive contributions preserved in the

Digest, which include injunctions to proconsuls to protect the poor and not to oppress the provincials (Howe 1942:45–46). Is it too far-fetched to look a century ahead and see the coming of Christianity as the overwhelming of the center of the Roman Empire by a sect from the eastern periphery? The Christian cultural revolution of the fourth century and the Severan political revolution of the third are certainly not unrelated. For one thing, without the political integration of the eastern and African peripheries where the Christian movement had gathered momentum, it is not easy to envision its impact upon the center of the Roman world. The relation is, however, much more complicated. The *constitutio Antoniniana*, by universalizing Roman citizenship, brought the Augustan notion of the Roman Empire as possessing fully autonomous universalism in and by itself closer to sociological reality than ever before. This political idea of universalism was buttressed by the cultural universalism of Iulia Domna's imperial cult, which was built on polytheistic diversity. The relationship between this political universalism that rested on religious diversity and the monistic religious universalism of Christianity as an integrative movement, which, needless to say, had political implications of its own, is interesting enough to require separate treatment.

Christianity was a universalist religion and an integrative movement. The monistic mode of integration it offered, however, was radically different from the mode present in the integrative reconstruction policies of the Severan imperial state. The Severan state had certainly been effective in exploiting the religious mode of integration. As we have seen, the eclectic imperial cult directed by Iulia Augusta during the first quarter century of Severan rule made for a definite kind of "polytheistic universalism." It can be said that "the center used it to assimilate the periphery and unify the empire" (Fowden 1993:38), with the reminder that the center itself had in practice shifted from Rome to Antioch. In 213 or 214, Caracalla annexed the kingdom of Edessa, accusing its Christian ruler, Abgar VIII, of mistreating his subjects who followed pagan customs, even though Abgar, like his father, had submitted to Severus and added the emperor's name to his own. The existence of a considerable Christian community is attested in the writings of one of its leaders, Bardesanes (Bar Daisan), "in the language of the Suroi [early Syriac]," translated by his followers into Greek. In *The Book of the Laws of the Countries*, Bardesanes speaks of "the new people of us Christians (KRSTYN'), that the Messiah has caused to arise in every place" (as cited in Millar 1993:463), while posing the problematic of unity *inter nationes* and thus presaging a Christian Roman Empire (Millar 1993:474–75; Buraselis 2007:46–47).

There was more going on in the religious scene: Mithraism, a syncretic religious movement of Persian origins, was probably the most important single cult during the Severan age and was particularly popular in the army. Its integrative potential, however, seems to have been limited, perhaps by the requirements of initiation, as no discovered Mithraeum could accommodate more than twenty-five persons (Frend 1984:276–77). Gnosticism also flourished as a rival to orthodox Christianity, as did a variety of other "heretical" Christian tendencies. There was also a distinct tendency toward philosophical monotheism among educated pagans (Frend 1984:278–79, 292). In Porphyry's Platonism and kindred rapprochement between Greek and Oriental wisdom, Fowden (1993:39–40) sees the search for a universal way to salvation and a centripetal perspective on polytheism that acknowledged local gods as "aspects of one universal god, satraps of a divine King of Kings." Orthodox Christianity, however, was more successful than its rivals as a universalist movement. The church fathers were increasingly appropriating the terms "universal" or "catholic" at the service of the Christian mission throughout the empire without fear of official persecution. Stimulated by the Severan Revolution, Origen was cognizant of the value of imperial political integration for the spread of the Christian faith: "Jesus was born during the reign of Augustus, the one who reduced to uniformity, so to speak, the many kingdoms on earth so that he had a single empire. It would have hindered Jesus' teaching from being spread through the whole world if there had been many kingdoms" (cited in Fowden 1993:89). In a similar vein, Saint Augustine (*City of God* 5.17) was to praise Caracalla's universalization of Roman citizenship without reservation.

What little evidence we have on Septimius Severus's own religious policy remains controversial; he may have consented to the persecution of Christians in Alexandria in 202 (Frend 1974:349; R. Grant [1970] 1990:99–100; dal Covolo 1989:ch. 2). The women of the imperial household, on the other hand, being from a Syrian priestly family, were keenly interested in religious issues. This was especially true of Iulia Domna's niece Iulia Mamaea, the powerful mother of Emperor Alexander Severus, whom Origen met (ca. 232) and described as "a most religious woman" (Frend 1974:350; 1984:272–73). Iulia Domna probably dominated the religious policy under Caracalla and may therefore be given credit for the cessation of persecution of the Christians. Caracalla, as we have seen, justified the issuance of the *constitutio Antoniniana* as being required by the majesty of the gods for the subjects of the empire. This is in line with the universalist tendency in his syncretic fusion of Zeus, Mithra, and Helios into the "invincible cosmocrator" (dal Covolo 1989:47–48, 52). Iulia Maesa's grandson Elagabalus (r. 218–22), who was the priest of the sun god Elagabalus in Emesa, ascended Caracalla's throne after the interruption of less than a year by

Macrinus, and launched a much more ambitious religious policy. He sought to extend political and legal centralization to the religious sphere but failed. It is only now, after nearly eighteen centuries of bad press, that Elagabalus's religious reforms have received an unbiased assessment (dal Covolo 1989). He attempted to subordinate other gods to his god, identifying the latter with the sun deity under a variety of names, and sought to integrate all the various cults of the empire, including the Jewish and Christian cults, into his syncretic solar monism and to establish some central control over them. To this end, in Rome itself, he married the sun god of Emesa, Elagabalus, to the moon goddess, named Urania in Carthage and Astoarche in Phoenicia, importing her statue from Africa (Herodian, 5.6.4; M. Grant 1996:25). As dal Covolo (1989:68) points out, Elgabalus's religious reform should in fact be seen as the culmination of the solar monism favored by Septimius Severus and Iulia Domna. Alexander Severus retreated from Elgabalus's brief and unpopular religious experiment, reestablished the traditional cults, and pursued a systematically pluralistic religious policy. In an inscription in Salon, he recognizes paganism, Judaism, and Christianity ("the third race") as the three religions of the empire. Alexander was benevolent toward Christianity and sought to integrate it within the syncretic imperial religion. He included an image of Christ in his laurel and is said to have wished to erect a temple for him as one of the gods (dal Covolo 1989:70). Christians had held important positions in the imperial household since Caracalla (Frend 1984:294–95). Under Alexander Severus, the benevolence of the imperial house was well noted in Rome. The Christian Julius Africanus was given the charge of building a library near the Pantheon and pioneered the writing of the entwined history of church and empire. The last Severan emperor's sympathy for Christianity was thus evident; and a Christian tract on resurrection is dedicated to his mother, Iulia Mamaea (dal Covolo 1989:74–79). *Didascalia Apostilorum* (1929:xc–xci), written in Syria, very probably in the first half of the third century and possibly under Alexander Severus, attests to the widespread existence of regular church buildings for good-size congregations. Indirect evidence for the spread of Christianity under the Severans dates from the 250s, when the Syrian deportees and prisoners of war settled in Iran by Shāpur I included a large number of Christians, including the patriarch of Antioch, Demetrius (Chaumont 1964b:169–74).

In the Severan age, Tertullian in Africa and Origen in the Near East sought to reconcile church and empire (R. Grant [1970] 1990:98–100). They were willing to compromise with certain demands of the imperial cult, with the clear hope of winning the ultimate loyalty of new recruits to Christianity as a universal integrative movement. That the integrative potential of

Christianity was greater than that of the Severan imperial cult is indicated by its systematic integration of women, especially widows, into the church hierarchy and services (*Didascalia Apostilorum* 1929:chs. 14–16).[20] We thus see both rivalry and rapprochement between the religious monotheism of Christianity and the political monism of the Severan postrevolutionary reconstruction. The marriage of these two modes of integration, as we shall see, was to be the mark of the teleology of the most important integrative revolutions to be considered in chapters 7 and 9.

Roman Revolutions in Perspective

In the Gracchan period, the Romans did discover the appeal to principles in politics and made their first attempt to justify political action theoretically (Nicolet 1967:144, 201). Religion was used tactically by various parties (Bowersock 1986a:298–304) but remained too insignificant to be drawn into the revolutionary process. Similarly, appeals to the republican tradition were frequently made, as was the case not only by Caesar's murderers but equally by his heir (Syme 1939). But neither religion nor the republican tradition determined the direction of the Roman revolutions. Nor did any new political ideology. The Roman revolutions, however, had two important unintended consequences: centralization of power and increasing integration of the periphery of the empire. In the long run, however, they were part of the process of expansion of the Roman Empire and the progressive and deepening integration of the periphery. The Roman revolutions were integrative revolutions par excellence. Syme (1939) called the transition from the republic to empire the "Roman Revolution" ironically, with Mussolini in mind. Yet the term is clearly applicable to the two other instances of violent transition in the process of enlargement of the Roman political community to include the outer peripheries through the expansion and finally universalization of citizenship, which was the social foundation of the Roman political order. The revolutions of Rome were indeed integrative revolutions.

The last Roman revolution was arguably the most interesting from a theoretical standpoint. Although the revolution that resulted from the fall of Commodus did not have Aristotelian-Paretan causes, it was unmistakably integrative in its consequences. Indeed, it was the ultimate integrative revolution that extended Roman citizenship to the entire free population of the empire. Rome, in the lapidary designation of the Severan jurists, became the *communis patria* (cited in Buraselis 2007:156). Two other consequences of the last Roman revolution were the autonomization and concentration of military power, on the one hand, and the centralization of the authority structure, on the other. This centralization marked the culmination of imperial autocracy under the rule of law, which had first been constitutionalized with the Flavian consolidation of the second Roman revolution.

The concentration and centralization of military power resulting from these revolutions have been well noted. What has not been so well noted in connection with the Roman revolutions is the legal consolidation of imperial autocracy. As we have seen, Augustus was keenly interested in the law, as were Galba and Vespasian, and Galba and Septimius Severus were actually lawyers. Their interest in developing constitutional law, far from being individual whims, represented a cultural trend; as individual emperors, they were clearly the tip of a slow-moving sociocultural iceberg. Although attempts to subordinate military power failed, they stimulated the development of Roman law and thus had far-reaching consequences in world history.

Two features of the Roman integrative revolutions stand out in world-historical perspective; one is vertically and the other horizontally integrative of Roman society. Vertically, the rise of the equestrian order, the Roman knights, is the leitmotif of the Roman revolutions—a *longue durée* process that took three centuries to unfold, from the protorevolutionary Social Wars to the Severan Revolution. Horizontally, the revolutions that integrated the peripheries of the Roman Empire show the increasing cultural influences of the eastern peripheries over the Roman center from Vespasian in 70 to Alexander Severus in 235. This makes Constantine's conversion to Christianity in 313 a foregone conclusion.

SIX

Rise of the Sasanian Empire: A Feudal Integrative Revolution in Late Antiquity

Cassius Dio, the Roman governor of Dalmatia and Pannonia and a contemporary witness to the destruction of the Parthian Empire and the rise of a far more threatening new one, was fully alert to the interimperial impact of these events. At the end of his history covering the years 222–29 BCE, Dio (80.4.1; 1927:282–83) records the alarming development in Mesopotamia that the Parthian Empire, having withstood the attacks of Caracalla and Alexander Severus, was overthrown now by a vassal king, one Ardashir (Artaxerxes), who "boasted that he would win back everything that the ancient Persians had once held, as far as the Grecian Sea, claiming that all this was his rightful inheritance from his forefathers."

The international context of this clash of empires was highlighted long ago by Altheim (1943), who saw the rise of the Sasanian Empire in Iran in the early decades of the third century as a revolution in response to "the crisis of the third century," which, according to him, encompassed all the ancient world. The idea of the crisis of the third century has more recently been revived with sharpened focus on the relationship between political integration through empire and the universalism of the world religions (Fowden 1993). The long third century—extending, from the Western viewpoint, from the fall of the Antonines (192 CE) to the conversion of Constantine (313)—witnessed not only the spread of two great universalist religions, Christianity and Manichaeism, but also massive strides in imperial political integration in the bipolar world of the Roman and Persian Empires. I have examined the universalization of Roman citizenship under the Severans, which was to be reinforced by the establishment of Christianity by Constantine exactly a century later. Shāpur I (240–72 CE), the second Sasanian emperor and the consolidator of our Sasanian Revolution, while continuing the revival of Zoroastrianism championed by his father and the empire's founder, Ardashir, toyed indecisively with the idea of adopting the world religion of Māni (216–76 CE)—the Prophet of Babylon—a move that would have anticipated the Constantinian solution to the problem of religion and empire by half a century. Ardashir's alternative solution to the problem of religion, making "the (Sasanian) state and (Zoroastrian) religion twins," had already been instituted and prevailed under Shāpur's successors, setting in motion a traditionalist developmental path of postrevolutionary reconstruction in Iran that contrasted sharply with that of the (Christian) Byzantine Empire.

Alexander and Anti-Alexander

The political culture of the third century, the common background to the Severan and the Sasanian Revolutions, is dominated by the scepter of Alexander the Great. It is perhaps no accident that the oldest extant Alexander romance is the one recorded by Pseudo-Cleisthenes in that century. We know as a matter of historical fact that Alexander's example of conquering the Orient had prompted Caracalla to invade the Parthian Empire and descend to the mouth of the Persian Gulf, whence he thought Alexander had embarked on the conquest of India (Dio, 78.7; Dabrowa 1984:158; Wiesehöfer 1987:373). The same idea of *imitatio Alexandri* also influenced the last Severan emperor and Alexander's namesake, Alexander Severus (Shayegan 2012:341–61). Dio's comment about Ardashir's ambitions is corroborated by other near-contemporary Roman sources and by the speech attributed to Ardashir in the *Nihāya* (fol. 90b): "We are the successors of those ancestors in their affairs and demanders of their rights." Ardashir (r. 224–40 CE), the founder of the Sasanian Empire, was the rising anti-Alexander. That he was fighting the Roman emperor Alexander Severus was incidental. Fundamentally, he had risen against the myth of Alexander. His feudal cavalry used conventional weapons against the Parthian and Roman emperors and their vassals, but at a deeper level, Ardashir's weapon in the mythic contest with the idea of Alexander was another idea: Iran (Ērānshahr, "empire of the Aryans"). The construction of this idea in the 220s and 230s CE was premised on the demonization of Alexander.

According to the historiography born in the Sasanian Revolution and faithfully transmitted by our Muslim sources, after defeating the last Achaemenid emperor, Darius III, Alexander sought the advice of his wise tutor, Aristotle, concerning the kind of political order he should establish in Iran. Aristotle advised him not to extirpate the Iranian nobility but divide and rule them. Alexander accordingly divided Darius's realm into a large number of petty kingdoms under his imperial rule and set up the Iranian grandees against each other as petty kings. This view encapsulated over five centuries of history into a grossly oversimplified schema which blended the Seleucid and the Parthian Empires into a single undifferentiated Hellenistic whole described as the regime of the petty kings—*muluk al-tawā'if* (kings of the tribes/parties).[1] The regime of petty kings was an accurate description of the late Parthian feudal empire, which had, according to Pliny, comprised eighteen kingdoms in the first century CE (Christensen 1944:19) but continued to break up into smaller petty kingdoms whose number reached two hundred and forty by the early third century (Lukonin 1983:701, 728). What was peculiar about this view of history, however, was the attribution of the advanced fragmentation of the late Parthian Empire entirely to Alexander's design five centuries earlier. In the opening line of the *Kārnāmak-e Ardashir-e Pāpakān* (Deeds of Ardashir, son of Pāpak), we thus read: "After the death of Alexander, the Roman, the Empire of Iran had two hundred and forty petty kings (*ktkhwt'y*)" (cited in Lukonin 1983:704).[2] Behind this Sasanian reconstruction of the historical memory lay the image of Alexander as the symbol of Hellenism, which was allegedly perpetuated by the Parthians and against which Ardashir rose in Persia (Persis or Fars), the heartland of the Achaemenid Empire, to avenge the blood of Darius III, whom Tabari (1.814) calls "his cousin, Dārā, son of Dārā, son of Bahman, son of Isfandiyār."

This symbolic violence was necessary for the success of the Sasanian Revolution. The revolutionary change brought about by Ardashir was indeed the marriage of the Achaemenid Empire and the Zoroastrian religion (Altheim 1943:18). The revolution can best and most efficiently be presented as the undoing of the work of Alexander. That is why Ardashir, our revolutionary *terrible simplificateur*, posed as the destroyer of Alexander's regime of the petty kings, the unifier of Iran, and the restorer of its true imperial tradition. Last but not least, Alexander had nearly succeeded in destroying the Zoroastrian religion along with the empire of Iran by burning 1,200 oxhides of sacred books and thereby opening the way for heresy and innovation. Ardashir was now claimed to be reviving and restoring Zoroastrian religion alongside the empire of Iran (Ibn Isfandiyār, 19).

The Political Structure of Parthian Feudalism

The Parthian Empire was highly decentralized and subject to continuous fragmentation of power. Furthermore, its authority structure was composite. In addition to the decentralized feudal polity—described as the regime of the petty kings (*muluk al-tawā'if*)—which varied considerably in different regions, it included a number of cities taken over from the Seleucids that had retained their Hellenistic constitution as poleis. These cities had their municipal councils and city magistracies. The most important city was the Parthian capital, the polis of "Seleucia on the Tigris," which was ruled by an elected Senate of three hundred representatives chosen, according to Tacitus (*Annals* 6.42), on the basis of "wealth and wisdom." The Parthian monarchs are shown as married to the city's goddess on some coins (Lukonin 1983:719).

Surviving constitutional documents record attempts by the powerful Parthian rulers such as Artabanus (Ardavān) III (10–36 CE) to encroach upon the autonomy of the city-states (Pigulevskaja 1963:86–89; Lukonin 1983:718). Although the weaker rulers of the late Parthian Empire were probably not in a position to continue this pressure, the already-weakened city-states did not regain their earlier importance (Pigulevskaja 1963:119). Furthermore, the most important of them suffered from constant warfare with the Romans. The agrarian component of the Parthian Empire was, by contrast, becoming increasingly preponderant, as was the dispersed military power of the feudal petty kings and their subordinates. Widengren's work on the subject (1956, 1967) leaves no room for doubt concerning the applicability of the term "feudalism" to Parthian Iran with regard both to its military organization and to its chivalresque political culture.

The domination of the feudal class rested on twin military and economic bases. Membership in the feudal cavalry (knights, *asβārān*, Arabic *asāwirah*) largely overlapped with the ownership of agrarian property by feudal nobility (*dehkānān*, Arabic *dahāqin*) (Widengren 1956:173–76). Their formal status was that of the free nobility. Two other estates are documented for the Parthian period: the priests (Magi) and the third estate, the subjects or "flock" (*ram*) (Perikhanian 1983:632). Strabo and early Sasanian documents also mention "scribes and judges," who clearly constituted a distinct social group and were ranked above priests (Widengren 1967:138), even though they do not seem to have constituted an estate in Parthian law. The feudal class itself was stratified. After the kings (*shahrdārān*, Middle Persian *štldl'n* = MLK') and the princes (*vaspuhrakān*) of the Arsacid dynasty came the grandees (*vazurkān*, Middle Persian *wčlk'n*), for whom we can now identify five great families in the Parthian era (Pourshariati 2008:42). Below them were the great majority of ordinary nobility: "the free" (*āzātān*, Middle Persian *'z'tn*) (Lukonin 1983:698–707). Each feudal lord had two categories of dependent followers in the feudal status hierarchy: helpers or aides (*hadyavarān*, Arabic *'ayyārān*) and bondsmen (*bandakān*).[3]

Royal authority in the Parthian Empire was vested in the Arsacid clan. The nomadic tribal tradition of the choice of the chief from the royal clan by the tribal assembly had, through the centuries, blended with the Hellenistic idea of representation to produce two councils that played the decisive role in the election of the Parthian ruler, or king of kings. We read in Strabo (11.9.3, cited in Lukonin 1983:689): "According to Poseidonius, the supreme council (*synedrion*) of the Parthians consists of two groups: one that of the [king's] kinsmen and the other that of wise men and magi, from both of which groups the kings were appointed." The existence of two councils can also be inferred from the *Annals* of Tacitus (6.42): "When people and senate agree, they can defy the Parthian king, but as soon as they fall out, each side calls on him for help against the other, and the ally called in to help the one ends by lording it over both" (as cited in Lukonin 1983:720). The valuable information transmitted by Justin Martyr further proves that the king could be deposed by "the Parthian Senate" (cited in Widengren 1967:109). In short, the two councils in the Parthian realm were a royal council representing the Arsacid clan and the army and an assembly of estates, wherein the priests and scribes predominated over some form of popular and city representation (Christensen 1944:1921; Widengren 1967:ch. 5).

An important element of the Parthian idea of kingship, which was later taken over by the Sasanians and assumed greater significance with the postrevolutionary centralization of power, derived from the Zoroastrian religion: cults of divine ancestors of the royal clan and the souls of paternal ancestors (Lukonin 1983:696).

The reproduction of Parthian feudalism was ensured by an elaborate system of military education centered on the institution of *dāyeak* (guardianship). The young princes were brought up by a guardian (*dāyak, dāyah*) who was a feudal lord. Guardianship could result in adoption, which, as we shall see, was the case with Ardashir. The central role of the *dāyeak* institution is demonstrated by the identification of the princes with their guardians (e.g., "Prince Sāsān, raised by Parrikan") in the royal inscriptions. Once the education of the young lord or prince was completed, he could serve at the court of the local king or of the Parthian ruler, the king of kings (Widengren 1967:ch. 3). In addition to such individual training, there is evidence from ancient times down to Parthian Armenia for military tutors training young men, who lived with them in bands of fifty, each of which constituted a brotherhood (Widengren 1967:88–92).

Parthian feudalism gave the free nobility local autonomy, while the relationship between the feudal lords and the kings, and between the latter and the king of kings, rested squarely on absolute loyalty and provision of military service. This central feature of Parthian feudalism explains the otherwise-baffling ability of the Arsacid rulers of the fragmented Parthian Empire to call together large armies that frequently defeated the Seleucids and the Romans.

Parthian armies consisted of the free noblemen, each with a number of bondsmen (*bandakān*), many of whom were on horse. According to the precious information given by Justin, the Parthian army that defeated Mark Antony consisted of fifty thousand bondsmen and four hundred free noblemen, the ratio being 125 to 1. In the case of the great lords, such as the house of Suren, which, according to Plutarch, mustered an army of ten thousand bondsmen against Crassus (Widengren 1967:30–31), the ratio could be even greater, though this particular report must have overlooked the Surens' free subfeudatories.

At the beginning of the third century at least one precondition of revolution was conspicuous: the Arsacid house was divided. The division had in fact begun in 191 when Vologases (Balāsh) IV wrested control of Seleucia from the aged Vologases III, who died a year or two later, and the tremors of the last Roman revolution, more specifically the civil war between Niger and Severus in Syria and the latter's invasion of Mesopotamia, deepened the Parthian political crisis in the late 190s (Debevoise 1938:255–58). Vologases IV ascended the throne in 207–8 only to face the insubordination of his brother Ardavān (Artabanus) IV, who had gained control of Media and declared his independence, striking his own coins in Ecbatana by 213, and appears to have extended his sway over Mesopotamia in the subsequent two or three years (Debevoise 1938:263–65). From about 213 onward, there were thus two Arsacid kings of kings, and the rift between them must have divided the entire nobility of the empire, with the consequence that once the Sasanian revolutionary counterstate began to seem a viable alternative, many feudal lords and even the three great feudal clans of the empire, the Surens, the Kārens, and the Varaz, defected to Ardashir (ŠKZ 2; Frye 1984:295).[4] Last but not least, the Parthian regime was badly shaken by Caracalla, who ravaged a large part of Media and dealt a heavy blow to its prestige by digging up the Parthian royal tombs and scattering the bones (Debevoise 1938:265).

The fragmented authority structure of the Parthian regime, however, made its collapse very, very slow. It took many years and numerous battles before Ardashir from Persia (Persis), a province on the southern periphery of the empire, could unify enough forces to overthrow the two Parthian kings of kings and conquer their respective capitals, namely Nihavand in Media and Seleucia in Mesopotamia.

Ardashir's Long Integrative Revolution

Though aptly characterizing the rise of Ardashir as a revolution, Altheim (1943:33) could think of revolution only in Marxian terms of class struggle and saw it as a reaction to the centuries-long domination of the mounted, northeastern, "Turanian" tribes, coinciding with the uprising of the Iranian urban and peasant strata against them. There is little evidence for this class interpretation of the Sasanian Revolution. Ardashir and the Sasanians were horsemen just like the Arsacids, and what undocumented peasant participation there may have been occurred under their aegis. The only clear evidence of the support of the urban strata for the Sasanian Revolution comes from Isfahan, where the people forced the local king to flee with his treasure to the Parthian court of Ardavān when they heard of the approach of Ardashir's army (*Nihāya*, fol. 91; Widengren 1971:769). But so did elements from the feudal nobility of the Isfahan region. The Sasanian Revolution was in fact not a class-based but an integrative revolution. The cornerstone of Ardashir's ideology—the destruction of the fragmented "regime of the petty kings" and the restoration of the unity of the Iranian empire—corresponds to the fundamental feature of the Sasanian Revolution which is admirably captured by the tenth-century historian al-Mas'udi, who contrasts the Sasanians as "the kings of integration" with the Arsacids as "the kings of the tribal parties (*muluk al-tawā'if*)" (al-Mas'udi 1970:2.238) and states more specifically about Ardashir that "it was he who overthrew the regime of the petty kings and whose regime is called the kingdom of integration (*mulk al-ijtimā'*)" (al-Mas'udi [1894] 1967:99).

The Process of Integrative Revolution in a Feudal Society

Ardashir's father, Pāpak, was the lord (*patikhshai*) and master of rites (*advenpat*) of the temple(-state) of Anahita at Stakhr (Chaumont 1959:176). Pāpak belonged to the warrior rather than the priestly estate and was in charge of the sacerdotal function of the temple of the war goddess, Anahita, where bloody sacrifice was offered and heads of enemies were sent as trophies once the revolutionary struggle began. The combination of temporal and sacerdotal authority appears to be in line with the exercise of authority on behalf of the gods by the *frataraka* of Persis under its Seleucid rulers before the Parthians. However, the fact that Pāpak was a lord with extensive temporal power over the domain and endowments of the temple at Stakhr and was clearly related on his mother's side to a dynasty of kings of Stakhr indicates the unusual extent of fragmentation of authority in the later Parthian feudal regime.

Pāpak was aided from the beginning by his sons, Shāpur and Ardashir, and began to struggle for the restoration of imperial unity at Stakhr, which was close to the ruins of the ancient Achaemenid Persepolis, where he is depicted in a graffito (Mosig-Walburg 1982:48n2). According to the versions of the fabricated genealogy of the dynasty, Pāpak's father was Sāsān.[5] A different version in the *Kārnāmak* interestingly makes Sāsān Pāpak's father-in-law and a shepherd and an ascetic who had hidden his descent from a more distant ancestor by the same name, Sāsān, said to be a Kayanid prince. These two different versions must have survived and been passed on to Ferdawsi's epic poem *Shāhnāma* (Book of kings; 7.131). Reflecting these two conflicting forged genealogies, Ferdawsi lists "the stock of Pāpak" and "the Sasanians" as two different groups and thereby considers Ardashir entitled to kingship by his "double origins."[6] The discrepancy between the two genealogies is interesting for showing that the official genealogy was a forgery intended to make Ardashir heir to the Achaemenids, the last of whom were later to be linked to the legendary Kayanids.[7] Instances of "Sāsān," attested from northeastern Iran in such combinations as *Sasandat* (Sāsān-given) and *Sasanbokht* (saved by Sāsān), establish Sāsān as a deity in the late Parthian period (Frye 1984:284–85). The older Sāsān who became an ascetic was the son of the legendary mysterious king Bahman and was probably considered the eponymous ancestor of the Sasanian lineage and identified with the god Sāsān. Given the Zoroastrian cult of the divine royal ancestors and the acceptance of Sāsān as a god in Parthia, it is probable that the founders of the rising dynasty called themselves Sasanians to establish their divine descent. This element of continuity with the Parthian ancient regime is worth stressing. Like the Arsacids, who bore the title *theos theopator* (god, of divine descent), Ardashir and Shāpur assumed the title of god (*bag*) in their inscriptions and claimed divine descent.[8] Ardashir thus styled himself "the Mazdā-worshipping god, Ardashir, who is descended from the gods." Given the inherent ambiguities in the symbolization of sacral kingship, one cannot say what this meant exactly. What I shall later claim strongly is that descent from the last Achaemenid was the cornerstone of Ardashir's pan-Iranian ideology for reintegrating Iran.

Ardashir, whose mother's lineage was nowhere considered worthy of mention, had been raised by a eunuch, Tayri, the commander of the citadel at Dārābjerd, who was his tutor (*dāyak*) according to the Parthian feudal tradition. Ardashir inherited Tayri's position after his death and appears to have launched his project for the unification of the feudal baronies on his own (Tabari, 1.814–15). Indeed, it is he who is credited with instigating Pāpak to kill his close relative Guchehr, the king of Stakhr, and ascend his throne.[9] This Pāpak did in 206, assuming the leadership of the rebel movement for unification.[10]

Pāpak remained the figurehead of the Sasanian revolutionary movement, while crowning his elder son, Shāpur, as the king and coregent of Persis. Numismatic evidence proves that, contrary to the literary accounts, Pāpak was still alive when a major power struggle broke out between Shāpur and Ardashir in the course of the revolution, and the former was mysteriously killed by a falling rock in an Achaemenid building en route to confronting Ardashir's forces (Tabari, 1.816; trans. 5.8; Christensen 1944:87). An assembly of the Sasanian clan and their feudatories then elected Ardashir king in place of his older brother. Pāpak remained on the throne as the figurehead of the Sasanian movement, surrounded by his court at Stakhr. Its modest size is shown in the royal inscription of his grandson, who finds only eight dignitaries worthy of mention (Chaumont 1959:180). Coins were now struck bearing the effigy of "god Pāpak, the king," with that of "god Ardashir, the king (*bag artakhshatr malka*)," whereas previously they had shown the coregent as "god Shāpuhr, the king" (Paruck 1924:305–7, nos. 1–12).

Ardashir was the real founder of the dynasty and the leader of the Sasanian Revolution. He had begun his bid for unification of Persis as soon as he had succeeded his tutor as the commander of the citadel (*argbad*) and feudal lord of Dārābjerd, and he had overcome and killed three local kings before urging his father, Pāpak, to do likewise with Guchehr in Stakhr. This would make Ardashir rather than Pāpak the initiator of the call to revolutionary struggle for unity. When the latter sought recognition from Ardavān IV, the Parthian king of kings, for transferring Guchehr's crown to his son Shāpur, his imperial overlord "wrote to him a harsh letter and let him know that he and his son Ardashir had made themselves guilty of insurrection by killing people." As long as his older brother was coregent with Pāpak, however, Ardashir did not control the Sasanian movement. The mysterious death of Shāpur removed the main obstacle to Ardashir's full control of the revolutionary movement. Immediately upon Shāpur's death, "a number of his brothers, some of whom were older than him, assembled and offered him crown and throne, so that everything came into the firm possession of Ardashir." Ardashir indeed wanted to make sure this possession would not be challenged and carried out the first purge of the Sasanian movement. He accused some of his "brothers" (i.e., vassals and fellow conspirators) "and killed (therefore) a great number of them." The purged vassals probably had sympathizers elsewhere, including Ardashir's original base, Dārābjerd, whose population "had risen against him, so he returned thither and conquered the town after killing a number of its citizens" (Tabari, 1.816–17;

trans. 5.9). Once firmly in control of the new revolutionary state, Ardashir immediately marched eastward beyond Persis. He defeated Balāsh (Vologases), the Parthian king of Kerman, and replaced him with one of his own sons, who was also called Ardashir (Widengren 1971:735–36, 761; ŠKZ 24–25). After this first major victory outside Persis, he proceeded to the coast of the Persian Gulf and defeated its petty king. Here the legend has completely metamorphosed the petty king of the coastline, whose name has been restored as Haftānbokht (saved by the seven [inauspicious stars / astral deities]), into a mythological monster, the dragon king (*kerm-kh*^{w}*atay*), who personifies the cosmic forces of evil and is slain by Ardashir (*artakhshatr*), the hero who champions Right Order (*arta*). Ardashir is presented both as the dragon-slaying hero and as the bringer of rain, fertility, and Right Order (Choksy 1988). Ardashir then returned to Persis with the treasures he had plundered.

With his defeat of Haftānbokht, evidence of Ardashir's activities as the leader of a revolutionary movement makes its way into our literary sources. Ardashir wrote to "Mehrak [the last independent petty king in Persis to be mentioned], who was king of Abarsus [*sic*] . . . and to a number of his equals in order to summon them to submit to him. But they did not submit. He marched against them and killed Mehrak. Then he marched to Jur [Firuzābād] and founded this city and started building the palace . . . and a fire-temple there." By now Ardashir had set up a bureau for writing letters and sending messengers to the petty kings and feudal lords of the Parthian Empire to join the cause of unification and submit to him. As for the founding of the city in Jur (Gur), which became the capital of the region he called Ardashir-khwarrah (the divine charisma of Ardashir), the significance of Ardashir's imperial gesture and utmost defiance was not lost on the Parthian king of kings, Ardavān, who reportedly wrote to Ardashir: "You have presumed beyond your rank in society . . . , O Kurd brought up among the tents of the Kurds! . . . And who ordered you to build the city which you have founded in the desert [Jur]?" (Tabari, 1.817; trans. 5.11). According to another tradition, Ardavān reminded the upstart Ardashir that he was the imperial sovereign of the regime of petty kings, "whereas four (kings) are (placed) over yourself" (*Nihāya*, fol. 91; Widengren 1971:768).

It will be noted that Ardashir built a fire temple in the first of the imperial cities he founded. At that point, he probably assumed the title of king of Iran. (He could not call himself king of kings, as two Parthian sovereigns still held that title.) A coin on which the title "king of Iran" occurs must belong to this period. It introduces the major symbols of the Sasanian Revolution and demonstrates the use of coinage as a means of revolutionary propaganda. One side of the coin shows the effigy of Ardashir with the legend "the Mazdā-worshipping god Ardashir, the king of Iran (*mazdāyasn bagi Artakhshatr malka irān*)," and the obverse, a fire altar with the inscription "Fire of Ardashir" (Paruck 1924:no. 13, pl. 1, xxxviii.5). The next fourteen coins in the same collection, which belong to the period after the overthrow of Ardavān, are identical except for the modification of Ardashir's title to "the king of kings of Iran" (Paruck 1924:307–10, 414; Taqizādeh 1943:29).

The election of Ardashir to coregent king and leader of the Sasanian movement, which was followed immediately by the first massive purge within the revolutionary movement, can reasonably be placed in the year 208 on the basis of Ibn al-Balkhi's statement on the length of the two phases of Ardashir's reign.[11] The epic reconstruction of these events by Ferdawsi in his *Shāhnāma* (7.130–31) captures some of the essential elements of Sasanian ideology that are corroborated by other evidence, such as the abovementioned genealogical claim recorded in the fourth-century *Kārnāmak*. According to Ferdawsi, the assembly was convoked by a wise sailor who saw "the Kay(anid) race and royal charisma" in Ardashir (*Shāhnāma* 7.130, v. 323). This reflects the fifth-century Zoroastrianization of the genealogy which linked the last Achaemenid, Darius III, to the Kavis of the Avesta who formed the legendary Kayanid dynasty after the fourth-century redaction of Zoroastrian texts by the hierocracy (Lukonin 1983:697–98). The rest of Ferdawsi's account, however, reflects the older, third-century layer: there gathered "men from rivers and mountains" and "sages and counsellors from every city" to what was in fact a feudal assembly of Pāpak's clan and the followers of Sāsān and their feudal dependents—"Every man at Stakhr who was of the stock of Bābak" and "those in the country who were of the seeds of Darius" (*Shāhnāma* 7.130, vv. 326–27). The speeches put in the mouths of Ardashir and the assembled men of the Sasanian party express the kernel of the movement's ideology. In his address to the assembly, Ardashir reminds them of "the base deeds the evil-natured Alexander perpetrated in the world. He slew every one of my ancestors and got the universe into his grasp by working injustice. I am of the seed of Esfandiār, yet Ardavān rules in the land. . . . If you will be my allies I will permit no one but myself to use my title or possess my lofty throne" (*Shāhnāma* 7.130, vv. 333–35; trans. Levy 1967:261–62). Thereupon, the assembled men respond: "those of us from the stock of Pāpak . . . , and those who are Sāsānians, gird up our loins for vengeance. . . . By your double origins are you of higher degree than any of us; kingship and sovereignty are your right" (*Shāhnāma* 7.131, vv. 341–45; trans. Levy 1967:262).

The rise of Ardashir in Persis and his revolutionary propaganda among the feudal class throughout the Parthian Empire were cause enough for alarm. I have mentioned Ardavān IV's insulting rebuke to Ardashir for founding a city. Ardashir's reported response was that he would build another city, to be called Rām-Ardashir, and "I very much hope to get my hands on you and then send your head and your treasures to the fire temple which I have founded in Ardashir-khwarrah" (Tabari, 1.818; trans. 5.11–12). Ardavān dispatched the king of Ahwaz to quell the rebellion in Persis, but the latter was defeated by one of Ardashir's "viziers," Abarsām. Ardashir's conquest of Kerman and the coastline on the farther periphery of the Parthian Empire had given him economic and military resources—treasury and cavalry—but was not strategically important for the purpose of imperial integration. For this purpose, Isfahan, the next province before Media, the central region of Ardavān's empire, was crucial. Banāk, a feudal lord from Isfahan, like many men of Persis who had by then offered Ardashir their "property and their own person and show[n] him obedience and vassalage," came to Ardashir "with six sons and a large army and troops." Ardashir was suspicious, thinking Banāk had been sent by Ardavān, but "Banāk came before Ardashir and took an oath with the solemn declaration: 'As long as I live, I myself with my children shall be your vassals'" (Antia 1900:18; Widengren 1971:776).

It goes without saying that Ardashir would not wait for the feudal lords of the Isfahan region to come to him with their retinues like Banāk one by one. He mobilized his forces and thrust northward from Persis toward Isfahan. The only piece of evidence we have of urban support for the Sasanian movement comes from a late source. According to the *Nihāya,* upon hearing the news that Ardashir and his army had advanced near the city, "the population of Isfahan . . . refrained from supporting their king's objective and deserted him, not being disposed to go to war with him." The king fled his province, taking with him "his following, his children, and his treasures" (*Nihāya,* fol. 91; Widengren 1971:769, trans. modified). After the conquest of Isfahan, Ardashir returned to Fars and proceeded to defeat Nirufar, the king of Ahwaz, in or after 221 (Pigulevskaja 1963:121). He annexed most of Khuzestan and founded the imperial city of Suq al-Ahvāz (Widengren 1971:762). Ardashir's possession of Isfahan in central Iran exposed the heartland of Ardavān's empire, extending from Rayy to northern Mesopotamia. The Parthian king of kings had to mobilize all the military resources at his disposal. According to the *Kārnāmak,* "Ardavān demanded army and horses," which means that he made a desperate effort to call the feudal cavalry into his army. Given the horse-producing potential of the areas by then under Ardashir's control and the fact that Ardavān was let down by many of his vassals, who were persuaded or intimidated by Ardashir, Ardashir's forces at the final battle, which Widengren's careful study locates at Golpaygan in the Median plain of Hormazjan and which took place in either

April or September 224 (Widengren 1971:744; Wiesehöfer 1987:372), must have had decisive superiority. Outright defections such as that of the great feudal family of Mehrān from Rayy apart, the armies of the petty kings of Hamadan and Rayy arrived when the battle was over. It is difficult to avoid the conclusion that they delayed joining Ardavān's army in collusion with his Sasanian rival, as these kings are later said to have sent him a messenger asking for safe conduct, and Ardashir confirmed them in their positions (*Nihāya*, fol. 92; Widengren 1971:770).

Be that as it may, Ardashir surprised Ardavān and occupied superior positions in the battlefield. Ardashir's son of the same name, who was appointed the first Sasanian king of Kerman, presumably after helping his father conquer it, has already been mentioned. In the account of the final battle, Tabari mentions Ardashir's other son and successor, Shāpur, for the first time. Shāpur commanded an advance guard and killed Ardavān's chief minister with his own hands. Ardashir attacked Ardavān and killed him. "It is said that Ardashir dismounted and trampled on the head of Ardavān with his foot. On that day of battle, Ardashir received the title of *Shāhanshāh* (King of Kings)" (Tabari, 1.819; trans. 5.14). The last should be read as Ardashir's acclamation as the king of kings on the battlefield. Some sources confirm that Persians and Parthians assembled on the battlefield and proclaimed Ardashir king of kings (Widengren 1971:781). After the defeat of Ardavān, Media submitted to Ardashir, who proceeded to occupy Ardavān's capital, Nihavand. There followed the swift conquest of Khorasan in the northeast. There can have been no time for preparatory mobilization of the feudal lords of the region, and the annexation must be considered the result of a direct military campaign in which Ardashir used the large cavalry army which he had amassed for confrontation with Ardavān and which remained largely intact.

Ardavān was by far the more powerful of the two Parthian kings of kings, and after his defeat, the balance of power in Mesopotamia decisively tilted in favor of Ardashir's insurgent state and against Vologases V. Some Parthian vassals evidently remained steadfast, but it is only in one source, *Nihāyat al-'irab*, that we are given the detailed information that a coalition of seventeen petty kings under the otherwise-unknown Shād-Mehr confronted Ardashir in Mesopotamia (Widengren 1971:751, text 770). On the other hand, the kings of Adiabene and Kirkuk defected outright and joined Ardashir in fighting the Parthians (Widengren 1971:778; Debevoise 1938:268–69). The defection of the local ruler of Babylon was more ambiguous but, I would argue, just as real. Bābā, the king of the Arameans (corrupted into "Armenians" and identified as "the Nabateans of the Sawād"), came to an understanding with Ardashir to stand by with his army when the latter attacked the Parthian monarch, who is incorrectly identified as the dead Ardavān (Nöldeke [1879] 1973:22; Widengren 1971:718–20) but must have been either Ardavān's son, Ardavazd (but Farrukhān in *Akhbār* 44; trans. Widengren 1971:772), or his brother Vologases V. Al-Mas'udi, who considered Bābā the last of the petty kings and the lord of Qasr Ibn Hubairah (Babylon), identified him by the puzzling proper name of Bābā (pope?) b. Bar Dina (son of religion), which may well be because the ruler of the Arameans of Sawād was the bishop and at the same time the temporal lord of Babylon.[12] The *Chronicle of Arbela* (Sachau, 60, as cited and translated in Widengren 1971:778) mentions the submission of Babylon immediately after the defection of the kings of Adiabene and Kirkuk.

It is a striking testimony of the force of dominant Hellenistic culture—and an attestation of a kernel of truth in the Sasanian demonization of Alexander—that the last stronghold of the Arsacid dynasty, established at the end of the second century BCE by the leaders of the Parni tribe (the first Parthians) who had rebelled against the Seleucid Empire in northeastern Iran, should be no other than Seleucia on the Tigris, which they had made their own capital and was the core of the metropolis known as Ctesiphon. The fall of this capital was a pathetic end to four hundred years of Parthian rule: "All the energy of the Parthians was in vain because their day had come and their hour arrived. At last they fled into the high mountains and handed over to the Persians all their countries and all their wealth which had been kept in the cities. The youngest son of Ardavān, called Arshak, was killed without mercy by the Persians in Ctesiphon" (*Chronicle of Arbela*; Sachau, 61; Widengren 1971:778). The last Parthian king of kings, Vologases V, must be presumed among those who fled to the mountains. The conquest of Ctesiphon occurred in 226, which was made the first regnal year of Ardashir, who had assumed the title of king of kings on the battlefield two years earlier and now officially crowned himself in the great capital (Wiesehöfer 1987:372). He founded his own imperial city, Veh-Ardashir, adjacent to the metropolitan conglomerate to the west and made Ctesiphon, later known as al-Madā'in (the cities), the capital of his new empire.

The triumph of the Sasanian Revolution under Ardashir's supreme leadership was complete: the empire of Iran was unified under one monarch. Pockets of resistance must nevertheless have persisted among the dispersed elements of the Parthian regime. More important, some Parthian vassals and princes had been drifting toward Parthian Armenia, which became the center of counterrevolutionary exiles after the fall of Ctesiphon. Ardashir and his army marched through northern Mesopotamia and Azerbaijan, whose conquest was later marked by a rock relief in Salmās (Luschey 1987:379–80), and launched an attack on Armenia in 227–28. The Parthian counterrevolutionary coalition, in whose forces the youngest class of feudal warriors, aged between fifteen and twenty, predominated, withstood Ardashir's attack and in fact defeated him (Widengren 1971:750, 758). On the strength of a coin of Vologases V as the king of kings in Ctesiphon, we are justified in assuming that, either through prior orchestration with the Parthian exiles or after hearing the news of Ardashir's defeat in Armenia, there was a Parthian counterrevolution in Ctesiphon in 228. Ardashir returned and suppressed it. No owl of Minerva was perched on the walls of Ctesiphon to take its flight as dusk set on the ruins of the Parthian civilization. Yet, it is perhaps more than a coincidence that in that year, as we shall see, Māni received his first revelation.

The Pace and Violence of Ardashir's Integrative Revolution

The long process of the Sasanian integrative revolution began in Fars (Persis) within the insurgent state while the Parthian regime of the petty kings was still in place, and so did some of the violence generated by the power struggle between the partners in the revolutionary coalition: namely, the two sons of Pāpak and their respective subfeudatories and bondsmen. As we have seen, Ardashir carried out a bloody purge of the Sasanian feudal party soon after he was elected king in 206. The *Kārnāmak* (13, 16) records another important instance of violence within revolutionary Persis in the case of Mehrak, a subordinate king who had turned against Ardashir, was accused of the feudal crime of breach of contract (*mihrān druzih*), and was killed with all his children by Ardashir (Widengren 1956:82).

Not counting the years before he was elected coregent with his father, it took Ardashir sixteen years—from 208 to 224—to integrate a strong territorial base around Persis for his insurgent state. The expansion of the new Sasanian state from that point on depended less on the mobilization of the indigenous feudal nobility and population and more on military superiority. The expedition to eastern Iran after the defeat of Ardavān in 224, in particular, was purely a military campaign. Ardashir's victorious cavalry marched from central Iran to conquer vast areas to the east: Gorgan, Khorasan, Khʷarazm, and Sistan in about a year (Widengren 1971:746). Indeed, the speed with which the conquest of the northeast was completed is barely credible, and had it not been for the numismatic evidence (Göbl 1971:42), we would have been inclined to dismiss the reports of our literary sources altogether.[13] The conquest of Mesopotamia does not seem to have taken more than a year even though it involved considerable propagandist and diplomatic activity. In short, the process of the integrative revolution in a highly fragmented feudal society was very slow at the beginning and required prolonged mobilization, in the course of which the ideology of the Sasanian movement was formulated and disseminated. As the integration continued and the military and economic resources of the insurgent state were augmented, the process of revolution gathered speed as it depended less and less on its mobilization and propagandist activities.

Both the long duration and the step-by-step, slow process of the Sasanian Revolution are largely due to the fragmented authority structure of the feudal Parthian Empire. For this reason, the Sasanian Revolution can be viewed as a long series of civil wars that ended with the conquest of Iran by Ardashir and Shāpur I. As we shall see, in regimes with more centralized structures of authority, revolutions are shorter, less violent and more distinct from civil wars.

The revolutionary unification of feudal Iran was violent. The *Nihāya* has the heading "The Story of Ardashir, son of Bābak, the Killer of the Persian Petty Kings," while the *Kārnāmak* speaks of his numerous "battles and combats against the local lords of the empire of Iran" (cited in Widengren 1956:82). Ardashir's chief propagandist, Tansar, admitted Ardashir's excessive bloodshed as alleged by the Parthian vassal, Goshnāsp, and he also partially quantified its extent in the statement that Ardashir seized Ardavān, the greatest of the petty kings, "together with ninety others who were the descendants of those enthroned by Alexander, and killed some of them by the sword and some by imprisonment" (Ibn Isfandiyār, 14). And again, Ardashir "overpowered all of the petty kings and killed them. Once he had liquidated eighty unruly kings, he liberated the world from one end to another" (*Fārsnāma*, Ibn al-Balkhi 1921:60).

In addition, the prominence of the theme of vengeance for the blood of Darius in the ideology of the Sasanian Revolution built considerable violence into its teleology. Ardashir extirpated the entire Arsacid royal clan, including its princesses. This is confirmed by the legendary accounts of the birth of Shāpur, whose mother was an Arsacid princess condemned to death by Ardashir but secretly saved by his wise counselors.[14]

The Pan-Iranian Ideology and the Restoration of Mazdian Religion as Instruments of Mobilization

The expansionist ideology of the Sasanian movement soon found expression in the conquest of Kerman and the foundation of the first imperial city in which a bureau of propaganda was set up to promote the cause of unification throughout the Parthian Empire. Either from the beginning or at some later point, an ascetic and *hērbad* (Zoroastrian cleric), Taōsar, more commonly known as Tansar, became the head of this bureau. Al-Masʿudi states that Tansar's father was one of the petty kings of Persis. He calls Tansar Ardashir's evangelist and missionary for his cause, as he sent messengers to different regions of the expanding empire to promote it (al-Masʿudi [1894] 1967:98–99). Tansar's bureau wrote letter after letter to the feudal lords of Iran to persuade them to join the Sasanian cause, and his activity to promote concord and unity in the fragmented land of Iran under Ardashir's rule is wishfully remembered in a Zoroastrian apocalyptic passage after the shattering of the Sasanian Empire (Boyce 1968:6–7). The letters from Tansar's bureau to the local rulers continued throughout the slow integrative process of Ardashir's revolution. The importance attached to this propaganda alongside warfare and intimidation is well brought out by Hamza Isfahāni (1844:45). The glory and prosperity of the ancient kings was due to their statecraft: "there was no more than one monarch and all the subjects obeyed him." To unify the subjects under the idea that there should be only one universal monarch, "Ardashir at the beginning wrote letters to the neighboring petty kings, and then used new stratagems until he had cleansed the empire of Iran from the petty kings by killing ninety of them." The letters to the petty kings must have conformed to the ethos of Parthian feudalism, their purpose being to induce the addressees to make a contract (*mihrān*) of fealty and become obedient vassals (*framān-burtār*). The new monarch and champion of imperial unity would then be paid homage (*parastishn*), and any subsequent disloyalty would be seen as a breach of contract (*mihrān druzih*) and justify violent retaliation (Widengren 1956:79–81, 91). One of Tansar's last letters and the only one that has reached us is in a heavily redacted sixth-century version through the Arabic translation by Ibn al-Muqaffaʿ. It is nevertheless an invaluable source on Ardashir's rise.

The promotion of Ardashir's claim to be the restorer of Zoroastrian religion, which Alexander had sought to destroy along with the empire of Iran, was of particular interest to Tansar. He was a religious authority and thus in an excellent position to guide the religious policy of the insurgent Sasanian state. At the final stage of the revolutionary power struggle,[15] Tansar wrote his only preserved letter to one of the last of the recalcitrant petty kings who ruled in the inaccessible region of Tabarestan as a Parthian vassal, Goshnāsp. In this letter, he appeals to the religious faith of Goshnāsp to persuade him to submit to Ardashir:

> If your concern is for religious matters, and you deny that any justification is found in religion, *know that Alexander burnt the book of our religion—1200 ox-hides—at Stakhr.* One third of it was known by heart and survived, but even that was all legends and traditions, and men knew not the laws and ordinances; until, through the corruption of the people of the day and the *decay of royal power* and the craving for what was new and counterfeit and the desire for vainglory, even those legends and traditions dropped out of common recollection, *so that an iota of the truth of that book remained.* . . . The revival of religion (*ehyā'-e din*) is therefore essential, and no king is better qualified than Ardashir for undertaking it. (Ibn Isfandiyār, 19; trans. Boyce 1968:37, emphasis added)

Furthermore,

> With the vanishing of religion you have lost also the knowledge of genealogies and histories and lives of great men, which you have let pass from memory. . . . [There can be no doubt concerning the] need of a ruler of understanding; for till religion is interpreted by understanding it has no firm foundation. (Ibn Isfandiyār, 19; trans. Boyce 1968:37)

Here we have the interweaving of the theme of religious revival into the ideology of universal monarchy. The new universal monarch had to be a man of understanding because only his correct interpretation can put religion on a firm foundation.

The genealogy of Ardashir as set out in the *Kārnāmak*, as we have seen, was of capital importance to his pan-Iranian ideology, as it was to his expansion into Roman Mesopotamia. Tansar's preserved letter provides additional evidence in this regard. Goshnāsp had sought to impress the Zoroastrian *hērbad* with the dignity of his royal rank by claiming descent from Bahman: "Then you declared: I have kinship and blood-ties with the king of kings through Ardashir son of Esfandiār who is called Bahman. My answer to you is that, for me, this latter Ardashir [i.e., the Sasanian] is of far greater dignity than the Ardashir of old" (Ibn Isfandiyār, 38; trans. Boyce 1968:66, slightly modified). This passage is remarkable for identifying the latter-day Sasanian king of kings as the namesake of a venerable Ardashir-Bahman. It thereby offers a clue that the mysterious Bahman was the Achaemenid Artaxerxes II. The *Bondaheshn* traces Ardashir's (Artaxsahr's) genealogy as follows: "Artaxsahr [MSS 'rt'ystl, 'rthstl] son of Pāpak, whose mother (was) the daughter of Sāsān, son of Vehafrit (son of) Zarir, son of Sāsān, son of *Artaxsahr [MSS 'rt''l = 'rtystl for 'rthstl?], who is called Vahuman, son of Spenddat" (cf. Anklesaria 1956:297–98).[16] The *Bondaheshn* makes a certain Sāsān Ardashir's maternal grandfather.

This Sāsān is the grandson of another Sāsān, who is the son of Ardashir-Bahman. Elsewhere, I have demonstrated that the "*Artaxsahr who is called Vahuman," and the spelling of whose name is curiously archaized, is indeed the Achaemenid Artaxerxes II, who was surnamed Mnemon (= Vahuman) in Greek (Arjomand 1998). The one thing we can safely infer from their coins about the obscure rulers of Persis under the Seleucids and Parthians is that they preserved and transmitted the Achaemenid heritage. After the first few who used the title *frataraka* (*prtk*, [sub]satrap) and, in some cases, "*frataraka* of god" (Soudavar 2009:422n12), Daryav (or Darius) assumed the title of king (*mlk*), and the last ones to assume this title were called Manuchehr (*mnčtry*) and Ardashir (*'rtxštr*) (Frye 1975:239). Through the mythical Bahman, Ardashir was thus connected with the other great historic patron-king of Zoroastrianism, his Achaemenid namesake, Artaxerxes II. The Islamic sources leave little room for doubt that the identification of Ardashir with Bahman was a core element of the Sasanian integrative ideology. One of Ardashir's decrees, transcribed by al-Masʿudi (1970:1.289), to give a crucial example, begins with the phrase "From Ardashir-Bahman, king of kings."

This teleology had a strong expansionist element built into it in the form of the claim to all the former lands of the Achaemenid Empire.[17] It redoubled the tendency toward export of revolution, a common consequence of successful and massive revolutionary mobilization (Skocpol 1988; Walt 1996), and resulted in the impressive imperial expansion under Ardashir's son Shāpur, who annexed Mesopotamia as "Non-Iran." In his imperial inscriptions Shāpur accordingly modified the idea of Ērānshahr into the "empire of Iran and Non-Iran [Anērān]" and styled himself "the Mazdā-worshipping god, Shāpur, king of kings of Iran and Non-Iran, of divine descent."

Ardashir may well have sent Ardavān's head as a trophy to the fire temple of Gur (Firuzābād), his first imperial city, as he had purportedly boasted he would do. A rock relief on the walls of a gorge that opens on to the plain where Ardashir built his city and palace no doubt depicts his victory over Ardavān. The rock relief uses the feudal symbolism of a tournament to show Ardashir's overpowering of Ardavān, while his son Shāpur overpowers the Parthian chief minister. The relief departs sharply in style and substance from Parthian reliefs (Yarshater 1971; Lukonin 1983:735) and marks the adoption of monumental representation for publicity. Following the example of the consolidators of the Akkadian Revolution two and a half millennia earlier, the Sasanian propaganda bureau in Persis chose monumental rock reliefs as a major medium for the glorification of the new imperial power. Its artists showed striking originality in adapting the techniques of mural painting to monumental sculpture in this first victory relief. Some decade and a half later, the same transfer of imperial power from the Arsacid to the Sasanian dynasty was to be represented in cosmological terms in the magnificent rock relief at Naqsh-e Rostam, in which a mounted Ardashir is invested with the diadem of sovereignty representing the royal glory (*khwarrah*) by Ohrmazd (Ahurā Mazdā), also on horseback. The king of kings and the Great God, identified in Middle Persian, Parthian, and Greek, are exactly the same size, and with perfect symmetry, the defeated Parthian Ardavān lies beneath the hoof of Ardashir's horse, and Ahriman (Ohrmazd's adversary) beneath that of Ohrmazd's horse. The Great God of Truth ordains the demise of the evil empire and invests the champion of Right Order with royal glory (Mosig-Walburg 1982:15–16; Choksy 1988:46). The Naqsh-e Rostam relief thus represents the consummate justification of Sasanian Revolution as the divinely ordained transfer of imperial power. Two investiture reliefs in the interim, however, are more revealing in detail. The earlier, which must have been carved shortly after the Firuzābād victory relief in the same city, shows Ohrmazd investing Ardashir with the Zoroastrian cultic bundle, Barsmān, which Ohrmazd holds in his left hand; there is a fire altar between the king and the god, who are the same size. The crown prince, Shāpur, and two other princes are also present (Mosig-Walburg 1982:1–5). The Firuzābād investiture rock relief thus brings out the significance of the fire altar and the Zoroastrian religion in the Sasanian ideology. The Zoroastrian symbol of the Barsmān bundle is also found in the second, later investiture relief at Naqsh-e Rajab but is not held by Ohrmazd. This rock relief emphasizes the dynastic principle and another important element of Sasanian ideology, one that has remained largely neglected. Ardashir's queen and another princess can be seen behind Ohrmazd, who hands the ring of sovereignty to Ardashir, while Shāpur stands behind his father. Shāpur's two young sons stand between the king and the god (Luschey 1987:379). The most significant feature of this investiture relief, however, is the representation of the god of war, Varhrān (Bahrām), identified with and symbolized by the legendary bird Verethragna (a falcon or an eagle); Ardashir had given the name of the god of war to the grandson standing before him under the ring of sovereignty (Mosig-Walburg 1982:6–13). Shāpur's two sons who were to succeed him were the namesakes of the gods represented in this relief: Hormazd (Ohrmazd) was named after the Great God, and Bahrām after the god of war. Ardashir had systematically established the fire of Bahrām ("the victorious fire") in every major city he had conquered; now it was appropriate to make room for the god of war and the prince who was his namesake.

Appeal to the Zoroastrian religion as a central element of Sasanian ideology is evident in the coins of Ardashir and Shāpur. Fire altars and fire temples appear on the reverse side of the early Sasanian coins with the legend "Fire of Ardashir/Shāpur." The obverse legend typically reads: "The Mazdā-worshipping god Ardashir/Shāpur, king of kings of Iran whose seed is from the gods" (Paruck 1924; Göbl 1971; Gnoli 1989:168). Ardashir's coins are particularly striking as proof of the interweaving of the revival of the Zoroastrian religion into the ideology of the restoration of the empire of Iran. The fire altar is combined with the Achaemenid throne and surrounded by royal diadem bands: the throne is the fire altar, and the fire altar is the throne (Mosig-Walburg 1982:26–29). The third crown of Ardashir depicted on his coins symbolizes his investiture by the Great God, Ohrmazd (Göbl 1971:table Ia). What is generally misunderstood and seems of equally great interest is that the eagle on Ardashir's fifth crown and on Shāpur's special investiture crown, which Göbl (1971:tables Ia–II) mistakes for a symbol of Anahita, in fact celebrates the investiture of the two founders of the Sasanian Empire by Bahrām, the god of war. The falcon or eagle can be none other than one of the main forms of Verethragna, whose wings were adapted for the crowns of Bahrām I and Bahrām II, the war god's namesakes who ruled shortly after Shāpur I (Mosig-Walburg 1982:37). This promotion of the god of war to the same rank as the war goddess Anahita by the leaders of the Sasanian Revolution is consistent with the evidence of the Naqsh-e Rajab investiture rock relief and indicative of the ethos of the feudal warriors who joined the movement for the restoration of the empire of Iran.

One of the great inventions of Ardashir's propagandists was the coining of the title "the Mazdā-worshipping . . . king of kings of Iran [Ērān]," which Shāpur modified to "Iran and Non-Iran [Anērān]" in tandem with the imperial expansion that followed the consolidation of revolution. Three important points should be noted. First, in the Parthian text of Shāpur's trilingual royal inscription at the Kaʿba-ye Zardusht, this title appears as "the king of kings of Aryans and non-Aryans," and the empire of Iran (Ērānshahr) to which it corresponds appears as "the Aryan empire [*aryānkhshatr*]," being rendered "the Aryan nation [*ethnos*]" in the Greek version (ŠKZ 1–2; Sprengling 1953:2, 14). Second, Gnoli (1987; 1989:136–51) has established that *ēr Mazdēsn* (Aryan, Mazdā-worshipping) was a royal title in which the use of "Aryan" (Ēr) in the singular was stylistically preferable to "Aryans" (Ērān). The connection of the two terms "Aryan" and "Mazdā-worshipping" indicates that the primary significance of "Aryan" is religious rather than racial.[18] Third and most important, again as Gnoli (1974; 1989:193, 175) proves, the political idea of Iran and the title "king of kings *of Iran*" have no Achaemenid or Arsacid precedent and are a Sasanian invention. These significant facts all point to the grandiose invention of a tradition by the ideologues of the Sasanian Revolution.

Birth of the Idea of Iran

I have sought to highlight the elements of novelty in the ideology of the Sasanian Revolution that had far-reaching consequences in postrevolutionary reconstruction and made its teleology distinctive. But this does not mean that everything in the tradition the Sasanians championed was invented or, more specifically, that the tradition and idea of universal monarchy were without firm historical roots. We met the idea of universal monarchy as the moving force in the teleology of the Akkadian integrative revolution in chapter 1. The idea of universal monarchy was, however, foreign to the world of Avesta. Original Zoroastrianism had demonized as the creatures of Wrath (*axšma; xšm*) the warriors who, according to Widengren (1967:33–36), were organized into cultic communities or bands with their hair parted in tresses. Furthermore, like the ancient priests (*karapān*), one of whom murdered Zoroaster, the warriors of the *kavi* estate are said to have opposed Zoroaster and been responsible for his imprisonment (*Dēnkart*, in Boyce 1989:76–77); and "the tyrants and *kavi*s" are regularly condemned alongside the ancient priests in the hymns attributed to Zoroaster himself (Gnoli 1974:186). With the conversion of Vishtāsp, however, a line of heroic *kavi*s is legitimated and endowed with the Kayanid or royal charisma (*kavaēm xvarenah* [= *farnah*]), but the notion of kingship remains essentially tribal, as one would expect from the pre-imperial organization of the Aryan tribes of northeastern Iran around 1000 BCE (Gnoli 1974:165, 171–72). The Achaemenids took over the Akkadian idea of universal monarchy in its form at the time of their conquest of Mesopotamia as the "great king" (*šarru rabu*) and the "king of kings" (*šar šarrāni*), replacing the Akkadian "lord of the Four Quarters." The syncretism of the new Achaemenid royal ideology was limited to the introduction of Ahurā Mazdā as the greatest god and, after Xerxes, the supremacy of the law (*dāt*) established by him. In the Achaemenid royal ideology, the king of kings was the Great King (*xshāyathya vazrka*), who was granted sovereignty over the earth (*bumi*) by the Great God (*baga vazrka*) (Gnoli 1974:152–65; 1989:6–7): "The Great King on earth represented the Great God in heaven: just as Ahurā Mazdā is the keeper of *aša* [cosmic order] in the universe, so the Achaemenian king is the keeper of *rta* [right order] in his kingdom." From this it follows that he who rebelled against the Right Order is the follower of the Lie and the worshipper of the evil demons (*daevas*) (Gnoli 1989:86–87). The absorption of the Mesopotamian idea of universal monarchy did not eliminate the tribal idea of kingship by hereditary blood right but was rather superimposed on it in the form of sovereignty "by the will of Ahurā Mazdā" and through investiture by the supreme god. This conception was compatible with the assimilation of the gods of different subject populations of the empire; Cyrus could thus be the "chosen of Marduk" (god of Babylon) and the anointed (messiah) of the God of heaven (Yahweh) (Gnoli 1974:150–67). Darius I (522–486 BCE) called himself the "Great King, King of Kings, King of countries containing all kinds of men" (Root 1990:120). This idea of imperial monarchy, it should be noted, was in marked contrast to the heroic idea of Kayanid or royal charisma of the old Aryan tribal society, terms that are remarkably absent in the Achaemenid inscriptions (Gnoli 1974:171–73; 1989:95–96).

What was new among the fundamental concepts of the Sasanian ideology, as propagated on the early coins, was expressed in the description of the king of kings as "Mazdā-worshipping" (*mazd ēsn*) and the specification "of Iran." From these phrases it is clear that Ardashir and Shāpur posed not only as restorers and protectors of the Zoroastrian religion but also, and above all, as the kings of kings of a new political entity, an integrated Iran.

Gnoli's forceful demonstration leaves no room for any doubt that there was no Parthian precedent for the notions of Ērānshahr (*ʿryʾnxštr*, empire of the Aryans) and the corresponding Aryan king of kings and the (Aryan) glory of Iran (*Ērān xvarrah*). The concept of Iran, as he points out, was a typical elaboration of the third century and a striking instance of invention of tradition effected by Ardashir as the core of the Sasanian religiopolitical propaganda (Gnoli 1989:103, 129, 175–77). This "invention," needless to say, did not mean pure fabrication. In fact, certain aspects of the Zoroastrian tradition were developed in the so-called Younger Avesta, where the archaic hostility to the *kavi*s had given way to the praise of the exploits of the (later) *kavi*s (kings) as defenders of the faith. The idea of "the glory of the Aryans (*airyanem x*^{v}*areno*)" had become "an organic part of Zoroastrianism, and that of *airyanēm vaēji* (*ērān-vēž*, the land of the Aryans), with its rivers and mountain peaks, had assumed a central position in Zoroastrian cosmology and sacred geography as the center of the earth" (Gnoli 1989:32–67). The ideologues of the Sasanian Revolution inventively drew on this religious tradition to create the political concept of Iran. This entails a significant pan-Iranian modification of the Achaemenid idea of universal monarchy.

The religious tradition of western Iran and Mesopotamia had been somewhat different. Major changes in Zoroastrianism had taken place during the reign of Ardashir's Achaemenid namesake, Artaxerxes II (404–358 BCE), one of its most important royal patrons (Boyce 1982:263). The most important change was the assimilation of the Babylonian war goddess,

Ishtar (= Venus), to the old Iranian goddess of waters and fertility, Ardevi Sura Anahita. The image cult of Anahita was established in this period, and the war goddess remained popular for centuries with the feudal lords. The headgear (*kolāh*) of the feudal nobility became her symbol, and she appears as the goddess investing the later Arsacids with sovereignty. We know that in at least one of her main temples, the fire temple at Stakhr, the feudal lord Pāpak was the sacerdotal master of ceremonies and officiated at her cult personally. Furthermore, in marked divergence from original Zoroastrianism, bloody sacrifice was offered at the temple, and the feudal lords and petty kings were not averse to sending the heads of their vanquished opponents to be displayed at the temple of the sword- or club-bearing goddess "whose four stallions Ahurā Mazdā created: Wind, Rain, Clouds, and Hail" (*Ābān Yasht* 28.120; trans. Malandra 1983:129). We know that Ardashir filled the temple at Stakhr with the heads of the petty kings he felled during his swift campaign in Khorasan in the mid-220s (Tabari, 1.819).

Another major feature of Zoroastrian religion probably datable to the reign of Artaxerxes II is the temple cult of fires. Unlike the image cult of Anahita, which disappeared after the Zoroastrian reforms of the Sasanian era, fire temples survived and indeed became the defining feature of Zoroastrianism. This was of course consonant with the deep roots of the association between Fire and Truth / Right Order, which made Fire (*ātar*) one of the two partners in the defeat of the Lie, the overcoming of the enmity of Ahriman (Anra Mainyu), and endowed it with divine glory. The *Zādspram* could thus write, "the *khvarenah* which dwells in the Victorious Fire (*vahrām ātakhsh*) battles with the invisible Lie (*drug*)" (Boyce 1982:224).

The fire altar appears on the coins of Seleucid Persis as the earliest symbol of Zoroastrian traditionalist response to Hellenistic domination in the third century BCE. The kings of the Parthian Empire founded royal fires for the benefit of the souls of their ancestors. Ardashir seized upon this politically important symbol of the Zoroastrian faith in his ideological campaign and made centralized control of the fire temples a major focus of his integrative revolutionary policy. The political motive behind this policy of religious centralization is explained by Tansar. After the death of the last Achaemenid, Darius II, each petty king established his own fire: "This was pure innovation, introduced by them without the authority of kings of old. The King of Kings has razed the temples, and confiscated the endowments, and had the fires carried back to their places of origin" (Boyce 1968:47).

Ardashir's policy of religionational integration through centralized control of the fire temples was closely associated with the establishment of the "Victorious Fire," or the Fire of Bahrām (Varhrān/Vahrām), upon the conquest and foundation of royal cities. The regular establishment of the Fire of Bahrām must have gone hand in hand with the promotion of the god of victory, a rank similar to that of Anahita, the goddess of war. Although a minor divine figure in the Avesta, Verethragna (i.e., Bahrām), the ancient god of victory, had the unique distinction of possessing the epithet "*xvarenah*-bearing," bearing the symbol of divine glory as his battle standard. In a more mythical vein, Verethragna transformed into a falcon (*vareghna*) for the purpose of transferring *xvarenah* (divine glory) from one hero to another (Malandra 1983:82). In addition, Verethragna gave men sexual potency in their testicles. All these features must have made the god of victory an appealing figure to the warriors who constituted the feudal nobility and can account for his popularity in Armenia and Asia Minor by the first century BCE. Verethragna (Artagnes) is thus doubly identified with Hercules and Ares as one of the three great gods in the cult of King Antiochus I of Commagene (69–31 BCE) and is prominently depicted at Nimrud Dagh (Boyce and Grenet 1991:322–24). This appeal cannot by itself account for the "promotion of Bahrām" into the Zoroastrian heptad of the Seven Bounteous Immortals (Menasce 1948; Boyce and Grenet 1991:64–65n67). The puzzle can, however, easily be solved by connecting the god of victory with the Sasanian idea of establishing a fire "victoriously" (*pad varahrānah*) (Boyce 1982:223–24). In other words, the Sasanian Revolution is by far the most likely historical juncture for this departure from the Zoroastrian tradition.

The texts in question have Ahurā Mazdā make the following declarations in favor of the god Bahrām (*Bahrām yazat*): "From the beginning I declared you victorious, now you have acquired victory, I confer the title of Bounteous Immortal (*amshasfand*) upon you" (Menasce 1948:7). This revolutionary promotion of Bahrām endows him with prime cosmological significance. He is made to succeed where other Bounteous Immortals have failed—namely, in overcoming the enmity of Ahriman. "I name you," declares Ahurā Mazdā, "the Seventh Bounteous Immortal, god Bahrām, the destroyer of my Adversary." It is even claimed that at the time of resurrection, it is Bahrām who will bind Ahriman together with the devils (*daevas*) and the Lie (Menasce 1948:15).

In the later reforms of the third and fourth centuries, as the Zoroastrian hierocracy grew stronger and less dependent on royal tutelage, this idea was rejected. Bahrām was demoted from the heptad but remained a very important god, much more so than he had been under the Achaemenids. The literary sources apart, the inscriptions of Shāpur and Kartir (Sprengling 1953:17, 49–50) leave no room whatsoever for doubting the utmost significance of establishing the Fire of Bahrām to mark the victory of the Sasanian Revolution.[19] The Fire of Bahrām/Victory was established as the fire of the victory of the Sasanian Revolution. On the rock relief in the imperial city Shāpur founded, Veh-Shāpur (Bishāpur), we read: "We have gone to so many countries and taken possession of so many of them with the help of gods, therefore we founded a great number of Vahrām fires in each country" (Wiesehöfer 2001:166).

The key to the importance of the god of victory in the Sasanian ideology is the *khvarenah* of Verethragna. As Gnoli (1974:173) points out, "the *khvarenah* has a special and intimate association with Verethragna and the Fire of Varhrčn, the royal fire par excellence." The *khvarenah*, as was pointed out, was an attribute of the Aryans and the Kayanids in the eastern tradition and was conspicuous by its absence in the Achaemenid inscriptions. The Sasanian ideologues discovered it in the form of *khwarrah* in the Zoroastrian tradition as developed in eastern Iran and, drawing on the Avestan reference to *khvarenah* as "a burning fire" (*Mehr Yasht* as cited in Gnoli 1974:173), must have found the double connection of Bahrām with fire and with *khvarenah* irresistibly attractive. This second favorite god of the feudal nobility thus became a dominant figure in Sasanian ideology. The fires of Bahrām were established in major cities. Ardashir used Bahrām's name alongside that of Ohrmazd for the two grandsons in the projected line of succession, and the god of victory became a god of royal investiture before long. Bahrām's most crucial function was to strengthen the Sasanian use of *khwarrah* as the principle of legitimacy of the new monarchy (Gnoli 1990:87–88).

Reform of Zoroastrianism

As we have seen, Taōsar, better known as Tansar, the head of Ardashir's propaganda bureau, was a man of religion, a *hērbad*. Al-Masʿudi considered him to be a feudal aide to Ardashir and a descendant of a Persian petty king. Although some authorities have questioned the evidence for the adherence of the Achaemenids to Zoroastrianism as distinct from Mazdaism, there is no doubt that the Parthians were Zoroastrians, and the Arsacid Vologases I is credited with the first attempt at religious reform and creation of a Zoroastrian canon on the basis of what had survived Alexander either "in writing or . . . in an authoritative oral tradition" (*Dēnkart*, cited in Zaehner 1955:32; trans. 8). What was certainly missing, however, as we find no evidence for it, is any organized religious hierarchy. Zoroastrianism appears to have had two somewhat distinct bearers: the western Iranian priestly estate of Magi (*magus*), called *magbads* in the Parthian period (Gnoli 1974:148), and two kinds of religious functionaries: fire temple guardians and teachers who trained novices in Zoroastrian lore and learned tradition, called *hērbads*, and masters of image shrines, called *bagnapads* (Chaumont 1960b; Boyce 1979:97–98). The "orthodox, righteous" Tansar was a feudal lord by birth and a *hērbad* by profession (*Dēnkart*, cited in Boyce 1968:6). Given the blanket of ignorance that covers the period, we have no choice but to consider him the chief architect of the Sasanian ideology of imperial integration through the revival of Zoroastrian religion disestablished by the evil Alexander. By then, the most advanced religious idea was that of a revealed religion based on a scripture, and the Sasanian Revolution had to create its own scriptural canon.

Tansar's distinctly religious task was the compilation of the Zoroastrian canon. To serve as the foundation stone for any further elaboration and invention of Zoroastrian tradition, however, the preexistence of the canon had to be established. According to the *Dēnkart*, the last Darius, before his defeat by Alexander, had "commanded that two copies of all the Avesta and Zand should be written, *even as Zoroaster had received them from Ohrmazd*, and that one should be preserved in the Royal Treasury and one in the National Archives (*diz-i nipisht*, literally, the fortress of writing)" (Zaehner 1955:7–8, 31). As this canon was allegedly destroyed by Alexander and the Macedonians, the Arsacid Vologases, as we have seen, had sought to reassemble its fragments, but the passage of time had partly obliterated whatever success he may have had in this task. Ardashir, the champion of the revival of the Zoroastrian faith for the revolutionary reintegration of the empire of Iran, authorized Tansar to collect the scattered works again in one place and to undertake their official edition: "His Majesty, the King of Kings, Artakhshatr (Ardashir) son of Pāpak, following the just authority of Tansar, commanded all those scattered teachings to be brought to the court. Tansar undertook the task and selected that one [set] and rejected the other from the canon, issuing this decree: 'The interpretation of all the teachings from the Mazdā-worshipping religion is our responsibility: from now on there is no lack of certain knowledge concerning them'" (*Dēnkart*, cited in Zaehner 1955:32; trans. 8, modified).[20]

Tansar's edition of the Avesta was of utmost importance in synthesizing the two concurrent Zoroastrian traditions, which Widengren (1968:ch. 7) identifies as the written Magian tradition of Shiz and the oral tradition of Stakhr transmitted by the Zoroastrian schools of the *hērbads*. There is no indication, however, that Ardashir set up a separate religious hierarchy to integrate the Magi priestly estate and the Zoroastrian teachers (*hērbads*). Nor was Tansar's attempt to close the canon definite. On the contrary, the openness of the Zoroastrian canon in the mid-third century is evident from what will be said below about religious reforms under Shāpur I. According to Christensen (1944:142), the edition of the Avesta prepared by Tansar was completed under Shāpur I and was deposited in the fire temple of Adhur Goshnāsp in Shiz in Azerbaijan. This, however, did not put an end to religious controversy, and it was only in the mid-fourth century that the text of the Sasanian Avesta was fixed definitively by an ecclesiastical council. The religious reform of Tansar was an important component of the Sasanian mobilizational ideology, but under Ardashir and Shāpur I, it remained under complete royal tutelage and subordinate to the integrative policy of the new state. Tansar's own account of religious reforms confirmed the supremacy of temporal authority over religious matters by stressing that the people had "need of a ruler of understanding; for till religion is interpreted by understanding it has no firm foundation" (Boyce 1968:37).

Consequences of the Sasanian Revolution

We know from the numismatic evidence that Ardashir had made Shāpur coregent even before crowning him as the king of kings (Paruck 1924:310–16, 416), and Shāpur's prominence in the epigraphic and literary accounts of the decisive battle of 224 against Ardavān V proves that he shared the leadership of the Sasanian revolutionary movement for a considerable time before completing the consolidation of the Sasanian Revolution on his own. Ardashir crowned Shāpur as the king of kings with his own royal fire (Paruck 1924:416; Göbl 1971:table Ia, last column) and retired in 241 shortly before his death in (probably) 242 (Wiesehöfer 1987:374).

Political Integration of the Empire of Iran and the Building of Its State

In the course of the Sasanian Revolution, the idea of Iran acted as a constitutive myth, motivating the creation of a unified empire of Iran (Ērānshahr). To call it a nationalist ideology would be anachronistic, and to call the political community it created, Iran, a nation would be misleading. Anachronism could be attenuated by calling the idea "protonationalist," but even that should be avoided by referring to the Sasanian postrevolutionary political community simply as Iran.

Ardashir and Shāpur I embarked on a vigorous policy of founding royal cities, distinct from the existing chartered cities of the Parthian Empire. At the time of their foundation the royal cities were administrative, and military centers in newly conquered kingdoms converted to administrative districts (Lukonin 1983:723). The encouragement of crafts and commerce in these royal cities, which were directly taxed by the central treasury, gave rise to important urban strata. These cities were, however, under the direct authority of the king of kings, and their names were often compounds of Ardashir, Shāpur, and *ērān* (Pigulevskaja 1963:123; Gnoli 1989:131, 157), and the urban strata had no political autonomy. As with all revolutions, continuity with the past is ensured by the unacknowledged appropriation and modification of the institutions of the old regime. The policy of foundation of cities eloquently attests to the lasting influence of Hellenism. In marked contrast to the declining chartered Seleucid cities, however, the royal cities were under central imperial authority and indeed were the main instrument of centralization of authority. The policy of foundation of cities altered the social structure of Iran considerably, giving greater weight to its urban elements at the expense of its agrarian elements. It opened a new era of integration and urban growth in Iranian history (Pigulevskaja 1963:ch. 2).

The promotion of urbanization and growth of the urban strata as a consequence of a revolution led by the feudal nobility would seem completely paradoxical from the viewpoint of a class-centered theory of revolution. By contrast, it is fully compatible with my structural model of an integrative revolution and can be further explained by the teleology of the Sasanian Revolution, and more specifically by the ingenious compiling of the idea of imperial integration with the Hellenistically inspired policy of founding imperial cities that bore the names of Iran and its unifying rulers in theirs. Ferdawsi frequently refers to representation in the highest councils of the state (*anjoman*), which played an important role at the time of succession and election of a new monarch. Narseh was elected king by the councils of state in 293, and Shāpur II was so designated before his birth in 307. But these were undoubtedly feudal assemblies of the grandees, even though it is possible that there was some form of popular representation from the newly founded imperial cities. We also find references to collective decisions of the army (*lashkar*) and the subjects (*ra'iyya*)—which corresponds to the Parthian *ram(ak)* (flock) and the people (*'amma*)—which are indicative of a measure of political integration of the lower strata (Widengren 1967:129). But the Sasanian imperial cities, far from being self-governing Seleucid ones, were in fact founded as sources of revenue through taxation and were centers of imperial administration.

In contrast to this pale imitation of the Hellenistic founding of cities, continuity with the Parthian feudalism of the immediate past was far greater. As Pourshariati (2008) proves convincingly, our Goshnāsp, who can be presumed to have been a member of the later dynasty of the Espahbadhs of Tabarestan, was by no means the only Parthian petty king to survive and be incorporated into the Sasanian imperial regime. Many members of the abovementioned families of Parthian grandees, the Suren, Kāren, Mehrān, and Kārang dynasties, were sooner or later co-opted and in fact came to constitute the Parthian (*pahlav*) grand nobility of the Persian (*pārsig*) Sasanian dynasty. As Pourshariati also shows, these Parthian families brought about the downfall of the Sasanian Empire after 628 CE, enabling the Muslim conquerors to pick up the pieces. In our terms, the Parthian feudal grandees set in motion an epicycle of centrifugal revolutions in reaction to the celebrated (re)centralizing reforms of Khosraw I, Anushirvān (531–79), which Gibbon (1932:413ff.) interestingly dealt with in a chapter (48) of the *Decline and Fall* entitled "The Revolutions of Persia after the Death of Chosroes or Nushirvan"!

Nevertheless, reversible though it may have proved, the Sasanian integrative revolutionary power struggle could be brought to an end only by military victories and centralization of the structure of authority. The center of the new empire of Iran was the imperial court. The most revealing and parsimonious index of the growth of the centralized state is the enumeration in Shāpur's inscription at Kaʿba-ye Zardusht of the state officials and functionaries with fixed ceremonial positions at the Sasanian court through three generations. From the abovementioned eight dignitaries at the court of Pāpak, we move through the thirty-one members of the royal family, governors, and state functionaries at the court of Ardashir to sixty-five at the court of Shāpur himself (Sprengling 1953:18–19). The same listing proves the successful integration of the feudal nobility into the state structure by an ingenious combination of socioceremonial rank (*gāh*) and office (*kārdārih*) (Perikhanian 1983:645). Only one dignitary is designated by an official title at the court of Pāpak, whereas the officeholding titles abound in Ardashir's court, the most notable being the commander of the army (*spāhpat*), followed by the commander of the thousand, the master of the bureaucracy (*dapirupat*), the judge, and the master of endowments. The multiplication of offices under Shāpur is proven by the appearance of additional military and bureaucratic offices and by the first appearance of a religious functionary, Kartir, who is identified as *hērbad* in Persian and as Magus in Greek (Sprengling 1953:19, 38). Like any patrimonial court, the majority of officials performed functions related to the household of the ruler, such as master of the hunt, master of (hunting) wild boar, cupbearer, sword-bearer, caller to the meals, and the like (Wiesehöfer 2001:183–89). The lowest-but-one functionary mentioned in the inscription is a judge (*dādvar*). As we shall see, a new high office, that of *mubad*, was created for Kartir, and on the basis of what we know about the judiciary function of this office later, it is reasonable to assume that he brought the function of the judge under his authority and in fact made himself the supreme judge of the realm.

Sasanian state building, however, did not have an impact on the feudal social structure of the Parthian regime or on its culture of chivalry. The empire remained divided into kingdoms, Sasanian princes were appointed kings subservient to the king of kings, and the Persian and Parthian nobility and grandees were co-opted. The one significant measure of feudal centralization, nevertheless, was Shāpur's appointment of the members of the royal family as subordinate kings, which gradually converted vassal kingdoms into provinces (Morony 1997:72). More crucially, military organization was not centralized. The grandees and the lesser nobility, the freemen (*āzātān*), maintained their extensive landholding domains and estates in exchange for military service and constituted the Sasanian armies and, when called upon by the king of kings ad hoc and for a campaign, gathered their bondsmen into contingents under the command of noble grandees (*vazurkān*). In sharp contrast to the Severan Revolution in the Roman Empire, the Sasanian Revolution did not result in permanent centralization of military power.

Continuities with Parthian feudalism also explain the limitations to the integrative impact of the Sasanian Revolution restricting the vertical social integration that might have resulted from the growth of imperial cities. In horizontal terms, there was significant territorial or geographical integration, but that, too, was subject to the inherent tendency of the ancient empires to fragment into a core, a periphery, and an outer periphery of vassal states (Mann 1986:1.ch. 5; Steinkeller 1987). The core of the Sasanian Empire was Persia (Fars), to which Mesopotamia was annexed and speedily integrated with the foundation of most, though not all, of the imperial cities. The empire's inner periphery consisted of Media (in the Western Quarter [*kust-e khwarbarān*]) and central Iran to the Alborz Mountains, on the one side, and the Southern Quarter (*kust-e nēmrōz*, including Kerman and Sistan), on the other (Pourshariati 2008:111–18). Hira and Edessa (the kingdom of the Abgārs) in Mesopotamia, Armenia, Azerbaijan (in the *kust-e ādurbādagā*, or Northern Quarter), Tabarestan, and probably most of the Eastern Quarter (*kust-e khwaorasan*), including Kushan, were the vassal states of the loosely held outer periphery, or the frontier (*marz*) (Chaumont 1975).[21]

Expansion of Ērānshahr to the Empire of Anērān (Non-Iran)

The Sasanian Revolution was a phenomenon inextricably interwoven with the international politics and political culture of the bipolar Perso-Roman world. Ardashir and Shāpur left their inscriptions in the languages of the ancien régime, Parthian and Greek, to which they added the Middle Persian of the Sasanian Revolution. In fact, the Parthian text is probably the original of Shāpur's "Res gestae" (Sprengling 1953:2, 21). Like Augustus, he chose to write on the walls of a sanctuary, the Kaʿba-ye Zardusht, which he built in full view of the Achaemenid reliefs at Naqsh-e Rostam to recount his conquests in the Achaemenid Non-Iran. With an ambivalence typical of revolutionaries, the Sasanians used the Greek of Hellenism, whose symbol, Alexander, they demonized, and the Parthian of the Arsacids, from whom they appropriated the claim to Achaemenid descent and, with it, to the western lands of the Achaemenid Empire. They further appropriated the fire altar as the symbol of Zoroastrianism, whose scripture the Arsacid Vologases I was the first to assemble. These appropriations were accompanied by the vilification of the ancien régime and vehement denial of any debt to its culture.

Kartir, who later rose to such prominence that he was allowed to leave his own inscriptions, provides us with invaluable information on the ideological aspect of Shāpur's policy of imperial expansion. Pursuant upon the claims to Achaemenid lands recorded in the late 220s by the well-informed Roman governor and historian Cassius Dio, the victorious and intensely mobilized feudal armies of Ardashir conquered northern Mesopotamia and ravaged Syria in the 230s. Shāpur defeated the Roman army, killing the young emperor Gordian III in 243 near al-Anbār (Massice), which he renamed Pēroz Shāpur (victorious Shāpur), and he conquered much of Syria in the 250s. Antioch fell in 253 or 256 and was reconquered in 260, when Shāpur used Emperor Valerian and other Roman captives to build Veh-Antiok Shāpur (whose name means "better than Antioch of Shāpur") back in Khuzestan (Morony 1997:71). In that year, he had defeated and captured Emperor Valerian "by our own hands" (*Res gestae Saporis*, in Shayegan 2012:11) and conquered thirty-five other cities besides Antioch (Millar 1993:159–66). The Mazdian revolutionary propaganda by the Magi that accompanied these campaigns is no less interesting than their spectacular military success. Chaumont (1973:669) observes that Shāpur entered the city of Antioch "less as a conqueror than a liberator." The revolutionary ferment in the region is confirmed by *Sibylline Oracle* 13 and numismatic evidence. Emesa, which had produced three empresses in living memory, was not likely to submit to alien rule. During the Persian invasion of Syria in 253, a priest (improbably of Aphrodite according to the sources) who bore the ancestral name of the priest-rulers of Emesa, Sampsigeramus,[22] proclaimed himself emperor in Emesa, assuming the imperial title on his coins of Imperator Julius Aurelius (Sulpicius) (Uranius) Antoninus. He was the source (Millar 1987:158–59) of this apocalyptic Roman response to the Sasanian Revolution:

> Again the world will be in chaos as men perish
> by pestilence and war. Persians will again set out
> to the tumult of Ares. . . .
> Then there will be a flight of Romans, but afterward
> the last priest of all will come, sent from the sun,
> appearing in Syria, and he will accomplish everything without deceit
> . . . then will come, sent from the sun,
> a lion, terrible and frightful, breathing a great flame. . . .
> He himself intact, unblemished and great
> will rule over the Romans, and the Persians will be powerless. (*Sib. Or.* 13.147–71)

The last priest was later crushed by Shāpur, and the lion never came, and the havoc caused by Shāpur's invasion of Syria continued after the death in captivity of Valerian, giving rise to the ephemeral empire of Queen Zenobia in the latter part of the 260s and its fall in 271. Palmyra was "located near barbarous *gentes* and nations" (Ulpian as cited in Millar 1993:141), or more precisely near the desert between the Roman and the Persian Empires, and inhabited by Arabs. Deeply rooted in the Syro-Roman aristocracy, Zenobia declared herself Augusta but did not neglect to call her late husband king of kings posthumously, while the governors she appointed after 267 bore the Persian title *argapētes* (*argbad*, meaning "citadel commander") in inscriptions (Millar 1993:170). Her son, Vaballatus (Wahb-Allāh), called himself not only "Imperator Caesar . . . Aurelius Septimius Vaballatus Augustus" but also the king of kings (Millar 1993:171).

The apocalyptic response of the Sibylline oracle had been provoked by the Mazdian propaganda, and the establishment of fire temples of "the Mazdā-worshipping religion" constituted an essential part of the early Sasanian imperial expansion. In Shāpur's account of his victories we read: "The gods have made us their ward, and with the aid of the gods we have searched out and taken so many lands, so that in every land we have founded Bahrām fires and have conferred benefits upon many Magi-men, and we have magnified the cult of the gods" (*Res gestae Saporis*, trans. Frye 1984:372).

The evidence from Armenia (Chaumont 1973:693) and the statement in the *Chronicle of Arbela* (Widengren 1971:778) that "king Ardashir gave orders for the construction of fire temples in honor of the gods. . . . and has forced many followers of other religions to worship the sun and the fire" strongly suggest that the practice of establishing fires of Bahrām in major cities upon victory was extended beyond Iran proper during the Sasanian Revolution. Shāpur continued this policy of establishing fires of Victory in the empire of Non-Iran, and the invaluable information we are given in the inscriptions of Kartir, whose career and rise to power were due to the policy of establishing fire temples in the conquered lands and putting Magian priests in their charge, strongly suggests that Zoroastrian ideological commissars accompanied Shāpur's armies. He appointed Kartir, who claimed to have begun his career under Ardashir, presumably as a religio-ideological commissar,[23] the head of a religio-ideological bureau, and authorized him to recruit men from the estate of the Magi as commissars and put them in charge of the newly established fire temples. "Shāpur, the king of kings, gave one power and authority over the estate of the Magi" (ŠKZ 1.1; Chaumont 1960a:341, 345). The purpose of this appointment is made clear immediately. "Upon the order of the king of kings, in country after country and place after place, there grew many religious offices, many fires of Varhrān were founded, many men of the Magi estate (*magumart*) became happy, and many fires and Magi were installed by imperial edict" (ŠKZ 1.2; Sprengling 1953:49; Mosig-Walburg 1982:61). We are indeed justified in assuming that Kartir "himself accompanied [Shāpur's] expedition at the head of a contingent of Magi" (Chaumont 1973:667). Kartir's own words are more boastful:

> And as for me, Kartir, from the earliest time onward for the gods and the lords, and for my own soul's sake, much trouble and pain were undergone: many fires [of Varhrān] and Magi in the empire of Iran I made prosperous; and in the empire of Non-Iran, too, wherever the horses and men of the king of kings arrived—the city of Antioch, etc., etc.—[wherever] Shāpur, king of kings, with horses and men inflicted pillage, fire, and havoc, there also, by command of the king of kings, I organized the men of the Magi estate and the fires [of Victory] installed in those countries. (ŠKZ 11–13; Sprengling 1953:51–52; Chaumont 1960a:347–48)

Religion and the Reconstitution of Political Order: Emergence of a Zoroastrian Hierocracy

With his great success in extending the Ērānshahr realized by his father to his own empire of Non-Iran, Shāpur became less ambivalent and more open toward international culture and experimented with new universalist cultural modes. This was the case with his religious policies after the conquests, which were open and experimental in a unique situation of religious pluralism and competition among universalist religions. The Roman prisoners of war and Syrian deportees who settled in the royal cities included a large number of Christians, including a patriarch of Antioch. Furthermore, Christian missionaries appear to have had considerable success in the royal and other cities, including even Stakhr (Chaumont 1964b:169–80). With his project of imperial expansion successfully completed, Shāpur issued an edict of religious tolerance which stands in sharp contrast to the persecutions of the Christians in the Roman Empire, granting religious freedom not only to the Christians but also to the Manichaeans and the Jews (Chaumont 1964b:183–84).

It appears that while Tansar had turned from revolutionary propaganda for the unification of the empire of Iran to compiling the edition of the Avesta, as recorded in the *Dēnkart,* Shāpur's attitude was much more liberal and eclectic:

> The King of Kings, [Shāpur], son of [Ardashir], further collected those writings from the Religion which were dispersed throughout India, the Byzantine Empire, and other lands and which treated of medicine, astronomy, movement, time, space, substance, creation, becoming, passing away, change in quality, growth (?), and other processes and organs. These he added to the Avesta and commanded that a fair copy of all of them be deposited at the Royal Treasury: and he examined (the possibility) of bringing all systems (?) into line with the [Mazda-worshipping] Religion. (Zaehner 1955:8, 32)

Shāpur ruled a world empire and had to confront the problematic relation between political universalism of empire and the religiocultural universalism of the world religions, which Fowden (1993) correctly identifies as the central issue in the crisis of the third century. On the political level, U. Bianchi (1988) rightly considers Shāpur's "halfway" universalism as reactive insofar as it portrays the rival Roman imperial order as the expression of the Lie. It should further be added that the introduction of the contrasting notion of Non-Iran casts the nationalist idea of the empire of Iran into a hardened anti-universalistic mold. In the religious sphere, however, the passages quoted above prove that Shāpur's response was to make the Zoroastrian canon more open and universalistic. But the religious question was more complicated, because he also had to respond to the contrasting universalism of the great world religion of his era, Manichaeism, the religion of a new Babylonian prophet, Māni.

Māni was born, lived through, and had his two revelations during Ardashir's Sasanian Revolution. He was a descendant of a Parthian feudal family from Mesopotamia which may well have participated in the abortive counterrevolution of 228, and he received his first revelation in that very year, at the age of thirteen. The Manichaeism he subsequently developed is tinged with "profound pessimism related to that dynasty's loss of power," and its scriptures have preserved a rich and variegated linguistic heritage, including the Parthian language itself. The revelation he received in that year can thus be seen as the first step in an integrative trajectory that contrasted sharply with Ardashir's political project, and along which the young prophet "resolved to found a world-wide movement which would reassert Arsacid values in the spiritual sphere" (Bivar 1983:97). Religious pluralism, too, was a salient feature of the late Parthian era. Māni's own name is Semitic-Aramaic, and his father's name, Pattēg, is Greek. His father had moved from Hamadan (Ekbatana) to southern Babylon and married a Parthian woman of royal descent. There is no doubt that the original inspiration for Māni's prophetic enterprise came from a gnostic, Judaizing baptist (*ghassāliyun*) sect founded in Mesopotamia by Elkasai, in which his father had raised him but which he later violently rejected and was expelled from. This is proven by the Christian origin of the names of the dramatis personae of Māni's salvation drama in Syriac (Sundermann 1979:99–100) and more explicitly by his calling himself the Messenger of Jesus Christ, along with his primary self-designation as the Messenger of Light. But immediately after his second revelation at the age of twenty-four, the Messenger of Light embarked for India, where he assiduously learned Buddhism, and on the way back from northern India, he converted the Sasanian kings of Turanistan/Baluchestan and of the Kushan to his new faith. As he embarked on his universal mission, the Semitic, Christian background of his teaching was dimmed, and he and his missionaries reconceptualized fundamental Mazdian beliefs in Parthian and Persian (instead of Aramaic and Syriac), freely assimilating the figures and concepts of his sacred cosmogony to those of the Mazdian pantheon in their various local incarnations (Boyce 1982; Sundermann 1979).

The young Māni was not just a survivor of the old Parthian regime trapped in morose nostalgia; rather, he vigorously seized the opportunity offered by the new and fast-expanding Sasanian regime. So he asked Pēroz, the king of Kushan, to introduce him to his brother, Shāpur, and presented an elegant expression of his creed, the *Shābuhragān*, to the latter on the occasion of his coronation as the king of kings.

The evidence suggests that despite its youth, the people of the new religion had already been active clandestinely, and Gnoli (1984:32, 38) speculates that Shāpur's appointment as the king of Kushan before becoming king of kings must have exposed him not only to Buddhism but also to Manichaeism in that region, as his successor in the post was a convert and follower of Māni. Be that as it may, Māni made an open bid to win over Shāpur and reportedly gained some favor with him as his physician. In the *Shābuhragān*, a book dedicated to and named after the new king of kings, which is Māni's only work written in Middle Persian, the language of the Sasanian Revolution, Māni set forth the general conception of his new universalistic religion, which would not be limited to one country and one language. In the book's preface, Māni had to establish the superiority of his religion over its rivals in a situation of religious pluralism. Al-Biruni's translation of the opening section of *Shābuhragān* reveals Māni's keen sense of the competitive situation of religious pluralism in which he was offering his religion as the best: "Wisdom and deeds have always from time to time been brought to mankind by the messengers of God. So in one age they have been brought by the messenger, called Buddha, to India, in another by Zarādusht to Persia, in another by Jesus to the West. Thereupon this revelation has come down, this prophecy in this last age through me, Māni, the Messenger [*fryštg* in the original] of the God of Truth to Babylonia" (al-Biruni 1879:190). Whatever the power of his inspired religious thinking, it was only Māni's unbounded confidence of a prophet that made him ignore the fact that Ardashir had already proposed the empire of Iran (Ērānshahr) as the realized millennial kingdom in his ideology. How otherwise could Māni expect the master of this new postmillennial empire to ignore the vested interests of the guardians of his victorious fires and just be converted to Māni's new apocalyptic faith in yet another New Empire (*š[h]r ʿy nwg*) (*Shābuhragān*, ll. 180–81; MacKenzie 1979:510), especially since this empire was to come about through the cosmic "conflagration of the demons of wrath (*swcyšn ʿy xšmyn*)" (*Shābuhragān*, ll. 269–76; MacKenzie 1979:514–15)? No winner of a revolution would trade in his reconstructed earthly political order for Māni's apocalyptic vision of the "empire of wisdom (*khradeshahr*)":

> God Khradeshahr (emperor of wisdom) . . . in that last [age], close to the Renovation (*prsqyrd, frashkert*) . . . will then stand up in the [heaven], and a great call will resound and it will become known to the whole universe. And these gods which in the cosmos of heavens and earths are lords of the house, of the village, of the tribe, and of the land, border-guard and demon-tormenter will praise that Khradeshahr. . . . And then god Khradeshahr will send messengers to east and west, and they will go and [bring] the pious (*dynwr*) with their helpers (*hyʾrʾn*). (*Shābuhragān*, ll. 17–45; MacKenzie 1979:504–5)

Not only the "helpers" of the messengers of (the god of) the empire of wisdom on earth but also his hierarchy of divine lords of heavens and earths, whose functions in the new empire after the Renovation are later described (Mackenzie 1979:512–13), are the exact replicas of the feudal lords and helpers whom Ardashir and Shāpur had integrated into the social hierarchy of the unified empire of Iran. Furthermore, the fragments reconstructed by MacKenzie from the manuscripts discovered in Central Asia at the beginning of the twentieth century are remarkable for showing the centrality of the idea of Renovation / New Creation after a cosmic conflagration, which Māni adopts from Zoroastrianism. One could not ask for a more striking contrast with the complete absence of Zoroastrian apocalyptic millennialism in the ideology of the Sasanian Revolution.

Two pieces of evidence demonstrate that the ideologues of the Sasanian Revolution were familiar with ancient apocalyptic beliefs and did their best to de-emphasize them in their reconstruction of the Zoroastrian tradition.[24] According to al-Masʿudi ([1894] 1967:98), Ardashir deliberately shortened the period of 513 years since the death of Alexander to 260 in order to make the millennium more distant, because Zoroaster had taught that "with the completion of the millennium religion and sovereignty would perish together." This contention is indirectly corroborated by Tansar's claim that the new empire established by Ardashir would last a thousand years (Ibn Isfandiyār, 39), which by implication dates the beginning of the new millennium to the foundation of Ardashir's empire. In any case it is evident that the millennial motif was subordinate in the ideology of the Sasanian Revolution, because the idea of "the empire of Iran" was the earthly substitute for the millennial kingdom. For this reason, as Gnoli (1989:161) maintains, "the idea of Iran also served as an antidote to Manichaean universalism."

Nevertheless, Shāpur did not proscribe Manichaeism, but on the contrary, he received Māni into his court as his physician and was accompanied by him on some of his campaigns, as was Kartir. It is reasonable to argue that he at least contemplated the kind of compromise with it as a universal religion that Constantine effected with respect to Christianity half a century after Shāpur's death. The nascent Zoroastrian hierocracy acted otherwise—that is, with alarm—and Kartir, who became its head and acquired great power and influence under Shāpur's successors, persistently sought Māni's destruction. He succeeded when Bahrām II (276–93) ascended the throne. Māni was summoned and made his last journey to appear before the new monarch. "Kartir the Magbed (*mubad*) planned with his friends who served before the king, and . . . jealousy and cunning . . ." (cited in Henning 1942:948–49). If we may be permitted to complete the broken Manichaean fragment, jealousy and cunning did their work: Māni was executed by the order of Bahrām II, and his followers were fiercely persecuted.

This brings us to the last and most intriguing of the consequences of the Sasanian Revolution. It is the most unexpected of all its consequences and the one that took the longest to unfold: the growth of the Zoroastrian hierocracy. Religion, as we have seen, was used in a minor key and as ancillary to the primary idea of Iran and had a relatively minor impact on the immediate political reconstruction.[25] I have suggested that the decision to export the Mazdā-worshipping religion alongside the revolution to the "empire of Non-Iran" was the main factor in the emergence of the Zoroastrian hierocracy. Once Ardashir and Shāpur proclaimed themselves to be the restorers of the Zoroastrian religion, however, they unleashed a social force they could not control forever. To be more precise, the Sasanian revolutionary ideology had given the custodians of restored Zoroastrianism a reserved niche built in advance into the teleology of the Sasanian Revolution. They had a tremendous cultural asset which could be converted to permanent authority by institution building. Within half a century, Kartir achieved this by organizing a Zoroastrian hierocracy and incorporating it into the structure of domination of the Sasanian Empire. Kartir's inscriptions in fact show the growth of a Zoroastrian religious organization, or hierocracy, out of the policy of propagation of the Mazdā-worshipping religions in the wars of conquest of Mesopotamia that aimed at the creation of the empire of Non-Iran. In them we have the earliest occurrence of the term "Chief of the Magi" (*magupat; mobad* in Persian) and the first mention of religious offices (*kertakān-e yazdān*; literally, "divine offices") (ŠKZ 1.1; Chaumont 1960a:345).

Shāpur's successors, whom the royal restorers of Zoroastrianism had named after the gods Ohrmazd and Bahrām, could not refuse support to Kartir. Ohrmazd I (272–73) appointed Kartir "the Mobad (head of the Magi) of Ohrmazd," a title that suggests the increasingly distinct organization of a religious hierarchy, and furthermore, Kartir was promoted to the rank of the nobility upon being bestowed with the "hat" and the "girdle" (Mosig-Walburg 1982:96). He was confirmed in this position by Bahrām I (273–76). But Kartir's great triumph came under Bahrām II (276–93), his spiritual ward who promoted him to the social rank of grandee and appointed him the chief judge of the empire in addition to his headship of the Zoroastrian hierarchy. Particularly important for the future growth of a Zoroastrian hierocracy was the transfer of the lordship and priesthood of the fire temple of Anahita—the Anahita-Ardashir and Lady Anahita at Stakhr—which had been invested in the monarch (Morony 1997:72). Kartir was also personally honored with the augmented title "the Savior of the Soul of Bahrām and the Mubed of Ohrmazd" (Mosig-Walburg 1982:100).[26]

Kartir, by necessity, went along with the election of Narseh (292–303) after the failed attempt to maintain Bahrām III on the throne, but he fell out of favor, as probably did the hierocracy as a whole. But temporary reversals under individual monarchs could not check the institutional growth of the Zoroastrian hierocracy, which was strong enough, under Shāpur II (307–79), to establish the definitive Sasanian Avesta, reform the Sasanian-revolutionary cults of Anahita and Bahrām, and purge those elements in them that were contrary to Zoroastrianism. The head of the hierocracy and architect of the reforms, Adhurpād Mehrāspand, convened a council that approved the Avestan canon and reportedly underwent the ordeal of molten bronze to prove its authenticity (Boyce 1979:118). Further growth of the Zoroastrian hierocracy is proven by the establishment, in the fifth century, of a Chief Mobad (*mubadān mubad*), who was also the Chief Justice of the late Sasanian Empire (Gnoli 1989:168).

To ensure the safeguarding of its vested institutional interest, the Zoroastrian hierocracy allied itself with the feudal nobility, which was well integrated into the Sasanian state by the end of Shāpur I's reign. Like the other universalist religion of the era, Christianity, Manichaeism favored the urban strata and showed an aversion to agriculture (*varz*). The Zoroastrian hierocracy sought to destroy Manichaeism by courting the feudal nobility and lavishing praise on agriculture and "relegated trading to the lowest rung of their ethic" (Gnoli 1989:161).

Through its permanent institutional power, the Zoroastrian hierocracy in turn had a profound impact on the social structure of Iran. As we have seen, it brought the interpretation of royal genealogy under its jurisdiction and, through it, the canonization of mythical northeastern lore as the epic of kings—*Khʷatay-nāmag*, translated into the New Persian *Shāhnāma*. The impact consisted in the translation of the Avestan term for castes into social reality. We can read that among the (Indian) ideas that Shāpur II sought to include in the Zoroastrian canon was the following: "Among them the body of man is, as it were, divided between the four castes on earth; Priesthood (corresponds) to the head, Warriorhood to the hands, Husbandry to the belly, and Artisanship to the feet" (Zaehner 1955:139).

It was not long before the fifth century, under the impact of the canonization and revival of the Avesta by Adhurpād Mehrāspand, that religiolegal reforms established the four estates (*pēšak*)—"priests" (*āšrōn*), "warriors" (*artēštārān*), "scribes" (*dipīrān*), and a fourth estate comprising "cultivators" (*vāstryōšān*) and "craftsmen" (*hutuxšān*) (Perikhanian 1983:633)—all of which are transcribed Avestan terms. The four estates represented the "clericalization of Sasanian society" (Widengren 1967:138), which was carried into the

Islamic era and was thus a very long-term consequence of the adoption of the Zoroastrian religion in Ardashir's revolutionary ideology.

Conclusion

To conclude, the unification and political integration of Iran have been shown to have been guided by the regulative idea of Ērānshahr as the central element in the teleology of the Sasanian Revolution. It acted as the constitutive principle of the integrative revolution that created a new political community, Iran, whose social solidarity and integration were enhanced by an official religion, Zoroastrianism, chosen as a result of Shāpur I's historically contingent decision during the exportation of the revolution. This makes the Sasanian Revolution an interesting case in that its teleology intensified and reinforced the common unintended consequence of all revolutions: namely, the enlargement and integration of the political community.

SEVEN

Rise of Islam: The Constitutive Revolution of Late Antiquity

What Cleisthenes had done in Athens by means of democratic political reform Muhammad did in Arabia as a by-product of a religious revolution. Muhammad led a constitutive revolution in a segmentary, tribal society that created a unified Arabia whose nomadic tribes, bound by religious solidarity, were transformed into armies of conquest and scattered into garrison towns from the heartland of the Sasanian Empire in Mesopotamia to the Nile and then farther west to North Africa. I shall draw on the embarrassingly rich primary and secondary sources on the rise of Islam to reveal the unappreciated implications of its historicocultural context of late antiquity and to analyze its process and consequences as a political revolution of the constitutive type in the peripheries of the Roman, Persian, and Ethiopian Empires.[1]

Preconditions of a Constitutive Revolution on the Periphery of Empires

The Roman province of Arabia is officially recorded in 111 CE by Emperor Trajan, who had served Vespasian as governor in Antioch as early as 75 and annexed Petra and its Nabataean Kingdom in 106 (Bowersock 1983:82–84). Later in the second century Septimius Severus divided Syria into two provinces, Syria Coele (north) and Syria Phoenice (south), and created the province of Mesopotamia. Philip the Arab became Roman emperor in 244 and ruled for five years, in which he founded his own city, made his son coregent to establish his own dynasty, and must have had time to enhance the integration of the province of Arabia through its provincial equestrian aristocracy. Meanwhile, Mesopotamia and Syria were conquered by Shāpur I (240–72) and constituted into his "empire of Non-Iran." He set up a vassal state in Hira on the western bank of the Euphrates. He made the chief of the tribe of Lakhm, Jadhima al-Abrash, "king [*basileus*, MLK] of the Tanukh," a tribal confederation that had recently settled in Mesopotamia in the area around Anbār, where the Roman emperor Gordian III had been defeated and killed in 243. Jadhima's nephew ʿAmr b. ʿAdi established himself in Hira and was given the title "king of the Lakhmids" by Narseh (293–302), one of Shāpur I's sons (Hoyland 2009:377). ʿAmr was succeeded by his son Imrau'l-Qays, who famously described himself on his tombstone, dated 328 and found in Roman Arabia, as the king of the Arabs and bearer of the crown (*tāj*). The Romans, meanwhile, recovered from defeat and retook Syria and parts of Mesopotamia, which became the main bone of contention and the central arena of conflict in the bipolar Perso-Roman world of the next four centuries. The Roman emperor Julian fell in battle against Shāpur II (307–79), who wrested control of the Arabs in Mesopotamia from the Romans and also campaigned in the Arabian Peninsula, subjugating its northern shores on the Persian Gulf. Meanwhile, a new imperial power was asserting itself in southern Arabia. Ethiopian incursions were becoming frequent, and Ezana, the king of Axum, laid claim to the Himyarite Kingdom in his inscriptions from the mid-fourth century (Hoyland 2009:382).

For the next two centuries, Hira flourished as a crossroad of trade, cultures, and civilizations on the border of the desert and the sown (Toral-Niehoff 2013). The development of the Arabic language received a tremendous boost from the poets gathered at the court of the Arab kings of the house of Nasrid in Hira in the fifth century, one of whom established his father's former ward, Bahrām V (420–38), on the Sasanian throne.[2] The Ethiopians overthrew the royal house of Himyar, which had converted to Judaism, and occupied southern Arabia in the mid-sixth century, attacking Mecca in the Year of the Elephant, so named after their war elephants. The Arab kingdom of Kinda presumably became an Ethiopian vassal state. The Persians conquered southern Arabia in the latter part of the sixth century, driving out the Ethiopians, and left a Persian colony, known as "the sons" (*al-abnāʾ*). In the sixth century, Mundhir b. Nuʿmān of Hira (504–54) was appointed the sole overlord of the Arabs in Persian territories, and he and his descendants, the Nasrids, brought parts of Hijaz, including Yathrib, the future Medina, into the sphere of Persian suzerainty. In the last quarter of the sixth century, Khosraw I (531–79) occupied southern Arabia after a maritime expedition, and it was put under direct Sasanian rule, with a garrison under the command of the governor (*marzbān*), in 599 (Al-Azmeh 2014:120). On the Roman side, Justinian made his main Arab client, al-Hārith b. Jabala (569–700), the phylarch of the Arabs as the Roman counterpart to Mundhir, and his descendants, the Jafnid dynasty, continued to rule the Roman vassal state (Hoyland 2001:81). They appear to have reacted to the Persian occupation of the Yemen by appointing a king over Mecca (Al-Azmeh 2014:112–14, 160–61).

Foreign political domination of Arabia is an important feature of the historical background of the rise of Islam. Arabia was on the periphery of the most powerful empires of late antiquity, the Persian and the Roman/Byzantine, to which Ethiopia must now be added. The Persians also occupied the southern shores of the Persian Gulf and dominated much of northeastern and north-central Arabia, including Yathrib (the future Medina), through their Nasrid Arab client state in the Hira (near the future Kufa). They also ran the silver mines of the Hijaz (Crone 2007:64). In short, most of the Arabian Peninsula came under Persian domination. The Byzantines dominated northwestern Arabia through their Jafnid client dynasty and its tribal confederation, and their influence in the south seems to have increased through their Christian Ethiopian ally under Justinian (Hoyland 2009:382). "And remember when you were few and abased in the land and were fearful that the people (*al-nās*) would snatch you away," so the Qur ͗ān (8.26) reminds the Arabs. "The people" was taken by the earliest commentators to refer to the Persians (or the Persians and the Byzantines) (Kister 1968a:143–44). The poet Qatāda affirms: "the Arabs were confined between the lions of Persia and Byzantium" (cited by Crone 1987:249).

Persian authorities or their clients in Hira favored the Jews of Yathrib for much of the sixth century. The Jewish tribes of Nadir and Qurayza dominated Yathrib (they were said to be its "kings") as tax collectors for the Persian emperor through the Sasanian governor (*marzbān*) of Zāra (Qatif) on the Persian Gulf. Their economic power declined when they lost this important fiscal function (Kister 1968a:147; 1979:330). This seems to be connected with a shift to direct control of Medina from Hira as a result of Khosraw's appointment of Mundhir b. Nu ͑mā in the midcentury, because in the last quarter of the sixth century, we hear of the appointment of an Arab from the Khazraj tribe as king of Hijaz (Lecker 2002:114–15). The political status of the Jews declined more sharply. By the time of the migration of Muhammad in 622, the Jews of Yathrib, though still considerably richer than the Arabs (Serjeant 1978:3; Newby 1988:17), were either the allies or clients of the Arab tribes of Aws and Khazraj. The Christians of Najran and southern Arabia were under Byzantine domination.

There is nothing new in the above summary of the political environment of Islam in late antiquity except perhaps for the insertion of Ethiopia in a minor key. The full implications of this politicohistorical context as the cultural precondition of the rise of Islam are only beginning to be worked out. The persistent prejudice of seeing Islam as a Judaeo-Christian heresy in the history of religions has to some extent been remedied by Fowden (1993, 2014) and Al-Azmeh (2014), who put its rise in the context of late antiquity. Their conception of late antiquity, however, remains heavily westward looking or Romanist. The old history of religions approach was useful for showing the well-documented early spread of sectarian forms of Judaism and Christianity from Judaea and Syria in the Roman sphere of influence to Arabia. But a serious corrective is still needed, and we must look eastward to the Persian Empire, whose political domination of the Arabian Peninsula was clearly preponderant by the end of the sixth century. The presence of Manichaeism in the Persian sphere of influence in Arabia has been minimized, if not denied altogether. This must be corrected. There is no reason to deny the presence of some Manichaean influence in seventh-century Arabia except for the deep-rooted, common scholarly prejudice of seeing late antiquity exclusively from the Judaeo-Christian and Romanist viewpoint.[3]

Muhammad's ancestor Qusayy had settled the Quraysh tribe in the sacred enclave (*haram*) of Mecca just over a century before Muhammad's birth. The custodianship (*hijāba*) of the House of Allāh, the Kaʿba, was secured for the Quraysh and gave them sacred immunity from attacks by other tribes (Peters 1994:26, 69). Even though the custodial functions became divided among his descendants through the lines of Hāshim and ʿAbd al-Dār, Qusayy's cultic reforms had a lasting effect, making him the "unifier" (*mujammaʿ*) of the tribal union of the Quraysh on behalf of Allāh. Furthermore, Qusayy's descendants succeeded in creating a supratribal collective identity by founding or reconstructing a cultic union, the *hums*, possibly in response to the unsuccessful invasion of Mecca by Abraha, the Christian Ethiopian viceroy of the Yemen in the mid-sixth century CE (Dostal 1991:197–98, 216). Be that as it may, the Quraysh linked their claim to be "the people [*ahl*] of Allāh" to a covenant (*ʿahd*) made by their putative ancestor, Abraham, whose image in the Kaʿba, holding arrows for the ritual of casting arrows in front of the idol Hubal, was erased only later by Muhammad's order (Rubin 1990:104–7).

The fact that the gods and their sanctuaries were usually shared by tribes made for a measure of religious and cultural unification. The religious unity of the Arab tribes of the Hijāz, western Arabia, was thus periodically reaffirmed by their pilgrimages to the divine sanctuaries around Mecca. These gods offered their worshippers protection (Q. 8.72) and could intercede on their behalf with the higher god, Allāh (Q. 10.18, 30.12) (Watt 1988:32–33). Invaluable information preserved in the pilgrimage formula of ritual invocation (*talbiya*) for the pre-Islamic Arab tribes proves that the relationship between the supreme god, Allāh, and the gods of the tribes was conceived as a partnership (*shirk*). Deities were embodied in idols (*asnām, awthān*) or sacred stones (betyls; *ansāb/nusub*). Each tribe had its own invocation formula. That of the Nizār was "Here I am, O God, here I am; Thou hast no partners except such partners as Thou hast; Thou possessest him and all that is his [i.e., the partner's]" (Ibn al-Kalbi 1965:7; Kister 1980:33, 50–51), while the Quraysh's was cited in the Qur'ān (and became known as "the Satanic Verse"): "To the Lat and the 'Uzza, and Manāt, the third and the other! Verily they are the high-flying cranes; and their intercession [with Allāh] is to be hoped for" (Ibn al-Kalbi 1965:19). The idol of the tribe of Khawlān, 'Umyānus, appears to have been associated with Allāh on a more equal footing, as the Khawlān divided their cattle and harvest between the two (Ibn al-Kalbi 1965:43–44). There was also the nameless god of Dhu'l-Khalsa (Al-Azmeh 2014:218). The Qur'ān characterizes the Arabian form of polytheism as "associationism" (*shirk*); its description of the Arabian tribes as "associationists," or believers in divine partnership (*mushrikun*), is quite precise. *Shirk* defines a precise variety of polytheism in which tribal and confederal gods of different ranks are associated with a higher God that thereby acquires a measure of transcendence. As such, it should be more specifically translated as "associationist polytheism." The Arabs admitted the supreme authority of Allāh but associated other astral and clan deities with him; as associates, the lesser deities could intercede with Allāh (Watt 1970; Kister 1980:48–49). In Q. 29.6, 63, the polytheists are shown to acknowledge Allāh as the higher God, the creator of the heavens and the earth, and the sender of rain to revive the earth after its death, but they refuse to carry out the implications of this belief in practice: "And when they sail on the ship, they pray to God as sole object of worship, but when he has brought them safe to land, they then associate [*hum yushrikun*]" (Q. 29.65). Associationism was thus the precise form of Arab polytheism and the linchpin of the religious unity of the segmented society of politically autonomous Arabian tribes.

The polytheistic cult of idols that persisted beneath the Allāh-dominated henotheism was deeply rooted in the social organization of tribal Arabia and cemented it. Not only each tribe but each clan (*batn*) within it had its own idol. Lesser idols pertained to the lower echelons of social organization: noblemen of the clans had their own idols, and domestic idols symbolized and cemented the unity of the family (Ibn al-Kalbi 1965; Lecker 1993:332, 342). This polytheistic tribal idolatry was hedged by a cult of vengeance (*tha'r*) with elaborate rituals that fostered clan solidarity (Chelhod 1955:101–4).

Furthermore, their social grounding gave the idols great political significance: in each clan, the idol was associated with its leader and with the clan assembly (*majlis*) near his house (Lecker 1993:342).

Despite Arabia's segmentary structure as a tribal society, its cultural unity was ensured by the common recognition of a pantheon of higher gods and a modicum of linguistic unity. The tribes of the Hijaz were unified by one of the two *lingue franche* of the peninsula, the other being the language of the northern and central Arabian tribes. During the century preceding the rise of Islam, the organization of the local trade by the Quraysh in the linguistically unified Hijaz had made for considerable economic integration of western Arabia. Trade fairs had grown in the protected environs of the divine sanctuaries in western Arabia, especially those around Mecca in conjunction with pilgrimage rites (Kister 1972:76–77; Crone 1987:177–85). The Quraysh became traders under the leadership of Qusayy's grandson Hāshim and played an important role in the growth of the caravan trade in the region. Meccan trade was greatly stimulated by the need for leather created by the Roman army in the province of Syria after its devastation by the Perso-Roman wars (Crone 2007). The Quraysh were thus "the merchants of Arabs" (Crone 1987:153), and their trade acted as a force for economic unification of the Hijaz. Furthermore, it had important political implications. The Quraysh created a military force consisting of mercenary Bedouins and Ethiopians (*ahābish*) to protect the caravans, which also enhanced its political predominance (Fahd 1989).[4] Meccan trade was also based on pacts (*ilāf*) among the clans of the Quraysh and the Bedouin tribes, not only of mutual help and protection but also for the guarding of caravans on a profit-sharing basis (Peters 1994:58–59, 68–69). The pacts amounted to a "Pax Meccana" in the Hijaz (Kister 1965:120–21). The situation was, however, rife with tension and conflict. The disparate and heterogeneous coexistence of the commercial ethos of the city of Mecca and the superimposition of religious unions on kingship ties did not always work smoothly. Rival religious and tribal cleavages could overlap, producing intermittent conflict, as they did between Mecca and Tā'if (Chelhod 1958:97, 113). This was inevitable as long as the religioculturally unified and economically integrated tribal society of western Arabia remained segmented and without any central or otherwise-unified political authority structure.

The above internalist view of religion in pagan Arabia is certainly not without sociological cogency and reveals the social functions of religion in tribal society. It needs to be supplemented by the ecumenical context of peripheral Arab paganism. The Arabian religion embedded in peninsular kinship and tribal institutions, as depicted above, did not in fact remain immune from ecumenical religious aspirations to transcendence and universalism. Clan and local deities and their cults coexisted with translocal, ecumenical deities of late antique paganism, with or without their cults and shrines but certainly with horizontal and vertical transfer of free-floating names and attributes (Al-Azmeh 2014). Furthermore, the evidence from the Qur'ān itself leaves no room for any doubt about the inroads made by Manichaean and Jewish (and perhaps Gnostic Christian) angel worship and the mélange of their respective, mitigated monotheistic traits (Crone 2010). Foreign—indeed, extraterrestrial—angels had deeply penetrated the cracks between the segments of the pagan religion embedded in Arabia's tribal social structure. Messianism was implanted within these cracks with Muhammad's monotheistic revolution. This implantation and its consequences require a different chapter and are therefore treated elsewhere (Arjomand, forthcoming:ch. 2). What I propose to do here is to analyze the foundation of a new religiopolitical community on the basis of his "realized messianism" as a constitutive revolution that resulted in the unification of Arabia.

Revolutionary Mobilization: Holy Struggle (*Jihād*) in the Path of God

The evident demise of mediated Persian authority in Yathrib had aggravated the endemic violence typical of segmented "stateless societies," setting its main tribes of Aws and Khazraj in unresolved deadly conflict. What was needed for its resolution was a holy judge-arbiter (*hakam*), the only native extratribal authority known in Arabia and one similar to the judges of the Old Testament. A number of aldermen (*naqib*s) from Yathrib were in charge of the search for one and met Muhammad at a trade fair. According to the earliest account of the meeting between Muhammad and the Yathribites in 'Aqaba, the aldermen gave Muhammad the following pledge: "We are of you and you are of us, whoever comes to us of your companions, or you yourself if you come to us, we shall defend you (*numni'ka*) as we would defend ourselves" (Tabari, 6.136; Mélamède 1934). They probably also gave him an armed escort of four or five bodyguards who later migrated with Muhammad (Lecker 2000:164–65). As the heavenly counterpart to the pledge at 'Aqaba, Muhammad received permission to fight (Q. 22.40–42), whereupon he ordered his companions to migrate from Mecca to the future Medina (*Life* 213). The prophet thus chose his sacred enclave and embarked on the "migration" (to a sacred enclave) (*hijra*) that was to mark the beginning of the Islamic era. Those who undertook *hijra* and joined him in the sacred enclave had the special status of Migrant (*muhājir*). God's permission to fight was probably first given to the Migrants "who have been expelled from their dwellings without any cause" (Q. 22.39) and then to all Muslims "to fight in the path of God" (Q. 2.244).[5] The coincidence of the two orders is not an accidental event in Muhammad's biography but was essential to his struggle for this-worldly translation of the apocalyptic vision that began in Medina. This is proven by the striking association between migration (*hijra*) and the struggle (*jihād*) "in the path of God" (Q. 8.71–73, 9.19–20) in the Qur'ān (Crone 1994a:354–55).

Migrating to the sacred enclave of Allāh meant forgoing the protection of the partner-god and thus discarding associationism in favor of monotheism (Watt 1988:20, 25). This was the condition sine qua non of Islam or submission to God: "To those who believed but did not make the *hijra* it is not for you [pl.] to give 'protection' [*wilāya*] until they do make the *hijra*" (Q. 8.72). Muhammad also had to derive his own authority exclusively from Allāh. It is striking how the many references to Muhammad as the Messenger of God occur exclusively in the Medinan verses of the Qur'ān (Welch 1983:43). Nevertheless, the Meccan verses of the Qur'ān had already developed the monotheism that formed the basis of Mohammad's struggle in the path of God and his concurrent construction of a community of believers.

The evolution of the conception of the one God without partners from its earliest identification with the "Lord [*rabb*] of this house [Kaʿba]" and the southern Arabian Rahmān, through the "Lord of the creatures" (*rabb al-ʿālamayn*) and to the Allāh without any sons, daughters, and partners was complete by the time of Muhammad's migration, thus culminating in the universal monotheism. By the same time, the notion of the Qur'ān had evolved from its literal meaning of "recitation"—recitation of the revealed word of God corresponding to a celestial register (*lawh al-mahfuz*), where everything is enumerated in the writing of scripture (*kitāb*) (Q. 78.29)—to something of both Scripture/Book and its interpretation (Sinai 2006:116, 120, 124). Nevertheless, the Qur'ān remained oral recitation, and the Qur'ānic message as a whole was not yet identified with the Book (*kitāb*), which denoted its biblical narratives and allusions (Neuwirth 2006:102). Upon his arrival, according to the traditionist Bayhaqi, Muhammad found the inhabitants of Medina "a mixed lot, consisting of the believers united by the mission (*daʿwa*) of the Messenger of God, the polytheists who worshiped idols, and the Jews who were the armored people of the forts and the allies (*halifs*) of the tribes of Aws and Khazraj, and wished to establish concord among all of them" (as translated in Lecker 1995:31). Muhammad's emigrants were supported by the Medinan believers and organized several raids, typically by a handful of Muslims, against the caravans of the Quraysh to sustain themselves from booty.

Muhammad, the prophet of the end of time, began the conquest of Arabia as the Prophet of the *malhama* (war); his apocalyptic battle was no other than the battle of Badr in Ramadan of year 2 (March 624), when God, according to the Qur'ān (3.123–25), sent down three thousand angels to fight alongside Muhammad's army.[6] Just as God had sent Michael to help in the great apocalyptic battle of the book of Daniel, the Muslim tradition has Gabriel and Michael each lead a thousand angelic troops to the right and left of Muhammad (and the archangel Isrāfil is added at the head of another thousand to reach the number given in the Qur'ān) (al-Wāqidi 1966:1.57–71, 113; Ibn Sa'd 1917:3.9) and considers the battle of Badr as "the day of redemption/deliverance [*furqān*]" mentioned in Q. 8.41 as a parallel to Exodus 14.13. With the help of the angelic host, Muhammad's three hundred or so holy warriors, who constituted almost the entire body of male Muslims at the time, defeated an army consisting of three times as many Meccans and their allies. The rich booty was distributed among the 313 or 314 holy warriors, three-quarters of whom were Medinan converts (al-Wāqidi 1966:1.23; *Life* 336).[7]

The battle of Badr also sealed the institutionalization of holy warfare as the distinctive Islamic path of revolutionary struggle for the religion of God (*din Allāh*): "Fight them until there is no more persecution and religion, all of it, is God's" (Q. 8.39). In fact, sura 8 of the Qur'ān (*Anfāl*), believed to have been revealed as divine commentary on the battle of Badr (al-Wāqidi 1966:1.131–32), or a section thereof, was often read to the Muslim armies before battle during the Muslim conquests.

Most of the Badr prisoners were ransomed to support the new Muslim community. The victory was also used by Muhammad to have two Medinan pagan intellectual opponents of Islam executed by their own converted clansmen (to avoid vengeance and payment of blood money) (Watt 1956:178–79).[8] A few months later (625/3), Muhammad besieged the fortification of the rich Jewish clan of Qaynuqā', who were goldsmiths and whose strength is put at three hundred armored men and four hundred men without mail, until they surrendered unconditionally (*Life* 363; Donner 2010:35). Their Arab protector from the tribe of Khazraj, 'Abdallāh Ibn Ubayy, who almost passed for a king before Muhammad's arrival (*Life* 279), interceded for them. He reportedly felt confident enough to grab the Prophet by the neck until the latter said, "You can have them!" (*Life* 363). The lives of the Jewish clan were spared, but their belongings were expropriated and they were expelled from the Medina settlement. This alarmed a half-Arab nobleman of the Jewish clan of Nadir, Kaʿb b. al-Ashraf, who went to Mecca to confer with the Quraysh and began composing anti-Muslim satires. Muhammad sanctioned a conspiracy involving Kaʾb's half brother to assassinate him and absolved the conspirators from the sin of lying. After the assassination of Kaʿb b. al-Ashraf, he reportedly added the injunction, "Kill any Jew that falls into your power," whereupon an Arab wantonly murdered his Jewish ally. The murder of Kaʿb b. al-Ashraf "cast terror among the Jews, and there was not a Jew in Medina who did not fear for his life" (*Life* 367–69). At this point some less important Jewish leaders approached Muhammad, and he seized the opportunity to conclude a pact with them that reaffirmed the status of the Jews as members of the unified community of Medina but also obligated them to pay the war tax (Serjeant 1978:32). The pact, which was kept by ʿAli b. Abi Tālib (Lecker 1995:26), formed the nucleus of what modern scholars have referred to as "the constitution of Medina" (CM) to be analyzed presently (Wellhausen 1975; Humphreys 1991: 92–98).

While proselytizing and winning new converts who would accept his prophetic authority on the basis of the new revelation, Muhammad wasted no time consolidating his authority as a judge-arbiter (*hakam*) according to Arabian customary law, which included legislative authority (Serjeant 1978:1–2). In doing so, he needed divine succor, and the phrase "obey God and his Messenger" appears some forty times in the Qurʾān in verses that are mostly dated to his first three years in Medina (Watt 1956:233).

The next battle, ʿUhud, in March 625/3,[9] went badly for the Muslims. The Helpers (the Medinans who supported the Migrants when they arrived in Medina), who bore the brunt of casualties, found the support of their Muslim brethren burdensome. ʿAbdallāh Ibn Ubayy openly criticized Muhammad for following the hotheaded youths against his own better judgment and Ibn Ubayy's advice and thereby bringing disaster to the Medinan Helpers, seventy of whom were killed. The power struggle between ʿAbdallāh Ibn Ubayy and Muhammad intensified as the tension between the Prophet and his Jewish clients increased. No longer trusting the Jews of Medina, Muhammad asked his young secretary, Zayd b. Thābit, to learn Hebrew and the Jewish script in 625/4, which the latter did in seventeen days (N. Abbott 1967:247, 257). That short time, however, must have been spent brushing up on the Hebrew and Aramaic that Zayd, who was teased as "a Jew with two sidelocks," had already learned at a Jewish school (*maktab/ midrās*), most likely in the quarter of the Qaynuqāʿ goldsmiths, together with the literates among the elite of the Khazraj such as Ibn Ubayy and Saʿd b. ʿUbāda (Lecker 1997).

Some five months after the battle of ʿUhud, Muhammad decided to expel Ibn Ubayy's other Jewish allies, the Banu al-Nadir, and sent them an ultimatum. Ibn Ubayy encouraged the Jewish clan to resist, saying to them, according to a common Qurʾān interpretation, "Surely, if you are expelled, we shall go out with you, and if you are attacked in war, we shall help you." This is immediately denied by the Qurʾān (59.11): "God testifieth that they are lying." Following two serious setbacks which cost the lives of nearly fifty missionaries sent by Muhammad to the nomads, he accused the Banu al-Nadir of conspiracy to kill him and attacked their oasis, destroying their palm trees. One of the two former "kings" or fiscal agents of the Persian Empire were members of the Banu al-Nadir. The clan surrendered in August 625/4, on the condition that they would keep their movable property, except for their weapons; they were deported, some to Syria, others to Khaybar. Two of them reportedly "became Muslims in order to retain their property." The rest packed their belongings on camels and left "with such pomp and splendor as had never been seen in any tribe in their days." Their land was distributed among the Migrants. The Medinan Helpers were excluded, presumably because they did not need land, except for two who pleaded poverty (*Life* 437–38).

The Nadir exiles from the Jewish settlement of Khaybar approached the Meccan pagans in the hope of being restored to Medina, and Muhammad dispatched a team including a converted son of a Jewish woman of Khaybar to assassinate their leader, Abu Rafiʾ Sallām b. Abi'l-Huqayq, most probably in 626/5 (Watt 1956:30–31; Newby 1971:217–20). Meanwhile, Ibn Ubayy persisted in his opposition and, over a year or so later, spread scandalous rumors about Muhammad's young wife, ʿĀyisha. Muhammad summoned a meeting of Ibn Ubayy's fellow Khazraj tribesmen to strip him of his tribal protection from punishment but did not succeed. But soon thereafter, Ibn Ubayy ceased his opposition and made a lasting peace with Muhammad, who performed his funeral rites himself (Watt 1956:185–87).

As the mobilization for holy struggle continued and the number of holy warriors increased from about three hundred in 624 (Badr) to three thousand with thirty-six horsemen in 627, the war levy and booty from raids on the Quraysh caravans became inadequate and there was an evident need for additional fiscal prey (*tuʿma*) (Kister 1986:88–89). According to some reports, the other kingly Jewish clan, the Banu Qurayza, had at first joined the Banu al-Nadir in the summer of 625/4 but then had come to terms with Muhammad, concluding a pact of peaceful coexistence (*muwādaʿa*) (Kister 1986:82–85). Coexistence, however, turned out to be neither easy nor peaceful, and the Qurayza, the strongest of the Jewish clans of Medina, became Muhammad's most lucrative fiscal prey in 627/5, immediately after the battle of the Trench. Perhaps as a vestige of their former status as the agents of Persia, the Qurayza possessed a large number of weapons in their storehouses and lent the Muslims tools to dig a trench around Medina, which was besieged by the Quraysh and its allied tribes. However, the Qurayza also established contacts with the Quraysh through instigators from the Nadir exiles. After some inconclusive fighting, the Quraysh and their allies lifted the siege and left in disarray. Muhammad at once laid siege to the fortification of the Qurayza two miles from Medina. The Qurayza surrendered unconditionally after two or three weeks, even though one companion of the Prophet had indicated by a gesture that their lives would not be spared. The number of Muhammad's holy warriors now exceeded three thousand. To arm them he confiscated 1,500 swords and shields, 300 coats of arms, and 200 spears from the Banu Qurayza. Insisting on observance of the legal formality of arbitration by a man from the protecting Arab tribe of Aws, Saʿd b. Muʿādh, a man who had previously managed the assassination of Kaʿb b. al-Ashraf and was severely wounded during the siege, approved the judicial murder of the Jewish captives. Some four hundred men, constituting almost the entire male population, were executed by the Migrants; six were spared by their three Medinan Arab confederate clans so as to avoid vengeance and payment of blood money (Watt 1956:214–16). The Qurayza women and children, numbering about one thousand, were taken captive and sold into slavery. The proceeds went to Muhammad's new treasury, while he made grants of their land and palm trees to the Migrants, who were to give back the trees allotted to them by the Medinan Helpers (Kister 1986:90–96). Medina was thus cleared of the Jewish clans and Muhammad became the undisputed ruler of the united community he had set up there.

Political success did not lessen Muhammad's sense of living at the end of time and preparing for the Last Judgment. For this reason, he insisted that his mosque be built, in accordance with Gabriel's instructions, as "a booth like the booth of Moses thy brother" (Kister and Hiskett 1962:154) and without a roof. When the palm branches that served as its walls were replaced by bricks about the time of the battle of the Trench, he refused to add a roof and retained the Mosaic form appropriate for the end of time. Nevertheless, success also sharpened the Prophet's political pragmatism. After the battle of the Trench, Muhammad married the widowed Muslim daughter of his distant cousin Abu Sufiyān, the leader of the pagan Quraysh, who gradually ceased to take part in its military operations and was conspicuously absent during the negotiations for the treaty of al-Hudaybiyya in March 628/6 between Muhammad and the Quraysh. Some three months later, Muhammad attacked the rich Jewish settlement of Khaybar, rewarding some 1,600 Muslims who had pledged their steadfastness in an anxious moment before the truce of Hudaybiyya with booty and land.[10] Despite its disadvantages, notably the undertaking to return Muslim refugees to the Quraysh, which the Quraysh did not capitalize on (Görke 2000), the truce of Hudaybiyya enabled Muhammad to take part in a pilgrimage and thus paved the way for the taking of Mecca in January 630/8 and for him to realize his dream of the believers "entering the Holy Mosque in security, God willing, with your heads shaven, not fearing" (Q. 48.27). The importance of appropriating the hajj for clearing Islam of the suspicion of foreignness and making it firmly Arabian cannot be overemphasized. Muhammad marched into Mecca with some ten thousand armed men (as compared to the three thousand he could muster three years earlier). Abu Sufiyān visited his camp secretly and arranged for a general amnesty. Within a month of the conquest of Mecca, Muhammad added some two thousand men to his army and defeated a coalition of the old opponents of the Quraysh in Hunayn. The wholesale conversion of the old Quraysh oligarchy took place rapidly, with the "winning of [their] hearts" (Q. 960) with a generous distribution of the booty from Hunayn. In the following year, he drew heavily on the Quraysh aristocracy for sending his first governors / fiscal agents to different tribal areas of Arabia (Shoufani 1973:26). This policy of "winning the hearts" caused considerable resentment among old Muslims, especially the Medinan Helpers, who reportedly got nothing in Hunayn (*Life* 594–97; Watt 1956:348–53). Nevertheless, the wisdom of Muhammad's policy was proven by the subsequent fact that the Quraysh leaders, despite their late conversion, remained faithful to the new Islamic state and made a major military contribution to the reunification of Arabia immediately after his death.[11] The conquest of Mecca and the defeat of the pagan tribal confederation in Hunayn made Muhammad the undisputed master of Arabia, and the close and distant tribes hastened to send "delegations" to him in Medina to accept Islam and join his unified polity (Ibn Saʿd 1917:1.2.38–86).[12] In the last months of 630/9, he was able to send an army of thirty thousand to Tabuk.

With the change in the composition of Muhammad's polity in the last five years of his life came a corresponding change in the pattern of motivation. Like any leader of a socioreligious movement, Muhammad always had to face the typical dilemma of "mixed motivation" by offering his followers rewards in both this and the other world.[13] The apocalyptic vision that motivated the battle of Badr, and found confirmation in victory attributed to God's dispatch of the army of angels, was punctured in the next battle, the battle of ʿUhud, when God let his gentile prophet be defeated and sent no angels to help him. According to Ibn Ishāq (*Life* 395), this mixture of rewards in both worlds had been reinforced after the disastrous battle of ʿUhud: "And he who desires the reward of this world We will give him it; and he who desires the reward of the next world We will give him it and We shall reward the thankful" (Q. 3.145).

Now the mix of motives had to be made considerably more this-worldly for the tribesmen who had joined the original holy warriors. This was to be expected. With Muhammad's increasingly realized messianism, the apocalyptic battles of the end of time as *malāhim* (the plural of *malhima*, meaning "war" in Hebrew) went dormant and were relegated to the millennialist reservoir, to be reactivated by the opponents of the Umayyad caliphate decades later. The more routine idea of endeavor or struggle (*jihād*) on the path of God came to the forefront. The holy warriors (Migrants) had been maintained on booty from the tribes, but as the Pax Islamica expanded and the confiscation of Jewish settlements was completed, northward expansion was the only remaining outlet for raids and booty (Watt 1956:145).

From the viewpoint of the teleology of Muhammad's revolution, this unification of Arabia was an incidental result of the triumph of the religion of God. Muhammad undertook the breaking of the idols of the Kaʿba himself, beginning with the destruction of Hubal, the red amber statue in human form. Abu Sufiyān had led the pagan Meccans at ʿUhud, their most successful battle against Muhammad, with the cry "Hubal be exalted!" to which Muhammad had responded, "Allāh is more exalted and more glorious!" (Ibn al-Kalbi 1965:28). Muhammad sent ʿAli b. Abi Tālib, Mughira b. Shuʿba, and Khālid b. al-Walid to destroy, respectively, the three goddesses, Manāt, the Lāt, and the ʿUzza (Ibn al-Kalbi 1965:15–17, 25–28). The idol of the tribes of Khathʿam and Bajila, Dhu'l-Khalsa, stood until the last year of Muhammad's life, when he commissioned Jarir b. ʿAbdallāh to lead the delegation from Bajila to destroy it (Ibn Saʿd 1917:1.2.78). The Khathʾam fiercely defended their idol, and one hundred of them were killed before the idol was destroyed (Ibn al-Kalbi 1965:35–36). The destruction of the idols meant the liquidation of the social organization of tribal Arabia and, above all, of autonomous tribal political leadership (Lecker 1993:343). What was left to complete the unfolding of the religious *telos* of Muhammad's revolution was the destruction of a handful of rival Arabian monotheistic prophets, the most important and powerful being Musaylima of Yamāma, the prophet of al-Rahmān, in an area close to Mecca (around present-day Riyadh). This was done by his successor, Abu Bakr (632–34) (Kister 2002).

The destruction of the old, segmentary political order was thus complete. The construction of a new political community and government had barely begun, however. As we shall see, these tasks, especially the second—

the construction of a new authority structure and government—remained incomplete at Muhammad's death. The unfolding of the teleology of the revolution was thus to continue under his successors.

The Construction of a New Community (*Umma*) in Medina

The greatest achievement of Muhammad's constitutive revolution in Arabia was the foundation of a universalist community of believers whose potential for territorial expansion resulted in the creation of a vast Muslim empire not long after his death. This achievement went hand in hand with and was indeed subordinated to the elaboration of Islam as the universalist religion of Muhammad's community of believers.

The Medinan verses of the Qur'ān become markedly different, both in form and in substance. The mysterious letters at the opening of the early suras, taken by some to be transcribed from the celestial register, give way to the introductory phrase "these are signs of God," while the community of Muhammad's hearers who appeared as part of pagan Arabia and "outside the Judaeo-Christian tradition gradually acquire a 'Biblicizing' outlook on many things" (Sinai 2011:414). The Qur'ān is now the Book of God par excellence. Islam, originally meaning "surrender" and "submission," as with Abraham's submission to God, is first differentiated from faith (*imān*) as a specific religion (Cantwell Smith 1978) and then from Judaism and Christianity as the restoration of the original and unadulterated Abrahamic monotheism. Infidelity (*kufr*) is increasingly coupled with pagan associationism (*shirk*), now describing Jews and Christians as well as pagan Arabs, and both notions are used as antonyms for Islam, the universal religion of Muhammad as the Seal of the Prophets (Izutsu [1966] 2002:187–202).

The idea of the *umma* as a community designated for salvation through a prophet is already strongly present in the Meccan verses of the Qur'ān (Denny 1977). Such a community, however, could not be constituted in Arabia without a revolution as I have defined the term: it required a radical transformation of the politically segmented tribal society and the structure of authority that held them apart. Although the Meccan converts had been individuals, Medina witnessed the phenomenon of acceptance of Islam by whole clans (Watt 1956:170–71).

The constitutive revolution began with Muhammad's migration to Medina. Muhammad had taken cognizance of the existing kinship and tribal solidarities and sought to harness them for the propagation of his religious mission. His missionaries to Medina had been sent to the Banu al-Najjār clan of Khazraj, the clan of his maternal grandmother (*Life* 199;

Mélamède 1934:48), and he himself resided with them when he migrated and built his mosque in their quarter (Tabari, 8.xvii, 4–5). Indeed, what must be considered his first act of foundation of a community based on faith, but also buttressed by clan solidarity according to customary law, may even have preceded the Constitution of Medina slightly. Probably one of Muhammad's first acts of legislation for his Muslim followers in Medina was the institution of Brotherhood (*muʾākhāt*) between the Migrants from Mecca and their local hosts, the Helpers.[14] The Helpers had provided their emigrant "brothers" with land and palm trees (*Life* 231–35). Muhammad's adoption of the rite bonding men into brotherhood through the mixing of their blood dates from before the migration to Medina and continued throughout the rest of his life. Muhammad's institution of fraternization between the Migrants and their Yathribite hosts was in fact a constitutional act, and its legal implications, notably mutual inheritance, were spelled out (Wellhausen 1883:554; Amir-Moezzi 2006:39–40).

Shortly after his arrival in Medina in 622/1, "the Messenger of God wrote a document (*kitāb*) between the Emigrants (*muhājirun*) and the Helpers (*ansār*), and in it he made a peace and a covenant with the Jews, establishing them in their religion and possessions, and stated the reciprocal obligations" (*Life* 231, slightly modified). This document or set of documents written between 622/1 and 627/6 is in fact the oldest Muslim historical document preserved, being even older than most verses of the Qurʾān. It is described in Islamic sources as Muhammad's pact with the Jews of Medina but is called the Constitution of Medina by modern scholars.[15] Although the notion of constitution can be accepted despite its obvious anachronism, it is very clear that the document says nothing about a *state* or form of government. Its greatest significance, by contrast, stems from its constitution of the *umma*, the consequent Muslim community of believers.

The Constitution of Media consists of a series of pacts, which were correctly executed and through which "Muhammad the Prophet [*al-nabi*]" (CM A.1) secured recognition of his authority as the judge-arbiter to whom all disputes were to be referred on behalf of Allāh (CM B.4).[16] One of the later clauses reiterates the requirement of referring disputes "to Allāh and to Muhammad, the Messenger of Allāh" (CM F4). The potentially expansive quality of this authority is evident. Those subject to this authority are constituted as "a unified community [*umma wāhida*] set apart from [other] people" (CM A.2a). The Qurʾān (21.92) duly sanctioned the new social compact for the believers: "This community of yours is a unified community, and I am your Lord, so worship me."[17] In fact, the unified community was religiously plural and "a rather loose heterogeneous political entity," comprising not only Muslims but also non-Muslim clans. As the Muslims were its soul, "the more the new faith grew, the more the *umma* overshadowed the clans" (Wellhausen 1975:131). Individuals who lost the protection of their tribes by joining "the united community" (*umma wāhida*) were the beneficiaries of a novel contractual solidarity. They were protected by its security under God but compensated according to the customary blood money and ransom rates (CM A.2c–j), and the Jews joining it were assured of parity in this regard (CM A.3a, 8). All the faithful covenanters with Muhammad (*mu'minin*)[18] were thus put under the protection (*dhimma*) of God, which the least of them could extend on behalf of all (CM A.7), and none of them could be killed in retaliation for the killing of any infidel (CM A.6). The united community was given collective responsibility for the punishment of crimes and treason among its members (CM A.5).

The tribal social structure of Medina formed the basis for the construction of Muhammad's *umma*. Under the Constitution of Medina, each clan kept "its organization and leadership." The "Emigrants from the Quraysh" were constituted into a clan (CM A.3), alongside the clans of the Aws and the Khazraj. The inner part of Medina was declared a sacred place (*haram*) for the covenanters (CM F, H; Denny 1977:45), just as Abraham had reportedly declared Mecca a sacred area (Rubin 1985:11). A pact of tolerance allowed the Jewish covenanters of the united community to practice their religion, as the Muslims did theirs, as long as they paid the war levy (*nafaqa*) alongside the other covenanters and refrained from treason (CM E.3–3b, G; Rubin 1985:12).

This last clause points to the crucial fact that, from the moment of creation of the new community, Muhammad was also making constitutional provisions for the revolutionary struggle (*jihād*) on the path of God. That a levy was imposed on the covenanters and their Jewish affiliates for the purpose is a minor aspect of this development. The general peace and security of God eliminated the legitimacy of the use of violence by politically autonomous segments of Arabian tribal society. The monopoly on the legitimate use of violence was in principle invested in the united community, thereby laying the foundation for a unified structure of authority—a state—devoted to the realization of the final end of the prophetic mission: "The covenanters shall make peace only in unity. No covenanter shall make peace apart from other covenanters in fighting [*qitāl*] on the path of God—and that only as a just and equitable decision by them. And all raiding parties shall fight with us one after another. And the covenanters shall execute retaliation on behalf of one another with respect to their blood shed on the path of God" (CM A.9–11).

Elsewhere, I have argued for the division of this composite document into three parts, as each part has its formal coherence as a legal deed (Arjomand 2010). The first part is interpreted as the deed of foundation of Muhammad's *umma*, not yet a community of individual believers but a confederation of clans and their clients unified in the struggle on the path of God. The second part of the Constitution of Medina guaranteed religious freedom to Jewish confederates, thus laying the foundation of the later Muslim system of religious pluralism; it created the first Muslim sanctuary (*ḥaram*) and introduced elements of individual responsibility. The third part, considered a supplement to the second, concerned the defense of the city of Medina against the Quraysh and added one new Jewish clan to the confederation. Taken altogether, the Constitution of Medina thus transformed pagan tribal vengeance into holy warfare and amounted to a pact of tolerance that allowed Jewish covenanters of the united community to have their religion, as Muslims had theirs, as long as they paid the war levy and refrained from treason.

The Unification of Arabia and the Emergence of a Composite Muslim Polity

The decade of struggle and warfare on the path of God had set sons against fathers and kinsman against kinsman. Muhammad's followers were each other's avengers of blood on the warpath of God, ignoring tribal customary law and family attachment (Wolf 1951). The Constitution of Medina displaced, desacralized, and subordinated the old ties of kinship. This was duly confirmed in the Qur'ān: "Verily, they who have believed and fled their homes and spent their substance for the cause of God, and they who have taken in the Prophet and been helpful to him, shall be near of kin to the other" (Q. 8.73). It also brought Muhammad's own migrant community in line with the earlier Qur'ānic conception of a new community of salvation. When the term *umma* regained currency after the death of the Prophet, however, it no longer meant the unified political community of Medina but the Islamic community of believers. Each *umma* was now a community of salvation constituted by a divine messenger. The Jews and Christians were the *umma*s of Moses and Jesus, respectively, as the Muslims were the *umma* of Muhammad. Furthermore, the peace and security of God eliminated the legitimacy of violence by clans as autonomous segments of Arabian tribal society. The near monopoly of the legitimate internal and external use of violence was in principle invested in the united community under the authority of "Muhammad the Prophet." Muhammad's authority thus instituted was, however, not developed by him or in the Qur᾽ān with the purpose of providing constitutional foundations for a state.

Muhammad's tribal policy was an aspect of creating a society and polity on a religious foundation around the belief in one God and Muhammad as his Messenger. As Muhammad's power grew in Medina, Arabian tribes in the surrounding deserts could put themselves under the protection of God and his Messenger without professing Islam. In this way, Muhammad created an intertribal security system, a Pax Islamica, around the growing polity in Medina. The Pax Islamica had a religious kernel: it was a system based on "the security of God and his Messenger." As he grew stronger, he demanded conversion to Islam from prospective allies brought under God's protection but continued to make purely political alliances with distant and powerful tribes that came to submit to the Pax Islamica on the basis of the Arab norms of tribal alliance (Watt 1956:144–46). In the year 626/5, he made a special arrangement with four hundred men from the Muzayna tribe, granting them the status of "emigrants" (*muhājirun*) within their own territories—which meant they would not have to join the *jihād*, thereby making an exception to the coupling of *hijra* with *jihād* as a condition of Islam (Madelung 1986:231–32). The *umma* was not a suitable term to apply to this confederate polity, and as Watt (1956:247) points out, it no longer appears in the Qur᾽ān or the treaties.

The reason was the radical change in the basis of Muhammad's domination in Arabia. Khālid b. al-Walid and ʿAmr b. ʿĀs, two important tribal leaders of the Quraysh, who were late converts like Abu Sufiyān, had already joined Muhammad in Mecca during the summer before the fall of Mecca and had taken part, with three thousand men, in the campaign of Mu᾽ta in September and October 629/8. Only seven hundred of the twelve thousand men who fought in Hunayn, the decisive battle for unification of Arabia under Muhammad, were Migrants (Watt 1956:53–59). Although their number had multiplied almost tenfold since the battle of Badr six years earlier, these early Muslims or members of Muhammad's charismatic religious movement were now a small minority in his armed forces.

Mohammad's unification of Arabia was by no means complete at the time of his death, and his success as a prophet had engendered a number of counterclaims to prophecy among the tribes resisting integration.[19] The most important rival claimant was Musaylima, who presented himself as the prophet of al-Rahmān among the tribe of Banu Hanifa. An exchange of letters between him and Muhammad, even if apocryphal, illustrates the integrative teleology of Muhammad's monotheism in contrast to the tribal autonomist one of the rival prophets of dissident tribes. Musaylima:

"To Muhammad the Prophet of God. Greeting unto thee! Etc. God has made me partake with thee in the rule. One half of the earth belongs to us [i.e., Banu Ḥanifa] and one half to the Quraysh." Muhammad: "From Muhammad the Prophet of God to Musaylima the liar. Greeting unto those who follow the right guidance! Etc. The earth belongs to God, he gives it as an inheritance to whosoever of his servants he pleases. And the end will be in favour of the pious" (al-Biruni 1879:192).

Muhammad did not live long enough to settle the constitution of the new polity or to lay down a set of rules for its government. This contrasts sharply with Muhammad's regulation of warfare, which formed the basis of the Muslim conquests, or what we might call "the export of the Islamic revolution" that resulted from the mobilization of the Arab tribes. One curious consequence of this failure is that, by the middle of the seventh century, "the Muslim state appears as a huge army accompanied by the most rudimentary civil bureaucracy" (Donner 1993:312).

Consequences of Muhammad's Constitutive Revolution in Arabia

As many of the long-term consequences of Muhammad's constitutive revolution in Arabia were not completely realized until its social revolution, examined in chapter 8, had occurred, I shall in this final section point out its important consequences in the short run.

Succession to Charismatic Leadership

The biggest unsettled questions at the time of the Prophet's death were those of legitimate rulership and organization of the state. The absence of reference to the form of government and political leadership in the Qurʾān is truly astonishing. Donner explains it as a consequence of Muhammad's apocalyptic expectation of the Day of Judgment, which would obviate the need for laying down norms of government. This forced his successors "to develop a theory of political legitimacy with almost no Qurʾānic basis" (Donner 1998:45). Madelung (1997:16–17), by contrast, argues that Muhammad saw the precedent of the rulership of the families of the earlier prophets mentioned in the Qurʾān as applying to his family as well, seeing a Hashemite monarchy as the obvious solution to the problem of succession after his death. Although Madelung may be right in arguing that this hierocratic principle of kinship to the Prophet was closest to Muhammad's intention of transforming his prophetic charisma to the charisma of his lineage by establishing a house of Muhammad on the biblical model of the house of David and the house of ʿImrān (Moses), for his *umma* three other principles were also imperfectly adumbrated in the sayings and deeds that had the potential for further logical development and corresponding institutionalization. The most important of these was the principle of seniority or precedence (*sābiqa*) in Islam. There was also the entirely new principle of consensus (*ridā wa'l-jamāʾa*). The weakest in terms of prophetic endorsement was the surviving pre-Islamic principle of nobility and leadership (*sharaf wa'l-riyāsa*) (Sharon 1984). This last principle was, however, favored by the Quraysh oligarchy of late converts whose hearts Muhammad had won at the final stage of the unification of Arabia.

Muhammad's male offspring had predeceased him, and Madelung (1997: 253) follows the Shiʿa in seeing his famous designation of his son-in-law and cousin ʿAli at Ghadir Khumm—"ʿAli is the patron [*mawlā*] of whomever I am a patron of"—as his succession appointment. He points out that the oath of allegiance to ʿAli as the fourth caliph matched this formula. The position argued by Madelung became the principle of Hashemite legitimism when ʿAli's son succeeded him as the caliph after his assassination with the proclamation "I am al-Hasan, the son of Muhammad" and was so addressed by the leading member of the Hashemite clan, ʿAbdallāh b. ʿAbbās, somewhat later during his brief tenure as caliph (Madelung 1997:311, 313). Paradoxically, however, the hierocratic model found relatively little support in the revolutionary power struggle after Muhammad's death and was developed only much later by the Shiʿite sects into the doctrine of the imamate. ʿAli, its main beneficiary, in fact gave his pledge of allegiance to Abu Bakr and ʿUmar, and it was his seniority in Islam that primarily ensured his succession as the fourth caliph, though he also claimed consensus as the basis of his legitimacy in the civil war with Muʿāwiya (Sharon 1984:130–32). The latter greatly reinforced the policy of the third caliph, ʿUthmān, and subordinated the principle of precedence in Islam to that of nobility and leadership.

Immediately after the death of the Prophet, Abu Bakr and ʿUmar were clearly apprehensive about the hierocratic principle, which would result in the caliphate and prophethood being reunited in the same family, meaning that the Banu Hāshim would monopolize both (Lammens 1910:16–17; Madelung 1997:22). Abu Bakr and ʿUmar were of very modest origins and must have counted on the support of "the disinherited" (*mustadʿafun*), who, as we shall see, were numerous among the early converts. They broke into a meeting of the Helpers led by Saʿd b. ʿUbāda and pushed them into accepting Abu Bakr as the *khalifa* (successor) of the Messenger of God. ʿUmar managed the streets of Medina and secured the allegiance of the residents, making an alliance with the obscure Fihrite on the margin of Quraysh, Abu ʿUbayda b. al-Jarrāh, who was later designated as his successor but killed in battle (Lammens 1910:116–17, 142; Madelung 1997:44–46). The Hashemite clan had the satisfaction of burying Muhammad and excluding Abu Bakr and his daughter ʿĀyisha from attending his funeral, and they unanimously refused to take the oath of allegiance to Abu Bakr for six months (Madelung 1997:43).

Abu Bakr, seconded by ʿUmar and supported by the early converts, claimed legitimacy on the basis of their precedence in Islam and developed the idea of the successorship (*khilāfat*) of the Prophet. They thus instituted the caliphate and fought the Arab tribes which refused to accept that the Prophet had founded a state authorized to receive taxes, as well as those who followed rival Arabian prophets in what became known anachronistically as the wars of apostasy (*ridda*). On pragmatic grounds, Abu Bakr argued that only the tribe of Quraysh could rule a unified Arabia, and therefore, the caliphate belonged to it (Madelung 1997:31, 37). Continuing Muhammad's policy of "winning the hearts," he used the leaders of the clans of Quraysh to subdue Arabia, alienating the Helpers, from whose leader he had snatched the caliphate. Like the Hashemites, the Helpers "tried to restore their faded fortune by backing" ʿAli, and when he lost the First Civil War, they were no longer part of the political elite (Donner 1981:274). When readmitting the defeated "apostate" tribes, meanwhile, Abu Bakr, the first caliph, and ʿUmar, his successor, exacted from their members, upon (re)conversion to Islam, the pledge to obey "whomever God had invested with authority" (*wallā Allāhu'l-amr*) (Kister 1994:100–101).

Like the Hashemites, the old oligarchy of late converts opposed ʿUmar's caliphate and appealed to the "house of Qusayy"; they gained ascendancy under the third caliph, ʿUthmān. After persuading ʿAli's son, al-Hasan, to abdicate the caliphate, Muʿāwiya greatly reinforced ʿUthmān's policy and subordinated the principle of precedence in Islam to that of nobility, and was accused by later generations of thus turning the caliphate into kingship (*mulk*) with the establishment of the Umayyad dynasty.

Religious Settlement

In contrast to his lack of attention to the normative regulation of the political order, Muhammad did institute a system of religious pluralism as part of the realistic modification of the Meccan apocalyptic vision. The gentile prophet of the Meccan period, devoted to the restoration of the primal religion of Abraham, whose "recitation" (*qurʾān*) consisted of the communication of the Enochic "preserved tablet," became "the Messenger of God" in the Medinan verses, and the Torah and the Gospel are explicitly recognized as holy scriptures: "For each of you [i.e., Jews, Christians, Muslims] we have appointed a path and a way, and if God had so willed, He would have made you but one community" (Q. 5.48). The Qur'ān (3.64) also came up with the formula for integrating the Jews as anti-associationist monotheists into the united community: "Say: 'O People of the Book, come to a word (which is) fair between us and you, (to wit) that we serve no one but God, *that we associate nothing with Him,* and that none of us take others as Lords beside God'" (emphasis added). This accommodative pluralism was endorsed by divine revelation: "There is no compulsion in religion [*lā ikrāh fi'l-din*]" (Q. 2.256). According to one important tradition, this verse was revealed on the occasion of the Prophet's decision to accept poll tax from the Magians (Zoroastrians) rather than requiring their forced conversion. This gave the Zoroastrians the same de facto status as the "people of the Book" (*ahl al-kitāb*). This decision provoked the indignation of a group of Muslims, including ʿAbdallāh Ibn Ubayy, who criticized Muhammad for granting the Zoroastrians the privilege he had denied the Arab polytheists. He and his followers were called the "hypocrites" (*munāfiqun*) on account of this opposition. Muhammad remained adamant, however, and reaffirmed that the Arab polytheists would be fought until they professed Islam (Kister 1994:89–91).

There is no evidence that the term *umma* was ever used to refer to the unified Islamic Arabia, nor, a fortiori, to the vast political society unified by the Muslim state after the conquests. The notion of *umma* reverted to its original meaning of a community designated for salvation through a prophet. Competing proselytizing religious communities were the striking feature of the religious situation in late antiquity, and Muhammad conceived of his own *umma*, or community, of believers along the same lines, albeit as the best of them (Q. 3.110) and their (golden) mean (Q. 2.143). The Qur'ān also links the notion of religious community with the "people of the Book" (Q. 2.63, 65; 5.69–70; 22.18). According to the earliest and strangely exclusivist Qur'ān commentaries, the *umma* of Muhammad consisted of the Muslims not contaminated by a pre-Islamic birth (Bashear 1997:44). The Muslim *umma* was thus completely distinct from the society ruled by the caliphate, which comprised other religious communities of the people of the Book. This enabled Muhammad's successors to turn the de facto recognition of different religious communities in the late Sasanian Empire into the pluralistic system of autonomous "protected" religious communities that was distinctively Islamic and eventually developed into the Ottoman millet system (Fowden 2014:97–98). The notion of a political community subject to a ruler entered Islam much later with the reception of Persian political lore. This was the ancient idea of subjects as the flock (*ra'iyya*) of their ruler, who was to govern them with justice (Arjomand 2003).

Absence of Mass Conversions after the Arab Conquests

The social background of the first Muslims who composed the core of Muhammad's charismatic movement was very different from those of either the Quraysh oligarchs or the tribesmen of Arabia who pledged allegiance to Muhammad in his last years. The first Muslims were individual converts. They included six or seven slaves, five women, four brothers of low status, and one man (Bilāl) freed by Abu Bakr. One of the slaves spoke a foreign (Ethiopian) tongue and was a Christian and was said by Muhammad's detractors to have taught him the Qur'ān. Of the eighty-two who migrated to Ethiopia to escape Meccan persecution, five were freedmen or clients (*mawāli*) and the rest were from Meccan clans and included some of Muhammad's cousins (*Life* 143–48, 179–80; Ibn Sa'd 1917:3.1282–83). The Migrants who fought in the battle of Badr included eleven slaves and freedmen (Watt 1956:344). Abu Bakr and 'Umar were merchants who, unlike Muhammad himself and his cousin 'Ali and his son-in-law 'Uthmān, did not belong to the tribal elite. The first clan conversion is reported to have occurred in Medina a little before the Prophet's migration, when, following their leader, Sa'd b. Mu'ādh, "every man and woman among the Banu 'Abdu'l-Ashhal joined Islam" (*Life* 201). Conversion by clans in Medina and among the northern Arabs continued under Muhammad. The second major change came after the conquest of Mecca and the battle of Hunayn, when tribes of southern Arabia and other regions pledged allegiance to Muhammad. As the wars immediately following the death of the Prophet demonstrated, quite a few of these tribes did not acknowledge Muhammad's prophecy and did not convert to Islam, some of them professed Islam but did not want to pay taxes to the nascent Islamic state, and yet others were followers of rival "false prophets" (Kister 2002:13–26).

The changed social composition of the Arab Muslims in the last years of Muhammad's life goes a long way toward explaining the lack of conversion of non-Arab peoples brought under Muslim rule with the Arab conquests following his death. Here we have the crucial factor behind the nature of the export of revolution from Arabia that explains why, contrary to a widespread misperception, it was not accompanied by the mass conversion of the conquered populations. As we shall see in the next chapter, it took another revolution a century and a quarter later to bring this expected consequence to realization.

EIGHT

Islam's Integrative Social Revolution

In the introduction, I alluded to the ancient notion of transfer of sovereignty by God from one nation to another in the book of Daniel; this idea later became known as *translatio imperii*. We find an early proof of the transmission of this notion to the Muslim world in a rousing speech given in July 748 by Qahtaba b. Shabib (d. 749/132), an Arab settler in Khorasan who commanded the revolutionary army advancing to Iran against the Umayyads:

> Men of Khorasan, this land belonged to your forefathers before you, and they were given victory over their enemies on account of their justice and righteous manners, until they changed and became unjust. . . . The God Most High was enraged with them and took away their authority (*soltān*) and gave the humblest nation on earth under their rule [i.e., the Arabs] domination over them. . . . The latter nation ruled with justice and remained faithful to the covenant for a while . . . [but] then they became oppressive in their rule. . . . Therefore [God] has empowered you against them [i.e., the Arabs turned oppressive]. . . . God will give you victory over them. (Tabari, 2.2005)

Qahtaba overran Iran but drowned in Iraq before the final victory of his revolutionary forces in the following year. A decade and a half later, Caliph Abu Jaʿfar al-Mansur celebrated his victory in the revolutionary power struggle and the establishment of the ʿAbbasid Empire by founding a new capital, City of Peace (*madinat al-salām*). Full astrological and geomantic apparatus were used for siting it, and the Zoroastrian astrologer Nawbakht cast the horoscope for the most auspicious hour for its founding. The parameters for the application of astral and geomantic sciences were, however, set by a historical given: the remnants of the Sasanian capital in the fertile black land of Iraq, Ctesiphon, now called al-Madāʾin. The turning point in world history thus celebrated was God's transfer of divinely ordained power (*dawla*, "empire") from the Persians to the Arabs.

The account of the self-destruction of the Umayyad imperial state and the details of the many-sided revolutionary power struggle that resulted in the victory of the ʿAbbasids in the Hashemite revolutionary power struggle are given elsewhere (Arjomand, forthcoming). The goals of this chapter are more limited: I intend to demonstrate, first, that the ʿAbbasid Revolution was an integrative revolution displaying features of both the Aristotelian-Paretan (I.2) and the Khaldunian (I.3) types; and, second, that the revolutionary process can be historicized through periodization.

The Revolution of the Eastern Periphery: Khorasan

When the self-destruction of the Umayyad Empire began with what Muslim historians consider the third *fitna* (civil war) in 744/126, Khorasan, on the northeastern periphery of the empire, was especially ripe for revolution for several reasons. Foremost among these were the social preconditions. Arab tribes had migrated there in large numbers—much larger than to Egypt, by comparison—resulting in considerable Islamicization and mixing of the conquerors and the conquered. Over three generations, the Arab settlers mingled with the non-Arab converts to Islam, who constituted the class of clients (*mawāli*) and whose names appear frequently in our historical texts. Despite the extensive Islamicization and the high proportion of clients, the governors were unwilling to release the new converts from their tax obligation (Dennett 1950:118–19). In 738/120, Nasr b. Sayyār al-Kināni became the Umayyad governor of Khorasan. According to Tabari (2.1665; trans. 26.192), for the next four years "Khorasan throve with a prosperity the like of which it had not enjoyed before that." This enabled Nasr to lower the taxes and nevertheless put together a sumptuous accession gift of a thousand slaves, five hundred maidservants, musical instruments, gold and silver ewers, horses, and falcons for al-Walid II in 743/125 (Tabari, 2.1766; trans. 26.116–17). Surprising as it may seem, a common pattern found in the sociology of revolution is for such an abrupt rise in prosperity to enhance the sense of entitlement among the classes benefiting from it, such as the Khorasanian clients, and to increase their sense of relative deprivation, possibly leading to revolution. The pattern is built into my Aristotelian-Paretan model, which makes the narrowness of the political class and the exclusion of a rising, socially qualified class a cause of revolutions.

The path for the revolutionary movement on the eastern periphery of the Umayyad Empire that finally triumphed in the mid-eighth century had been paved by earlier integrative movements that had arisen in the course of conversion of the region to Islam. The Umayyad governors of Khorasan refused to lift the poll tax (*jizya*) on the new converts, thus stimulating the growth of movements that articulated their grievances and sense of injustice. The missionary activity in Khorasan and Transoxania was mainly the work of the Murji'a movement, which was eventually brought under the leadership of the founder of the first main Sunni school of Islamic law, Abu Hanifa (d. 767/150). The Murji'a became known as the people of equality and justice, and their key ideas were reflected in the teachings of Abu Hanifa, who promulgated the doctrine of *irjā'*, which involved leaving judgment of the worth of Muslims to God while accepting their profession of Islam at face value. Just as notable was the acceptance of the recitation of the Qur'an in Persian, which was even more clearly meant to establish the equality of Arab and non-Arab Muslims (van Ess 1991–97:1.183, 2.491). The first major political manifestation of unrest among the new converts to Islam was the great Murji'ite revolt, led by al-Hārith b. Surayj, which began in 734/116 (Sadighi 1938:35–37).

Al-Hārith arose in Tukharistan and occupied Faryab and conquered Balkh, later known as Murji'ābād (Murji'aville), with four thousand men. He then proceeded in a triumphant march to Gorgan (Jorjan), Taleqan, and Marw al-Rudh. Near Balkh, he was confronted by Nasr b. Sayyār, who was a seasoned Umayyad official and who was jointly in charge of the city. Al-Hārith tried to win over Nasr's troops by summoning them to "the Qur'an, the Sunna and allegiance to the acceptable one (*al-ridā*)" (Tabari, 2.1567; trans. 25.105). This is the first we hear of the Murji'ite idea of a caliphate based on popular consent (the caliph should be "acceptable" to the people). By the time al-Hārith was approaching the capital of Khorasan, Marw, some sixty thousand men—including important *dehqāns* (noblemen and petty kings) of Khorasan and Transoxania and Arab horsemen from his tribe of Tamim and from the Yemenite tribe of Azd—had joined him (Gabrieli 1935a:53–62). The governor of Khorasan confronted him with all his troops. The Arabs in al-Hārith's camp defected and joined the Tamim and Azd contingents of the governor's army, causing al-Hārith's defeat. "The *dehqāns* returned to their own lands" (Tabari, 2.1569–70; trans. 25.107–8). Al-Hārith returned to Balkh, however, to establish his own government and judiciary and resided in the Tobushkān castle in Upper Tukharistan (Tabari, 2.1589–91; trans. 25.126–27). By the time the newly reappointed governor of Khorasan, Asad b. 'Abdallāh al-Qasri, arrived, only Marw and Nishapur remained under Umayyad control (Tabari, 2.1582; trans. 25.119), Transoxania having already been lost at the beginning of the rebellion. The uprising led by al-Hārith spread in the same area covered by the Murji'a movement and can be considered a Murji'ite revolt (Madelung 1982; 1988:18).

It took Asad until the end of 737/118, nearly three years after the outbreak of the rebellion, to suppress it and retake Khorasan. Although al-Hārith b. Surayj fled to the Turks after the failure of his rebellion, he remained active in Turkistan, and appeared well ensconced in the city of Shash (present-day Tashkent) in 739/121. Nasr b. Sayyār, now the governor of Khorasan, persuaded the king of Shash to expel al-Hārith. To take the wind out of al-Hārith's sails, Nasr renewed ʿUmar II's policy of not taxing the converts while proclaiming himself the "protector of the [new] Muslims," in an effort to win over some newly converted noblemen (*dehqāns*). His fiscal commissioner removed the poll tax from thirty thousand converts and imposed it on eight thousand non-Muslims who had been exempted from it (Tabari, 2.1688–89; trans. 26.24–25). Nasr's policy of establishing close ties with the local nobility and royal families, including marrying the daughter of the king of Bukhara, can also be construed as similarly motivated to preempt oppositional mobilization (Sadighi 1938:38; Zakeri 1995:250).

The ʿAbbasid missionary Qahtaba b. Shabib[1] had refused to support al-Hārith in the last months of crisis (van Ess 1991–97:2.492), though his agents wooed some of the Murjiʾites in the years after the latter's death. The Murjiʾite Ibrāhim b. Maymun al-Sāʾigh and his followers joined the ʿAbbasid mission (Agha 2003:164–65), and some of the "people of insight" joined the rival, Hashemite revolutionary movement, led in Khorasan by ʿAbd al-Rahmān, who was known as Abu Muslim and later hijacked the movement for the ʿAbbasids, at the outbreak of revolution in 747/129 (*Akhbār* 280, 285). In the earliest stage of this power struggle, however—in Balkh in 748/130 and in Marw in the following year—the Murjiʾites not only refused to join Abu Muslim's coalition but, on the contrary, fought him. In Balkh, the Arabs and the *mawāli* were joined under the leadership of Muqātil, son of the famous client general Hayyān al-Nabati, who unfurled the Murjiʾite's own black banners. Abu Muslim sent the Arab-Khorasanian missionary Abu Dāwud Khālid b. Ibrāhim al-Dhuhli to put down the uprising (Tabari, 2.1997–98; trans. 27.104–5). Two Murjiʾite leaders who were disciples of Abu Hanifa, including the abovementioned Ibrāhim b. Maymun al-Sāʾigh, were executed in Marw by Abu Muslim's agents (Madelung 1988:20).

The revolutionary movement from the periphery that finally overthrew the Umayyads was that of the Hashemites. There can be little doubt, however, that it was greatly influenced by the Murjiʾite revolt. The Hashemites adopted the black banner of the Murjiʾites, although they modified al-Hārith's "the acceptable one" to "the acceptable one (*al-ridā*) from the House of Muhammad," and they also modified al-Hārith's battle cry *"Yā mansur!"* (O Victorious!) to *"Yā Muhammad, yā mansur!"* (Tabari, 2.1921, 1972; trans. 27.31, 82).

According to the insider history of the ʿAbbasid movement, until the third ʿAbbasid caliph, al-Mahdi, propounded the idea that his ancestor, the eponymous ʿAbbās, was the heir to the Prophet as the latter's uncle, "the original ʿAbbasid Shiʿism (partisanship), to which Abu Muslim called, was from Muhammad b. al-Hanafiyya [d. 700/81]." The Shiʿite sect is correctly identified as Kaysāniyya; they were the followers of the Kufan rebel Mukhtār, who is anachronistically said to be the first to recognize the imamate of the ʿAbbasid Muhammad b. ʿAli (d. 744/126) (*Akhbār* 165). The Kaysāniyya were in fact an extremist Shiʿite group who believed that Muhammad b. al-Hanafiyya had not died but was in "occultation" (*gayba*) on Radwa Mountain, and they considered his son Abu Hāshim ʿAbdallāh their imam. When Abu Hāshim died, a little before the apocalyptic year AH 100 (718–19) (Arjomand 2000), two of his relatives claimed they had been designated by him as his successor: the ʿAbbasid Muhammad b. ʿAli and the Talibid ʿAbdallāh b. Muʿāwiya (Moscati 1952). Although Abu Hāshim's followers were called the Hāshimiyya as well as the Kaysāniyya in heresiography, some modern scholars have misunderstood the term as the self-designation of the Hashemite revolutionary movement a quarter of a century later by deriving it from Abu Hāshim rather than Banu Hāshim. ʿAbdallāh b. Muʿāwiya launched an ideological campaign to broaden the legitimism of the descendants of ʿAli to that of the Banu Hāshim as the clan of the Prophet and created a sizable state in Fars and central Iran from 744 to 747. The ʿAbbasid Muhammad b. ʿAli recruited his partisans among the Kaysāniyya and reorganized them as a clandestine group in Kufa, focusing their chiliastic expectation on himself or his offspring, and sent a man to Khorasan, allegedly ordering him to call the people to "the acceptable one from the House of Muhammad" without naming anyone specifically (*Ansāb* 3.82). Another report confirms the calling to the acceptable one from the house of Muhammad, whose name was to be kept secret, and records the disappointment with the mission in Kufa at the passing of the second apocalyptic opportunity: "the year hundred passed and the partisans [*shiʿa*] did not number thirty men" (*Akhbār* 194).

The Hashemite revolution, however, had to relocate the main field of its activity from metropolitan Kufa to the Khorasanian periphery. The reason for the choice of Khorasan after the disappointment in Kufa, as the ʿAbbasid imam put it, was that "most of the people of Iraq adhere to the House of Abu Tālib" (*Akhbār* 173, 205–6).

The man sent to set up the clandestine ʿAbbasid mission in Khorasan shortly after the beginning of the new century was soon discovered and executed by the governor, and the mission was taken over by an Iranian client sent from Kufa, nicknamed Khidāsh (the damager), who turned the Hashemite cause into a neo-Mazdakite or Khorrami religion before being killed by the governor in 736/118. The stimulus to renew the Hashemite mission in Khorasan came from Bukayr b. Māhān, a native of Hormozfarrah (glory of the god Hormazd) in Khorasan and a client who had prospered as a fiscal agent of the Umayyad government and had joined the movement in Kufa. Bukayr told the ʿAbbasid imam Muhammad b. ʿAli that the people of Gorgan and Khorasan were his party (*shiʿa*) and the area his abode of migration (*dār hijra*); the latter replied, "indeed our mission is Oriental [*daʿwatuna sharqiyya*], our helpers the people of the Orient, and our banners are black" (*Akhbār* 198–99). Bukayr was accordingly sent to Khorasan to pick up the pieces of the mission wrecked by Khidāsh and reorganize it. He set up a clandestine hierarchy of a twelve divisions corresponding to the twelve tribes of Israel, each under a chief missionary (*naqib*) commanding subordinate ranks of alternate chiefs (*nāzir/naqib*s), of which there were about twenty, missionaries (*dā ʿī*), and junior missionaries (*dāʿi duʿāt*), of which thirty-seven are named. The seventy (or sixty-five) missionaries constituted the high council of the ʿAbbasid mission in Khorasan (*Akhbār* 213–23; Agha 2003:25).

In 747/129, the disintegration of the Umayyad central authority must have become increasingly evident. All accounts agree that the ʿAbbasid Ibrāhim al-Imam sent his new freedman (or client) to Khorasan as "a man from his household" (Moscati 1949–50:482) to take over the leadership of the mission and prepare for revolution. Abu Muslim arrived in Khorasan, producing Ibrāhim al-Imam's letter, and skillfully wrenched the leadership of the Khorasanian chapter from the disgruntled Sulaymān b. Kathir, who was nominally the chief missionary after Bukayr b. Māhān (*Akhbār* 271–73; Sharon 1983:214–24). As indicated by the name he is most generally known as, Abu Muslim al-Khurāsāni, he was probably a native of Khorasan, though one Khorasanian is said to have disputed that and said he was from Isfahan (to which his ʿIjli former masters were closely connected); he certainly proved knowledgeable enough about the topography of the region to micromanage some of his generals' strategic moves.

Outbreak of the Revolution

On the night of June 9, 747,[2] Abu Muslim, the freed slave serving Ibrāhim b. Muhammad, the imam (leader) of the ʿAbbasid clandestine mission, "unfurled the banner sent to him by the imam," together with the flag upon which was written the Qurʾanic verse (22.30) "Permission is given to those who fight because they have been oppressed; surely God has the power to aid them [to victory]!" (Tabari, 2.1954; trans. 27.67). This was in the village of Sefidhanj, one of the villages belonging to the Khuzāʿa, the Arab tribe of the senior ʿAbbasid missionary, Sulaymān b. Kathir. Abu Muslim and the missionaries surrounding him had put on black garments distinctive of the revolutionary party (*shiʿa*) and awaited the recruits to the cause of revolution from the surrounding villages in the Marw agricultural region. The call to uprising immediately spread beyond the partisans. "In one day, the people of sixty villages joined him" (Tabari, 2.1952; trans. 27.64). And thus began the revolution of Abu Muslim al-Khurāsāni in the rural periphery of the Umayyad Empire.[3] Rural support for Abu Muslim's revolt in this decisive early stage is evident.[4] The overwhelming majority of those who started the revolution were peasants on foot, wielding clubs. The paucity of horsemen among them is in striking contrast to the prominence of the landed nobility in the preceding Murjiʾite rebellion of al-Hārith. The peasant support for Abu Muslim also contrasts with the urban, petty-bourgeois profile of Abu Salama and his followers in Kufa. Of the two missionaries whom al-Tabari identified by their native villages without any tribal identification, the first was a client of one of the clans of Nasr b. Sayyār's tribe of Kināna (Agha 2003:376), the second a convert who did not even have the status of a *mawlā*. Soqādem was the agricultural district in which the Kharijites had been converting the population to Islam[5] and where their rebellion had been so successful as to induce the Yemenite tribal leader Judayʿal-Kirmāni to defect to them (Balʿami 2003:2.998, 1009). The ʿAbbasid missionaries evidently had great success in taking advantage of the path paved for them by the Kharijites, and probably in winning over some of their converts. Furthermore, wearing black in Khorasan had the double connotation of the messianic black banner and of mourning for the family of the Prophet killed by the Umayyad tyrants, notably Yahyā b. Zayd, whose murder and crucifixion in 743 had produced enormous popular sympathy and thus a fertile ground for recruitment.[6] The crucifixion of Yahyā b. Zayd was singled out as "the cause of mobilization of the people of Khorasan and their missionaries," whereupon the ʿAbbasid imam charged Qahtaba b. Shabib, returning from hajj, with calling the people of Khorasan "to obedience to the House of the Messenger of God" (*Akhbār* 167).

As a freedman or, at best, a servile client, Abu Muslim did not neglect the integration of slaves and their equal treatment. He welcomed slaves and they flocked to his camp as soon as they had dug the trench around it at the outbreak of his rebellion. He ceremoniously manumitted a slave who was joining them, saying that God, whose right over him was prior to his owner's, had liberated him. "He gathered the heads of the party [*shiʿa*] and its elite on that day and said, 'Verily has God made your mission safe and powerful for whoever seeks protection in it. Whoever enters it, be she or he free or a slave, obligates you. . . . We accept every slave who comes to us zealous for our cause, and his rights shall be observed as ours'" (*Akhbār* 280). There had been a "missionary to the slaves" and a commander was appointed over them. As the number of slaves in the camp grew rapidly, the prosperous among the supporters of the revolution must have been alarmed, and they made Abu Muslim send out callers to tell the slaves to return to their owners. By this time, the slaves who had joined the revolution had a leader (*qā'id*), who protested vigorously: "How should they return to those [the owners] who opposed them and are angry with them because of the love for the House of Muhammad? As God Most High said, 'The Prophet has greater authority over the believers than they themselves have'" (Q. 33.6). The slaves returned to their camp, and as their number increased further, they were sent westward to the revolutionary army of Abivard and Nesa under the command of the Arab missionary Musā b. Ka'b (*Akhbār* 281).

Nor did Abu Muslim neglect the incorporation of women into the revolutionary movement, his austerely ascetic attitude notwithstanding.[7] From the *Akhbār al-dawla* we learn of a group of "women from the people of the mission" who were followers of Abu Muslim and claimed to have been abducted by a Khidāshist (Khorammi) 'Abbasid agent, Abu Khālid, who had formed his own sect, the Khālidiyya, and rebelled on behalf of an 'Alid "acceptable one" against Abu Muslim. Abu Khālid was summoned by Abu Muslim but escaped and remained a fugitive through the course of the revolutionary power struggle. Abu Muslim sent one of the women, called Umm al-'Alā, with a number of horsemen in pursuit of Abu Khālid, who killed them all. Another woman, Umm al-Fawāris, who was the manager of Abu Muslim's own household, however, rose to admonish Abu Muslim, presumably in sympathy with Abu Khālid or the 'Alid candidate and was beaten by clubs and stoned by order of Abu Muslim (*Akhbār* 403–4). Women must have remained prominent among the Iranian followers of Abu Muslim after his death; they became known as the Fātimiyya and are said to have absorbed the Khālidiyya sect (*Akhbār* 403). Women mobilized by Abu Muslim during the revolution must be presumed responsible for the designation of his daughter Fatima as their imam and leader (Sadighi 1938:212–14).

Revolutionary State Building, Export of Revolution, and Imperial Expansion

Abu Muslim began his open rebellion somewhat ahead of schedule to take advantage of the near breakdown of state authority in Marw, the capital of

Khorasan, as a result of the rebellion of the Kharijites and conflict among the Arab tribes that had made the Yaman under Kirmāni their allies. Six months later, the governor, Nasr b. Sayyār, fled Marw. He was chased from city to city, and his son was killed by Qahtaba. Nasr, sheikh of the northern Arabs of Khorasan, left its soil, fleeing to Rayy in central Iran and died in nearby Sāva at the age of eighty-five in October 748 (Rabi ʿ I, 131). Meanwhile, Abu Muslim had ordered the agents of the revolutionary party to administer an oath of allegiance to "the acceptable one from the House of God's Messenger!" (Tabari, 2.1989; trans. 27.98). Such a convenient oath of allegiance to an unknown Hashemite acceptable as caliph would be puzzling indeed if we assume that the revolutionary movement was controlled by the ʿAbbasid Ibrāhim al-Imam, who had not yet been arrested by Marwān II.[8]

Abu Muslim acted independently and autocratically as the "master of the mission/revolution" (*sāhib al-dawla/da ʿwa*) to set up his own Hashemite state. His first appointments were those of a chief of his guard, a police chief, a head of state bureaucracy (*diwān*), and a judge, with salaries of four thousand dirhams each (Tabari, 2.1989; trans. 27.98). These four officials operated from Abu Muslim's fortified camp in Mākhovān and supervised the affairs of the missionaries, who were turning into officials, and organized the volunteers who were flooding the revolutionary camps (Sharon 1990:102–7). They were thus forming the nucleus of Abu Muslim's state, which, as we shall see presently, was able to serve as an instrument of conquest and imperial expansion in Transoxania in just a few years.

At this time, Qahtaba b. Shabib returned from Arabia, bringing a covenant and new banners from the new imam, Ibrāhim b. Muhammad. Abu Muslim dispatched Qahtaba to Iran and Mesopotamia as the head of a revolutionary army, with a few Arabs and some of the *mawāli* in the inner circle in positions of command. Another revolutionary army was organized for the conquest of Transoxania under the Arabs and client missionaries.

Although Arabs who had settled in Khorasan were predominant among the commanders of the revolutionary armies recruited by Abu Muslim, the lower ranks were overwhelmingly non-Arab, and if there were any settled Arabs and clients among them, their tribal affiliation was not recorded in the army registry (*diwān al-jund*), and they were identified only by their native villages (Sharon 1986:116–17; 1990:97–102; Daniel 1997:545). Abu Muslim ordered the commissioners appointed for the registration of the volunteers who had joined the revolutionary camps "to enter them in a register with their names, their fathers' names and their villages" (Tabari, 2.1957; trans. 27.68). It is likely that most of the men thus recruited to the revolutionary army had no tribal affiliation of any sort, and it is certain that the vast majority of them fought on foot and with axes and, especially, clubs known as *kāfirkubāt* (infidel smashers). The informed depiction of the revolutionary volunteers by Nasr b. Sayyār and Marwān II's secretary, ʿAbd al-Hamid, affirms not only their religious zeal indicated by this appellation of their main weapon but also the non-Islamic character of their religious beliefs and strongly anti-Arab animus (Daniel 1997:545–46).

The recruitment of the Khorasanian army was a revolutionary departure from the Umayyad pattern of military recruitment by tribal affiliation, either directly or through clienthood. Abu Muslim's institutionalization of nontribal recruitment of soldiers from villages was one of the most important integrative aspects of the ʿAbbasid Revolution. It put an end to the Arab domination of Muslim armies and opened military organization first to the Persians and shortly thereafter to the Turks.

Qahtaba's revolutionary army was intensely ideological. The imam's banners were carried, and frequent assurances and predictions of victory were made by the imam when the Khorasanians were greatly outnumbered by the enemy (Tabari, 2.2005; trans. 27.111). Qahtaba routinely issued "the invitation to the acceptable one" (*daʿwa ila'l-ridā*) to the Umayyad forces before battle (*Akhbār* 335, 340, 365). At least on one important occasion in Gorgan, as we have seen at the beginning of this chapter, he propounded a theory of revolution, telling the men of Khorasan that their turn to wield power, forfeited by their fathers (the imperial Persians), had come again, because the Arab nation had gone astray in their governance (Tabari, 2.2004–5; trans. 27.110–11).

Qahtaba conquered Rayy for Abu Muslim. In that year (749/131), Abu Muslim coins were minted in Rayy, continuing to use the Hashemite legend "Say: 'I ask you no recompense for this other than the love of my kin'" (Q. 44.23), while adding "by order of Abu Muslim the *amir* of the House of Muhammad" (Wurtzel 1978:191). Qahtaba's revolutionary army swept through the rest of Iran, defeating the greatly superior reformed armies of Marwān in Isfahan and Nahavand, and reached Mesopotamia in March 749 (Rajab 131). By that time, Abu Muslim himself was primarily oriented eastward. Transoxania did not participate in the Hashemite revolution but was rather the object of the imperial expansion of Abu Muslim's revolutionary state.[9] As soon as Abu Muslim set up his revolutionary state in Marw, however, he appointed his agents as governors of Bukhara and Samarqand, which had been governed from Khorasan under Nasr b. Sayyār. Neither Samarqand nor Bukhara, however, played any role in the revolutionary mobilization and uprising that occurred in Khorasan. Karev's (2002) careful analysis of two hitherto-unexamined sources as well as his excavations of the palace and new wall built by Abu Muslim in Samarqand clearly shows the imperial nature of the annexation of Transoxania by Abu Muslim and his generals.

A major rebellion in Bukhara against Abu Muslim was suppressed by his general Ziyād b. Sālih in the summer of 750. At that time, the ruler (*ekhshid*) of Farqana, farther east in Transoxania, had accepted vassalage to the emperor of China, who had sent an army of one hundred thousand men under General Kao-Sien-che to help him against the pro-Muslim ruler of Shash, with whom he was in conflict. Kao-Sien-che sacked Shash and killed its king, whose son fled to the Muslims. Abu Muslim decided to exploit the situation for imperial expansion and sent Ziyād b. Sālih against the Chinese. Ziyād reached the Chinese army at the banks of the river Tarāz. Abu Muslim moved from Marw to Samarqand to be closer to the scene and reinforced Ziyād's troops by some ten thousand men in May 751. In the major battle of Taraz (Talas) in July 751 (Dhu'l-Hijja 133), Ziyād defeated the Chinese army, reportedly killing fifty thousand men and taking another twenty thousand captive (Karev 2002:11–15).[10] The battle of Talas decided the fate of Central Asia, closing it to the Chinese empire and opening it to Abu Muslim's imperial expansion.

Abu Muslim spent most of the next year or two in Samarqand, building a new wall and fortifications for the city as the capital of the new empire and a grand palace for himself as its ruler, while conducting the campaigns against China and its Transoxanian vassals (Karev 2002:27–36). He had arrived there in the company of his Arab-Khorasanian general Abu Dāwud Khālid b. Ibrāhim, who had suppressed the Murji'ite rebellion in Balkh for him. He sent Abu Dāwud on a campaign against the king of Khuttal, who fled with his armed retinue of *chakar*s and his *dehqān*s to Farqana and thence to Turkistan and China (Tabari, 3.74; trans. 27.197). By this time, the local rulers of Transoxania were fully alarmed by Abu Muslim's presence in Samarqand, and eleven of them put themselves under the protection of the emperor of China, repeatedly begging him to attack "with hearts united those in black garments" (cited in Karev 2002:17). This was after the crushing defeat at Talas, and Chinese help never came. Abu Muslim overcame the rebellion of the kings. In 752/134, Abu Muslim sent Abu Dāwud against Ekhrid, the ruler of Kashsh. "Abu Dāwud slew the *dehqān* of Kashsh along with a number of other *dehqān*s, but spared . . . the brother of Ekhrid, and made him ruler of Kashsh." He sent the imperial booty, including captured ornaments and gilded Chinese vessels, to Abu Muslim in Samarqand (Tabari, 3.79–80; trans. 27.202).

At about this time, Abu Muslim executed the ruler of Bukhara (Bokhārātkhodā), who had helped him against the rebels in 750, and his son and family, leaving only a brother to take his place. According to Maqdisi, "Abu Muslim came to Bukhara from Samarqand" and "extended his power over the kings of Transoxiana and their *dehqāns*, executing them, taking their children into captivity and confiscating their goods. He made the captives cross the river [Oxus] in groups of 50,000." He goes on to say that Abu Muslim had been intending to invade China when his governor of Soghdia rebelled against him (in 753/135) (cited in Karev 2002:7).[11]

The Revolutionary Power Struggle and the Reintegration of the Khorasanian Periphery

The revolutionary power struggle among the members of the ʿAbbasid family and the crisis of succession following the death of the first ʿAbbasid caliph, Abu'l-ʿAbbās, in 754/136, followed by that against Abu Muslim, who had been lured to Iraq in that same year, have been treated in the companion volume (Arjomand, forthcoming). Suffice it to say here that these power struggles ended with the murder of Abu Muslim in February 755. His murder by the new caliph, Abu Jaʿfar, who also defeated his uncle ʿAbdallāh b. ʿAli at the same time, revealed the heterogeneity of the social forces that had backed the revolution in a series of rebellions against ʿAbbasid rule in Iran and Khorasan and an attempt to assassinate Abu Jaʿfar by an Abu Muslimite fifth column in his palace in Hāshimiyya—the city and palace of the treacherously murdered last Umayyad governor of Iraq, Ibn Hubayra. These preoccupied Abu Jaʿfar in the first five years of his insecure rule, and he postponed dealing with the unresolved issue of the legitimacy of the ʿAbbasid caliphate as the fulfillment of the promise of the Hashemite revolution. Despite his limited military power and resources, in 762/145 the new caliph daringly provoked the rebellion of his ʿAlid cousins who claimed better title to the promised Hashemite caliphate. After suppressing it, he succeeded in appropriating the Hashemite revolution and thus bringing it to an end, and moved on unchallenged to consolidate the ʿAbbasid caliphal autocracy.

There can be little doubt that the critical turning point in the mass conversion of Khorasan to Islam was the seven or eight years of Abu Muslim's revolutionary government as the "master of revolution." The astrologer Ibn Abi Tāhir Tayfur clearly saw this and stated categorically: "the Zoroastrian religion expired among the *dehqāns* and they accepted Islam during the period of Abu Muslim. This was a general revolution [*inqilāb*] in [both] religion and the state [*mulk*]" (cited also in van Vloten 1894:67n4). The conversion of the rest of Iran to Islam also happened during this period. The conversion was as superficial, however, as it was swift (Bulliet 1979:45, 55).

Unlike the deceased ʿAbbasid caliph Abu'l-ʿAbbās and his uncle and brother contending to succeed him, Abu Muslim was not only the head of the Khorasanian state and its officials but also a genuine charismatic leader surrounded by disciples. After his murder, Abu Muslim's numerous followers began to organize themselves throughout Iran and Khorasan into sects in opposition to ʿAbbasid rule. This meant developing Persianate religious beliefs and practices in the syncretic Islam they had professed under Abu Muslim's leadership during the revolution. This is clearly reflected in a number of pejorative apocalyptic traditions that call Abu Muslim "scoundrel, son of scoundrel" (*lukaʿ b. lukaʿ*) and worse, one of which seems worth quoting: "He will hoist the black; his beginning is victory, his end, unbelief. He will be followed by the scum of the Arabs, the lowliest of the *mawāli*, runaway slaves and unbelievers (*murrāq*) of the provinces. His face will be black and his religion, polytheism" (Agouadé 1979:105, citing Nuʿaym b. Hammād).

The sectarian formation that thus emerged was called Abu Muslimiyya by later heresiographers. This umbrella term should not obscure the fact that Abu Muslim's followers organized themselves into sectarian groups locally and rebelled in a number of different locations. "Abu Muslimiyya," affirms one heresiographer, "are called by different names in different locations: they are called the Khorramiyya in the region of Isfahan, Mazdakiyya and Sonbadiyya in Qazvin and Rayy, the Reds [*muhammira*] in Mahin, Quliyya in Azerbaijan, and the Magians [*moghān*] [variant, the Whites (*mubayyida*)] in Transoxania."[12]

As soon as the news of Abu Muslim's murder reached Iran, al-Masʿudi (1970:4.144) tells us, "the Khorramiyya (neo-Mazdakites) became agitated. They constituted a sect called the Muslimiyya [also Abu Muslimiyya], believing in the imamate of Abu Muslim, and fell apart after his death. Some of them maintained that he was not dead and would not die before becoming manifest again to fill the earth with justice." Others held kindred millennial beliefs concerning him, and yet others believed that his daughter, Fatima, inherited his imamate (Sadighi 1938:140–41). The first of Abu Muslim's officials and disciples who rose to avenge his blood was a Zoroastrian called Sonpadh.[13] He may have been at Nishapur or Hulwan and had been entrusted with Abu Muslim's treasury as the latter left Iran for his pilgrimage to Mecca. Sonpadh's rebellion spread quickly, and he defeated the governor of Rayy and captured the city. Sonpadh assumed the title Victorious General (*piruz espahbadh*), and during the seventy days of his rebellion, he reportedly amassed an army of some eighty thousand for marching on Iraq. Abu Jaʿfar dispatched Jahwar b. al-Marrar al-ʿIjli, "a partisan of the revolution" (*ahl al-dawla*), to put down the rebellion. After a fierce battle, some sixty thousand of Sonpadh's followers were killed, and he fled to the king of Tabarestan, whose brother killed him (Sadighi 1938:132–35, 148).

Without subscribing to Sonpadh's theory of the imminent demise of the Arab empire, Jahwar nevertheless judged Abu Jaʿfar's hold on power shaky enough to refuse to send him the captured treasury of Abu Muslim, and he rebelled openly. In the following year, 756–57/138, he minted coins in his own name "by the order of Amir Jahwar b. al-Marrar" (Miles 1938:22, no. 41). Abu Jaʿfar now turned to another one of the "sons of the revolution" (*abnāʾ al-dawla*), Muhammad b. al-Ashʿath al-Khuzāʾi, Abu Muslim's first governor of Fars who had forced Abu Jaʿfar's uncle ʿIsā to forswear an administrative-military career. Al-Ashʿath defeated Jahwar despite his considerable military force, and the latter fled to Azerbaijan and was killed there (Tabari, 3.122; trans. 28.49–50). The social support for Jahwar's revolt is as interesting as that for Sonpadh's. On the one hand, he clearly had the support of the local population. He had defeated Sonpadh with the help of the local opposition against Sonpadh in Rayy under the leadership of a butcher, ʿUmar b. al-Aʿlāʾ. On the other hand, Jahwar's supporters included "the elite of the Persian cavalry, Ziyād [b. Moshkān] and al-Ishtakhanj," and the Transoxanian *dehqān* Zubāra al-Bukhāri (Tabari, 3.122; trans. 28.50; *Ansāb* 3.247; Crone 1998:17).

The political mobilization of the Iranian nobility and bourgeoisie in ʿAbbasid Iran had important further integrative consequences and led directly to the incorporation of Tabarestan into the ʿAbbasid Empire and its conversion to Islam. The region of Tabarestan on the Caspian coast had remained under the rule of its dynasty of local kings, the Espahbadhs. We have no other evidence to verify Balādhuri's statement that Sonpadh wrote to the local king of the nearby Daylam, but we know that he sent or carried at least a part of Abu Muslim's treasury to Espahbadh Khorshid, whom he must have considered instrumental for the overthrow of the empire of the Arabs. Khorshid, however, sent Sonpadh's head to Abu Jaʿfar but refused to return Abu Muslim's treasury or give his son to the new caliph as a court hostage. By this time, 758/140 or the following year, Khorasan was out of control, and its governor, as we shall see, had joined the Abu Muslimite rebels. Abu Jaʿfar was persuaded by the advisers to his son (who had taken over the governorship of Rayy after the rebellions of Sonpadh and Jahwar and was soon to assume the title Mahdi) to come to terms with Khorshid, who agreed to pay him the tribute of 300,000 dirhams, as in the Sasanian era, and to help the caliph with the passage of the army he wanted to send to Khorasan (Ibn Isfandiyār, 174–75). That army was commanded by Marzuq al-Sindi. Abu Ja'far also moved Abu 'Awn from Egypt to Gorgan to deal with the multiple crises. The army's secret order was to annex Tabarestan first. To do so, Marzuq recruited 'Umar b. al-A'lā', the butcher who had helped Jahwar defeat Sonpadh. 'Umar was recommended by Parviz (Abarwiz), the brother of the local ruler of Damavand and the Espahbadh's enemy, who knew him from some intrigue related to Sonpadh and the Rāwandiyya (Tabari, 3.137; trans. 28.73) but was now a refugee with the Espahbadh in Tabarestan because of some subsequent mischief in Gorgan. 'Umar was a ruthless soldier of fortune with thorough knowledge of the local conditions and passes. He joined the caliph's army and helped it conquer Tabarestan in 759–60/142,[14] and he was appointed governor of Amol. "'Umar b. al-A'lā' took the seat of government, proclaimed justice, and called to Islam, and the people . . . , group after group and tribe after tribe, came to him and accepted Islam" (Ibn Isfandiyār, 176).[15] Abu Ja'far thus began the export of the 'Abbasid Revolution from Iraq. Imperial expansion continued in the following year with raids into Daylam. He ordered the governor of Basra and Kufa to enlist the affluent citizens for an expeditionary force for jihad in Daylam, following the original pattern of Muslim conquests from those garrison cities (Tabari, 3.142; trans. 28.82–83).

The connection between the followers of Abu Muslim in Khorasan and those in Iraq, who constituted something of a "fifth column," is obscure, and all we can tell is that the key network was an extremist Shi'ite group recorded in heresiography as the Rāwandiyya, especially its core group, called Rizāmiyya after its leader, Rizām b. Sābiq, an Abu Muslim disciple who narrowly escaped death after the massacre of the Rāwandiyya. The group shared the general belief of Abu Muslim's followers in imamate through incarnation. The Rizāmiyya among them "appeared in Khurasan in the days of Abu Muslim . . . and conferred the Imamate on Abu Muslim, attributing the fortune of Imamate to him and claiming that the spirit of God was incarnated in him" (Shahrastāni as quoted in Moscati 1949–50:476). It is interesting to note that they are said by one heresiographer to have believed that the imamate had passed from the 'Alids to the 'Abbasid Muhammad b. 'Ali, then to his brother 'Abdallāh b. 'Ali al-Saffāh, and finally from him to Abu Muslim. According to al-Madā'ini, "the Rāwandiyya were a Khurasanian group who followed Abu Muslim, the Master of the Hashemite mission (*sāhib da'wa Banu Hāshim*)" (Tabari, 3.129; trans. 28.62–63).

The first indication we have of Abu Ja'far's link with the extremist Rāwandiyya of Taleqan in Tokharestan is during the revolutionary struggle with Abu Muslim instigated by him and his brother, Abu'l-'Abbās, in the first years of the latter's caliphate. In subsequent years, a number of Rāwandis moved to Iraq among the "sons of revolution." Abu Ja'far's success in recruiting one of their prominent members, 'Uthmān b. Nahik, and his brother 'Isā into the conspiracy to murder Abu Muslim was a major coup. After the murder of Abu Muslim, they are said to have worshipped Abu Ja'far as a divine incarnation and Abu Muslim's successor, but we must conclude that was a pretense that allowed them to remain near the new caliph and keep their access to him. Some six hundred of the Rāwandiyya organized a procession around the caliph's palace in Hāshimiyya chanting, "This is the palace of our Lord" (Tabari, 3.130; trans. 28.61–62; Browne 1902:1.316–17), but their secret aim was in fact to kill him.

The assassination attempt failed.[16] Abu Ja'far, who had very few guards on the occasion, escaped death narrowly, with the help of the Umayyad general Ma'n b. Zā'ida, who came out of hiding to save the new caliph's life and was later handsomely rewarded for his bravery with the governorship of the Yemen. The Rāwandiyya surrounding the palace were massacred by troops brought by Khāzim b. Khuzayma. 'Uthmān b. Nahik's betrayal and murder of Abu Muslim was evidently a great shock to the Rāwandiyya, and their reverence for him as incarnating the spirit of Adam notwithstanding, they shot him with an arrow and killed him. Abu Ja'far appointed 'Isā b. Nahik commander of the guards in his place, and 'Isā held the command for the rest of his life (Tabari, 3.130–32; trans. 28.63–66). The caliph did not eradicate the rest of the Rāwandiyya. Harb b. 'Abdallāh al-Rāwandi was Abu Ja'far's man for easing his uncle Ismā'il out of the governorship of Mosul in 759/142 and was appointed chief of the militia in the city. During the Hashemite Ibrāhim's rebellion in 762–63/145, Harb al-Rāwandi killed five hundred inhabitants of the city who wanted to prevent him from reinforcing the caliph (Tabari, 3.296; trans. 28.268). Harb al-Rāwandi was killed fighting the Khazars in Armenia two years later (H. Kennedy 1981:30–31).

Another missionary of Abu Muslim in Khorasan who moved to Transoxania and rose to avenge him was Ishāq the Turk, so nicknamed because his mission was in Turkistan. He organized his supporters on the basis of a variant admixture of neo-Mazdakite ideas and the cult of Abu Muslim and tore down the 'Abbasid black banners and replaced them with white ones (Mélikoff 1962:56). Ishāq's followers also dressed in white and became known as the Whites (Mubayyida or Sepid-jāmagān), and their beliefs were in line with the Abu Muslimiyya millenarian movement initiated by Sonpadh. Ishāq considered Abu Muslim in occultation (*gayba*) in the mountains of Rayy and expected his manifestation, this time in the company of Zoroaster, whose prophet he was said to be. To reinforce his own authority and gain the support of the 'Alid partisans, he also claimed to descend from Zayd b.

'Ali (Browne 1902:1.314–15 *apud* Ibn al-Nadim). A group of Whites killed the governor of Khorasan, Abu Dāwud Khālid b. Ibrāhim, in July 757 (Rabiʿ I 140) (Gardizi 1984:273), doubtless because he had betrayed Abu Muslim to the ʿAbbasid caliph three years earlier. There were also strong indications of the clandestine spread of the ʿAlid mission on behalf of the fugitive sons of ʿAbdallāh b. al-Hasan (*Ansāb* 3.229–30; Tabari, 3.146; trans. 27.89–90; Balʿami 2003:2.1102). Abu Jaʿfar sent ʿAbd al-Jabbār al-Azdi, a seasoned Arab-Khorasanian Hashemite missionary and the first ʿAbbasid revolutionary police chief in Kufa, back to his native land to deal with the situation, despite or perhaps because of his known ʿAlid inclination.

Upon arrival, ʿAbd al-Jabbār must have judged the ʿAbbasid cause a lost one against the combined force of the Abu Muslimite and ʿAlid movements, and he rebelled against the ʿAbbasid caliph when a Persian hulk (*ʿilj*) who became his court astrologer told him that a great kingdom for him in Khorasan was writ in the stars (*Ansāb* 3.229). He arrested and executed the pro-ʿAbbasid army commanders, while torturing his predecessor's fiscal agents to extract for himself the tax they had collected. The caliph, who anticipated his imminent rebellion, told an adviser that "ʿAbd al-Jabbār has just destroyed our party (*shiʿa*)" (Tabari, 3.128, 134; trans. 28.59–60, 69–70). ʿAbd al-Jabbār then forswore his allegiance to Abu Jaʿfar and raised the white banner of the rebel Mubayyida and made an alliance with a *dehqān* called Barāz-banda, who claimed to be the Hashemite Ibrāhim (i.e., Ibrāhim b. ʿAbdallāh b. al-Hasan) (Gardizi 1984:274–75). At this point, the Khālidiyya (named after their leader, Abu Khālid), who continued the tradition of the Persian archheretic Khidāsh under Abu Muslim (see above), resurfaced, arguing that the testamentary designation of Abu Hāshim reverted to the ʿAlids after the death of Ibrāhim al-Imam. Abu Khālid, who had been in hiding for a long time, rose with five hundred of his followers during the rebellion of ʿAbd al-Jabbār, presumably siding with the Whites and Barāz-banda, but was killed (*Akhbār* 403–4). ʿAbd al-Jabbār's rebellion lasted almost exactly two years, but his hopes were finally dashed when the inhabitants of Marw al-Rudh rebelled against his misrule. The ʿAbbasid forces defeated the pretender Barāz-banda and captured ʿAbd al-Jabbār after most of his troops deserted in July 759 (Rabiʿ I 142) (Gardizi 1984:275). He was sent to Abu Jaʿfar and in vain appealed to his revolutionary comradeship and pleaded first for mercy and then for a merciful death because of his contribution to "this revolution and mission." Abu Jaʿfar called him a son of a whore who had killed Qahtaba's missionaries; he ordered his hands and feet to be cut off before killing him and displaying his corpse on the cross (Moscati 1947:614–15). Abu Jaʿfar dismissed and arrested ʿAbd al-Jabbār's brother, ʿAbd al-ʿAziz, who was also a member of the revolutionary elite and a "preacher inclined toward Muʿtazilism," serving as the governor of Basra (*Ansāb* 3.230). The old Khorasanian missionary and first ʿAbbasid governor of Egypt, the client Abu ʿAwn ʿAbd al-Malik b. Yazid, who must have completed his assignment in Tabarestan, arrived in Marw in the following year as ʿAbd al-Jabbār's replacement and remained governor of Khorasan until 766/149 (Gardizi 1984.276).

The murder of Abu Muslim burst asunder the conglomeration of social groups he had gathered under the banner of the Hashemite revolution. A sharp ethnic rift appeared, separating the Persian masses from the Arabs, which replicated itself to some degree within the Khorasanian revolutionary elite, the *abnāʾ al-dawla* (sons of the revolution). The caliph's response was to step up efforts to co-opt the Umayyad Arab elite. Muhammad b. al-Ashʿath, the Arab-Khorasanian who had served as Abu Muslim's revolutionary governor of Fars and barred Abu Jaʿfar's uncle from entry to the province, now switched to his side and served him for the rest of his career. In Egypt, the local Arab aristocracy consolidated their hold on power for the coming generations (H. Kennedy 1981:33–36). After Khorasan was recovered from ʿAbd al-Jabbār and the Whites, members of the Arab-Khorasanian revolutionary elite, Abu ʿAwn and Humayd b. Qahtaba, governed Khorasan for Abu Jaʿfar al-Mansur and his heir apparent, Muhammad al-Mahdi, with Khāzim b. Khuzayma al-Tamimi commanding the major military campaigns; even some survivors from the Umayyad elite, such as Layth, son of Nasr b. Sayyār and father of the future rebel Rafiʿ, were co-opted (Barthold [1928] 1968:201).

Revolutionary Leadership and the Appropriation of the Hashemite Revolution

The last in the series of events that decisively closed the revolutionary power struggle and can thus be considered the end of the Hashemite revolution was the defeat and elimination of the most serious contender to the title "the acceptable from the House of Muhammad," the idea that had set the revolution in motion two decades earlier.

The ʿAlids had to accept the ʿAbbasid coup of 749/132 as a fait accompli. The head of the Husaynid branch of the family, Jaʿfar b. Muhammad, did not trust the Khorasanians and did not respond to their overtures, concentrating his efforts on organizing his following into a sect with distinct religious discipline and law and developing a corresponding theory of the imamate (Hodgson 1955). Abu Jaʿfar developed good relations with him, consulted him on some legal matters (Ya'qubi 1960:2.369), and called him al-Sādiq (the truthful) (al-Isfahani 1949:256). The Hasanid branch, headed by 'Abdallāh b. al-Hasan, was more reluctant to give up the claim to the Hashemite caliphate, a claim that had been acknowledged in 744/126 by the 'Abbasids themselves (Nagel 1970), and appeared more responsive to the Khorasanians who wanted an 'Alid caliph. Nevertheless, he came to terms with Caliph Abu'l-'Abbās, though without revealing the whereabouts of his sons, Muhammad and Ibrāhim, and without explicitly giving up the latter's claim to the caliphate. According to one report, Abu'l-'Abbās bought 'Abdallāh b. al-Hasan with one million dirhams (*Fragmenta* 1871:214). Abu Ja'far, however, did not think the legitimacy of the 'Abbasid caliphate was secure from the Hasanid challenge. He could not find the Hashemite Mahdi, Muhammad b. 'Abdallāh, or his brother, Ibrāhim, but he rounded up thirteen prominent Hasanids, including 'Abdallāh b. al-Hasan. When Abu Ja'far returned to Mecca years later to lead the hajj in 762/144, they were led from prison and paraded in a most humiliating fashion in chains before being transported to Iraq.

In September 762,[17] Muhammad b. 'Abdallāh b. al-Hasan rose in the city of the Prophet, Medina, as the Hashemite Mahdi with 250 men and proceeded with cries of "God is great!" to storm the prison and release the prisoners, including the former governor Muhammad b. Khālid al-Qasri. Like Yazid III, he rode on a donkey but, this time, in a white shirt and with a white turban, and his men availed themselves of the two loads of swords smuggled in by the agents of his brother, Ibrāhim. Like the Khorasanian rebels after the murder of Abu Muslim, the Hashemite rebels in Medina and Mecca donned white, as they were to do in Basra when Ibrāhim began his ill-timed uprising shortly before the death of Muhammad (Tabari, 3.193, 223; trans. 28.147–48, 185). Muhammad b. Khālid al-Qasri later admitted that he offered armed support to the rebel Mahdi. The latter did not take up this offer, as he did not trust Qasri, who soon established secret contact with the caliph (Tabari, 3.201, 215–16; trans. 28.157–58, 176–77). Muhammad b. 'Abdallāh sent his brother Musā in an abortive attempt to extend the rebellion to Syria (Tabari, 3.216–17; trans. 28.177–78), while Ibrāhim was preparing to do so in Iraq, and appointed to his government prominent members of the politically disposed aristocracy of Medina—not just 'Alids and Talibids but also descendants of 'Umar and Zubayr and other companions of the Prophet. Only one client, the Khorasanian traditionalist resident in Medina, 'Abd al-'Aziz b. al-Darawardi, the head of the arsenal, was appointed to an important office (Tabari, 3.202; trans. 28.159; al-Isfahani 1949:282–83, 296).

Two sons of Zayd b. ʿAli and their families and followers supported the rebellion of Muhammad b. ʿAbdallāh, as did at least two sons and a nephew of their cousin, Jaʿfar b. Muhammad al-Sādiq, despite the latter's disapproval. Many of the most learned scholars of Medina also supported the rebellion, including Ibn Hurmuz and Ibn ʿIjlān. Mālik b. Anas, founder of the Maliki school of law, issued a fatwa absolving the inhabitants of Medina from their oath of allegiance to Abu Jaʿfar (Tabari, 3.200, 252, 258–59, trans. 28.156, 216, 223–24; al-Isfahani 1949:252, 28–91). According to one report, "none of the leading citizens stayed away from Muhammad except a small group" (Tabari, 3.199; trans. 28.154–55). There is some exaggeration in this claim, as Muhammad b. ʿAbd al-ʿAziz promised to help Muhammad b. ʿAbdallāh but slipped away, and Ibn al-Zubayr's grandson Nāfiʿ b. Thābit told Muhammad b. ʿAbdallāh that he was a bad bet: "You have made an uprising in a region in which there is no money or troops or mounts or weapons" (Tabari, 3.217; trans. 28.178).

Muhammad b. ʿAbdallāh sent his Talibid cousin Hasan b. Muʿāwiya to take Mecca as its governor from the incumbent, who offered no firm resistance. Hasan quickly established himself in Mecca and appears to have mustered 2,700 men at the height of the rebellion, including his trumpeter, Wāthiq, who was soon to lead a rebellion of black slaves in Medina (Tabari, 3.218–21; trans. 28.179–83). But when news of Muhammad's death arrived, "people began to slip away," and Hasan and his men, who were on their way to Medina to help him, marched on and joined his brother Ibrāhim, who had risen in Basra (Tabari, 3.221; trans. 28.183).

In sharp contrast to the freedman Abu Muslim, Muhammad b. ʿAbdallāh, scion of the holiest lineage and a descendant of the Prophet on his mother's as well as his father's side, the most "blue-blooded (*sarih*) of the Quraysh," completely lacked personal charisma. He was the Mahdi and allegedly had the same black mole between his shoulders as the Prophet's[18] (al-Isfahani 1949:243), was corpulent, and had a very swarthy complexion, being variously nicknamed "Tar Face" and "Charcoal Face." In fact, his face was scarred by smallpox, and he was a stutterer who had to beat his chest to make his voice come forth (Tabari, 3.203–6, 223; trans. 28.160–63, 185). He did not display much competence in statecraft and did not manage tribal sensitivities well either. He tried to make up for what he lacked as a charismatic leader by imitating his namesake and forefather Muhammad. He carried the Prophet's sword and spoke from his pulpit; he began his rebellion where the Prophet had dug the famous trench to defend his city against the Quraysh and adopted the Prophet's war cry in the battle of Hunayn: "One [God] and one alone!" Indeed, against better strategic advice, he began digging the trench again with his hands, shouting, "God is great," with the people chiming in and exclaiming, "Rejoice in victory. This is the trench of your forefather, the Messenger of God!" (Tabari, 3.228–29, 237, 247; trans. 28.191–92, 201, 210–11).

Muhammad b. ʿAbdallāh's conduct of the final battle demonstrated an obsession with divine preordainment and a lack of common sense. He mounted the pulpit to announce, "I hereby absolve you of your oath of allegiance to me. Whoever wishes to stay may do so. Whoever wishes to leave may do so." According to another report, he added, "Victory comes from God, and the affair is in His hand." This pious indulgence and exhortation backfired disastrously. As an eyewitness admitted, "A world of people left, including me" (Tabari, 3.230; trans. 28.193). Meanwhile, the caliph had moved to Kufa himself, putting it under military occupation to forestall a sympathetic rebellion, and sent for Salm b. Qutayba al-Bāhili, who was with his son in Rayy, to come to Iraq immediately with as many troops as he had. He also sent his nephew, ʿIsā b. Musā, accompanied by his other nephew, the son of Abu'l-ʿAbbās, with Humayd b. Qahtaba and the Khorasanian troops at the vanguard. He also attached a trusted member of his secret service who later carried the head of the Hashemite Mahdi to him and identified that of his brother, Ibrāhim. At that time, Abu Jaʿfar could spare only four thousand troops for the expedition to Medina and was desperate for reinforcement by Salm b. Qutayba (Tabari, 3.223–25; trans. 28.185–88).

The decisive fighting for the caliph against the ʿAlid anti-caliph was done by the Khorasanian troops, who spoke Persian, and their generals, such as Māhān b. Bakht and Asad b. Marzbān. Asad was among those who would shortly help the caliph, now al-Mansur, by forcing his current commander, ʿIsā b. Musā, to abdicate in favor of Mansur's son, now Muhammad al-Mahdi, as the successor-designate for the caliphate (Tabari, 3.238–39, 244; trans. 28.202–3, 208). The Khorasanian generals were indeed the *abnāʾ al-dawla*, but in a quickly changing sense—no longer the sons of revolution but sons of the (ʿAbbasid) state.

Muhammad b. ʿAbdallāh was killed on December 12, 762 (14 Ramadan 145), his rebellion in Arabia having lasted two and a half months. Just two weeks before his death, his brother Ibrāhim began his uprising in Basra. The Hashemite Mahdi's revolt was rich in religious motivation but poor in material ones. Sociologically, this feature goes a long way toward explaining its failure. The uprising of his brother was also rich in religious symbolism, but this time far more successfully combined with material incentives. Ibrāhim assumed the title al-Hādi (dispenser of divine guidance) and termed his brother's rising in Medina as a manifestation (*zuhur*), and the coins he struck in Basra correspondingly bore the Qur'anic verse (17.83): "Truth has come, and falsehood is perishing!" (Lowick 1979:220).

Ibrāhim did take the opportunity to marry the most decked-out woman of Basra, who "would come to him with her cosmetics and many-hued garments" (Tabari, 3.309; trans. 28.282), and set up headquarters in the wine house on the former Persian encampment, where he could hear the sounds of mandolins and singing (Tabari, 3.309; trans. 28.282–83). More important, he immediately reconstituted ʿAbdallāh b. Muʿāwiya's Hashemite state in southern Iran and Iraq, which, in contrast to his brother's Arabia, was rich in fiscal and military resources and offered Ibrāhim the possibility of rewarding many of his supporters with government offices. In the treasury of Basra alone, he found six hundred thousand dirhams (two million, according to another report) and could pay his soldiers fifty each (Tabari, 3.300; trans. 28.272). He thus faced Abu Jaʿfar with an army at least as large as and very probably larger than the caliph's.[19] Ahwaz, Fars, and Wasit fell to the ʿAlid rebels one after another. The evidence for popular support for the ʿAlid revolt is incontestable. Ahwaz was taken by a small force, numbering 250 against the governor's forces, which were "said to number 4,000" (Tabari, 3.300; trans. 28.272). The rest of southwestern Iran joined the rebels just as quickly (Arjomand, forthcoming).

The caliph knew Ibrāhim's military superiority and sent for Salm b. Qutayba al-Bāhili in Rayy. He also ordered Khāzim b. Khuzayma to move from Rayy to Ahwaz with four thousand men. Abu Jaʿfar spent the most anxious time of his reign waiting for Salm b. Qutayba's troops and for the additional ones under ʿIsā b. Musā he had recalled from Medina: "By God, there are only 2,000 men in my force. I have scattered my army. . . . If I am to come safely out of this, my forces [here] should not be 30,000 short." He accordingly recruited "some blacks and a few other people" and "regularly ordered firewood to be stacked and kindled at night" to give the impression that the camp was much larger than it was. Furthermore, he vowed to have nothing to do with women "until I know whether Ibrāhim's head is mine or my head belongs to Ibrāhim" (Tabari, 3.304–6; trans. 28.277–79). A companion at the time found him like "a lion, a restless wild cat, a predator to his peers who robs them of their spirit" (Tabari, 3.282; trans. 28.252). Abu Jaʿfar confided his anxiety that "Ibrāhim has now really recognized how ragged my flank is" to Salm b. Qutayba's brother Hajjāj, who had evidently come with him from Rayy. Hajjāj wrote later that he found the caliph like " a solitary hawk, intensely concentrated": "I judged him incapable of returning the salutation because of the uninterrupted rips and rents in his regime, the armies surrounding him, as well as the 100,000 swords lying in wait for him in Kufa . . . , all waiting for him in one ferocious horde, ready to pounce" (Tabari, 3.307–8; trans. 28.280–81).

All was not lost, however. About this time, his man in Mosul brought Abu Jaʿfar the heads of some five hundred Ibrāhim sympathizers of that city who had tried to prevent him and his troops from leaving, and the caliph said, "This is the beginning of victory" (Tabari, 3.296; trans. 28.268). Abu Jaʿfar's uncle ʿAbdallāh b. ʿAli, who was soon to perish in the house the nephew made to collapse on him, had put victory within reach for the caliph by advising him to move to Kufa personally and keep Kufa under tight repression[20] and to bring to the arena of confrontation the former governor of Basra, Salm b. Qutayba, who not only came with vital military reinforcements but was also joined by his tribe in the city of Basra—namely, the Bāhila, "both Arabs and clients" (Tabari, 3.304–6; trans. 28.277–79).

Ibrāhim's generals advised him to consolidate his power in the new Hashemite state and avoid immediate confrontation: "May God prosper you! You have gained control of Basra, Ahwaz, Fars and Wasit, so stay where you are and send the armies. . . . All we need is your [good] judgment." Yet, good judgment is the hardest thing to have in a situation of revolutionary mobilization. Ibrāhim was pressured to confront the caliph's army by zealots who counted on the rising of the Kufan partisans (Tabari, 3.309; trans. 28.282). But the zealots' proposed instigation of rebellion in Kufa was foiled by the equally doctrinaire stand of Bashir al-Rahhal, a Muʿtazilite ascetic known for his sociopolitical reading of the Muʿtazilite theological principle of *ʿadl* ([divine] justice) (van Ess 1991–97:2.329), who issued a fatwa against endangering the lives of the Kufans, who were "the people of our religious community (*milla*), our mission (*daʿwa*) and our prayer orientation (*qibla*)" (Tabari, 3.311; trans. 28.284–85). Among those who joined Ibrāhim's rebellion, al-Tabari also names five prominent traditionalists "and a numerous group of religious jurists and scholars" (Tabari, 3.298; trans. 28.269–70).

Ibrāhim agreed to confront the enemy anyway. By then, ʿIsā b. Musā and Humayd b. Qahtaba had arrived from Arabia with fifteen thousand men, outnumbering Ibrāhim's ten thousand men, whose number dwindled to four or five hundred[21] when the dams were broken and their fields was flooded. Fate sealed this strategic advantage of the caliph with an arrow lodged in Ibrāhim's head during the battle of Bākhamrāʾ on February 18, 763 (25 Dhu'l-Qaʿda 145) (Tabari, 3.309–10, 316; trans. 28.283, 289). Khāzim b. Khuzayma retook Ahwaz (Tabari, 3.306; trans. 28.278), and the rebellion collapsed in Wasit and Fars.

After the suppression of the ʿAlid rebellion, Abu Jaʿfar gave the governorship of Basra to Salm b. Qutayba and that of Kufa to ʿIsā b. Musā. In that year, early 763/145, the Hashemite revolution was thus irreversibly appropriated by the ʿAbbasid house. This accomplishment was sealed by the appropriation of contested charismatic titles. As Balʿami (2003:2.1102) put it in his concise rendition of Tabari's sprawling reports, having killed the original charismatic claimant to the title Mahdi, to whom he himself had pledged allegiance during the late Umayyad period of multiple sovereignty, Abu Jaʿfar appropriated it for his own son: "Abu Jaʿfar gave him the title of Mahdi and said: 'Muhammad b. ʿAbdallāh, the Mahdi of the House of Muhammad, is this my son, not that Muhammad b. ʿAbdallāh b. al-Hasan.'" On the same occasion, he himself assumed the messianic title Mansur (al-Masʿudi [1894] 1967:341). This left the title of the slain brother of the Hasanid Mahdi, Ibrāhim—namely, *al-hādi* (the righteous guide)—to be appropriated by his grandson in due course.

The victor of the Hashemite revolution, a revolution now definitely made ʿAbbasid, proceeded to complete the foundation of his own imperial city at the center of the world, near the Sasanian capital and on land still belonging to *dehqān*s. He first called it the City of the Victor (*madinat al-mansur*) (Tabari, 3.271–74, 279; trans. 28.237–42, 248) and then the City of Peace (*madinat al-salām*).[22] Abu Jaʿfar allotted a huge estate by the Jawhar canal connecting the Tigris and Euphrates below the former Sasanian capital, al-Madāʾin, to Nawbakht, the Zoroastrian astrologer who had predicted the fall of Ibrāhim and cast the horoscope for the foundation of the City of the Victor (Tabari, 3.318; trans. 28.291). Of its four gates facing the four quarters of the universe, the most important was the Khorasan gate, which became known as Gate of the Revolution (*bāb al-dawla*) (Mottahedeh 1975:65). And to celebrate the ʿAbbasid Revolution as the social revolution of the clients, the new capital included a quarter of the clients (*darb al-mawāli*) (Omar 1976:50) as well as land granted to the "sons of revolution."

Consequences of the ʿAbbasid Revolution: Caliphal Absolutism and the Integration of the Persian *Mawāli*

Abu Mansur Muhammad b. Ahmad, who became the caliph al-Qahir in 932/320, asked his companion, Muhammad b. ʿAli al-Misri al-Khurāsāni al-Akhbāri, to tell him about his ancestor al-Mansur, and here is what that Khorasanian expert in historical traditions had to say:

> He was by God the first to create a split between the descendants of al-ʿAbbās b. ʿAbd al-Muttalib and the house of Abu Tālib [b. ʿAbd al-Muttalib]; until then their cause was a single cause. And he was the first caliph to surround himself

> with astronomers and act according to astronomical ordinances; the Zoroastrian astronomer Nawbakht, ancestor of the Nawbakhtis, was with him and accepted Islam from his hand. . . . And he was the first caliph for whom books were translated from the Persian language into Arabic, . . . and other ancient books from Greek, Latin, Pahlavi, Persian, and Syriac. . . . And he was the first caliph to employ his clients and slaves in his government, appoint them to important functions, and give them precedence over Arabs. The caliphs who succeeded him among his descendants followed this example until the domination of the Arabs collapsed, their leadership disappeared, and their status lapsed. (al-Masʿudi 1970:5.211)

One cannot ask for a more concise summary of the consequences of the ʿAbbasid Revolution than what its consolidator, Abu Jaʿfar al-Mansur, is given the credit for being the first to institute.

Caliph al-Mansur himself celebrated the new principle of autocracy that discarded the Hashemite revolutionary principle of the caliphate of the "acceptable one" (*al-riḍā*) for a new version of the caliphate as the absolute rule of God's deputy. In the final oration of his reign, modeled on the Prophet's so-called farewell speech delivered on the day of the ʿArafat in 775/158, he thus asserted his claim to divinely ordained autocracy: "I am the authority (*sultan*) of God upon his earth, and I govern you through his guidance and his direction to what is right" (Tabari, 3.426; trans. 29.131, modified slightly). Paradoxical as it seems, compared with the Arabist doctrine of caliphal absolutism elaborated by the Marwanid caliphs, which was based exclusively on Islam (Tabari, 2.1756–64; Crone and Hinds 1986:118–26), the ʿAbbasid doctrine of the autocracy of God's caliph reflected the integrative dimension of the ʿAbbasid Revolution, systematically incorporating the Persian theory of kingship.

The ʿAbbasid autocracy resulting from the consolidation of power that ended the revolutionary process fostered the growth of the secretarial class, which exercised administrative and political power insecurely, depending on the will and whim of the caliph, but enjoyed enormous cultural dominance independently. The famous Persian secretary ʿAbdallāh b. al-Muqaffaʿ perished during the revolutionary power struggle among the contenders for succession to the first ʿAbbasid caliph, but not so the political culture he propagated. Some important elements of the outlook of the Persian secretarial class (*kuttāb*) became permanently embedded in the new Islamic society ushered in by the integrative revolution of the Persian *mawāli*.

The incorporation of the Persian client secretaries into an expanded caliphal bureaucracy was made definite by the son and grandsons of the

Hashemite missionary Khālid b. Barmak under Caliph Hārun al-Rashid, during the period referred to as "the rule of the house of Barmak" (*sultān al-Barmak*) (786–803/170–187) (Sourdel 1959:1.179). A Basran Manichaean and protégé of the Barmakis rendered Ibn al-Muqaffaʿ's prose translations of *Kalila wa Dimna* and of the *Book of Mazdak* in Arabic verse for the pleasure of the Caliph Hārun al-Rashid (Arjomand 1994). Even the great ʿAbd al-Hamid al-Kātib, the staunchest supporter of the last Umayyad caliph, Marwān II, was rehabilitated, and his administrative epistles became the object of emulation for the subsequent generation of secretaries. The reason for this rehabilitation, which is also the key to the continuity between the pre- and the postrevolutionary regimes, was revealed to ʿAbd al-Hamid's son Ismāʿil by no less a person than the great Yahyā b. Khālid al-Barmaki: "We never seek an argument in support of sovereignty (*mulk*) without finding that your father had preceded us in adducing it" (cited in al-Qādi 1993:237).

Some decades later, in the ninth (third) century, al-Jāhiz gives us the following portrait of a secretary:

> [He] has learnt the maxims of Bozorgmehr, the Covenant of Ardashir, the Epistles of ʿAbd al-Hamid and the Adab of Ibn al-Muqaffaʿ, and has taken the *Book of Mazdak* as the fountainhead of his learning and the *Kalila wa Dimna* collection as the secret treasury of his wisdom. . . .
>
> His first task is to attack the composition of the Koran and denounce its inconsistencies. . . . Then he straightaway interrupts the conversation to speak of the policies of Ardashir Papakan, the administration of Anushirvan, and the admirable way the country was run under the Sasanians.[23]

Al-Mansur also put the ʿAbbasid caliphal absolutism on a solid sociological foundation, reaching beyond the secretarial bureaucracy to an Islamic society that was rapidly expanding among the subjects of his empire and was soon to encompass the great majority of them. The son of a Berber concubine who upheld the honor of fellow half-breeds in his last letter to the ʿAlid challenger to his rule (Arjomand, forthcoming), Abu Jaʿfar was the perfect first consolidator and centralizer of power after the revolution of the non-Arab clients, whose call to Islam in the Hashemite mission swept aside the Arabism of the Umayyad Empire and established the equality of all Muslim subjects of the ʿAbbasid Empire as a matter of principle. This far-reaching passive democratization of Islam's integrative revolution in mid-eighth-century Iraq, where the garrison city of Basra was soon outdone by Baghdad as a melting pot of the *mawāli* and even newer converts (Hoyland

2001:245, *apud* the Syrian John bar Penkaye), had far-reaching sociocultural consequences that are generally acknowledged.

From Basra, Abu ʿAmr b. al-ʿAlāʾ (d. 770/154) added the promotion of Arabic grammar to the study of the Qurʾan by dispatching his students to tribal informants to gather information on "the speech of the nomadic Arabs" (*kalām al-ʿArab*), and the information was fed by the Persian client Sibawayh (d. 796/180) into the construction of the first grammar of classical Arabic (Hoyland 2001:245–46). Another Persian client, Muqātil b. Sulaymān (d. 767/150), wrote the oldest surviving commentary on the Qurʾan. Yet another client, at the courts of Abu Jaʿfar's brother in Mesopotamia and of his son in Rayy, who finally moved to and died in al-Mansur's City of Peace, Ibn Ishāq, was the great-grandson of a certain Yasār (a typical name for the earliest converts) who had been captured in one of the early battles against the Sasanian Empire (Zaryab-Khoʾi 1989:81–94). Ibn Ishāq produced the definitive *Life of the Prophet* as part of his world history of salvation (Khoury 1983:esp. 22) and thus completed the ad hoc reconstruction of the history of Islam by preceding generations of the *mawāli* by portraying it as a universalist, world religion rather than an Arab one (Noth and Conrad 1994:157–67). The gibe against the client secretaries by al-Jāhiz notwithstanding, the *mawāli* in general thus handsomely repaid their debt to the Islamic society they were appropriating by making its language and culture ecumenical and its religion universal.

NINE

The Papal Revolution and Its Export: The Crusades

"The oldest revolutionary in Europe is the pope!" declared Eugen Rosenstock-Huessy in 1931 in *Die europaïschen Revolution und der Charakter der Nationen* ([1931] 1951:11). Five years later, Gerd Tellenbach ([1936] 1970:1, 111) similarly called the reform movement for "the freedom of the Church" that began in 1058 and reached its peak under Gregory VII (1073–85) "a struggle for right order in the world" and "a great revolution in world history" unforeseen by any. Since then, the idea of the papal revolution has been used to designate Gregory VII's struggle for the freedom of the church from temporal powers, also known as the Investiture Contest. Berman (1983:85–113) presents the reform movement as a total revolution that culminated in the First Crusade (1096–99) as its "foreign war."[1] Despite this last observation, however, this widely shared reading of the papal revolution is internalist, focused exclusively on the developmental path of Western Christianity, and ignores the church's entangled history with the struggle against the surrounding Muslim world. No serious attempt to understand the episode as a revolution has been made from the viewpoint of entangled histories and comparative sociology. This chapter is the first such attempt and focuses on constitutive historical connections as well as implicit comparisons between revolutions in medieval Islam and Christianity.

It is worthwhile, however, to preface my analysis with a note on counterfactual analysis of adequate causation. One student of Max Weber's who applied Weber's idea of counterfactual causal adequacy to the study of Islam, C. H. Becker ([1932] 1967:1.16), came up with a noted counterfactual statement to highlight Islam's Hellenistic heritage: "Without Alexander the Great, no Islamic civilization!" A more compelling world-historical counterfactual conditional came a little later in another major study of the entangled history of Islam and the West. In *Mohammed and Charlemagne*, the completed manuscript left on his deathbed in May 1935, Henri Pirenne (1957:234) summed up his conclusion: "It is therefore strictly correct to say that without Mohammed Charlemagne would have been inconceivable!" Anticipating the conclusion of this chapter, we may phrase a contrasting counterfactual conditional of equal or greater world-historical significance: "Without Islam, no papal revolution!"

Geopolitics of the Reform of the Church in the Second Half of the Eleventh Century

The export of the Fatimid Revolution from the Maghreb to Egypt, Syria, and Sicily in the last quarter of the tenth century made Sicily a province of the Fatimid empire, whose governors were now and then recalled to Cairo. The Muslims also overran southern Italy, especially Calabria, in the closing decade of the tenth century, and it was Calabria that was used in 1020 as the base for what was in effect a reconquest of Sicily by Ahmad al-Akhal (r. 1019–38), who made Palermo his capital (Brett 2010:50). It was in the decades preceding the Byzantine invasion of Sicily in 1040 and the overrunning of Apulia by Norman tribesmen in 1042 that the dire Saracen menace to Rome disturbed the exclusive appropriation of the papal pontificate by the parochial and otiose Roman aristocracy and prompted two Italian popes, Benedict VIII (1012–24) and his brother, John XIX, to reform the Roman church in order to make it administratively more efficient, while putting the papacy under the protection of the rising German Salian dynasty. Benedict VIII used his military skills as a count to organize an expedition against the Muslims in Sardinia in 1015–16 and launched the reform movement in a council at Pavia in 1018. His brother, John XIX, crowned the Salian Conrad II as emperor in Rome in 1027, becoming increasingly subservient to him. The reform movement continued under another Roman patrician who bought the papacy to fix it, Gregory VI (1044–46), whose attempts at reform drew their impetus from his young deacon, and possibly relative, Hildebrand (Ildebrando) (Whitney 1926:15–22).

Meanwhile, Emperor Conrad II's forceful successor Henry III (1039–56) decided that neither he nor the project of reform of the church had any need for Italians. While acting as the Vicar of Christ to depose three popes in 1046 (Berman 1983:578n3), Henry III also made the Roman Senate grant him the status of *patricius* to enable him to "nominate" popes, and he used it to install a series of German popes in Rome, the greatest of whom was his friend Bruno of Toul, who became Pope Leo IX (1049–54). In a few years, Leo IX and Henry III secured the emancipation of the church from the

Roman aristocracy. Leo created his own court, curia, and packed it with a brilliant generation of ecclesiastical reformers, mostly German and French, whom he brought to Rome with him. He did, however, have the good sense to recall to Rome the Italian Hildebrand, who had accompanied Gregory VI into his German exile after deposition. Henry III died unexpectedly in 1056, just as his friend Leo IX had two years earlier, but the Duke of Lotharinga, Godfrey, ignored the rights of the *patricius* inherited by the new king, Henry IV (1056–1106), who was a child of six or seven, and managed the election of his own brother, as Stephen IX, to the papal throne (Tellenbach [1988] 1993:148–49). Stephen's papacy lasted less than a year, and Nicholas II (1059–61) and his two Italian successors, Alexander II (1061–73) and Gregory VII (1073–85), had to develop a new, nonterritorial basis for the papacy, as the city of Rome was geopolitically a very uncertain, unreliable, and unsustainable base for it (Tellenbach [1988] 1993:153–57). As Gregory confided to his friend Abbot Hugh of Cluny in January 1075, "those among whom I live, Romans, Lombards and Normans, are worse than the Jews and the infidels [Saracens]!" (cited in Fliche 1946:75).

Leo IX's pontificate ended tragically with his imprisonment by the Normans before his sudden death in April 1054. Nevertheless, Nicholas II found it expedient to make an alliance with the Normans that was negotiated by Hildebrand and by Desiderius, the abbot of Monte Cassino, his successor as Pope Victor II (1086–87) (Whitney 1926:36). Just as they had done for Nicholas II, Norman troops installed Alexander II in Rome against an antipope, who nevertheless continued to sign bulls as Pope Honorius II for the next eight years (Whitney 1926:42–45). Insecure in Rome, Alexander II sought an alternative and a more abstract base for papal authority by championing the Christian world against the Saracens in Spain and Sicily (Fliche 1946:48–54).

With the fragmentation of Muslim rule in Sicily, the Normans were invited by one of the local Muslim rulers as mercenaries in 1061 but began the piecemeal conquest of the island for themselves with full papal endorsement, capturing Palermo in 1072. The Norman conquest of Sicily was sanctified by the popes as a holy war against Muslims in the name of Saint Peter. Count Roger I of Sicily was given the banner of Saint Peter (*vexillum sancti Petri*) to protect him in the war against the Muslims (Robinson 1990:324). As allies, Normans were indeed unruly, however. They sacked Rome to save Pope Gregory VII from Emperor Henry IV in 1084, and the outraged Roman populace forced Gregory VII to take refuge in Norman-ruled Salerno. The Normans protected him until his death on May 25, 1085. Gregory's successors, Victor II and Urban II (1088–99), also lived under Norman protection.

Rome was certainly not safe as the pope's residence for the decade after its sack and devastation by the Normans. Gregory VII died in Salerno, and Victor II in Monte Cassino, his real home. All the while, the anti-pope Guibert, Clement III (1080–1100), who had been brought to Rome by Henry IV to crown him emperor in 1083, controlled Rome. Urban II spent less than a third of his pontificate in Rome, and while there he lived in a mean state. In 1094, a fellow French abbot, Geoffrey of Vendôme, was distressed to find him living in the house of a certain Frangipani and bought the Lateran Palace for him from Clement III's agent. Nevertheless, Urban II died in the private home of Pierleoni and was buried under cover of darkness, leaving Rome once again to Clementine control (Brooke 1926:91; Tellenbach [1988] 1993:254).

In short, in the two crucial decades of the papal revolution, the pope had ceased to be the *Roman* pontiff in the strict sense and was increasingly the Vicar of Saint Peter at the Apostolic See. It is remarkable that without any secure territorial base, Pope Gregory VII nevertheless presumed to judge the earth, to use his words, and declared his court to be "the court of the whole of Christendom" (cited in Berman 1983:99). Furthermore, he explicitly claimed suzerainty over Spain, Corsica, Sicily, and Hungary as properties of Saint Peter. This sovereign authority over all the lands of Saint Peter was exercised from the Holy See, at once ubiquitous and without any secure terrestrial base—and certainly not one in Rome. As Gregory told the French princes setting out against the Moors in Spain at the very beginning of his papacy in April 1073, "the kingdom of Spain was from ancient times subject to St Peter in full sovereignty [*proprii juris*], and . . . it belongs of right to no mortal, but solely to the Apostolic See" (*Gregory* 6).

Hildebrand, his name notwithstanding, was an Italian who had lived his formative life and career in Rome under the same Saracen menace that had forced his compatriots to initiate the reform of the Roman church before it was taken over by the German popes. Somewhat later, as a close adviser to Alexander II, he took part in organizing holy wars against the Saracens in Sicily to the south and Spain to the west. He eagerly followed his predecessor on those fronts, despite his hallmark struggle with temporal powers in Germany, France, and Italy. The major Christian victory of the period in Spain, the capture of Toledo, did not take place until a year after Gregory's death. Meanwhile, a disastrous turn of events had forced his attention eastward. In 1071, the Seljuk Turks inflicted a decisive defeat on the Byzantine emperor in the battle of Manzikert/Malazgird, which threw the Eastern Roman Empire into a decade-long convulsion and opened Anatolia to the continuous inflow of Turkish tribes. Gregory became pope two years later and wasted no time in planning a campaign against the Seljuk Turks as "commander and pontiff" (Robinson 1990:325). Writing to the German king, Henry IV, in December 1074, Gregory set forth his plan for a crusade so "that the religion of Christ may not utterly perish in our time" (*Gregory* 57). Although the plan had to be aborted because of his subsequent problems with Henry IV, Gregory never lost interest in the Byzantine struggle against the Seljuks, who intensified his aversion to the Saracens (Cowdrey 1998:489–90). He sought an understanding with the Byzantine emperor Michael VII and excommunicated those who overthrew him, including Alexius Comnenus, who came to power in 1081 (Runciman 1957:98–99). He also wrote to the Christian bishops and clergy under the rule of the Saracens in Carthage, Mauritania, and elsewhere in North Africa (*Gregory* 16–17, 94–95; Cowdrey 1998:491–94). In one of his last and bitterest letters admitting defeat in 1084, Gregory would announce the approach of Antichrist, declaring that "the true Christian faith . . . is turned over to evil fashions of this world and is alas! alas! almost annihilated. Its ancient colors are changed, and it has become the laughingstock, not only of the Devil, but of Jews, Saracens and pagans" (*Gregory* 194).

Constitutional Politics of the Revolutionary Struggle for the Freedom of the Church

Saint Jerome's Latin translation of the Bible had drawn on the terminology of Roman law, employing such terms as *potestas*, *imperium*, and *iurisdictio*. In establishing the Apostolic See and the primacy of its bishop, the pope, over those of Constantinople and Alexandria in the mid-fifth century, Pope Leo I, the Great (440–61), claimed that, as the successor of Saint Peter, he inherited the "plenitude of power" (*plenitudo potestatis*) given to Saint Peter by Christ (Ullmann 1976:84). What was now needed was the transcendent abstraction of the Holy See of Saint Peter from Rome to wrest it from the claws of the Roman aristocracy and, with it, that of the Vicar of Saint Peter from the narrower conception of the Roman pontiff as the bishop of Rome. This was done by amplifying the constitutional implications of *plenitudo potestatis* and is reflected in the appearance of the designation of *papatus* (papacy) alongside *pontificates* (pontificate) from the mid-eleventh century onward, marking the emergence of the papacy as such (Tellenbach [1988] 1993:186). Cardinal Peter Damiani had argued for the primacy of the pope over the universal church rather than over temporal powers. Gregory VII highlighted the identification of Saint Peter's Apostolic See with the universal church and Mater Christianitas, thus making it subject to the pope exclusively (Ladner 1954:52–53, 60–61).

This fundamental conceptual breakthrough, in turn, had to be sustained institutionally. The Curia and the College of Cardinals, or the Sacred College, were the two institutions on which the new papacy could be based independently of the Roman aristocracy and clergy, on the one hand, and the German king, on the other. These institutions had to be developed by the reforming popes. Leo IX cleared the Roman church of the local clergy and administrative staff who were guilty of simony (purchase and sale of clerical offices) and ordained the foreign clerics he had brought with him as cardinal bishops and priests, giving a new meaning to the very term "cardinal" (a derivative of *cardo*) by seeing Saint Peter's See as the "head and pivot (*cardo*) of the Universal Church" and thereby adding to it the connotation of participation in the government of the universal church (Kuttner 1945:172, 176). He also created two new "liturgical" cardinals in Besançon and Cologne and reserved the observance of liturgy "according to the custom of the Roman Church" for seven monks who later became known as cardinals (Kuttner 1945:165, 167). Nicholas II privileged the seven suffragan cardinal bishops of metropolitan Rome in the canonical election of the pope. Alexander II referred to the latter as the seven cardinals of Saint Peter's and augmented the jurisdiction of cardinal priests (Kuttner 1945:152, 176). At the same time, the differentiation between the cardinal bishops and the cardinal priests began to disappear. In the competitive mobilization by Gregory VII and anti-pope Clement III, who gave his deacons the title of cardinal deacons (Kuttner 1945:197), cardinals were courted by both sides, and counterfeits of Nicholas II's decree extended the prerogative of the seven to all cardinals, whom Peter Damiani called the "Senators of the Universal Church" (Kuttner 1945:174). The original meaning of the term "cardinal" was forgotten, and a *collectio canonum* from 1087 declared the cardinals to be "the cardines (pivots) who rule and guide God's people," and a description of the Lateran church from the same period mentions the seven cardinal bishops and twenty-eight others as cardinal bishops and priests who have the power of judgment over all bishops of the empire (Kuttner 1945:152, 176–77). In the course of the struggle for the freedom of the church, the cardinals thus emerged as the highest dignitaries of the Catholic Church, who constituted the Sacred College and eventually claimed the exclusive right to elect the pope.

The papal revolution grew out of the reform movement with the election of Archdeacon Hildebrand as Pope Gregory VII in April 1073. Hildebrand chose to have himself proclaimed Gregory VII out of loyalty to his fellow Italian and former reformist pope Gregory VI, under whom he had begun his career and with whom he had gone into exile (*Gregory* 150). But his program of church building also had great affinity with that of Gregory I, the Great (590–604), whom he followed in calling himself the "Servant of the servants of God." As the archdeacon (after 1059) of the nascent Roman Curia, he was the ablest administrator of the church reform movement. Nevertheless, and his papal office notwithstanding, he displayed what must be typologically classified as the charisma of the Prophet.

Hildebrand had been closely involved with the constitutional politics of the reform movement long before he became pope. Though probably not yet archdeacon, Hildebrand was clearly the Curia's kingmaker, as already in 1057, Stephen IX had left instructions before his death that the election of his successor be delayed until Hildebrand's return from Germany. Even though these instructions were ignored and Benedict X was elected pope in April 1058, Hildebrand did not accept the fait accompli on his return, and as soon as he had reached Florence, he had its bishop, Gerhard, elected Pope Nicholas II in Sienna (Tellenbach [1988] 1993:149). Fully aware of these irregular elections, and of his own dependence on Norman troops for overcoming the rival anti-pope, Nicholas II promulgated the decree on the election of the pope by the cardinal bishops at the Lateran Council in April 1059. The decree was confirmed by a second, a year later, when its formulation was tightened by using the term "canonical election" (*canonica election*), while declaring null and void the "enthronement on the Holy See for money, men's favor following any popular or military sedition, and without unanimity, canonical election and benediction of the cardinal-bishops, and then of the lower orders of clergy" (cited in Fliche 1946:20). Two fundamental conceptual breakthroughs were needed before further reform of the church could be seriously pursued, however.

Although the papal constitutional prerevolution was set in motion by the 1059 decree of Nicholas II, neither of the two subsequent elections of 1061 and 1073 conformed to it (Tellenbach [1988] 1993:154–55). In fact, the election of the revolutionary pope on April 22, 1073, was reasonably said to have been by the Holy Spirit through the Roman plebs! According to Gregory's own account written on the following day, and a fuller eyewitness account written a decade or so later, a tumult broke out during the funeral of Alexander II, and men, including the clergy, and women shouted, "Hildebrand Bishop!" Hildebrand tried to reach the pulpit, but a certain Hugo Candidus reached it first and gave a fiery speech that prompted the clerics to call out "God has chosen Pope Gregory." The people then dragged Hildebrand and put him on the papal throne despite his resistance (Tellenbach [1988] 1993:155–56). Gregory collapsed but wrote on the following day from his bed that "a great tumult of people rushed upon me like madmen," adding nevertheless that "it was evidently done by a special act of divine grace" (*Gregory* 2).

Once he recovered from the turmoil of his election, the Curia bureaucrat emerged as a reconstructed prophet, lamenting the fall of the church from its pristine sacrality to the present ignominious status of subjection to profane, mundane interests and temporal powers. He wrote letter after letter to the rulers of feudal Europe and to the clergy and people of its various dioceses fulminating against the sins of simony and clerical fornication, calling for the "Freedom of the Church," its "restitution to a glorious pristine state," and "the restoration of that old and holy Church, so that it would be torn loose from servile oppression, nay tyrannical servitude, and restituted to its old liberty" (cited in Ladner 1956:18–19). "Because of sin," he wrote to Geoffrey, the Duke of Lorraine, in May 1073, the whole world is "set in malice against us!" (*Gregory* 7); and to his Patarine supporters in Lombardy some two months later, "Also saith the prophet, 'Cursed be he that keepeth back his sword from blood!'" (*Gregory* 11). Gregory's prophetic style emerges clearly when, urging reform on the archbishop of Magdeburg in 1075, he quotes Jeremiah 1.10: "Lo, I have set thee this day over the nations to waste and destroy, and to build and to plant" (cited in Ladner 1956:21–22). In a letter to the clergy and people of Aquileia in 1077, he urged them to suppress the evil customs that have corrupted the church by restoring the practice of canonical election of bishops while assuring them that he "only seeks what is necessary for the salvation of all" (cited in Ladner 1956:22). His prophetic style is similarly shown in a late letter from 1084, where he cites from the Psalms: "the kings of the earth set themselves and the rulers take counsel together against the Lord and against his anointed" (*Gregory* 193).

The manifesto of the papal revolution was a lost canonical collection, whose twenty-seven chapter headings were also cited separately as *dictatus papae* (Ullmann 1975:135). It was published in 1075 to demonstrate that the only form of government for a Christian society that was permitted by canon law was a papal monarchy. Remembering doubtless his old patron Leo IX's excommunication of the bishop of Compostela for arrogating to himself the title "the bishop of the Apostolic See," which belonged to the pope alone (Tellenbach [1988] 1993:190), Gregory's dictates begin with the assertion of his primacy within the church over all other bishops: that the bishop of Rome alone is by right called universal (title 2) and that he may depose and absolve any bishop (no. 25). Exclusive legislative power is claimed for the pope: he alone is permitted to "make new laws according to the needs of the times" (no. 7). Then we have the most revolutionary claims of all for papal supremacy over temporal authority: that he may depose emperors (no. 11) and that he may absolve subjects of unjust men from their oath of fealty (no. 27) (Fliche 1946:79–80).

Gregory himself summarized the *dictatus papae* manifesto in a decree of February 1075, which amounted to the declaration of the rule of God on earth. This proclamation of Christian theocracy was made by Gregory, installed on the seat of Saint Peter, "sinful and unworthy though we are." Any Christian ruler wishing to save his soul, "according to the Christian faith and the constitution of the Church, cannot refuse obedience, not to us but to God Almighty. . . . Whoever wishes to execute God's orders faithfully cannot despise ours, as they interpret the decisions of the holy fathers, and they must be received just as if they came from the mouth of the Apostle [Saint Peter] himself" (cited in Fliche 1946:133).

In his other pronouncements and correspondence, Gregory expanded titles 2, 7, and 25 to mean that the sovereign status of the pope entitled him to unquestioning obedience by all bishops and, further, that he had full freedom to change any law issued by his predecessors (Ullmann 1965:107). His expansive interpretation of titles 11 and 27 was that the papal plenitude of power made him the judge of the proper discharge by kings of their divine trust and enabled him, as he claimed when deposing Emperor Henry IV, to take away "empires, kingdoms, principalities, dukedoms, marquisates earldoms and the properties of all men" (*Gregory* 152). Justifying the excommunication of the emperor in terms of the pope's authority to "judge the earth," Gregory maintained in March 1081 "that the priests of Christ are to be considered as fathers and masters of kings and princes and of all believers" (*Gregory* 169).

Gregory VII derived his revolutionary claim to spiritual, temporal, and *territorial* authority as the Vicar of Saint Peter from the power of the keys given to Peter by Jesus Christ when saying, "I shall give you the keys of the kingdom of heaven, and whatever you bind on earth will be bound in heaven and whatever you loosen on earth will be loosened in heaven" (Matthew 16.18–19). Having asserted that kings surely "belong to the sheep which the Son of God committed to St Peter," Gregory asks, "Is he to whom the power of opening and closing heaven has been given not permitted to judge the earth? Far from it" (cited in Robinson 1990:295). And in a similar vein, "For if the See of St Peter decides and judges celestial things, *how much more* does it decide and judge the earthly and the secular" (cited in Ullmann 1965:103, emphasis added).

I have added to the well-recognized spiritual and temporal dimensions of the authority of Saint Peter the territorial one. This was especially important for the feudal society of Western Europe. According to the most famous of the medieval forgeries, the Donation of Constantine, that emperor had given sovereignty over the western part of the Roman Empire to

Pope Sylvester, the bishop of Rome—that is, the See of Saint Peter—and given him additional landed estates elsewhere and in various islands "for the upkeep of the church of St Peter." Gregory included among the duties of the king he presumed to judge the protection not only of the See of Saint Peter but also of his lands, the claim to which he ever expanded into Saracen territories in Spain, Sicily, and other islands around Italy, notably Corsica, where he delegated his "vicariate" to the archbishop of Pisa as an "Apostolic Vicar" (*Gregory* 126, 135). Two important consequences follow from this. The feudal principle of grounding authority in landed property was harnessed to the hierocratic theme and became increasingly important for the justification of papal authority and eventually papal monarchy (Ullmann 1970:331–32).

In the 1060s, the reforming popes who had recruited Normans as their allies in southern Italy made them vassals (*fidelis*) of the Holy See and continued to give them fiefdoms as they advanced in Sicily; and Alexander II "conferred a banner on William as a token of kingship" when he embarked on the conquest of England in 1066. Gregory VII likewise granted his Norman allies fiefdoms on behalf of Saint Peter. In 1080, the Norman Robert Guiscard swore a feudal oath of allegiance as the Duke of Apulia, Calabria, and Sicily to be "the vassal [*fidelis*] of the Holy Roman Church and of the Apostolic See and of you, my lord Gregory, universal Pope," promising to "protect the revenues [*regalia*] and the property of St Peter" (*Gregory* 158). Furthermore, Gregory extended the feudal principles of feudal vassalage to create vassal kingdoms in Croatia, Dalmatia, and Hungary as "the property of the holy Roman church," and when writing to the Christian kings and princes of Spain, he claimed that "Spain was surrendered to the jurisdiction and proprietorship of St Peter and the holy Roman church" (Robinson 1990: 306–7).

When renewing Gregory VII's claim to Corsica in 1091, Urban II, good canon lawyer that he was, explicitly cited *Constitutum Constantini*: all islands were bestowed by "Emperor Constantine on St Peter and his vicars as their property." In the same year, Urban grounded his own claim to the islands of Lipari on clauses 13 and 17 of the *Constitutum* (Robinson 1990:310).

Revolutionary Mobilization of Italian Cities and Frankish Feudal Society

The course of the conflict between Pope Gregory VII and King Henry IV, with its spectacular ups and downs, from the barefoot appearance of Henry at Canossa in the winter of 1077 to beg the pope's forgiveness and thereby forestall his joining the elected anti-king in Germany, to Henry's deposition by the pope in February 1080, and finally his triumphant entry to Rome and his imperial coronation on March 31, 1084, has been exhaustively studied (Tellenbach [1988] 1993:185–252). In the course of this struggle, Gregory mobilized the laity in Italian cities against the nonreformist clergy; in December 1080, to give a noted example, he wrote to "the clergy and the people" of Ravenna seeking to rouse them against their royalist archbishop Wibert (anti-pope Clement III) and the clergy loyal to the latter, "who are the enemies of the cross of Christ!" (*Gregory* 165). Gregory also sought to persuade the great feudal lords to use force to prevent simoniac and unchaste clergy from celebrating the mass (Tellenbach [1988] 1993:208–9).

From our point of view, two remarkable features of this decade of conflict between the church and the empire must be highlighted. Pamphleteering spread widely in support of the pope, in what has been described as "the first great age of propaganda in world history" (Tellenbach 1940:14–15). The polemical writing campaign began with the reform movement and was promoted by the reformists, who provoked responses and counterattacks by their opponents. It gathered great momentum under Gregory VII, when lay investiture and the conflict with Henry IV were added to the older themes of simony, lay domination of the church, and clerical marriage. The publicists were almost exclusively monks and priests, who disseminated handwritten manuscripts in networks of close association in monasteries, churches, scholarly circles, and even occasionally in the street (Mirbt 1894:96–110). Monastic networks with major abbeys as their nuclei were of particular importance in the dissemination of the propagandist literature (Mirbt 1894:110–12). Many of the polemicists wrote anonymously, some pseudonymously, and the Gregorians outnumbered their opponents (Mirbt 1894:86–95). The pamphlets popularized the cause of church reform in tandem with Gregory's concrete measures such as the order to boycott married priests and those with concubines, which in the words of one pamphleteer, caused "the confusion of all human laws, . . . sudden unrest among the populace, new treacheries of servants against their masters and masters' distrust of their servants, abject breaches of faith among friends and equals, conspiracies against the powers ordained by God . . . and all this backed by those who are called leaders of Christendom" (cited in Berman 1983:95).

Many of Gregory's own letters can be counted as elements of the mobilizational propaganda. From the beginning, he fulminated against his clerical opponents as "precursors of Antichrist" (*Gregory* 9) and "ministers of Satan and heralds of Antichrist" (*Gregory* 11) and did not hesitate to demonize his temporal foes in equally forceful terms, as in the following letter: "Who does not know that kings and princes derive their origins from men ignorant of God who raised themselves above their fellows by pride, plunder, treachery, murder—in short, by every kind of crime—at the instigation of the Devil . . . ?" (Berman 1983:110).

The second feature is the two very different social groups that Gregory's propaganda campaign sought to mobilize as partners in the revolutionary papal coalition: first, the Frankish, German, and Italian feudal knights; and, second, the urban strata in Milan and other cities of Lombardy consisting of the barons (*capetanei*), the minor patriciate, the so-called lesser vavasors (*vavassores minors*), and plebeians (*popolani*). Together with his Norman allies in southern Italy, they constituted the heterogeneous Gregorian revolutionary coalition.

Mobilization of the knights of Christendom against the Saracen peril was one of the main goals of Gregory VII's voluminous correspondence. He called these knights the troops of Saint Peter (*militia sancti Petri*) (*Gregory* 181), frequently summoning them to war as liege men or vassals (*fideles*) of Saint Peter (*Gregory* 154, 163). The widespread recruitment of Christian knights was completely detached from the specific local goals of the papacy and its investiture contests but instead created an otherwise-heterogeneous constituency that could remain united only by the export of the papal revolution. Besides the knights he was recruiting for holy warfare against the Saracens, Gregory also wrote to those of Milan and other northern Italian cities.

Mobilizing urban support followed a very different trajectory. The confluence of the incipient urban revolution in Lombardy with the struggle for the freedom of the church began in the mid-eleventh century and continued for some two decades, but their respective developmental paths diverged in the early years of Gregory VII's papacy. In a posthumously published 1913 manuscript comparing Occidental and Oriental cities, Max Weber attributed the world-historical significance of urban revolutions in Italy to the political autonomy and self-government of the cities that developed on the basis of the "revolutionary usurpation" of power by the communes (Weber 1978:1253), or of "non-legitimate domination," to use the phrase supplied by the editors of *Economy and Society*, which nevertheless later spurred the growth of urban law—"the codification of a special rational law for citizens which the courts of the consuls were to apply" (Weber 1978:1254). For Weber, the starting point of the urban revolutions was the *coniuratio*, or oath-bound association of arm-bearing burghers. He identified the *coniuratio* of Milan in 980 as the earliest instance of such sworn urban leagues; around 1100, such leagues had developed into city assemblies, as in Genoa and elsewhere (Weber 1978:1226, 1252).

The Milanese sworn associations come into clearer view in 1035–37 during the civil war between the barons (*capetanei*), headed by Archbishop Aribert (1018–45), and the lesser vavasors, in which the latter gained the upper hand with the help of Emperor Conrad II. Conrad imprisoned Aribert for about two months, and in his *Constitution de feudis* of 1037 he made the vavasors a separate feudal estate under the jurisdiction of the emperor and with their own committee (Violante 1953:196–204). Feeling threatened by the upper stratum of the plebeians—the *cives*, comprising owners of landed property inside the city and in the surrounding countryside, merchants, and some craftsmen (Violante 1953:209–13)—the two parties made an uneasy peace, and Aribert made a significant step in incorporating the feuding parties into a somewhat unified political community that also included the plebeians in its de facto tripartite constitutions and invented the standard of the Milanese commune (Prévite-Orton 1926:217–19). Nevertheless, a revolt of the *cives* broke out in the last year of Aribert's rule, triggered by a violent incident between a vavasor and a plebeian. Continuing his father's middle course, Emperor Henry III appointed a vavasor, Guido Velate (1045–71), to succeed Aribert as archbishop of Milan in 1045. For the next decade, Guido saw growing discord among the three groups, which drew in reformist dissidents from the Milanese, nobility-dominated, Ambrosian clerical establishment.

As the See of Saint Ambrose, the patron saint of Milan, the church of Milan was virtually independent of Rome and the See of Saint Peter in the first half of the eleventh century, and Archbishop Aribert was the perfect embodiment of the Ambrosian tradition. Although invested by the emperor, Archbishop Aribert successfully fought Emperor Conrad and his subservient pope, John XIX, not only to preserve the autonomy of metropolitan Milan but to extend its domination over Lombardy through suffragan bishops and by the direct appointment of the bishop of Lodi (Violante 1953:169–76).

There were heretical movements in Lombardy under Archbishop Aribert, but it was in the second decade of Archbishop Guido's rule that a major religious movement was launched in Milan itself. Arialdo, a deacon and a vavasor, and another cleric from the nobility, Landolfo, who belonged to the La Cotta family of *capetanei*, began preaching to the *popolani* against simony and clerical marriage and concubinage—the major themes of the church reform movement. People from the surrounding countryside flooded to Milan to hear them. By 1055, they were joined by another wellborn cleric, Anselm of Baggio, who had imbued the monastery of Bec, under its prior, Lanfanc of Pavia, with reformist ideas. Together, the three are credited as founders of the movement known as the Pataria or Patarines (literally, "ragpickers"). The Pataria movement soon spread from Milan to the rest of Lombardy and to Tuscany. The diocese of Lucca fell vacant in 1055, but it was not until 1056, probably in September, that Archbishop Guido gave it to Anselm to get him out of Milan. As bishop of Lucca, however, Anselm of Baggio made the city hospitable to reformers and continued as an ecclesiastical leader of the Patarines (Violante 1955:160–72). Patarine activism took the form of harassment of married clergy and disruption of their services and the boycott of simoniacs. In May 1057, Patarine demonstrations against simony and clerical concubinage turned violent, and popular tumult spread to other cities, such as Pavia and Asti, where the plebeians rose against the nonreformist bishops. One result was a war between Milan and Pavia in 1059 (Whitney 1926:40–41; Prévite-Orton 1926:219; Vio lante 1955:182–89).

During the short pontificate of Stephen IX in 1057, we find Hildebrand and the new bishop of Lucca, Anselm of Baggio, acting closely together in Rome, where they presented the Patarine leader Arialdo to the pope. They were charged with a double mission to the city of Milan and thence to the imperial court in Germany, which they undertook in November and December of 1057 (Violante 1955:201–9). This was followed by a much longer mission in which Anselm was joined by the reformist cardinal Peter Damiani (d. 1072), who was sent as the papal legate to control the Patarine movement in Lombardy and to steer it in the direction of ecclesiastical reform—that is, clerical celibacy and militancy against the royalist, antireformist clergy (Whitney 1926:41–42; Violante 1955:212–13). Meanwhile, Hildebrand maintained his cordial relationship with Anselm and, through him, kept an eye on urban mobilization and agitation as a means of promoting reform of the church. Upon the sudden death of Nicholas II on July 27, 1061, Hildebrand lobbied for and finally managed the election of his friend Anselm of Baggio as Pope Alexander II, putting him on the papal throne in Rome with the help of Norman troops (Whitney 1926:39, 43). During his relatively long pontificate, 1061–73, Alexander II gave continuous support to the Patarines, thereby harnessing the incipient urban revolution to the goals of ecclesiastical reform.

Meanwhile, Arialdo continued to lead the Patarines in Milan, while Landolfo was wounded in one of the many clashes with the defenders of the Ambrosian clerical establishment and lost his voice. His place was taken by his brother, Erlembald, who combined the zeal of a pilgrim to the Holy Land with the political skills of an urban patrician and the military leadership of a baron. He has been described as the "real founder of the Italian commune." Erlembald visited Rome in 1065 and was honored by his fellow

Patarine and Milanese nobleman, Pope Alexander II, with a white banner of Saint Peter and made the knight of the Roman and the universal church (Whitney 1926:47). Erlembald gathered a band of knights around him and ineffectively ruled Milan throughout a severe and violent investiture contest over the succession to Archbishop Guido that began in the last year of Alexander II (1072) and continued under Gregory VII. In 1073, Erlembald was emboldened by the new pope's enthusiastic support and began the persecution of the simoniac and married clergy, using coercion increasingly, forbidding them from performing their function, and replacing them by his own priests. This provoked a violent reaction by the nonreformist and royalist clergy that resulted in Erlembald's murder and the collapse of the Patarine movement in 1075. Gregory would not give up quickly, though. Writing to a Patarine knight whom he perhaps expected to take Erlembald's place in 1076, Gregory claimed that his Norman allies desired to have Saint Peter "as their sole lord and sovereign under God" (*Gregory* 91). He praised the knight for "comforting the soldiers of Christ" and promised him military support "when we have conferred with the liegemen [*fideles*] of St Peter" (*Gregory* 92). Although Pope Gregory VII continued to encourage the Patarines for a while longer, the course of urban revolution was veering irreversibly in a different direction (Cowdrey 1998:281–84).

In the last quarter of the eleventh century, a new institutional pattern for the communes was taking root not only in Lombardy but also in the rest of northern Italy and Tuscany. The *coniurationes* were coalescing with and being transformed into the *commune colloquium*, the *parlamento*, or the *arengo* and were electing consuls (*consules*) to govern their cities (Prévite-Orton 1926:220–21). The appearance of elected consuls in the last decades of the eleventh century was, incidentally, noted by Weber (1978:1253). The period of the birth of the commune in Italy coincided with increased study of the rediscovered Justinian Code, which influenced early urban constitutional law and explains the choice of the term "consul" for the highest urban magistrates. "With the establishment of consuls two oaths were taken in the *arengo*, the one by each consul binding him to certain duties for his term of office, the other by the representatives in the name of the assembled people, which must have included from the first a promise to obey the consuls" (Prévite-Orton 1926:221–22). As the revolutionary, nonlegitimate domination of the *coniuratio* gave way to the rule of law in the commune, the teleology of the urban revolution in Italy followed its distinctive developmental path, one that contrasted sharply with the developmental path of papal revolution that was set in motion by Gregory VII's struggle for the freedom of the church.[2]

Teleology of the Papal Revolution

In a letter to Emperor Anastasius I written in 496 CE, Pope Gelasius I (492–96) made a distinction between the "sacred authority" (*auctoritas sancta*) of the priesthood and the "royal power" (*regalis potestas*) of the kings as the two swords "by which this world is chiefly ruled" (cited in Tellenbach [1936] 1970:33). It was not until the movement for the reform of the church in the mid-eleventh century that this distinction was made into an invidious contrast in order to prove the superiority of the pope as the Vicar of Saint Peter and bishop of his Apostolic See—that is, Rome—over kings and emperors. This invidious reading of the metaphor of the two swords, the spiritual and the temporal, by Pope Gregory VII was indeed revolutionary, and it was established by a revolution in world history that set a subsequent developmental path that was fully distinctive of Western Christianity.

The mission of this pope, elected by divine grace, was "the freedom of the church," a deceptively modest starting point whose telos was, however, nothing short of the creation of a theocratic monarchy in a consistently coherent new Christian world order. As Tellenbach ([1936] 1970:164) put it, even better than Max Weber might have, "Gregory stands at the greatest . . . turning point in the history of Catholic Christendom; in his time the policy of converting the world gained once and for all the upper hand over the policy of withdrawing from it: the world was drawn into the Church, and the leading spirits of the new age made it their aim to establish the 'right order' in this united Christian world . . . [by] asserting the supremacy of the 'Servant of the servants of God' over the kings of the earth." The only thing this admirable internalist viewpoint leaves out is that the unified Christian world in which this transformation took place required the export of the papal revolution—that is, the Crusades—into the Muslim world that encircled it. To this I shall return.

The key element in the teleology of the papal revolution had already been identified by Cardinal Humbert in his major contribution to reform, *Adversus simoniacos*, completed shortly before his death in 1061. It consisted in a radically novel reading of Gelasius's two-swords dictum: "Just as the soul dominates and commands the body, so is the sacerdotal dignity superior to royal dignity, as heaven is to earth" (cited in Fliche 1946:82). Gregory VII advanced the slogan "Freedom of the Church!" for the abolition of the fundamental evil of the investiture of clergy by laymen. With the consolidation of the papal revolution under Urban II, however, lay investiture was quietly dropped to the second order of priority. It was in effect disposed of by one of Urban's successors, Paschal II, in the 1122 Concordat of Worms.

A distinction was made between the temporalities and the spiritualities of the church and thus between the investment of bishops with "*regalia*" by the king and their consecration by the pope (Tellenbach [1988] 1993:279–81).

This important shift in the goals of the Gregorian Revolution in the face of the practical impossibility of some of those goals marks its distinctive developmental path. More consequential in the long run, albeit a failure in the short run, was the second element in its teleology: namely, the idea of papal *plenitudo potestatis* as the conceptual basis of Gregory's program of hierocratic monarchy. Thus began the expansive reinterpretation of the concept, which lasted into the twelfth century and resulted in the transfer of Christ's statements to the pope through his vicarious Petrine powers and finally made the pope the Vicar of Christ. Gregory VII coupled this reinterpretation with his new reading of Gelasius, in which he asserted that if Saint Peter was given authority in matters spiritual, *how much more* did that entail authority over matters temporal (Tellenbach [1936] 1970:153)? This made for an invidious contrast between *auctoritas sancta* and *regalis potestas* in the reading of Gelasius's dictum on the two swords and would eventually lead to the conclusion that every human creature was a subject of the pope and dependent on him to achieve salvation. As suitable historical conjunctions arose, steps were taken, albeit in spurts, toward that conclusion, which found its fullest expression in Boniface VIII's *unam santam* bull of 1302, which famously made all human creatures subject to the pope's *plenitudo potestatis* and claimed for spiritual power the right to institute "earthly power" (*potestas terrena*) (Ladner 1954:75). In other words, spiritual authority must institute royal power (Ullmann 1965:115).

Consolidation of the Papal Revolution by Urban II (1088–1099)

Like most revolutions, not only did the papal revolution have a charismatic leader who initiated it, but it also had a consolidator without whom it would have remained incomplete or have failed. The consolidator of Gregory's papal revolution was Urban II (1088–99), a Frenchman whose formative life experience as a Cluny prior gave him both the necessary personal detachment from Rome and the most sophisticated administrative skills of the age. Urban also had one further qualification for the task of consolidation: he was a good canon lawyer. When he was elected pope by the Gregorians, Rome was under the control of Henry IV's anti-pope, Clement III, who selectively appropriated the reformist agenda (Fliche 1946:206), and the struggle to free the church from temporal powers seemed all but lost.

Under Abbot Odilo, who died in 1049, the year of the election of Pope Leo IX, the de facto unification of a large number of priories into the first translocal organization in Christendom took place, even though the terms *ordo, res publica, universitas,* and *corpus* were not to be applied to it until a century later. Odilo had also sought to harness the so-called Peace of God, the first general movement in feudal Europe to limit warfare among Christians by establishing a Truce of God between Saturday noon and Monday (Berman 1983:88–90). As pope, Urban II sought to consolidate the unity of Cluny as a translocal corporation not only by referring to its subordinate monasteries as its limbs (*membra*) but also by bringing the appointment of clerics to its churches under papal supervision (Constable 1996:174, 247). Much more consequentially, Urban employed the Cluniac model for the administrative centralization of papal authority, while using monks as an instrument of reform of the church (Fliche 1946:221–25). To achieve this latter end, he made the College of Cardinals into the pope's advisory body, consecrating a considerable number of bishops. His cardinal deacons become more conspicuous in papal documents, as he promoted seven of them in a bid to mobilize more supporters in his competition with the anti-pope Clement III (Kuttner 1945:178, 198).[3] He also used his skills as a canon lawyer, issuing bulls to extend and centralize papal authority. His early councils confirmed the Gregorian condemnation of simony, clerical marriage, and lay investiture, though in practice he was not nearly as combative toward temporal powers as Gregory VII (Fliche 1946:207–9).

One of Urban II's great successes was the final integration of the church of Milan into the mother church of Rome under Saint Peter's Vicar. After the Patarine fiasco of Erlembald, Gregory relied on his friend Countess Matilda, whom he called Saint Peter's daughter (*Gregory* 46). He was also fortunate to have for his last legate in Lombardy Bishop Anselm II of Lucca (1081–86), who was from the same Baggio family of Milanese *capetanei* as Alexander II (Cowdrey 1968:41–42). No sooner had he become pope in 1088 than Urban II began his successful effort to win over the new archbishop of Milan, Anselm III (1086–93), to the cause of Saint Peter (*causa sancti Petri*), reminding him that Saint Ambrose had considered it heretical to be separated from Rome. He won over Anselm III's successors to Saint Peter's cause as well. He reconstructed the memory of the Patarines, calling Erlembald the revered "soldier of Christ" and moving his remains and then Arialdo's to the monastery of Saint Dionysius and directing the local canonization of Patarine saints. His sermons revived the Patarine movement and inspired them to launch a militant campaign against the unchaste clergy in 1097 and dominate a reforming council of Milan that condemned simony and lay investiture in the following year. Under Urban II, the Ambrosian church finally gave up its tradition of autonomy and became papalist, championing the cause of Saint Peter in Lombardy (Cowdrey 1968:45–48).

Urban II's geopolitical situation remained precarious, however. The pious Countess Matilda of Tuscany remained a faithful supporter of the papacy after the death of Gregory VII. In her struggle against Henry IV, she married the young son of the Duke of Bavaria, less than half her age, machinated the revolt of Henry's son, Conrad III, in 1093 and the treachery of his current (Russian) wife, and helped create a pro-pope Lombard League, which included Cremona, Piacenza, and Lodi as well as Milan, and was headed by Archbishop Anselm III, who crowned the young Conrad III in Milan (Cowdrey 1968:45). All this suddenly improved Urban II's political situation. Urban II was quick to seize the opportunity offered by his success in Lombardy to make himself the master of Christendom and leave his mark on world history. He began by reconquering his fatherland, France, for the papacy and using it as the solid basis for reviving Gregorian mass mobilization while channeling it to the export of the papal revolution in the form of the First Crusade, which was proclaimed by him at the Council of Clermont in November 1095.

Export of the Papal Revolution

In 1054, Leo IX tried to make the patriarch of Constantinople accept the primacy of the See of Saint Peter. "Like the immovable pivot (*cardo*) which sets the door forth and back," he wrote, "thus Peter and his successors have the sovereign judgment over the entire church. . . . Therefore his clerics are named cardinals, for they belong more closely to the pivot by which everything is moved" (cited in Kuttner 1945:176, translation slightly modified). The failure of Gregory VII's old friend Cardinal Humbert to bring Eastern Christianity into the reformist fold by peaceful negotiation as Leo IX's legate to Constantinople in fact caused the schism of 1054, when Humbert broke off negotiations and excommunicated the patriarch of Constantinople. Gregory VII, the last surviving member of Leo IX's circle,[4] could not have forgotten any of these facts. In fact, he promoted the organization of an army under the pope to achieve the same purpose by military means. Within a year of his election, Gregory planned an expedition of Christian knights and fifty thousand men under his personal command to Asia Minor (*Gregory* 25; Tellenbach [1988] 1993:231). After driving out the Saracens, he would then hold a council in Constantinople to save Byzantium and the supremacy of the pope (Runciman 1957:99). According to Ullmann (1976:99), the establishment of Roman primacy in Byzantium was Gregory's principal aim. This would clearly mean the extension of the reform of the church to Eastern Christianity. Berman (1983:579n21) is therefore correct in pointing out that a major initial goal of the Crusades "was to export the Papal Revolution to Eastern Christendom." Gregory's propaganda campaign had sought to mobilize temporal powers against heretics (Mirbt 1894:456–62). In the course of their struggle for "the freedom of the church" from temporal power, the Gregorian canonists had developed the doctrine of "righteous persecution" by the end of Gregory's papacy. The idea of righteous persecution was further developed to justify both the Crusades and the subsequent persecution of the heretics in the twelfth century. In both cases, the pope took command in a holy war against the infidels or heretics, using the Christian princes and the knights as the "secular arm" of the church (Robinson 1990:318–21). The export of the papal revolution thus established the principle that the pope as the wielder of supreme spiritual authority had the right to direct the kings and feudal rulers as holders of temporal power.

Urban II had been keenly interested in Muslim Spain before becoming pope and had helped organize a French holy war for Alexander II while he was still at Cluny. But the export of revolution to Spain was checked by the Almoravid Revolution of the Berber tribesmen in North Africa, who crossed the Straits of Gibraltar and were solidly ensconced in Andalusia by 1091 (Fliche 1946:229–31, 273–74, 291). Sicily was already captured by his Norman allies, who gave Urban a free hand in creating monasteries and bishoprics as an important element of his project of extension of centralized papal authority; and he rewarded the Norman Count Roger of Sicily with the hereditary status of papal legate in the subsequently notorious bull of 1098 (Berman 1983:411). Urban II could not use the Gregorian mobilizational mechanisms for any southward move but had to look eastward for the export of the revolution of the Holy See of Saint Peter. Meanwhile, the Truce of God was not holding, and even pilgrims to the Holy Land were being attacked and robbed. Violence had to be deflected elsewhere and a new holy war launched.

According to his biographer, Urban II had heard that his predecessor "Pope Gregory had preached . . . an expedition to Jerusalem for the defense of the Christian faith and the liberation of the Lord's Sepulcher," and he organized the First Crusade on the model of his predecessor's holy wars in the name of Saint Peter (cited in Robinson 1990:325). He left Rome for northern Italy and France, where he enjoyed greater popularity, and as a dress rehearsal for his greatest council, he called one for the month of March 1095 in Piacenza, where he could rely on the support and the league of Lombard cities and the archbishop of Milan. Bishops apart, the lower clergy, numbering about four thousand, and the laity, numbering over thirty thousand, attended (Fliche 1946:265). After stopping for some three weeks in May in Milan, a papal stronghold, Urban II left for France, visiting Le Puy and Saint-Gilles in August and September, and reached his beloved Cluny in October. There, he unveiled his plan for a crusade and convoked the Council of Clermont for the following month (Fliche 1946:264–78).

On the last but one day of the Council of Clermont, on November 27, 1095, the mass of people gathered to hear the pope was far too large to be accommodated in any church, and so the papal throne was set up in an open field. There Urban II summoned the rich and the poor to take up the cross and march to Jerusalem to liberate the Holy Sepulcher (Runciman 1957:106–7). The Council of Clermont granted the first "plenary indulgence," absolving the crusaders from liability to punishment in Purgatory for sins committed prior to joining the holy army of Saint Peter (Berman 1983:171). As the words of the pope spread through the "Frankish lands, the Franks, hearing them, straightaway began to sew the cross on the right shoulder of their garments, saying that they would all with one accord follow the footsteps of Christ" (*Gesta Francorum* 1962:2). Urban picked a French nobleman, Adhemar de Monteil, bishop of Le Puy, as his legate to accompany the expedition and Raymond of Saint-Gilles, Count of Toulouse, who was celebrated for leading holy wars in Spain, as his military commander. Raymond took the cross on December 1 and accompanied Urban on a preaching tour of Toulouse and the rest of southern France in 1096. He then followed the legendary trail supposedly built by Charlemagne to the Holy Land, catching up with Peter the Hermit and his band of millennialist pilgrims turned crusaders in anticipation of the Second Coming (Runciman 1957:115). Urban II followed the chaotic course of the First Crusade (1096–99) through his legate but died in Rome on July 29, 1099, without hearing the news of the capture of Jerusalem.

Pilgrimage to Jerusalem is well attested for the third quarter of the eleventh century and was growing independently of holy warfare. The Cluniac monk Rudolf Glaber was a typical leader of pilgrims, expecting the imminent appearance of the Antichrist and braving the perilous road to the city of Jerusalem, imagined as the promised land of the end of time according to the book of Revelation. Knights were joining the pilgrims in an increasing number. The Patarine leader Erlembald of Milan was a holy knight when called by Gregory VII to lead the struggle for the freedom of the church in his city, and Salerno was freed for Gregory from the Muslims by the Norman knights returning from pilgrimage to the Holy Land (Erdmann 1935:280–83).

As we have seen, the recruitment of knights for holy warfare had become systematic with Gregory VII's *militia sancti Petri*, the forerunner idea of the Knights Templar and other knightly orders (Erdmann 1935:250–51). Urban II's genius consisted in the marriage of the pilgrimage movement with the holy warfare of the knights. He combined the traditional Christian vow (*votum*), in which a man staked his salvation on the fulfillment of a promise to God, and the powerful symbol of the cross into *votum crucis*, and he issued crosses that were borne in the First Crusade "by command of the Pope" (Robinson 1990:331–32).

Consequences of the Papal Revolution

When the papal revolution began, mid-eleventh-century Rome was surrounded by Muslim dominions in southern Italy and southern Europe and was alarmed in the third quarter of that century by the victory of the Seljuk Turks in the Eastern Christian Roman Empire, over which it claimed primacy. The export of the papal revolution therefore shaped its character to a far greater extent than did the export of the other revolutions that we have studied, and I have accordingly treated it as one of its constitutive elements rather than a consequence.

Integration of Fragmented Feudal Society through Christianization

Like our other revolutions, the papal revolution was an integrative revolution, but its mode of integration was distinctively different, indeed unique. It consisted in the integration of politically fragmented feudal communities into the Catholic (Universal) Church through Christianization.

It has often been crudely asserted that church and state are one in Islam, in contrast to the separation of church and state in Christianity in accordance with the Gelasian doctrine of the two swords. The historical picture of the contrasting paths of integration and differentiation in Islam and Christianity is much more complicated. The Christianization of the Roman Empire went hand in hand with its disintegration in the West and did not extend far beyond the cities into the pagan countryside. Even in the cities, the mode of integration of Christian society was highly localized and depended primarily on the spread of the cult of saints, some of whom were transformed former city gods (Brown 1981). Localized integration on the basis of Christian solidarity was centered on the patron saints of the cities, the most important of whom, by the eleventh century, was arguably Ambrose, the patron saint of metropolitan Milan.

The religious organization of Latin Christianity took the form of proprietary churches of the feudal lord, who appointed the clergy and invested its chaplains, while the investiture of the archbishops of the cathedral cities devolved on kings. Thus, for the six centuries following Gelasius, Western Christian kings remained Vicars of Christ, as the Umayyad and ʿAbbasid caliphs were Vicars/Deputies (*khalifa*) of God (Crone and Hinds 1986). As Charlemagne reminded Pope Leo II, who crowned him, the king's business as the Vicar of Christ was to govern and defend the church, while the pope's duty was to pray for it (Berman 1983:66). Furthermore, the system of localized proprietary churches and monasteries differed little from the system of privately endowed mosques, Sufi convents, and *madrasa*s in the Muslim world (Arjomand 1999), except that neither the Sufis nor the *ʿulamā*ʾ in the *madrasa*s constituted a "clergy" invested with authority by the founder of the endowment (*waqf*) or by anyone else. As we have seen, it was not until the eleventh century that Gelasius was read in conjunction with the other key fifth-century idea, the *plenitudo potestatis* of Leo I, sharply deepening the differentiation between spiritual and temporal authority, between church and state, along a developmental path that has no parallel in Islam or, for that matter, in Eastern Christianity.

This momentous long-term consequence of Gregory VII's revolution was already implied by his idea of the freedom of the church at the outset and underlies its significance in world history. It could not be achieved without the centralization of authority in the Holy See of Saint Peter as the first critical step in the rise of papal monarchy in Western Europe through the twelfth and thirteenth centuries.

Centralization of Papal Authority and the Development of Canon Law

We have also seen the centralization of authority and power structure as a consequence of all our revolutions, but once again, we here have a mode of centralization of authority that is very distinctive, creating the Catholic Church as a bureaucratic hierarchy unique among the hierocracies of the world religions. It is a mode of centralization premised on the differentiation of religious and political authority, consistent with the nonterritorial mode of integration of the feudal society of Western Europe through Christianization but buttressed by a comparatively remarkable growth of the law of the universal church. Last but not least, it is the consequence of the distinctive form of the export of the papal revolution as the Crusades.

Max Weber (1978:829) correctly identifies the Gregorian age as the period of critical transition in which the "occidental church traveled the path of legislation by rational enactment," the decisive factor in the transition being "the unique organization of the Catholic Church as a rational institution [*Anstalt*]." He adds, admittedly with anachronistic hindsight, that "the character of ecclesiastical law-making was influenced by the fact that the church's functionaries were holders of rationally defined bureaucratic offices" (Weber 1978:828). As we have seen, Gregory's *dictatus papae* (title 7) gave the pope the exclusive right to "make new laws according to the needs of the times." These new laws were called decretals. The decretals thus represented the new papal legislation and could be collected as the law of the church.

Collection of canons had been under way as part of the reform movement, and a collection of seventy-four titles (decretals) had been published under Leo IX. Anselm of Lucca and Cardinal Deusdedit published other collections, and Ivo of Chartres edited *Pannormia* (All laws) under Urban II, who was himself an accomplished canon lawyer. In 1140, Gratian published his great treatise in which he divided the sources of canon law into the old canons and the new papal decretals, and his student Hugguccio ruled that "a decretal prevails over a canon" (cited in Berman 1983:202). A century later, in 1234, Pope Gregory IX published the *Decretals*, which remained the basic corpus of canon law until the twentieth century.

As we have seen, the study of the Justinian Code had an impact on the development of urban constitutional law. Its impact on the development of canon law was much greater. Papal canonists applied what Roman law had said about the emperor (*princeps*) to the pope: "The Pope is the *princeps* of the church. *Quod principi placuit legis habet vigorem*" (cited in Maitland 1898:16). The pope also assumed the imperial function of issuing rescripts (T. Honoré 1981:102). These rescripts were in fact the decretals and provided the means for converting the law-finding typical of religious laws of the world religions into lawmaking by the pope. A decretal was not necessarily or usually a decision on a concrete case but rather was an abstract answer to an abstract question, just like those posed to and answered by a mufti in Islamic law. But as the questions were submitted to the pope by the bishops, as "holders of rationally defined bureaucratic offices," the rescripts could in fact be said to have declared "the common law (*jus commune*) of Christendom, the law of the Universal Church" (Maitland 1898:16). The mode of centralization of papal authority was thus closely patterned on the mode of integration of the politically fragmented Western Christendom.

The export of Muhammad's revolution, as we hinted in chapter 7, was territorial, based on military conquest and without any differentiation between religious and political authority, which would appear much later.

Gregory VII and Urban II planned, and the latter executed, the export of their revolution without any secure territorial base anywhere. The Crusades certainly did not secure the Holy Land as a territorial base for the papacy but rather made its authority over Christendom entirely independent of its real estate in the city of Rome. Only much later was the spiritual authority of the pope as the monarch of the universal church partially converted to the creation of a Papal State around Saint Peter's earthly church, the Vatican.

TEN

The Mongolian Integrative Revolution in Eurasia

Our last great medieval revolution is that of Chinggis Khan (d. 1227), scion of a Mongol noble clan who unified the Turko-Mongolian tribes of eastern Eurasia and used the military might of his nomadic confederates to build a vast empire of conquest comprising Iran and northern China. It was the repeat of a pattern of constitutive revolution found among the ancient Turks, but with significant alterations that mitigated its inherent instability and greatly increased its absorptive capacity for building an empire of conquest. The empire of conquest he built, the Great Mongol Empire (Yeke Mongghol Ulus) (1206–59), fragmented under his grandsons but, in doing so, gave birth to lasting new nomadic-sedentary compound societies that covered the Chinese and the Persianate ecumenes. The establishment of the Great Empire of the Mongols, extended through Russia to Hungary under his son Ögedei (1229–41), was thus doubly an integrative revolution in that it unified Eurasia as never before, albeit briefly, and then permanently restructured Eurasia into three ecumenical zones, each with a distinctive compound society and developmental path.

The expansion of the Great Mongol Empire was abruptly halted in 1259, when Chinggis Khan's grandson, the Great Khan / Möngke Qa'an (1251–59), died unexpectedly during his campaign against the Southern Sung in China, backed by his brother Qubilai, while their other brother, Hülegü, was leading the western campaign of conquest that had overthrown the ʿAbbasid Caliphate in 1258 to reach the Mediterranean and was continuing southward against Egypt. It was de facto divided into three empires. Two of them consolidated enduring restructured nomadic-sedentary societies in two different cultural ecumenes, one Uighur-Chinese under Qubilai, the other Persianate under Hülegü. The third region of the Great Mongol Empire was the Ulus Jochi, meaning the tribes and country assigned to Chinggis Khan's eldest son,

Jochi (d. 1227). This area was ruled by Chinggis's oldest grandson, Jochi's son Batu (d. 1256), and its people became known as the Golden Horde. The nomadic empire of the Golden Horde lasted for another two and a half centuries, but with minimal cultural interaction with the settled population.

As one would expect, the Mongol Revolution had very different consequences in the regions that it could not hold together for more than a generation. In each region, the Mongol rulers created compound societies in which the nature and mutual influence of nomadic rulers and sedentary subjects varied greatly, as did the patterns of social integration and stratification. The khanate of Chinggis Khan's second son, Chaghadai (d. 1241), sprawled across large steppes lacking natural boundaries and any ecumenically unified culture, and it was not until the latter part of the fourteenth century that the *ulus* (nation, inclusive of land and people) of Chaghadai was transformed into an empire of conquest by Temür/Tamerlane (d. 1405).

Jochi's khanate followed a different path of development. The Russian princes (*knjaz'ja*) surrendered and became tributaries of the Golden Horde as Saray was built as its capital on the Volga in 1243. The princes' fiscal obligation as vassals of the Golden Horde was a comprehensive, grand tribute (*alba qubchiri* / *qalan yāsā*). The Russian Orthodox Church was exempted from paying the tribute and given juridical autonomy by a series of edicts (*yarlighs*) issued by the Golden Horde khans (Schurmann 1956b:340–52). In 1251, Batu helped install Möngke as the Great Khan for what was an effective condominium over the Qipchaq Steppe (*dasht*) in western Eurasia (Jackson 1978:207, 224–27). The Golden Horde integrated Mongolian and Turkic tribesmen by converting to the latter's religion, Islam,[1] under Batu's brother and successor, Berke (1257–67), and thus reinforced its nomadic pattern of life without any deep penetration of the sedentary societies of the region (Allsen 1979). Although the extensive dominion of the Golden Horde included Russia, Russia was marginal to it, as were Georgia and Armenia. Russian, Georgian, and Armenian princes remained vassals of the Mongols, collecting the annual tribute for them. The Mongols did not garrison these vassal principalities, as China, Inner Asia, and Iran were garrisoned,[2] and the Golden Horde did not need any fiscal administration of its own beyond a very minimal one in its capital, Saray, again in sharp contrast to China and Iran (Halperin 1983:247–50).[3] The successor states of the Great Mongol Empire in China and Iran, as we shall see, had a completely different developmental path and created new compound nomadic-settled societies under the Yuan and Il-khanid dynasties, which were shaped by two distinct political cultures.

The Prototype: Ancient Constitutive Revolutions of the First and Second Turk Empires

The presence of nomadic Turks, all bearing the surname A-shih-na, in Juan-juan state in northern China is recorded in the fifth century CE. The Juan-juan state weakened in the early sixth century and disintegrated by the middle of that century, being replaced by the first empire of the Turks (Hephthalites) in 552 (Sinor 1990:295–97). Its two cofounders, according to the Orkhon inscriptions of the first half of the eighth century, "established the political organization and laws of the tribal union" (cited in Golden 1982:51). "These were wise Kaghans," the inscription continues. "All their officers, . . . the nobles, . . . the entire people were just. This was the reason why they were able to rule . . . [and] could uphold the laws" (cited in Sinor 1990:297). According to this old Turk political theology as recorded in the Uighur script, the "Heaven-like, Heaven conceived, wise Turk Kaghan" was no other than the Son of Heaven, and his charisma as the imperial ruler was transferred to the royal clan, any member of which could be elevated to the kaghanate (Golden 1982:45).

By the end of the sixth century, the empire was divided into western and eastern halves, and the kaghan of the Eastern Turks, presumably adopting the neighboring Iranian cosmology, styled himself the "master of the seven climes" (Sinor 1990:306). The first kaghanate was destroyed by wars of succession and internomadic warfare. According to the Sui Chinese annals (ca. 600), "the Türks prefer to destroy each other rather than to live side-by-side. They have a thousand, nay ten thousand clans who are hostile to and kill one another" (cited in Sinor 1990:307). The Turk kaghanate was revived by Elterish, the Kutlugh (Fortunate) (682–92), scion of the A-shih-na clan, who led the uprising of the *qara budun* (black commoners) after a long period of Chinese servitude, and the kaghanate reached its peak of imperial power under Bilgä (Wise) Kaghan (716–34), who thus describes his achievement in the Orkhon inscriptions: "When I became Kaghan, the people . . . had dispersed . . . on foot [i.e., without horses], and naked. To reestablish the nation [polity] I led twenty-two campaigns. . . . Then, by the grace of Heaven [*Tngri*], and because of good fortune [*Kut*] . . . , I brought back to life the dying people, the naked people I clothed, and I made the few many" (cited in Sinor 1990:313).

The great Turk kaghanates or empires, like the Khitan empire of the Liao dynasty and the Mongol Empire later, were created by a confederation of Turkic tribes under a supratribal leader. Their emergence depended largely on the conditions of the two neighboring empires, the Chinese and the Persian, and they drew on these neighbors' center-building symbolic and administrative resources to transform their conquest-driven confederations into lasting empires. Foremost among these were symbols and terminology of imperial legitimacy. The word *kaghan* is no more Turkish than the names of the two founders of the kaghanate and can plausibly be read as the khan of khans, modeled on the Persian *shāhanshāh* (king of kings). The kaghans also assumed the Chinese imperial title Son of Heaven (Tian = Tngri), interestingly rendered in the Persianate and Soghdian areas by the Persian theophoric *bagapuhṛ* (Arabized as *faghfur*, "son of god"),[4] which survived only in the devaluated form of *bāghatur/bahādor* ("brave"—a lower noble rank than *khān*) (Chen 2002).[5] Tian (Heaven), if not identical to, was easy to identify with the Turkic Tngri (sky god), and the principal requirement of the Son of Heaven, that of being "correct" (*zheng*), was compounded with that of the king of kings, namely justice.[6] The Turkic innovation was to restrict the Mandate of Heaven to descendants of a single royal clan, the A-shih-na.

The supratribal polities formed at the inception of the Turko-Mongolian empires were formed out of the union of Turkic tribes. Each tribe was an autonomous polity (*budun*) headed by a khan (*qan*) and consisting of clans, each clan (*oboq*) or kinship group headed by a hereditary chieftain (*noyan*) and divided into lineages (*urugh*). The stratification was a simple one, consisting in the division between the nobles (*bäglär*) and the commoners (*haran*, also *budun*). Each stratum was conceived as a kinship group with shared "bone": white for the nobility and black for the commonalty (Krader 1958:90). Several clan chieftains could meet in an assembly (*quriltai*) to elect a khan (*qan*), who led them in raids and to whom they swore loyalty. Tribes formed and decomposed around the khans as fragile political entities. On rare occasions, several tribes could also form a supratribal confederation. If unified into a supratribal polity under a kaghan, the tribes would stand in a relation of super- and subordination (Farquhar 1990:1–2). The subordinate authority of a khan of a submitted tribe was expressed as *ēl/il* ("Heaven which gives the *il*").[7] The unsubmitted tribes were pejoratively called *bulgha*. Any unification could not, however, be taken for granted. On the contrary, in light of the abovementioned Sui official's observation, it was a wonder, and it was unstable primarily due to the problem of succession, which meant chronic contestation and internecine wars after the death of the supratribal kaghan. The adoption of the terminology of imperial kingship, in other words, could do little to modify the structure and dynamics of predatory Turko-Mongolian imperial polities, whose mythical founding ancestor, as Edward Gibbon remarked, was suckled by a she-wolf, just like Romulus, the legendary forebear of another empire-building martial race, the Romans.

There was also, however, a built-in, endemic instability of imperial polity in the Turk empires due to the unchanged rules of nomadic patrimonialism for the division of conquered lands and peoples, which made the empires relatively ephemeral. They were prone to crises of succession that stemmed from the principle of succession by contestation. Joseph Fletcher, using a Celtic analogy, calls this principle "tanistry." The khan of any Turko-Mongolian tribe was an ad hoc chief, elected from a noble clan for his martial competence, which was tested by contestation and proven by the elimination of rival contenders. This rule applied to the supratribal leader of a conquest-oriented confederation and remained unchanged for his successors. As Fletcher (1979–80:240–41) put it, tanistry "politicized society, and it personalized monarchy. . . . An active, personal military leader was essential to the cohesion of his people. His person—indeed his personality—was the linchpin of society." Through loyalty to the kaghan, the divine legitimacy of supratribal, imperial leadership thus cemented supratribal solidarity. That this legitimacy and consequent solidarity penetrated deep into the Mongol polity is demonstrated by the routine expression recorded by a Sung envoy in 1237: "They always say: 'Relying on the might of Eternal Heaven and the protective good Fortune of the Emperor!'" (cited in Allsen 1991:223). Nevertheless, the structure of Turko-Mongolian imperial domination remained a personal system of authority, just like Weber's ideal type of patrimonialism. It can be qualified further as nomadic patrimonialism to highlight its other characteristic: namely, the conception of the conquered lands and peoples as the patrimony (i.e., property) of the imperial conqueror to be divided by him among his heirs (Aigle 2004:52–53). This conception is endorsed as a principle of public law in the Great Yasa (law code) of Chinggis Khan, who divided his vast empire into four and gave each of the four *ulus*es as patrimonies to his four sons from his principal wife, thus also perpetuating the institution of tanistry. The system of tanistry at the imperial level for succession to the kaghanate (the Mongol qa'anate) in the Great Mongol Empire, as we shall see, involved very considerable bloodshed and protracted wars of succession, as was the case among the contenders from the four Chinggisid *ulus*es.

In short, the epicycle of integrative prototypes of the Mongol Revolution—the rise and fall of nomadic confederal empires—fits our Khaldunian type. Furthermore, the history of Turkic state formation in northern China also provides us with compelling evidence for Ibn Khaldun's corollary conception of the civilizing process as consisting of the loss of martial valor and solidarity and the mellowing of the manners and morals of nomadic tribesmen as a result of settlement and seduction by the learning and luxuries of civilized, urban life. The deep ambivalence of the assimilationist, great Mongol qa'an Qubilai (d. 1294) indicates his instinctive awareness of the process, which is succinctly expressed by the earlier Khitan empire builder and founder of the Liao dynasty (907–1127), Abaoji (d. 926), who told a Chinese envoy, "I can speak Chinese, but I never speak it in the presence of my tribal people. I fear that they may emulate the Chinese and grow soft and timid" (cited in Mote 1999:47). Furthermore, like the Il-khans in Iran, the Turko-Mongolian rulers of China were selective in their appropriation of Chinese political culture. Yuanhao (d. 1048), the founder of the Xi Xia state, which preceded the Mongols in adopting the Uighur script, had a decisive preference for the ancient Chinese Legalist statecraft tradition over Confucian humanism, which he considered unsuitable for his warlike steppe people (Mote 1999:181).

Chinggis Khan's Integrative Revolution and the Establishment of the Great Mongol Empire

Learning the pattern of nomadic empire building by trial and error, the greatest Turko-Mongolian supratribal empire builder of all time, Temüjin, a Mongolian tribal leader who became known as Chinggis Khan, embarked on the centralization of military power around the turn of the thirteenth century before he could take advantage of the integrative symbolism of the imperial ruler as the Son of Heaven. He began to expand his own nomadic patrimony by defeating, breaking up, and absorbing the major tribes of Mongolia in 1203 and 1204. Temüjin first attacked his former allies, the Kereid. According to the *Secret History of the Mongols*:

> For three days and three nights they fought,
> Until the third day [the Kereid leader] Ongkhan's army surrendered.
> . . .
> Then they took all the Kereid people
> And dispersed them among us,
> Taking all their possessions as spoils.

Then came the Merkit's turn.

> This time Chinggis Khan made a decree:
> He ordered that the Merkit be disbanded,
> Distributing their people among all the other divisions,
> so that they ceased to exist as a people. (cited in Mote 1999:420–21)

In 1204, the Naiman confederation, the most powerful in Mongolia, was similarly shattered. Partly in preparation for the campaign against the Naiman,

Chinggis Khan founded the first distinctive institution of his empire, the Keshig guard, in 1203—the date can accordingly be taken as the beginning of his military revolution.

Mongol custom allowed for two types of personal ties other than clan relations: sworn brotherhood (*anda*) and, more important, the institution where a man could forswear loyalty to his own clan to become an associate or comrade (*nöker*) of a leader (O. Lattimore 1962; Morgan 2007:34–35). By 1203, Temüjin, the rising Mongol supratribal leader, had drawn on the latter customary bond to organize a corps of 150 guards (*keshigten*; "the guards who serve in turn"), whose commander held one of the foremost two of the ten court offices Temüjin had created, and to recruit a bodyguard (*qorchi*s) consisting of 1,000 braves (*bāghatur/bahādor*) in the following three years (Barthold [1928] 1968:382–91). The immediate model for the Keshig was the organization of the Kereid tribe, to which Temüjin had been affiliated as a client and an ally (de Rachewiltz 1983:284–85).

According to the military treatise contained in the fourteenth-century *Yuan shih* (2a–b; *Yuan shih* 1937–85:92–93), the founding emperor appointed the Four Heroes—Borgul, Borǰu, Muqali (d. 1223), who later commanded the Mongol armies in the conquest of northern China, and Chila'un—to command the Keshig. When Borgul died early, he assumed its command himself. "For this reason, it was called Great [*yeke*] [since] the Son of Heaven commanded it by himself." The guards took turns, eighty of them were night guards (*kebtegül*), and seventy were day guards (*turghagh*). The latter group included sons of affiliated clans who were hostages, including Söbötei (d. 1248), who became a *bāghatur* and one of the Four Hounds and led the Mongol armies in the western conquests (Buell 1993b). The significance of Chinggis Khan's personal guard was by no means restricted to military organization. The Keshig of the supreme commander were also members of the royal household and became high officials of the imperial conquest state when their functions were extended beyond the household of the ruler to the administration of the fast-expanding realm (Hsiao 1978:34–38; Melville 2006:136–37, 142–43).[8]

Chinggis Khan's revolutionary military reorganization that created the Mongol army of conquest came in 1206. He adopted the ancient imperial Chinese decimal system of army ranks, modeled more immediately on that of the Turkic Jurchen empire he conquered. Chinggis Khan delinked the old Turkic decimal military organization from tribes, and his new decimal units of ten, a hundred, a thousand, and ten thousand men comprised nomads from various tribes, each under the command of one of his *nöker*s (associate, comrade), who was now called *noyan*. Affiliated tribal leaders who had enjoyed that title now lost the traditional power to detach themselves from the supratribal leader and were subjected to his strict military discipline as the supreme commander. Defeated nomads and subjugated tribes were also organized into new decimal units under Mongol commanders. Units of a hundred were commanded by a centurion; of a thousand, by a chiliarch; and the new divisions of ten thousand (*tümen*), by a myriarch (*tümen-ü noyan*). The new divisions were composites of various tribes and unaffiliated nomads whose secondary collective solidarity congealed around their new commanders. Muqali's division, which was passed on to his son and grandson, for instance, included a unit of one thousand from his own Jalair tribe (de Rachewiltz 1993). All soldiers' loyalties were transferred to Chinggis Khan as the supreme leader through these commanders, who were his personal appointees (Biran 2004:340, 346–49). The Keshig was also enlarged by the recruitment of the sons and younger brothers of commanding officers of the new army (Hsiao 1978:36), and the bodyguard was expanded to ten thousand (Farquhar 1990:2).

This unparalleled centralization of military power also meant the transformation of a grand tribal coalition into a hierarchical army of conquest. The engine of expansion and the closest equivalent of a government in this new nomadic patrimonial empire was the decimal military organization. It was a constantly mobile government from the tents of the world conqueror's *ordo* (camp). Unlike the earlier steppe conquest confederations such as the Khitan state, the tribes that composed the army had lost their autonomy, were disbanded and regrouped alongside the absorbed conquered peoples, and thus fused into the new Mongolian nation whose army consisted of ninety-five chiliarchies (units of one thousand).[9] In exchange for this loss of independence and unquestioning loyalty to the supreme leader and commander of the nation, they were assured of the latter's justice in the equitable distribution of booty, of posthumous recognition as heroes if they fell in battle, and of the security of their descendants (Mote 1999:405, 422–23). "I look upon the nation," dictated Chinggis Khan in a letter, "as a new-born child and I care for my soldiers as if they were my brothers" (cited in Mote 1999:433). His unification of many previously distinct tribes and peoples into a new nation under arms expanded the meaning of "Mongol," thus creating a new warrior national identity, and can therefore be taken as the act of foundation of the Great Mongol Empire.

The revolutionary military reorganization in 1206 was matched by a tremendous symbolic upgrading of Temüjin in the *quriltai* of the assembled Mongolian tribes in the same year. Already considered the legitimate successor of the semilegendary twelfth-century Kutlugh Kaghan, he upgraded his status with the help of the chief shaman, Teb Tengri Kököchü, who conveyed the Mandate of Heaven to him and most probably coined Chinggis (a Turkish term meaning "oceanic," "universal," or "fierce") Khan as his throne name. "After he had thus subjected all the nations with felt tents," according to the *Secret History*, "they gave to Chinggis Khan the title of Khan." Kököchü then repeated the prophecy revealed to him by the "order-king of Eternal Heaven" (*möngke tengri-yin jarliq qan*) (cited in Franke 1978:20–21):

> "God has spoken with me," Kököchü proclaimed, "and has said: 'I have given all the face of the earth to Temüjin and his children and named him Chinggis Khan. Bid him administer justice in such and such fashion.'" (Jovayni, as cited in Fletcher 1986:34)

Once the Mandate of Heaven was conveyed in this Mongolian fashion by the shaman, however, Chinggis Khan converted it to the imperial, unmediated variant and wasted no time in eliminating the intermediary, Teb Tengri Kököchü, who was "no longer loved by Tengri" (cited in Fletcher 1986:35). The Chinggisid house replaced the old Turkic A-shih-na clan as the recipient of the Mandate of Heaven in perpetuity. All the Mongol edicts in the thirteenth and fourteenth centuries were accordingly issued "through the power of Eternal Heaven" (*möngke tengri-yin kücündur*) (Franke 1978:15; Golden 1982:72). The Il-khans in Iran could augment the formula by their claim to the charisma of the Chinggisid lineage by adding "the good royal Fortune of the Khan" (*qan-u suudur*) (Aigle 2004:36). We know from the coinage of the Iranian vassal states that Chinggis Khan assumed the title *qa'an* (i.e., the old Turkic *kaghan*). What is more remarkable is that these coins also prove the immediate adoption of the main attribute of Persian kingship: namely, justice. We thus have "The Just / the Great Chengiz Khan" and "Qā'ān / The Just" (Allsen 1991:224–25). After his death, Chinggis Khan was deified as an ancestor spirit—"Heaven-born Chinggis Khan, born of the decree of Eternal Heaven"—and four shrines for sacrificing to his memory were built within the Mongol Empire (Heissig 1980:60–61). He remained the celestial ruler of the Great Mongol Empire alongside the earthly qa'ans who were his sons and grandsons (Franke 1978:24).

Chinggis Khan adapted the Uighur alphabet, probably in 1204 (de Rachewiltz 1983:283), and appointed Uighur tutors to teach it to his four sons. He also created the office of chief justice (*yeke jarghuchi*), whose function was to administer the Mongolian customary law (*yosun*) and the ruler's decrees (*jasagh*). The chief justice used the Uighur alphabet to record

Chinggis's military regulations (*jasagh*) as imperial law, to which Mongol custom was later added (Manz 2010:131). Thus was born what was arguably Chinggis Khan's most enduring institution, his Great Yasa, or law code.

With the Mandate of Heaven, the law code, and, above all, his formidable nation of horsemen in arms, Chinggis Khan proceeded to conquer northern China from 1211 to 1227 and the rising nomadic empire of the Khʷārazmshāhs in Central Asia and Iran from 1218 onward. In the course of these conquests, Chinggis Khan reorganized the defeated armies of the conquered nations into *tümen* divisions and compelled them to fight alongside the Mongols.

After the conquest of China, Chinggis Khan appointed unsalaried Mongolian or Khitan governors (*dārughas*) in some cities of China, and so did his general, Muqali. The *dārugha* carried out civil administration of occupied territories and passed on his office to a son or a brother (Endicott-West 1989:25–28). *Dārughas* were also appointed in some major cities in Central Asia and Iran, but the Uighur and Kharaluk principalities in Central Asia (Allsen 1983), two kingdoms in Korea, and parts of Iran, notably Yazd, Fars, Kerman, and eventually Herat, remained under local rulers who had submitted and became vassal states. Other cities and states were put under military occupation, with each of the four *uluses* of Chinggis Khan's sons having its own garrisons (Manz 2010:136). State building proceeded amid conquest. Within a decade, Chinggis Khan had established an Uighur-Mongol secretariat or chancellery under the Kereid Chinkhali for his war state to administer the logistics of conquest, the booty, and confiscated land and estates (de Rachewiltz 1983:284). In the administration of conquered China, he was joined by Yeh-Lü A-hai (d. 1223), a Sinicized Khitan official who had defected early to Temüjin with his brother, Yeh-Lü T'u-hua (d. 1231), who succeeded him after serving on the staff of the supreme commander (*yeke noyan*) (Buell 1993c). The Khʷarazmian Mahmud Yalvach (meaning "envoy") (1254) organized the administration of Central Asia and was succeeded by his son, Masʿud Beg (d. 1289). Mahmud had served as Chinggis Khan's ambassador to his homeland to negotiate trade with Khʷārazmshāh just before the murder of the former's merchants in Atrar, which triggered the outbreak of war (Allsen 1993). Last but not least, there was Chinggis Khan's astrologer, secretary, and adviser Yeh-Lü Ch'u-Ts'ai (d. 1243), a Buddhist Khitan and scion of a distinguished Sinicized family of Chin officials tracing its descent to the Liao royal house, who joined the khan's *ordo* in 1218 and remained with him in Central Asia until 1226 (de Rachewiltz 1993:136–41).

With the conquest of northern China, many Khitan, Jurchen, and Chinese local officials and garrison commanders defected or surrendered, bringing with them the entire populations under their control as well as the Chinese-style officials who administered sedentary territories. The ranks of the chancellery secretaries (singular, *bichigchi/bitikchi*) were augmented, and a more differentiated Chinese official titulature began to be used (Farquhar 1990:3).

The Great Mongol Empire under Ögedei and Möngke

Chinggis Khan divided his empire among his four sons from his principal wife, each of whom governed his own *ulus* (nation). His third son and successor as khan, Ögedei (1229–41), overthrew the Chin dynasty in 1234 and extended his conquests through Iran and Russia to Hungary and Poland with the second western campaign (1236–41). Each of the four *ulus*es collected both the regular tribute (*alban*), which included a poll tax, taxes on herds and craft production, a gradated household tax, and a property tax in Chin territories, and extraordinary levies (*qubchiri/qubchur*), which were, however, quite frequent and numerous. The Turko-Mongolian ruling estate was exempt from taxation (*dragan/tarkhān*) (Schurmann 1956b:312–29). Both these categories of taxes were collected by tax farmers who were, as a rule, Central Asian Muslims, Soghdians, Uighurs, and Turks who were agents of the *ortaq*—commercial partners of the Mongolian royal family and nobility in international trade.

Yeh-Lü Ch'u-Ts'ai, who rose to be Ögedei's chief administrator as the chief of the newly established Secretariat, rescued many former Chinese and Jurchen officials who had been enslaved and given to their Mongol captors. Ch'u-Ts'ai's reforms amounted to a rough adaptation of the Chinese secretariats and ministerial hierarchy for the imperial chancellery (de Rachewiltz 1993). The National College (Kuo-tzu xüeh), attached to the Confucian temple, was founded in Yen-ching (Beijing) in 1233, and a civil service examination was held in 1237 (Dardess 2003:119). Ögedei appointed Yang Wei-chung, who spoke Mongolian and later succeeded Ch'u-Ts'ai as the first Chinese chief of the Secretariat in 1243, director of the National College, and Yang admitted eighteen students, including Yao Shu (d. 1278), a refugee from a prominent family of former Chin officials, who helped him found a private Academy of the Supreme Ultimate committed to the (Neo-)Confucian Daoxue (Dao Learning, or Learning of the Way) in 1238 (de Bary 1981:20–22). In 1236, Yao, dressed like a Mongol, rushed to meet the captives of a Mongol raid in order to rescue the renowned neo-Confucian teacher Chao Fu, who was on the verge of suicide, and brought him back to Yen-ching; over a hundred of Chao's disciples soon followed. Yao was appointed the first secretary of the Yen-ching Regional Administration (Chan 1980:17–21). Four thousand and thirty candidates had meanwhile passed the 1237 civil service examination and were allowed to serve in local governments and were given the title "officials who advise on affairs." Those enslaved former officials who passed were manumitted (Farquhar 1990:45). The civil service examination met with the fierce opposition of the Mongol nobility, however, and was not repeated.

More consequential than administrative reform was the systematization of the distribution of the conquered lands in China, Central Asia, and Iran as enormous appanages to the members of Chinggis Khan's royal family and his top generals. Fourteen of these, granted by Chinggis Khan himself, were called the Original Appanages. An appanage (*ayimagh; suyurghal*) included the cultivators and the resident craftsmen. The Chinggisid empresses, princes, and princesses appointed their own managers and administrators to their appanages, which were sometimes also called *uluses*. Myriarchs and chiliarchs held less extensive fiefs (*qubi*) (Farquhar 1990:3, 17).

The qa'anate of Möngke (1251–59) saw the greatest consolidation of the Great Mongol Empire and a much improved centralization of government and fiscal administration that allowed a vigorous resumption of conquests. More relevant to the organization of new armies of conquest was his formation of new divisions by breaking up and reconstituting tribal contingents following Chinggis Khan's model. The precedent was Chinggis Khan's expeditionary army to India, to which each of his four sons contributed a chiliarchy commanded by its own *noyan* (Vassāf 1852–53:12; Āyati 1993:2–3). This method was combined with the so-called *tama/łama* system of forming new units from the centuries and chiliarchies of the central army for expeditions to provinces (Aubin 1969:74–76; Jackson 1978:192–93). In government administration, however, Möngke replaced the representatives of the four imperial lines by those of the four sons of Tolui—that is, the qa'an himself and his three brothers (Aubin 1995:19). This must be seen as a measure of concentration of power in imperial administration.

In 1253, he thus created an *ulus* for his brother Hülegü, who was to lead the western campaign, while ordering his other brother, Qubilai, to invade western China. Given the character of the Great Mongol Empire of conquest, planned expansion went hand in hand with consolidation. As we shall see, Qubilai embarked on the Sinicization and rationalization of his large appanage, and Möngke attended to the greater integration of Iran from Karakorum in anticipation of Hülegü's expedition, making fresh appointments to ensure greater representation of the imperial subjects by setting up a triumvirate consisting of a Mongol, a Central Asian, and a Persian at the apex of the fiscal administration of Iran (Aubin 1995:19–20).

The army of some seventy-five thousand men (Mote 1999:440) under Hülegü's command had representatives from each of the three other branches of the Chinggisid imperial family, each bringing his own contingent (Aubin 1969:74–78). He moved it at a leisurely pace through Central Asia, subdued the Ismāʿili fortresses in Iran in 1256, and overthrew the ʿAbbasid caliph and sacked Baghdad in 1258. Möngke Qa'an himself, aided by Qubilai, had launched the massive campaign against the Southern Sung when he fell ill on the southern Chinese front. Hülegü was campaigning against Ayyubid Syria and Egypt, taking Damascus in April 1260, when the news of Möngke's death impelled him to return to Iran with the bulk of his army; the small force that he left behind was defeated in ʿAyn Jālut shortly thereafter.

Even Chinggis Khan's development of instruments of military centralization of power and the establishment of martial regulations as imperial law could not remedy the endemic instability of Turko-Mongolian regimes resulting from tanistry. As the charismatic leader of the Mongol Revolution, he managed to avoid the usual consequences of tanistry by eventually designating his third son, Ögedei, as his successor, while giving Mongolia itself to his youngest son, Tolui (d. 1232). Chinggis had wanted to designate his oldest son, Jochi, but his choice was rejected by Chaghadai, who called Jochi "that Merkit bastard," as he had been conceived during his mother's captivity by the Merkits. Tanistry was avoided also because Jochi predeceased his father. Nevertheless, the crises of succession that produced the Ögedei-Tolui condominium took two years to resolve, and then only as a result of pressure from Chinggis Khan's chief secretary and astrologer, Yeh-Lü Ch'u-Ts'ai, who assembled the *quriltai* that elected Ögedei qa'an in 1229 (Jackson 1978:197). After Ögedei's death in 1241, the effects of tanistry were also minimized by his powerful widow, Töregene, who became regent. It was not until the much delayed *quriltai* of 1246 that she managed to have her son Güyük elected qa'an. Batu of the Golden Horde was not a good loser, however, and was prepared for a major war against Güyük when the latter died in 1248. Then tanistry, so far restrained, came to the Great Mongol Empire with a vengeance between 1249 and 1251, causing an unprecedented bloodbath that virtually eliminated the line of Ögedei and greatly weakened that of Chaghadai. Since the bloodiest contest among the divisions of the winners of Chinggis Khan's revolution clustered around his four sons, this crisis of succession can be treated as the revolution's decisive power struggle. As such, it deserves to be examined in some detail alongside how the tanistry system after Möngke's death in 1259 led to the definitive fragmentation of the Great Mongol Empire.

The mastermind throughout the succession struggle that followed Güyük's death in 1248 was Tolui's widow, the matriarch of his line and a Kereid princess, Sorqaqtani Beki (d. 1252). Starting her bid for supremacy from the backseat, she capitalized on her relationship with her nephew Batu, who was the ruler of the Golden Horde. Her sister had been Jochi's senior wife and was Batu's mother (Jackson 1978:196), and Batu was now the senior male member, *āqā*, of the Chinggisid house. The aunt and the nephew coordinated their machinations for over two years. Batu's main interest seems to have been to secure the extensive Jochid steppe dominions. He declined the Great Qa'anate for himself and supported Sorqaqtani's promotion of her son Möngke and helped her carry out the Toluid coup of 1251. Güyük's widow and Ögedei's grandson Shiremüo, whom he had designated his successor, were put to death in Sorqaqtani's *ordo* on the discovery of a "plot" by the Ögedeids, in which the Chaghadaids also allegedly conspired. The bloodbath extended to many more Ögedeids and to quite a few victims from the Chaghadaid line (Jackson 1978:198–207).

Discounting the Chinese record doctored by Qubilai Qa'an, we know from the history of the Persian bureaucrat Vassāf that, upon Möngke's death in 1259, Tolui's youngest son, Arigh-böke, who was in charge of Mongolia according to the Mongol tradition, assumed the qa'anate in Karakorum in alliance with Alghu, the scion of the Chaghadaid line whose life had been spared in the Toluid coup of 1251 on account of his youth and who was now made the governor of Almaliq. Arigh-böke ruled for two and a half years, while Qubilai held China. There followed a four-way succession struggle that resulted in the definitive fragmentation of the Great Mongol Empire. Arigh-böke's khanate collapsed internally in 1262/658 as a result of the rebellion of Alghu, who switched to Qubilai's side in 1262. According to Vassāf, it was only after Alghu had decisively defeated Arigh-böke that Qubilai's force reached the latter and finished him off, forcing him to throw himself on his elder brother's mercy (Vassāf 1852–53:13–14). More consequential was the three-sided succession struggle between Jochid Berke, who had succeeded Batu as the khan of the Golden Horde, and the Toluid brothers Qubilai and Hülegü. Unlike Qubilai, Hülegü was not a major figure in Mongol history until the death of his brother Möngke, and his status would have depended on the success of the western campaign. In 1260, he remained in Iran with his *ulus* and did not attend either Arigh-böke's *quriltai* or the rump one assembled by Qubilai that elected him qa'an. He knew, however, that his greatest enemy was Berke to the west and figured that his best course of action was to remain subordinate to whichever brother prevailed in Karakorum. Hülegü eventually supported his brother Qubilai Qa'an, who rewarded him with the title Il-khan in 1262 (Manz 2010:144–45). All the while, his struggle was with Berke and the Golden Horde in the west and for the lush pastures around the Caspian Sea.

The established Jochid *ulus* had a stronger claim than Hülegü's upstart one, not only to those pastures but to the whole of Iran. Although all the four imperial Chinggisid lines had garrisons and fiscal agents in occupied Iran before the arrival of Hülegü, those of the Jochids were predominant. As we shall see presently, Chin Temür, who governed Iran from 1230 to 1235, was one of Jochi's men, as were his chief secretary and the chief secretary of his successor. It may have been in recognition of this fact that the Jochid relatives of Batu outnumbered other princes who brought contingents to Hülegü's expeditionary army (Jackson 1978:215–20). Their liquidation was therefore Hülegü's first task in establishing his complete mastery over Iran and thereby elevating his status as the head of his *ulus* to that of the ruler of the Golden Horde. This struggle had in fact begun before the crisis of succession. No sooner had he received a decree from Möngke giving him the authority over the province he had captured by overthrowing the ʿAbbasid caliph in 1258, than Hülegü convened a local *quriltai* to endorse it. The four Jochid princes in attendance demurred, and the three senior ones were strangled with bowstring. A great slaughter of Jochid troops followed, and Berke's man in Anatolia, Baichu, was executed. War broke out between Berke and Hülegü in 1261, and at that time the latter chose Qubilai over Arigh-böke as his sovereign and asked for his support. Qubilai appointed both Alghu and Hülegü Il-khans over their respective provinces. Hülegü finally attacked and defeated Berke in 1263, thereby securing his mastery over Iran. In preparation, Hülegü wrote to Alghu, who had just married Orghina Khatun, who was a granddaughter of Chinggis Khan's, the former regent on behalf of Chaghadai's great-grandson, and also the sister of Hülegü's wife, Öljei Khatun (Vassāf 1852–53:14; Āyati 1993:4; Manz 2010:161).[10] Alghu responded by purging Berke's representatives and governors from his own domain (Jackson 1978:232–35) and did not even spare Berke's favorite Sufi, Shaykh Sayf al-Din Bākharzi, for whom Sorqaqtani Beki had built a madrasa in Bukhara (Afshār 1980:11). The tanistry struggle for the succession to Möngke thus ended. Acknowledgment of Qubilai as the Great Qa'an notwithstanding, the Mongol Empire was now de facto divided into three: the Golden Horde, the Hülegü *ulus*, and the Great Khanate in China and Mongolia.

Consequences of the Mongol Revolution I: Emergence of the Compound Society in Iran

Eastern Iran was conquered, along with the Central Asian parts of the Khʷārazmshāh's rival Turkic empire, by Chinggis Khan in the first Mongol western campaign (1218–25). The cities refused to surrender, and their massacre and devastation were far greater than in northern China. Unlike the Chin Empire, whose garrisons often defected or surrendered, Sultan Mohammad b. Tekish Khʷārazmshāh's was a Turkish empire vigorously on the rise, and his major cities paid the deadly price. The last Khʷārazmshāh, Jalāl al-Din, in fact reconstituted the empire in western Iran and the Caucasus between 1224 and 1231 but then was defeated by the new army sent by Ögedei under the command of Chormaghun and was killed by Kurdish bandits (Boyle 1968:322–35). The Mongols then ruled Iran directly from Mongolia, through imperial decrees (*yarligh*) carried by an *ilchi* (envoy), while the Mongol princes, as we have seen, each appointed their own scribes/secretaries (*bitikchi*) under a chief secretary (*ulugh bitikchi*).

The first governor was the Khitan Chin Temür, a Jochid *nöker* who brought his administrative staff with him from Khʷarazm (1230–35), where he had been a governor (*basqaq*). The main secretaries of his bureau were Sharaf al-Din Khʷārazmi, a Turk, and Körgüz, an Uighur. But he also co-opted a few families of Persian bureaucrats to administer fiscal matters. His secretary Körgüz in effect succeeded him as de facto governor. He demoted Sharaf al-Din, who nevertheless remained Batu's *bitikchi* in Iran and in fact survived Körgüz. Sharaf al-Din in turn appointed another Batu man, Nezām al-Din, as the chief *bitikchi*. Körgüz continued his master Chin Temür's policy of co-opting the Iranian nobility and invited the landed notables of Khorasan to restore their ruined estates, until he was arrested and executed by the Chaghadaids for insulting their recently deceased father in 1242. Arghun Aqa, an Oirat *nöker* of the deceased qa'an Ögedei who led the Chaghadaid representatives to arrest Körgüz, survived the purge of the Ögedeids and ruled Iran as the last Mongol governor of the Great Mongol Empire from 1243 until 1255. There was little military or administrative centralization, as each of the four Mongol *ulus*es had its own occupying troops and its own *bitikchi* (Aubin 1995:11–17). When Hülegü came to Iran in 1253, he brought a number of *noyan*s with him who did not return at the end of his campaigns in 1260 but remained in Iran to become grandees of the new Il-khanid regime. An administratively somewhat more centralized but equally deadly pattern of patronage, protection, and cross-caste political alliances developed among Mongol princesses, amirs (as the *noyan*s were now called), and rival bureaucratic Persian families. The Persian families nevertheless managed to centralize the administration through the vizierate and to form a number of short-lived factions around prominent viziers such as Majd al-Molk Yazdi, Sadr al-Din Khāledi Zanjāni (vizierate, 1291–98), Saʿad al-Dawla b. Safi al-Din Abhari, and Tāj al-Din ʿAli-Shāh Tabrizi and around vizierial dynasties, notably those of the Sāheb-Divān Jovayni

(1233–84) and of Rashid al-Din (1295–1336) (Aubin 1995). The women of the royal household—notably the Kereid princess Doquz Khatun, wife of Hülegü's father and then Hülegü's chief wife, whose *ordo* bore her name to the end of the dynasty while being reassigned to successive queens; Öljei Khatun, wife successively of Hülegü, Abaqa, and Arghun; and two Bulughan khatuns, the second of whom was married to Arghun and Geykhatu before becoming Ghāzān's favorite wife and (re)marrying him as a fellow Muslim when he converted to Islam (Lambton 1988:292–94 and table 8)—played a very important political role in succession crises and in routine factional politics throughout the reigns of successive Il-khans who all died young. They had their own camps (*ordo*s) and military retainers, were frequently visited by the Mongol amirs and Persian viziers, and had appanages and allowances from Crown land (*inju, dalay*) to maintain them (Manz 2010:146).

The Constitutionalist Reading of the Rise of the Mongols by Persian Bureaucrats

The structure of the polity Hülegü made independent and began to rule certainly favored the major attempt by the Persian bureaucrats to Persianize it by grafting on to it the unifying ideology of the "kingship of the land of Iran" (*pādshāhi-ye Irān-zamin*). The idea of undivided and territorial sovereignty in the Persian political tradition as represented to Hülegü by his Persian bureaucrats must have seemed to him and his successors an attractive antidote to tanistry—the central fault line of the Il-khanid political structure as of all Turko-Mongolian nomadic empires. Hülegü died in 1265, almost thirty years before his brother Qubilai Qa'an, and four of his sons and grandsons had succeeded him as Il-khan before Qubilai's death in 1294. This made the crises of succession due to tanistry chronic in the Il-khanid regime, with the worst following the death of his son Abaqa in 1282, when the Mongol princesses and amirs and the Persian viziers, as well as the fiscal resources of the realm, were fairly equally divided between his other son, Tegüder, and his grandson Arghun (Manz 2010:148–49). While Il-khanid rulers eagerly received the idea and claimed the title of king of kings (*shāhanshāh*) or imperial monarch, they nevertheless continued to emphasize their conquest right to rule their compound societies by minting coins as "possessor of the necks of [submitted] nations" (*mālek al-reqāb al-omam*) (Seĭfeddini 1978–81:1.2337, 2.29).

Two years after the death of the last Khʷārazmshāh, Jalāl al-Din, and after the second Mongol devastation of Khorasan in 1233, Bahā᾿ al-Din Jovayni, who had succeeded his father as the chief secretary, defected to the Mongols and was appointed chief *bitikchi* by Chin Temür and entrusted with a mission to Ögedei Qa'an in 1235–36/633. The qa'an issued a *yarligh* appointing him the highest Persian official in the Mongol imperial administration in Iran, in which the Persian title *sāheb-divān-e mamālek* (master of the bureau of the realm [of Iran]) was reportedly used instead of the Mongolian title of chief *bitikchi*. He typically remained, however, under the nominal supervision of a Mongol *noyan*/amir (Lambton 1988:52). Toward the end of his life, Bahā' al-Din sent his young son 'Atā-Malek (Prince 'Atā) to the imperial capital, Karakorum, where he remained from 1249 to 1253, with only a brief return to his estate in Jovayn, Khorasan. 'Atā-Malek Jovayni (d. 1283) took part in the enthronement of Möngke as the imperial qa'an in 1251, where he was told to write a history of the rise of the Mongols within the Persian statecraft and historiographic framework of kingship for the edification of the young *pādshāh* (imperial king) (Jovayni, 1.3).

Jovayni's *Tārikh-e Jahān-goshā* (History of the world conqueror), completed in 1260, begins with the foundation of the Mongol Empire or, in his words, "the rules established and the commandments [*yāsās*] decreed by Chinggis Khan (d. 1227) after his uprising [*khoruj*]," and with the mention of Alexander as the prototypical world conqueror (Jovayni, 1.16):

> According to his determination and judgment, he set a regulation for every expediency, made a punishment for every crime; and as the Tartar nations did not have a script, Mongolian children learned the script from the Uighurs and wrote down those commandments and ordinances on scrolls and called it the great Book of Yasas [*Yāsā-nāma*][11] . . . and whenever a khan ascends the throne or brings together a large army or assembles the princes for deliberation in the affairs of the realm, they bring out those scrolls and base their policies on them. (Jovayni, 1.17–18)

He then uses *yāsā* as a generic term for (public) law: "Whatever is in the *yāsā* of Chinggis Khan was free of bias, and treated all tribes equally" (Jovayni, 1.18). Chinggis Khan had dictated the following in a letter taken down by a Daoist sage: "I am from the barbaric North. . . . I wear the same clothing and eat the same food as the cowherds and the horse-herders. We make the same sacrifices and we share the same riches" (cited in Mote 1999:433). Jovayni attests to the persistence of this remarkable egalitarianism of Mongolian political culture half a century after the foundation of the empire: "For whoever ascends the throne of the khanate, they merely add the one title of khan or qa'an to their names and no more . . . , and in their decrees and letters they write only the name of the person concerned and make no distinction between rulers and commoners" (Jovayni, 1.19).

Jovayni's next task is to provide a constitutional reading of the succession to the khanate among the descendants of Chinggis Khan. He freely avails himself of the testamentary designation (*vasiyyat*) of a successor by ancient Persian kings and the appointment of a successor as the *vali al-ʿahd* by Muslim caliphs. Chinggis Khan is thus said to have called the four sons from his main wife and told them that one of them had to take charge of the government of the whole empire, and he was therefore designating Ögedei (d. 1241) as his successor (*vali al-ʿahd*) (Jovayni, 1.146–47).

This promotion of the Muslim conception of successorship in Jovayni's constitutionalist reading of Mongol history evidently aimed at undermining what I have called tanistry, which was sustained by at least two contradictory Mongolian customary practices: inheritance of the heartland of the empire of conquest by the youngest son and the principle of seniority and preeminent right of the senior male member (*āqā*) of the ruling house in succession. Jovayni predictably highlights the former on behalf of the Toluid house of his royal patron while minimizing the principle of seniority. To establish the legitimacy of the sons of Tolui—Möngke and Hülegü—Jovayni (1.146) has Ögedei, after his nomination by Chinggis Khan, state the principle that "the youngest son is the lieutenant of the father," adding that because "the youngest son of the great *ordo*, chief prince [*ulugh noyan*]—that is, Tolui—has been in [your] service day and night and has seen and heard and learned the *yāsā* and the *yosun*," he is more deserving of the qa'anate. Half a century later, Rashid al-Din is even more emphatic about Toluid legitimacy but makes no allusion to the principle of seniority in the context of succession (Jackson 1978:195).

In Jovayni's account, the first and most significant law that Ögedei promulgated as the new qa'an was that "all the commands and decrees issued earlier by Chinggis Khan be valid and immune and protected [*mahrus*] from all change, alteration, and disturbance." This constitutional entrenchment of the laws of Chinggis Khan carried the sanction that "whoever initiates an act which is not in accord with the old and new laws should be punished" (Jovayni, 1.149).

Ögedei's son and successor, Güyük (d. 1248), is also reported to have issued upon succession a law entrenching all the laws of the earlier emperors—that is, his grandfather and his father. They were valid and protected from alteration, and there was no need to obtain the signature of a new qa'an for their renewal (Jovayni, 1.211).

The last but not the least important component of Jovayni's Persianate constitutionalist reading of Mongol customary and public law consisted of anecdotes on the normative deeds of Ögedei Qa'an in the style of the *sira*, or normative precedents, set by ancient kings as in the Muslim "mirrors for princes"—that is, books on statecraft and political ethics (Jovayni 1.158–91). Ögedei is, furthermore, portrayed as favoring his Muslim subjects especially.

While Jovayni was writing his history in Persian, the first Il-khans themselves showed a keen interest in the epic of the ancient kings of Iran. Hülegü and his successor, Abaqa (d. 1282), had the palaces at the Sasanian coronation site of Takht-e Solaymān decorated with verses of the *Shāhnāma* on tiles (Melville 2013). The later Il-khans promoted Persianate kingship by producing lavishly illustrated manuscripts of the *Shāhnāma* and, as we shall see, commissioned their high fiscal official Hamdallāh Mostawfi to write their own supplementary epic of kings, *Zafarnāma*, which devoted more verses to the kingship of Chinggis Khan and his descendants than to that of either the Arabs or the Persians.

Meanwhile, other bureaucrats from the co-opted Persian nobility were seeing to the political education of their new master in the languages with which he was familiar. Thus, one Malek Eftekhār al-Din Bakri Qazvini translated the classics of Indo-Persianate statecraft *Kalila o denmah* into Mongolian and *Sendbādnāma* into Turkish (Aubin 1995:26). The Il-khanid bureaucrat Vassāf (484–99) appended a short treatise, "Ethics of Sovereignty" (Akhlāq-e saltanat), to his continuation of Jovayni's *Tārikh-e Jahān-goshā* for the new kings of Islam, Sultan Mahmud (Ghāzān Khan) and Sultan Mohammad Khodā-banda (Öljeitü). It contains no acknowledgment of the Mongol political tradition and places the legitimacy of monarchy squarely on justice in the classical Persian tradition. Vassāf, however, endorses his fellow Persian colleague's constitutionalist reading of Mongol history and has Ghāzān assemble the elite of the realm before his death, urging them to obey his brother Öljeitü, his *vali al-ʿahd* (heir apparent), "for three of four years," as his successor "and not to infringe my ordinance [*āʾin*] and law" (Vassāf 1852–53:457; Āyati 1993:270).

Rashid al-Din Fazlallāh Hamadāni (d. 1318), the famous vizier of the last Il-khans, developed Jovayni's constitutionalist reading of Jovayni and extended it to cover the reigns of his royal patrons. His political theology incorporates Jovayni's account that the first successor of the founder of the Mongol Empire, Ögedei, decreed in his first law (*yāsāq*) that "all the commandments of Chinggis Khan hitherto remain in effect and valid and protected against all alteration and variation." When reporting Chinggis

Khan's designation of Ögedei and his line as his successors, Rashid al-Din elaborates one of Jovayni's remarks on Möngke Qa'an's correction of a constitutional infringement (Jovayni, 1.143) by attaching a significant condition to the designation, namely, "that you do not alter any law [*yāsāq*] after me" (Rashid al-Din, 1.529). This is picked up by Rashid al-Din to reconstruct constitutional debates between Möngke's brother and successor, Qubilai Qa'an, which could equally serve the establishment of independent Il-khanid rule in Iran by his other brother Hülegü (d. 1265).[12] When the legitimacy of the succession of the late Möngke Qa'an (d. 1259), and by implication that of his brother, is challenged by the pretenders from the line of Ögedei, Qubilai is made to reply that the designation was conditional upon not altering "the ancient law," which they had done by killing a certain Alta Luqān without due process of law (Rashid al-Din, 1.69).

Rashid al-Din also elaborated on Jovayni's account of the foundation of the Mongol Empire: "As with the passage of time, worldly affairs and laws decay . . . and the situation of states and nations becomes disturbed and shaken, there will rise a Lord of Auspicious Conjunction [*sāheb-qerān*—i.e., a world conqueror] of great and awe-inspiring majesty who enjoys heavenly backing." And so rose Chinggis Khan, who "conquered many kingdoms in a short period and ordered and codified the laws and customs [*yāsāq o yosun*] of kingship and established procedures for the spread of justice and protection of the subjects" (Rashid al-Din, 1.287–88).

To be more precise, Chinggis Khan appointed his sons as commanders of ten thousand, a thousand, and a hundred men, organized the army/nation (*jam'iyyat*), convened the *quriltai*, and established for them, once again, the constitution, customs, and laws (*ā'in o yosun o yāsāq*). In other words, he restored the constitution of the old Turkic empires preceding his own. Rashid al-Din has his royal patron follow the tradition of his illustrious ancestor by teaching his associates Mongol custom and law and assigning their ranks accordingly as elders, youngsters, sworn brothers, and relatives by marriage (cited in Aigle 2004:37). Chinggis Khan's own acts of foundation included the appointment of the first imperial chief justice, *yārghuchi*, who, according to Rashid al-Din, set the pattern for Mongol legal procedure. According to a later Il-khanid source, the record of the cases involving Mongols was kept in a book, *yārghu-nāma* (Morgan 2007:86).

The most important component of Rashid al-Din's political theology, however, was original. He introduces a distinctive teleological twist that made the Mongol conquests the instrument not only of the restoration of Persianate royal justice but also, and more important, of the spread of Islam. His royal patron, Ghāzān Khan (r. 1295–1304), had converted to

Islam, adopting the title and name of Sultan Mahmud, and Rashid al-Din accordingly proceeded to give an Islamic twist to the Turko-Mongolian political theology. He gives an account of his enthronement as the "king of Islam" upon "the throne of the khanate" on the astrologically auspicious Sunday, November 10, 1295 (Dhi'l-hijja 23, 694), and by the "honest and nonhypocritical consensus of the [Mongol] pillars of the state and the court notables" (Rashid al-Din, 2.1261).[13] This historical fact gave our vizier a basis for constructing his Islamicate cosmic teleology: "The far-reaching divine wisdom thus required that the cure of the ailment [presumably massacre and destruction of cities] for those peoples be Islam . . . so as to make clear to the inhabitants of the earth the prevalence of God's eternal command. And this meaning was embodied in the generous presence of the king of Islam, the king of kings of peoples, the Shadow of God, and the helper of his religion, Sultan Mahmud Ghāzān Khan. . . . 'This is God's bounty. He vouchsafes it to whom he wills (Q. 3.26)'" (Rashid al-Din, 2.1289–90). On the mundane level, Rashid-al-Din mentions the legal reforms of the king of Islam, which meant the restoration of the *shari'a* alongside the *yāsā* and the appointment of kadis to implement it, as well as that of a council of administrators, judges, and descendants of 'Ali to meet two days a week at the research bureau (*divān*) at the congregational mosque to issue responses to legal queries (Rashid al-Din, 2.1287–90).

Rashid al-Din had the satisfaction of remaining in office to take part in the enthronement of yet another "king of Islam," Ghāzān Khan's brother Öljeitü on July 27, 1304 (Dhi'l-hijja 15, 703). The succession was according to Ghāzān's testament (*vasiyyat-nāma*),[14] which designated his "noble brother, and great sultan, the noble qa'an, the king of kings of Islam, . . . the most just of the Il-khans . . . Sultan Mohammad Khodā-banda Khan, . . . who is the telos [*maqsud*] of the manifestation of the Chinggis-Khanid state and the promised instrument of the removal of the decline of the Muslim religion" (Rashid al-Din, 1.2–3).[15] The new Il-khan nevertheless adhered to Mongol constitutional principles by examining the "*yāsāq* and *yosun* and customs and norms [*rosum*] of his brother" and predecessor (Rashid al-Din, 1.7).

As Rashid al-Din was beginning his political career as deputy vizier under Ghāzān, Sadr al-Din Khāledi, known as the Sadr-e Jahān (president of the world),[16] narrowly escaped death in 1296 thanks to the intercession of one of the Il-khan's wives and held his second vizierate for some two years before his enemies in the bureaucracy, at Rashid al-Din's instigation, persuaded Ghāzān that he was guilty of peculation. The Il-khan had him cut into two halves in May 1298, before the investigation was complete.

During his first vizierate, from 1291 to 1295, however, Sadr al-Din had persuaded the debauched Geykhatu (1291–95), who had little interest in governing, to make him an amir, as well as the vizier, thereby removing the nominal subordination of the Persian vizier to the Mongol amir, and to make agents of the Mongol princesses and princes directly responsible to him. With the absolute power thus granted him, Sadr al-Din embarked on significant centralization of government through fiscal control of Crown lands in Fars and Iraq. Aubin (1995:46–68) rightly considers him the first upholder of the Il-khanid concept of "absolute vizierate," a position that Rashid al-Din secured for himself before long and held until his execution in 1318. Rashid al-Din then embarked on his own administrative and fiscal reforms, which are much better known than Sadr al-Din's, because Rashid al-Din wrote about them extensively in his history of the reign of Gāzān, *Tārikh-e mobārak-e Ghāzāni*, where he supplemented his Persianate theory of monarchy with a strong emphasis on the rationalization of state finances. Furthermore, in the letters of instruction he issued to his governors, ten of whom were his own sons, he elaborated the Perso-Islamicate conception of political economy (Petrushevsky 1970; Rajabzāda 1977). According to this conception—the so-called circle of justice—the justice of the ruler is the center of a virtuous circle of good government, contentment of the subjects, prosperity, and military might (Rashid al-Din 1979:113).

Hamdallāh Mostawfi (d. 1340/740), the last architect of the Il-khanid political theology, offered a somewhat different constitutionalist interpretation of Mongol history that stemmed from a teleology centered on Iran rather than Islam. This teleology was embodied in an epic of kings, adding Chinggis Khan and his descendants to the dynasties of ancient Persian and medieval Islamic world empires. His *Zafarnāma* (Book of victories) thus marked the culmination of the Persianate acculturation of the Il-khans. Hamdallāh Mostawfi equates the Mongol *quriltai* as well as their ad hoc councils (*kengāč*) with the *anjoman* (council) of the ancient kings in Ferdawsi's *Shāhnāma* (Aubin 1995:55). While confirming the testamentary designation of Ögedei as Chinggis Khan's successor (*vali al-ʿahd*) (Mostawfi, 8.2–3), he is careful to constitutionalize the legitimacy of the Il-khans by enumerating the rights of their ancestor, Tolui, as the youngest son and associate (*nöker*) of Chinggis Khan. Tolui had learned the legal code from his father (Mostawfi, 8.3). The conditions of Ögedei's designation are, furthermore, accorded a Persianate constitutionalist reading as a "covenant" (*paymān*, yet another term from the *Shāhnāma*) to observe the "laws of the king [*shāh*]" (Mostawfi, 8.4). The account of the first law of Güyük is likewise cast in constitutional terms, and the continued legitimacy of his (Ögedeid) line is made dependent on observing the covenant not to violate the legal code, because the world order depended on its correct observance by the descendants of Chinggis Khan (Mostawfi, 8.123). More to the same point, the ascension of the Toluid Möngke Qa'an is presented as the restoration of this constitutional principle (Mostawfi, 8.138, 141–42). All this is the prelude to the restoration of royal justice of the ancient kings in the land of Iran.

Like Rashid al-Din, Mostawfi (10. 261–65, vv. 627, 681, 693) celebrates the conversion of the Il-khanids to Islam as a historic landmark:

> As he was a companion of divine charisma [*farr-e Izadi*]
> He [Ghāzān] became desirous of Islam.
> . . . .
> As Ghāzān became Muslim at the time,
> So did everyone who was with him.
> . . . .
> As Islam was revealed among the Mongols,
> The world became secure from war and violence!

Mostawfi's most important contribution, however, consists in binding the Persianate theory of monarchy inseparably to the land of Iran. Faithfully to the Persianate tradition, the king's divine charisma is made transitive and spread to the realm of Iran, making it prosperous and luminous. Mostawfi alternately calls the territorial empire of the Il-khanid king "the land of Iran" (*Irān-zamin*) and the "realm of Iran" (*molk-e Irān-zamin*).[17] Like the owl of Minerva, our Hamdallāh Mostawfi lived on to see the disintegration of the Il-khanid empire in the late 1330s. And the two components of his Persianized Turko-Mongolian political theology survived with him. Dreams of Persianate imperial kingship, and the reality of imperial Turko-Mongolian nomadic patrimonialism, both survived, though their synthesis occasionally burst asunder.

Paradoxical as it may seem, the rebirth of Iran was thus an unintended consequence of Mongol imperial domination. The rise of the "national state" in Iran, wrongly placed by Walter Hinz (1933) at the beginning of the Safavid era, was in fact the consequence of the division of the Great Empire of the Mongols (Yeke Mongghol Ulus) after the death of Möngke Qa'an between his brothers Qubilai and Hülegü. It consisted in the transformation of Hülegü's *ulus*, constituted by Möngke in the mid-1250s, into the independent Il-khanid imperial kingdom of *Irān-zamin* (the land of Iran). This transformation was clearly the goal of Hülegü and his Il-khan successors but was wrought, as we have seen, by the Persian state builders of the subsequent three-quarters of a century. The unifying idea of the "realm(s) Iran" (*mamlakat/mamālek-e Irān-zamin*) (Nakhjavāni 1964:9–10, 40, 75ff.) survived the fragmentation of the Il-khanid empire after 1335. The highest office of the state held by a Mongol in the mid-fourteenth century was the "amir of the *ulus*," although the title alluded to the time when Iran was a mere part of Hülegü's *ulus*; an exemplar of the decree of appointment to the office from 1360/761 now defined the *ulus* under his authority as coextensive with the land of Iran—"*ulus dar mamlakat-e Irān-zamin*"—that is, "from the boundaries of Egypt to the Oxus valley and from the Straits of Hormuz to Bāb al-Abwāb [Darband]" (Nakhjavāni 1964:10).[18] Indeed, the imperial kingdom of *Irān-zamin* as best delineated by Hamdallāh Mostawfi was both the revival of the Sasanian idea of Iran and the prototype of modern Iran as a nation-state (Fragner 1997; Lane 2003).

We must now contrast this idealized constitutionalist reading of the Persian bureaucrats with the real constitution of the Turko-Mongolian compound polity in Iran from 1260 to 1405. Although the Persian bureaucrats had no trouble selling the Il-khans the Persian idea of kingship over a territorial empire, Iran, the gap between the Turko-Mongolian itinerant conception of the khanate and the Persianate territorial idea of kingship was enormous. Hülegü welcomed the latter as the means for transforming his subordinate tribal khanate or chiefdom into an independent monarchy over a specific territory. The actuality of the itinerant kingship of the Il-khanids, who resided in their camp enclosure (*ordo; ordu* in Persian) and gave audiences in their palatial tent (*khargāh*) (Melville 2013), no less than the itinerant kingship of the Turkish Seljuks before them, who were also idealized as Persian kings by their vizier Nezām al-Molk,[19] was at great variance with the ideal of Persianate imperial kingship.

The viziers and high officials received no personal or professional appreciation from the Il-khans as recompense for promoting their overlords' sovereignty over the undivided land of Iran. They remained squarely within the estate of the conquered Persian subjects, and their Mongol masters, as "possessors of their necks," had nothing but contempt for them. Each time they were summoned to the *ordo* of the Il-khan or even that of one of the princesses, they went trembling and hoping to come out alive. Vassāf recounts the harrowing story of how, during a banquet, three years before his final destruction by Arghun, the great Sāheb-Divān Shams al-Din Mohammad Jovayni offered Abaqa a cup of wine three times, and the khan refused to take it and picked up a piece of pork on the tip of a sharp knife and told him to eat it. The Muslim vizier obeyed, and the khan finally accepted his cup of wine, telling those present that he had intended to gouge the Sāheb-Divān's eyes out if he had refused (Vassāf 1852–53:96; Āyati 1993:58–59). The emergence of the absolute vizierate under the late Il-khans did not give the viziers any greater security of life.

Vassāf and Mostawfi were both seasoned bureaucrats who served rival viziers and survived their downfalls. Their lack of professional security and confidence is striking, though hardly surprising. Vassāf (1852–53:488–89) ended his tract on political ethics with a long poem on "the unfaithfulness of the world," highlighting the impermanence of earthly sovereignty from the legendary Persian kings to the Mongols, including Ghāzān. Much more poignantly and precisely, Mostawfi reflects on not just the impermanence but the dire perils of the vizierate. He describes the execution in 1284 of the powerful Sāheb-Divān Shams al-Din who was, for thirty years, "the king's minister in the land of Iran" (*dar Irān-zamin bud dastur-e shāh*) (Mostawfi, 10.161, v. 214) and who

> For thirty full years in the realm of Iran [*molk-e Irān*],
> The world was under the reins of his competence.
> With justice, knowledge, and golden judgment,
> He made the world more pleasant than paradise. (Mostawfi, 10.156, vv. 109–10)

Yet his unbounded ambitions brought about his own martyrdom and the annihilation of his entire family (Mostawfi, 10.161, vv. 210–11). The demoralizing lesson drawn by Mostawfi from the fate of the vizierial dynasty of Sāheb-Divān (and, closer to him, that of Rashid al-Din), as well as the torture and execution of almost all the Il-khanid viziers, is that servile humility is the key to survival in government service:

> Let us not attempt to achieve superiority
> As seeking such superiority may cost one's life.
> We should seek but lowly work,
> Tending to the worship of the Just One [*dādgar*—i.e., God].
> . . . .
> As your being appeared from earth
> Be like dirt, my son, lying lowly everywhere. (Mostawfi, 10.162, vv. 227–28, 236)

The most glaring discrepancy between the ideal and the real constitutions of the Il-khanid regime was, however, due to the unaltered Turkic custom of contestation for succession to the khanate. The imposing facade of Persian kingship notwithstanding, tanistry, never acknowledged as a constitutional principle, was nevertheless impossible to eradicate from nomadic patrimonialism. Rashid al-Din is silent on the violent crises of succession following the deaths of Abaqa and Arghun, as he is on the principle of seniority conflicting with that of the designation of a *vali al-ʿahd*, which underlaid the election of Hülegü's eldest surviving son, Tegüder (Ahmad) in 1282 (Boyle 1968:364–79). As a vizier, he himself managed to hold it at bay for the last three Il-khanid "kings of Islam," but it returned with a vengeance when the last of these, Abu Saʿid, died without any male offspring at the end of November 1335. The Chinggisid royal family did not breed well in Iran. Hülegü had fourteen sons, but Abaqa had only two sons, Tegüder three, Geykhatu three, and Ghāzān one. Abu Saʿid was the only one of Öljeitü's sons to survive childhood. In the ferocious tanistry that followed Öljeitü's death, Ghiyāth al-Din, Rashid al-Din's son, quickly put Prince Arpa, a Toluid descendant of Arigh-böke, on the throne, but the vizier and his khan perished within five months, as did Solaymān, who was a descendant of Baidu and several other Chinggisid pretenders. Of the main Mongol tribes, the Jalayer backed some of them until their leader, Shaykh Hasan-e Bozorg, decided to rule in his own name and founded the Jalayerid dynasty (1336–1432), while the Oirat tribe, after failing to establish their own pretender, rallied briefly behind Sultan Abu Saʿid's sister, Sati Beg, as the widow of Amir Choban, until the Chobanid leader, Hasan-e Kuchak, who was also a grandson of Geykhatu through his mother, decided to rule in his own name and founded the Chobanid dynasty (1336–56) (Boyle 1968:413–16; Manz 2010:159). It was not until Temür (Tamerlane), a descendant of Chaghadai's chief *yārghuchi* and scion of the Barlas clan, which stemmed from Chinggis Khan's Keshig (Subtelny 2010:170–72), revived and reunified the decaying *ulus* of Chaghadai and transformed it from a tribal confederation into an army of conquest that Turko-Mongolian imperial rule found stability for a quarter of a century (Manz 1983). To legitimate his deed of unification of the Chaghadaid *ulus* and expansion of his empire to Iran in the 1380s, Temür married a Chinggisid princess and assumed the title "imperial son-in-law" (*güregen*) while making another Chinggisid, a certain Shah Mahmud Khan, the figurehead king of his new nomadic empire, styling him the "king of Islam" in the late Il-khanid fashion, and ordering coins struck and the Friday sermon (*khotba*) delivered in his name (Manz 1988). This makeshift combination of the Chinggisid and late Il-khanid symbols of sovereignty, however, was no more successful than the Persianate constitutionalism of Jovayni and Rashid al-Din in holding tanistry at bay. On the contrary, tanistry returned after the second world conqueror's death in 1405 to bedevil the Timurids and other Turko-Mongolian successor states for the rest of the fifteenth century and beyond (Arjomand 2016b:15–16).

Consequences of the Mongol Revolution II: The Yuan Polity in China

We have seen how Qubilai won the struggle for succession by 1264 and became the Qa'an of the Great Mongol Empire, granting de facto independence to Berke as the khan of the Golden Horde and to Hülegü as the Il-khan of Iran. He had wrested Mongolia from Arigh-böke and struggled for over a decade to secure it definitively, as he had Central Asia, which, however, he lost to Ögedei's grandson Qaidu by 1279 (Rossabi 2009:104–14). By contrast, he held northern China firmly, declaring himself in 1271 the emperor of a new Chinese dynasty, Yuan (meaning "chief" but with the connotation, in the *Book of Changes*, of the origins of the universe) (Chan 1967:133), and proceeding to overthrow the Southern Sung in 1279, thus incorporating the rest of China into the Yuan Empire, which lasted to 1368.

Already as a young prince during the qa'anate of Ögedei in the late 1230s, Qubilai had begun recruiting Chinese advisers and experimenting with Sinicizing his government in his appanage in the district of Xingzhu in northern China, just as his mother, Sorqaqtani Beki, was doing in her neighboring appanage (Mote 1999:446–47). He continued to receive Chinese visitors in Karakorum in the early 1240s, while Ögedei's reforms were unraveling in the face of a hostile dowager regent, Töregene (1241–46), and later her son, Güyük Qa'an (1246–48). The Buddhist monk Liu Ping-chung (d. 1274), who had met Qubilai in Karakorum in 1242, submitted a "ten-thousand-word" memorial on future government policy and administration to him around 1249 (Chan 1967:118). At about the same time, Qubilai sought advice on government from another Chinese scholar, Tou Mo (d. 1280), who became one of his political counselors (Chan 1993b).

In 1251, Qubilai sent a special envoy to invite Yao Shu to meet him and give him advice on government, and Yao submitted a lengthy memorial on the basic principles of government and was ordered to set up a Pacification Bureau in Ching-cao. When Qubilai became qa'an in 1260, he set up ten more Pacification Bureaus and appointed Yao Shu the pacification commissioner (Chan 1980:22–30). In 1253, Qubilai took Liu Ping-chung on the campaign against the Ta-li Kingdom as his military adviser, and in 1256, he commissioned him to draft a blueprint for his summer capital, which was to be named, first, K'ai-p'ing fu and then (in 1264) Shang-tu (Xangdu) (Chan 1967:125–27). All these northern Chinese literati introduced the Chinese tradition of statecraft and its political ethic to Qubilai in the 1250s and 1260s. His conquest of southern China in the 1270s brought the southern literati and their Daoxue, or Learning of the Way, into Yuan political culture. Nevertheless, the Chinese input was exaggerated by later Confucian scholars like the compilers of the *Yuan shih*, according to whom Qubilai (Emperor Shizu) "placed trust in Confucian techniques (*rushu*) and so was able to Sinify barbarian ways (*i hua bian i*) and set up canons and regulations" (cited in Dardess 2003:129). In fact, Qubilai was careful to counterbalance his rapidly growing Chinese officialdom by doubling the number of offices to which he appointed Mongols and Central Asians. During his qa'anate (1260–94), he appointed 163 Central Asian Turks to high office, almost half of whom (73) were Uighurs. This was twice as many individuals as those appointed during the Great Mongol Empire (1200–1259) (de Rachewiltz 1983:285).[20] But he also had Chinese works on administration and statecraft translated for them into Mongolian (Franke 1982; Rossabi 2009:138–39).

Although the Il-khans became de facto independent in Iran as a result of the struggle with Möngke for succession, they were nevertheless "subordinate Khans" and fully acknowledged Qubilai's sovereignty, continued to affix the qa'an's seal on their documents (Schurmann 1963:27), and did whatever he ordered them to do. Bayan (d. 1295), known, according to Marco Polo, as Bayan Hundred Eyes, was the grandson of one of Chinggis Khan's commanders and had accompanied his father in Hülegü's Persian campaign. Bayan returned to Qubilai and was appointed Left Chancellor in the newly reorganized Secretarial Council in 1265. He was assigned to the Sung campaign in 1273, became commander in chief of the Yuan army in the conquest of Hang-Chou, and, in February 1276, as the Myriarch of the Left and Right, received the seal of the Sung dynasty and accepted the surrender of the last emperor (Hsiao 1993). In 1267, the Persian astronomer Jamāl al-Din arrived in the imperial capital from the observatory of Hülegü's adviser Nasir al-Din Tusi in Maragha to design Qubilai Qa'an's new calendar, just as the Muslim architect "Yeh-hei-tieh-erh" and his staff were beginning the construction of Ta-tu (Great Capital, Beijing) (Rossabi 2009:125, 132, 136). A few years later, when the Southern Sung campaign revealed the deficiency of Mongol siege techniques, Abaqa Il-khan sent his uncle Qubilai two Persian military engineers, Ismā'il and 'Alā' al-Din, who went to the besieged Xiang-yang early in 1273. They "set up an engine at the south-east corner of the city. The missile weighed 150 catties. When the machinery went off the noise shook heaven and earth" (cited in Rossabi 2009:86). This was evidently too much for the Sung commander, who surrendered.

The most prominent among the Central Asian Muslims who attained high office in the Great Mongol Empire and become Qubilai's men were Shams al-Din Sayyid Ajall Bukhāri (d. 1279), also known as Sayyid Elchi (envoy) Shams al-Din, and Ahmad Fanākati (d. 1282). Sayyid Ajall's family were Bukharan notables who entered Mongol service under Chinggis Khan in the 1220s—that is, shortly after Mahmud Yalvach and his sons, and a decade and a half before the elder Jovayni. Sayyid Ajall served as *yeke darughachi* (imperial chief justice) already under Ögedei, and subsequently became a *yārghuchi* (chief justice) more or less as that office was becoming differentiated from that of the *darughachi*. He played an important role in securing Qubilai's succession (Buell 1993a:467–71). Having served Qubilai in the Secretarial Council in 1261, Sayyid Ajall was commissioned to set up and head the Regional Secretarial Council for western China in 1264. This made him in effect the proconsul for western China, including Szechwan, Shensi, and Yunnan, the province created after the annexation of the Kingdom of Ta-li (Qara Jang). In 1273, Sayyid Ajall established himself in Yunnan with a small Mongol garrison and spent the last years of his life there, leaving its government to his sons when he died at the age of sixty-eight in 1279. Sayyid Ajall and his dynasty promoted Islam in Yunnan but, more important, ensured the Sinicization of western China and its integration into the Yuan Empire (Buell 1993a:472–79).

Ahmad Fanākati, known in Chinese sources simply as Ahmad, had been a *nöker* of Alchin Noyan (d. 1237) and was in Alchin Noyan's daughter's *ordo* when Qubilai married her in 1239. Ahmad moved with her to Qubilai's court. He was promoted to the Secretarial Council in 1262 and, despite receiving corporal punishment for irregularities in 1264, succeeded in creating the new Office for Regulating State Expenditure in 1266 (Franke 1993:539–42). Qubilai made him the chief finance minister as the head of a new Presidential Council in 1270. Ahmad in turn put the financial administration of the empire mainly in the hands of Central Asian Muslims (Chan 1980:41). Like his contemporary Sāheb-Divān Shams al-Din Mohammad Jovayni in Iran, Ahmad sought to establish his own vizierial dynasty in the next decade and a half. He put one son in charge of the imperial capital, Ta-tu, appointing another the *darughachi* of the commercial center of Hangchow and yet another a military commander (Rossabi 2009:181).

Qubilai Qa'an needed Ahmad to raise revenues for the building of his summer and imperial capitals, Sang-tu and Ta-tu, for supplying them with grain, and then for his expeditions in the south and later to Japan. Moving the capital from Karakorum to Beijing drastically changed the structure of Qubilai's empire. Between 1261 and 1274, Ahmad added half a million households to the tax register, bringing the number close to two million, established a network of state monopolies (Schurmann 1956a:146–89; Rossabi 2009:180), and taxed international trade—something he knew well as an *ortaq* trading partner to the imperial family. Ahmad also supervised the conversion of the tribute and levies of the Mongol Empire to Chinese taxes: land tax, head tax, grain tax, and household taxes (Schurmann 1956a:8, 65–107). A decree of 1264 introduced a variable scale for the land tax payable by different classes of people, noting that under Chinggis Khan it had been uniform regardless of the class of subjects. In 1280–81, following the conquest of the Southern Sung, a new land tax altered the tax regulations of 1260 by introducing four rates for different categories of subjects created in the censuses (Schurmann 1956a:68–70).

Qubilai had used his Chinese advisers for the acts of foundation of the Yuan dynasty, the building of an ancestral temple, the geomantic location of the new capital, a new calendar, and ceremonial court music. His giving control of the empire's finances to Ahmad and his Semu retinue created mounting tension between them and the Chinese members of the Secretarial Council. Although his old and irreplaceable advisers were dead by 1280, other Chinese officials had moved up to the Secretarial Council and found powerful support among the Mongols, notably General Bayan and Noyan An-tung (d. 1293). On April 10, 1282, a group of low-ranking conspirators bludgeoned Ahmad to death in the presence of the Secretarial Council members, and on June 4, all who had offered Ahmad wives, daughters, and sisters to obtain posts in the administration were dismissed. Altogether 714 of his men were purged, Ahmad's property was confiscated, and several of his sons were executed (Franke 1993:550–52).

Nevertheless, Qubilai did not yet cede imperial finances to Chinese officialdom and appointed as finance ministers, successively, the two other "villainous ministers"—first, Ahmad's Chinese underling Lu Shih-jung and then the Tibetan (and probably also Uighur) Buddhist monk Sangha—to continue Ahmad's revenue-raising policies. Crown Prince Chen-chin and Noyan An-tung, however, continued to lead the Chinese opposition faction and brought about Lu's execution in 1285 and Sangha's in 1291. Qubilai reluctantly went along, thus terminating the control of imperial finances by the Central Asian faction and ceding the upper hand in fiscal administration to the Chinese imperial bureaucracy (Rossabi 2009:190–99).

The dominance of Chinese Confucian officialdom was thus ensured for the rest of the Yuan period. The distinctively Mongol office of the *darughachi* continued to be quite important, but it was deeply penetrated by the Chinese at the local level (Mote 1999:493–95). The absolute number of Turks in high office, including *darughachi*s (and the preponderance of Uighurs among them), remained remarkably constant throughout the Yuan period (de Rachewiltz 1983:284–85), while the Chinese bureaucracy expanded enormously after the overthrow of the Southern Sung.

The conquest of southern China created an altogether different polity. Qubilai—problem following Liu Ping-chung's advice—ordered his generals to respect the property rights of the Chinese gentry (Schurmann 1956b:306). Some large estates were confiscated, but these were made into government-controlled military colonies (*t'un-t'ien*) to protect the southern border, and part of the revenue from the land was used to pay government officials who received salaries, unlike the high officials of the Great Mongol Empire, such as the *darughachi*s and the *yārghuchi*s who were nonsalaried. Furthermore, he ordered his generals to refrain from massacres and released tens, if not hundreds, of thousands of Sung soldiers and civilian war captives who had been enslaved according to the Mongol law code. Lastly, Qubilai adopted the village-led Sung agrarian organization of the *she*, extending its functions to include the management of charitable granaries and schools for peasant children (Rossabi 2009:120–21, 185–86). It should be noted that, except for respecting the *waqf* property that sustained the charitable endowments and that was put under the supervision of Hülegü's Persian counselor Nasir al-Din Tusi (d. 1274), the conquest of the Southern Sung contrasted sharply with Hülegü's conquest of Iraq, when Baghdad was sacked and its population massacred, and conquered agrarian land either became Crown land under the Sāheb-Divān or was alienated as large *siurghāl*s (large land grants) to the Turko-Mongolian military elite.

The demographic and consequently economic changes resulting from the conquest of the Southern Sung were immense. To northern China's population of under 9,000,000 (1,700,000 households) were added over 40,000,000 people (8,000,000 households). The most fertile agricultural land was located in the Yang-Tzu basin, and great centers of maritime commerce, such as Hangcow and Kan-fu, were located on the South China coast (Schurmann 1956a:10). Arguably of even greater significance was the sudden and massive retention of the Chinese bureaucracy to allow the orderly fiscal exploitation of the fivefold increase in the population and the even greater increase in the economic resources of the empire. Thus, according to *Yuan shih*, "when the new era of the Yuan was established, and the Central Secretariat and the Pacification Bureaus were set up, all the old officials of the Court, all the gentlemen in retirement, were now reappointed to civil positions" (157.6497, as cited in Schurmann 1963:26–27).

Confucian Statecraft under the Yuan

Just as his subordinate brother and nephew Il-khans were doing in Iran, Qubilai lived and gave audience in tents not only in his summer capital,

Shang-tu, but also in the Imperial Park in Ta-tu, where grass, dirt, and other pastoral memorabilia were transported from Mongolia (Rossabi 2009:133). His powerful wife Chabi had her own *ordo*. Nevertheless, Qubilai was also the founding Chinese emperor of the Yuan dynasty and was receptive to the Chinese political and religious culture, which was, however, more pluralistic than that of Il-khanid Iran. Yuan constitutionalism and imperial rule of law, accordingly, developed along a more pluralistic path.

The predominant political ethic in China was Confucianism, as is evident in its endorsement by the Buddhist monk Liu Ping-chung. Already in the earliest extant memorial to Qubilai, Liu's "ten-thousand-word" memorial, we have Chinggis Khan and Prince Qubilai placed in the Confucian constitutional history alongside the ancient emperors of China and their wise counselors:

> Government institutions, rites, music and the teaching . . . were completed in the reigns of Yao and Shun. . . . Since the restoration of the Han, . . . rulers who followed the Path . . . were only to be found among five emperors: Wen, Ching and Kuang-wu of the Han Dynasty, and T'ai-Tsung and Hsüan-tsung of the Tang Dynasty. . . . [Then] the Heaven-sent Emperor Chinggis Khan . . . , with only a brigade of men, . . . subdued the whole world in less than a few years. . . . I, your humble servant, have heard that "even though the empire can be conquered on horseback, it cannot be administered on horseback." In ancient times [the Kingdom of Chou was governed by] King Wu, who was assisted by his younger brother, the Duke of Chou. (cited in Chan 1967:119)

Liu ends his preface by urging Qubilai to be to his older brother Möngke the wise counselor that the Duke of Chou was to the legendary King Wu. What this preface alludes to is Tang statecraft and the Confucian political ethic, recast in the late Southern Sung period as the "Learning of the Sage-Emperors and Kings." According to this tradition, which is packaged, perhaps misleadingly, as "neo-Confucianism," it was the duty of the ministers, versed in this learning, to impart it to the ruler as his counselors. The late eleventh-century author of the *Mirror of Tang* and the *Learning of the Emperors* (*Ti-xue*) maintained that the "Learning of the Emperors and Kings was the Great Learning," consisting of the steps taken in self-governance that lead to the governance of the state and virtuous management of the world and that indeed "are none other than the Way of Yao and Shun" (cited in de Bary 1981:96–97). Furthermore, "order and disorder in the world all depend on the heart-and-mind of the ruler. If his heart-and-mind are correct, then the myriad affairs of the court will not be incorrect" (cited in Bary 1981:30). Qubilai's Confucian ministers followed Liu in reminding him of his responsibility as the new Chinese emperor for maintaining the world order through enlightened government.

Liu himself then proceeds to outline a program of government in detail: a hierarchical bureaucracy of civil and military officials, taxation, a code of law, expenditure of the wealth of the empire on its subjects, decoration of the high-ranking officials, standardization of units of measurement, a school system, official management of land assigned to the raising of military horses, renewal of ritual sacrifice and its music and of the calendar, and the writing of the history of the preceding Jurchen Chin dynasty for his own edification and that of his officials (Chan 1967:120–21).

Yao Shu's 1251 memorial on the basic principles of government was also mainly concerned with practical statecraft, even though as a Learning of the Way adept he prefaced it with eight points on enlightened rule based on Confucian morals. It contained some thirty recommendations for administrative reform, including the expansion of military colonies (*t'un-t'ien*), suggestions for Grand Canal transportation, and a law code modifying the penal system. Qubilai carried out some of the recommendations in his princely appanage and commissioned Yao Shu and another Confucian adviser, Shih T'ien-tse, to prepare a new code of law for his Chinese subjects in 1262 (Chan 1980:22–24, 32–33). Meanwhile, in 1260, another convert to Learning of the Way, Hao Ching (d. 1275), submitted a memorial sketching a constitutional history of China against the yardstick of the golden age of the Han sage-rulers and recommending the unification of China under Sinicized administration. Qubilai took note (de Bary 1981:25).

While the idea memorialized by Liu Ping-chung and a similar one by Tou Mo drew on the older Confucian tradition of statecraft, Yao Shu's protégé and colleague Xu Heng (d. 1281), who was from peasant stock but had passed the civil service examination of 1237, introduced the so-called neo-Confucian Learning of the Way of Zhu Xi (d. 1200), which was destined to become the established orthodoxy when the civil service examinations were restored in 1313 (Elman 1997:60). Although Zhu Xi highlighted the more philosophical "Learning of the Mind-and-Heart" (Xin-xue), Xu Heng slanted it toward the more general Confucian statecraft and political ethic by defining the Way as "the study of the affairs of the country" (de Bary 1981:24). In 1266, Heng submitted a lengthy "five-point" memorial on state organization, central administration, the difficulties facing a ruler, agriculture, schools, and attention to minor matters, which was read to Qubilai in Shang-tu. Xu maintained that the success of a ruler depended on his ability to win the hearts of his subjects. Learning the major differences between the Mongol and Chinese cultures for policy making, he estimated, would take thirty years. The essential element of central administration was effective legislation, as laws governed men, but men maintained them. His political economy was not dissimilar from Rashid al-Din's in the Il-khanid empire, but he explicitly added the importance of schools to the promotion of agriculture. As a master of Learning of the Mind-and-Heart (Xin-xue), Xu Heng also emphasized that self-improvement was the basis of government according to the Way (Dao). The memorial on the five points included a number of specific recommendations that Qubilai implemented in the following three years: fixed salaries and land grants to local officials, hereditary appointments and appointments by recommendation (*yin*), decrees promoting regional agriculture and the institution of a censorate, and the imperial (re)institution of the National College (Chan 1993a:428–31).

Substantial as this immediate impact of the five-point memorial was on state policy, Xu Heng's most long-lasting impact on Yuan political culture was as the educator of the civil servants. He promoted Zhu Xi's *Elementary Learning* (*Xiao-xue*), which was a summary of the Four Classics—*Analects, Mencius, Doctrine of the Mean*, and, the key text, the *Great Learning*—and wrote a commentary on it in vernacular Chinese which soon replaced Zhu Xi's text as the basic textbook in the National College and Confucian academies, adding to it his individual textbook commentaries on the *Great Learning* and the *Doctrine of the Mean* (de Bary 1981:136–37, 146–47). Under his extensive posthumous influence, the imperial edict (*yarligh*) of 1313 made the Four Classics required texts for the civil service examination, which was thereby restored (Chan 1982:211–14).[21] The 1313 civil service examiners' take on Learning of the Way put considerable emphasis on statecraft studies (Bol 1997:52).

The reception of Learning of the Way in the Yuan Empire was indeed the high point of Sinicization. In 1233, with the Mongol menace aggravated by the fall of the Chin dynasty in northern China, the Southern Sung emperor Li-tsung appointed Chen Te-xiu (d. 1235), a follower of Zhu Xi's Learning of the Way and a leading proponent of Confucian reform, finance minister and spokesman for the Hanlin Academy. In the following year, Chen presented to the emperor the monumental *Extended Meaning of the Great Learning*. The emperor was enjoined to "take the ancient sage-kings as his model and mentors" (de Bary 1981:85). After the Three Dynasties, this "learning of the emperors and kings was lost" (de Bary 1981:107), however, and needed to be recovered.

The *Great Learning*, Chen told the emperor, demonstrates that the governance of the emperors and kings of antiquity took the human person as its basis and extended it to all-under-Heaven, and it sets priorities for the ruler as follows: extending knowledge, making the will sincere, rectifying the mind-and-heart, cultivating the person, regulation the family, ordering the state, and pacifying all-under-Heaven (de Bary 1981:107).

The person of the ruler is, needless to say, the starting and central point of the process:

> The person of the ruler is the true root of the empire and dynasty, and . . . "careful circumspection" is the root of cultivating the person. . . . From one's own family this can be extended to the state, and from the state to all-under-Heaven. . . .
>
> The court is the basis of the empire, the ruler the basis of the court, and the mind-and-heart the basis of the ruler. . . . It all goes back to the mind-and-heart of the ruler. (deBary 1981:115)

Lastly, Chen did not fail to offer what would later be seen as a remedy to Mongolian tanistry, which was the greatest threat to imperial stability: the sage-emperor should settle the dynastic succession by the installation of an heir apparent (de Bary 1981:110). Qubilai followed this last principle, going against Mongol *yāsā* and *yosun* (law and custom), appointing his son Chen-chin (Jingim) his designated successor in 1276.

Qubilai commissioned a translation of Chen's *Extended Meaning*, which was read to the Sinophile Ayurbarwada, Emperor Jen-tsung (r. 1312–20), a contemporary of Il-khan Üljeitü, who was renamed Sultan Mohammad Khodā-banda (God's bondsman) and celebrated as the second "king of Islam." The Yuan emperor ordered its publication and abridgement for a Mongolian translation (de Bary 1981:125). *Extended Meaning of the Great Learning* thus took its place alongside the Four Classics and Xu Heng's commentaries as the basis of the political culture of the Yuan literati.

Dao-xue, who was supported by the so-called Chin-hua[22] Confucianism of the endangered Chinese literati, faced the problem of governance in an age when sage-emperors and kings no longer ruled. He solved it by highlighting the political role of the "authentic scholar" (*chen-ju*) as the master of the Confucian tradition and of the law to guide the imperfect emperors (Langlois 1981:137). The responsibility of the Confucian scholar as counselor to the ruler was to speak out with utmost candor and to refuse to serve a ruler who departed from virtue. As Mencius (2B.2) had insisted, "unless the ruler honors virtue and delights in moral principles, . . . it is not worthwhile to have anything to do with him" (cited in de Bary 1981:28). The lapse in the transmission of the true Way and confusion of teachings make the authentic scholar responsible for guiding government policy. "Even without good governance, scholars could explain the way of good government for the benefit of mankind and transmit it to later generations, but without scholars the world fell into darkness and people lost their way" (cited in de Bary 1981:94–95). This resonated well with Chen Te-xiu's idea of the Confucian literati as teachers of the rulers. The Confucian scholar had the function of teaching the ruler the forgotten learning of the emperors and the duty of remonstrating with him when he deviated from it (de Bary 1981:118). The Chinese bureaucrats, who gained unexpected power after the collapse of the Southern Sung, were thus provided with a strong professional ethic. Their Il-khanid counterparts lacked a similar reassuring professional ethic, as was evident in the moral despair of Vassāf and Mostawfi, and they certainly lacked any formal right of remonstrance, which Empress Chabi enjoined the Chinese literati to exercise as Qubilai's counselors (Rossabi 2009:67).

Important though the Learning of the Way through the cultivation of the mind-and-heart was for the general development of Chinese culture, its bent was more philosophical and speculative than practical, and even its "learning of the emperors" was too idealized for practical government and daily exercise of authority. The more practical concerns required far closer attention to statecraft (*ching-chi*) and the study of law. The transmitter of the Chinese tradition of statecraft to the Yuan dynasty, Wang Yün (d. 1304), was not a major Confucian thinker, and many of his voluminous writings are lost. He came from a family of government clerks (*li*) and was a judge before and after his appointment to the Hanlin Academy in 1277 (Franke 1982:156–60). Following the literati of the preceding Chin dynasty in northern China such as the author of the *Concise Mirror for Emperors and Kings*, Wang drew heavily on the Tang tradition of statecraft, notably the political and ethical analects (*Chen-kuo cheng-yao*) and *Examples of the Emperor* (*Ti-fan*) attributed to Emperor Tang Tai-zong (d. 649) himself.

In 1282, Wang Yün presented *Summaries of Actions of a Crown Prince* to Qubilai's heir apparent, Chen-chin. It is a compilation of Han and Tang political analects from classical sources arranged under twenty topics or chapters. The third chapter has the teacher of a Tang prince appropriately say, "If the basis is correct all affairs will be in order. The crown prince is the basis of the state," while the fifteenth traces the institution of "gentle remonstrance" (*chi-chien*) to the Eastern Han emperor Kuang-wu (r. 25–57) (Franke 1982:167–69).[23] Prince Chen-chin, however, predeceased his father in 1286, and when Qubilai's grandson Temür succeeded him as Emperor Ch'eng-tsung (1294–1307), Wang presented him with the more substantial *Mirror of Action for Preserving the Achievements in the Yüan-chen Era* and was ordered by the new emperor to compile the "Veritable Records" (*shih-lu*) of his grandfather's reign, which was duly presented to the court in July 1295

(Franke 1982:161). The *Mirror* consists in the enumeration of fifteen categories of action befitting a ruler. Six of these categories, as summarized by Franke (1982:173–77), are the following:

> 2. *Fa-tsu.* Take Ancestors as models.
>
> The state was never before as big as now and never was there a ruler as holy as Shih-zu (Qubilai). Temür should continue his exemplary actions and statutes. . . .
>
> 3. *Ai-min.* Love of the People.
>
> Heaven in his benevolence (*jen*) produces the myriad beings and the ruler governs them as the viceroy of Heaven. His priorities should be benevolence and love. Shih-zu (Qubilai) completed the conquest of all-under-Heaven which Tai-zu (Chinggis Khan) had begun. Now the emperor should act like . . . emperors Wen and Ching of the Han. Love can be realized by letting the army rest, decreasing punishments and reducing taxes. . . .
>
> 9. *Chin-ling.* Be Careful with Ordinances.
>
> Ordinances proclaim virtues and warnings. They should take Heaven as model and conform to the People. . . . "When issuing commands they should be considered as eternal models not just lightheartedly." (T'ang T'ai-tsung) It is important that the ruler and his government remain credible in the eyes of the people. Precedents should be changed only after due deliberation.
>
> 10. *Li-fa.* Establish laws.
>
> Laws are tools of orderly government and therefore indispensable. Now our state is over 60 years and yet does not have any fixed laws. . . . Take the statutes and ordinances of former dynasties and proclaim them as "New Laws of the First Year."
>
> 11. *Chung t'ai-chien.* Respect the Censorate's Criticism.
>
> Censors are the eyes and ears of the Son of Heaven. . . .
>
> 12. *Hsüan-shih.* Selection of Scholars.
>
> Qubilai Qa'an had, both as heir apparent and as emperor, continuously summoned worthy men to his court. . . . The recent decrees on local recommendations were a good start. [However,] Qubilai Qa'an and Chen-chin had such ideas but did not put them into effect.

Categories 2, 3, and, to some extent, 12 of royal actions show the important role that Wang played in constitutionalizing the rule of Qubilai and his grandfather Chinggis Khan as Chinese emperors, or Sons of Heaven, something he had done and continued to do more extensively elsewhere. In 1263, Qubilai had set up a Confucian-style ancestral temple with tablets for Chinggis Khan, the latter's sons, and his parents (Franke 1978:30–31). He had also ordered the compilation of Veritable Records of his four predecessors, beginning with Chinggis Khan (Elman 1997:71). Wang had collected the *Holy Injunctions of Qubilai* (*Shih-zu sheng-hsün*). Some of Qubilai's edicts compiled by Wang doubtless made their way to the state handbook (*Yüan-tien chang*) in the 1330s, including those establishing a national capital (1264), introducing a new national Mongolian script (1269), adopting Yüan as dynastic name (1271), and the appointment of empress and crown prince (1276) (Franke 1978:25). It is important to note that Wang had the distinction of having two of his treatises, the *Actions of a Crown Prince* and the *Holy Injunctions*, translated into Mongolian, along with the two above-mentioned classics of Tang statecraft,[24] a collection of edicts and admonitions by Mongol emperors (mostly Qubilai's), and administrative handbooks (Franke 1982:153–54, 181). These translations, it should further be noted, were important for the political and cultural integration of northern and western China into the unified Yuan Empire.

Wang Yün's attention to statecraft must have been particularly appealing to government clerks (*li*), who were said to be twenty times as numerous as Confucian scholars in the Yuan bureaucracy (Langlois 1981:140) and must be considered the force behind the wide spread of the study of law and, in particular, the republication of the *Tang Code* in the last half a century of the Yuan Empire. The collation *Tang Code with Commentary* was published under the auspices of the court in the 1320s and stimulated efforts to codify the laws of the empire (Langlois 1981:165–68).

Qubilai's assumption of Chinese emperorship, thus legitimated on Confucian grounds, in no way interfered with his claim to universal monarchy as the heir to the world conqueror, Chinggis Khan, and in his own right as the conqueror of southern China. He continued to be called the Wise Qa'an (*sechen qaghan*) and the universal monarch in Mongolia and western China. When he converted to Buddhism, the Buddhists legitimated him as the Bodhisattva and Chakravartin (savior and universal monarch) far beyond China—in fact, throughout the world, on the periphery of the empire among the Tibetans, the Nepalese, the Kiliyeds, and the Tasig (Persians) and in the center among "the forty myriarchies of Blue Mongols and the Oirats" (cited in Franke 1978:59). In a 1345 inscription, the Wise Qa'an appears as the "Chakravartin who lets turn one thousand golden wheels" (cited in Franke 1978:68).

Buddhist legitimation was particularly significant, as Mongolia was following him in accepting Buddhism, just as the Golden Horde and the Il-khans were turning to Islam. A Buddhist chronicle from 1333 places the Mongols in world history thus: "At that time a king was born in the Northern Mongol state. . . . His name was Chinggis." Then came his grandson, Qubilai: "He adopted the teaching and the Law of the Buddha and civilized (*hua*) his people according to the Law" (cited in Franke 1978:55).

Compound Societies in Il-Khanid Iran and Yuan China: A Comparison

As Herbert Spencer noted ([1876] 1972:145–46), military conquest creates compound and doubly compound societies. Chinggis Khan's empire of conquest had already complicated the social stratification of the Mongolian polity by adding categories of *noyan* (prince) and *tarkhān* ([military] elite exempt from taxation) as the upper strata of its compound society, making a Turko-Mongolian military ruling caste dominant over several conquered, subject societies. This stratification survived the fragmentation of the empire into Yuan China and Il-khanid Iran after 1260 and was inherited by the Timurid and other successive Turko-Mongolian nomadic empires in Central Asia and Iran. The consequences of the Mongol integrative revolution after the fragmentation of the Great Mongol Empire unfolded in these two great neighboring Eurasian ecumenes. Their divergent developmental paths were equally independent of the factors accounting for the formation of the original Turko-Mongolian predatory confederation. Rather, each path depended on the conditions of the two civilizational zones, the Chinese and the Persianate, in which the compound societies developed.

The Yuan and Il-khanid state structures evolved along sharply divergent paths. Bureaucratization and centralization of the Il-khanid state remained primitive. Rashid al-Din's administrative reforms, whatever the extent of their implementation, were reversed after the fall in 1336 of his son, Ghiyāth al-Din. The bureaucracy of the Turko-Mongolian successor states in mid-fourteenth-century Iran, taxing and administering a sparsely populated and predominantly nomadic pastoralist society, remained roughly at the same minimal level of organization as that of the Great Mongol Empire under Ögedei a century earlier (Nakhjavāni 1964). With Qubilai's conquest and incorporation of the populous and sedentary southern China in the 1270s, Yuan state structure expanded enormously and became considerably more hierarchical and bureaucratic (Farquhar 1990). It gave the Yuan regime not only a compound society but also a compound—that is, dual—state not found in the Turko-Mongolian empires of fourteenth- and fifteenth-century Iran. The Yuan Mongolian monarchy and army coexisted with Chinese bureaucratic tax collection and local government, creating a dual military (*wu*) and bureaucratic (*wen*) system (Schurmann 1963). The Yuan Empire acquired a more stable and orderly fiscal base and became much less haphazardly predatory than the Il-khanid state.

From the third postconquest generation onward, and as sociocultural integration increased in the fourteenth century, we can speak of caste societies in both China and Iran. In the Il-khanid and Timurid empires in Iran and Central Asia, society was rigidly stratified into an upper military-political Turko-Mongolian caste, later termed the *ʿaskeri* (military), and the non-Turkish or Tajik subject caste, the *raʿiyyat/reʿāyā* (the flock). The two estates were subject to two different laws and their respective courts, the Mongol military estate to the *yāsā*, the Tajik, Muslim estate to the shariʿa. The chief administrator of the law code, apart from the Il-khan himself, was the *yārghuchi*, and his jurisdiction extended to all state officials in fiscal and administrative matters; the chief administrator of the shariʿa was the *qāzi al-qozāt* (chief justice). Nakhjavāni's (1964) manual of administration, however, makes it amply clear that several other military Turko-Mongol officials of the state were expected to be familiar with Mongolian law and customs (*yāsā o yosun*), and various civil officials with the shariʿa and law of justice (*qānun-e maʿdalat*). In principle, there were no intermarriages between the elite and the subject castes. There could be rare exceptions such as marriages between members of the Il-khanid royal house and those of local dynasties—notably, Princess Kürdüjin was the offspring of the marriage between one of Hülegü's sons and the last ruler of the Salghurid vassal state in Fars, Abïsh Khatun (d. 1286); Princess Kürdüjin governed Kerman briefly as the widow of the local ruler, Soyurghātmish, around 1295 (Vassāf 1852–53:284; Āyati 1993:172) and governed her own ancestral Fars for a much longer period in the fourteenth century (Lambton 1988:272–87). Another exception was the tax exemptions to top bureaucrats, such as Tāj al-Din ʿAli-Shāh and Vassāf, which elevated them to the status of *tarkhān* (Vassāf 1852–53:523, 631; Āyati 1993:295, 361–62).

A major change in the Il-khanid legal system resulted from the conversion of Ghāzān Khan to Islam, which made the regulation of the extensive charitable-educational endowments of the last Il-khans subject to the Islamic law of *waqf* (Arjomand 1999). But the major change in the social order—namely, the abolition of caste pluralism—was left to the Ottomans, who extended tax exemption as well as the status of *ʿaskeri* to all government employees, including the judges and the bureaucrats.

Yuan stratification and the juridification of ethnic status were more complicated: there were four estates. The Mongols predictably constituted the legally most privileged estate, and below them were the Semu, who were Central Asian Turks and Persians; below the Semu were the northern Chinese, who were called Han in the Yuan period, and the southern Chinese, called Nanren, who constituted the most disprivileged estate (Mote 1999:489–90). It is quite likely that the estate stratification was not as rigid as Iran's two castes, as the fourfold distinction was in practice harder to enforce. The

Semu, paradoxically because of their easier access to the bureaucracy, became culturally Sinicized (Mote 1999:493), and intermarriage with them became increasingly common among the Turko-Mongolian soldiers, and probably more generally.

In theory, the Mongols were the only estate allowed to bear arms in both the Yuan and the Il-khanid Empires, and in the former Chinese civilians were even forbidden to learn Mongolian (Schurmann 1963:27). Nevertheless, the Yuan regime quickly became dependent on armed Chinese militarily, making the ban on the spread of arms to non-Mongol populations ineffective. More important, the Mongol armed forces began to lose its ethnic insulation. The Great Mongol Empire was the result of the military conquest of a nation-in-arms. The Keshig was preserved as the imperial elite force but was supplemented by the more numerous *tammachi* (*tamghachi*) troops recruited mainly among the Khitans, Uighurs, and Turks and by Chinese contingents. With the growth of Chinese bureaucracy in the fourteenth century, the *tammachi* armed forces declined because of the depletion of the resources of the military colonies, which were put under civil administration. Impoverishment resulting from the corporate nature of their economy was aggravated by the levies imposed by the bureaucracy on the military's extended families (*a'rugh*), to such an extent that, already by 1299, the wives and children of some *tammachi* troops were sold. There were also flights of families and desertion of soldiers (Hsiao 1978:27–30). No longer a privileged ethnic estate, the Turko-Mongolian soldiers mingled with the general population. The same intermingling must have occurred with the Turko-Mongolian officials. We have illustrative evidence for intermarriage from the fifteen Mongolian and Semu candidates in the 1333 civil service examination: ten of them had Chinese mothers, and eight had Chinese wives (Hsiao 1978:32).

In Iran, all Turko-Mongolian tribesmen bore arms. However, although the one attempt to disarm the non-Mongols among the population in Fars under Ghāzān Khan is described by Vassāf as a complete failure, the sedentary population of Iran could never challenge the firm domination of the Turko-Mongolian ruling caste, which was reinforced by the reconquest achieved by Temür's Chaghadaid confederal tribes in the closing decades of the fourteenth century. Consequently, the rigid dual Turko-Mongolia/Persian caste system prevailed to the end of the fifteenth century.

CONCLUSION

World-Historical and Theoretical Significance of Premodern Revolutions

What sets this study apart from others in the sociology of revolution is the subordination of causal analysis to typological taxonomy, on the one hand, and the shift of focus from the causes to the consequences of revolutions in order to assess their significance in world history. The subordination of causality to typology provides a framework for studying structure in world history; my selection of cases on the basis of their significance realized a major methodological principle for understanding meaning in history that was cherished and preached by Max Weber but not much practiced by him. The concluding remarks that follow are intended as brief summaries of these two novel aspects of the study.

Premodern Revolutions and the Pattern of World History

The significance of the Near East can properly be attributed to its two major contributions to world history: world religions and empires (Lapidus 1988:1–11). Our first constitutive revolution—that of Sargon of Akkad in the mid-third millennium BCE, created empire as a political regime on the basis of the idea of universal monarchy. Our Roman and Persian integrative revolutions in antiquity created a variety of imperial orders by different military, political, and legal means and through different processes of revolutionary power struggle and constitutional politics. Muhammad's constitutive revolution in Arabia gave birth to the last universal religion of pure monotheism, while achieving the unification of Arabia on the periphery of the Ethiopian, Persian, and Roman Empires as the prelude to the rapid creation of an empire comprising all of the Persian and much of the Roman predecessor empires. I have highlighted the theoretical significance of the integrative revolution that followed the rise of Islam in the mid-eighth century, the

Hashemite or ʿAbbasid Revolution, as a subtype of integrative revolution (I.3) that begins in the geographical and social peripheries of the Muslim empire and results in cementing their incorporation into the center.[1]

The ancient world also offers the case of an integrative revolution that produced a diametrically opposite type of political regime to empire—namely, the establishment of democracy in ancient Athens by the Cleisthenian constitutive revolution in the mid-first millennium BCE. Democracy did spread beyond Athens to other parts of the Hellenic ecumene, but no further. It had bad press for the next two millennia and was certainly considered an inferior type of political regime by the Muslims who transmitted the Greek cultural heritage, and by the Christians in Western Europe who received it. It was left to the French Revolution of 1789 to revive the idea, welding it to national sovereignty and integration as well as modernity, and it took another century and a half and two world wars for democracy to be equated with political modernity and prevail globally as the "best" type of political regime. But this subsequent history by no means exhausts the significance of the Athenian constitutive revolution. As we have seen from the example of the short-lived Italian federal state in the first century BCE in chapter 3, two modalities of integrative revolution are possible as alternatives. The constitution of a then-new Italian federal political order was a substitute for integration into the old Roman one for the aristocracies of the twelve allied cities whose demand for Roman citizenship was denied. In this respect, the short-lived Italian confederacy, which I have called the first new nation, was the forerunner of the American Revolution and all subsequent wars of national liberation.

There is no denying the world-historical significance of the conversion of Constantine, and subsequently and gradually the whole Roman Empire, to Christianity, but the major transformation of the ancient world occurred a century earlier. Two revolutions in the bipolar world of western Eurasia redrew its map; they took place one after the other, each over a relatively short span of a third of a century, which justifies calling them revolutions. The Severan Revolution in the last decade of the second century and the first decades of the third century, analyzed in chapter 5, shifted the center of the Roman Empire from the city of Rome to its eastern periphery a century before Constantine, while making it truly ecumenical by universalization of Roman citizenship, whose expansion I have highlighted as the leitmotif of the earlier Roman revolutions. The Sasanian Revolution, subject of chapter 6, begun in 208 at the foot of the ruins of Persepolis, burned by Alexander half a millennium earlier, was an integrative revolution in the highly decentralized feudal empire of the Parthians. It was the revolution that gave birth to the idea of Iran—Ērānshahr—and whose export into the eastern territories of the Roman Empire between 242 and 260 created an "empire of Iran and Non-Iran" that lasted until its conquest by the Arabs after the death of Muhammad.

Muhammad's revolution in the third decade of the seventh century in Arabia, on the periphery of the two empires of the bipolar western Eurasian world and of Ethiopia, as analyzed in chapter 7, was constitutive of an entirely new ecumenical community that required a very long time to construct and another revolution to complete. As shown in chapter 8, this second revolution was integrative in the social sense of integrating the vast population of the converted subjects of the Muslim empire and in the geographical sense of beginning on the northeastern periphery of that empire and shifting its center eastward to Baghdad, close to the ruins of the Sasanian capital, Ctesiphon. As I discuss in chapter 8, the Hashemite, or ʿAbbasid, Revolution did result in centralization of power according to my Tocquevillian model and indeed gave birth to the remarkably secular bureaucratic elite that constituted the administrative cadre of the ʿAbbasid Empire and reproduced itself in all the subsequent Turko-Mongolian and early modern Muslim empires.

In contrast to earlier revolutions, however, religion was the driving force in the teleology of the rise of Islam and its social revolution. The same is true of our next revolution, the revolution set in motion by Pope Gregory VII in Western Christendom and discussed in chapter 9. It integrated Western Christendom as never before, and it detached the Catholic Church from imperial and feudal powers to a considerable extent. It did result in centralization of the authority structure, but the authority structure not of the Holy Roman Empire but of the Catholic Church, making the next European revolution, the Reformation, primarily against the pope and the centralized church and only secondarily a revolution in the Holy Roman Empire. Last but not least—a consequence rarely seen in this light, the Crusades were indeed the export of the papal revolution.

In contrast to Muhammad's successful revolution in the seventh century, the religious revolution led by Pope Gregory VIII after his election in 1074 was immediately a failure. Not only did he have to share the city of Rome for much of the time with a rival pope, but he was in the end expelled from it and died under the protective custody of the Normans in 1085. In the long run, however, it achieved its goal of the "freedom of the church" from earthly powers and laid the foundations of the medieval papal monarchy. Like earlier ones, the world-historical significance of this case that qualifies it as a revolution by my definition is due entirely to its long-term consequences.

The Mongol Revolution, presented as such in chapter 10 for the first time, was an integrative revolution that unified the Mongol tribes of Inner Asia, but its unforeseen consequences integrated almost the entire Eurasian landmass as never before in history. Chinggis Khan's integrative revolution in thirteenth-century Mongolia created the greatest Eurasian empire, comprising Iran and China and stretching into Russia and Hungary. As a unified empire, it lasted for a generation after its founder's death in 1227, but the fragmentation of Chinggis Khan's empire thereafter had even greater significance in world history. No revolution in world history has suffered as much neglect in modern scholarship as the Mongol Revolution; this is due to the parochial character of social theory as well as the normative distance of its warrior culture from modern sensibilities. Eurocentrism in the West and Sinocentrism in the East militate against its proper appreciation. Stanislav Andreski's pioneering work in comparative military sociology, written in 1954, has but a single allusion to the Mongols ([1954] 1968:159), and closer to our time, one would look in vain for the word in the index to Geoffrey Parker's celebrated *Military Revolution* (1988). Sinocentrism in modern scholarship is no less guilty. Volume 6 of *The Cambridge History of China,* covering the period 907–1368, which includes a century and a half of Mongolian rule from 1211 to 1368, is shamelessly subtitled *Alien Regimes and Border States*. As the less parochial approach to social theory advocated by this study can demonstrate, the national integration of modern China and modern Iran are clearly traceable to the Mongol Revolution in Eurasia and must be treated among its long-term consequences.

A Typology of Premodern Revolutions

The surprising theoretical conclusion of this comparative study is that the ancient and medieval revolutions, although they share the definition of abrupt political change with major sociocultural consequences with modern revolutions, display a contrasting set of causes and consequences. Their primary feature defines them as integrative. I offer three ideal (sub)types of integrative revolution in the introduction to highlight the range of variety in the ancient and medieval revolutions considered. I also offer a contrasting ideal type of modern revolutions as centralizing or Tocquevillian, to throw light on a secondary feature of some of these premodern revolutions, as can be seen in the summary table of typology of premodern revolutions (table 3).

As this typological summary table shows, all but three of our ancient and premodern revolutions begin in the periphery, and all but two of them result in some measure of centralization of power and authority. Without any

Table 3 Typological summary of ancient and medieval revolutions

		Causes							Consequences	
		Structure of authority				Political community				
Cases	Starting point	Intermittence, incongruence	Divided ruling class	Fragility	Loss of legitimacy	Segmentation, fragmentation	Restrictiveness	Retrenchment	Integration	Centralization
Akkadian Sargon ca. 2400 BCE	P	+	–	–	–	+	–	–	+	+
Athenian Cleisthenes ca. 500 BCE	P (exiles)	–	+	–	–	+	–	+	+	–
Roman I Social Wars to Augustus 91 BCE–14 CE	C	+	+	–	–	–	+	–	+	+
Roman II Flavian 68–70 CE	P	–	+	+	+	–	–	+	+	+
Roman III Severan 193–235 CE	C	–	–	+	+	–	–	+	+	+

(*continued*)

Table 3 (*continued*)

Cases	Starting point	Causes							Consequences	
		Structure of authority				Political community				
		Intermittence, incongruence	Divided ruling class	Fragility	Loss of legitimacy	Segmentation, fragmentation	Restrictiveness	Retrenchment	Integration	Centralization
Sasanian Iran 208–272 CE	P	+	–	–	–	+	–	–	+	+
Rise of Islam Muhammad 610–44 CE	P	+	–	–	–	+	–	–	+	+
ʿAbbasid Hashemite 744–63 CE	P	–	+	–	+	–	+	+	+	+
Papal (Investiture Contest) 1075–1122 CE	C	+	–	–	–	+	–	–	+	+
Mongol Chinggis Khan 1200–1259 CE	P	+	–	–	–	+	–	–	+	–

Note: C = center; P = periphery.

exception, these revolutions result in the greater integration of the political community. In short, all premodern revolutions are integrative revolutions.

This study of the structure and meaning of revolution in history leaves out the motivation to revolution as social action, whose examination requires a somewhat different analytical framework. My discussion of the teleology of revolutions in this volume is restricted by structural considerations largely to the unintended consequences of the revolutionary process. In *Apocalypse and Social Revolution in Islam,*[2] my focus on teleology is sharpened and inclusive of millennial expectations and intended consequences of revolution as social action. Revolution in Islamic history is accordingly considered alongside political messianism, which is traced back to its origins in the Maccabean revolt against the Seleucid Empire in the second century BCE.

EPILOGUE

Revolutions of the Last Hundred Years in the Light of My Typology

Since the Russian Revolution of 1917, there have been major instances of revolution according to my definition—of the replacement of one political order by another or, in other words, the transformation of the structure of authority and its social foundations. It is therefore appropriate in this epilogue to see what light can be thrown on them by the typology based on this definition.

The Epicycle of Revolutions Motivated by the Modern Myth of Revolution

As we have seen, the Aristotelian-Paretan, integrative model of revolution fits the revolutions of the ancient and medieval world very well. Furthermore, the English and French Revolutions had their integrative aspect, as did the Latin American revolutions in the early nineteenth century and the revolutions of national liberation in the twentieth century, which set up new political communities under native elites. The Aristotelian-Paretan ideal type of integrative revolution therefore throws considerable light on these revolutions. The relatively disprivileged, Creole colonial upper class who supplied the leaders of the Spanish American revolutions against the peninsular Spaniards from 1808 to 1826, such as the liberators José de San Martín and Simón Bolivár, indeed belonged to a revolutionary counter-elite as described by that model (Lynch 1973:18–23).

In the introduction, I mentioned the birth of revolutionary professionals as bearers of the myth of revolution in nineteenth-century Western Europe. In the twentieth century, not only had the number of revolutionary professionals grown throughout the world but other revolutionary counter-elites were imitating them as leaders of mass mobilization according to my Aristotelian-Paretan type of integrative revolution. By informing the meaning of social action for world revolutionaries, the modern myth of revolution was thus appropriated throughout the world and constituted a powerful source of motivation for the growing number of revolutionary professionals. The intelligentsia supplied the cadre of the Communist Party in twentieth-century China, as it had that of Russia earlier. In the former case, however, they were forced to abandon the cities captured by the Kuomintang and withdraw to the countryside in the Long March of 1934–35, where they continued to mobilize the peasantry under Japanese occupation, leading a revolution that fits my structural model of Khaldunian integrative revolution. The Khaldunian type (I.3) fits the epicycle of Asian communist revolutions in Vietnam just as well.

The intelligentsia that supplied the bearers of the modern myth of revolution in Vietnam were the provincial Confucian literati who lived close to the peasants in villages but had shared power with the court mandarins in the bipolar structure of authority characteristic of the Vietnamese kingdom (Woodside 1989). Not unlike the provincial nobility of "the two Russias" of the second half of the nineteenth century that gave birth to a revolutionary counter-elite (Shapiro 1967:85–113; Tucker 1969:117–21), the Vietnamese provincial mandarinate elite became prone to revolutionary activism. Unlike in Russia, however, the dispossession of this elite was not due to differential modernization (Tucker 1969:117–21) but to the colonization of Indochina by the French. Let us begin our concluding narrative with them.

In his very last essay written in March 1923, Lenin anticipated the emergent new form of the modern myth of revolution. In "the revolutionary and nationalist East," the overwhelming majority of the world's population "has been drawn into the struggle for emancipation with extraordinary rapidity, so that . . . there cannot be the slightest shadow of doubt what the final outcome of the world struggle will be. In this sense, the complete victory of socialism is fully and absolutely assured" (as cited in Tucker 1969:132–33).

The project of socialism by revolution is hereby merged with that of national liberation through war against Western imperialism. The respective weight of these two heterogeneous components of this agenda for revolutionary professionals made for varying teleologies of revolution in different world regions (Knight 1990b:181–82). In the year after Lenin's death, the young professional revolutionary from Indochina who was then living in Paris and who settled for Ho Chi Minh as his name after many changes wrote in an essay entitled "Lenin and the Peoples of the East" that Lenin was revered by the Asians because he exemplified the imposing and beautiful "morality of the teacher" (as cited in Woodside 1989:153). The son of a mandarin who had passed the Confucian national examination in 1901 and grew up in the imperial capital, Hue, Ho Chi Minh was honoring Lenin as the archetypal ascetic Confucian teacher and, as such, made him his own role model by creating the Indochina Communist Party in 1930 and establishing a communist republic in Hanoi in September 1945.

During the struggle for the national liberation of Vietnam from the French, whom he defeated in 1954, and its unification with the South in continuation of the people's war ending with the defeat of the Americans in 1975, he combined nationalism and communism in the manner typical of the post-1945 war-born communist revolutions (Johnson 1962; Tucker 1969:155–57). In this people's war, Ho Chi Minh selectively highlighted elements of Confucianism in the Vietnamese national culture that he found compatible with science and Marxism-Leninism. In the long run, the Confucian components of the synthesis appear to have become preponderant in veering the teleology of the Vietnamese revolution. From 1990 on, Ho has been lionized for his Confucian spirituality, and in 1991, the Hanoi government ordered the "restoration" of the national examination for civil servants (Woodside 2006:80–81).

The teleology of the Cuban Revolution, by contrast, was squarely set in the socialist direction, albeit with a nod to the Latin American tradition. The revolutionary struggle of today's generation in Latin America against Yankee imperialism, asserted Fidel Castro, "was ever greater and more decisive for humanity" than "the great epic of Latin American Independence." Therefore, "[t]he duty of every revolutionary is to make the revolution. It is known that the revolution will triumph in America and throughout the world, but it is not for revolutionaries to sit in the doorways of their houses waiting for the corpse of imperialism to pass by" (as cited in Halliday 1999:117). There was, however, no war of liberation, as the Yankees never occupied Cuba, and the theorists of revolution were quick to replace the juridical colonial status with economic dependency (Knight 1990b). Just as the Eleventh World Festival of Youth and Students in Havana in 1978 was celebrating the last Marxist-Leninist revolution in the Brezhnevite version lavishly supported by the Soviet Union (Meeks 1993:192), however, a communist revolution of the Maoist variety was unfolding in Cambodia, and an Islamic revolution as its alternative was unfolding in Iran.

Writing about the Central American and Caribbean revolutions of the second half of the twentieth century, including the Cuban Revolution, Brian Meeks substituted "post-colonial revolution from the middle" for Skocpol's "class-based revolts from below," highlighting the revolutionary leadership of the middle-class and lower-middle-class intellectuals in Cuba, Nicaragua, and Grenada, who are described as "young, *potential* state-builders, whose avenue to power has been blocked" (Meeks 1993:189, emphasis in the original). It should be evident that, here too, Pareto's notion of a revolutionary counter-elite built into my Aristotelian-Paretan ideal type of integrative revolution is a far more accurate description of the social group in question.

The myth of communist revolution was a powerful source of motivation in the struggle against French colonialism not only for the Vietnamese but also for the Cambodian students in Paris after World War II. In describing Saloth Sar (better known by his nom de guerre as Pol Pot), a former companion and lifelong full-time revolutionary described him by appropriating the remark made by Axelrod about Lenin: that he was "the only man who had no thoughts but thoughts about the revolution, and in whose sleep dreamt of revolution" (as cited in Chandler 1991:239). Pol Pot and the Communist Party of Kampuchea under his leadership made the proletarian revolution explicitly aspirational. The sons of poor peasants were to be the vanguard of communist revolution and commissars of proletarianization by reeducating older men and women of other social classes. Following the militarization of the idea of revolution in war-born communism in Asia, revolutionary violence was extolled as the foremost virtue, and the revolutionary struggle was called waging war.

The Khmer Rouge cannot be said to have swallowed the myth of revolution without adding their own ingredients to it. It is true that they followed Mao's militarization of the myth of revolution religiously (Chandler 1991:241–42) and indeed made "fighting men and women" the third social class of the people to be represented in their National Assembly, besides workers and peasants (Constitution of 1976, 1, 7; Burgler 1990:64). All other classes were abolished. Furthermore, Mao's Great Leap Forward also inspired their even more disastrous Super Leap Forward (Chandler 1991:245). It is also true that the very word for "revolution" (*padevat*) to which they gave currency was unwonted and somewhat strange in the Khmer language (Chandler 1991:250). Their nationalism, too, was typical of the post-1945 war-born communist revolutions. But they pushed the mixture of nationalism and communism to very great lengths, seeking to isolate themselves from foreign nations, especially from Vietnam.

They sought to revive the Angkor Empire of the Khmer nation, calling the party to which "the perfect revolutionary must submit . . . to become a perfect tool of the Revolution" *angkar* (organization) (Burgler 1990:62). Their invisible government that ruled Democratic Kampuchea after its establishment in 1975 was called the Revolutionary Angkar/Organization of the Higher Angkar/Organization, and the counterrevolutionaries were called the "enemies of the Angkar/Organization" (Chandler 1991:242–53). In a speech to army representatives in July 1975, Pol Pot claimed that "we have waged our revolutionary struggle basically on the principles of independence, sovereignty and self-reliance." Likewise, in a major radio broadcast in April 1976, Khieu Samphan celebrated the return of the Khmer nation and people to glory and self-esteem: "Now with victory we have regained our honor, our dignity, and now we smell good again" (as cited in Burgler 1990:58–59).

Ieng Sary contended in 1977 that "the Khmer revolution has no precedent. What we are trying to do has never been done before in history" (as cited in Chandler 1991:240). His claim deserves credence. The systematic evacuation of Phnom Penh and other cities and the decimation of the country's population were completely at odds with the aspirational goal of creating a proletariat consisting of an industrial working class forged out of the poor peasantry. After overseeing this bizarre experiment in revolutionary social engineering, Pol Pot invited the former king, Norodom Sihanouk, to dinner on January 5, 1979. Pol Pot, whose aunt had been a dancer in the Royal Ballet and borne a child to Sihanouk's predecessor, King Monivong (r. 1927–41), used the royal language he had learned in his youth to apologize for failing to talk to the gourmet prince in five years and offered him a delicious dinner, impeccably served (Chandler 1991:311). Two days later, he ignominiously fled Phnom Penh by helicopter. Democratic Kampuchea thus collapsed on January 7, 1979, and with it died the myth of communist revolution, forged a third of a century earlier, while the two-centuries-old original myth of revolution was undergoing its last modification in the incipient Islamic revolution in Iran.

When the myth of revolution became an autonomous modern cultural form, it was transformed from a consequence of one (French) revolution to a cause of subsequent ones. Reverse causality obtained, and the idea of revolution became one of its causes. After causing revolution after revolution that aimed to create a proletariat rather than seeking to mobilize one, the reverse causality introduced into world history by the modern myth of revolution went haywire in Cambodia, claiming one million lives, or one in eight of the Cambodian population, in less than four years.

With the advent of modern mass politics, observed Max Weber, "hierocracy has no choice but to establish a party organization and to use demagogic means, just like all other parties" (cited in Arjomand 1988:200). This explains why a Shiʿite Grand Ayatollah decided to take a leaf from the revolutionary professional's book to mobilize the Iranian masses for a revolution against the shah in the 1970s. If the first European revolutionary had been a pope, as Rosenstock-Huessy ([1931] 1951) asserted and I have shown in chapter 9, then the leader of the first modern Islamic Revolution was a Shiʿite Grand Ayatollah who had assumed the title of imam. Under his leadership, the task of revolutionary mass mobilization was taken over by militant clerics from the Communist (Tudeh) Party.

Elsewhere, I have analyzed the Islamic Revolution of 1979 in Iran, which disrupted half a century of state building and modernization by the Pahlavi shahs, as a Tocquevillian revolution. The Islamic Revolution, however, clearly brought to light the deficiency of Skocpol's state-centered theory due to her neglect of Tocqueville and the encumbering of the model instead with the burden of war and financial crisis owing to international power politics. I concluded my book on the Islamic Revolution of 1979 in Iran, *The Turban for the Crown* (1988:191), with the following remarks: "The Shah's regime collapsed despite the fact that his army was intact, despite the fact that there was no defeat in war, and . . . despite the fact that the state faced no financial crisis and no peasant insurrection. Where does all this leave the usual generalizations about revolutions? Mostly in the pits." In a footnote I referred to Theda Skocpol and her still-fashionable theory of revolution that Collins hailed as a new paradigm. I added another critical point on the same page: "the collapse of the political order in Iran demonstrates that there is more to a system of authority than coercion. There is also the normative factor of legitimacy. What brought the Pahlavi regime down was not the disintegration of its army but rather its loss of legitimacy and a massive nationwide campaign of civil disobedience."

In contrast to Skocpol's theory, my state-centered Tocquevillian ideal type of revolution can accommodate this loss of legitimacy, which highlights the role of the elite, dispossessed through the centralization of power in a modernized state, in leading the revolution against it—in this case the Shiʿite religious elite, which had retained full control over an autonomous hierocracy. There was no "class-based revolt from below," as she had predicted.[1]

With the remotely possible exceptions of financial crisis, the East European revolutions run even more clearly counter to the current theories of revolution than did the Iranian Revolution a decade earlier.

Negotiated, Dystopian Revolutions of Central Eurasia after 1989

By my definition, there have been revolutions in South Africa, Poland, Hungary, Czechoslovakia, the Soviet Union, and Albania, and a stalled revolution in Romania, in the closing decade of the twentieth century. The most striking feature of the political systems of the Soviet Union and Eastern

Europe, to belabor an obvious point, was the overcentralization of the state, which is the focal point of the Tocquevillian model. The loss of legitimacy that makes the imposing edifice of absolutist states hollow at the time of revolution should also be considered a feature of the Tocquevillian type. The second important, and equally obvious, feature of these regimes was that the Communist Party constituted the political society, and there was no meaningful political enfranchisement of the nominal citizens. The party was the oligarchy that restricted access to various levels of political power and excluded a large and constantly growing number of educated people from the political community. This feature made the regimes of the Eastern bloc prone to revolution according to my Aristotelian-Paretan model.

Last but not least, the East European revolutions were preceded by what one analyst has described as "collective claims of faith" (Di Palma 1991:49), which I would prefer to describe as the first example in world history of a complete collapse of a world religion from within (Gellner 1992). Let me dwell briefly on each of these three points.

Collapse of the Soviet Monolith

The collapse and reconstitution of the USSR was eminently Tocquevillian as a type of revolution. Revolutionary situations occur because of the disintegration of central authority. With the disintegration of central authority, other forms of legitimate authority, including those with a hitherto-shadowy existence, come to life and assume greater importance. These include both formal political institutions, such as parliament, and nonpolitical academic and professional ones whose authority is extended into the political sphere in emergency.

In a work published over a decade ago, a Lithuanian émigré social scientist recognized the importance of these alternative structures of authority as a kind of "second pivot" for transition from totalitarianism. The significance of the *perestroika* reforms of 1988 lies precisely in the creation of such a second pivot, notably in the form of such institutions as the All-Union Congress of People's Deputies and in the revival of the Russian Supreme Soviet, and so forth. This second pivot quickly became the institutional frame of reference in which "the outbreak of dissension within the Soviet political elite occurred. The Soviet elite became divided, and some apparatchiks of the republic crossed the line to the opposition within this framework" (Hosking 1992b:34).

Constitutions are more than scraps of paper; and the fact that Lenin had in theory divided the monolithic power structure under the control of the

Bolshevik party into a federation of nominally sovereign republics which were increasingly staffed by indigenous cadres made it possible for the Soviet bureaucracy to split along republican lines seventy years later and for the paper republics suddenly to come to life and embark on assiduous legislation (Motyl 1991:1).

The formal institutional arrangement was embodied in the constitutions in which the dissidents, in a variety of nonpolitical institutions or informal gatherings, and the republican apparatchiks, for whom sovereignty meant real power, could find points of common interest and form the political coalitions that carried out the dismantling of the Soviet Union (Hosking 1992a).

Enlargement of the Political Community

The consolidation of the revolution of 1917 meant the destruction and/or bureaucratic subjugation of those organs of civil society that had been the agents of the revolutions of 1905 and 1917—namely, the institutionalized Zemstvos assemblies and the spontaneous Soviets councils. At the same time, the Communist Party of the Soviet Union became a closed oligarchy. In Stalin's words, "the party has become in all respects like a fortress, the gates of which are opened only to those who have been tested" (cited in Jowitt 1990:271). Completing the process under way since World War II, Khrushchev fully opened the gates of the fortress and presided over a significant influx, mainly of working-class representatives, into the party. This influx continued under Brezhnev: the party became something of a "lazy monopoly," and its "proletarianizations" continued. Gorbachev's goal for the restructuring and enlargement of political society required controlled opening of the party as well as the working out of a linkage between it and the newly resuscitated political institutions. During the *perestroika*, various attempts at controlled enlargement of political society failed, including proposals for preserving factory constituencies alongside residential ones (Cappelli 1990). In the end, to quote Motyl (1991:3): "Gorbachev destroyed the system, and he did so by fatally weakening the Communist Party. . . . [and] failing to replace it with a meaningful institutional substitute."

The result, as we know, was the crumbling from within and collapse of the imposing but hollow Soviet monolith in a way highly reminiscent of Tocqueville's description of the collapse of absolutism in France that had helped my own understanding of the collapse of the centralized and equally hollow structure of the shah's state in Iran.

Let us look at the integrative dimension of the East European revolutions. Three points are worth mentioning: (1) the opening up of the political community was the major motive of the oppositions everywhere; (2) the challengers who "wanted in" were the intelligentsia, and the political elite whose monopoly they wanted to break were the political class and their co-optees, who came predominantly from the working class; and (3) the clash of citizenship and nationality as competing criteria for membership in the newly constructed political communities is at the root of the tragic paradox of the East European revolutions against the communist oligarchies.

During 1988, the dissident movement in the Soviet Union, like its counterparts in other East European countries, began to attack the central tenet of Marxism-Leninism—namely, the monopoly of the Communist Party. Gorbachev himself did not contemplate the abolition of the one-party system and as late as October 1989 would dismiss the radicals' proposal to abolish the monopoly of the Communist Party as rubbish. Yet he was forced to introduce the same proposal himself, and the amendment of article 6 of the Soviet Constitution in March 1990 disestablished the Communist Party. By then, the Communist Party was already disestablished as the first major step in the Velvet (or Constitutional) Revolution in Czechoslovakia, and also in Hungary and Poland (or it had changed its name).

What did the composition of the communist parties look like in the late 1980s, and who were the challengers who wanted in and were advocating the political enfranchisement of civil society? Brezhnev's "proletarianizations" policy was meant to confirm "the claim that Soviet authority is derived from the people" (Bialer 1982:181). The working-class background of the political elite and the sub-elites was a source of ideological legitimation for the communist regimes. It was particularly important given the nondemocratic character of the selective co-optation process. In Poland in 1970 under Gierek and in Czechoslovakia after 1968, a similar process of "proletarianization" occurred, while in Romania under Ceauşescu, recruitment of some peasants into the cadres performed a similar ideological function (Deák 1992). Here are some arresting statistics (there was of course a large measure of self-reproduction among cadres). Workers constituted 63 percent of new Communist Party–Czechoslovakia members between 1971 and 1976. In Hungary in 1985, 40 percent of party members were workers; in their congress in 1989, the proportion of working-class delegates had dropped to only 9 percent (Cappelli 1990). In the Soviet Union in 1985, when Gorbachev came to power, workers made up 44.5 percent of the total number of deputies (whereas 30.7 percent of the deputies were from the intelligentsia).

Who were the challengers? The intelligentsia, former premier Mazowiecki in Poland, the presidents of Czechoslovakia and Hungary, and the mayors of Moscow and Saint Petersburg are obvious examples. And just one particularly salient statistic: in Hungary's 1989 party congress 90 percent of the delegates were intellectuals (compared to 9 percent workers). In the Soviet Union the composition of the Communist Party remained unchanged down to the last Congress of People's Deputies, but then the party candidates were battered in various kinds of elections and the party itself was swept away after August 1991.

This brings me to citizenship and nationality as the two contradictory bases for membership in the newly enlarged political societies after the East European revolutions. Citizenship and nationhood are alternative principles of political integration. The latter principle is in fact disintegrative in the multinational, multiethnic context of Eastern Europe and Eurasia. The Austro-Hungarian and Ottoman Empires disintegrated after World War I, and the Russian Empire was the only territorially contiguous empire to survive. One of the most striking failures of the communist regimes has been to foster the notion of citizenship and a sense of collective identity on the basis of membership in the nation-state as a socially constructed, or to use Benedict Anderson's expression, "imagined," community in the Soviet Union, Czechoslovakia, Romania, and elsewhere. The consequence is the breaking up of the Soviet empire and various nationality problems for other East European countries that were part of the Ottoman and/or Hapsburg Empires.

Loss of Legitimacy

We now come to the most important cause of the collapse of communism that even now has no place whatsoever in Skocpol's (1979) or Goldstone's (2014) theories: namely, its complete loss of legitimacy. A political order is a structure of authority that may be upheld by coercion but requires legitimacy for its long-term stability. Loss of legitimacy therefore makes it vulnerable by undermining what Weber (1978:31) called its "validity" (*Geltung*). Given the nondemocratic nature of communist regimes and their form of government, this validity depended less on popular belief and support than on the faith of its administrative staff. Loss of faith and cynicism among the members of communist parties has been widely acknowledged (Di Palma 1991). The late Ernest Gellner, after several trips to Russia, estimated that the percentage of the faithful among the communist elite of the Soviet Union was no more than 1 percent. (Imagine what would happen to Catholicism and Islam if the proportion of the faithful was no higher among the Catholic priests or the Muslim mullahs.)[2] This is not to say that popular support for the regime was not eroded. Obviously, it was. Poggi (1990:168–69) is right in identifying this cause of the East European revolutions: "While [the state] is committed to economic success, it is doomed to economic failure, at any rate insofar as its economic performance is measured against that of advanced capitalist economies." The economic failure that came to light in the 1980s therefore was devastating: "because for too long . . . the Soviet state had sold itself to its citizens by promising to catch up with and [go] over . . . the standard of living of advanced capitalist countries."

This amounts to saying that it was not the economic crisis per se but its devastating impact in undermining the ideology and legitimacy of the communist regime that can account for its collapse. Economic success was necessary for the validation of the communist faith; and economic failure devastated it because the worldly faith lacked the safety valves of the world religions. Economic failure, in other words, did not cause the collapse of the communist regime per se but only because it was required by the principles of legitimacy of that type of regime and therefore it resulted in its loss of legitimacy.

The Distinctive Feature of the East European Revolutions in World History

The striking feature of the loss of legitimacy of the East European regimes is the utter devastation of the very idea of *ideology*. The opponents of the regime rejected the idea of ideology and ideological politics alongside the totalitarian culture. To live with them was, to use Havel's famous phrase, to "live within a lie" (cited in context in Goldfarb 1990:539). It is significant that as its last act on September 5, 1991, the Congress of People's Deputies of the Soviet Union issued a Declaration of Human Rights that included the following proviso: "There should be no statist ideology made incumbent upon citizens" (cited in Hazard 1992:5). Not only does this vehement rejection of ideology make the East European revolutions without ideology—which is by no means unprecedented—but it also gives them a pronounced *anti*-ideological, indeed dystopian, character (Eisenstadt 2006:198–203). This last stunning feature of the East European revolutions does make them unique in world history.

The postcommunist revolutions in Eastern Europe suggested that the era of chiliastic revolutions may have come to an end with the Islamic Revolution of 1979 in Iran. The revolutionary transformations witnessed in the East European revolutions were, however, changes in the political order which qualify them as revolutions in that they fit both the state-centered Tocquevillian and the integrative Aristotelian-Paretan models. Yet they are revolutions *without* ideologies serving as a political religion. The modern myth of revolution as the salvation of mankind, which produced its cycle of ideological revolutions ending with the Islamic Revolution in Iran, played no role in them. I hope the broadening of our historical perspective on revolution, which is the primary goal of this study, will establish the fact that there were indeed revolutions in the premodern world as major changes in the political order and its social base without the modern myth of revolution and the ideologies it engendered.

The Arab Revolution of 2011

The Arab Revolution of 2011 not only ignored the myth of revolution of its 1789-based script but was a throwback to the untheorized European revolutions of 1848. As a revolutionary wave in a cultural/civilizational zone or world region, the Arab Revolution of 2011 is strikingly similar to the European revolutions of 1848. The "Springtime of Peoples" (Rapport 2008) was indeed sociologically similar to the "Arab Spring" in many ways. The revolutions of 1848 and 2011 were constitutional revolutions in their teleologies. In both cases, however, the revolution spread over several different polities and its outcome varied accordingly. We may thus speak of different outcomes of a single revolution in different countries. Last but not least, we find a very interesting parallel in terms of both the rapid spread and generality of revolutionary mobilization and the alternation of revolution and counterrevolution.

In the so-called Great Revolutions, the old regime collapsed and was replaced by a new revolutionary state. This conception is seriously brought into question by the Arab Revolution of 2011, in which the old state structures survived. The one exception is Libya, where the old regime was totally destroyed as a result of its military defeat by NATO forces. In reopening the book of history in search of parallels that can help our understanding, we find more than one. In 1848, the old European states did not collapse, except in France, but survived to reconstitute themselves, as happened with the Tunisian and Egyptian states in 2011. The same is true of the post-1989 revolutionary transformation in Central and Eastern Europe. Notable among a number of similar terms coined to characterize this feature of political transformation in Central and Eastern Europe and South Africa are "self-limiting" and "negotiated revolution." This same feature is, however, found not only in most instances of the European revolutions of 1848 but also in the constitutional revolutions of 1906 and 1908 in Iran and the Ottoman Empire, respectively.

A recent study of the constitutional revolutions of the first decade of the twentieth century in Iran and the Ottoman Empire shows that the seizure of state power became a major element of the revolutionary repertoire (and subsequently ingrained in the notion of revolution) only after the Bolshevik Revolution of 1917 (Sohrabi 2011). It was strikingly absent in these earlier constitutional revolutions and in those of China and Mexico that followed shortly thereafter. Self-limitation is thus a necessary consequence of the constitutionalist ideology and makes all constitutional revolutions "negotiated revolutions," if the state does not collapse internally or as a result of external military defeat. Each constitutional revolution, however, sets in motion a historically contingent pattern of negotiated constitutional settlement with the involvement of surviving state institutions in response to popular protests and mobilized groups in civil society. Though suggestive, neither "negotiated" nor "self-limiting" captures the main characteristic of what is better typified as "constitutional revolution"—the type that is primarily marked by the survival of the old state and therefore a varying balance between the state and the revolutionary opposition.

Like the European revolutions of 1848, the teleology of the Arab Revolution of 2011 unfolded in the constitutional counterrevolutions of Morocco in 2011 and of Egypt in 2013, and finally in the Tunisian constitution of January 2014 (Arjomand 2014).

Conclusion

Max Weber noted in the preface to *Ancient Judaism* that modern revolutionary ideology is rooted in the Judaeo-Christian and Islamic world religions of salvation. Islam is the youngest of these; and Mohammad saw his prophecy as the final revelation and the Seal of Prophecy. Will the intensely ideological Islamic Revolution in Shiʿite Iran that triggered the wave of Sunni revolutionary jihad, from al-Qaeda in the 1990s to the Islamic State in Iraq and Syria (DAʿESH, 2013–17), turn out to be the Seal of Revolutions[3] in the apocalyptic sense? The postcommunist revolutions of Eurasia suggest an answer in the affirmative. If so, the coming revolutions will be closer to Aristotle's more limited and political conception than to the modern myth of revolution as dressed up by Marx. But whatever type of revolution the future may hold in store for us, there is no excuse for ignoring the typological and teleological diversity of revolutions, any more than for neglecting the primacy of political factors in vain, positivistic pursuit of predictive models.

In offering the "disenchantment of the world" as the diagnosis of his time, with ghosts of religious ideas masquerading under the guise of scientific determinism, Max Weber acknowledged his agnosticism concerning any future prophecy that could reclothe these zombies in proper religious form (Weber 1948). In concluding this survey of the post-1989 dystopian and anti-ideological revolutions of 1989, we may wonder if the charismatic modern myth of revolution will one day revive in full force as a political religion. S. N. Eisenstadt suggests that such a revival has indeed been in the making in the form of revolutionary religious fundamentalism as the Jacobinist component of multiple modernities. If so, we have already had the Islamic Revolution in Iran, with its vigorous synthesis of religion and political religion, as its prototype (Eisenstadt 2006:203–11). The Sunni Islamic revolution of DA'ESH, however, violently rejected ideology as foreign to Islam, and their leader affirmed their anti-ideological atavism by assuming the name of the first caliph to succeed Muhammad, Abu Bakr, as the first and last ruler of the Islamic State in Iraq and Syria.

Beyond these speculations, it is safe to assume that, as long as centralized states remain important in world history and there is room for greater integration of the politically disenfranchised, there will be revolutions that produce far-reaching consequences, with or without apocalyptic millennialism and with or without revolutionary ideologies. And they are likely to follow the Tocquevillian centralized ideal type in their causation and/or the Khaldunian model in their process and/or the Aristotelian-Paretan integrative type in their consequences.

NOTES

INTRODUCTION

1. Among other paintings, in *The Lictors Bring Home the Sons of Brutus* (1784). David's student François-Joseph Navez continued the master's tradition of Classicist pictorial republicanism, notably in *The Oath of Brutus (upon the Foundation of the Roman Republic on Liberty)* (see below, pp. 65, 89, 117). I cannot find a date for *The Oath of Brutus*, but it was contemporary with Musset's *Lorrenzaccio*, mentioned immediately below, which was written in the aftermaths of the 1830 French revolution.
2. This modification of the script dated from a decade earlier but was completed just before the Russian Revolution of 1917 (Tucker 1969:126–27, 148–52).
3. This type of explanation is familiar to social scientists, especially in the form of functional explanation (Stinchcombe), but it is equally appropriate for all kinds of planned social action, including medieval and modern revolutionary action.
4. Ricoeur (1984–88:3.21–22) sees "narrative mediation" as the tool for reconciling, on the one hand, the Aristotelian perspective on the extension of time as objective succession and, on the other, the Augustinian perspective on internal time-consciousness as the constitution of "the present of attention" with essential reference to "the past of memory and the future of expectation."
5. Fustel had apparently imposed on himself the stricture of not reading Mommsen until his own book was almost finished (Momigliano 1977:337).
6. The interview is summarized in Arjomand 1988:148–49 and discussed at full length in "Through Persian Eyes," BBC Radio 4 (http://www.bbc.co.uk/programmes/b01kbq9p).
7. My email of November 10, 2006, and Tilly's response.
8. Emperor Augustus, who completed the revolutionary transformation of Rome from republic to empire, as we shall see, took great care in covering this transformation with a constitutional facade; Hitler arguably came to power through regular channels and observed certain constitutional formalities in the 1930s; and Hungary after 1989 underwent what László Sólyom (2007), later its president, called a "rule of law revolution," which was subsequently reversed by similarly legal means by the Fidesz Party under the leadership of Viktor Orbán. Yet in all these cases, there was unusual political mobilization of society and radical transformation of the political order.
9. Practically speaking, in the studies of single Great Revolutions, there is a tendency toward excessively long periodization (Krejčí 1983) that cannot be justified on theoretical comparative grounds.

10. This idea was already current in the mid-fifth century BCE (Finley 1986:50, 58n9). In the mid-second century BCE, Polybius (1962:1.466) formulated the notion of *anacyclosis*: "the regular cycle of constitutional revolutions, and the natural order in which constitutions change, are transformed and return to their original stage."
11. As the above discussion indicates, some of Aristotle's ideas about revolutions are fruitful. Others, however, have proved misleading. Foremost among the latter is the plausible but unhelpfully vague idea that disputes over equality and justice are the general causes of revolutions. He asserts categorically that "the cause of sedition is always to be found in inequality" (*Politics* 6.1; 1962:205–6). Marx turned this idea into a purportedly scientific theory of revolution as caused by economic exploitation and class struggle, while Tocqueville seems to be paraphrasing another assertion of Aristotle's on the same page: "It is the passion for equality which is thus at the root of sedition!" However, as Friedrich (1966:6–7) points out, disputes over justice and equality necessarily enter the revolutionary process only because they motivate all politics. There is therefore no warrant for considering them grounds or general causes of revolutions. For a general discussion of Aristotle's treatment of revolution, see Lintott 1982:ch. 7.
12. See chapter 8.
13. See Arjomand, forthcoming:ch. 9, for a full discussion.
14. See chapter 8.
15. The literature abounds in confusion resulting from the failure to distinguish the outbreak, process, and outcome as three separate components of the idea of revolution. The conditions leading to the outbreak of revolutions do *not* determine either the revolutionary process or the outcome of the revolutionary struggle.
16. See chapter 1.
17. Krejčí (1983:15–16) and Rule (1988:79–90) have noted the underutilization of Pareto's idea by the students of revolution.
18. It should be noted that Linz (1975) proposes his typology of political regimes with no particular regard for revolutions. In other words, proneness to revolution is not a definitional property of the types.
19. It is not Pareto's debunking of ideology—which we need not give much attention to—but his division of the supporters of revolution into an insurgent elite and their mobilized constituencies that makes his model superior to the Marxian model. The latter is hopelessly encumbered by the assumption of the identity of class interest—identical for both the insurgent elite and the mass of their supporters—which is far too strong to fit any known case. Lenin's distinction between the working class and the party as its vanguard can be taken as an implicit acknowledgment of the superiority of the Paretan model.
20. More precisely, during the Social War (91–88 BCE) and after the fall of Nero (70 CE).
21. See chapters 7–9.
22. According to Pareto, ideologies are variables ("derivatives") corresponding to certain constants ("residues"), which are the true social forces. He writes: "a derivative is accepted not so much because it convinces anybody as because it expresses clearly ideas that people already have in a confused sort of way—the latter fact is usually the main element in the situation" ([1917–19] 1968:1086, no. 1747). The insurgent elite create an emotional bond with their supporters by articulating derivatives that correspond to the residues of deep sentiment. The Khaldunian *'asabiyya*, mechanical group solidarity typical of tribes, is clearly one such residue. To call the religious reform and revitalization that supplement *'asabiyya* and thus overcome the divisive,

segmentary character a "derivative" is therefore misleading. Other derivatives are also misleadingly labeled, as they, too, play a major role in the motivation of revolutionary action. They concentrate the sentiments and intensify the residues associated with them, and in doing so they serve as a potent tool for mobilization. Religion and nationalism are important in part because the strongest sentiments that can bind the revolutionary counter-elite and their supporters derive from collective identity. Religion emphasizes the identity of the counter-elite and their constituency as members of a community of faith; nationalism, as members of a putative primordial community of blood.

23. The failure of the Maccabean revolt accounts for its exclusion from this volume because it does not fit any of my structural models of revolution. Owing to its world-historical significance as the origin of messianism, it is, however, included in the companion volume, *Apocalypse and Social Revolution in Islam* (Arjomand, forthcoming).

CHAPTER ONE

1. In the city-state of Lagash, the temple of the goddess Baba, the consort of the city god, was managed by the wife of the *ensi*, the god's steward (Gadd 1971a:126).
2. We should offer our thanks to Enlil and the Mesopotamian pantheon that all details of specific antecedents of Sargon's success are irretrievably lost, thus saving much printers' ink and readers' eyesight for posterity by making the historian's typical infinitely regressive listing of the causes of the Akkadian Revolution impossible.
3. For a general account of later parallels to the idea of the universal monarch as the lord of the four quarters in other civilizations by a nonspecialist, see Perry 1966.
4. The etymology of the new notion of totality (*kishshatu*) shows its derivation from Kish, where the idea of strong kingship originated (Steinkeller 1993:120).
5. For the analytical significance of this point, see above, pp. 26–28.

CHAPTER TWO

1. Traill (1975:101) points out that setting up the demes amounted to breaking up dense clusters within the city, while it also meant unifying scattered small communities in the countryside. The overall integrative consequence of these two opposite effects should, however, be evident.
2. See chapter 5.
3. English translations are from Thucydides 1954.
4. This was certainly the case with the *comitia centuriata*, one of the two popular assemblies. The organization of the other assembly, the *comitia tributa*, is more obscure and probably did not have a military basis. The *comitia centuriata*, on the other hand, was organized and voted in centuries—that is, military formations of a hundred men—and continued to meet with full military ceremonial, usually in the Campus Martius outside the walls of the city (Jolowicz and Nicholas 1972:20–21, 26; Lintott 1982:71–75).
5. The largest number recorded before the crisis of the late republic is 337,000 in 163 BCE (Rostovtzeff [1927] 1960:87). For further details, see table 1.
6. He was also doing so with the late fourth-century hindsight of the Persian monarchy his student Alexander was appropriating through conquest.

CHAPTER THREE

1. Gracchus's argument that the ten tribunes as representatives of the plebs were removable by them at will was in accordance with the Greek principle of absolute

sovereignty of the people (Betti and Crifò [1914] 1982:70–71), a principle that never took hold in Rome and did not supply the teleology of the Roman revolutions.

2. The Gracchi episode has received much attention because it can be interpreted in terms of class struggle. This interpretation focuses on Tiberius Gracchus and his agrarian law at the expense of his younger brother, Gaius Gracchus, whose reform program was much more elaborate and comprehensive. It neglects the latter's granting of important judiciary and fiscal functions to the knights as well as his late attempt to revive an earlier proposal for the extension of Roman citizenship. The class struggle interpretation also ignores the fact that the agrarian law had weighty support among the aristocracy and in fact remained in force after the bloody suppression of Tiberius Gracchus. Although broader economic interpretations of the Gracchan episode can be offered (Boren 1957–58), they have to be supplemented by taking into account the serious military crisis of the period (Badian 1972b).
3. The right of *provocatio* was a reasonable alternative to citizenship, as it conveyed an important benefit enjoyed by the citizens: namely, protection against improper subjection to the unchecked *imperium* of the Roman magistrates (Sherwin-White 1973a:135).
4. A lack of *concordia* was Plato's condition for revolution. See the introduction above.
5. As we shall see later, the gradual but decisive transfer of military functions to increasingly professionalized career officers (L. de Blois 1987:13–21) played no small part in the incipient exclusion of the knights from political power and created a need for their consequent reintegration.
6. This is documented by the charter granting Tarentum the status of a *municipium* (Lewis and Reinhold 1951:1.414–16).
7. The tribunes continued to play a political role, ancillary to the generals, for two more decades before their power, *tribunicia potestas*, was abstracted from their office and attached to the *princeps*. See below.
8. Crassus was in Syria, as proconsul.
9. The office of interrex was formally entrusted to the tribunes.
10. A plebiscite, it will be recalled, is a law passed by the plebeian assembly.
11. As a patrician, he was not eligible to hold the office of the tribune of the plebeians.
12. Consul Marcellus sought to annul these reforms in 51 or 50 BCE (Suet., *J. Caesar* 28).
13. The analysis presented in this section is based on Syme's (1939:chs. 7–15) meticulous account. Syme tells the story from the viewpoint of the triumvir, though it can and should also be read from the viewpoint of the republican constitutionalists.
14. See chapter 5.
15. In addition to holding these offices, Augustus was given the power, formerly enjoyed by the Senate, of declaring war, making peace, and concluding treaties.
16. The most important of these uncertainties is due to the forty-one-year gap between the censuses of 70–69 and 28 BCE and raises serious doubts about the compatibility of the republican and the Augustan figures. The census of 70–69 was the first to include the citizens enfranchised as a result of the Social War, and it shows a doubling of the number of registered citizens. Many new citizens must have remained unregistered, and resistance to their registration must be presumed to be the main cause of suspension of the publication of the official census (*lustrum*) by the Romans for four decades. Undoubtedly, different criteria were used for registration in 70 and in 28, and this creates difficulties from the demographic point of view (Wiseman 1969). From our point of view, however, the mere fact of greatly increased municipal registration on the basis of new criteria is politically significant.

17. This incorporation can be explained by competitive mobilization during civil strife and revolution. For parallel democratization of local politics in areas dominated by conservatives in revolutionary France, see Hunt 1984:169.

CHAPTER FOUR

1. These events are not identified as revolutions by historians, but they do fit my definition of revolution.
2. The consuls chose the Capitol to avoid meeting at the Senate House, which had been renamed the Julian Building.
3. Augustus had applied the law of treason to curb freedom of expression and as an instrument of censorship for the first time (*Annals* 1.72, also 2.50).
4. According to the designation for the Roman state, the Senate should have come before the people.
5. These are Seneca's own words (*Annals* 14.53).
6. His last name, as we shall presently see, was equally appropriate for his historical role.
7. The human race was used as an equivalent of the Roman Empire. Other noteworthy legends are *Salus et Libertas* and *Pax et Libertas* (Nicolas 1979:2.1314–17).
8. Galba also punished those Gallic states that had opposed Vindex. A year or so later, these sought to break away from Rome and set up an independent Gallic empire. See below.
9. According to Josephus (*Jewish War* 259), Vespasian wrote to Tiberius Alexander as soon as he had been acclaimed emperor and received his enthusiastic support. Tacitus doubtless had the more reliable information, as coordination between Tiberius Alexander in Egypt and Mucianus and Vespasian in Syria becomes evident in my analysis of the Flavian propaganda below.
10. That is, the legions in Pannonia and Dalmatia. The first of these was under the command of another protégé of Galba, Cornelius Fuscus (Nicolas 1979:2.1200).
11. Seven according to Nicolas (1979:1.281), eight according to Wells (1984:163).
12. This was done with the collusion of the proconsular commander of the German armies, Hordeonius Flaccus.
13. See chapter 3, pp. 76–77, above.
14. Primus left Rome under pressure to complain to Vespasian in person.
15. The poverty of its ideology is evident in the coinage of the German armies, which contrasts sharply in this respect with those of Vindex and Galba. Such legends as "*Fides Exercituum*" and "*Concordia Praetorianorum*" were exclusively military. Only "*Concordia Provinciarum*" had broader significance in that it contained the undecoded secret of the empire (Nicolas 1979:2.1328–29).
16. Brunt's (1977) argument that the *lex de imperio* was already institutionalized and that the *l.d.i.V.* is "tralatician" would seem to apply with any force to the usual honors voted by the Senate for Vitellius, and perhaps Otho, in which case it does not affect my statement on its definitive establishment in the course of consolidation of the revolution of 68–69. In any event, Lucrezi's contrary view (1982:182–88) seems more plausible.
17. Clause 4 had been exercised de facto by Augustus in 7 CE (Lucrezi 1982:161) and by Vitellius (Suet., *Vitellius* 11).
18. Caesar's exceptional *commendatio* of 44 BC was thus made into the legal institution of *commendatio* and *suffragatio* of the imperial era with radically changed meaning (Levi 1938a).

19. The assumption of tribunician power came much later and was made retroactive; and the tribunician day was made to coincide with the *dies imperii* (Lucrezi 1982:132–36).
20. The number of Praetorian cohorts was reduced from sixteen to nine.
21. Clause 6 and the sanction of the *l.d.i.V.* seem to imply as much. As we shall see, as a consequence of the next Roman revolution, Domitian's interpretation would become a legal principle.
22. Even after the destruction of the Temple in Jerusalem, messianism flared up in Cyrenaica in 73 (Hengel 1974:1.254).
23. This can be inferred from Josephus's detailed description of the itinerary of Titus's journey back from Alexandria to lay siege to Jerusalem, where Josephus appears as the chief collaborator in the Roman camp, where he discharged his main function, which was to persuade the Jews to submit to Rome.
24. The Pharisee leader Rabbi Johanan ben Zakkai, who fled the besieged Jerusalem, which was under Zealot control, is reported to have similarly saluted Vespasian as emperor in his camp (Roth 1962:74–75). The *Sibylline Oracles* (5.36, 152–54, pp. 394, 396), however, preserve a different picture of Vespasian as a "great destroyer of pious men," telling us that when Nero died, "the whole creation was shaken and kings perished, and those in whom sovereignty remained destroyed a great city and righteous people" (Lanchester's emendation [396n12] should be accepted). In a later oracle, the attitude toward Vespasian is softened considerably. Though still "a great destroyer of pious men," he is now also "a noble great-spirited king" (*Sib. Or.* 12.99–100, 115, pp. 447–48).

CHAPTER FIVE

1. Two consuls implicated in the conspiracies of 182 were Didius Julianus, governor of Lower Germany, and Helvius Pertinax, governor of Syria. They had been made consuls together by Marcus in 175; and they were to be successively murdered as emperors in 193. Septimius Severus, the third emperor of that year, was serving under Pertinax in Syria and was dismissed with him or shortly after (Birley 1971:105–6).
2. Severus was among the senators who had to suffer the indignity of being "unconstitutionally" tried by equestrian prefects (Howe 1942:33n4).
3. Thus, a Sibylline oracle (4.119–21, p. 387) contends that "a great king will flee from Italy like a runaway slave . . . over the channels of the Euphrates, when he dares to incur a maternal curse for repulsive murder."
4. Mithradates IV of Pontus may have used the Oracle of Hystaspes against Sulla in his anti-Roman propaganda. Also, an oracle had foretold the return of Nero already in the time of Marcus Aurelius (*Sib. Or.* 8.68–72, p. 419).
5. See R. Grant (1970) 1990:198. In a later oracle, Niger himself is, *ex eventu*, "a warlike Ares," the warrior "roused from the East for the sake of lordship" (*Sib. Or.* 12.250–53, p. 451).
6. Except for insignificant exclusions according to some readings of line 9, but not even that according to Oliver's (1989:504) reading on the basis of a parallel phrase in Tabula Banasitana.
7. This was his second marriage and took place in the summer of 187.
8. Dio also throws in the cowardice and rashness of Gaul for good measure. In fairness, it should be pointed out that Dio qualifies the statement by saying that Caracalla had the vices but not the virtues of the three races he belonged to.
9. See the next subsection.

10. Birley (1971:336) considers Papinian to have been Syrian on account of his relation to the family of Iulia Domna. This made his son a Syrian senator (Bowersock 1982:667), but this relation, like Severus's, may well have been through marriage.
11. In the later part of his reign, Caracalla delegated the authority to issue rescripts to his mother, Iulia Domna (T. Honoré 1994:21).
12. Severus's rationalization of law also affected reform of the calendar. In the interest of efficiency and rationalization, he made the tribunician year in which the reign of the emperor was counted correspond to the calendar year and begin on January 1 (Hock 1984).
13. As a result of the addition of these judicial functions, it became usual practice to appoint two prefects to deal with military and judicial matters respectively. Through a process of piecemeal delegation and as a result of the superintendency of the provincial armies, the legal business of the office had grown, and one of the two prefects was sometimes a lawyer (T. Honoré 1982:3).
14. Ulpian's glosses on the legal powers of the emperor are incorporated into the Justinian *Digest* as follows:

    (*On the Julian-Papinian Law XIII*) The emperor is not bound by statutes. The empress to be sure is bound by statutes, but the [reigning] emperor grants her the same privileges that he himself enjoys.

    (*Institutes I*) What the emperor has determined has the force of a statute; seeing that by a royal law which was passed concerning his authority the people transfers to him and upon him the whole of its own authority and power. (Lewis and Reinhold 1951:1.492)

15. Among the many indicators of this reduced importance is the statement by the jurist Paul that a senator has a double domicile, in Rome and in his *patria*; compare this with Trajan's requirement that all senators own property in Rome (Millar 1964:10, citing *Digest* 1.9.2).
16. The discharge premium was increased from 12,000 to 20,000 sesterces for the legionaries. The Praetorians received a higher discharge premium.
17. Severus allowed all centurions and *principales* to wear the equestrian status symbol of a gold ring (Alföldy 1988:171).
18. He was later made a senator, very probably by Septimius Severus.
19. Justinian attributed the *constitutio* to Antoninus Pius, evidently not considering Caracalla worthy of it, and the latter is not mentioned by Aurelius Victor either (Buraselis 2007:3–5).
20. The *Didascalia Apostilorum*, however, gives precise instructions about the position of the bishop's throne (ch. 12), with no mention, needless to say, of the imperial throne or the emperor. Anticipating chapter 9 of this study, I can say that implicit in the Christian monistic mode of integration was the revolutionary potential realized in the papal revolution of the late eleventh century.

CHAPTER SIX

1. The term was to enter Spanish as *reyes des taifas* to describe the fragmented political regime in eleventh-century Andalusia.
2. Christensen (1944:19) takes *ktkhwt'y*, which means "head of the [noble] house" and designates the feudal lords (Widengren 1956:96–97), to be the Pahlavi original of the Arabic *muluk al-tawā'if*.

3. The service due to the feudal lord was symbolized by the tying of the belt (*kamar bastan*). On the nature and ancient roots of the feudal bond between the lord, the helper, and the bondsman, see Widengren 1967:ch. 1.
4. Citations of ŠKZ are to paragraph (and, where applicable, line) numbers, and translations are my own. Pourshariati (2008) has compellingly argued for the addition of the Mehrān and the Kanārangiyān clans on the basis of later evidence.
5. Ardashir's inscriptions do not mention Sāsān, but according to the official Sasanian genealogy reported by the historians, notably Tabari and Hamza, and implicitly confirmed by Shāpur's inscription (ŠKZ 4.5), Sāsān was the father of Pāpak (Shaki 1990).
6. See below, p. 159.
7. For possible implications of this forged genealogy, see Soudavar 2014:141–72. He speculates that the Sasanians were followers of an ascetic named Sāsān who had founded a religious order later taken over by Pāpak.
8. Frye (1962:414) asserted that the word *bag* (god) for Pāpak and Ardashir in the early Sasanian inscriptions meant a sort of "Your Majesty!" but without any justification, and I am not aware that his later finding that Sāsān was a god modified his position. Somewhat similarly, Soudavar (2014:141) is content to say that the title *bag* assumed by the first Sasanians was "in ancient times only used to qualify deities," while further denying that the Sasanians claimed divine descent by disputing the scholarly consensual reading of *chehr* (of gods) as "seed" and proposing "radiance" instead.
9. Following Nöldeke's annotation, this spelling, Guchehr, which assumes a corrupt Arabic transliteration of Juzhir, must represent Old Persian *gao-čiθra*, as discussed by Soudavar (2009:427–28).
10. The beginnings of the Sasanian Revolution are shrouded in complete obscurity except for the dim light thrown on it by Tabari (Nöldeke [1879] 1973:1–22) and an inscription from the city of Bishāpur from which 206 CE can be inferred as the year of the establishment of the Sasanian dynasty. The inscription is dated "the year 58, forty years of the fire of Ardashir, twenty-four years of the fire of Shāpur, the king of fires." This would fix the date of the inscription at 264 and the beginning of the era at 206. It is reasonable to assume that the beginning of the era was reckoned from the coronation of Pāpak (Frye 1984:292). If we were to accept the legend and the Muslim sources that Ardavān IV was the monarch against whom he rebelled, however, we would have to place his declaration of independence after 212–13 (Taqizādeh 1943:40).
11. *Fārsnāma*, Ibn al-Balkhi 1921:61: "The duration of his reign from the time he rose in Persis to the end was thirty-two years, which includes kingship in full integrity after the overthrow of the petty kings for fourteen years."
12. The name Bābā (pope) for a bishop is also attested in the same source, which informs us of the promotion of the bishop of Seleucia in 310 (al-Biruni 1879:16).
13. Another indication of the purely military character of the Khorasan campaign is the large number of heads of vanquished kings sent to the fire temple of Anahita (Tabari, 1.819; trans. 5.15).
14. According to a similar legend recorded in the *Kārnāmak*, a daughter of Mehrak was secretly saved to become the wife of Shāpur and mother of Hormazd.
15. This was before Ardashir made Shāpur his coregent, as proven by the letter's extensive discussion of appointing a successor (it turned out that Ardashir did not follow the recommendations given in the letter).
16. This is the second genealogy reported by Tabari, who continues the line through Vishtāsp and Lohrāsp. The one he prefers and reports first has two unidentifiable figures after Lohrāsp and significantly qualifies Bahman as king (*al-malik*) (Tabari, 1.813).

17. It is very interesting that this was in fact a central element of Parthian foreign policy explicitly attested by Tacitus (*Annals* 6.31, p. 213) for Artabanus II (11–36 CE). Ardashir appropriated this policy without acknowledgment and instead vilified the Parthians, who had claimed Achaemenid descent and risen against and ousted the Seleucids, the heirs of Alexander's conquests.
18. The racial connotation becomes accentuated with the addition of the contrasting phrase "and of Non-Iran" after the imperialist expansion.
19. To this day, "when a sacred fire is installed the priests who escort it to the sanctuary carry weapons, that is maces and swords; and some of these ceremonial weapons are hung thereafter on the sanctuary walls to symbolize the warrior-nature of the fire" (Boyce 1982:224).
20. For another *Dēnkart* text, see Zaehner 1955:145; trans. 139.
21. For a detailed breakdown, see Chaumont 1975.
22. His son, interestingly, bore another name associated with the family: Sohaemus, that of one of the four Julias (Teixidor 1997–98:717)!
23. The reference to Ardashir may well be an afterthought (Sprengling 1953:38).
24. Despite lack of scholarly consensus, the "antiquity of the Zoroastrian apocalyptic" is well established (Boyce 1984; Widengren, Hultgård, and M. Philonenko 1995).
25. Unlike Kartir, there is no contemporary epigraphic evidence of the existence of Tansar.
26. This agrees with Skjærvø's 1983 reading of Kartir's inscription. Skjærvø later (1997:316) altered his reading to make Bahrām the savior of Kartir's soul. The new reading still gives Kartir unprecedented honor.

CHAPTER SEVEN

1. The examination of its teleology as a revolution motivated by the ecumenically shared late antique apocalyptic vision that unfolded in transcendental monotheism will be left to the companion volume (Arjomand, forthcoming).
2. Mundhir b. Nuʿmān succeeded his father, who had been Bahrām's tutor (*dāyak*) according to the Persian feudal tradition and had raised him in his legendary palace of Khᵛarna(q) in Hira (Tabari, 1.850–51, 855; trans. 5.75, 82–83).
3. See Arjomand, forthcoming:ch. 2 for a discussion of Manichaeism in Arabia.
4. Some Ethiopian military presence is still found in Mecca during the Second Civil War, half a century after Muhammad's death (Bashear 1997:99–100).
5. Other—presumably somewhat later—verses promise paradise as a reward (Watt 1956:4–5).
6. According to Ibn ʿAbbās, the angels wore white turbans in the battle of Badr and red turbans a few years later at Hunayn (where they helped but without fighting) (*Life* 303–4).
7. According to al-Wāqidi, their number was 313, 5 of whom were not present during the distribution of booty.
8. They belonged to the Aws Manāt, the majority of whose clans broke their idols and converted to Islam, changing its name to Aws Allāh (Watt 1956:178–79).
9. I follow the chronology of J. Jones (1957), which is basically al-Wāqidi's.
10. The division of booty and fiscal levies imposed on the Khaybar were formally recorded and served as the legal model for treaties with the Jewish colonies of Fadak, which followed immediately, and with those of Wadi al-Qurāʾ and Taymāʾ later, all of which stipulated payment of regular levies to the Muslim state (*Life* 521–23; Watt 1956:218).

11. See chapter 8.
12. Muhammad had the satisfaction of seeing "men entering God's religion in throngs" (Q. 110.2). Many tribes had a pragmatic motive, as the control of Mecca made him the most powerful man in Arabia. One delegate stated explicitly, however, that his tribe took the conquest of Mecca as proof of Muhammad's Prophethood and hastened to declare their submission (Ibn Sa'd 1917:1.2.80). Another delegate, from the Yemen, where Jewish messianism was strong, similarly declared:

 > You are the Prophet about whom we were informed,
 > And the Torah and the Prophets gave the good news of you[r coming]!
 > (Ibn Sa'd 1917:1.2.80)

13. Sa'd b. Khaythama had insisted on drawing lots with his father because only one of them could participate in the battle of Badr, saying he would have let his father go had it not been for the promise of going to heaven (al-Wāqidi 1966:1.20). By contrast, a holy warrior evidently not so impressed by the latter promise during the battle of the Trench complained that "Muhammad used to promise that we would eat the treasures of Khosrow and Caesar [the Persian and Roman emperors]" (*Life* 454).
14. Ibn Ishāq (1858–60:344–45; trans. 234–35), however, reports that the Brotherhood was formed immediately after the first section of the Constitution of Medina (pact with the Jews of Yathrib) was concluded.
15. The first modern critical analysis of the Constitution of Medina, by Julius Wellhausen in the late nineteenth century, did not use the term "constitution" but referred to it as the "municipal charter [*Gemeindeordnung*] of Medina" (Wellhausen 1889). It was in the mid-twentieth century and in the context of the Indian Muslims' search for an Islamic model of the nation-state that Muhammad Hamidullah (1968) called it "the earliest written constitution of a state in the world."
16. The references are to Abu 'Ubayd's text of the Constitution of Medina (CM) as edited by Lecker (2004). The translations are mine (Arjomand 2010).
17. Serjeant (1978:5–7) sees Q. 3.101–3 as a further reference to the new social pact. The term *umma wāhida* occurs eight times in the Qur'ān. See Rubin 1995:134–38 for citations.
18. I am following Serjeant's (1978:12–15) suggestion that the term *mu'minin,* which later acquired the meaning of "the believers," originally meant parties to / beneficiaries of the covenant (*amān*) that put them under God's protection.
19. See p. 212 below.

CHAPTER EIGHT

1. His given name was Ziyād (Sharon 1990:445).
2. 25 Ramadan 129.
3. Contradictory reports on his humble background notwithstanding, Abu Muslim was evidently sent to Khorasan by Ibrāhim al-Imam to start the revolution because he was a native and knew its remote rural hinterland well.
4. As Daniel (1996:178) points out on the basis of the above and other passages in the sources, "the villages that can be identified are consistently located in the deep countryside."
5. As in Sistan and other parts of Iran (Madelung 1988).
6. According to al-Mas'udi (1970:4.50), all children born in Khorasan in that year were named Yahyā or Zayd!

7. He considered sexual intercourse temporary insanity and would allow it only once a year (Yusofi 1989:39, citing Ibn Khallakān).
8. Blankinship's (1988:601–3) careful examination of the sources leads him to the conclusion that Ibrāhim was arrested in the following year, 130, or in early 131 (748–49).
9. This point is correctly underlined by de La Vaissière (2007:54–57). On the basis of the identification of a Transoxanian nobleman among the Hashemite missionaries, al-ʿAlāʾ b. Hurayth b. Qutbah, Agha's (2003:150–51) somewhat fantastic statements to the contrary must be rejected. ʿAlāʾ's mission was not in Transoxania proper but in Khʷarazm to its northwest, and Amol, which is on the Khorasanian side of the river Oxus.
10. Karev (2002) establishes the dates through the correspondence of independent Chinese and Muslim sources.
11. See, further, Arjomand, forthcoming.
12. *Tabsirat a-ʿawāmm* as cited in Mashkur 1948:32. The variant *mubayyida*, for *moghān*, is given by Shahrastāni as cited in Browne 1902:1.311.
13. His name is variously recorded as Sonbād/Sunbād, Sonbādh/Sunbādh, and Sunfādh. I follow the form suggested to Sadighi by the linguist Émile Benveniste: a theophoric name corresponding to the Pahlavi *son-* or *san-* (of unknown meaning) and *pāt* (protected by) (Sadighi 1938:135n2).
14. Or a year later, in 760–61/143, according to some sources (Tabari, 3.140; trans. 28.80).
15. ʿUmar b. al-Aʿlāʾ and his descendant remained and served Caliph al-Mansur and his successors as governors and did not return to the bourgeois profession of butchery.
16. Tabari makes the revolt of the Rāwandiyya the first event under the year 141 (756–57), but other sources date it earlier (Tabari, 3.129; trans. 28.62n286).
17. 27 Jumada II or 1 Rajab 145 (Tabari, 3.195; trans. 28.150).
18. It was also called a seal (*khatim*), like the Prophet's Seal of Prophecy (Arjomand 1988), and the poet accepted his claims on the basis of predictions by "the non-Arabs [*aʿājim*] in the books" (al-Isfahani 1949:243).
19. Ibrāhim probably had 4,000 men, while the caliph had 1,500 in Hāshimiyya (Tabari, 3.290, 293; trans. 28.261, 264).
20. He had done this by occupying Kufa and forcing its inhabitants to wear black (Tabari, 3.294; trans. 28.265).
21. Or perhaps reduced to as few as seventy! See Tabari, 3.315; trans. 28.288.
22. The old Persian name of the city, Baghdād (given by god), survived, however.
23. Translation from Pellat 1969:274, with "Testament" modified to "Covenant" (of Ardashir).

CHAPTER NINE

1. The Crusades are presented as the export of the papal revolution also in Rosenstock-Huessy ([1931] 1951:150–53), who further considers (162–68) the development of Catholic ritual over the next two centuries its liturgical consequences.
2. The two trajectories remained entangled in the next two centuries, but each maintained its distinctive direction.
3. Under his successor, Paschal II (1099–1118), the number of papal cardinal deacons increased to eighteen.
4. Leo's reformist German successor, Pope Victor II (1055–57), suggested Humbert or Hildebrand as his possible successor on his deathbed (Whitney 1926:32).

CHAPTER TEN

1. The conversion of Berke and the Golden Horde to Islam predated Il-khan Tegüder's indecisive conversion in Iran in 1282 and the decisive conversion of Ghāzān Khan, who "ordered all the Uighurs and Mongols to accept Islam" in 1295 (Vassāf 1852–53:324; Āyati 1993:198).
2. Turko-Mongolian garrisons were set up in the interior of northern China under Ögedei, and in greater number in Southern Sung territories by Qubilai, who established twenty-eight of them along the Yangtze in 1282 (Hsiao 1978:53–57).
3. Perry Anderson (1974:227) is therefore right in attributing the longevity of the Golden Horde nomadic empire to its ability to subject Russia to "tributary rule . . . from the borderlands of pastoral territory [around the Caspian], while itself remaining within steppe country." This is not to say, however, that the Golden Horde did not influence the developmental path of Russia itself; in fact, it did (Ostrowski 1990).
4. The Chinese transcriptions, *mohefu* and *mofu*, were borne by the chiefs of Khitan and Juan-juan but disappear by the time of the Liao dynasty (916–1125).
5. Compare how the Persian *bag* (God) gets devalued in being transformed into the Turkish *bäg* (lord).
6. According to Chen (2002:289–90), Tian started as a deity imposed by the invading Zhou tribes from Inner Asia who overthrew the Shang dynasty ca. 1122 BCE.
7. Over the centuries, the term *ēl/il* came to refer to the tribal polity as well.
8. This is another characteristic that Weber found to be a defining feature of patrimonialism.
9. By the time of Chinggis Khan's death in 1227, the number had reached 129,000 (Mote 1999:427). Barthold's ([1928] 1968:404) estimates are higher, and he puts the number of troops used against the Khʷārazmshāh and for the conquest of Iran at 150,000–200,000.
10. A third sister was married to one of Batu's sons.
11. See Morgan 2005:296 for the significance of this phrase.
12. Rashid al-Din also seeks to justify the independence of the Il-khanids since Hülegü by having the great Möngke Qa'an tell his brother to return to Mongolia after accomplishing his mission just for appearance's sake (*zāheran*) (Allsen 1991:234).
13. The first Il-khan to convert to Islam and assume the title Sultan Ahmad was Hülegü's son Tegüder in 1282. His rule was, however, contested in less than a year by his nephew Arghun, who accused him of abandoning the Mongolian tradition for Islam and replaced him as Il-khan in 1284.
14. For the interesting details of Ghāzān Khan's testament, see Melville 2006:152–54.
15. When commissioning the Mosul Qur'an of 1311–12/711, Öljeitü calls himself "Shadow of God on Earth, and His Caliph" (Allsen 1991:232).
16. His appellation may well be the progenitor of the title Sadr-e Aʿzam for the grand vizier, later prime minister.
17. Irān-zamin (land of Iran) was the conceptual creation of Ferdawsi in preference to the Sasanian idea of Ērān-shahr (empire of Iran), but it was not coextensive with the territory of the Samanid, Ghaznavid, or Buyid Kingdoms, and the main Seljuks did not show much interest in it. Fortunately for its Persian bureaucrats, the Il-khanid territory roughly corresponded to that of the Sasanian Empire.
18. The same fourteenth-century manual of administration (Nakhjavāni 1964) uses the term *mamālek-e mahrusa* (the [divinely] protected realms) as a synonym for "the land of Iran." A further attestation of continuity between the Mongol regime and modern Iran is the use of this alternative term down to the end of the nineteenth century.

19. The Seljuks, too, had resided and given audience in their pavilions (*kushk*) in military camps (*lashkargāh*) outside cities (Durand-Guédy 2013).
20. Out of 163 high officials under Qubilai, 43 were *darughachi*s.
21. Also required as texts were the Five Classics: *Classic of Poetry, Book of Documents, Book of Rites, I Ching,* and *Spring and Autumn Annals.*
22. Chin-hua is the area some 110 kilometers to the south of the former Sung capital of Hangchow.
23. Wang Yün also wrote *Mirror for a Prime Minister,* which is not extant (Franke 1982:162).
24. The T'ang political analects were translated into Khitan, Tangut, and Jurchen as well (Franke 1982:155).

CONCLUSION

1. The ʿAbbasid Revolution is generally recognized as Islam's social revolution. I have not highlighted the distinction between "social" and "political" revolutions in this study, as all early revolutions begin with revolutionary political change, as distinct from other kinds of political change that lack important social consequences.
2. Shortly to be published by Oxford University Press.

EPILOGUE

1. See the introduction, p. 10.
2. Private communication with author. See also Gellner 1995.
3. According to Muslim conventional wisdom, Muhammad was the Seal of the Prophets.

REFERENCES

Ābān Yasht. 1983. Translated by W. W. Malandra. *See* Malandra 1983.

Abbott, A. 1992. "What Do Cases Do? Some Notes on Activity in Sociological Analysis." In *What Is a Case? Exploring the Foundations of Social Inquiry*, edited by C. C. Ragin and H. S. Becker, 53–82. Cambridge: Cambridge University Press.

———. 1995. "Sequence Analysis: New Methods for Old Ideas." *Annual Review of Sociology* 21:93–113.

Abbott, N. 1967. *Studies in Arabic Literary Papyri*. Vol. 76. Chicago: University of Chicago Press.

Adcock, F. E. 1959. *Roman Political Ideas and Practices*. Ann Arbor: University of Michigan Press.

Afsaruddin, A. 2010. "Where Heaven and Earth Meet: Remembering Muhammad as Head of State." In *The Cambridge Companion to Muhammad*, edited by J. E. Brockopp, 180–98. Cambridge: Cambridge University Press.

Afshār, I. 1980 (AH 1358). Introduction to *Awrād al-ahbāb o fosus al-ādāb*, by Abu'l-Mafākher Yahyā Bākharzi, 3–35. Tehran: Farhang-e Irān Zamin.

Agha, S. S. 2003. *The Revolution Which Toppled the Umayyads Neither Arab nor ʿAbbāsid*. Leiden: E. J. Brill.

Agouadé, J. 1979. "Messianismus zur Zeit der Frühen Abbasiden." Islamisches Seminar Dissertation. Tübingen: University of Tübingen.

Aigle, D. 2004. "Le grand jasaq de Gengis-Khan, l'empire, la culture mongole et la sharīʿa." *JESHO* 47 (1): 31–79.

Akhbār al-dawla al-ʿAbbāsiyya wa fihi akhbār al-ʿAbbās wa waladihi. 1971. Edited by ʿA.-ʿA. al-Duri and ʿA.-J. al-Mutallabi, Beirut.

Al-Azmeh, A. 2014. *The Emergence of Islam in Late Antiquity: Allah and His People*. Cambridge: Cambridge University Press.

Alföldy, G. 1971. "Cassius Dio und Herodian über die Anfänge des neupersischen Reiches." *Rheinisches Museum für Philologie* 114 (H. 4): 360–66.

———. 1988. *The Social History of Rome*. Translated by D. Braund and F. Pollock. Baltimore, MD: Johns Hopkins University Press.

Allsen, T. T. 1979. "Batuʾids." In *Encyclopedia of Islam*, 1:1106–8. New ed. Leiden: E. J. Brill.

———. 1983. "The Yüan Dynasty and the Uighurs of Turfan." In *China among Equals: The Middle Kingdom and Its Neighbors, 10th–14th Centuries*, 243–80. Berkeley: University of California Press.

———. 1991. "Changing Forms of Legitimation in Mongol Iran." In *Rulers from the Steppe: State Formation on the Eurasian Periphery*, edited by G. Seaman and D. Marks, 223–41. Los Angeles: University of Southern California.

———. 1993. "Mahmūd Halavač (?–1254), Mas'ud Beg (?–1289), 'Ali Beg (?–1280): Bujir (fl. 1206–1260)." In *In the Service of the Khan: Eminent Personalities of the Early Mongol-Yüan Period (1200–1300)*, edited by I. de Rachewiltz, H.-L. Chan, C. Hsiao, and P. W. Geier, 122–35. Wiesbaden: Harrassowitz.

Alram, M., M. Blet-Lemarquand, and P. O. Skjærvø. 2007. "Shapur, King of Kings of Iranians and Non-Iranians." *Res Orientales* 17:11–40.

Altheim, F. 1943. *Die Krise der alten Welt: Im 3. Jahrhundert n. Zw. und ihre Ursachen*. Berlin-Dahlem: Ahnenerbe-Stiftung.

Amir-Moezzi, M. A. 2006. *La religion discrete: Croyances et pratiques spirituelles dans l'islam shi'ite*. Paris: Librairie philosophique J. Vrin.

Anderson, P. 1974. *Passages from Antiquity to Feudalism*. London: NLB.

Andreski, S. (1954) 1968. *Military Organization and Society*. 2nd ed. London: Routledge and Kegan Paul.

Anklesaria, B. T. 1956. *Zand-Ākāsīh: Iranian or Greater Bundahišn*. Bombay: Shahnamah Press.

Antia, E. K., ed. 1900. *Kârnâmak-i Arthakhshîr Pâpakân*. Bombay: Fort Printing Press.

Arendt, H. (1963) 1979. *On Revolution*. Harmondsworth, UK: Penguin.

Aristotle. 1962. *Politics*. Translated and edited by E. Barker. New York: Oxford University Press.

———. 1984. *The Athenian Constitution*. Translated by P. J. Rhodes. New York: Penguin Books.

Arjomand, S. A. 1980. "The State in Khomeini's New Islamic Order." In "Iranian Revolution in Perspective," special issue, *Iranian Studies* 13 (1–4): 147–64.

———. 1986. "Iran's Islamic Revolution in Comparative Perspective." *World Politics* 38 (3): 383–414.

———. 1988. *The Turban for the Crown: The Islamic Revolution in Iran*. New York: Oxford University Press.

———. 1992. "A Demographic Theory of Revolution; or, Sociology as Sorcery?" *Contemporary Sociology* 21 (1): 3–8.

———. 1994. "'Abd Allah ibn al-Muqaffa' and the 'Abbasid Revolution." *Journal of Iranian Studies* 27 (1–4): 9–36.

———. 1998. "Artaxerxes, Ardašīr, and Bahman." *JAOS* 118 (2): 245–48.

———. 1999. "The Law, Agency, and Policy in Medieval Islamic Society: Development of the Institutions of Learning from the Tenth to the Fifteenth Century." *Comparative Studies in Society and History* 41 (2): 263–93.

———. 2000. "Ğayba." In *Encyclopaedia Iranica* 10:341–44.

———. 2003. "Law, Political Reconstruction and Constitutional Politics." *International Sociology* 18 (1): 9–34.

———. 2006. "Revolution in Early Islam: The Rise of Islam as a Constitutive Revolution." *Yearbook of the Sociology of Islam* 7:125–57.

———. 2009. "The Constitution of Medina: A Socio-legal Interpretation of Muhammad's Acts of Foundation of the *Umma*." *International Journal of Middle East Studies* 41 (4): 555–75.

———. 2010. "Legitimacy and Political Organisation: Caliphs, Kings and Regimes." In *The New Cambridge History of Islam*, 4.225–73. Cambridge: Cambridge University Press.

———. 2012. "The Conception of Revolution in Persianate Political Thought." *Journal of Persianate Studies* 5 (1): 1–16.

———. 2014. *Social Theory and Regional Studies in the Global Age*. Albany: State University of New York Press.

———, ed. 2015. *The Arab Revolution of 2011: A Comparative Perspective*. Albany: State University of New York Press.

———. 2016a. "State Formation in Early Modern Muslim Empires: Common Origin and Divergent Paths." *Social Imaginaries* 2 (2): 35–51.

———. 2016b. "Unity of the Persianate World under Turko-Mongolian Domination and Divergent Development of Imperial Autocracies in the Sixteenth Century." *Journal of Persianate Studies* 9 (1): 1–18.

———. Forthcoming. *Apocalypse and Social Revolution in Islam*. Oxford: Oxford University Press.

Arjomand, S. A., and E. A. Tiryakian, eds. 2004. *Rethinking Civilizational Analysis*. London: Sage.

Aubin, J. 1969. "L'ethnogenèse des Qaraunas." *Turcica* 1:65–94.

———. 1995. *Émirs mongols et vizirs persans dans les remous de l'acculturation*. Paris: Association pour l'avancement des études iraniennes.

Augustan History: The Scriptores Historiae Augustae. 1924. Vol. 2. Edited by D. Magie. Loeb Classical Library. Cambridge, MA: Harvard University Press.

Averroës. 1966. *Averroes' Commentary on Plato's "Republic."* Edited by E. I. J. Rosenthal. Cambridge: Cambridge University Press.

Āyati. 1993 (AH 1372). *Taḥrir-i tārikh-i Vaṣṣāf*. Tehran: Mu'assasah-'i Muṭāla'āt va Taḥqiqāt-i Farhangi (Pazhuheshgāh).

Bacon, Francis. 1994. *Essays*. New ed. London: J. M. Dent.

Badian, E. 1958. *Foreign Clientelae (264–70 B.C.)*. Oxford: Clarendon Press.

———. 1962. "From the Gracchi to Sulla (1940–1959)." *Historia: Zeitschrift für Alte Geschichte* 11 (2): 147–245.

———. 1972a. *Publicans and Sinners: Private Enterprise at the Service of the Roman Empire*. Ithaca, NY: Cornell University Press.

———. 1972b. "Tiberius Gracchus and the Beginning of the Roman Revolution." In *Aufstieg und Niedergang der römischen Welt*, vol. 1.1, edited by H. Temporini. Berlin: Walter de Gruyter.

Badie, B. 1985. "Formes et transformations des communautés politiques." In *Traité de science politique*, vol. 1, edited by M. Grawitz and J. Leca, 599–663. Paris: Presses universitaires de France.

Baker, K. M. 1990. *Inventing the French Revolution: Essays on French Political Culture in the Eighteenth Century*. Cambridge: Cambridge University Press.

Balādhuri, Ahmad b. Yahyā b. Jābir al-. 1866. *Kitāb Futuh al-Buldān*. Edited by M. J. de Goeje. Leiden. Translated by P. K. Hitti (pt. 1) and F. C. Murgotten (pt. 2) as *The Origins of the Islamic State* (New York: Columbia University Press, 1916–24).

———. 1978. *Ansāb al-Ashrāf*. Vol. 3. Edited by 'A.-'A. al-Duri. Beirut.

Bal'ami, Abu 'Ali. 2003 (AH 1382). *Tārikh-e Bal'ami*. Edited by M. T. Bahār. 3 vols. Tehran.

Balandier, G. 1985. "Le politique des anthropologues." In *Traité de science politique*, vol. 1, edited by M. Grawitz and J. Leca. Paris: Presses universitaires de France.

Baneth, D. Z. H. 1971. "What Did Muhammad Mean When He Called His Religion Islam? The Original Meaning of *Aslama* and Its Derivatives." *Israel Oriental Studies* 1:183–90.

Barthold, V. V. 1925. "Musaylima." *Bulletin de l'Académie des sciences de Russie* 19:482–512.

———. (1928) 1968. *Turkestan Down to the Mongol Invasion*. Translated by H. A. R. Gibbe. Reprint, London: Luzac.

Bashear, S. 1997. *Arabs and Others in Early Islam*. Princeton, NJ: Darwin Press.

———. 2004. "*Hanifiyya* and *Hajj*." In *Studies in Early Islamic Tradition*, 1–21. Jerusalem: Max Schloessinger Foundation.

Becker, C. H. (1932) 1967. *Islamstudien*. 2 vols. Reprint, Hildesheim: Georg Olms.

Benveniste, E. 1929. *The Persian Religion according to the Chief Greek Texts*. Paris: Librairie orientaliste Paul Geuthner.

Berman, H. J. 1983. *Law and Revolution: The Formation of Western Legal Tradition*. Cambridge, MA: Harvard University Press.

Betti, E., and G. Crifò. (1914) 1982. *La crisi della repubblica e la genesi del principato in roma*. Curated by Giuliano Crifó, with a presentation by Emilio Gabba. Rome: Pontificia Universitas Lateranensis.

Bialer, S. 1982. *Stalin's Successors: Leadership, Stability, and Change in the Soviet Union*. Cambridge: Cambridge University Press.

Bianchi, U. 1988. "Zoroastrian Elements in Manichaeism: The Question of Evil Substance." In *Manichaean Studies: Proceedings of the First International Conference on Manichaeism*, edited by P. Bryder, 13–18. Lund: Plus Ultra, 1988.

Bickerman, E. J. 1947. *The Maccabees: An Account of Their History from the Beginnings to the Fall of the House of the Hasmoneans*. New York: Schocken Books.

Bienen, H. 1968. *Violence and Social Change*. Chicago: University of Chicago Press.

Billington, J. H. 1980. *Fire in the Minds of Men: Origins of Revolutionary Faith*. New York: Basic Books.

Biran, M. 2004. "The Mongol Transformation: From the Steppe to Eurasian Empire." *Medieval Encounters* 10 (1/3): 339–61.

Birley, A. R. 1971. *Septimius Severus: The African Emperor*. Abingdon, UK: Taylor and Francis.

———. 1972. "The Lacuna in the *Historia Augusta*." In *Bonner "Historia Augusta" Colloquium*, 1974.55–62. Bonn: Habelt.

———. 1976. *The Third Century Crisis in the Roman Empire*. Manchester: John Rylands University Library of Manchester.

Biruni, Abu Rayhān al-. 1879. *The Chronology of Ancient Nations*. Edited and translated by C. E. Sachau. London: W. H. Allen.

Bivar, A. D. H. 1983. "The Political History of Iran under the Arsacids." In *The Cambridge History of Iran*, vol. 3.3, edited by E. Yarshater, 21–99. Cambridge: Cambridge University Press.

Blankinship, K. Y. 1988. "The Tribal Factor in the ʿAbbasid Revolution." *JAOS* 108 (4): 589–603.

———. 1994. *The End of the Jihâd State*. Albany: State University of New York Press.

Blenkinsopp, J. 1981. "Interpretation and the Tendency to Sectarianism: An Aspect of the Second Temple History." In *Jewish and Christian Self-Definitions*, vol. 2, edited by E. P. Sanders, 1–26. Philadelphia: Fortress Press.

Blois, F. de. 1995. "The 'Sabians' (*Sābiʾun*) in Pre-Islamic Arabia." *Acta Orientalia* 56:39–61.

———. 2002. "Nasrāni and Hanif: Studies on the Religious Vocabulary of Christianity and of Islam." *BSOAS* 65 (1): 1–30.

Blois, L. de. 1987. *The Roman Army and Politics in the First Century before Christ*. Amsterdam: J. C. Gieben.

Bol, P. K. 1997. "Examinations and Orthodoxies: 1070 and 1313 Compared." In *Culture and State in Chinese History: Conventions, Accommodations and Critiques*, edited by T. Huters, R. B. Wong, and P. Yu, 29–57. Stanford, CA: Stanford University Press.

Boren, H. C. 1957–58. "The Urban Side of the Gracchan Economic Crisis." *American Historical Review* 63 (4): 890–902.

Borkenau, F. 1937. "State and Revolution in the Paris Commune, the Russian Revolution, and the Spanish Civil War." *Sociological Review* 29 (1): 41–75.

Bowersock, G. W. 1965. *Augustus and the Greek World*. Oxford: Clarendon Press.

———. 1973. "Syria under Vespasian." *JRS* 63:133–40.

———. 1975. "Herodian and Elagabalus." *Yale Classical Studies* 24:229–36.

———. 1982. "Roman Senators from the East: Syria, Judaea, Arabia and Mesopotamia." *Atti del Colloquio internazionale AIEGL su epigrafia e ordine senatorio, Roma, 14–20 maggio 1981*, 651–68.

———. 1983. *Roman Arabia*. Cambridge, MA: Harvard University Press.

———. 1986a. "From Emperor to Bishop: The Self-Conscious Transformation of Political Power in the Fourth Century AD." *Classical Philology* 81 (4): 298–307.

———. 1986b. "The Mechanics of Subversion in the Roman Provinces." In *Entretiens sur l'antiquité classique*, vol. 33, *Opposition et resistances a l'Empire d'Auguste a Trajan*, 291–317. Geneva: Fondation Hardt.

———. 2003. "The Nabataeans in Historical Context." In *Petra Reconsidered*, edited by G. Markoe, 19–25. New York: Abrams.

Boyce, M. 1968. *The Letter of Tansar*. Rome: Istituto italiano per il Medio ed Estremo Oriente.

———. 1979. *Zoroastrians: Their Religious Beliefs and Practices*. London: Routledge and Kegan Paul.

———. 1982. *A History of Zoroastrianism*. Vol. 2, *Under the Achaemenians*. Leiden: E. J. Brill.

———. 1984. "On the Antiquity of Zoroastrian Apocalyptic." *BSOAS* 47 (1): 57–75.

———. 1989. *A History of Zoroastrianism*. Vol. 1, *The Early Period*. Leiden: E. J. Brill.

Boyce, M., and F. Grenet. 1991. *A History of Zoroastrianism*. Vol. 3, *Zoroastrianism under Macedonian and Roman Rule*. Leiden: Brill.

Boyle, J. A. 1968. "Dynastic and Political History of the Il-Khāns." In *The Cambridge History of Iran*, vol. 5, *The Saljuq and Mongol Periods*, 303–422. Cambridge: Cambridge University Press.

Brett, M. 2010. "The Central Lands of North Africa and Sicily until the Beginning of the Almohad Period." In *The New Cambridge History of Islam*, vol. 2, *The Western Islamic World, Eleventh to Eighteenth Centuries*, edited by M. Fierro, 48–65. Cambridge: Cambridge University Press.

Brinton, C. (1938) 1965. *The Anatomy of Revolution*. New York: Vintage.

Brooke, Z. N. 1926. "Gregory VII and the First Contest between Empire and Papacy." In *The Cambridge Medieval History*, vol. 5, *Contest of Empire and Papacy*, edited by J. R. Tanner, C. W. Prévite-Orton, and Z. N. Brooke, 51–111. Cambridge: Cambridge at the University Press.

Broughton, T. R. S. 1962. Comment on P. A. Brunt, "The Equites in the Late Republic." In *Deuxième conférence internationale d'histoire économique*, 1:150–62. Aix-en-Provence.

Brown, P. R. L. 1981. *The Cult of the Saints: Its Rise and Function in Latin Christianity*. Chicago: University of Chicago Press.

Browne, E. G. 1902. *A Literary History of Persia: From the Earliest Times until Firdawsi*. 4 vols. London: T. F. Unwin.

Brunt, P. A. 1957. "Athens and Sicily." *Classical Review* 7 (3–4): 243–45.

———. 1959. "The Revolt of Vindex and the Fall of Nero." *Latomus* 18 (fasc. 3): 531–59.

———. 1977. "Lex de Imperio Vespasiani." *JRS* 67:95–116.

———. 1988. *The Fall of the Roman Republic and Related Essays*. Oxford: Clarendon Press.

Buell, P. D. 1993a. "Saiyid Ajall (1211–1279)." In *In the Service of the Khan: Eminent Personalities of the Early Mongol-Yüan Period (1200–1300)*, edited by I. de Rachewiltz, H.-L. Chan, C. Hsiao, and P. W. Geier, 466–79. Wiesbaden: Harrassowitz.

———. 1993b. "Söbötei Ba'atur (1176–1248)." In *In the Service of the Khan: Eminent Personalities of the Early Mongol-Yüan Period (1200–1300)*, edited by I. de Rachewiltz, H.-L. Chan, C. Hsiao, and P. W. Geier, 13–26. Wiesbaden: Harrassowitz.

———. 1993c. "Yeh-Lü A-Hai (ca. 1151–ca. 1223), Yeh-Lü T'u-Hua (d. 1231)." In *In the Service of the Khan: Eminent Personalities of the Early Mongol-Yüan Period (1200–1300)*, edited by I. de Rachewiltz, H.-L. Chan, C. Hsiao, and P. W. Geier, 112–21. Wiesbaden: Harrassowitz.

Bulliet, R. W. 1979. "Conversion to Islam and the Emergence of a Muslim Society in Iran." In *Conversion to Islam*, edited by N. Levtzion, 30–51. New York: Holmes and Meier.

Buraselis, K. 2007. *Theia Dōrea: Das Göttlich-Kaiserliche Geschenk*. Vienna: Österreichischen Akademie der Wissenschaften.

Burgler, R. A. 1990. *The Eyes of the Pineapple: Revolutionary Intellectuals and Terror in Democratic Kampuchea*. Nijmegen Studies in Development and Cultural Change, vol. 3. Saarbrücken: Breitenbach.

Cahen, C. 1963. "Points de vue sur la 'Revolution 'abbaside.'" *Revue historique* 230:295–338.

Campbell, J. B. 1984. *The Emperor and the Roman Army, 31 BC–AD 235*. Oxford: Clarendon Press.

Cantwell Smith, W. 1978. *The Meaning and End of Religion*. San Francisco: Harper and Row.

Cappelli, O. 1990. "Comparative Communism's Fall: The First Phase; The 'Intelligentsia Revolution' of 1989–1990." *Harriman Institute Forum* 3 (6): 5–6.

Carson, R. A. G., P. Berghaus, and N. M. Lowick, eds. 1979. *A Survey of Numismatic Research, 1972–1977*. Bern: International Numismatic Commission.

Casanova, P. 1911. *Mohammed et la fin du monde*. Paris: Paul Guethner.

———. 1924. "Idris et 'Uzair." *Journal asiatique* 205:357–60.

Chan, H.-L. 1967. "Liu Ping-chung (1216–74)." *T'oung Pao* 53 (1/3): 98–146.

———. 1980. "Yao Shu (1201–1278)." *Papers on Far Eastern History* 22:17–50.

———. 1982. "Chu Hsi and Yuan Neo-Confucianism." In *Yuan Thought: Chinese Thought and Religion under the Mongols*, edited by H.-L. Chan and W. T. de Bary, 197–231. New York: Columbia University Press.

———. 1993a. "Hsü Heng (1209–1281)." In *In the Service of the Khan: Eminent Personalities of the Early Mongol-Yüan Period (1200–1300)*, edited by I. de Rachewiltz, H.-L. Chan, C. Hsiao, and P. W. Geier, 416–47. Wiesbaden: Harrassowitz.

———. 1993b. "Tou Mo (1209–1281)." In *In the Service of the Khan: Eminent Personalities of the Early Mongol-Yüan Period (1200–1300)*, edited by I. de Rachewiltz, H.-L. Chan, C. Hsiao, and P. W. Geier, 407–15. Wiesbaden: Harrassowitz.

Chandler, D. P. 1991. *The Tragedy of Cambodian History*. Cambridge: Cambridge University Press.

Charlesworth, J. H. 1983. "Sibylline Oracles." In *The Old Testament Pseudepigrapha*, 1.317–472. Garden City, NY: Doubleday.

Chaumont, M.-L. 1959. "Pāpak, roi de Staxr et sa cour." *Journal asiatique* 247:175–91.

———. 1960a. "L'inscription de Kartir à la Ka'bah de Zoroastre." *Journal asiatique* 248:339–80.

———. 1960b. "Recherches sur le clergé zoroastrien: Le *herbad*." *Revue de l'histoire des religions* 158:55–80, 161–79.

———. 1964a. "Où les roi sassanides étaient-ils couronnés?" *Journal asiatique* 252:59–75.

———. 1964b. "Les Sassanides et la christianisation de l'empire iranien au IIIe siècle de notre ère." *Revue de l'histoire des religions* 165:165–202.

———. 1973. "Conquêtes sassanides et propagande mazdéenne." *Historia* 22:664–710.

———. 1975. "États vassaux dans l'empire des premiers Sassanides." *Acta Iranica* 4:89–156.

Chelhod, J. 1955. *Le sacrifice chez les Arabes*. Paris: Presses universitaires de France.

———. 1958. *Introduction á la sociologie de l'Islam: De l'animisme á l'universalisme*. Paris: G.-P. Maisonneuve.

———. 1962. "Mythe chez les Arabs." *L'homme* 2 (1): 66–90.

Chen, S. 2002. "Son of Heaven and Son of God." *Journal of the Royal Asiatic Society* 12:289–325.

Choksy, J. K. 1988. "Sacral Kingship in Sasanian Iran." *Bulletin of the Asia Institute* 2:35–52.

Christensen, A. 1944. *L'Iran sous les Sassanides*. Copenhagen: Ejnar Munksgaard.

Collins, J. J. 1984. "The Sibylline Oracles." In *Jewish Writings of the Second Temple Period: Apocrypha, Pseudepigrapha, Qumran, Sectarian Writings, Philo, Josephus*, edited by M. E. Stone, 357–82. Minneapolis, MN: Fortress Press.

Collins, R. 1999. *Macrohistory: Essays in the Sociology of the Long Run*. Stanford, CA: Stanford University Press.

———. 2005. "Weber and the Sociology of Revolution." In *Max Weber's Economy and Society: A Critical Companion*, edited by C. Camic, P. D. Gorski, and D. M. Trubek, 297–321. Stanford, CA: Stanford University Press.

Colpe, C. 1983. "Development of Religious Thought." In *The Cambridge History of Iran*, vol. 3.2, *The Seleucid, Parthian and Sasanian Periods*, edited by E. Yarshater, 819–65. Cambridge: Cambridge University Press.

Constable, G. 1996. *The Reformation of the Twelfth Century*. Cambridge: Cambridge University Press.

Cooper, J. S. 1990. "Mesopotamian Historical Consciousness and the Production of Monumental Art in the Third Millennium B.C." In *Investigating Artistic Environments in the Ancient Near East*, edited by A. C. Gunter. Washington, DC: Arthur M. Sackler Gallery, Smithsonian Institution.

———. 1993. "Paradigm and Propaganda: The Dynasty of Akkade in the 21st Century." In *Akkad: The First World Empire; Structure, Ideology, Traditions*, edited by M. Liverani, 11–23. Padua: Sargon.

Covolo, E. dal. 1989. *I Severi e il Cristianesimo*. Rome: LAS.

Cowdrey, H. E. J. 1968. "The Papacy, the Patarenes and the Church of Milan." *Transactions of the Royal Historical Society* 18:25–48.

———. 1998. *Pope Gregory VII (1023–1085)*. Oxford: Clarendon Press.

Crone, P. 1980. *Slaves on Horses: The Evolution of the Islamic Polity*. Cambridge: Cambridge University Press.

———. 1987. *Meccan Trade and the Rise of Islam*. Princeton, NJ: Princeton University Press.

———. 1994a. "The First-Century Concept of *Hiǧra*." *Arabica* 41:352–87.

———. 1994b. "Were the Qays and the Yemen of the Umayyad Period Political Parties?" *Der Islam* 71:25–57.

———. 1998. "The ʿAbbāsid Abnāʾ and Sāsānid Cavalrymen." *Journal of the Royal Asiatic Society* 8 (1): 1–19.

———. 2007. "Quraysh and the Roman Army: Making Sense of the Meccan Leather Trade." *BSOAS* 70 (1): 63–88.

———. 2010. "The Religion of the Qurʾānic Pagans: God and the Lesser Deities." *Arabica* 57 (2): 151–200.

———. 2013. "The *Book of Watchers* in the Qurān." In *Exchange and Transmission across Cultural Boundaries: Philosophy, Mysticism, and Science in the Mediterranean World*, edited by H. Ben-Shammai, S. Shaked, and S. Stroumsa, 16–51. Jerusalem: Israel Academy of Sciences and Humanities.

Crone, P., and M. Hinds. 1986. *God's Caliph: Religious Authority in the First Centuries of Islam*. Cambridge: Cambridge University Press.

Cumont, F. 1909. "La plus ancienne géographie astrologique." *Klio* 9 (9): 263–73.

———. 1931. "La fin du monde selon les mages occidentaux." *Revue de l'histoire des religions* 104:29–96.

Dabrowa, E. 1984. "Le programme de la politique en Occident des derniers Arsacides." *Iranica Antiqua* 19:149–65.

Dahl, R. A. 1975. "Democratic Regimes." In *Handbook of Political Science*, vol. 3, *Macropolitical Theory*, edited by F. I. Greenstein and N. W. Polsby. Reading, MA: Addison-Wesley.

Dale, S. F. 2006. "Ibn Khaldun: The Last Greek and the First Annaliste Historian." *International Journal of Middle East Studies* 38 (3): 431–51.

Daniel, E. L. 1979. *The Political and Social History of Khurasan under Abbasid Rule, 747–820*. Minneapolis, MN: Bibliotheca Islamica.

———. 1996. "The *'Ahl al-Taqādum'* and the Problem of the Constituency of the Abbasid Revolution in the Merv Oasis." *Journal of Islamic Studies* 7 (2): 150–79.

———. 1997. "Arabs, Persians, and the Advent of the Abbasids Reconsidered." *JAOS* 117 (3): 542–48.

Danto, A. C. 1985. *Narration and Knowledge: Including the Integral Text of Analytical Philosophy of History*. New York: Columbia University Press.

Dardess, J. W. 2003. "Did the Mongols Matter?" In *The Song-Yuan-Ming Transition in Chinese History*, edited by P. J. Smith and R. von Glahn, 111–34. Cambridge, MA: Harvard University Press.

Daryaee, T. 2007. "Imitatio Alexandri and Its Impact on the Late Arsacid and Early Sasanian and Middle Persian." *Plectrum* 12:89–97.

———. 2014. "Historiography in Late Antique Iran." In *Perceptions of Iran: History, Myths and Nationalism from Medieval Persia to the Islamic Republic*, edited by A. M. Ansari, 65–76. London: I. B. Tauris.

Deák, I. 1992. "Survivors." *New York Review of Books* 39 (5): 8.

de Bary, W. T. 1981. *Neo-Confucian Orthodoxy and the Learning of the Mind-and-Heart*. New York: Columbia University Press.

Debevoise, N. C. 1938. *A Political History of Parthia*. Chicago: University of Chicago Press.

de La Vaissière, É. 2007. *Samarcande et Samarra: Élites d'Asie centrale dans l'empire Abbasside*. Paris: Association pour l'avancement des études iraniennes.

DeNardo, J. 1985. *Power in Numbers: The Political Strategy of Protest and Rebellion*. Princeton, NJ: Princeton University Press.

Dennett, D. C. 1950. *Conversion and the Poll Tax in Early Islam*. Harvard Historical Monographs, vol. 22. Cambridge, MA: Harvard University Press.

Denny, F. M. 1977. "*Umma* in the Constitution of Medina." *JNES* 36 (1): 37–47.

de Rachewiltz, I. 1983. "Turks in China under the Mongols: A Preliminary Investigation of Turco-Mongol Relations in the 13th and 14th Centuries." In *China among Equals: The Middle Kingdom and Its Neighbors, 10th–14th Centuries*, 281–310. Berkeley: University of California Press.

———. 1993. "Yeh-Lü Ch'u-Ts'ai (1189–1243), Yeh-Lü Chu (1221–1285)." In *In the Service of the Khan: Eminent Personalities of the Early Mongol-Yüan Period (1200–1300)*, edited by I. de Rachewiltz, H. L. Chan, C. Hsiao, and P. W. Geier, 136–75. Wiesbaden: Harrassowitz.

Didascalia Apostilorum. 1929. Edited and translated by R. H. Connolly. Oxford: Clarendon Press.

Dio, Cassius. 1927. *Dio's Roman History*. Loeb Classical Library, vol. 9. Cambridge, MA: Harvard University Press.

Di Palma, G. 1991. "Legitimation from the Top to Civil Society: Politico-cultural Change in Eastern Europe." *World Politics* 44 (1): 49–80.

Djaït, H. 1989. *La grande discorde: Religion et politique dans l'Islam des origines*. Paris: Gallimard.

Donner, F. M. 1981. *The Early Islamic Conquests*. Princeton, NJ: Princeton University Press.

———. 1986. "The Formation of the Islamic State." *JAOS* 106 (2): 283–96.

———. 1993. "The Growth of Military Institutions in the Early Caliphate and Their Relation to Civilian Authority." *Al-qantara: Revista de estudios árabes* 14:311–26.

———. 1998. *Narratives of Islamic Origins: The Beginnings of Islamic Historical Writing*. Princeton, NJ: Darwin Press.

———. 2010. *Muhammad and the Believers at the Origins of Islam*. Cambridge, MA: Harvard University Press.

Dostal, W. 1991. "Mecca before the Time of the Prophet—Attempt of an Anthropological Interpretation." *Der Islam* 68 (2): 193–231.

Doyle, W. 1991. "Counter-Revolution." In *Revolution and Counter-Revolution*, edited by E. E. Rice. Oxford: Basil Blackwell.

Drinkwater, J. F. 1983. *Roman Gaul: The Three Provinces, 58 BC–AD 260*. Ithaca, NY: Cornell University Press.

Duncan-Jones, R. 1967. "Equestrian Rank in the Cities of the African Provinces under the Principate: An Epigraphic Survey." *Papers of the British School at Rome* 35:147–88.

Durand-Guédy. 2013. "Ruling from the Outside: A New Perspective on Early Turkish Kingship in Iran." In *Every Inch a King: Comparative Studies on Kings and Kingship in the Ancient and Medieval Worlds*, edited by L. G. Mitchell and C. Melville, 325–42. Boston: E. J. Brill.

Eddy, S. K. 1961. *The King Is Dead: Studies in the Near Eastern Resistance to Hellenism*. Lincoln: University of Nebraska Press.

Edwards, L. 1927. *The Natural History of Revolution*. Chicago: University of Chicago Press.

Eickelman, D. F. 1967. "Musyalima: An Approach to the Social Anthropology of Seventh Century Arabia." *JESHO* 10:17–52.

Eisenstadt, S. N. 1978. *Revolution and the Transformation of Societies: A Comparative Study of Civilizations*. New York: Free Press.

———. 2006. *The Great Revolutions and the Civilizations of Modernity*. Leiden: E. J. Brill.

Elman, B. A. 1997. "Formation of 'Dao Learning' as Imperial Ideology during the Early Ming Dynasty." In *Culture and State in Chinese History: Conventions, Accommodations and Critiques*, edited by T. Huters, R. B. Wong, and P. Yu, 58–82. Stanford, CA: Stanford University Press.

Emerton, E., ed. (1932) 1969. *The Correspondence of Pope Gregory VII: Selected Letters from the Registrum*. New York: W. W. Norton.

Endicott-West, E. 1989. *Mongolian Rule in China: Local Administration in the Yuan Dynasty*. Harvard-Yenching Institute Monograph Series, vol. 29. Cambridge, MA: Harvard University Press.

Erder, Y. 1990. "The Origins of the Name Idris in the Qur'ān: A Study of the Influence of Qumran Literature on Early Islam." *JNES* 49 (4): 339–50.

———. 1994. "The Karaites' Sadducee Dilemma." *Israel Oriental Studies* 14:195–226.

Erdmann, C. 1935. *Die Entstehung des Kreuzzuggedankens*. Stuttgart: Kohlhammer.

Fahd, T. 1989. "Rapports de la Mekke préislamique avec l'Abyssinie: Le cas des *ahâbîš*." In *L'Arabie préislamique et son environnement historique et culturel*, edited by T. Fahd, 537–48. Strasbourg: E. J. Brill.

Fallers, L. 1968. "Political Anthropology and Anthropological Study of African Politics." In *State and Society*, edited by R. Bendix et al. Boston: Little, Brown.

Farhi, F. 1990. *States and Urban-Based Revolutions: Iran and Nicaragua*. Urbana: University of Illinois Press.

Farquhar, D. M. 1990. *The Government of China under Mongolian Rule: A Reference Guide*. Stuttgart: F. Steiner Verlag.

Fears, J. R. 1977. *Princeps a Diis Electus: The Divine Election of the Emperor as a Political Concept at Rome*. Rome: American Academy in Rome.

Ferdawsi. 1995 (AH 1374). *Shāhnāma*. Moscow ed. 8 vols. Tehran: Nashr-e Dād.

Finley, M. I. 1986. "Revolution in Antiquity." In *Revolution in History*, edited by R. Potter and M. Teich, 47–60. Cambridge: Cambridge University Press.

Flaig, E. 1992. *Den Kaiser herausfordern: Die Usurpation im römischen Reich*. Frankfurt: Campus.

Fletcher, J. 1979–80. "Turco-Mongolian Monarchic Tradition in the Mongol Empire." *Harvard Ukrainian Studies* 3–4:236–51.

———. 1986. "The Mongols: Ecological and Social Perspectives." *Harvard Journal of Asiatic Studies* 46 (1): 11–50.

Fliche, A. 1946. *La réforme grégorien et la reconquête chrétienne (1057–1123)*. Paris: Bloud et Gay.

Foran, J. 1993. "Theories of Revolution Revisited? Toward a Fourth Generation." *Sociological Theory* 11 (1): 1–20.

———. 2002. *Taking Power: On the Origins of Third World Revolutions*. Cambridge: Cambridge University Press.

Foster, B. R. 1993. "Management and Administration in the Sargonic Period." In *Akkad: The First World Empire; Structure, Ideology, Traditions*, edited by M. Liverani, 25–40. Padua: Sargon.

Fowden, G. 1993. *Empire to Commonwealth: Consequences of Monotheism in Late Antiquity*. Princeton, NJ: Princeton University Press.

———. 2014. *Before and after Muḥammad: The First Millennium Refocused*. Princeton, NJ: University Press.

Fragmenta historicorum arabicorum, et quidem pars tertia operis Kitábo 'l-Oyun wa 'l-hadáïk fi akhbári. 1871. Edited by M. J. de Goeje. Leiden: E. J. Brill.

Fragner, B. G. 1997. "Iran under Il-Khanid Rule in a World-Historical Perspective." In *Iran face à la domination mongole*, edited by D. Aigle, 123–31. Tehran: Institut français de recherche en Iran.

Franke, H. 1978. *From Tribal Chieftain to Universal Emperor and God: The Legitimation of the Yuan Dynasty*. Munich: Verlag der Baerischen Akademie der Wissenschaften / C. H. Beck.

———. 1982. "Wang Yun (1227–1304): A Transmitter of Chinese Values." In *Yuan Thought: Chinese Thought and Religion under the Mongols*, edited by H. L. Chan and W. T. de Bary, 152–93. New York: Columbia University Press.

———. 1993. "Ahmad (?–1282)." In *In the Service of the Khan: Eminent Personalities of the Early Mongol-Yüan Period (1200–1300)*, edited by I. de Rachewiltz, H. L. Chan, C. Hsiao, and P. W. Geier, 539–57. Wiesbaden: Harrassowitz.

Franke, H., and D. Twitche, eds. 1994. *The Cambridge History of China*. Vol. 6, *Alien Regimes and Border States, 907–1368*. Cambridge: Cambridge University Press.

Frankfort, H. 1948. *Kingship and the Gods: A Study of Ancient Near Eastern Religion as the Integration of Society and Nature*. Chicago: University of Chicago Press.

———. 1951. *The Birth of Civilization in the Near East*. New York: Barnes and Noble.

Frend, W. H. C. 1974. "Open Questions concerning the Christians and the Roman Empire in the Age of the Severi." *Journal of Theological Studies*, n.s., 25, pt. 2: 333–51.

———. 1984. *The Rise of Christianity*. Philadelphia: Fortress Press.

Friedrich, C. J. 1966. "An Introductory Note on Revolution." In *Revolution*, edited by C. J. Friedrich. Nomos, vol. 8. New York: Atherton Press.

Frye, R. N. 1962. *The Heritage of Persia*. London: Weidenfeld and Nicolson.

———. 1975. "The Rise of the Sasanians and the Uppsala School." *Acta Iranica* 4:239–46.

———. 1984. *The History of Ancient Iran*. Munich: C. H. Beck.

Furet, F. 1981. *Interpreting the French Revolution*. Cambridge: Cambridge University Press.

Fustel de Coulanges, N. D. (1864) 1900. *The Ancient City: A Study of the Religion, Laws, and Institutions of Greece and Rome*. Boston: Lee and Shepard.

Gabba, E. 1976. *Republican Rome, the Army, and the Allies*. Translated by P. J. Cuff. Berkeley: University of California Press.

Gabrieli, F. 1935a. *Il califfato di Hishām*. Alexandria, Egypt: Société royal d'archéologie.

———. 1935b. "Al-Walīd ibn Yazīd: Il califfo e il poeta." *Rivista degli studi orientali* 15:1–64.

Gadd, C. J. 1971a. "The Cities of Babylonia." In *The Cambridge Ancient History*, vol. 1, pt. 2, *Early History of the Middle East*, ch. 13. 3rd ed. Cambridge: Cambridge University Press.

———. 1971b. "The Dynasty of Agade and the Gutian Invasion," In *The Cambridge Ancient History*, vol. 1, pt. 2, *Early History of the Middle East*, ch. 19. 3rd ed. Cambridge: Cambridge University Press.

Gallie, W. B. 1968. *Philosophy and the Historical Understanding*. 2nd ed. New York: Schocken.

Gardizi, Abu Sa'id 'Abd al-Hayy b. Zahhāk. 1984 (AH 1363). *Tārikh-e Gardizi*. Edited by 'Abd al-Hayy Habibi. Tehran: Donya-ye Ketāb.

Gaudemet, J. 1982. *Institutions de l'antiquité*. 2nd ed. Paris: Sirey.

Gellner, E. 1995. "Fundamentalism as a Comprehensive System: Soviet Marxism and Islamic Fundamentalism Compared." In *Fundamentalisms Comprehended*, edited by M. Marty and R. S. Appleby, 277–87. Chicago: University of Chicago Press.

Gelzer, M. (1912) 1969. *The Roman Nobility*. Translated by R. Seager. Reprint, Oxford: Basil Blackwell.

Gerth, H. H. and Mills, C. W. 1948. Introduction to *From Max Weber: Essays in Sociology*, edited by H. H. Gerth and C. W. Mills. London: Routledge and Kegan Paul.

Gesta Francorum et aliorum Hierosolymitanorum / The Deeds of the Franks and the Other Pilgrims to Jerusalem. 1962. Edited by Rosalind Hill. Oxford: Clarendon Press.

Ghedini, F. 1984. *Giulia Domna tra Oriente e Occidente: Le fonti archeologiche*. Rome: La Fenice.

Ghirshman, R. 1971. *Persia: From the Origins to Alexander the Great*. London: Thames and Hudson.

Gibbon, E. W. 1932. *Decline and Fall of the Roman Empire*. 2 vols. New York: Modern Library.

Gil, M. 1987. "The Medinan Opposition to the Prophet." *JSAI* 10:65–96.

———. 1992. "The Creed of Abu 'Āmir." *Israel Oriental Studies* 11:9–57.

Gluckman, M. 1965. *Politics, Law and Ritual in Tribal Society*. New York: Mentor Books.

Gnoli, G. 1974. "Politique religieuse et la conception de royauté sous les Achéménides." *Acta Iranica* 2:117–90.

———. 1984. "Universalismo e nazionalismo nell'Iran del III secolo." In *Incontro di religioni in Asia tra il III et il X secolo d.C.*, edited by L. Lanciotti, 31–54. Florence: Leo S. Olschki Editore.

———. 1987. "Ēr Mazdēsn: Zum Begriff Iran und seiner Entstehung im 3. Jahrhundert." *Studia Iranica* 5:83–100.

———. 1989. *The Idea of Iran: An Essay on Its Origin*. Rome: Istituto italiano per il Medio ed Estremo Oriente.

———. 1990. "On Old Persian *Farnah*." In *Iranica Varia: Papers in Honor of Professor Ehsan Yarshater*. Leiden: E. J. Brill.

Göbl, R. 1971. *Sasanian Numismatics*. Braunschweig: Klinkhardt und Biermann.

Golden, P. B. 1982. "Imperial Ideology and the Sources of Political Unity amongst the Pre-Činggisid Nomads of Western Eurasia." *Archivum Eurasiae Medii Aevi* 2:37–77.

Goldfarb, J. C. 1990. "Post-totalitarian Politics: Ideology Ends Again." *Social Research* 57 (3): 533–54.

Goldfrank, W. L. 1979. "Theories of Revolution and Revolutions without Theory: The Case of Mexico." *Theory and Society* 7 (3).

Goldstone, J. A. 1982. "The Comparative and Historical Study of Revolutions." *Annual Review of Sociology* 8 (1): 187–207.

———. 1991a. "An Analytical Framework." In *Revolutions of the Late Twentieth Century*, edited by J. A. Goldstone, T. R. Gurr, and F. Moshiri, 37–51. Boulder, CO: Westview Press.

———. 1991b. *Revolutions and Rebellions in Early Modern Europe*. Berkeley: University of California Press.

———. 2001. "Toward a Fourth Generation of Revolutionary Theory." *Annual Review of Political Science* 4 (1): 139–87.

———. 2014. *Revolution: A Very Short Introduction*. Oxford: Oxford University Press.

Goodwin, J. 2005. "Revolutions and Revolutionary Movements." In *Handbook of Political Sociology*, edited by T. Janoski, R. Alford, A. Hicks, and M. A. Schwartz, 404–22. Cambridge: Cambridge University Press.

Görke, A. 2000. "Historical Tradition about al-Ḥudaybiya." In *The Biography of Muhammad: The Issue of the Sources*, edited by H. Motzki. Boston: E. J. Brill.

Gottschalk, L. 1944. "Causes of Revolution." *American Journal of Sociology* 50 (1): 1–8.

Gouldner, A. 1965. *Enter Plato: Classical Greece and the Origins of Social Theory*. New York: Basic Books.

Granovetter, M. 1978. "Threshold Models of Collective Behavior." *American Journal of Sociology* 83 (6): 1420–43.

Grant, M. 1996. *The Severans: The Changed Roman Empire*. London: Routledge.

Grant, R. M. (1970) 1990. *Augustus to Constantine: The Rise and Triumph of Christianity in the Roman World*. Reprint, San Francisco: Harper and Row.

Griffin, M. T. 1985. *Nero: The End of a Dynasty*. New Haven, CT: Yale University Press.

Gruen, E. S. 1974. *The Last Generation of the Roman Republic*. Berkeley: University of California Press.

Gurr, T. R. 1968. "Urban Disorder: Perspectives from the Comparative Study of Civil Strife." In *Riots and Rebellions: Civil Violence in the Urban Community*, edited by L. H. Masotti and D. R. Bowen. Beverly Hills, CA: Sage Publications.

———. 1980. "On the Outcome of Violent Conflict." In *Handbook of Political Conflict*, edited by T. R. Gurr. New York: Free Press.

Gyselen, R. 2008. "The Great Families in the Sasanian Empire: Some Sigillographic Evidence." In *Current Research in Sasanian Archaeology, Art and History: Proceedings of a Conference Held at Durham University, November 3–4, 2001*, edited by D. Kennet and P. Luft, 1810.107–13. Oxford: Archaeopress.

Halliday, F. 1999. *Revolution and World Politics: The Rise and Fall of the Sixth Great Power*. Durham, NC: Duke University Press.

Halperin, C. J. 1983. "Russia in the Mongol Empire in Comparative Perspective." *Harvard Journal of Asiatic Studies* 43 (1): 239–61.

Hamidullah, Muhammad. 1968. *The First Written-Constitution in the World*. 2nd ed. Lahore: Sh. Muhammad Ashraf.

Hamza Isfahāni, Abu'l-Hasan. 1844. *Ta'rikh sani muluk al-ard wa'l-anbiyā'*. Edited by I. M. E. Gottwaldt. Petropli.

Hazard, J. N. 1992. "Soviet Law Takes a Fresh Breath." *Harriman Institute Forum* 5 (6).

Heissig W. 1980. *The Religions of Mongolia*. Berkeley: University of California Press.

Henderson, M. I. 1963. "The Establishment of the *Equester Ordo*." *JRS* 53 (1–2): 61–72.

Hengel, M. 1974. *Judaism and Hellenism: Studies in Their Encounter in Palestine during the Early Hellenistic Period*. 2 vols. London: SCM Press.

Henning, W. B. 1942. "Mani's Last Journey." *BSOAS* 10 (4): 941–53.

———. 1944. "The Murder of the Magi." *Journal of the Royal Asiatic Society* 76 (3–4): 133–44.

Herodian. 1969. *History of the Empire*. Loeb Classical Library. Cambridge, MA: Harvard University Press.

Herodotus. 1972. *The Histories*. Harmondsworth, UK: Penguin.

Heuss, A. 1973. "Das Revolutionsproblem im Spiegel der antiken Geschichte." *Historisches Zeitschrift* 216 (1): 1–72.

———. 1974. "Theodor Mommsen und die revolutionäre Struktur des römisches Kaisertums." *Aufstieg und Niedergang der römischen Welt* 2 (1):77–90.

Hilali, A. 2010. "La palimpseste de San'a et la canonization du Coran: Nouveaux éléments." *Cahiers du Centre Gustave Glotz* 21:443–48.

Hinnells, J. R. 1973. "The Zoroastrian Doctrine of Salvation in the Roman World: A Study of the Oracle of Hystaspes." In *Man and His Salvation: Studies in Memory of S. G. F. Brandon*, edited by E. J. Sharpe and J. R. Hinnells. Manchester: Manchester University Press.

Hinz, W. 1933. "Schah Esma'īl II: Ein Beitrag zur Geschichte der Ṣafavīden." *Mitteilungen des Seminars für orientalische Sprachen* 36:19–100.

Hobsbawm, E. J. 1986. "Revolution." In *Revolution in History*, edited by R. Porter and M. Teich, 5–46. Cambridge: Cambridge University Press.

Hock, R. P. 1984. *The "Historia Augusta," Septimius Severus and Roman Britain: A Select Commentary of the Vita Severi*. Ann Arbor, MI: University Microfilms International.

Hodgson, M. G. 1955. *The Order of Assassins . . . : The Struggle of the Early Nizârî Ismâ'îlîs against the Islamic World*. The Hague: Mouton.

Honoré, A. M. 1962. "The Severan Lawyers: A Preliminary Survey." *Studia et Documenta Historiae et Juris* 28:162–232.

Honoré, T. 1981. *Emperors and Lawyers*. London: Duckworth Press.

———. 1982. *Ulpian*. Oxford: Clarendon Press.

———. 1994. *Emperors and Lawyers*. 2nd ed. Oxford: Clarendon Press.

Hopkins, K. 1978. *Conquerors and Slaves: Sociological Studies in Roman History*. Cambridge: Cambridge University Press.

Hopper, R. D. 1950. "The Revolutionary Process: A Frame of Reference for the Study of Revolutionary Movements." *Social Forces* 28 (3): 270–79.

Hornblower, S. 1992. "Creation and Development of Democratic Institutions in Ancient Greece." In *Democracy: The Unfinished Journey, 508 BC to AD 1993*, edited by J. Dunn, 1–16. New York: Oxford University Press.

Hosking, G. A. 1992a. "Independent Political Movements in the USSR since 1985." Lecture delivered on February 5, 1992, as reported in *At the Harriman Institute* 5 (5).

———. 1992b. "Roots of Dissolution." *New York Review of Books* 39 (1/2): 34–38.

Howe, L. L. 1942. *The Pretorian Prefect from Commodus to Diocletian (A.D. 180–305)*. Chicago: University of Chicago Press.

Hoyland, R. G. 2001. *Arabia and the Arabs from the Bronze Age to the Coming of Islam*. London: Routledge.

———. 2009. "Arab Kings, Arab Tribes and the Beginning of Arab Historical Memory in Late Roman Epigraphy." In *From Hellenism to Islam: Cultural and Linguistic Change in the Roman Near East*, edited by H. M. Cotton, R. G. Hoyland, J. J. Price, and D. J. Wasserstein, 374–400. Cambridge: Cambridge University Press.

Hsiao, C. C. 1978. *The Military Establishment of the Yuan Dynasty*. Cambridge, MA: Harvard University Council on East Asian Studies.

———. 1993. "Bayan (1236/7–1295)." In *In the Service of the Khan: Eminent Personalities of the Early Mongol-Yüan Period (1200–1300)*, edited by I. de Rachewiltz, H. L. Chan, C. Hsiao, and P. W. Geier, 584–607. Wiesbaden: Harrassowitz.

Humphreys, R. S. 1991. *Islamic History: A Framework for Inquiry*. Princeton, NJ: Princeton University Press.

Hunt, L. A. 1984. *Politics, Culture, and Class in the French Revolution*. Berkeley: University of California Press.

Huntington, S. P. 1968. *Political Order in Changing Societies*. New Haven, CT: Yale University Press.

Ibn Abi Tāhir Tayfur. OR Ms British Library Oriental Ms. Add 7473.

Ibn al-Balkhi. 1921. *Fārsnāma (The Fársnáma of Ibnu 'l-Balkhí)*. Edited by G. Le Strange. London: Luzac.

Ibn al-Kalbi. 1965. *Kitāb al-asnām*. Cairo: Dār al-Qawmīyah lil-Ṭibā'ah wa-al-Nashr.

Ibn Isfandiyār, Muḥammad Ibn al-Ḥasan. 1941 (AH 1330). *Tārikh-e Tabarestān*. Tehran: Ramazāni.

Ibn Ishāq, Muhammad. 1858–60. *Sīrat Rasūl Allāh*. Edited by F. Wüstenfeld. Göttingen. Translated by A. Guillaume as *The Life of Muhammad* (London: Oxford University Press, 1955).

Ibn Khaldun, 'Abd al-Rahmān. 1992. *Kitāb al-'ibar (Tārikh Ibn Khaldun)*. 7 vols. Beirut: Dār al-kutub al-'Ilmiyya. Vol. 1 edited and translated by F. Rosenthal as *The Muqaddimah*, 3 vols. (Princeton, NJ: Princeton University Press, 1967).

Ibn Sa'd. 1917. *Kitāb al-Tabaqāt al-Kabir (Biographien)*. Edited by E. Mittwoch and E. Sachau. 8 vols. Leiden: E. J. Brill.

Isfahani, Abu'l-Faraj al-. 1949 (AH 1368). *Maqātil al-Ṭālibiyyīn*. Cairo.

Izutsu, T. (1966) 2002. *Ethico-religious Concepts in the Qur'ān*. Montreal: McGill-Queens University Press.

Jackson, P. 1978. "The Dissolution of the Mongol Empire." *Central Asiatic Journal* 22:186–244.

Jacobsen, T. 1939. "The Assumed Conflict between the Sumerians and the Semites in Early Mesopotamian History." *Journal of the American Oriental Society* 59 (4): 485–95.

———. 1943. "Primitive Democracy in Ancient Mesopotamia." *JNES* 2 (3): 159–72.

———. 1976. *The Treasures of Darkness: A History of Mesopotamian Religion*. New Haven, CT: Yale University Press.

Janos, A. C. 1964. "Authority and Violence." In *Internal War: Problems and Approaches*, edited by H. Eckstein, 130–41. New York: Free Press of Glencoe.

Jaspers, K. 1949. *Vom Ursprung und Zeil de Geschichte*. Zurich: Artemis.

Johnson, C. A. 1962. *Peasant Nationalism and Communist Power: The Emergence of Revolutionary China, 1937–1945*. Stanford, CA: Stanford University Press.

———. 1966. *Revolutionary Change*. Boston: Little, Brown.

Jolowicz, H. F., and B. Nicholas. 1972. *Historical Introduction to the Study of Roman Law.* 3rd ed. Cambridge: Cambridge University Press.

Jones, A. H. M. 1960. *Studies in Roman Government and Law.* Oxford: Basil Blackwell.

Jones, J. M. B. 1957. "The Chronology of the Maghāzī—a Textual Survey." *BSOAS* 19 (2): 245–80.

Josephus, Flavius. 1971. *The Second Jewish Commonwealth (Being Books XII–XX of the "Jewish Antiquities").* Translated by N. N. Glatzer. New York: Schocken.

Jouvenel, B. de. 1949. *On Power: Its Nature and the History of Its Growth.* Translated by J. F. Huntington. New York: Viking Press.

Jovayni, ʿAlāʾ al-Din ʿAtā-Malek. 1911. *Tārikh-e Jahān-goshā.* Edited by M. Qazvini. 3 vols. Leiden: E. J. Brill.

Jowitt, K. 1990. "Gorbachev: Bolshevik or Menshevik?" In *Developments in Soviet Politics,* edited by S. White, A. Pravda, and Z. Y. Gitelman, 270–91. Durham, NC: Duke University Press.

Karev, Y. 2002. "La politique d'Abū Muslim dans le Māwarāʾannahr: Nouvelles données textuelles et archéologiques." *Der Islam* 79 (1): 1–46.

Kassis, H. E. 1983. *A Concordance of the Qurʾān.* Berkeley: University of California Press.

Keaveney, A. 1987. *Rome and the Unification of Italy.* London: Croom Helm.

Kedourie, E. 1991. "The Third World and the Idea of Revolution." In *Revolution and Counter-Revolution,* edited by E. E. Rice. Oxford: Basil Blackwell.

Kemezis, A. M. 2014. *Greek Narratives of the Roman Empire under the Severans: Cassius Dio, Philostratus and Herodian.* Cambridge: Cambridge University Press.

Kennedy, H. 1981. "Central Government and Provincial Élites in the Early ʿAbbāsid Caliphate." *BSOAS* 44 (1): 26–38.

Kennedy, M. D. 1999. "Contingencies and the Alternatives of 1989: Toward a Theory and Practice of Negotiated Revolution." *East European Politics and Society* 13 (2): 293–302.

Khoury, R. G. 1983. "Les sources islamiques de la 'Sîra' avant Ibn Hishâm (m. 213/834) et leur valeur historique." In *La vie du prophète Mahomet: Colloque de Strasbourg, octobre 1980.* Paris: Presses universitaires de France.

Kister, M. J. 1965. "Mecca and Tamīm (Aspects of Their Relations)." *JESHO* 8 (2): 113–63.

———. 1968a. "Al-Hīra: Notes on Its Relations with Arabia." *Arabica* 15:143–69.

———. 1968b. "*Al-tahannuth*: An Inquiry into the Meaning of a Term." *BSOAS* 31:223–36.

———. 1972. "Some Reports concerning Mecca: From Jāhiliyya to Islam." *JESHO* 15:61–93.

———. 1977. "The Battle of The Harra: Some Socio-economic Aspects." In *Studies in Honor of Gaston Wiet,* edited by M. Rosen-Ayalon, 33–49. Jerusalem: Hebrew University Press.

———. 1979. "On the Wife of the Goldsmith of Fadak and Her Progeny: A Study in Jāhili Genealogical Tradition." *Muséon* 92:321–30.

———. 1980. "*Labbayka allāhumma, labbayka*. . . : On a Monotheistic Aspect of a Jāhiliyya Practice." *JSAI* 2:33–57.

———. 1981. "'O God, Tighten Thy Grip on the Mudar . . .': Some Socio-economic and Religious Aspects of an Early *Hadīth*." *JESHO* 24 (1): 242–73.

———. 1984. ". . . *illā bihaqqihi*. . . : A Study of an Early *Hadīth*." *JSAI* 5:33–52.

———. 1986. "The Massacre of the Banu Qurayza." *JSAI* 8:61–96.

———. 1994. "Social and Religious Concepts of Authority in Islam." *JSAI* 18:84–127.

———. 2002. *Studies in Jāhiliyya and Early Islam.* Aldershot, UK: Ashgate Variorum.

Kister, M. J., and M. Hiskett. 1962. "'A Booth Like the Booth of Moses . . .': A Study of an Early Ḥadīth." *BSOAS* 25 (1): 150–55.

Knight, A. 1990a. *The Mexican Revolution*. Lincoln: University of Nebraska Press.

———. 1990b. "Social Revolution: A Latin American Perspective." *Bulletin of Latin American Research* 9 (2): 175–202.

Kornhauser, W. 1964. "Rebellion and Political Development." In *Internal War: Problems and Approaches*, edited by H. Eckstein, 142–56. New York: Free Press of Glencoe.

Koselleck, R. 1984. "Revolution. IV. Von der Frühen Neuzeit bis zur Französischen Revolution." In *Geschichtliche Grundbegriffe*, vol. 5, edited by O. Brunner, W. Conze, and R. Koselleck, 689–788. Stuttgart: Klett-Cotta.

———. 1985. *Futures Past: On the Semantics of Historical Time*. Translated by Keith Tribe. Cambridge, MA: Harvard University Press.

Kraay, C. M. 1949. "The Coinage of Vindex and Galba, A.D. 68, and the Continuity of the Augustan Principate." *Numismatic Chronicle and Journal of the Royal Numismatic Society* 9 (3/4): 129–49.

Krader, L. 1958. "Feudalism and the Tatar Polity of the Middle Ages." *Comparative Studies in Society and History* 1 (1): 76–99.

Kraminick, I. 1972. "Reflections on Revolution: Definition and Explanation in Recent Scholarship." *History and Theory* 11 (1): 26–63.

Krejčí, J. 1983. *Great Revolutions Compared: The Search for a Theory*. New York: St. Martin's Press.

Kunkel, W. 1972. *An Introduction to Roman Legal and Constitutional History*. Translated by J. M. Kelly. 2nd ed. Oxford: Clarendon Press.

Kuran, T. 1989. "Sparks and Prairie Fires: A Theory of Unanticipated Political Revolution." *Public Choice* 61 (1): 41–74.

———. 1992. "Why Revolutions Are Better Understood than Predicted: The Essential Role of Preference Falsification." *Contention* 1 (3): 199–207.

Kuttner, S. 1945. "Cardinalis: The History of a Canonical Concept." *Traditio* 3:129–214.

Ladner, G. B. 1954. "The Concepts of 'Ecclesia' and 'Christianitas' and Their Relation to the Idea of Papal 'Plenitudo Potestas' from Gregory VII to Boniface VIII." *Miscellanea Historiae Pontificae* 18:58–77.

———. 1956. "Gregory the Great and Gregory VII: A Comparison of Their Concepts of Renewal." *Viator* 4:1–26.

Lambton, A. K. S. 1988. *Continuity and Change in Medieval Persia*. Vol. 2. Albany: Bibliotheca Persica at State University of New York Press.

Lammens, H. 1910. *La république marchande de la Mecque vers l'an 600 de notre ère*. Alexandria.

Lane, G. E. 2003. *Early Mongol Rule in Thirteenth-Century Iran: A Persian Renaissance*. London: Routledge.

Langlois, J. 1981. "Political Thought in Chin-hua under Mongol Rule." In *China under Mongol Rule*, edited by J. Langlois, 137–85. Princeton, NJ: Princeton University Press.

Lapidus, I. M. 1972. "The Conversion of Egypt to Islam." *Israel Oriental Studies* 2:248–62.

———. 1988. *A History of Islamic Societies*. Berkeley: University of California Press.

Lasky, M. J. 1976. *Utopia and Revolution: On the Origins of a Metaphor*. Chicago: University of Chicago Press.

Lassner, J. 1980. *The Shaping of ʿAbbasid Rule*. Princeton, NJ: Princeton University Press.

———. 1984. "Abu Muslim al-Khurāsān." *JAOS* 104 (1): 165–75.

———. 1986a. "Abu Muslim, Son of Salit: A Skeleton in the ʿAbbasid Closet?" In *Studies in Islamic History and Civilization in Honour of Professor David Ayalon*, edited by M. Sharon. Leiden: E. J. Brill.

———. 1986b. *Islamic Revolution and Historical Memory: An Inquiry into the Art of ʿAbbasid Apologetics*. New Haven, CT: American Oriental Society.

———. 1989. "The ʿAbbasid *Dawla*: An Essay on the Concept of Revolution in Early Islam." In *Tradition and Innovation in Late Antiquity*, edited by F. M. Clover and R. S. Humphreys, 251–55. Madison: University of Wisconsin Press.

Lattimore, O. 1962. *Inner Asian Frontiers of China*. Boston: Beacon Press.

Lattimore, R. 1960. *The Greek Lyrics*. Chicago: University of Chicago Press.

Lawson, G. 2005. *Negotiated Revolutions: The Czech Republic, South Africa and Chile*. Aldershot, UK: Ashgate.

———. 2016. "Within and Beyond the 'Fourth Generation' of Revolutionary Theory." *Sociological Theory* 34 (2): 106–27.

———. 2017. "A Global Historical Sociology of Revolution." In *Global Historical Sociology*, edited by J. Go and G. Lawson, 76–98. Cambridge: Cambridge University Press.

Lecker, M. 1993. "Idol Worship in Pre-Islamic Medina (Yathrib)." *Le muséon* 106:331–46.

———. 1995. *Muslims, Jews, and Pagans: Studies on Early Islamic Medina*. Leiden: E. J. Brill.

———. 1997. "Zayd b. Thabit, 'a Jew with two sidelocks': Judaism and Literacy in Pre-Islamic Medina (Yathrib)." *JNES* 56 (4): 259–73.

———. 2000. "Did the Quraysh Conclude a Treaty with the Ansār prior to the Hijra?" In *The Biography of Muhammad*, edited by H. Motzki, 157–69. Leiden: E. J. Brill.

———. 2002. "Levying of Taxes for the Sasanians in Pre-Islamic Medina." *JSAI* 27:109–26.

———. 2004. *The "Constitution of Medina": Muhammad's First Legal Document*. Princeton, NJ: Darwin Press.

———. 2014. "Three Parties for a Single Pact." *Oasis* 19:100–106.

Lenin, V. I. 1936–38. *Selected Works*. 12 vols. London: Lawrence and Wishart.

Levi, M. A. 1938a. "La legge dell'iscrizione C.I.L. VI,930" (*Lex de potestate Vespasiani*). *Athenaeum* 26:85–95.

———. 1938b. "I principii dell'imperio di Vespasiano." *Rivista di filologia* 16:1–12.

Levy, R., trans. 1967. *Firdawsī's "The Epic of Kings": "Shāhnāma," the National Epic of Persia*. Chicago: University of Chicago Press.

Lewis, N., and M. Reinhold, eds. 1951. *Roman Civilization*. 2 vols. New York: Columbia University Press.

Lintott A. 1968. *Violence in Republican Rome*. Oxford: Clarendon Press.

———. 1982. *Violence, Civil Strife, and Revolution in the Classical City, 750–330 BC*. Baltimore, MD: Johns Hopkins University Press.

Linz, J. J. 1975. "Totalitarian and Authoritarian Regimes." In *Handbook of Political Science*, vol. 3, *Macropolitical Theory*, edited by F. I. Greenstein and N. W. Polsby. Reading, MA: Addison-Wesley.

Liu, J. T. C. 1988. *China Turning Inward: Intellectual-Political Changes in the Early Twelfth Century*. Cambridge, MA: Harvard University East Asian Studies.

Liverani, M., ed. 1993. "Models and Actualization: The Kings of Akkad in the Historical Tradition." In *Akkad: The First World Empire; Structure, Ideology, Traditions*, edited by M. Liverani, 41–68. Padua: Sargon.

Lowick, N. M. 1979. "Une monnaie ʿAlide d'al-Basrah date de 145 H (762–3 après J.-C.)." *Revue numismatique*, 6 ser., 218–24.

Lucrezi, F. 1982. *Leges super principem: La "Monarchia costituzionale" di Vespasiano*. Naples: Pubblicazioni della Facolta giuridica dell'Universita di Napoli.

Lukonin, V. G. 1983. "Political, Social and Administrative Institutions: Taxes and Trade." In *The Cambridge History of Iran*, vol. 3.2, *The Seleucid, Parthian and Sasanian Periods*, 681–746. Cambridge: Cambridge University Press.

Luschey, H. 1987. "Ardašir I. Rock Reliefs." In *Encyclopaedia Iranica*, vol. 2, edited by E. Yarshater, 377–80. Boston: Routledge and Kegan Paul.

Lynch, J. 1973. *The Spanish American Revolutions, 1808–1826*. New York: W. W. Norton.

MacIver, R. M. (1942) 1964. *Social Causation*. Reprint, New York: Harper and Row.

———. 1948. *The Web of Government*. New York: Macmillan.

MacKenzie, D. N. 1979. "Māni's *Šābuhragān*." *BSOAS* 42:500–534.

———. 1980. "Māni's *Šābuhragān*." *BSOAS* 43:288–310.

Madelung, W. 1965. *Der Imam al-Qāsim Ibn Ibrāhim und die Glaubenslehre der Zaiditen*. Berlin: Walter de Gruyter.

———. 1982. "The Early Murji'a in Khurasan and Transoxania and the Spread of Hanafism." *Der Islam* 59:32–39.

———. 1986. "Has the *Hijra* Come to an End?" *Revue des études islamiques* 54:225–37.

———. 1988. *Religious Trends in Early Islamic Iran*. Vol. 4. Albany: State University of New York Press.

———. 1997. *The Succession to Muhammad: A Study of the Early Caliphate*. Cambridge: Cambridge University Press.

Mahdi, M. 1957. *Ibn Khaldun's Philosophy of History*. Chicago: University of Chicago Press.

Maitland, F. W. 1898. *Roman Canon Law in the Church of England*. London: Methuen.

Malandra, W. W. 1983. *Introduction to Ancient Iranian Religion: Readings from the Avesta and the Achaemenid Inscriptions*. Minneapolis: University of Minnesota Press.

Mann, M. 1986. *The Sources of Social Power*. 2 vols. Cambridge: Cambridge University Press.

Manz, B. F. 1983. "The Ulus Chaghatay before and after Temür's Rise to Power." *Central Asiatic Journal* 27 (1–2): 79–100.

———. 1988. "Tamerlane and the Symbolism of Sovereignty." *Iranian Studies* 21 (1–2): 105–22.

———. 2010. "The Rule of the Infidels: The Mongols and the Islamic World." In *The New Cambridge History of Islam*, vol. 3, *The Eastern Islamic World, Eleventh to Eighteenth Centuries*, edited by D. O. Morgan and A. Reid, 128–68. Cambridge: Cambridge University Press.

Mao Tse-tung. 1970. *Papers*. Edited by J. Ch'en. New York: Oxford University Press.

Mashkur, M. J. 1948 (AH 1327). "Sondbādh." *Pashutan* 1 (7): 31–34.

Mas'udi, Abu'l-'Ali b. al-Ḥusayn al-. (1894) 1967. *Al-Tanbih wa'l-Ishrāf*. Reprint, Leiden: Brill.

———. 1970. *Muruj al-Dhahab wa Ma'din al-Jawhar*. Edited by C. Pellat. 11 vols. Beirut.

Matthew, D. 1992. *The Norman Kingdom of Sicily*. New York: Cambridge University Press.

McDaniel, T. 1978. "Meaning and Comparative Concepts." *Theory and Society* 6 (1): 93–117.

McNeill, W. H. 1963. *The Rise of the West*. New York: Mentor Books.

Meeks, B. 1993. *Caribbean Revolutions and Revolutionary Theory*. London: Macmillan.

Meier, C. 1984. "Revolution II. 'Revolution' in der Antike." In *Geschichtliche Grundbegriffe*, vol. 5, edited by O. Brunner, W. Conze, and R. Koselleck, 656–70. Stuttgart: Klett-Cotta.

Mélamède, G. 1934. *The Meetings at al-'Akaba*. Uppsala: A.-B. Lundequistska Bokhandeln.

Mélikoff, I. 1962. *Abu Muslim: Le "porte-hache" du Khorassan dans la tradition épique turco-iranienne*. Paris: Librairie d'Amerique et d'Orient Adrien Maisonneuve.

Melville, C. 2006. "The *Keshig* in Iran: The Survival of the Royal Mongol Household." In *Beyond the Legacy of Genghis Khan*, edited by L. Komaroff, 135–66. Leiden: E. J. Brill.

———. 2013. "The Royal Image in Mongol Iran." In *Every Inch a King: Comparative Studies on Kings and Kingship in the Ancient and Medieval Worlds*, edited by L. G. Mitchell and C. Melville, 343–69. Boston: E. J. Brill.

Menasce, P. J. de. 1948. *Arabische Philosophie*. Bern: Francke.

Michalowski, P. 1987. "Charisma and Control: On the Continuity and Change in Early Mesopotamian Bureaucratic Systems." In *The Organization of Power: Aspects of Bureaucracy in the Ancient Near East*, edited by M. Gibson and R. Biggs, 45–57. Chicago: Oriental Institute.

———. 1993. "Memory and Deed: The Historiography of the Political Expansion of the Akkad State." In *Akkad: The First World Empire; Structure, Ideology, Traditions*, edited by M. Liverani, 69–90. Padua: Sargon.

Miles, G. C. 1938. *The Numismatic History of Rayy*. Vol. 2. New York: American Numismatic Society.

———. 1957. "Some Arab-Sasanian and Related Coins." *A.N.S. Museum Notes* 7:187–209.

Millar, F. 1964. *A Study of Cassius Dio*. Oxford: Clarendon Press.

———. 1971. "Paul of Samosata, Zonobia and Aurelan: The Church, Local Culture and Political Allegiance in Third-Century Syria." *JRS* 61:1–17.

———. 1987. "Empire, Community and Culture in the Roman Near East." *Journal of Jewish Studies* 38:143–64.

———. 1993. *The Roman Near East, 31 BC–337 AD*. Cambridge, MA: Harvard University Press.

Millward, W. G. 1964. "The Adaptation of Men to Their Time: An Historical Essay by al-Ya'qubi." *JAOS* 84:329–44.

Mirbt, C. 1894. *Die Publizistik im Zeitalter Gregors VII*. Leipzig.

Momigliano, A. 1934. "Nero." In *The Cambridge Ancient History*, vol. 10, *The Augustan Empire, 43 BC–69 AD*. Cambridge: Cambridge University Press.

———. (1934) 1961. *Claudius: The Emperor and His Achievement*. Translated by W. D. Hogarth. Reprint, New York: Barnes and Noble.

———. 1975. *Alien Wisdom: The Limits of Hellenization*. Cambridge: Cambridge University Press.

———. 1977. *Essays in Ancient and Modern Historiography*. Oxford: Basil Blackwell.

Mommsen, T. 1854–56. *The History of Rome*. 3 vols. Glencoe, UK: Free Press.

———. 1887. *Roemisches Staatsrecht*. Vol. 2.2. 3rd ed. Leipzig.

———. 1965. "Der letzte Kampf der römischen Republik." In *Gesammelte Schriften*, vol. 4, *Historische Schriften, I*. Berlin: Weidmannsche Verlagsbuchhandlung.

———. 1968. *The Provinces of the Roman Empire*. Translated and edited by T. R. S. Broughton. Chicago: University of Chicago Press.

Monneret de Villard, U. 1948. "'Aksum e i quattro re del mondo." *Annali Lateranensi* 12:125–80.

Morgan, D. O. 2005. "The 'Great Yasa of Chinggis Khan' Revisited." In *Mongols, Turks, and Others: Eurasian Nomads and the Sedentary World*, edited by D. O. Morgan, R. Amitai-Preiss, and M. Biran, 291–308. Leiden: E. J. Brill.

———. 2007. *The Mongols*. Oxford: Blackwell.

Mørkholm, O. 1989. "Antiochus IV." In *The Cambridge History of Judaism*, vol. 2, *The Hellenistic Age*, edited by W. D. Davies and L. Finkelstein. Cambridge: Cambridge University Press.

Morony, M. G. 1984. *Iraq after the Muslim Conquest*. Princeton, NJ: Princeton University Press.

———. 1997. "Sasanids." In *Encyclopedia of Islam*, 9.70–83. Leiden: E. J. Brill.

Mosca, G. 1939. *The Ruling Class*. Translated by H. D. Kahn. Edited by A. Livingston. New York: McGraw-Hill. (English translation of *Elementi di scienza politica*.)

Mosca, P. G. 1986. "Ugarit and Daniel 7: A Missing Link." *Biblica* 67:496–517.

Moscati, S. 1947. "La rivolta di 'Abd al-Ǧabbār contro il califfo al-Manṣūr." *Rendiconti Lincei*, ser. 8, 2:613–15.

———. 1949–50. "Studi su Abu Muslim." *Rendiconti Lincei*, ser. 8, 4:323–35, 474–95.

———. 1950. "Per una storia dell'antica 'ši'a." *Rivista degli studi orientali* 30:251–67.

———. 1950–51. "Studi su Abu Muslim." *Rendiconti Lincei*, ser. 8, 5:89–105.

———. 1952. "Il testamento di Abu Hāšim." *Rivista degli studi orientali* 27:28–46.

Mosig-Walburg, K. 1982. *Die Frühen sasanidischen Könige als Vertreter und Förderer der zarathustrischen Religion: Eine Untersuchung der zeitgenössischen Quellen*. Frankfurt am Main: P. Lang.

Mostawfi, Hamdallāh. 2000 (AH 1389). *Zafar-nāma*. Vol. 8, *Qesm-e Soltāniyya*. Tehran: Pazhuheshgah-e ʿOlum-e Ensāni va Motāleʿāt-e Farhangi.

Mote, F. W. 1999. *Imperial China, 900–1800*. Cambridge, MA: Harvard University Press.

Mottahedeh, R. 1975. "The Abbasid Caliphate in Iran." In *The Cambridge History of Iran*, 4.57–89. Cambridge: Cambridge University Press.

Motyl, A. J. 1991. "Russian Hegemony and Non-Russian Insecurity: Foreign Policy Dilemmas of the USSR's Successor States." *Harriman Institute Forum* 5 (4).

———. 1999. *Revolutions, Nations, Empires: Conceptual Limits and Theoretical Possibilities*. New York: Columbia University Press.

Muller, E. N., and K.-D. Opp. 1986. "Rational Choice and Rebellious Collective Action." *American Political Science Review* 80 (2): 471–87.

Murphy-O'Connor, J. 1974. "The Essenes and Their History." *Revue biblique* 81:215–44.

———. 1976. "Demetrius I and the Teacher of Righteousness (I *Macc.*, x, 25–45)." *Revue biblique* 83:400–420.

Musset, A. de. 1991. *Lorrenzaccio*. Paris: Larousse.

Nagel, T. 1970. "Ein früher Bericht über den Aufstand von Muḥammad b. ʿAbdallāh im Jahre 145." *Der Islam* 46 (1): 227–62.

Nakhjavāni, Muḥammad ibn Hindūshāh. 1964. *Dastur al-Kāb fi taʿyyin al-marāteb*. Moscow: Nayk.

Neusner, J. 1963. "Parthian Political Ideology." *Iranica Antiqua* 3:40–59.

Neuwirth, A. 2006. "Structure, Linguistic and Literary Form." In *The Cambridge Companion to the Qurʾān*, edited by J. D. McAuliffe, 97–114. Cambridge: Cambridge University Press.

Newby, G. D. 1971. "Observations about an Early Judaeo-Arabic." *Jewish Quarterly Review* 61 (3): 212–21.

———. 1988. *A History of the Jews of Arabia*. Columbia: University of South Carolina Press.

Nicolas, É. P. 1979. *De Néron à Vespasien*. 2 vols. Paris: Les belles lettres.

Nicolet, C. 1967. *Les Gracques; ou, Crise agraire et révolution à Rome*. Collection Archives, 33. Paris: Julliard.

———. 1974. *L'ordre équestre à l'époque républicaine (312–43 av. J.-C.)*. 2 vols. Paris: Éditions de Boccard.

Nicols, J. 1978. *Vespasian and the Partes Flavianae*. Wiesbaden: Franz Steiner Verlag.

Nöldeke, T. (1879) 1973. *Geschichte der Perser und Araber zur Zeit der Sasaniden: Aus d. arab. Chronik des Tabari*. Leyden: E. J. Brill.

Noth, A., and L. I. Conrad. 1994. *The Early Arabic Historical Tradition: A Source-Critical Study*. Princeton, NJ: Darwin Press.

Oberschall, A. 1978. "Theories of Social Conflict." *Annual Review of Sociology* 4 (1): 291–315.

Oliver, J. H. 1978. Review of *Die Constitutio Antoniniana und Papyrus Gissensis 40.1*, by Hartmut Wolff. *American Journal of Philology* 99 (3): 403–8.

———. 1989. *Greek Constitutions of Early Roman Emperors*. Philadelphia: American Philosophical Society.

Omar, F. 1969. *The 'Abbasid Caliphate, 132/750–170/786*. Baghdad.

———. 1976. *'Abbasiyyat: Studies in the History of the Early 'Abbasids*. Baghdad: University of Baghdad.

Oppenheim, L. 1964. *Ancient Mesopotamia: Portrait of a Dead Civilization*. Chicago: University of Chicago Press.

Ort, L. J. R. 1967. *Mani: A Religio-historical Description of His Personality*. Leiden: E. J. Brill.

Ostrowski, D. 1990. "The Mongol Origins of Muscovite Political Institutions." *Slavic Review* 49 (4): 525–42.

Pareto, V. (1917–19) 1968. *Œuvres completes*, vol. 12, *Traité de sociologie générale*. Reprint, Geneva: Librairie Droz.

Parker, G. 1988. *The Military Revolution: Military Innovation and the Rise of the West, 1500–1800*. Cambridge: Cambridge University Press.

Parsons, T. 1966. *Societies: Evolutionary and Comparative Perspectives*. Englewood Cliffs, NJ: Prentice-Hall.

Paruck, F. D. J. 1924. *Sāsānian Coins*. Bombay: Times Press.

Payne, R. 2013. "Cosmology and the Expansion of the Iranian Empire." *Past and Present* 220 (1): 3–33.

———. 2014. "The Reinvention of Iran: The Sasanian Empire and the Huns." In *The Cambridge Companion to the Age of Attila*, edited by M. Maas, 282–99. Cambridge: Cambridge University Press.

Pellat, C., ed. 1969. *The Life and Works of Jāḥiẓ*. Berkeley: University of California Press.

Perikhanian, A. 1983. "Iranian Society and Law." In *The Cambridge History of Iran*, edited by E. Yarshater, vol. 3.2, *The Seleucid, Parthian and Sasanian Periods*, 627–80. Cambridge: Cambridge University Press.

Perry, J. W. 1966. *Lord of the Four Quarters: Myths of the Royal Father*. New York: G. Braziller.

Peters, F. E. 1994. *Muhammad and the Origins of Islam*. Albany: State University of New York Press.

Petrushevsky, I. P. 1970. "Rashid al-Din's Conception of the State." *Central Asiatic Journal* 14:148–62.

Pettee, G. 1966. "Revolution—Typology and Process." In *Revolution*, edited by C. J. Friedrich. *Nomos*, vol. 8. New York: Atherton Press.

Pigulevskaja, N. 1963. *Les villes de l'état iranien aux époques parthe et sassanide*. Paris: Mouton.

Pirenne, H. 1957. *Mohammed and Charlemagne*. Cleveland: Meridian Books.

Pizzorno, A. 1987. "Politics Unbound." In *Changing Boundaries of the Political*, edited by C. S. Maier, 27–62. Cambridge: Cambridge University Press.

———. 1994. *Le radici della politica assoluta e altri saggi*. Milan: Feltrinelli.

Plato. 1941. *The Republic*. Edited by F. M. Cornford. Oxford: Clarendon Press.

Plutarch. 1970. *De Iside et Osiride*. Edited and translated by J. G. Griffiths. Bangor: University of Wales Press.

Poggi, G. 1990. *The State: Its Nature, Development and Prospects*. Cambridge: Polity Press.

Polybius. 1962. *The Histories of Polybius*. Translated by E. S. Shuckburgh. Edited by F. W. Walbank. 2 vols. Bloomington: Indiana University Press.

Pourshariati, P. 2008. *Decline and Fall of the Sasanian Empire: The Sasanian-Parthian Confederacy and the Arab Conquest of Iran*. London: I. B. Tauris.

Prévite-Orton, C. W. 1926. "The Italian Cities till c. 1200." In *The Cambridge Medieval History*, vol. 5, *Contest of Empire and Papacy*, edited by J. R. Tanner, C. W. Prévite-Orton, and Z. N. Brooke, 208–41. Cambridge: Cambridge at the University Press.

Pritchard, J. B., ed. 1955. *Ancient Near Eastern Texts Relating to the Old Testament, with Supplement*. 2nd ed. Princeton, NJ: Princeton University Press.

Puech, E. 1994. "Messianism, Resurrection, and Eschatology at Qumran and in the New Testament." In *The Community and the Renewed Covenant*, edited by E. C. Ulrich and J. C. VanderKam, 235–56. Notre Dame, IN: University of Notre Dame Press.

Qādi, W. al-, 1993. "Early State Letters: The Question of Authenticity." In *The Byzantine and Early Islamic Near East*, edited by A. Cameron and L. I. Conrad. Princeton, NJ: Darwin Press.

Raaflaub, K. 2005. "Polis, 'the Political,' and Political Thought: New Departures in Ancient Greece, c. 800–500 BCE." In *Axial Civilizations and World History*, edited by J. P. Arnason, S. N. Eisenstadt, and B. Wittrock, 253–83. Leiden: E. J. Brill.

Rabin, C. 1957. *Qumran Studies*. Oxford: Oxford University Press.

Rad, G. von. 1967. *The Message of the Prophets*. San Francisco, CA: HarperCollins.

Radkau, J. 2009. *Max Weber: A Biography*. Cambridge, UK: Polity Press.

Ragin, C. C. 1987. *The Comparative Method*. Berkeley: University of California Press.

Rahman, F. 1976. "Pre-foundations of the Muslim Community in Mecca." *Studia Islamica* 43:5–24.

Rajabzāda, H. 1977 (AH 1355). *Ā'in-e Keshvar-dāri dar 'ahd-e Rashid al-Din Fazlallāh*. Tehran: Tus.

R.-Alföldi, M., K. Mosig-Walburg, and R. Walburg. 1983. "Aksumitische Münzstudien: Einleitung." *Paideuma* 29:221.

Rapport, M. 2008. *1848, Year of the Revolution*. New York: Basic Books.

Rashid al-Din Fazlallāh Hamadāni. 1979 (AH 1358). *Savāneh al-afkār-e rashidi*. Edited by M. T. Dāneshpazhuh. Tehran: Dāneshgāh-e Tehran.

Rawshan, M., and M. Musavi, eds. 1994 (AH 1373). *Jāme' al-Tavārikh*. By Rashid al-Din Fazlallāh Hamadāni. 4 vols. Tehran: Alborz.

Reid, S. B. 1989. *Enoch and Daniel: A Form Critical and Sociological Study of the Historical Apocalypses*. Berkeley, CA: Bibal Press.

Renfrew, C. 1986. Introduction to *Peer Polity Interaction and Socio-political Change*, edited by C. Renfrew and J. F. Cherry. Cambridge: Cambridge University Press.

Ricoeur, P. 1984–88. *Time and Narrative*. Translated by K. Blamey and D. Pellauer. 3 vols. Chicago: University of Chicago Press.

Robin, C. 2000. "Les 'filles de Dieu' de Saba á la Mecque: Reflexions sur l'agencement des pantheons dans l'Arabie ancienne." *Semitica* 50:113–92.

Robinson, I. S. 1990. *The Papacy, 1073–1198, Continuity and Innovation*. Cambridge: Cambridge University Press.

Root, M. C. 1990. "Circles of Artistic Programming: Strategies for Studying Creative Process at Persepolis." In *Investigating Artistic Environments in the Ancient Near East*, edited by Ann C. Gunter, 115–47. Washington, DC: Smithsonian Institution.

Rosenstock-Huessy, E. (1931) 1951. *Die europaïschen Revolution und der Charakter der Nationen*. Reprint, Stuttgart: Kohlhammer.

Rossabi, M. 2009. *Khubilai Khan: His Life and Times*. 2nd ed. Berkeley: University of California Press.

Rostovtzeff, M. (1927) 1960. *Rome*. Translated by J. D. Duff. Reprint, New York: Oxford University Press.

Roth, C. 1962. "The Pharisees in the Jewish Revolution of 66–73." *Journal of Semitic Studies* 7:63–80.

Rowland, R. J. 1965. "C. Gracchus and the *Equites*." *Transactions and Proceedings of the American Philological Association* 96:361–73.

Rowton, M. B. 1973a. "Autonomy and Nomadism in Western Asia." *Orientalia* 17:247–58.

———. 1973b. "Urban Autonomy in a Nomadic Environment." *JNES* 32:201–14.

Rubin, U. 1985. "The Constitution of Medina: Some Notes." *Studia Islamica* 62:5–23.

———. 1990. "Hanifiyya and Ka'ba: An Inquiry into the Arabian Pre-Islamic Background of *Din Ibrāhim*." *JSAI* 13:85–112.

———. 1995. *The Eye of the Beholder: The Life of Muhammad as Viewed by the Early Muslims.* Princeton, NJ: Darwin Press.

Rule, J. B. 1988. *Theories of Civil Violence.* Berkeley: University of California Press.

Runciman, S. 1957. *A History of the Crusades.* Vol. 1, *The First Crusade and the Foundation of the Kingdom of Jerusalem.* Cambridge: Cambridge University Press.

Russell, D. S. 1965. *Between the Testaments.* Philadelphia: Fortress Press.

Sachau, E. 1915. "Die Chronik von Arbela." *Abhandlungen des Preussischen (Deutschen) Akademie der Wissenschaften,* no. 6.

Sadighi, G. 1938. *Les mouvements religieux Iraniens au IIe et au IIIe siècle de l'Hégire.* Paris: Les presses modernes.

Saller, R. P. 1982. *Personal Patronage under the Early Empire.* Cambridge: Cambridge University Press.

Salmon, E. T. 1958. "Notes on the Social War." *Transactions and Proceedings of the American Philological Association* 89:159–84.

Saumagne, C. 1965. *Le droit latin et les cités romaines sous l'empire.* Paris: Sirey.

Schiffman, L. H. 1989. *The Eschatological Community of the Dead Sea Scrolls.* Atlanta, GA: Scholars Press.

Schluchter, W. 1988. *Rationalism, Religion and Domination: A Weberian Perspective.* Berkeley: University of California Press.

Schürer, E., G. Vermes, F. Millar, and M. Goodman. 1986. *The History of the Jewish People in the Age of Jesus Christ.* Vol. 3, pt. 1. Edinburgh: T. and T. Clark.

Schurmann, H. F. 1956a. *Economic Structure of the Yüan Dynasty: Translation of Chapters 93 and 94 of the "Yüan shih."* Cambridge, MA: Harvard University Press.

———. 1956b. "Mongolian Tributary Practices of the 13th Century." *Harvard Journal of Asiatic Studies* 19:304–89.

———. 1963. "Problems of Political Organization during the Yüan Dynasty." In *Trudy dvadtsat'piatogo Mezhdunarodnogo kongressa vostokovedov,* 26–31. Moscow: Nauka.

Schwartz, M. 1985. "The Religion of Achaemenian Iran." In *The Cambridge History of Iran,* edited by I. Gershevitch, vol. 2, *The Median and Achaemenian Periods,* 664–67. Cambridge: Cambridge University Press.

Seager, R., ed. 1969. *The Crisis of the Roman Republic.* Cambridge: Heffer.

Sealey, R. 1976. *A History of the Greek City States, 700–338 B.C.* Berkeley: University of California Press.

Seĭfeddini, M. A. 1978–81. *Monetnoe delo i denezhnoe obrashchenie v Azerbaĭdzhane,* v. 12.–15. Baku, Azerbaijan: Ėlm.

Selbin, E. 1999. *Modern Latin American Revolutions.* 2nd ed. Boulder, CO: Westview Press.

Sellheim, R. 1965–66. "Prophet, Chalif und Geschichte: Die Muhammed-Biographie des Ibn Ishāq." *Oriens* 18–19:33–91.

Sellwood, D. 1983. "Numismatics: Minor States in Southern Iran." In *The Cambridge History of Iran,* edited by E. Yarshater, vol. 3.1, *The Seleucid, Parthian and Sasanian Periods,* 299–321. Cambridge: Cambridge University Press.

Serjeant, R. B. 1978. "The *Sunnah Jāmi'a,* Pacts with the Yathrib Jews, and the *Tahrim* of Yathrib: Analysis and Translation of the Documents Comprised in the So-Called 'Constitution of Medina.'" *BSOAS* 41 (1): 1–42.

———. 1982. "The Interplay between Tribal Affinities and Religious (Zaydi) Authority in the Yemen." *Al-Abhāth* 30:11–48.

Seux, J. M. 1967. *Epithetes royales akkadiennes et sumeriennes*. Paris: Letouzey et Ane.

Sewell, W. 1995. "The Historiography of the French Revolution and the Comparative Sociology of Revolution: Disjunctions and Complementarities." Paper presented at the SCASSS Symposium on Social Theory and Revolutions, Uppsala.

Shaban, M. 1970. *The 'Abbasid Revolution*. Cambridge: Cambridge University Press.

Shaked, S. 1969. "Esoteric Trends in Zoroastrianism." *Proceedings of the Israeli Academy of Sciences and Humanities* 3:175–221.

———. 1997. "Popular Religion in Sasanian Babylonia." *JSAI* 21:103–17.

Shaki, M. 1990. "The Fillet of Nobility." *Bulletin of the Asia Institute* 4:277–79.

Shapiro, L. 1967. *Rationalism and Nationalism in Russian Nineteenth-Century Political Thought*. New Haven, CT: Yale University Press.

Sharon, M. 1983. *Black Banners from the East: The Establishment of the 'Abbasid-State; Incubation of a Revolt*. Leiden: E. J. Brill.

———. 1984. "The Development of the Debate around the Legitimacy of Authority in Early Islam." *JSAI* 5:121–41.

———. 1986. "Military Reforms of Abu Muslim." In *Studies in Islamic History and Civilization in Honour of Professor David Ayalon*, edited by M. Sharon, 105–43. Leiden: E. J. Brill.

———. 1990. *Revolt: The Social and Military Aspects of the 'Abbāsid Revolution*. Jerusalem: Magnes Press.

Shayegan, R. 2012. *Arsacids and Sasanians: Political Ideology in Post-Hellenistic and Late Antique Persia*. Cambridge: Cambridge University Press.

Sherk, R. K., ed. 1988. *The Roman Empire: Augustus to Hadrian*. Cambridge: Cambridge University Press.

Sherwin-White, A. N. 1956. "Violence in Roman Politics." *JRS* 46 (1–2): 1–9.

———. 1973a. *The Roman Citizenship*. Oxford: Clarendon Press.

———. 1973b. "The Roman Citizenship: A Survey of Its Development into a World Franchise." In *Von den Anfängen Roms bis zum Ausgang der Republik*. N.p.

———. 1973c. "The Tabula of Banasa and the Constitutio Antoniniana." *JRS* 63:86–98.

Shoufani, E. 1973. *Al-Riddah and the Muslim Conquest of Arabia*. Toronto: University of Toronto Press.

Simon, R. 1997. "Mani and Muhammad." *JSAI* 21:118–40.

Sinai, N. 2006. "Self-Referentiality as a Strategy of Self-Authorization." In *Self-Referentiality in the Qur'ān*, edited by S. Wild, 104–34. Wiesbaden: Harrassowitz.

———. 2011. "The Qurān as Process." In *The Qur'ān in Context: Historical and Literary Investigations into the Qurānic Milieu*, edited by A. Neuwirth, N. Sinai, and M. Marx, 407–39. Leiden: E. J. Brill.

Sinor, D. 1990. "The Establishment and Dissolution of the Türk Empire." In *The Cambridge History of Early Inner Asia*, vol. 1, *From Earliest Times to the Rise of the Mongols*, 285–316. Cambridge: Cambridge University Press.

Sirks, A. J. B. 2015. "Public Law." In *The Cambridge Companion to Roman Law*, edited by D. Johnston, 332–52. Cambridge: Cambridge University Press.

Skjærvø, P. O. 1983. "'Kirdir's Vision': Translation and Analysis." *Archaeologische Mitteilungen aus Iran* 16:269–306.

———. 1997. "Counter-Manichean Elements in Kerdir's Inscriptions. Irano-Manichaica II." In *Atti del Terzo Congresso Internazionale di Studi "Manicheismo e Oriente Cristiano Antico,"* edited by L. Cirillo and A. van Tongerloo, 313–42. Turnhout, Belgium: Brepols.

Skocpol, T. 1979. *States and Social Revolutions*. New York: Cambridge University Press.

———. 1988. "Social Revolutions and Mass Military Mobilization." *World Politics* 40 (2): 147–68.

Snodgrass, A. 1986. "Interaction by Design: The Greek City State." In *Peer Polity Interaction and Socio-political Change*, edited by C. Renfrew and J. F. Cherry, 47–58. Cambridge: Cambridge University Press.

Sohrabi, N. 2011. *Revolution and Constitutionalism in the Ottoman Empire and Iran*. Cambridge: Cambridge University Press.

Sólyom, L. 2007. "Role of Constitutional Courts in the Transition to Democracy with Special Reference to Hungary." In *Constitutionalism and Political Reconstruction*, edited by S. A. Arjomand, 258–314. Leiden: E. J. Brill.

Soudavar, A. 2009. "The Vocabulary and Syntax of Iconography in Sasanian Iran." *Iranica Antiqua* 44:417–60.

———. 2014. *Mithraic Societies: From Brotherhood Ideal to Religion's Adversary*. Houston: Lulu.com.

Sourdel, D. 1959. *Le vizirat 'abbaside de 749 à 936 (132 à de l'Hégire)*. 2 vols. Damascus: Institut français de Damas.

———. 1960. "Questions de cérémonial ʿabbaside." *Revue des études islamiques* 28 (1): 121–48.

Spencer, H. (1876) 1972. *Herbert Spencer on Social Evolution*. Edited by J. D. Y. Peel. Chicago: University of Chicago Press.

Sprengling, M. 1953. *Third-Century Iran: Sapor and Kartir*. Chicago: Oriental Institute.

Ste. Croix, G. E. M. de. 1981. *The Class Struggle in the Ancient Greek World from the Archaic Age to the Arab Conquest*. Ithaca, NY: Cornell University Press.

Steinkeller, P. 1987. "The Administration and Economic Organization of the Ur III State: The Core and the Periphery." In *The Organization of Power: Aspects of Bureaucracy in the Ancient Near East*, edited by M. Gibson and R. Biggs, 15–33. Chicago: Oriental Institute.

———. 1992. "Mesopotamia in the Third Millennium B.C." In *The Anchor Bible Dictionary*, vol. 4, edited by D. N. Freedman, 724–32. New York: Doubleday.

———. 1993. "Early Political Development in Mesopotamia and the Origins of the Sargonic Empire." In *Akkad: The First World Empire; Structure, Ideology, Traditions*, edited by M. Liverani, 107–29. Padua: Sargon.

Stinchcombe, A. L. 1968. *Constructing Social Theories*. New York: Harcourt Brace Jovanovich.

———. 1975. "Social Structure and Politics." In *Handbook of Political Science*, vol. 3, *Macropolitical Theory*, edited by F. I. Greenstein and N. W. Polsby. Reading, MA: Addison-Wesley.

———. 1978. *Theoretical Methods in Historical Sociology*. New York: Academic Press.

———. 1990. "A Critique of the Theory of Structuration." In *Anthony Giddens: Consensus and Controversy*, edited by J. Clark, C. Modgil, and S. Modgil, 47–56. London: Falmer Press.

Stockton, D. 1979. *The Gracchi*. Oxford: Clarendon Press.

Stroumsa, G. G. 1986. "'Seal of the Prophets': The Nature of a Manichaean Metaphor." *JSAI* 7:61–74.

———. 2007. "False Prophet, False Messiah and the Religious Scene in Seventh-Century Jerusalem." In *Redemption and Resistance: The Messianic Hope of Jews and Christians in Antiquity*, edited by W. Horbury, 285–96. London: T. and T. Clark.

Subtelny, M. E. 2010. "Tamerlane and His Descendants: From Paladins to Patrons." In *The New Cambridge History of Islam*, vol. 3, *The Eastern Islamic World, Eleventh to Eighteenth Centuries*, edited by D. O. Morgan and A. Reid, 169–200. Cambridge: Cambridge University Press.

Suetonius. 1957. *The Twelve Caesars*. Translated by R. Graves. Harmondsworth, UK: Penguin.

Sundermann, W. 1979. "Namen von Göttern, Dämonen und Menschen in iranischen Versionen des manichäischen Mythos." *Altorientalische Forschungen* 6:95–133.

Swain, J. W. 1940. "The Theory of the Four Monarchies: Opposition History under the Roman Empire." *Classical Philology* 35:1–21.

Syme, R. 1939. *The Roman Revolution*. Oxford: Clarendon Press.

———. 1958. "Imperator Caesar: A Study in Nomenclature." *Historia* 7 (2): 172–88.

———. 1982. "Partisans of Galba." *Historia* 31 (4): 460–83.

Tabari, Muhammad b. Jarir al-. 1879–1901. *Ta'rikh al-rusul va'l-muluk*. Edited by M. J. de Goeje. 15 vols. Leiden. Annotated English translation in *The History of al-Tabari*, 40 vols. (Albany: State University of New York Press, 1985–2007).

Tacitus, C. 1942. *The Complete Works of Tacitus*. Edited by M. Hadas. New York: Modern Library.

Taqizādeh, S. H. 1943. "The Early Sassanians." *BSOAS* 11.

Tarjoma-ye tafsir-e Tabari. 1977 (AH 1356). Edited by H. Yaghmā'i. 7 vols. in 4. Tehran: Tus.

Tavory, I., and S. Timmermans. 2014. *Abductive Analysis: Theorizing Qualitative Research*. Chicago: University of Chicago Press.

Tcherikover, V. 1959. *Hellenistic Civilization and the Jews*. New York: Atheneum.

Teixidor, J. 1997–98. "Antiquités sémitiques." *Annuaire du Collège de France*, 713–35.

Tellenbach, G. (1936) 1970. *Church, State and Christian Society at the Time of the Investiture Contest*. Translated by R. F. Bennett. Reprint, New York: Harper Torchbooks.

———. 1940. *Church, State and Christian Society at the Time of the Investiture Contest*. Translated by R. F. Bennett. Oxford: Basil Blackwell.

———. (1988) 1993. *The Church in Western Europe from the Tenth to the Early Twelfth Century*. Translated by T. Reuter. Reprint, Cambridge: Cambridge University Press.

Thucydides. 1954. *History of the Peloponnesian War*. Harmondsworth, UK: Penguin.

Tilly, C. 1978. *From Mobilization to Revolution*. Reading, MA: Addison-Wesley.

———. 1993. *European Revolutions, 1492–1992*. Oxford: Blackwell.

———. 2000. "Processes and Mechanisms of Democratization." *Sociological Theory* 18 (1): 1–16.

———. 2005. "Regimes and Contention." In *Handbook of Political Sociology*, edited by T. Janoski, R. Alford, A. Hicks, and M. A. Schwartz, 423–40. New York: Cambridge University Press.

Tilly, C., and J. B. Rule. 1965. *Measuring Political Upheaval*. Princeton, NJ: Princeton University Press.

Tiryakian, E. A. 1995. "Collective Effervescence, Social Change and Charisma: Durkheim, Weber and 1989." *International Sociology* 10 (3): 269–81.

Tocqueville, A. de. 1955. *The Old Régime and the French Revolution*. Translated by S. Gilbert. New York: Doubleday.

Toral-Niehoff, I. 2013. "Late Antique Iran and the Arabs." *Journal of Persianate Studies* 6 (1–2): 115–26.

Traill, J. S. 1975. *The Political Organization of Attica: A Study of the Demes, Trittyes, and Phylai, and Their Representation in the Athenian Council. Hesperia*, Supplement 14. Princeton, NJ: American School of Classical Studies at Athens.

Tucker, R. C. 1969. *The Marxian Revolutionary Idea*. New York: W. W. Norton.

Ullmann, W. 1965. *A History of Political Thought: The Middle Ages*. Harmondsworth, UK: Penguin Books.

———. 1970. *The Growth of the Papal Government in the Middle Ages*. London: Methuen.

———. 1975. *Law and Politics in the Middle Ages*. Cambridge: Cambridge University Press.

———. 1976. "The Papacy as an Institution of Government in the Middle Ages." In *The Papacy and Political Ideas in the Middle Ages*, ch. 18. London: Variorum Reprints.

Ulrich, E., and J. VanderKam, eds. 1994. *The Community and the Renewed Covenant: The Notre Dame Symposium on the Dead Sea Scrolls*. Notre Dame, IN: University of Notre Dame Press.

VanderKam, J. C. 1984. *Enoch and the Growth of an Apocalyptic Tradition*. Catholic Biblical Quarterly Monograph Series 16. Washington, DC.

———. 1994. "Messianism in the Scrolls." In *The Community and the Renewed Covenant*, edited by E. Ulrich and J. VanderKam, 211–38. Notre Dame, IN: University of Notre Dame Press.

van Ess, J. 1991–97. *Theologie und Gesellschaft im 2. und 3. Jahrhundert Hidschra*. 6 vols. Berlin: Walter de Gruyter.

———. 1992. "'Abd al-Malik and the Dome of the Rock: An Analysis of Some Texts." In *Bayt al-Maqdis: 'Abd al-Malik's Jerusalem*, edited by J. Raby and J. Johns, 33–58. Oxford: Oxford University Press.

van Vloten, G. 1894. *Recherches sur la domination arabe, le chi'itisme et les croyances messianiques sous le khalifat des Omayades*. Amsterdam: J. Mueller.

Vassāf, Shehāb al-Din 'Abd Allāh Sharaf Shirāzi. 1852–53 (AH 1269). *Tajziyat al-amsār wa tazjiyat al-a'sār*. Bombay.

Vermes, G. 1992. "The Oxford Forum for Qumran Research Seminar on the Rule of War from Cave 4 (4Q285)." *Journal of Jewish Studies* 43 (1): 85–94.

———. 1995. *The Dead Sea Scrolls in English*. 4th ed. London: Penguin Books.

Violante, C. 1953. *La socità milanese nell'età precommunale*. Bari, Italy: Gius, Laterza e Figli.

———. 1955. *La Pataria milanese e la riforma ecclesiastica*. Rome: Istituto storico italiano per il Medio Evo.

Voegelin, E. 1952. *The New Science of Politics*. Chicago: University of Chicago Press.

———. 1956. *Order and History*. Vol. 1, *Israel and Revelation*. Baton Rouge: Louisiana State University Press.

———. 1957. *Order and History*. Vol. 2, *The World of the Polis*. Baton Rouge: Louisiana State University Press.

Von Laue, T. H. 1987. *The World Revolution of Westernization: The Twentieth Century in Global Perspective*. Oxford: Oxford University Press.

Wacholder, B. Z. 1978. "The Letter from Judah Maccabee to Aristobulus: Is 2 Maccabees 1:10b–2:18 Authentic?" *Hebrew Union College Annual* 49:89–133.

———. 1983. *The Dawn of Qumran: The Sectarian Torah and the Teacher of Righteousness*. Cincinnati, OH: Hebrew Union College Press.

Walt, S. M. 1996. *Revolution and War*. Ithaca, NY: Cornell University Press.

Wāqidi, Muhammad b. 'Umar al-. 1966. *The Kitāb al-maghāzi*. Edited by M. Jones. 3 vols. London: Oxford University Press.

Watt, W. M. 1956. *Muhammad at Medina*. Oxford: Oxford University Press.

———. 1970. "The 'High God' in Pre-Islamic Mecca." *Actes du Ve Congrés international d'Arabisants et d'Islamisants*, 499–505.

———. 1988. *Muhammad's Mecca: History in the Qur'ān*. Edinburgh: Edinburgh University Press.

———. 1993. "Musaylima." In *Encyclopedia of Islam*, 6:664–65. Leiden: E. J. Brill.

Weber, M. (1904) 1949. "Objectivity in Social Science and Social Policy." In *The Methodology of the Social Sciences*, edited by E. A. Shils and H. A. Finch, 49–112. Glencoe, IL: Free Press.

———. (1906) 1995. *The Russian Revolutions*. Translated and edited by G. C. Wells and P. Baehr. Reprint, Cambridge: Polity Press.

———. 1948. *From Max Weber: Essays in Sociology*. Edited by H. H. Gerth and C. W. Mills. London: Routledge and Kegan Paul.

———. 1952. *Ancient Judaism*. Translated by H. H. Gerth and D. Martindale. New York: Free Press.

———. 1978. *Economy and Society*. Edited and translated by G. Roth and C. Wittich. 2 vols. Berkeley: University of California Press.

Welch, A. T. 1983. "Muhammad's Understanding of Himself: The Koranic Data." In *Islam's Understanding of Itself*, edited by R. G. Hovannisian and S. Vryonis Jr., 15–52. Malibu, CA: Undena Publications.

Wellhausen, J. 1883. "Mohammedanism." In *Encyclopaedia Britannica*, 10th ed., 26:544–65.

———. 1884–99. *Skizzen und Vorarbeiten*. 6 vols. Berlin: Reimer.

———. (1887) 1927. *Reste arabischen Heidentums*. Reprint, Berlin: Walter de Gruyter.

———. 1889. "Die *Gemeindeordnung von Median*." *Skizzen und Vorarbeiten* 4:65–83.

———. (1903) 1963. *The Arab Kingdom and Its Fall*. Translated by M. G. Weir. Reprint, Beirut: Khayyat.

———. 1975. "Muhammad's Constitution of Medina." Edited and translated by W. Behn. In *Muhammad and the Jews of Medina*, by A. J. Wensinck, 128–38. Freiburg: Klaus Schwarz Verlag.

Wells, C. 1984. *The Roman Empire*. Stanford, CA.: Stanford University Press.

Westenholz, A. 1993. "The World View of Sargonic Officials: Differences in Mentality between Sumerians and Akkadians." In *Akkad: The First World Empire; Structure, Ideology, Traditions*, edited by M. Liverani, 157–70. Padua: Sargon.

Whitney, J. P. 1926. "The Reform of the Church." In *The Cambridge Medieval History*, vol. 5, *Contest of Empire and Papacy*, edited by J. R. Tanner, C. W. Prévite-Orton, and Z. N. Brooke, 1–50. Cambridge: Cambridge University Press.

Widengren, G. 1956. "Recherches sur le féodalisme iranien." *Orientalia Suecana* 5:79–182.

———. 1967. *Der Feudalismus im alten Iran*. Cologne: Westdeutscher Verlag.

———. 1968. *Les religions de l'Iran*. Paris: Payot.

———. 1971. "The Establishment of the Sasanian Dynasty in the Light of New Evidence." In *La Persia nel Medioevo*, 711–84. Rome: Accademia nazionale dei lincei.

Widengren, G., A. Hultgård, and M. Philonenko. 1995. *Apocalyptique iranienne et dualism qoumrânien*. Paris: Adrien Maisonneuve.

Wiesehöfer, J. 1987. "Ardašir I: History." In *Encyclopaedia Iranica*, vol. 2, edited by E. Yarshater, 371–80. Boston: Routledge and Kegan Paul.

———. 2001. *Ancient Persia from 550 BC to 650 AD*. Translated by A. Azodi. London: I. B. Tauris.

Wiseman, T. P. 1969. "The Census in the First Century B.C." *JRS* 59:59–75.

Wolf, E. R. 1951. "The Social Organization of Mecca and the Origins of Islam." *Southwestern Journal of Anthropology* 7 (4): 329–56.

Wolski, J. 1974. "Arsace 1er, fondateur de l'état parthe." *Acta Iranica* 3:159–99.

Woodside, A. B. 1989. "History, Structure, and Revolution in Vietnam." *International Political Science Review* 10 (2): 143–57.

———. 2006. *Lost Modernities: China, Vietnam, Korea, and the Hazards of World History*. Cambridge, MA: Harvard University Press.

Woude, A. S. van der. 1982. "Wicked Priest or Wicked Priests? Reflections on the Identification of the Wicked Priest in the Habakkuk Commentary." *Journal of Jewish Studies* 33:349–59.

Wurtzel, C. 1978. "The Coinage of the Revolutionaries in the Late Umayyad Period." *Museum Notes* (American Numismatic Society) 23:161–99.

Ya'qubi, Ahmad b. Wadih al-. 1960. *Tārikh*. 2 vols. Beirut: Dār Sādir.

Yarbro Collins, A. 1993. "The Influence of Daniel on the New Testament." In *Daniel: A Commentary on the Book of Daniel*, edited by A. Y. Collins, J. J. Collins, and F. M. Cross, 90–112. Minneapolis, MN: Fortress Press.

Yarshater, E. 1971. *Were the Sasanians Heirs to the Achaemenids?* Accademia nazionale dei lincei.

———. 1983. "Mazdakism." In *The Cambridge History of Iran*, vol. 3.2, *The Seleucid, Parthian and Sasanian Periods*, edited by E. Yarshater. Cambridge: Cambridge University Press.

Yoffee, N. 2005. *Myths of the Archaic State: Evolution of the Earliest Cities, States and Civilizations*. Cambridge: Cambridge University Press.

Yuan shih. 1937–85. *Un code des Yuan*. Vol. 3. Paris: E. Leroux.

Yusofi, G. H. 1989 (AH 1368). *Abu Molem-e Khorāsāni*. Tehran: Ketāb-e Javānān.

Zaehner, R. C. 1955. *Zurvan: A Zoroastrian Dilemma*. Oxford: Clarendon Press.

Zakeri, M. 1995. *Sasanid Soldiers in Early Muslim Society: The Origins of 'Ayyārān and Futuwwa*. Wiesbaden: Otto Harrassowitz Verlag.

Zaryab-Kho'i, A. 1989 (AH 1368). "'Abu Hanifa." In *Bazmāvard*, 128–43. Tehran: Sokhan.

Zimmermann, E. 1983. *Political Violence, Crises and Revolution: Theories and Research*. Cambridge, MA: Schenkman.

INDEX